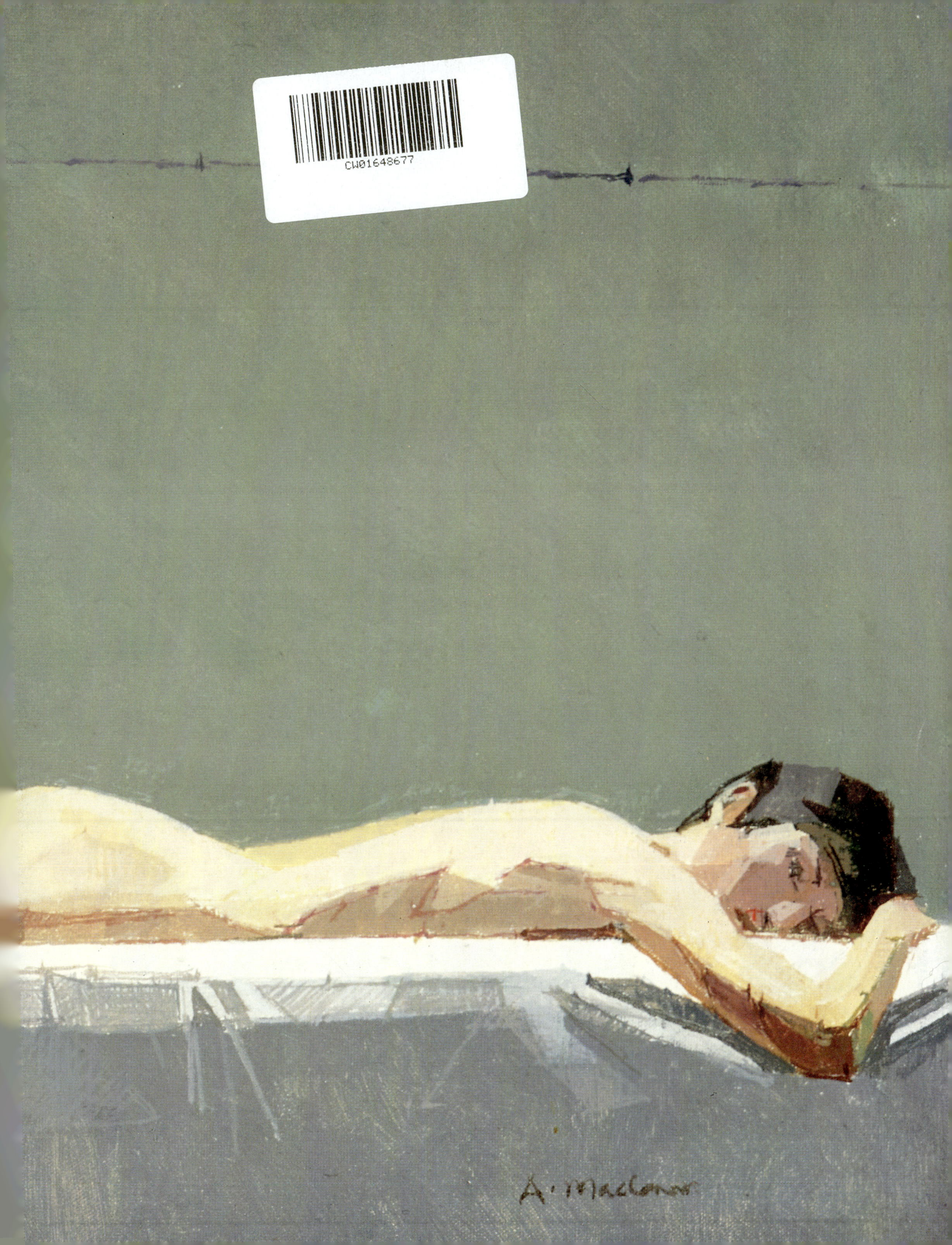

CAMBERWELL
SCHOOL OF ARTS & CRAFTS

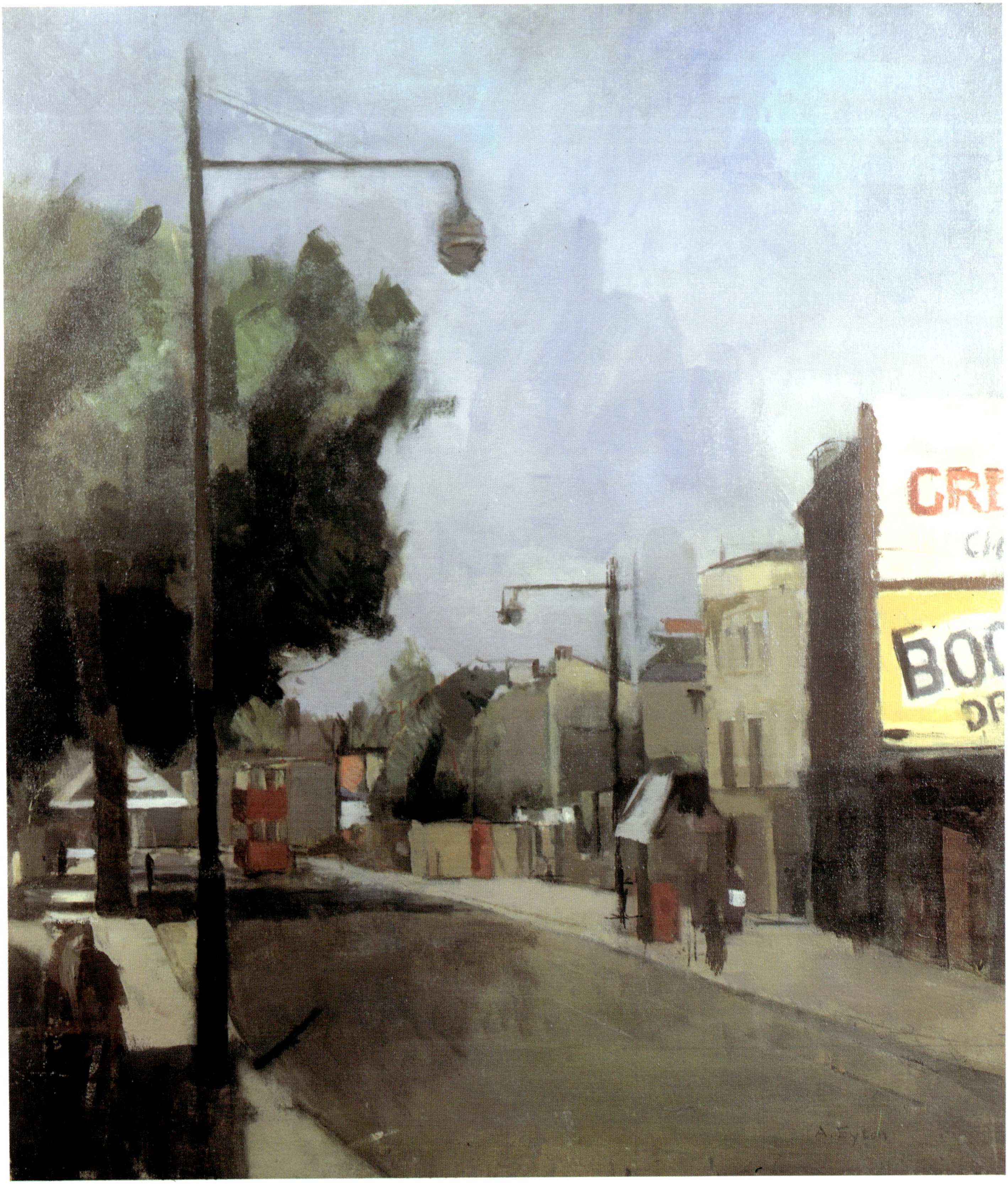

CAMBERWELL
SCHOOL OF ARTS & CRAFTS

ITS STUDENTS & TEACHERS
1943-1960

GEOFF HASSELL

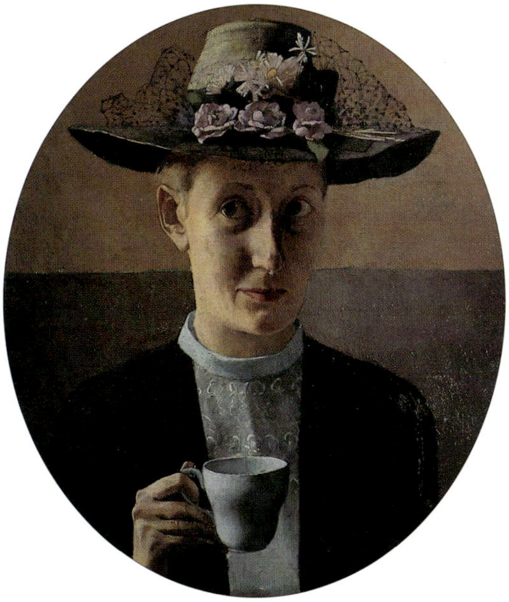

ANTIQUE COLLECTORS' CLUB

ISBN 1 85149 180 5

British Library Cataloguing-in-Publication Data
A catalogue record for this book is available from the British Library

Printed in England
by the Antique Collectors' Club Ltd., Woodbridge, Suffolk
on Consort Royal Satin paper
supplied by the Donside Paper Company, Aberdeen, Scotland

Endpapers: ANDREW MACLAREN, *Nude*, 1958. Oil on board, 11in x 16in.
Private collection.

Title page illustration: ROSA BRANSON, *The New Hat.* Oil on board, 24in x 18in.
Courtesy of Mr Lee Seaman.

Frontispiece: ANTHONY EYTON, *Peckham Road, Camberwell.* Oil on canvas, 29½in x 25in.
Private collection.

Contents

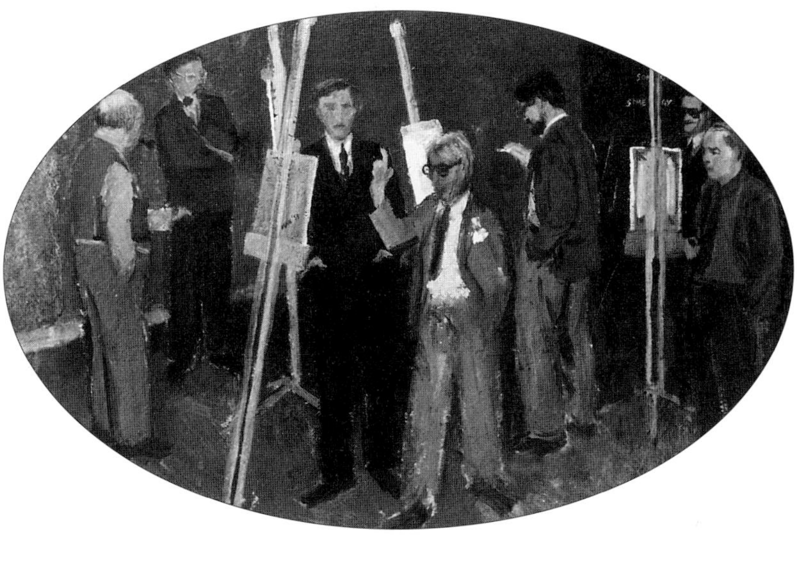

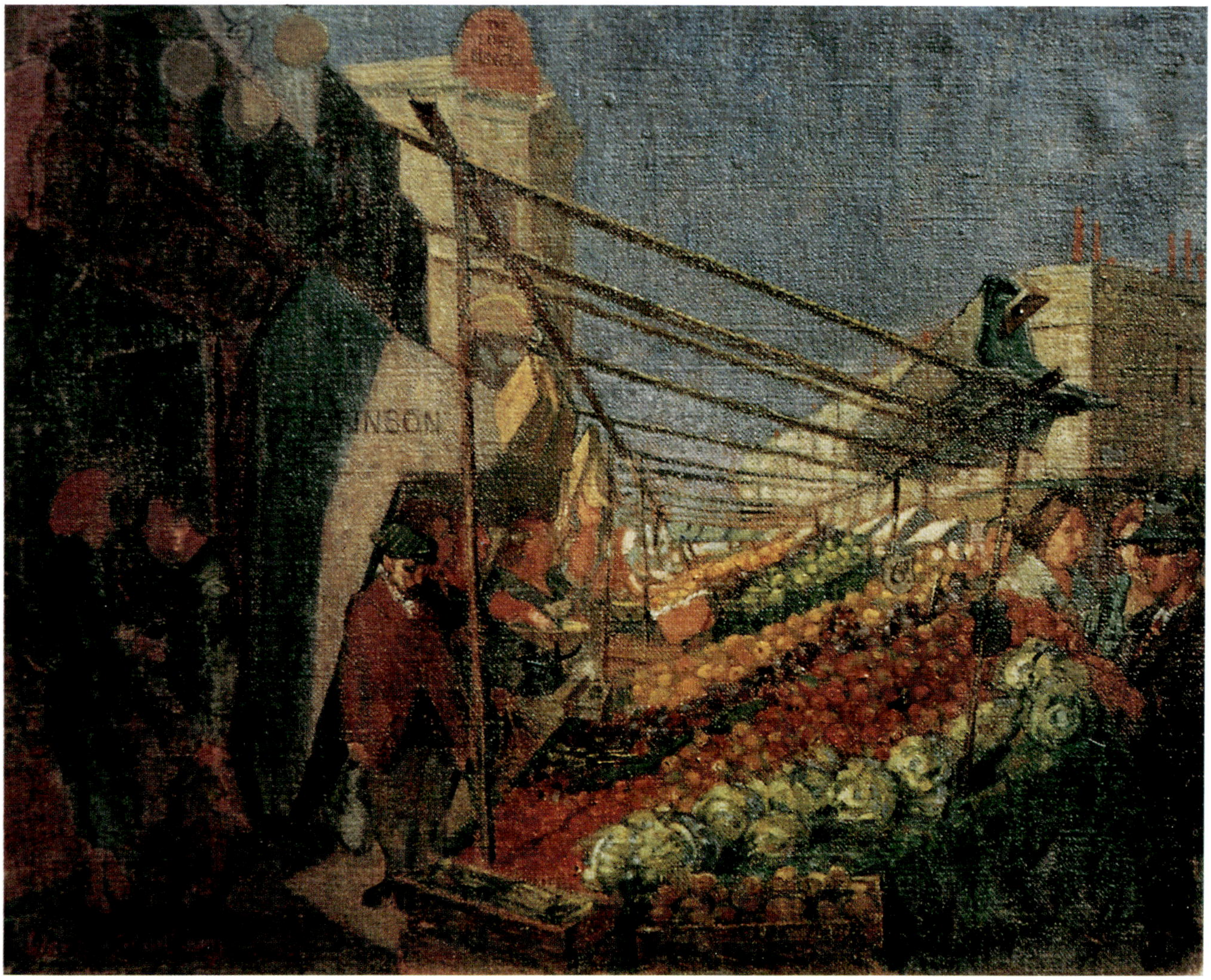

WOOLF GOLDBERG. *Hackney Market*, 1948. Oil on canvas, 25in x 30in. Artist's collection.

Dedication

To Cynthia, without whose initial help and hours pounding the keyboard, this book would never have got off the ground.

Apologia

During the several years it has taken to compile, I have attempted to make the Dictionary section of this book as comprehensive as possible. Inevitably, however, there will be errors and omissions and for these I apologise. There may also be a number of anomalies, particularly relating to the dates during which some artists and teachers were actually at the School; for example where no record cards exist, or where the School's records differ from those of the artist. Again, I apologise if my striving for accuracy has sometimes fallen short of expectations.

Introduction

It was towards the end of 1986, while having lunch at the studio of Anthony Eyton, that I first heard the name of Camberwell in an artistic context. Tony said to me "Have you ever heard of Dick Lee?" "No" said I, "Who is he?" Tony then informed me that in my capacity as an art dealer I should get to know him, as he was an interesting painter who had studied and taught at Camberwell with Eyton. So I made an appointment to visit Dick Lee at his home in Norfolk, not knowing what to expect. To my amazement I found an Aladdin's cave of largely unseen paintings, mainly small oils, on board or panel, painted 'plein air' with a freshness and spontaneity that I had rarely witnessed from a contemporary artist. Dick was most informative about Camberwell and the time he had spent there, both as a student and a teacher. I soon became as interested in this art school as I was in his ability as

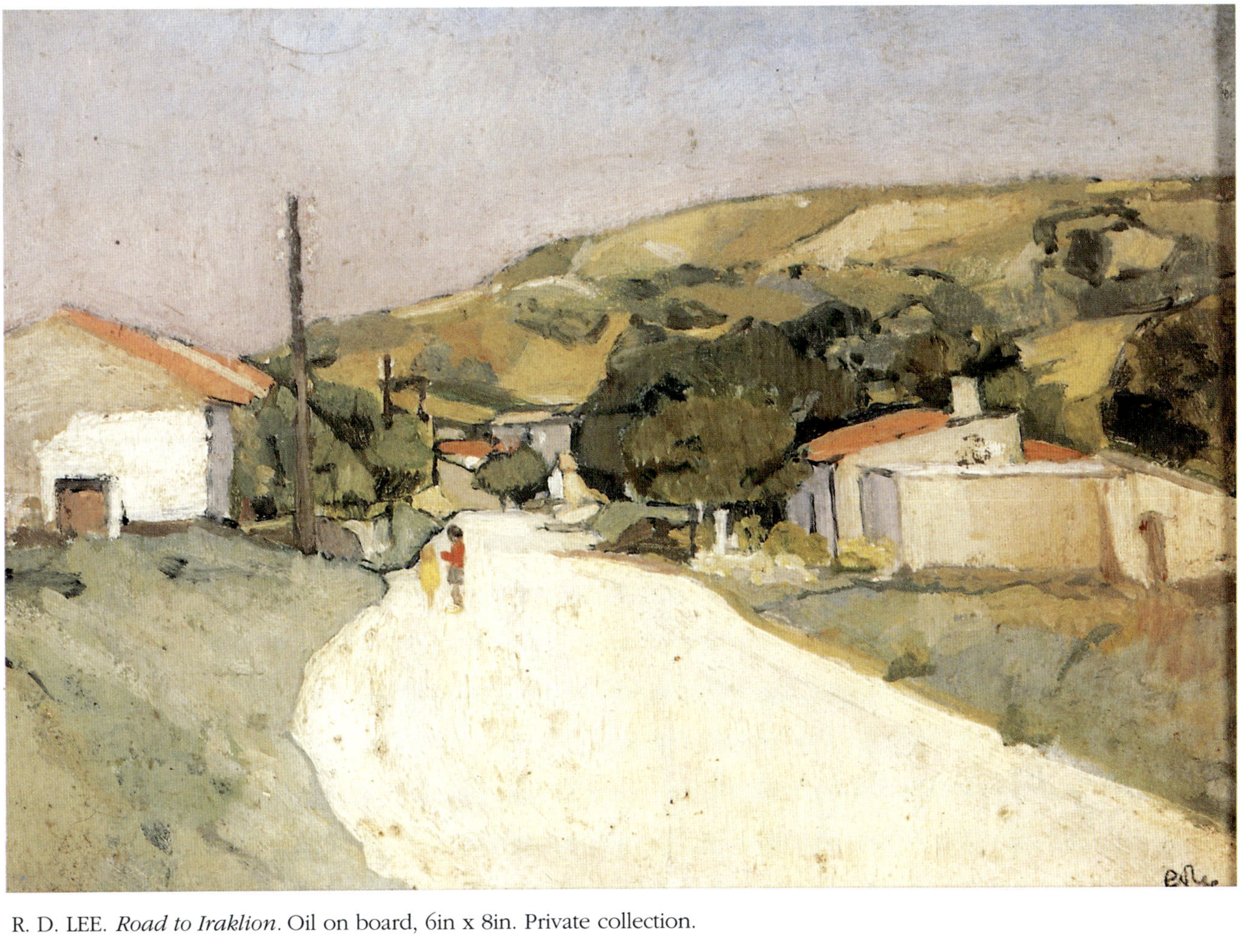

R. D. LEE. *Road to Iraklion*. Oil on board, 6in x 8in. Private collection.

an artist and was able to leave Norfolk with examples of his work, together with names of fellow Camberwellians.

Shortly after, my colleague and friend Irving Grose of Belgrave Gallery, London, visited me in the Cotswolds and happened to see a couple of Lee's paintings. He was as taken with his work as I had been. I had, meanwhile, read about the Euston Road School and realised that in some small way it had attempted to re-form itself at Camberwell School of Art in the immediate post-war years, and that Eyton and Lee were an obvious outcome. I conveyed this information to Irving Grose and we loosely discussed the possibility of acquiring work by teachers and students of Camberwell during the 1940s and 1950s, with the view to an exhibition in London at some future date. Obsession took over and, during the next eighteen months I visited artist after artist, accumulating not only contemporaneous paintings, but interesting anecdotes of their times at Camberwell.

In May 1988, the exhibition reached fruition and I quote from Max Wykes-Joyce's critique in the *Arts Review*, 20th May 1988: "It is strange how one always thinks of Schools, groups of major artists working within a common aesthetic, and usually in a particular locale, as belonging to one's parents' or grandparents' generation. It is with difficulty, no matter how clearly defined it is, to accept one's contemporaries and friends as constituting such a School. However, I shall have, to mix the metaphor, to bite the bullet. For this excellent show, splendidly catalogued, clearly establishes the Camberwell Group with as much significance in English painting as the Pre-Raphaelites or the Camden Town Group... The seventy works in this show establish the significance of the Camberwell School beyond doubt."

The obsession with Camberwell did not end with this exhibition, and it was suggested by numerous people that the information I had gleaned should be recorded in print for posterity. A further four years' work has been involved in attempting to locate as many ex-Camberwell students and teachers as possible, not only in this country, but all over the world. Many thousands of miles, hundreds of letters and telephone calls have resulted in an accumulation of information, not always flattering towards Camberwell, but relevant to the short period between 1943-60 that is covered by this publication. Thankfully, the vast majority of people I contacted were more than willing to give as much information as possible, and were so kind in supplying not only paintings for the exhibition at the Belgrave Gallery, but also photographs of their work and even personal photographs, some of which are reproduced here. It is sad, however, that a small minority refused to answer several written requests, and an occasional spoken one, even though I had taken much time in tracing their whereabouts. Furthermore, I would like to apologise to those people listed who, despite all my efforts, remain untraceable. No doubt this list is in no way definitive, as I am sure that many more students and teachers attended the School in those immediate post-war years, whose names did not appear on the register at Camberwell. My apologies to them also. I hope in some small way that this attempt on my part will help perpetuate what was indeed a golden era in British post-war art.

In conclusion, I should like to dedicate this book to the memory of Joe Dixon (1915-1991) whose help as an unpaid private detective in supplying me with names and addresses was so invaluable. Naturally, there are very many more people to whom I should like to express sincere thanks, but I am unable to list them individually; hopefully this publication affirms my gratitude to them all.

Geoff Hassell, Cheltenham, 1995

Abbreviations used in text

*An * used in the dictionary entries indicates that there is also an entry for the artist whose name is thus marked.*

A.	Associate
A.I.A.	Artists' International Association
A.T.C.	Art Teachers' Certificate
b.	born
B.A.	Bachelor of Arts
B.M.	British Museum
Bt.	Baronet
C.B.E.	Commander Order of the British Empire
C.H.	Companion of Honour
Dip.A.D.	Diploma in Art & Design
D.F.A.	Diploma of Fine Art
D.L.	Deputy Lieutenant
E.R.S.	Euston Road School
F.	Fellow
F.P.S.	Free Painters & Sculptors
F.R.B.S.	Fellow, Royal Society of British Sculptors
F.R.S.A.	Fellow, Royal Society of Arts
F.S.A.E.	Fellow, Society of Art Education
G.L.C.	Greater London Council
G.P.O.	General Post Office
Hon.	Honorary Member
I.C.A.	Institute of Contemporary Arts
I.L.E.A.	Inner London Education Authority
I.S.	International Society of Sculptors, Painters and Gravers
Kt.	Knight
L.A.A.	London Artists' Association
L.G.	London Group
M.A.	Master of Arts
N.D.D.	National Diploma in Design
N.E.A.C.	New English Art Club
N.S.	National Society
O.B.E.	Officer Order of the British Empire
P.	President
P.O.W.	Prisoner of war
Prof.	Professor
R.A.	Royal Academy, Royal Academician
R.A.F.	Royal Air Force
R.B.A.	Royal Society of British Artists
R.B.S.	Royal Society of British Sculptors
R.B.S.A.	Royal Birmingham Society of Artists
R.C.A.	Royal College of Art
R.Cam.A.	Royal Cambrian Academy
R.D.I.	Royal Designer of Industry
R.E.	Royal Society of Painter-Etcher & Engravers
R.H.A.	Royal Hibernian Academy
R.I.	Royal Institute of Painters in Watercolours
R.O.I.	Royal Institute of Oil Painters
R.P.	Royal Society of Portrait Painters
R.S.A.	Royal Scottish Academy
R.S.M.A.	Royal Society of Marine Arts
R.W.A.	Royal West of England Academy
R.W.S.	Royal Watercolour Society
S.G.A	Society of Graphic Art
S.I.A.D.	Society of Industrial Artists & Designers
S.W.A.	Society of Women Artists
S.W.E.	Society of Wood Engravers
U.A.	United Society of Artists
V.	Vice
V. & A.	Victoria & Albert Museum
V.P.	Vice President
W.A.A.F.	Women's Auxiliary Air Force
W.R.N.S.	Women's Royal Naval Service
W.V.S.	Women's Voluntary Service

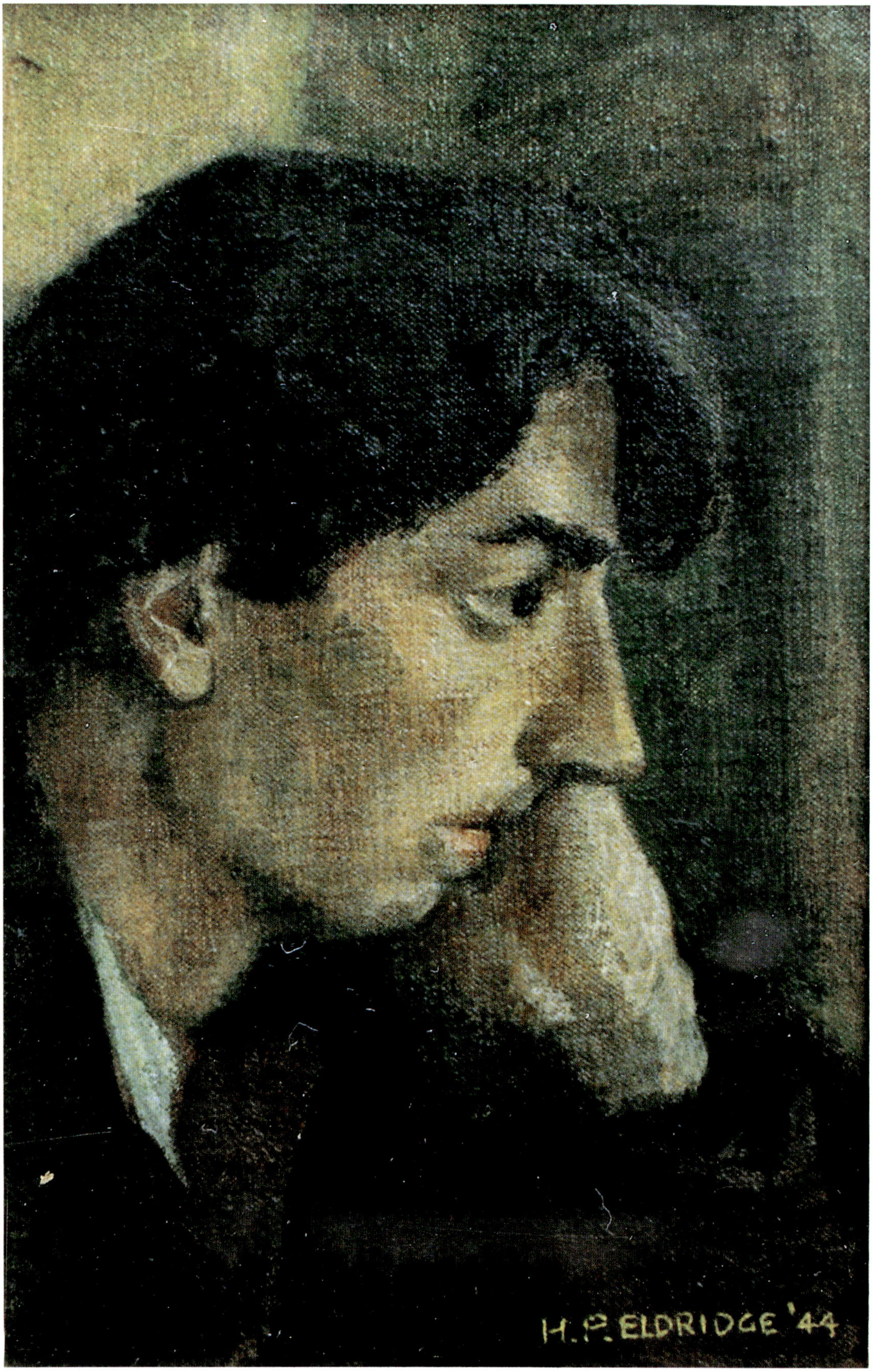

HAROLD ELDRIDGE. *Portrait of John Minton,* 1944. Oil on canvas board, 14in x 10in. Private collection.

Camberwell – a brief history

It was not until 1836 that active State support for art and technical education came into being. The initial grants were, by today's standards, incredibly small and by the year of the Great Exhibition (1851), the grant had been increased to the princely sum of £15,000. Although the Exhibition had been acclaimed as a great success, there were certain uneasy feelings in the corridors of power concerning the state of British industry (things seem not to have changed) and as a result, the Science and Art department was set up at South Kensington, eventually under the control of the Board of Education. Small annual grants were awarded in aid of privately conducted art and science classes based on annual examinations. Initially, these grants were very low, but by the end of the last century had risen to amounts of more than £150,000.

From the 1880s onwards, there was a sudden and rapid development in the field of art education. The many Livery Companies of London helped greatly by establishing the City and Guilds of London Institute in 1880, and by helping with the formation of various technical schools. In 1893 the London County Council established the Technical Education Board. At this time, the only provision for such technical education in the Borough of Camberwell was at the Camberwell Green

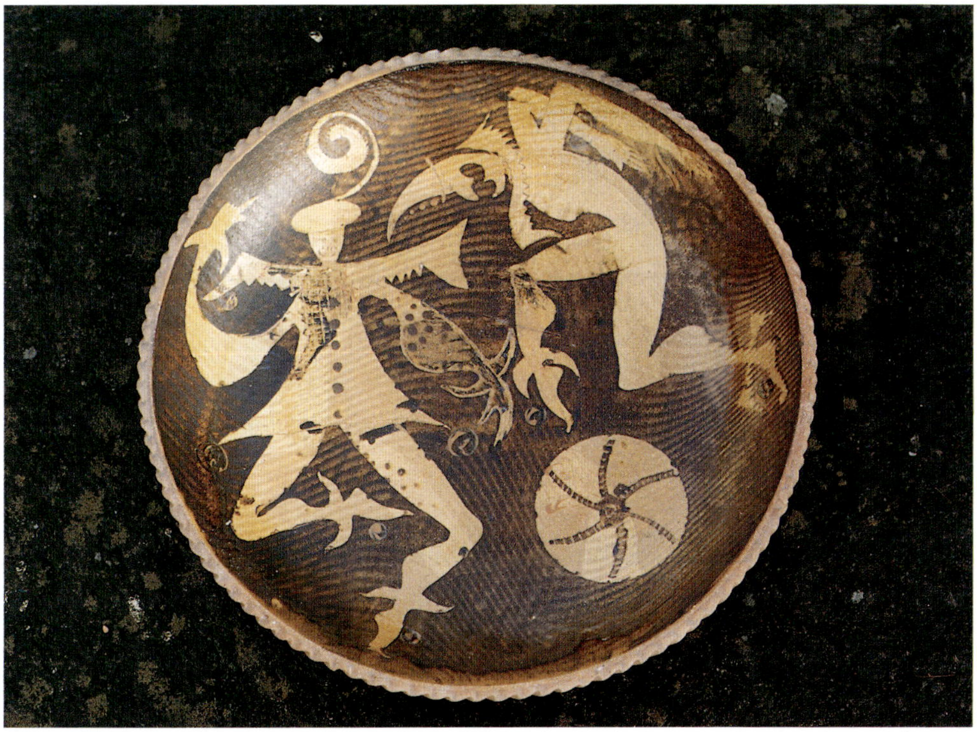

JOCK PURDIE. Earthenware 'clown' dish decorated with brushed slip and paper resist cut freehand, 18in wide, 1950. Courtesy of Margaret Kerr.

CAMBERWELL SCULPTURE SCHOOL, 1958. The unfinished figure on the stand is by Raphael Maklouf – the model in the background is Sylvia. Photo courtesy of Seth Cardew.

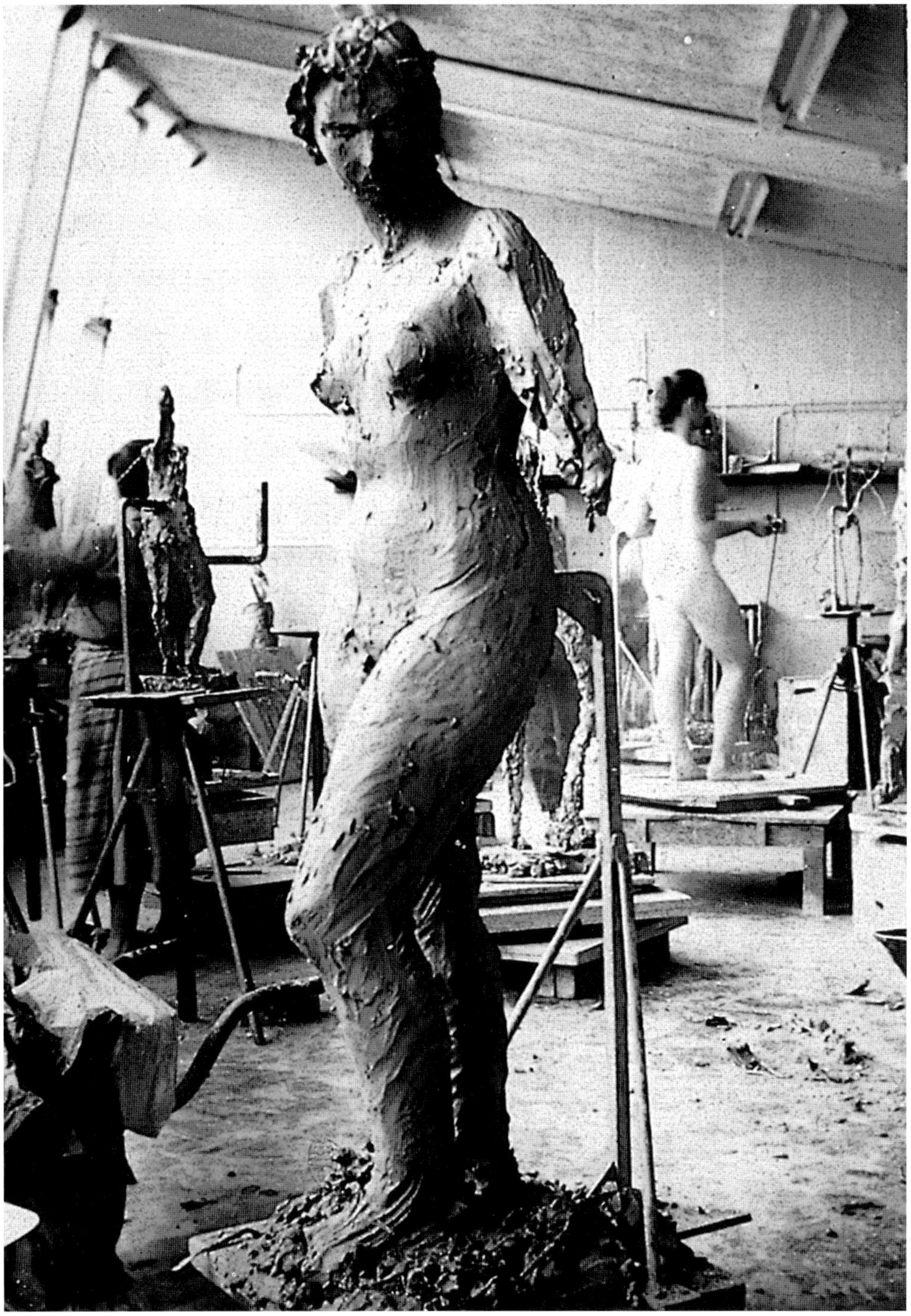

Science and Art Evening Class that provided tuition in joinery, carpentry and other building skills. By 1896, the Governors of the City Parochial Foundation transferred to the Vestry of Camberwell, the South London Art Gallery. The Library Commissioners proposed that a proportion of the building should be set aside for the formation of an art school.

That Camberwell School of Arts & Crafts also owes its existence to practising artists is no understatement. On Wednesday, 6th January 1898 the School was officially opened by Sir Edward Poynter, President of the Royal Academy. The movement for the foundation of an Arts Centre in South London had received the support of other artistic luminaries of the day, including Sir Edward Burne-Jones (1833-1898), Lord Leighton (1830-1896), Walter Crane (1845-1915) and George Frederick Watts (1817-

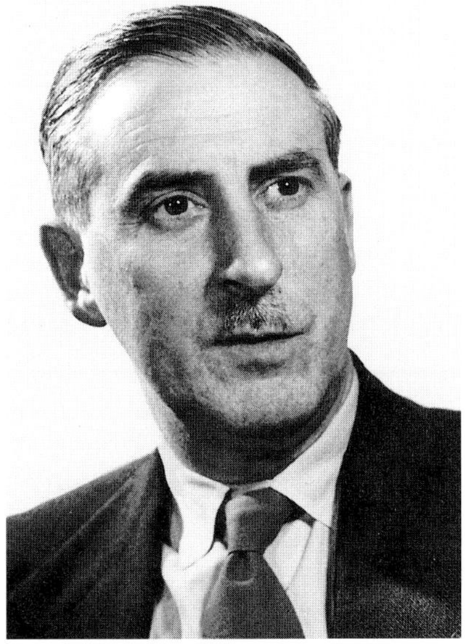

ALBERT HALLIWELL, c.1948.

1904). It was, however, due to the financial generosity of W. Passmore Edwards, whose gift of £5,000 in memory of the late Lord Leighton, finally gave birth to the Camberwell School of Arts & Crafts. The School's first Headmaster was Mr Cecil Laurence Burns (1863-1929), who stayed only a year and a half before being appointed Principal of Bombay School of Art. He was succeeded in September 1899 by Mr William B. Dalton (b.1868) who was a sculptor and ceramic decorator. He remained Principal until 1920, actively encouraging the Craft and Trades aspect of the curriculum.

Less than two hundred students enrolled for the first session but within three years this number had nearly doubled. By 1908 additional building was necessary to accommodate the increasing number of classes, which by then included a large Typography Department as well as, on the Crafts side, Building Trade Classes, Plumbing and Brickwork. By the end of 1913 the new extension had opened, which was primarily to contain the main Drawing and Painting rooms, the Pottery, Sculpture, Library, Wood & Metalwork shops and various specially equipped craft rooms. The School which, at its birth, possessed only eight workrooms, had now grown to thirty, therefore it was possible to add several subjects to the curriculum.

It was during this period that such students as Gerald Kelly, Gilbert Spencer, David Jones and Stanley Badmin passed through the School on their way to far greater horizons, Spencer, of course, returning several years later as a teacher. Stanley Thorogood (1873-1953) was appointed Principal in 1920, and it was he who had assisted in establishing, in that same year, the Junior Art School, providing not only an instruction in general education but also, from the age of thirteen, specialised art courses. The Junior Art School was to last for nearly forty years. Throughout its long productive life it successfully supplied the art world in its many areas with a steady stream of talented artists and craftspeople, richly imbued with the finest teaching the country had to offer. Sadly, in line with government policy, the Junior School closed in 1958.

A major force in contemporary British pottery also cut his teeth at Camberwell, namely William Staite Murray (1881-1962). Murray, born in Deptford, South London, enrolled as a student in 1909 and extended his interests from painting into ceramics. He worked with Bernard Leach (1887-1979) and Hamada and was later to become head of the Pottery School at the Royal College of Art.

During the next decade or so, very few practising artists were employed on the staff at Camberwell, S. W. Hayter (1901-1988), A. S. Hartrick (1864-1950), Walter Bayes (1869-1956), Randolph Schwabe (1885-1948), Vivian Pitchforth, Cosmo Clark (1897-1967), Eric Fraser (1902-1983) and McKnight-Kauffer (1890-1954) being the main exceptions. The only sculptor of any note to have taught at the School before the Second World War was Fred McWilliam (1909-1992).

In 1938, on the retirement of the Principal – Stanley Thorogood, who had held the post for eighteen years – William Johnstone was appointed. Johnstone, who had spent time during the 1920s studying in Paris under André L'Hôte (1885-1962), had observed that most teachers of art at the Atelier were indeed practising artists, and their abilities as teachers were of secondary importance. He noticed how their very presence excited and inspired the students. This was a lesson he never forgot and he vowed to himself that, if he ever held a position of responsibility in an art education establishment, he would employ similar methods. He had to wait some twenty years but, when his opportunity arose, he grabbed it without question. He set about changing and enhancing the staff at Camberwell by employing teachers only on their abilities as artists, irrespective of any teaching qualifications or experience that they may or may not have possessed.

In the years immediately before the Second World War, Camberwell had seen a

RICHARD KENDALL AND NORAH BRADON. Sketch of two comic figures, c.1950. Clay, 6½in high.
Courtesy of Rosamond Hayward.

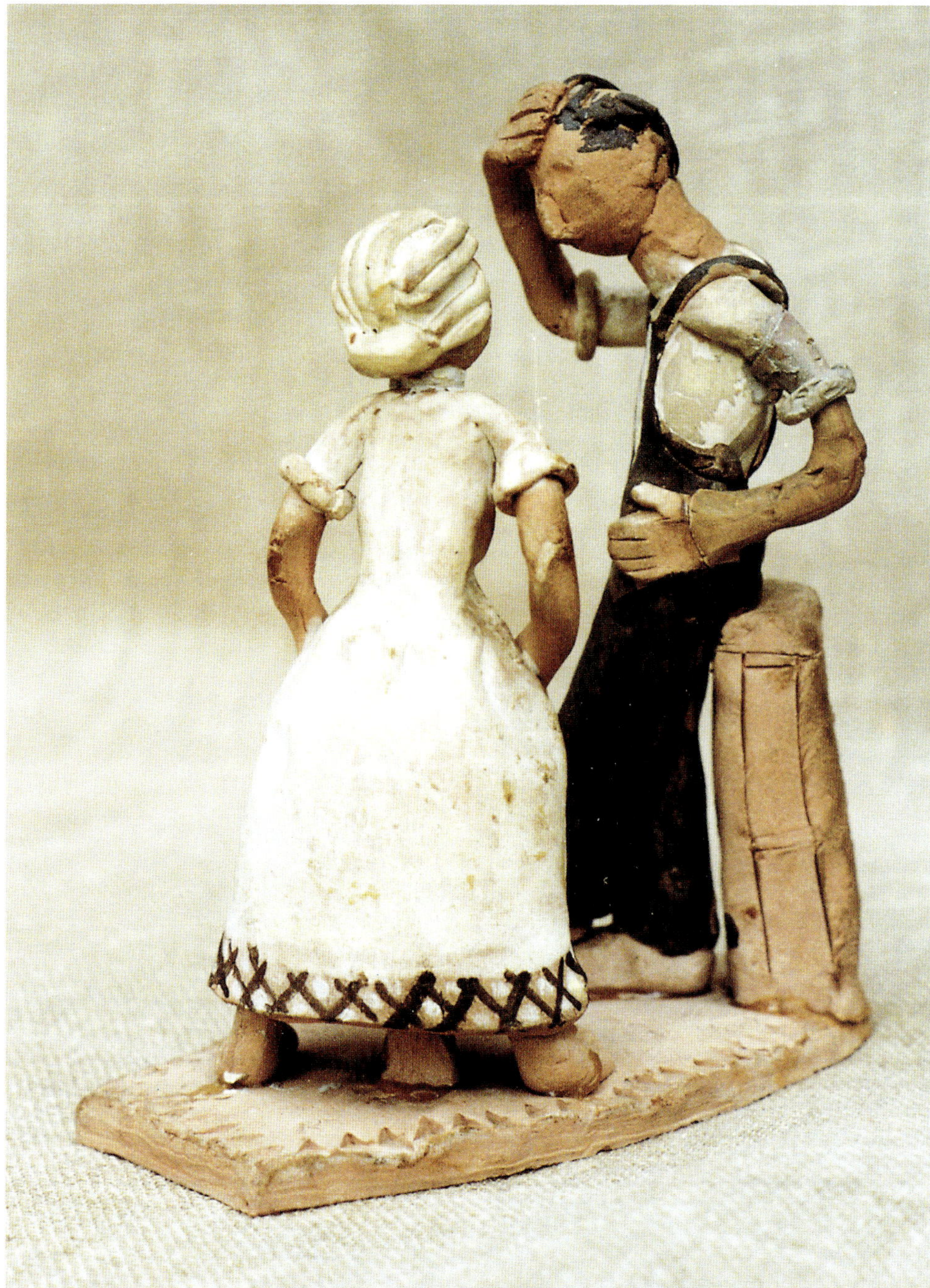

steady decline in its Building Trade Courses that had for so many years been a major part of its curriculum. Conversely, other courses, including Textiles, Printing, Bookbinding, Illustration, Design and Pottery, were beginning to expand. Camberwell therefore offered a great challenge to its new Principal, particularly as it possessed a somewhat unique, large and thriving Junior Arts School where he might be able to develop so many of his own ideas. Of great assistance to him in this were two of his early appointments: Albert Halliwell (later to become Vice-Principal) and Norman Dawson. Dawson had been appointed primarily because of his work with children and Halliwell because of interest in and development of his theories in Basic Design. These then far-sighted activities of Johnstone, including the teaching of film animation – not previously taught at an art school in England – made Camberwell known to an even wider circle of students. Student enrolments began steadily to increase.

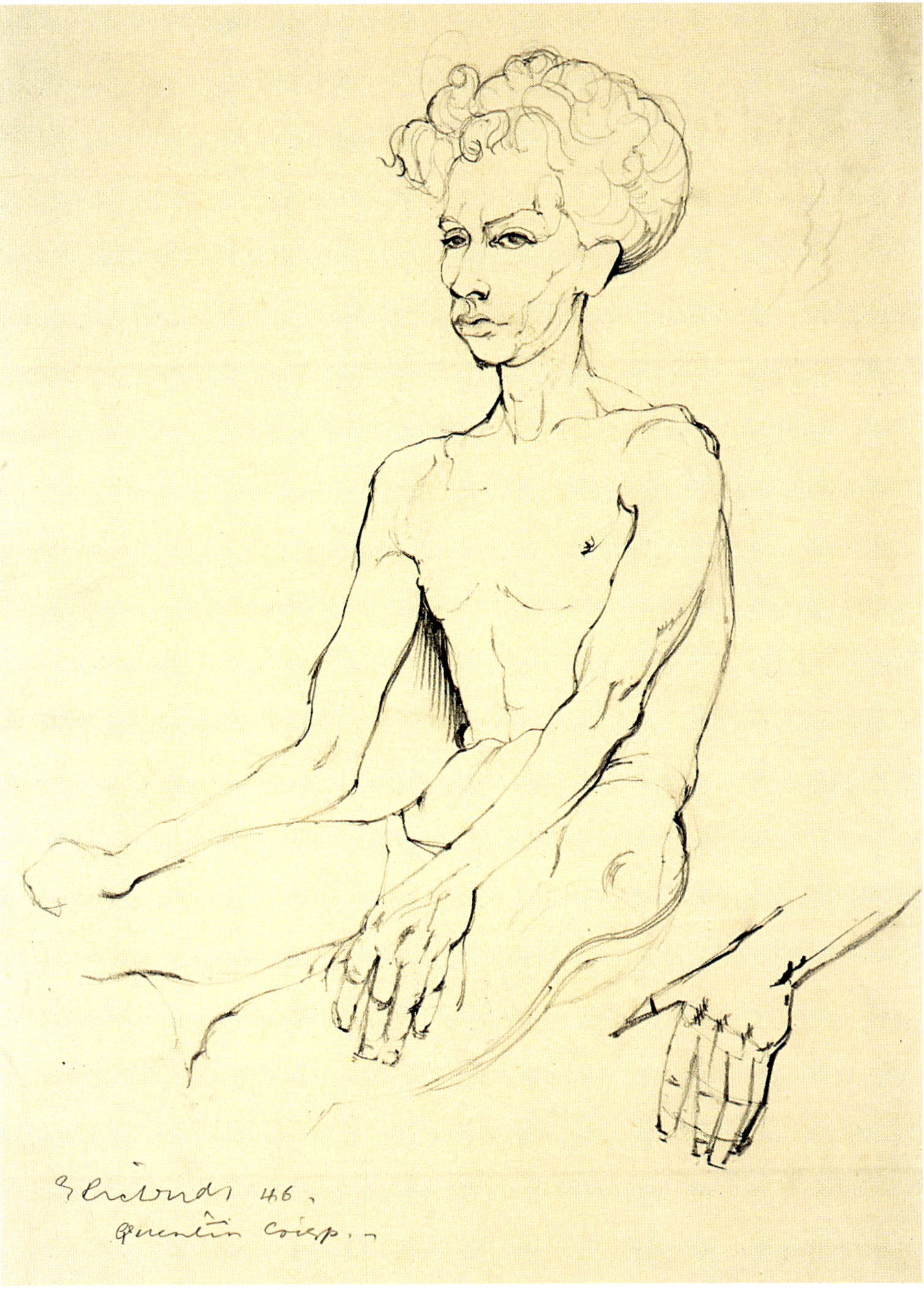

GORDON RICHARDS.
Quentin Crisp. Pencil, 15in x 11in. Artist's Collection.

At the outbreak of war in 1939, the School closed and the juniors were evacuated to Chipstead in Kent. In October of that year, as no bombing incidents had occurred, it was decided that the Typography Department and a few of the painting and drawing classes should be reopened at Camberwell. However, by the following August, as bombing raids began over London, it was agreed that the senior full-time students and the juniors already out of London should all be re-housed in Northampton. Here they joined up with similar evacuees from the Central School of Arts and Crafts and from Hammersmith School of Art. They were known collectively as the London Art School. The school was effectively closed apart from weekends, for the benefit of anyone wishing to relax from their war-time duties. Consequently, a few printing, drawing, painting and design classes, although frequently interrupted due to enemy action, continued until May 1941. Two near misses caused damage that took several weeks to repair, but by Easter 1942 a few full-time

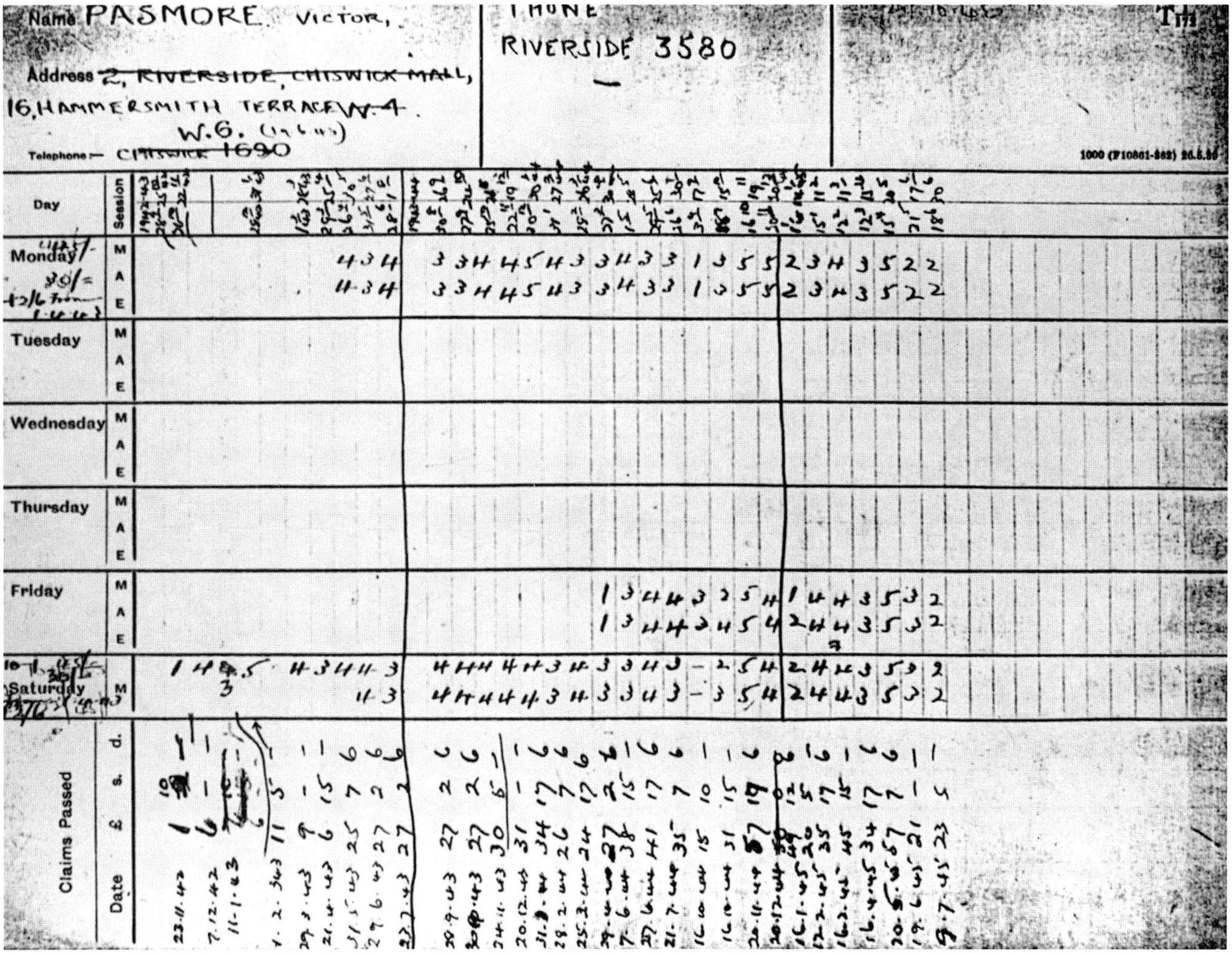
Name PASMORE. VICTOR,

Address ~~2, RIVERSIDE, CHISWICK MALL,~~
16, HAMMERSMITH TERRACE ~~W.4~~.
W.6.

Telephone:— ~~CHISWICK 1690~~

PHONE
RIVERSIDE 3580

Day | Session | Monday | Tuesday | Wednesday | Thursday | Friday | Saturday | M | A | E

Claims Passed | Date | £ | s. | d.

VICTOR PASMORE's record card, 1942-45.

students began to return from Northampton. Attendances began to increase, and it was not until 1944, when the flying bombs made their first appearance over London causing students to work in the cellars, that any further interruption occurred. During this period William Johnstone had gone some small way towards achieving his aims, having already on his staff artists of the calibre of Lawrence Gowing, Sam Carter, John Dodgson and Eric Fraser.

Towards the end of 1942, at the suggestion of Sir Kenneth Clark in his capacity as member of the Board of Governors of the school, Victor Pasmore was recommended for a teaching post in the Painting Department. Pasmore had spent 1941-42 in military service in Edinburgh and following his 'resignation' from the Army as a conscientious objector, had been arrested while on leave in London and subsequently jailed for six months. Although this newly appointed member of staff had received no formal art training William Johnstone, in his autobiography *Points in Time*, stated that Pasmore had "exquisite taste", and that "every bit of colour he put together was sensitive. If he could hand out a standard of taste he was bound to have a general effect for good in South-East London".

It is recorded in the Minutes of a meeting of the Joint Advisory Sub-Committee of the School in March 1943, that William Johnstone stated, "I am absolutely confident that should the Senior School be opened, I shall have no difficulty in obtaining students". The Minutes further record: "An added argument to the natural extension of Camberwell's work is the presence on the staff of such acknowledged experts as Mr Victor Pasmore and Mr Michael Ayrton, and it seems a pity that their services should not be more fully employed. In the opinion of Sir Kenneth Clark, Director of the National Gallery, Mr Pasmore is one of the six living painters who will have a

UNKNOWN CAMBERWELL STUDENT. *Four Teachers*, c.1948. Watercolour, 16in x 9½in.
The teachers are, clockwise from top: William Coldstream, Victor Pasmore, Claude Rogers and Lawrence Gowing.
Private collection.

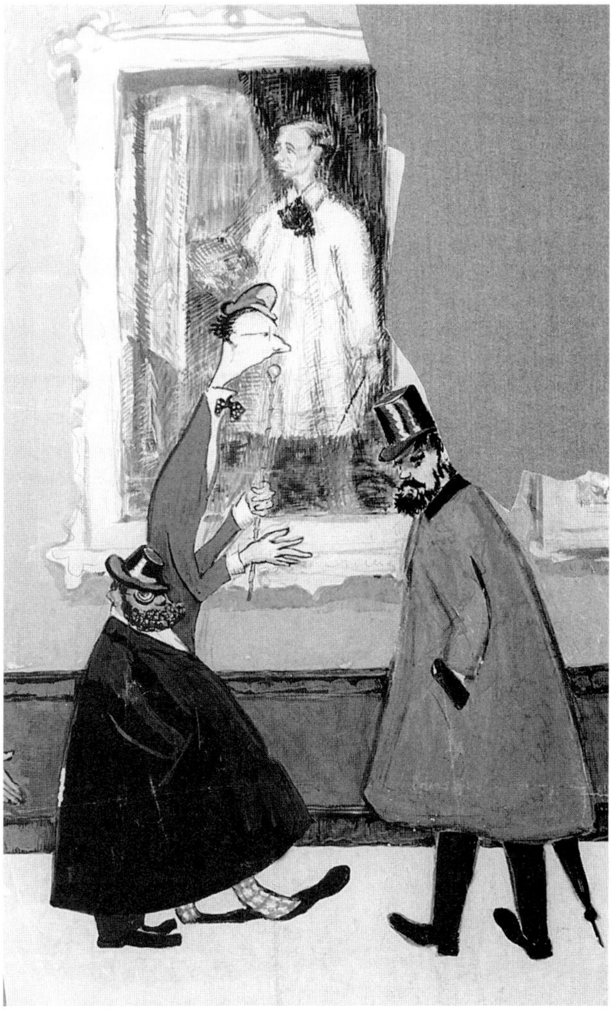

Unknown teacher and student, Camberwell Juniors, c.1946.

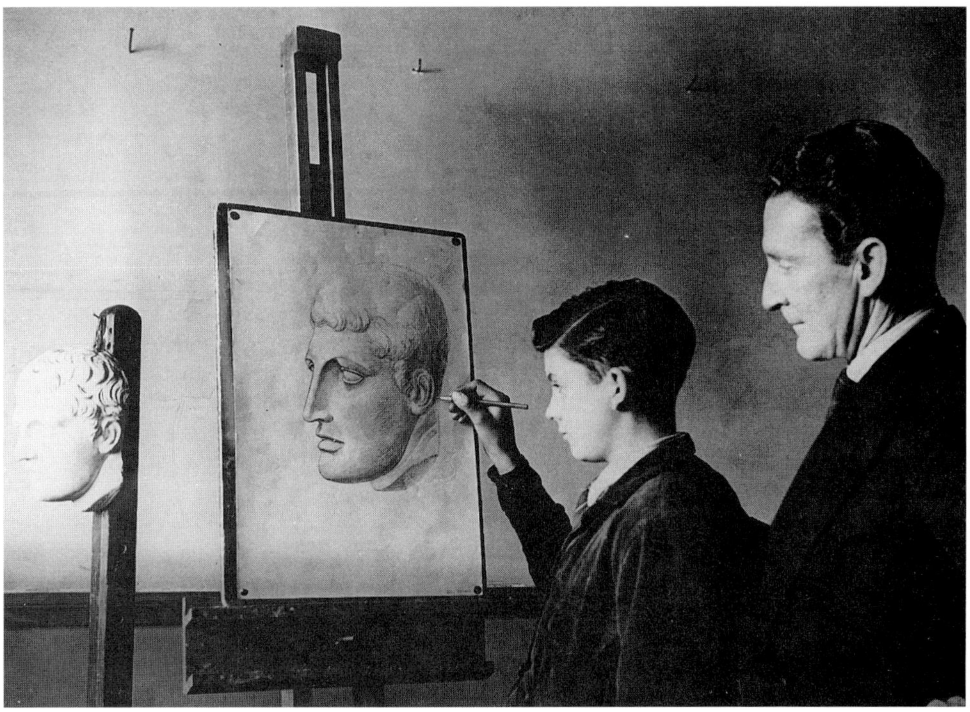

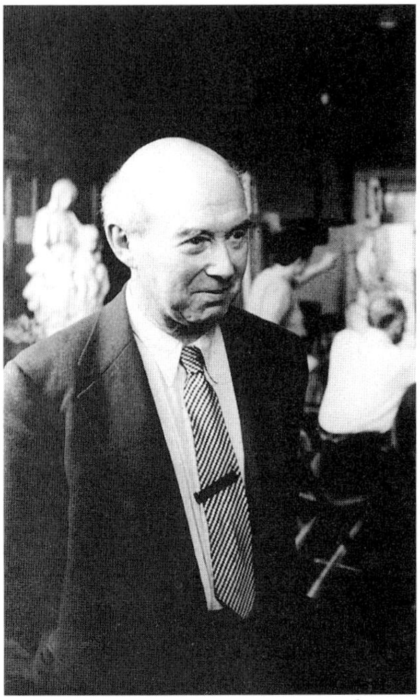

MARTIN BLOCH, Life Room at Camberwell, 1954.

marked influence on British Art. Mr Ayrton at twenty-two designed and carried out Mr John Gielgud's production of *Macbeth* at the Piccadilly Theatre recently and the designs and drawings for it have been purchased by the Victoria & Albert Museum." Johnstone, being a canny Scot, also realised that the war would eventually end and that all Pasmore's old pals from the Euston Road School and elsewhere would need jobs. One reason, that he never publicly admitted, for giving Pasmore a job was hopefully to entice other top-ranking artists to the School when they were free from active duty. This surely came to pass!

By the time the war had ended, the School had suffered considerable damage that took time to correct. The years 1945 and 1946 saw huge influxes of ex-service students who, with their grants, had decided to be teachers of art, commercial artists or follow some artistic career. It was at this point, as Bruce Laughton states in his book *The Euston Road School*, that the 'Reunification at Camberwell' began. Pasmore had advised Johnstone that two of his (Pasmore's) friends – Claude Rogers and William Coldstream – had been demobilised and were looking for a job. The fire began to rage, because of the established reputations of these artists, innumerable students and indeed other top-rate artists of the day were attracted to Camberwell. These members of the Euston Road Group, although only remaining at Camberwell for a relatively short period, had influenced their students to such a degree that the image of Euston Road painting was to remain long after the departure of Coldstream, Rogers, Pasmore *et al.* This, of course, is not to say that there were no other influential teachers at Camberwell during this period. John Minton – one of the bright young teachers of the day – joined the Camberwell staff in September 1943 and was to have a lasting effect on those students with whom he came into contact. He was generous not only in the way all teachers should be, giving of themselves, but in many other ways. Jazz was the music of the moment and he not only enjoyed listening and attending with his coterie of students, nicknamed 'Johnny's Circus', but he often gave money to students to help pay for their instruments. In other perhaps less financially significant but equally important acts did he show his readiness in giving. He would arrive at his classes laden with fruit and vegetables of the best quality (most food was still rationed) and after use by the students as still life compositions, he made sure that they had their share of the subject matter to take to their not so well-off homes to eat.

On speaking to many students and teachers, one gets the impression that the 'Euston-Roaders' always considered themselves artistically and intellectually a cut above designers, illustrators and printmakers. If this was so, then perhaps the students actually benefited from any division that may have been present, as the non-painters were not constrained by the bounds of artistic convention and so revealed to their charges a broader spectrum of expression.

The canny Scot, William Johnstone, found that his own managerial skills were not up to running a large number of staff and an even greater number of eager students. Due to government policy at the end of the war to give ex-servicemen grants – as much as £3-10-0d (£3.50) per week – normal student registration had trebled. Figures show that by the late 1940s over 1,600 full-time, part-time and junior students were on the register. The rooms available at the time were far too small to house the willing pupils and budding artists, regularly to be seen spilling into the corridors, especially when a good-looking female model was posing in the life class. William Coldstream and Johnstone never really saw eye to eye. Coldstream had already achieved a reputation as an artist and teacher through his much hailed Euston Road School and it has been suggested that Coldstream felt himself somewhat superior, both artistically and as an educator, to his Principal. It has also been suggested by many who were present at the time that Coldstream soon began

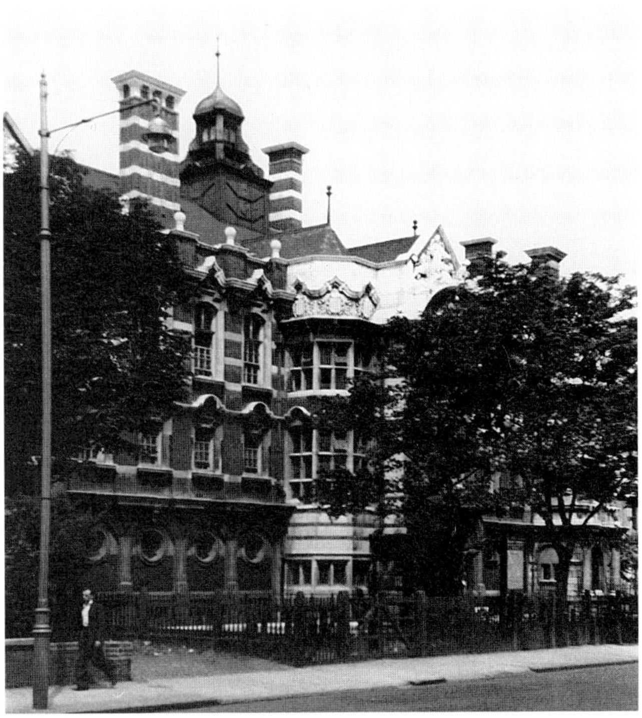

FRONT VIEW OF CAMBERWELL SCHOOL OF ART AND CRAFTS, 1952. Photo courtesy of A. Miller

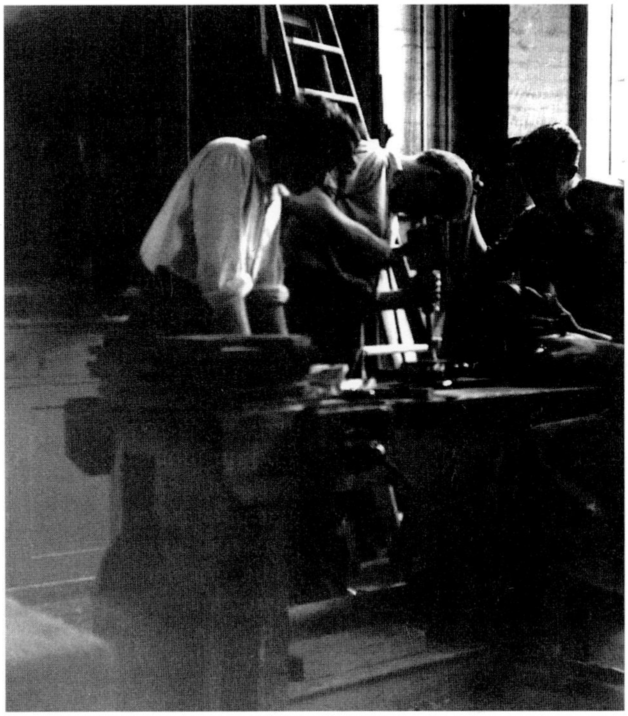

CABINET-MAKING WORKSHOP, c.1952.
Left to right: Paul Read, Maurice Irving, Roy Rayfield, Ray Little. Photo courtesy of A. Miller.

to act as though he was running Camberwell and not Johnstone. Many students would go to Coldstream with their personal problems and this rankled Johnstone. So the 'fighting' went on, and when the vacant position of Head of the Slade School of Fine Art arose, Coldstream was up and running. To make matters worse, some members of staff and some very good students were happy to follow their new-found mentor to greener pastures.

Johnstone's own departure to the Central School of Arts & Crafts was soon to follow, perhaps as a face-saving exercise. Following Johnstone's departure and Daniel's arrival, a brief interregnum occurred. During this period, George Richard Woolway (1879-1961) was called out of retirement and acted as Principal. An experienced artist and teacher, he had studied at the Royal College of Art 1899-1904. A friend of Philip Wilson Steer (1860-1942), he was supported by him in his application for the job of Principal of Clapham School of Art, which Woolway held in the early 1920s. About ten years later he was appointed Principal of St Martin's School of Art, a position he held until his retirement from teaching during the Second World War. In 1947 his successor – Leonard Daniels – was instrumental in the appointment of Martin Bloch. Bloch had studied in his native Germany under Lovis Corinth (1858-1925) in the early years of the century and had travelled throughout Europe, meeting and working with such people as Jules Pascin (1885-1930), Marie Laurencin (1883-1956), Robert (1885-1941) and Sonia Delauney (1885-1979), Karl Schmidt-Rottluf (1884-1976) and many others. He was thus able to bring to Camberwell a far broader outlook than many of his peers. Much loved by his students, his method of teaching and painting was often derided by some members of the staff. It has been suggested that perhaps he was ahead of his time. This aside, many students were devoted to him and his methods, and his masterful understanding of how colour and light affect atmosphere. Undoubtedly his success as a teacher was in no small way due to his persuasive persona. In his introductory speech at the opening of the Arts Council Touring Exhibition of 1958 at the South London Art Gallery, Leonard Daniels said: "Nobody could believe that he was anything but a serious artist." As soon as he was appointed to the staff he was to "add a touch of Franciscan gaiety to our supposedly Cistercian solemnity."

The year 1948 saw the Golden Jubilee of the School and, to mark the occasion, it was decided to produce a memento. The Typography Department, founded as long ago as 1905, was symptomatic of the school as a whole in its attitude towards the various parts of which it was composed. A large number of the students who attended its courses were apprentices working at the School during their employers' time. The School, equipped with the most modern letterpress machinery, had over the years achieved a reputation second to none in the British Isles and, arguably at that time, among the finest in the world. It was therefore fitting that they should produce *Jubilee*, a small succinct publication giving a brief history of the School in its first fifty years, with lithographic illustrations by Edward Ardizzone. Such first-hand experience for students of illustration, that is the technical side of book production, was of course to prove invaluable for them when they were to enter the commercial world. The School also ran courses on book-binding, printing techniques and layouts for the budding commercial book designer. Yet ironically, it was not until 1953 that the School was to have a dedicated Graphic Art course.

By the very early 1950s most of the Euston Road entourage had deserted the environs of Camberwell for (so they thought) brighter lights, but those few important years had left their indelible influence on many young students, some of whom themselves had joined the staff at the School. It was not until the appointment in 1958 of Robert Medley as Head of Painting that these influences began to wane. Medley who, in his days as a student at the Slade, had found the teaching methods and style of painting there not to his liking, had hardly changed his opinions over the subsequent thirty-five years. He clearly states in his autobiography *Drawn from the Life*: "By the end of the first year I had come to the conclusion that the teaching of painting in the school needed the added dimension of a tougher perceptual and intellectual discipline. The painting of sensitive pictures in an acceptable Sickert-Euston Road style that had become the norm at the School was all very well, but it left too much out of account, too many possibilities unexplored." He soon went some way towards exploring these possibilities by the appointment to the staff of the Anglo-American painter, Charles Howard. Medley had known Howard through brief meetings at Roland Penrose's Surrealist gatherings in 1936, the year of the first Surrealist Exhibition in England. On the same wavelength, they soon set about revising the students' curriculum: "The course we devised was made compulsory for all students who came to the first classes, a series of systematic colour exercises concentrating on the range of greys between black and white..."

Perhaps, however, the final nail in the coffin of the previous regime came with the appointment, albeit on a part-time basis, of Frank Auerbach. Again Medley states in his autobiography: "The other thing I felt was needed was to offer some real alternative to the Coldstream manner of drawing, which had become something of a formula at the school. Frank Auerbach, visiting once a week became the strongest antidote possible. The studio soon became deep in charcoal, heavily worked paper, and paint scrapings."

Auerbach's near obsession with agglomeration, rather than with form and shape, perhaps ended a period in the teaching of art that arguably has not been rivalled in post-war years. I have attempted to give as brief a background as possible to the period in time that this Dictionary covers. During my research I amassed a large amount of anecdotes from teachers and students and, with as little editing as possible, I reproduce a selection, hoping to convey the feeling of those post-war years when, as William Johnstone in his autobiography states: "Modern ideas spread round London like setting fire to dry hay, and everybody heard about

Camberwell. People forgot about the Royal College of Art, the Slade or the Central School of Arts & Crafts, they were completely 'out'".

Course Requirements

In the post-war years, anyone entering the School was expected to have passed the School Certificate Examination, preferably with Art as one of the subjects. In practice, however, there was a great deal of flexibility and latitude. The age range of students was considerable, as ex-service people in their mid- to late-twenties mixed in the same classes with fifteen and sixteen year olds. To achieve the National Diploma in Design (N.D.D.), a student had to complete a preliminary two year Intermediate Course of general studies. This included an extremely wide-ranging curriculum composed of Life Drawing, History of Art, Painting, Anatomy, Architecture, Fashion Design, Lettering and a craft – Pottery, Weaving or something similar. This was followed by a further two years in one or two specialised subjects. Students could, if they wished, take Intermediate in one school and move to another for the N.D.D., so not all the Camberwell students had been together for the full four years. Life Drawing and History of Art were an integral part of all courses, the latter included museum visits. Some of the more unusual visits in the case of the potters and ceramicists included trips to the South Eastern Gas Board in the Old Kent Road. Here students could observe various kilns. The Authority supplied not only industrial and studio kilns but also crematoria! Also nearby was the Pickford Furniture Repository at the Elephant and Castle, where many of the vehicles were still horse-drawn, thus affording the students a perfect opportunity to draw these wonderful beasts of burden. Few who know this area today would imagine that only forty years ago such activities, as well as a fully operational Blacksmiths' Forge just off Deptford High Street, were part of the everyday life of the post-war metropolis.

Ceramics

A largely unsung aspect of Camberwellian day to day life was its Pottery Department. Richard Kendall, who was the son-in-law of Bernard Leach, joined the staff at Camberwell in 1946. He was soon appointed Head of Department and his tremendous enthusiasm, sense of humour and skill spurred his students to great things. Arguably his greatest contribution was his ability to gather a team of singular talents to work with him, Lucie Rie and Hans Coper being the most famous. He had, however, already inherited such fine technicians as 'Jock' Purdie, Honora French and Norah Bradon. Purdie, a potter who is probably only now remembered by the people who knew him at the School, came to Camberwell after the war as a mature student. Probably already over forty years of age, he had worked for the G.P.O. before the war and had served in the Navy during the hostilities. A gifted student, he was experimenting with thin-cast bone china and porcelain years before it became fashionable to do so. So uninhibited was his work that, as a result of an enormous piece of terracotta tile executed for his N.D.D. examination, the authorities saw fit subsequently to lay down a maximum size for work submitted. Purdie undoubtedly had a considerably unacknowledged influence on the next generation of ceramic students at Camberwell. He was to turn down the opportunity of a full-time teaching post at the School, preferring to run the L.C.C. Schools' Pottery Firing Centre at Stockwell. He did, however, teach evening classes at Camberwell and would often be seen padding down the road at dusk, carrying a large carpet bag, having already had his tea at Lyons Café at Camberwell Green. He cut an impressive figure, tall, bearded, wearing a rather loud check jacket, flannel trousers and, irrespective of the climate, sandals and no socks. He was known to have terrified sedate ladies in his evening classes with a kindly-meant curse, which always sounded far worse in his broad Glaswegian accent. In 1959, he suddenly gave up all connections with London and retired to the Isle of Arran. His premature departure was arguably a great loss to British studio pottery. Try as I might, I have been unable to trace his present whereabouts assuming, that is, that he is still alive. I hope that, should this book reach a second edition, information will have come to light on one of Camberwell's greatest missing characters.

Honora French (Frenchie), was a Camberwell institution in her own right. She reigned as 'queen of the kiln room' for many years, always turning up dressed like a bird of paradise and never admitting to be being over fifty years of age. She is believed, as a young woman, to have worked for Charles Vyse and, through him, met George Eumorfopoulos. Much feared by the students, she had the power of life and death in the kiln room, by deciding which pots should be fired first. In her spare time, when not packing the kiln, she produced a stream of distinctive pots, some not without merit. She spent most of her earnings purchasing antique pots from the numberous shops then to be found in the Peckham area. She often said that her fine collection would eventually be donated to the School after her death. Unfortunately, she had a very generous nature under her fierce exterior and would tend, in moments of weakness, to give away many of her finest treasures. I believe that she lasted well into her nineties and died, unfortunately, in an alms house, where she spent her last few years. What became of her treasures is open to conjecture.

Bookbinding

The School ran courses in Bookbinding from before the outbreak of the First World War, the classes always being under the auspices of the Printing Department. Like the majority of trade and craft subjects taught at the School, it was attended by part-time students often in their own time after working hours. Members of staff had included George Sutcliffe, colleague and partner of the world-renowned bookbinder and designer, Francis Sangorski. Printing and Bookbinding at Camberwell therefore had a deserved reputation among its peers as well as arguably the added advantage of close association with a thriving art school. Other staff members of note included Alex J. Vaughan and his successor, John Corderoy. Corderoy had been a prize winner (1933-34) of the respected City & Guilds Technical Examination and was largely responsible for the post-war development of Printing and Bookbinding at Camberwell. Although remembered and highly regarded by his former students, I have unfortunately been unable to trace any close family or friends who might have supplied a detailed curriculum vitae of this fine bookbinder and teacher. It appears he died of cancer during the early 1970s, shortly after the commencement of the Paper Conservation course. I was, however, fortunate in making contact with two well-known bookbinders, Brian Hoy and American-born, Camberwell-trained Sally Lou Smith. Hoy joined the Printing department in the late 1950s as a full-time lecturer under James Wright, the departmental head. At this time Philip Hiseman was his second in command and John Corderoy was the teacher in charge of the bookbinding section. The printing department was housed in the building next to the Art Gallery and dealt with day release apprentices from the local printing industry, who followed a course leading to the City & Guilds of London Institute Certificate.

There was also a full-time course of three years duration for home and overseas students studying printing management. When the London School of Printing moved from Stamford Street to its present site at the Elephant & Castle, many London printing firms sent their apprentices to the new school and Camberwell lost out. Because of the uncertainty of falling numbers, the bookbinding section gave a lot of thought to starting a full-time course in 'Conservation of Paper Objects': books, archive documents, maps, prints and drawings, hopefully leading to employment in record offices, museums, archive departments and private collections in this country and abroad. Fortunately, the department had attained a reputation of such renown that when the Florence flood disaster occurred in 1966, it was able to supply expertise and assistance of the highest level. This natural calamity and misfortune strengthened the School's claim for a full-time course in paper conservation. Camberwell was eventually given permission to start a two year full-time course in 'Archive Preservation & Repair' with twelve students in September 1971. Today, the course is undoubtedly Europe's finest and ranks amongst the highest anywhere in the world.

The bookbinding section only occasionally accommodated a few full-time students, Sally Lou Smith being one of them. She arrived in London in late 1957 and, having heard of the bookbinding course, made her way to Camberwell. Interviewed by John Corderoy, she was surprised and pleased to be able to commence classes almost immediately at the beginning of 1958. The only full-time student, her part-time colleagues included Stefani (*sic*) Delbanco, wife of Gustav Delbanco, the well-known collector and partner in the Cork Street fine art gallery, Roland, Browse and Delbanco. Sally Lou Smith recalls Corderoy as being a kind and generous teacher who achieved much in his time, particularly by his design of the 'Camberwell' typeface, still very popular and used by bookbinders and many craftspeople making tooled letters today.

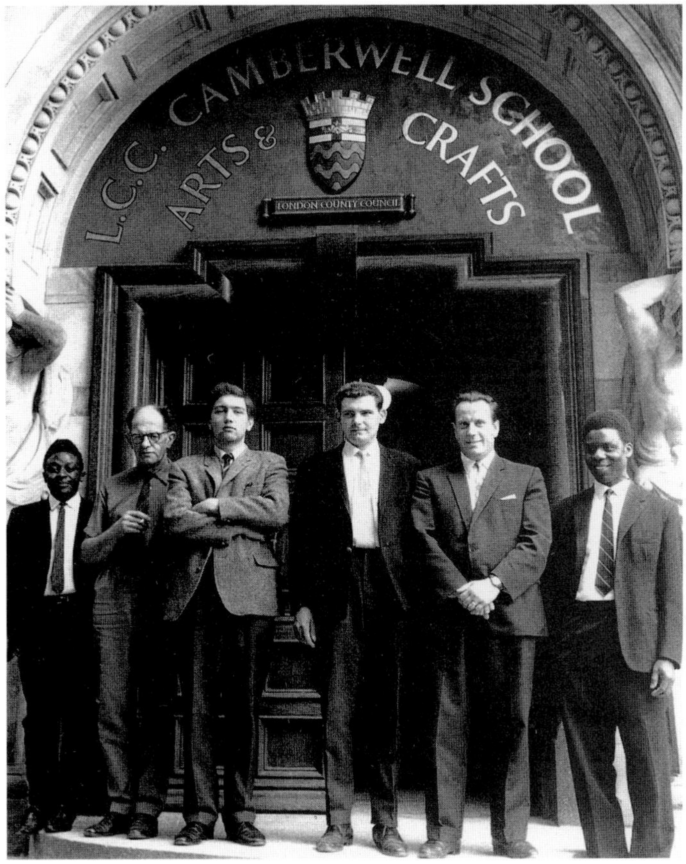

GROUP OF TEACHERS AND STUDENTS FROM PRINTING/BOOKBINDING DEPARTMENT c.1960.
2nd left John Corderoy, 4th left David Collins, 5th left Brian Hoy.
Photo courtesy Brian Hoy

Examination

The N.D.D. examination had two requirements. The first was a written and illustrated dissertation of about 2,500 words on some aspect of the candidates' main subject in which they held a particular interest. The second requirement was a timed paper that varied from course to course but which in the main asked the student to select three items from a choice of specified briefs to be executed over a given period, anything between one and three weeks. Once completed, the executed works and written papers were removed to such places as County Hall in the case of Fine Arts, and to the Royal College for the Ceramicists/Potters for marking. The logistics involved must have been tremendous as examiners, in those days, did not just visit the School to view the body of work that the students and staff these days display with such panache in today's art colleges. This archaic practice continued until the advent of the Diploma in Art and Design (Dip.A.D.), which was not introduced until the 1960s.

Lodgings

During many conversations with Camberwell teachers and students, the words 'Lower Marsh' arose on several occasions. Thanks are due to Christopher Pinsent who kindly supplied me with the following memoir concerning 22a Lower Marsh and information concerning the activities of Maurice Feild.

22a Lower Marsh is the living accommodation above corner shop premises in the market street on the south-eastern side of Waterloo Station. Part of an early Victorian terrace, the house was reconstructed in a discreet modern manner in the 1930s for a doctor who used the shop as a G.P.'s surgery. During the war a bomb destroyed the buildings opposite, leaving 22 in view of the approach ramp to Waterloo Station.

Patrick George, Andrew Forge and Christopher Pinsent, painting students at Camberwell, moved here in 1947 after Pinsent's father had negotiated the lease. In spite of this, they found themselves obliged to share the house with a friend of the landlord's, the philosopher Oswald Wauchope, his wife Jean and two small children, while Wauchope was completing a book for Faber & Faber. Wauchope's philosophy, put briefly, was something like 'take no thought for the morrow' or 'consider the lilies...', and that most of us ossify ourselves through preoccupations with how to avoid death. 'Death Avoidance' was thus presented as the cardinal deleterious disposition. He and Forge held long discussions, Forge at the time being preoccupied with the teachings of Martin Buber as set out in the book *I and Thou*. Wauchope would cheerfully relate his life history in illustration of his tenets. He had, for instance, set up a Preparatory School by popular demand of parents who admired his ability as a teacher. Since, however, like Ginger and Pickle in Beatrix Potter's shop, he never sent out bills, the enterprise had to close down. Having finished his book, he got a job as a labourer at the V. & A., who were so impressed by his ability that he was made Head of the Circulation Department. When 'Oz' left Lower Marsh, Forge still kept in touch on visits to the V. & A. to borrow slides for Evening Institute lecturing. It is said that during the war at a certain 'progressive' London School, the lady teachers kept sailors in the attic. These three Camberwell students, however, during their first year at Lower Marsh, harboured instead a special unofficial tutor. Some years after, 'Oz' returned from Kenya bringing them presents of sacks of sugar and coffee beans.

When the Wauchopes left, their children's little room was taken by a student of Anglo-Saxon literature, June Hodge. In 1948 she was succeeded severally by the painting students Anthony Eyton, Jo Higson and Anthony Fry, so that the premises were then occupied entirely by Camberwell students. Visitors included old friends of George's from Edinburgh Art School who had studied with him under Gillies. Among them were Craigie Aitchison, Jeffrey Camp and Robert Wragg of Belper, Derbyshire, who, befriended by Alfred Munnings, had already launched into a career as a country painter suggestive of that of George Morland. Wragg, it is believed, became Head of a Cornish art school before his early and tragic death.

Views from the upper floor, and of local street corners, became the chief motifs of George's work at the time. The other painters were in general less committed to such subjects and worked from portrait models, still-life, on copies of old masters and from drawings. There was a regular practice of grinding pigments in oil on marble wash-stands and keeping them in screw-cap jars topped up with water. The shop itself, its window area much reduced by corrugated iron shuttering, looked most like a studio but was least satisfactory owing to the distracting noises of the street. Beneath this was a large, windowless, concrete chamber that proved to be good for parties. Many other Camberwell students and some of the painting staff came on occasion. The poet, W. H. Auden, who had once taught George, Pinsent and Forge English at the Downs Preparatory School, and was an old friend of Maurice Feild and of Coldstream, came to lunch. Auden subsequently bought a painting by Andrew Forge.

By the end of the 1940s the three original residents had left Camberwell. Forge left to be married, Pinsent retained only his bed while teaching in the country and only

George stayed on whilst teaching at the Slade. Higson had left to teach in Leeds but Eyton and Fry continued to work there on *magnum opus* submissions for the Rome Scholarship. The shop premises were taken by the then Slade and ex-Camberwell student Robin Goldsbrough and subsequently by a medical student, Nicholas Brown. The Camberwell students Francis Hoyland, Tom Espley and David Hume also worked or lived here briefly at this time, together with an Arabic scholar, Patrick 'Oscar' Lewis. George became effectively resident administrator and during the first year of his marriage occupied more of the house. When he and his family moved out, Craigie Aitchison and Miles Murphy used the upper rooms in which to paint. It was in one of these rooms that Murphy was severely burnt when, in the absence of his model, he put on the wedding dress used for the bridal subject of his Rome Scholarship submission, and stepped back into the gas fire. Aitchison rushed to his assistance and flung pieces of flaming dress out of the window into the crowded market street. The premises were soon filled with ambulancemen, firemen and police and Murphy was taken to hospital. Not long after this incident, in about 1955, the lease ended, and with it the Camberwell connection.

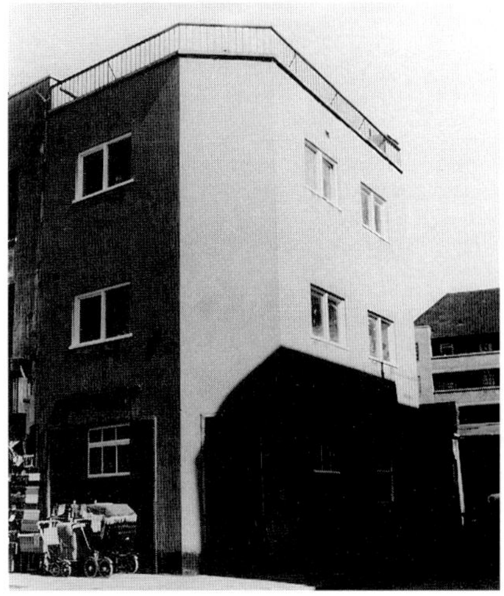

'LOWER MARSH', *the house of Christopher Pinsent, shared by his Camberwell colleagues.* Photograph courtesy of Tom Epsley.

A second property, 51 Wilson Road, barely two hundred yards from the School, was also occupied by many Camberwell students. Thanks are due to the late Patrick Symons for his assistance with recollections of the Camberwell connection. The house, an end of terrace near to Wilsons Grammar School and backing on to St Giles' Churchyard, was bought by Anthony Fry in the late 1940s. For the first eighteen years Symons lived on the top floor, where he was able to put in a studio window facing the churchyard when war damage was repaired.

The Frys moved mostly to Box, as Anthony was teaching at Corsham soon after leaving Camberwell. The rooms downstairs were variously occupied at different times by Francis Hoyland, Tom Espley, Pamela Haddon, Hilda Briddon, Christopher Chamberlain and Anthony Eyton. Eyton and Symons painted reciprocal portraits on the first floor of the house during the late 1950s. Countless other people visited and no doubt from time to time painted there. There are paintings behind the first floor shutters by Francis Hoyland and Tom Espley and a small painted frieze by Hoyland above the double doors. In those days milk was delivered by horse and there were horse-drawn rag-and-bone men and a real muffin man with a bell, carrying on his head a tray of muffins.

The name of Maurice Feild (1905-1988) occurs several times in the text and an explanation of his Camberwell connections are, I feel, relevant. He studied drawing and painting under Francis Stanislaus Robinson (b.1885) and Albert W. M. Rissik, later attending the Slade School, studying under Professor Henry Tonks (1862-1937) from 1924-26. It was here that he first met William Coldstream, also a student during the same period. He went into teaching at the age of twenty-three, joining the staff of the Downs School, Colwall, under Geoffrey Hoyland. In 1937 he organised an exhibition of the work of some of his pupils at the Redfern Gallery, and during vacations showed his own paintings with the Euston Road Group and the London Group. In 1948 he held a one-man exhibition at the City Art Gallery, Worcester and six years later was invited by his friend, William Coldstream, to join the staff of the Slade School of Art. Feild was never directly attached to Camberwell but from about 1943 to the present, pupils of his have either been teachers or students at the School. At the Downs Preparatory School he introduced his pupils to drawing from nature and to a professional technique in oil painting. At the same time, he embraced the differently orientated philosophy of the Society for Education in Art and was associated with Nan Youngman (b.1906) and the writer Herbert Read in the encouragement of young children's imaginative expression in art. In 1932 the poet W. H. Auden joined the staff at the Downs School and the two became devoted friends. Auden left in 1935 to work on documentary films under John Grierson and in doing so re-encountered his old acquaintance, the ex-Slade student William Coldstream. Auden returned briefly to the Downs and in 1937 Coldstream visited the School to paint his portrait (which is now in the collection of the University of Texas). The Euston Road School had opened in October, so that Feild was acquainted with it from the beginning, and he encouraged those of his ex-pupils with an evident commitment to painting, to pursue their apprenticeship at Euston Road.

The Downian Lawrence Gowing thus got to Euston Road, but in 1940 war interrupted this sequence. In the event, many of Feild's ex-pupils sought the teaching of Coldstream, Pasmore and Rogers as re-established at Camberwell in 1945, with Gowing already on the staff, having arrived during 1943. Ex-Downs' pupils who followed this migration as students were Patrick George, Andrew Forge, Christopher Pinsent, Anthony Fry, Francis Hoyland, Tom Espley, David Hume and Robin Goldsbrough.

One of Feild's special qualities was his sense of the independent nature of artistic making – whether pictorial, musical or literary. He thus inspired his pupils with this by the example of such painters as Whistler, Pissarro and Sickert, and he liked to read aloud to them from W. H. Davies's *Autobiography of a Supertramp.* He had an eye for distinguishing between ponderously half-baked intentions and truly-fledged lyricism, and he always anxiously applied this test to his own gracefully professional paintings. During most of his time at the Downs, Feild organised a painting week there for ex-pupils in the Easter holidays. In the late 1940s some of these returned from Camberwell, occasionally bringing colleagues who were not old Downians. Many more ex-Camberwell students came to know him when he subsequently taught at the Slade and St. Albans Schools of Art.

Some time after beginning this project, the name of Quentin Crisp appeared in several conversations with various students and teachers. Unknown then to most people outside the art circle, Quentin Crisp was a well-known life model during the post-war years. I set out to find him and hopefully persuade him to write a memoir from a model's point of view. His words, unedited, follow:

A Model's Eye View

As with every other job that I have ever done, I became an Art School Model by chance – almost by default. A friend of mine who was in this line of work couldn't fulfil an engagement at Toynbee Hall and implored me to go there in her stead. I went, thinking that if I didn't faint, this could become a whole new way of life. I remained more or less conscious and stayed in the business on and off for thirty-five years. It turned out to be what I was born to do. As an unkind acquaintance once said to me, "I suppose it's easier for you to pose than not". What every model needs are two apparently contradictory attributes – abject humility because, while at work, he is really only a thing, and unshakeable self-assurance without which he could never survive the contempt in which he is held by the students.

During my life as a model, I went to innumerable colleges, polytechnics and private studios thrown open to small huddles of housewives whom the washing machine had liberated from the gardens of domestic bliss, so that they might traverse the deserts of culture. I knew the set-up because in my youth, I had been an art student. That happened so long ago that I can remember my work being solemnly scrutinised by the Principal to see if I was worthy of a place in the Life Room. Once there, I became mad about drawing from the nude, but disappointed by the models. They were naked and they kept still, but they had obviously adopted a minimum risk policy; they were not like the work of Mr Buonarotti. Much

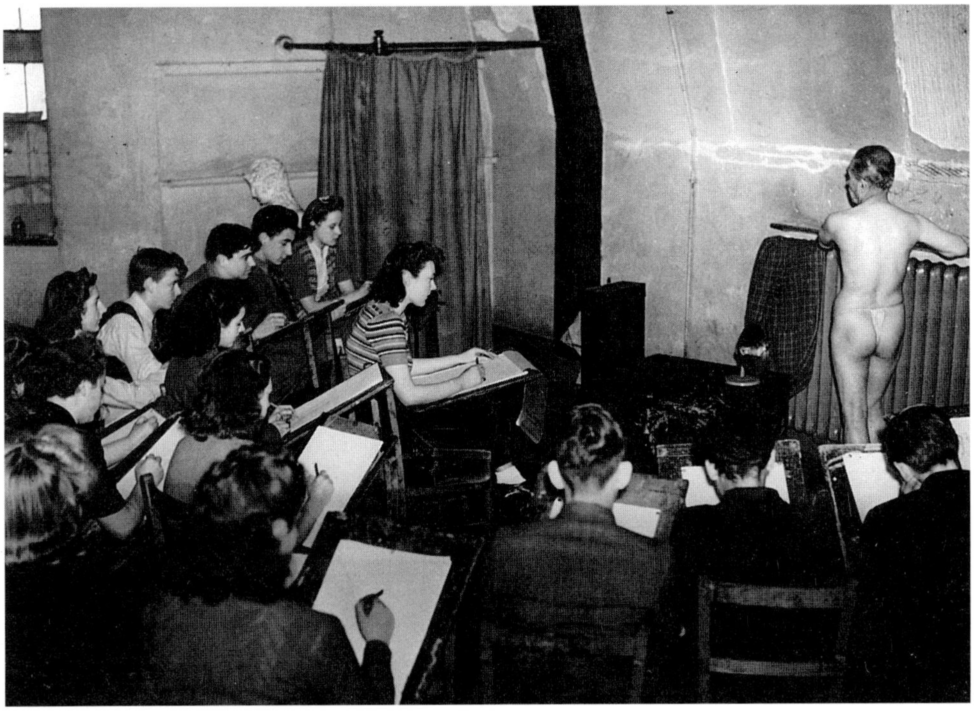

UNKNOWN LIFE CLASS, c.1946.

later, when I myself became more painted against than painting, I decided to be as Sistine as hell. I climbed up the walls; I rolled on the floor; I hung from beams; I held chairs over my head. The students were furious. Gradually I became aware that I was not posing for the pupils; I was working for the teachers.

Teenagers do not enter Art Schools running forward with little cries of ecstasy and arms outstretched toward art. They go in backwards – creeping away from real life. When some heavily mortgaged parent says to his daughter "...and you, Jennifer, what are you going to do when you leave school?" a cold wind blows through the room. For one terrible moment the girl envisages the horrors of adulthood. Then she says "I'll do art", and the dreaded day of reckoning is deferred for four irresponsible years. During that time, she sits in the canteen, dreaming, necking, playing her guitar and, as a last resort, occasionally attending a class. Then her Hungarian blouse wears out and she becomes a typist.

If taken seriously, the Life Room was always the home of the brave. During my years as a model, students became increasingly rebellious at being told to draw from the nude; it was difficult and there was no money in it. The word was out that art had gone abstract. To students this meant that it had become easy and it could make them rich. As they became more and more unruly, calling the Masters by their first names, ignoring their instructions and fighting in the Life Room until the easels fell on the floor, the teachers grew increasingly indifferent. At Goldsmiths' College a certain Mr McCullough used to make his first appearance of the day by putting his head round the Life Room door at half past three, and saying "T'kettle's on". Members of my profession preferred one school to another for the oddest reasons. In the bleak corridors of St Martin's School of Art, I passed a model who greeted me with the words "Isn't it awful?" "Isn't what awful?" I asked, assuming that the Principal had been stabbed or our wages had been cut. "It's so commercial", she replied. She evidently felt exiled from the *vie de Bohème*. To me, a good school was simply a warm school, preferably near home, but in fact, I worked mostly in suburban colleges or ones in the home counties – Watford, Willesden, Walthamstow and even Southend (self-immolation could go no further) because these were the assignments that other models would not accept.

A Camberwell Beauty* is a term only known to lepidopterists but I did occasionally go there. It was neither a suburban school nor was it in the heart of London – if such a place exists; it was lower in the hierarchy than the Royal College, but higher than some others. It had its own aura that I judged to be 'Arty' without being precious.

The front office was manned by the vilest people on earth. When I first went there, I was in lieu of another model. This did not daunt me particularly because models substitute for one another as often as orchestral musicians. To my consternation, I was rebuked – nay, reviled though, obviously, if blame was to be laid, it should have been heaped upon the head of the young man who sent me. When I offered to leave, I was grudgingly asked to stay and found myself in the presence of a Mr Gowing. I was later told that he was a famous artist who painted everything green. I took this information calmly, but a lot of models are keen to work for well-known painters; they seem to think that a little greatness may be reflected on to them. My indifference was due mostly to my natural detachment but also to my ignorance of art. When people ask me "What have you got against paintings?" I can only reply "What have you got against the wall?" The only well-known painter that I recognised immediately he entered the class in Camberwell was Mr Minton and that was because, when not at work, he used to spend his time in The Wheatsheaf – one of the more disreputable public houses in Fitzrovia.

When I was first a model, total anonymity was deliberately preserved. I was called 'Model' and addressed the teachers as 'Sir'. Like Miss Marsh in *Upstairs, Downstairs*, I knew my place and it saved me the bother of having to learn all their names. It is quite possible that I have stood naked in the presence of a succession of geniuses; they were almost all uniformly courteous but their methods of working varied considerably. Some teachers, arriving in the Life Room would say "Stay just as you are. That's it for the day, everybody." Others, handling my limbs with the least possible carnality, would rearrange them in accordance with some secret theory of aesthetics. The most difficult Master for whom I ever worked was a Mr Rogers. When I flung an arm into the air, he reeled backward, crying, "What on earth are you doing now?" He didn't approve of posing and wanted me to look like an ordinary mortal. I would not have found this easy in real life; when L.C.C. naked in the presence of my enemies and with nothing to reassure me but a board floor and a kitchen chair, I was completely at a loss. Mr Rogers was obviously working on the principle that his students were all talented or, at the very least, serious and that, therefore, to them everything in the world was of visual interest. I suspected that the class was made up entirely of incipient hooligans and that the model's function was to set before their sleepy eyes a series of anatomical riddles in the hope of forcing them, if not to understand, to look.

At the end of my career as an art school model, I returned to Camberwell and worked for a diminutive and charming young woman, whose name I can no longer remember. By that time permissiveness had spread like poison ivy over the entire body of education. She wanted me to talk to the students as much as to pose for them. I was glad to comply. At the end of each afternoon class, she was kind enough to drive me to The Duke of York's Theatre, where I was beginning my apprenticeship to the smiling and nodding racket. Soon, dividing my waning energy between the two jobs became too arduous. My Agent said "This is ridiculous". Camberwell was the last School at which I ever posed.

Quentin Crisp, New York

*A Camberwell Beauty is a nymphalid butterfly with dark purple wings and cream yellow borders. It is so called because it was first discovered in this country on an open top horse-drawn omnibus. This was in the countryside near London at a place called Camberwell!

A

AARONS, *Andrew Lewis* (b.1939)
He was at Camberwell School of Art from 1957-58 before moving to Manchester University as a post-graduate student in Textile Design. In the early 1960s he worked as a Textile Designer in the U.K., before emigrating to Canada, where he taught art and was eventually appointed Director of Fine Arts at the Sir Sandford Fleming College, Canada, an appointment he held for seven years before returning to the U.K. in 1977. He has continued to teach at the Anglia Polytechnic, Cambridge, where he currently lives. He has exhibited widely, including group exhibitions at the South London Art Gallery, The Usher Gallery, Lincoln and Heffers Gallery, Cambridge. His solo exhibitions have included shows at the Prince Arthur Galleries, Toronto, 'London Underground' Art Gallery of Hamilton, Ontario and Markswood Gallery, Essex. His publications include *A History of Canadian Painting* published by McIntyre Educational Media, 1981. His work is in many public and corporate collections, including the Canadian Broadcasting Corporation, York University, Toronto, British Rail, University of Cambridge and the Bank of Mexico, Mexico City.

ABRAHAMS, *Ivor* (b.1935)
Born in Wigan, he attended Southport Art School, where he studied anatomy and life drawing. After attending St. Martin's School of Art from 1952-54, he spent a three year period at Camberwell, during which time he was also apprenticed to the Fiorini Bronze Foundry. His early career followed the unlikely path of making mannekins for the London-based South African fashion guru Adel Rootstein, so prominent in the London fashion scene of the mid-1950s. He has also been visiting lecturer at Goldsmiths' College, Birmingham College of Art, the R.C.A. and the Slade School of Fine Art. His work has been shown extensively around the world and his one-man exhibitions include The Richard Feigen Gallery (New York), Arnolfini (Bristol), Aberdeen Art Gallery, Mappin Art Gallery (Sheffield) and Mayor Gallery (London). He has participated in many group exhibitions in the U.S.A., Israel, France and the Whitechapel Art Gallery, London. His work is in numerous public collections including The Arts Council of Great Britain, Bradford Art Gallery, Denver Museum (Colorado), Fort Lauderdale Museum (Florida), The National Gallery of Australia, The Museum of Modern Art (New York), The Tate Gallery, the V & A and the Walker Art Gallery (Liverpool). He now lives and works mainly in France and in 1994 held a solo exhibition at the Bernard Jacobson Gallery, London.

ALFORD, *John* R.B.A., N.E.A.C., N.D.D. (b.1929)
He was a student at Camberwell from 1949-53 and was most influenced by Dunstan* and Eurich*. He has exhibited at numerous mixed exhibitions including the R.A., R.S.M.A., N.E.A.C. and the R.B.A He has also shown his work extensively in the U.S.A., France and Canada. He is currently Director of Art at Shrewsbury School.

ARDIZZONE, *Edward Jeffrey Irving* C.B.E., R.A., R.D.I. (1900-1979)
He first studied art at Westminster School of Art, 1920-21, under Bernard Meninsky, but did not take up painting full-time until some years later. He was predominantly an illustrator of books from the mid-30s, and was an official War Artist from 1940-45. He taught illustration at Camberwell during the period 1948-51; and was responsible for the illustrations in *Jubilee*, a publication to commemorate the 50th Anniversary of Camberwell School of Arts & Crafts in 1948. He exhibited widely, including the R.A., the N.E.A.C., Leicester Galleries, Mayor Gallery, Leger Gallery, and the New Grafton Gallery.

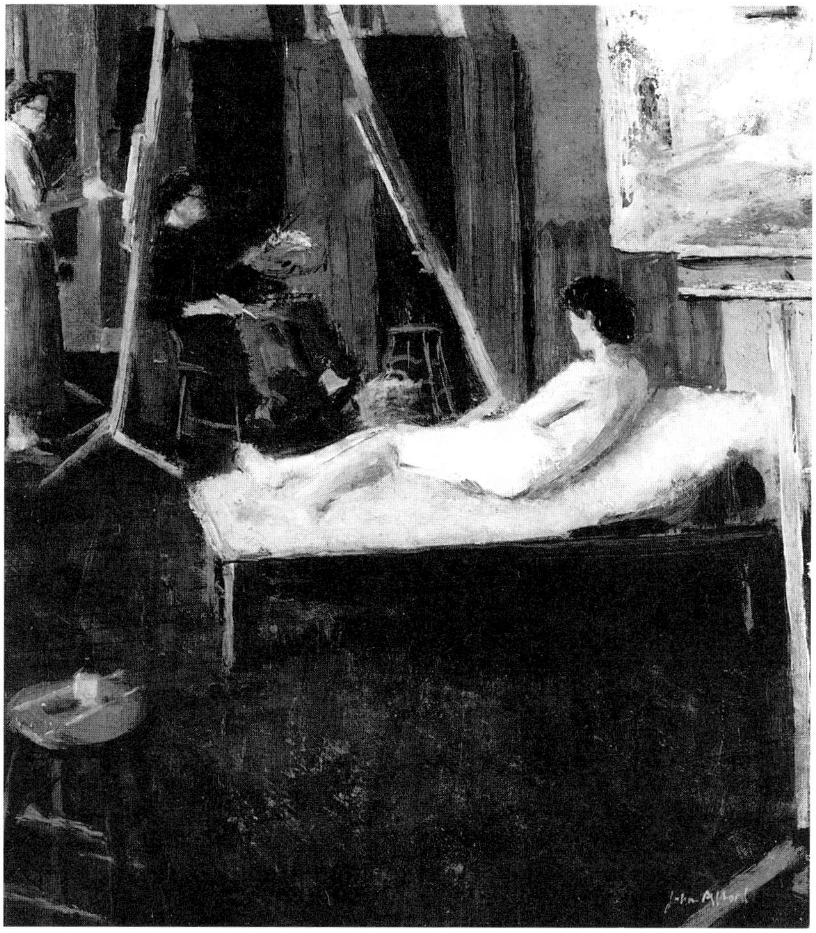

JOHN ALFORD. *Life Class at Camberwell*, c. 1950. Oil on board, 12¾in x 11in. Private collection.

ARDIZZONE, *Philip Augustin Irving* (1931-1978)
The son of Edward Ardizzone, he studied at the Slade School of Fine Art where he was mainly taught by Coldstream and Monnington. He gained the Slade Diploma in Fine Art and exhibited widely at the R.A., the Phoenix Gallery, Lavenham, Piccadilly Gallery, Roland Browse & Delbanco and Leicester Galleries. He taught at Camberwell from 1957-58.

ARNOLD, *Charles Geoffrey* A.R.W.A. (b.1915)
Painter, who first studied at Bradford College of Art 1931-34, and at Camberwell School of Art 1946-47. He also attended the Slade School of Art between 1947-50. He has exhibited at the R.A., R.W.A., L.G., and was elected A.R.W.A. 1952.

ARIMATSU, *Joyce Enid* (*née* Westwood) (b.1934)
Born and bred in Camberwell, she joined the school as a junior in 1947. during her five years there she was taught by most of the main drawing and painting teachers including Dunstan*, Rogers* and Gilbert Spencer*. Marriage to a Japanese diplomat meant extensive travel and only in the last decade or so has she followed her career as an artist. She has shown her work in Toronto, Canada and in Bunko-Ku, Tokyo. In 1922 she held a two-person show with her old Camberwell colleague Rachel Patterson* at the The Royal Bank of Canada in the City of London.

ARNUP, *Sally* (b.1930)
Sculptor, who studied at Kingston and Camberwell Schools of Art under Karel Vogel*, 1948-51. She later attended the R.A. Schools 1952-55, studying under Frank Dobson and John Skeaping. She first exhibited at the R.A. in 1957 and was, for many years, on the staff of York School of Art. Her work has also been seen in the R.S.A. R.B.A. Paris Salon and the R.B.S., of which she is a Fellow.

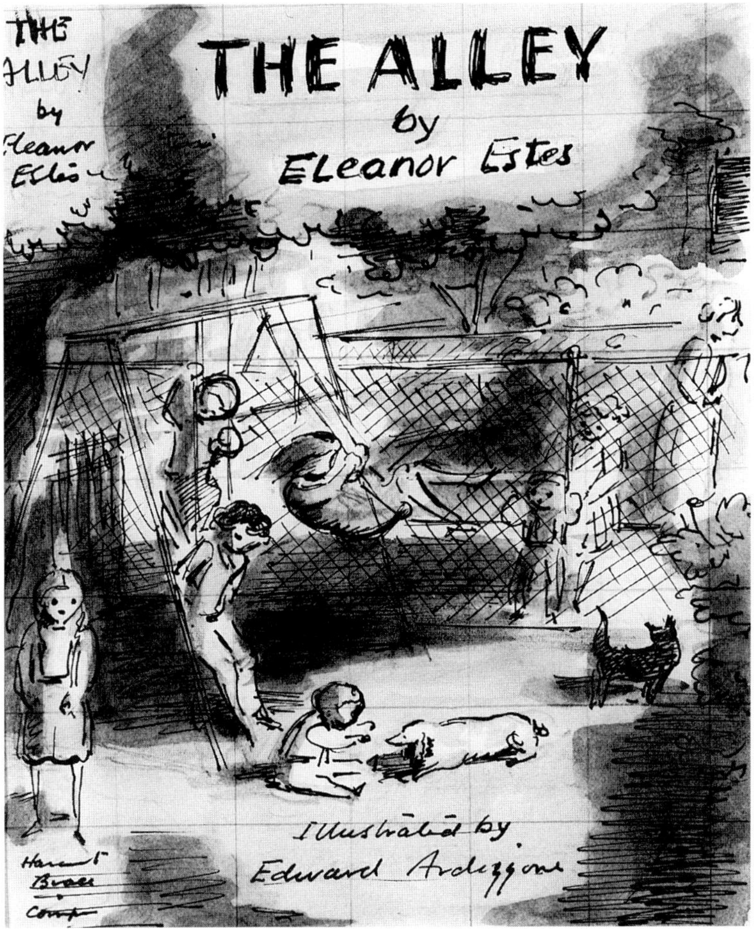

EDWARD ARDIZZONE. *Book jacket design for The Alley, by Eleanor Estes.* Pen, ink and watercolour, 8in x 6¼in. Private collection.

ATKINS, *Phoebe* (*née* Hopson) (b.1932)
A student at Camberwell from 1949-50, her work was mostly influenced by Christopher Chamberlain*. By her own admission she worked very little, and because of this she left the School some eighteen months later.

AUERBACH, *Frank* (b.1931)
Born in Berlin, he was sent to England in 1939, spending the war years at a Quaker school in Kent. He first attended art classes at the Hampstead Garden Suburb Institute and then at the Borough Polytechnic under his teacher and mentor David Bomberg. He furthered his studies at St. Martin's School of Art 1948-52, and at the R.C.A. 1952-55. Between 1958 and 1965 he was a member of staff at Camberwell, having been invited by Robert Medley on his appointment as Head of Fine Art. His one-man exhibitions include Beaux-Arts Gallery, Marlborough Fine Art, London and New York. His works are in many public collections including the Tate Gallery, Arts Council of Great Britain, Contemporary Arts Society, and museums and galleries around the world.

AULD, *Ian* (b.1926)
Although he trained as a painter, firstly at Brighton and then at the Slade School of Fine Art 1947-50, it is as a potter that he is best known. After spending three years in the Middle East where he established a ceramic department in Baghdad, he joined the staff at Camberwell in 1958, where he taught for seven years. In 1965 he left Camberwell to teach at the Bath Academy, returning ten years later as Head of the Department of Ceramics, where he stayed until his retirement from teaching in 1985. He has exhibited his work occasionally at Craft Centres, including Primavera during the 1960s. Since his retirement he has owned a shop specialising in tribal art and antiquities.

JOHN ALFORD.
The Teaching Staff at Camberwell, c.1952. Oil on canvas, 14in x 19in.
Collection of the late Richard Eurich.
From left to right: M. Bloch, R. Eurich, R. Macdonald, G. Spencer, P. Matthews, B. Dunstan and M. Salaman.

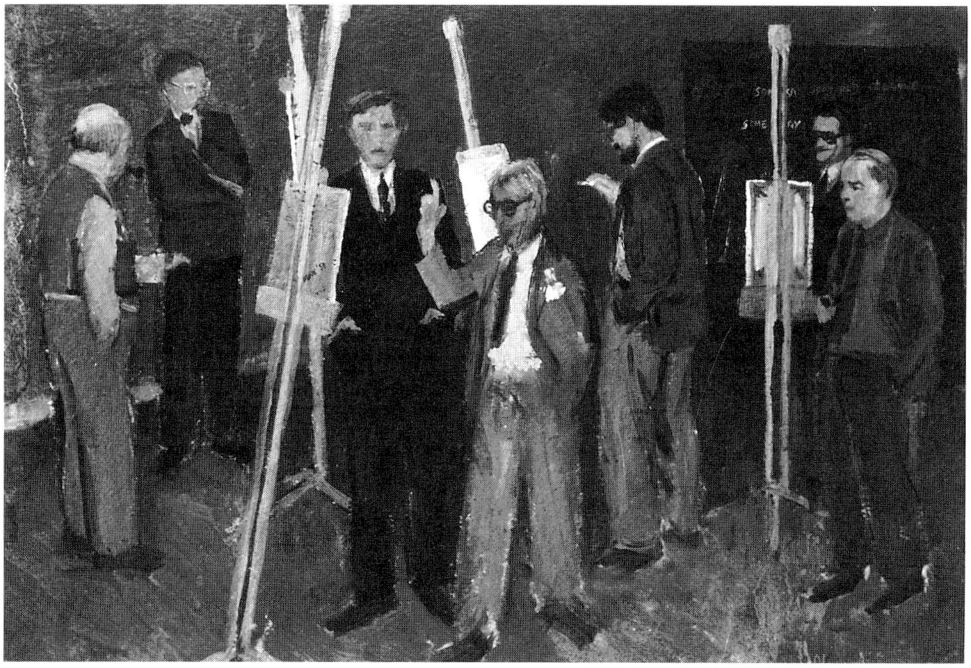

AUSTIN, *Lionel John* N.D.D. (b.1938)
A student at Camberwell from 1956-60. His main influences were Dixon*, Eyton*, Fry* and Lee*. Known as 'Leo', he married the artist Margot Noyes*. He exhibited at the Edinburgh Festival in 1960 before joining the B.B.C. as a designer. In the early 1960s he became a film and television production designer and is now freelance, working all over the world, like his Camberwell colleague Brian Eatwell*.

AVIS, *John Augustus* (b.1931)
A student at Camberwell from 1947-50, he was taught by Sam Carter*, John Minton* and Susan Einzig*, before winning a scholarship to the Slade School of Fine Art, where he was also taught by Coldstream*, Rogers* and Patrick George*. A winner at the Slade of the coveted Tonks Drawing prize, he has shown his work in numerous group exhibitions, including Young Contemporaries and at the R.B.A. at the Mall Galleries. He has held numerous teaching posts, including Senior Lecturer at the University of Kumasi (Ghana) and a Lecturer in Foundation Studies at Ipswich School of Art. He is currently Head of the Department of Foundation and Diploma Studies at the Chelsea School of Art.

AYRES, *Daphne Auriol* (*née* Echalaz) N.D.D. (b.1922)
A student at Camberwell from 1946-49, her main influences were Coldstream*, Gowing*, Pasmore*, and Rogers*. She exhibited with the L.G. during the early 1950s and is the sister of Opal Howard*.

AYRES, *Gillian* O.B.E., R.A. (b.1930)
Student at Camberwell 1946-50. After a year spent in Cornwall, she returned to London in 1951 when her work was included in the first Young Contemporaries exhibition. In 1959 she was appointed to the staff at the Bath Academy of Art (Corsham) where she was to remain until 1966. She has had numerous one-woman exhibitions, including the Redfern Gallery, Kasmin Gallery, Women's International Centre, New York, Knoedler Gallery and the Museum of Modern Art (Oxford). She had a retrospective exhibition at the Serpentine Gallery in 1983 and has exhibited several times at the Hayward Gallery. Her work is in public collections including the Tate Gallery, The Museum of Modern Art (New York) and the V. & A. She has won prizes at the Tokyo Biennale and at John Moores, Liverpool. She was for many years Senior Lecturer at St. Martin's School of Art and the Head of Painting at Winchester School of Art between 1978-81. She married the painter, Henry Mundy*.

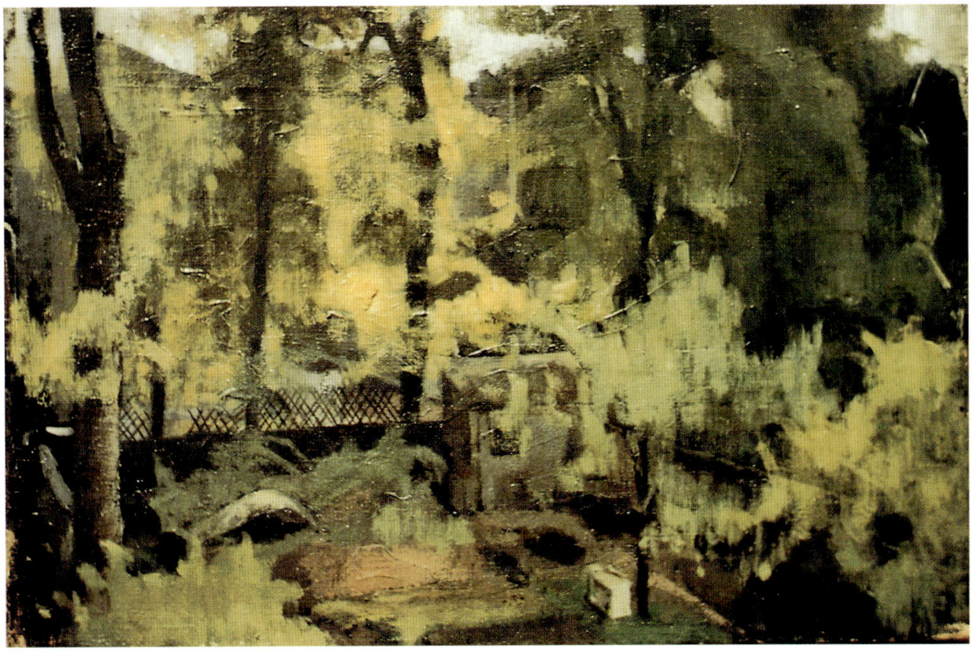

JOHN AVIS. *Back Garden, London*, 1949. Oil on canvas, 9½in x 14in. Artist's collection.

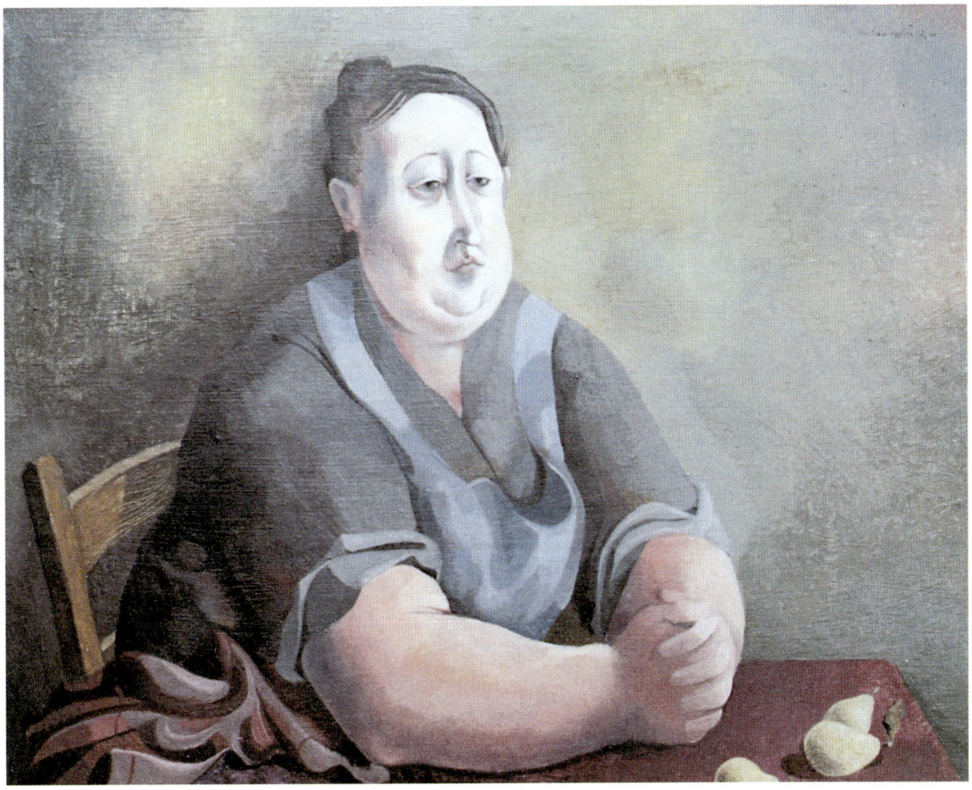

MICHAEL AYRTON. *Portrait with Pears*, 1943. Oil on canvas, 19½in x 23in. Private collection. (This is a portrait of Mrs Fursey, the cleaning lady at Camberwell Art School.)

AYRTON, *Michael* R.B.A. (1921-1975)
He first studied art at Heatherley's Art School in 1935. After a successful two-man exhibition with John Minton* and further success in designing for *Macbeth*, produced by John Gielgud, Ayrton was offered a post teaching Life Drawing and Theatre Design at Camberwell which he held between 1942-44. He was also well-known as a broadcaster on art, regularly taking part in B.B.C. radio's *Round Britain Quiz*. He illustrated numerous books and achieved an international reputation as an artist, illustrator and sculptor.

B

BAGUST, *Peter Stanley* (1901-1985)
A painter and art dealer, born in London, the son of the painter Frederick Bagust. Following regular family moves and evacuation during the war, he spent his National Service years 1948-49 in Holland and Germany. He briefly studied under the well-known German etcher, Otto Fischer, and in 1950 joined Farnham Art School where his formal education began. Further studies and travels throughout Europe followed, and in 1956 he enrolled as a part-time student at Camberwell Art School, where he spent the next four years studying painting and life drawing with Nuttall-Smith* and Anthony Eyton*, amongst others. By the early 1970s he had moved to South Devon, where he opened and still runs a successful art gallery. He has not exhibited his work other than in his own establishment, but continues to paint when time permits.

BAKER, *Eve* (*née* McMullin) (b.1925)
She attended Hastings Art School from 1942-43 and following war service continued her studies there and at Camberwell from 1949-52. The raising of a large family prohibited her from exhibiting for many years and she later turned to the making of pottery, a path which she has followed for many years.

BAKER, *Geoffrey* (b.1926)
He first studied art at Cardiff School of Art from 1950-52 before spending a year at the Ecole du Louvre in Paris. From 1958, for a ten year period, he taught Drawing and Painting at High Wycombe School of Art, at the same time teaching similar subjects at Camberwell, where for the next ten years he taught alongside Masterman* and Matthews*, who were to greatly influence him. During this period he showed his work extensively with the L.G., Leicester Galleries, South London Art Gallery, R.S.A., R.A. and in recent years the Unity Gallery in Fairfield, Iowa, where he is currently Professor of Art at the Maharishi International University, lecturing in numerous subjects, including research into Consciousness and the Arts. His work has been purchased by the President and Council of the R.A.

BANNISTER, *Georgina* (b.1930)
She studied at Camberwell from 1951-54, and was taught and influenced by Edward Ardizzone* and Bernard Dunstan*. She has had one-woman and mixed exhibitions in East Anglia, where she lives and works.

BARHAM, *Jean Mary* (*née* Plummer) (b.1924)
A student at Camberwell from 1947-50, whose main influences were Burn, Monnington* and Rogers*. She has exhibited her work at the World Trade Centre and Greenwich Theatre, the R.A. and N.E.A.C.

BARTLETT, *Adrian* (b.1939)
He was a student at Camberwell from 1958-61, where he was taught by Auerbach* and Medley*. He has had one-man exhibitions at Morley Gallery, St. Paul's School Gallery and The British Council Gallery in Athens. He has shown in group exhibitions in America, Italy, Belgium, Germany, Sweden and Australia, as well as the U.K. He is married to the artist Victoria Bartlett*.

BARTLETT, *Victoria* (née Howitt) (b.1940)
She was a student at Camberwell 1957-61, where she was taught by Auerbach*, Christopher Chamberlain*, Medley* and Vogel*. She has held one-woman exhibitions in Los Angeles and San Francisco in the mid-1970s and latterly has had exhibitions at Edward Totah Gallery and The Camden Arts Centre. She has also taken part in group shows in the U.S.A., Australia, France, Germany, Switzerland, Luxembourg, Hungary and Poland. She is married to the artist Adrian Bartlett*.

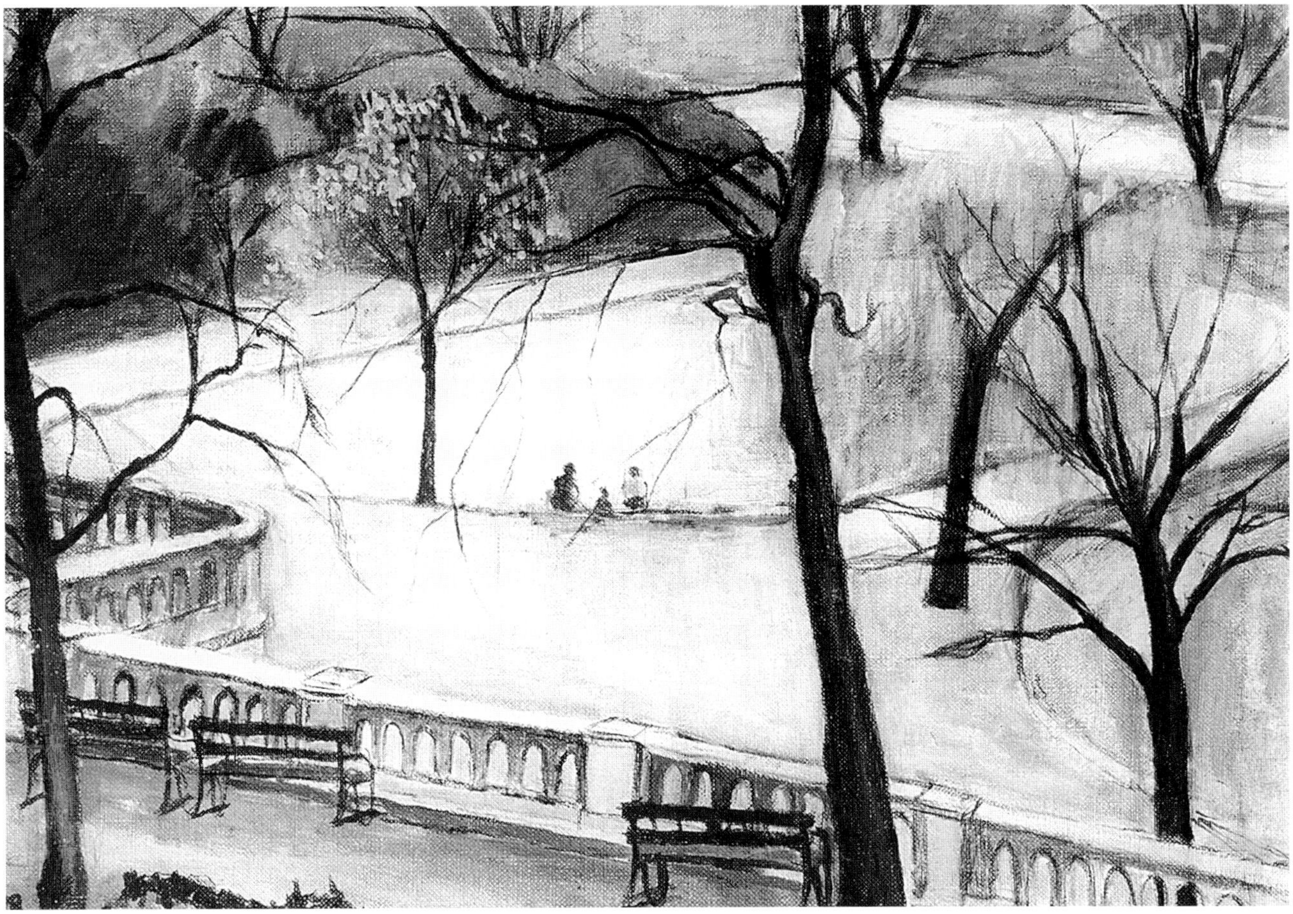

JEAN BARHAM. *Bishops Park, Fulham,* 1946. Oil on canvas, 12in x 16in. Private collection.

BATTY, *Dora M.* (c.1900-1966)
Very little is known about this artist but it was recently discovered that she taught Fabric Design and Illustration at Camberwell during the 1940s and was highly regarded by her students. It is also known that she illustrated several books, including *A Poet's Alphabet* and *The Giant Without a Heart.* She often worked in pen and ink as well as gouache and scraperboard. Numerous examples of her work were illustrated in the *Artist* magazine during the 1930s and 1940s. Recent research has discovered that Batty is thought to have designed pottery during the early 1920s, as she was a close friend of Harold Stabler (1872-1945), who taught at the R.C.A. Stabler was a partner in the ceramic firm of Carter, Stabler & Adams, who specialised in nursery scenes based on children's rhymes and toys and also in nursery tableware. This company was later taken over by Poole Pottery Limited. In 1925 she was commissioned by MacFisheries to design a number of marine themes for use on their fish-paste lids and packaging labels to promote the sale of these products amongst 'pot-lid' collectors. She also taught at the Central School of Arts and Crafts during the years prior to the Second World War and produced numerous posters for the London Passenger Transport Board (London Transport). We have yet to discover where she studied her art (although because of her association with Harold Stabler, the R.C.A. is a distinct possibility) or indeed exactly when she was born and died. There is no record of her having exhibited at any of the major venues of the day.

BAYLY, *Clifford John* V.P.R.W.S. (b.1927)
He studied at Camberwell from 1946-49 and was most influenced by Minton*, Monnington* and Pasmore*. He exhibited on numerous occasions in the late 1940s

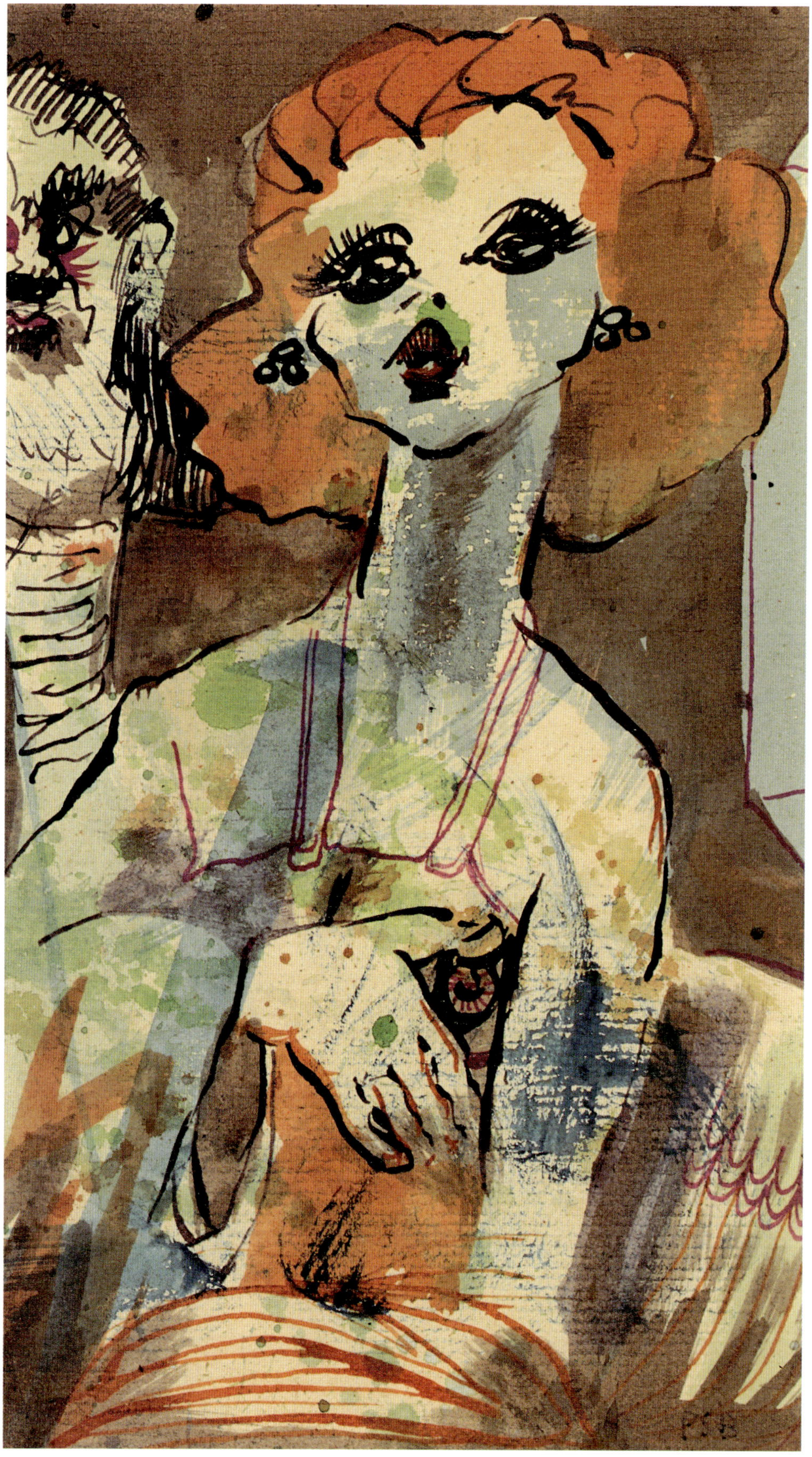

PETER BAGUST. *The Red Head.* Pen, ink and watercolour, 7½in x 4in.
Courtesy of Mr and Mrs R. Sansom.

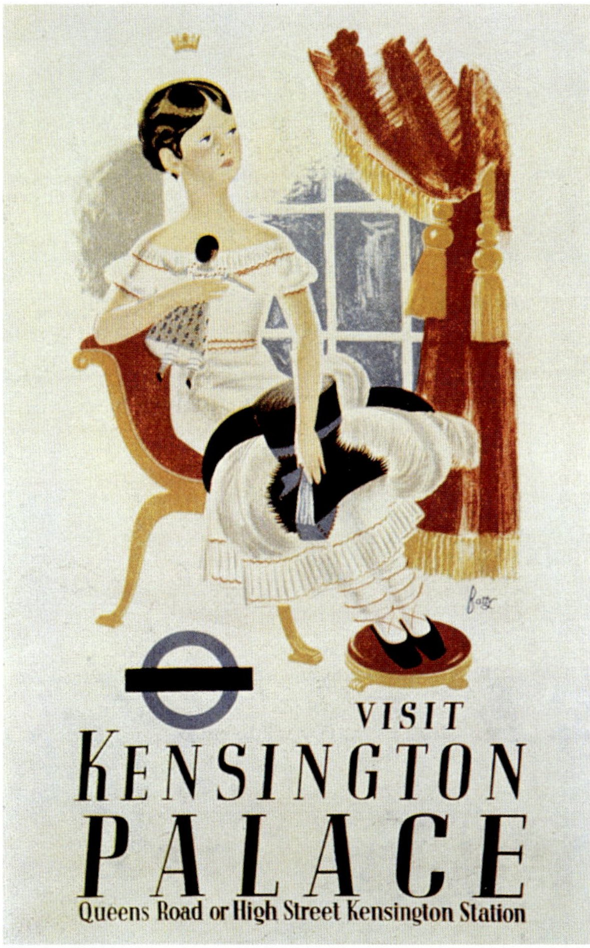

DORA BATTY. Transport poster. Lithograph, 30in x 20in. Courtesy of London Underground.

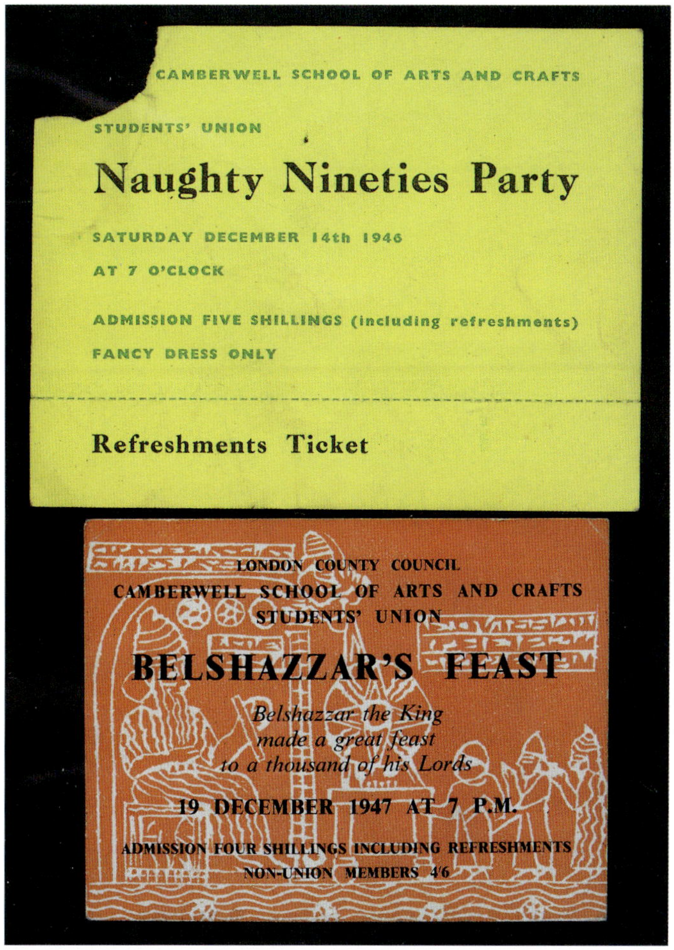

Tickets for student balls, printed in the Lithography Department. Courtesy of Clifford Bayly.

at the Young Contemporaries Exhibition and subsequently for many years at the R.A. For thirty years he taught and encouraged young graphic artists at Maidstone and Canterbury Colleges of Art. He travels extensively and has had one-man shows in Australian Galleries in Sydney, Adelaide, Melbourne and Queensland. He has been a member of the R.W.S. for a number of years.

BENDALL, *Sidney Ernest* (b.1925)
He enrolled as a student in 1948 and was to remain at Camberwell on a part-time teaching basis until his retirement forty years later in 1988. He has for many years followed a career as a freelance designer and is a member of the Guild of Lettering Craftsmen. His original teachers and greatest influences were Vernon Shearer* and John Buckland-Wright*.

BENNETT, *Valerie see DANIEL, Valerie*

BEUTLICH, *Tadek* (b.1922)
Born in Poland, he originally studied at the Poznan School of Art from 1937-39. Between 1945-46 he was in Italy furthering his studies at the Rome Academy of Art. He joined Camberwell as a student in 1949 but within two years had been appointed visiting lecturer, a position he was to hold until 1974. An acknowledged expert in the field of tapestry-weaving, he wrote *The Technique of Tapestry Weaving,* published by Batsford, in 1967. He has shown his work in the U.S.A. at the Smithsonian Institute and at prestigious venues throughout Europe and the U.K., including the V. & A.

BEVAN, *Dorothy* (*née* Johnson) (b.1928)
She attended Camberwell 1943-48 where her teachers and influences were Ayrton*, Dora Batty* and Gowing*. During the years immediately after Camberwell she was a fabric designer, working for companies including Marks & Spencer, Liberty's and Colefax & Fowler. She abandoned painting for many years, and it was only during the 1970s that she began to exhibit her work. She is now considered a botanical artist and has won many medals for her work, which is shown annually at the Royal Horticultural Society. She spends much of her time in California and her work is regularly published in American botanical magazines.

BEVIS, *Leslie Cubitt* (1890-1984)
It is believed that he was born in America, coming to Europe after the First World War. During the 1950s he was a lecturer in sculpture at Camberwell and a regular exhibitor at the R.A., N.E.A.C. and other major London venues. He had in the mid-1930s exhibited in the Paris Salon and in 1953 he was elected F.R.B.S. On his death he bequeathed his studio contents to the Society, many of which are currently under restoration. This fine portrait sculptor often used his students as models.

BIZON, *Edna* (*née* Uden) S.W.A. (b.1929)
She first studied art at St. Martin's from 1943-44 before becoming a student at Camberwell until 1947. She was taught and influenced by Burn*, Gowing* and Minton*. She exhibited widely, including the R.A., O'Nians King Street Galleries, Thorndike Gallery (Leatherhead) and in Munich.

BLOCH, *Martin* (1883-1954)
Following an early interest in music and architecture, he began studying art in Munich in 1905 and later in Berlin under Lovis Corinth. During the years prior to the Second World War he travelled extensively in Europe, working in Italy, Spain, Denmark and France. He came to England in 1934 and, together with Roy de Maistre, opened a School of Contemporary Painting. He held his first one-man exhibition in England at Alex Reid and Lefevre Gallery in 1939. In the mid-1940s he shared a studio with Josef Herman and by 1947 had become a naturalised British subject. During 1949, at the invitation of his friend and the Principal of Camberwell, Leonard Daniels*, he joined the staff as a guest teacher. He continued to exhibit widely in the few remaining years before his death. His works are in permanent collections throughout the world, including Arts Council of Great Britain, Berlinische Galerie (Berlin), B.M., Welsh Arts Council Collection, Museum of Harvard University (Cambridge, U.S.A.), Bristol Museum & Art Gallery, Leeds City Art Galleries, Leicester Museum & Art Galleries, Museum of Tel Aviv, National Gallery of Art (Washington, U.S.A.), San Francisco Museum of Art, Tate Gallery, V. & A. and the South London Art Gallery, where his Centenary Exhibition was held in 1984.

BOND, *Valerie see* PRESCOTT, *Valerie*

BOTHA, *David* (b.1921)
Born in South Africa, he first trained as an art teacher in Cape Town in 1950, spending twelve months at Camberwell during 1951 where he studied wood engraving and pottery. From here he spent a further twelve months travelling in Europe and worked in Paris, Rome and Madrid. He has shown his work widely in South Africa, as early as 1944, his first one-man exhibition being in Cape Town in 1956. His work is in the public collections of White Gallery (Bloemfontein), Pretoria Art Museum, Rand Afrikan University and Hester Rupert Art Museum (Graaf-Reinet).

BOULTON, *Janet* (b.1936)
Attended Swindon School of Art 1953-55 and then for the next three years at Camberwell. Her teachers included Pitchforth*, Fry* and Eyton* and in 1958 she was the winner of the David Murray Landscape Scholarship. In 1977 a retrospective exhibition was held at Swindon Museum and Art Gallery. She has exhibited at many galleries, including the A.I.A. Galleries, with the L.G., Browse Darby, Mercury Gallery (London) and the R.A. Summer Exhibition. During the 1980s she was Artist in Residence at Radcliffe Infirmary, Oxford, she also edited Paul Nash's letters to Mercia Oakley. A solo exhibition of her work was held at the Mercury Gallery in 1994.

BRADON, *Norah* (b.1901)
Ceramicist and potter who studied at the R.C.A. in the early 1920s. At the suggestion of Sir William Rothenstein, the Principal, she joined Bernard Leach in his St. Ives Pottery as a student/assistant in 1924. She was, he said, his most gifted pupil and she worked for him until 1928. She then joined Katharine Pleydell-Bouverie at the Coleshill Pottery in Wiltshire, where the two young innovators experimented with wood and vegetable ash glazes. She held her first exhibition with her partner in 1930 at Muriel Rose's Little Gallery in London followed by a second a year later at Paterson's Gallery in Bond Street. This second show was unusual in that it attracted a high praising critique in *The Times,* which for a show of pottery was almost unheard of in its day. In 1936 she left Wiltshire for Sussex, where she taught at Brighton Art School up to and during the war. In the late 1940s she joined the staff at Camberwell, where she passed on her tremendous skills and knowledge to a succession of grateful and gifted pupils. She remained there until her retirement in the early 1960s. Examples of her work are in the V & A and at the Crafts Study Centre, Bath.

BRANSON, *Rosa* (b.1933)
The daughter of Clive Branson, the artist and regular exhibitor with the A.I.A., she was surrounded by art as a young child. Following the death of her father in the war, she decided to take up art as a career, and she joined the Camberwell School of Arts & Crafts in 1949, where she was taught by Eurich* and Rogers*. She won a scholarship to the Slade School of Fine Art in 1953 where she was reunited with her father's pre-war colleague – Coldstream*. Her group exhibitions have included the R.A. Summer Exhibitions, R.O.I.; L.G. and the Young Contemporaries. She has held numerous one-woman exhibitions at the Woodstock Gallery (London), Barbican Centre and the Lyric Theatre (London). Her works are in the collections of the Marquise of Sligo, Nuffield Foundation and Lambeth Palace; as well as County Councils and Education Authorities.

BRASON, *John Ainsley* A.R.C.A. (b.1924)
He first studied at the R.C.A. during the war years at Ambleside under Percy Horton and Gilbert Spencer*. He was a teacher at Camberwell between 1949-54, during which time he was Head of the Intermediate Department. Shortly after leaving Camberwell he joined Pinewood Studios in the Special Effects Department, graduating to the position of Art Director. By the time the late fifties arrived he had become freelance and began working with such famous Directors as John Huston, David Lean, Fred Zinnemann and Stanley Donen. He eventually became a Producer/Director making feature films and over one hundred commercials. He became a screenwriter in the 1960s and has remained so ever since. His television credits include *Colditz, Secret Army, Diamonds, The Fourth Arm, Kessler, Special*

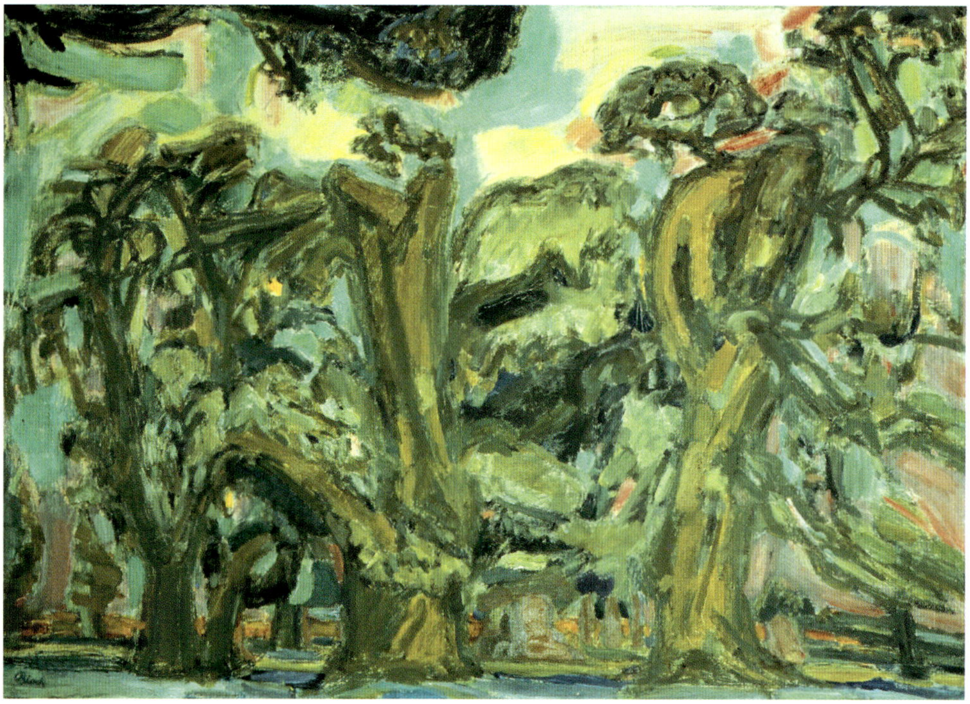

MARTIN BLOCH. *Trees in Greenwich Park*, 1949. Oil on canvas, 23in x 31½in. Private collection.

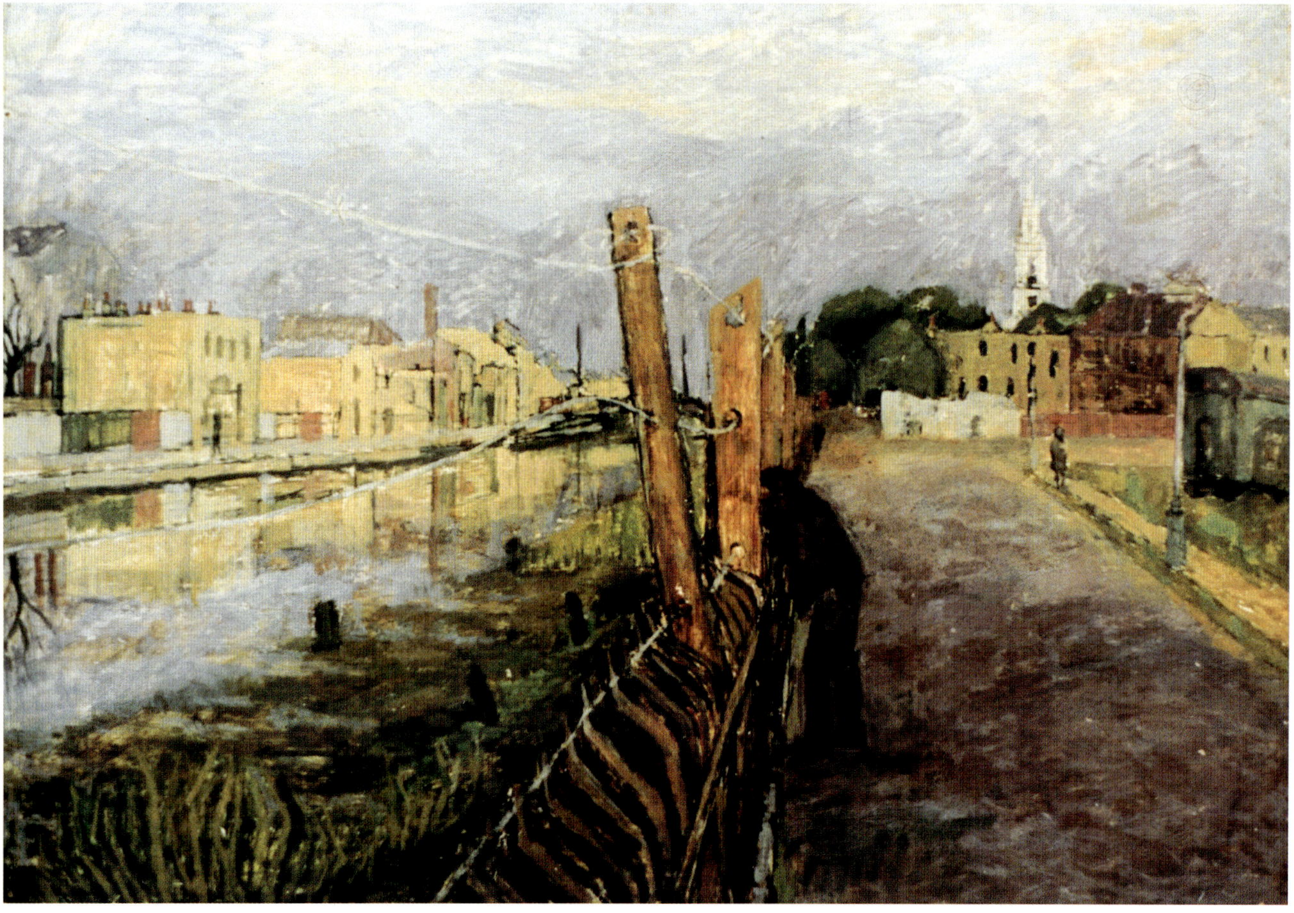

HILDA BRIDDON. *The Canal, Camberwell*, 1957. Oil on board, 36in x 48in. Artist's collection.

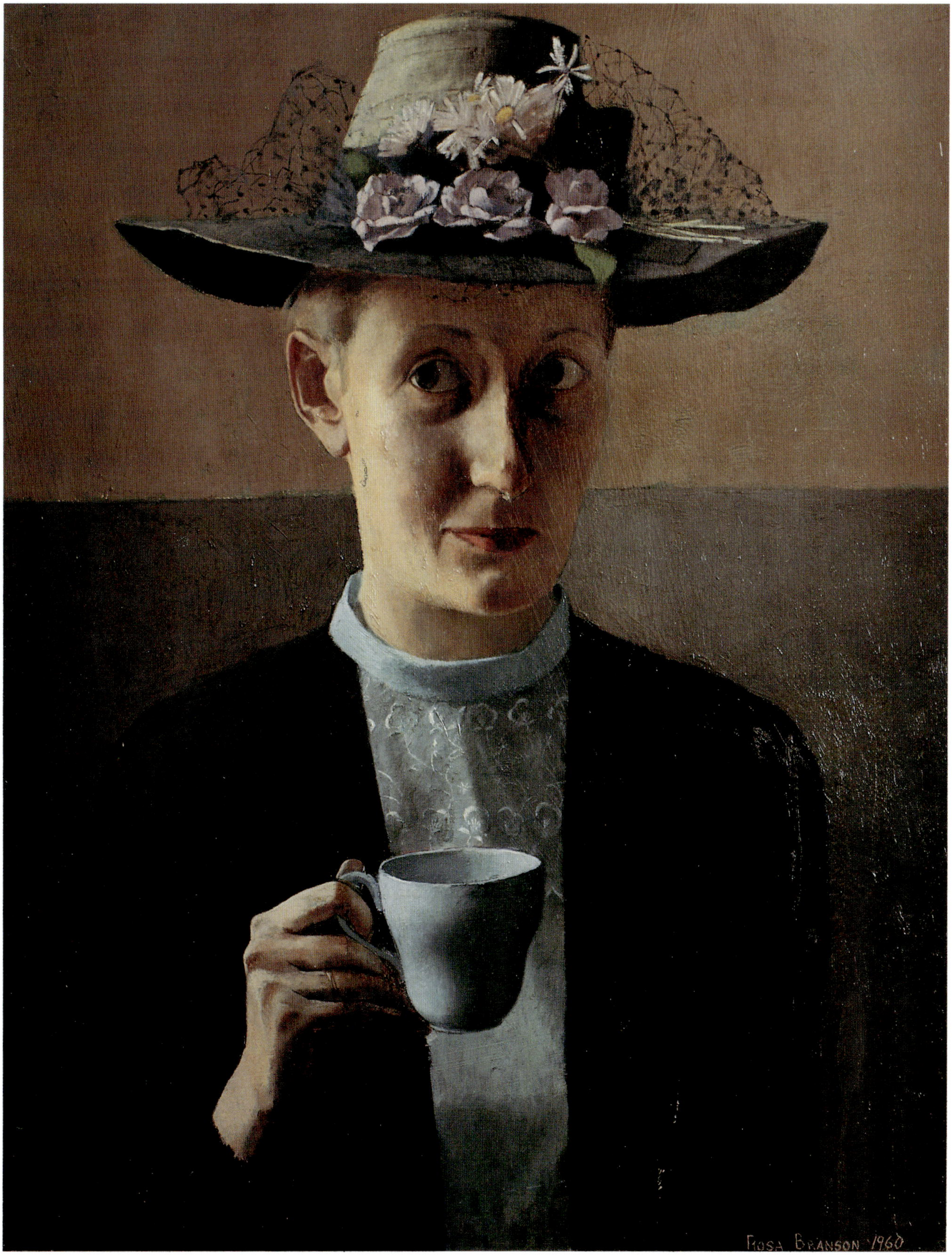

ROSA BRANSON. *The New Hat.* Oil on board, 24in x 18in. Courtesy of Mr Lee Seaman.

Branch and *Howard's Way*. He currently works mainly in Europe and was involved in a Centenary production on Vincent Van Gogh.

BREEDS, *Elizabeth Joan see* MASSY, *Elizabeth Joan*

BRIDDON, *Hilda* N.D.D. (b.1935)
Student at Camberwell 1954-58 where Anthony Fry*, R. D. Lee* and Vernon Shearer* had most influence on her career as a painter. Whilst at Camberwell she won a landscape scholarship which enabled her to have a further two years' study at the Slade School of Fine Art, during which time she won a second prize for her figure painting in one of her Diploma works. She returned for a short period to teach at Camberwell after leaving the Slade, and has also taught art privately. She had a spell of working for the Arts Council but due to family commitments ceased painting for many years until the early 1980s. As yet she has not exhibited but hopes to do so when sufficient work has amassed.

BROMFIELD, *Frederick Victor* (b.1942)
He was a student at Camberwell from 1958-64 where, as an intermediate, he was taught and influenced by Christopher Chamberlain.* He was also taught by R. D. Lee*, Uglow* and Auerbach*. He has exhibited in numerous mixed shows including the L.G., South London Group, R.A. Summer Exhibition and at the Piccadilly Gallery, Portal Gallery, Blackheath Gallery and the Greenwich Theatre Art Gallery.

BROUGH, *Alan* (b.1924)
He was a student at Camberwell 1946-51, where his main influence was Bernard Leach, with whom he worked for four years in the late 1960s. He has shown his work extensively, particularly in the Cornish Guild of Craftsmen Exhibitions and at the Newlyn Orion Gallery, Balloil College (Oxford) and at galleries in France and Sweden.

BROWN, *Rosamond Florence see* HAYWARD, *Rosamond Florence*

BUCHANAN, *Elspeth* (b.1915)
Born in Scotland, she won a scholarship in 1933 to Edinburgh College of Art. In 1935 she won travelling scholarships which enabled her to further her studies in London, Paris and Germany. In 1939 she was successful in applying for a place at the R.C.A., but the onset of the Second World War made her remain in Scotland, where she taught at Aberdeen. By 1941, however, she was seconded by the Admiralty and worked as a draughtswoman until the end of hostilities. She joined Camberwell School of Art in 1946, where she was taught by Gowing* and Pasmore.* At the end of 1947, she returned to teaching and held several posts in England before returning to Scotland during the late 1950s. She has exhibited her work many times at the R.A., R.S.A. and the Glasgow Institute of Fine Arts. In 1939 she was elected a Member of the Scottish Society of Woman Artists and in 1941 a Member of the Scottish Society of Artists.

BUCHANAN, *Lilian* (b.1914)
Coming from an artistic background (her father was the painter Alexander Buchanan) she arrived at Camberwell in 1947 as a mature student, having seen war service in the W.A.A.F.S. Her teachers included Coldstream* and Rogers*. Her ambition at the time was to be an illustrator and for a while she illustrated children's books. She is a member of the R.W.A. and has exhibited there regularly for a number of years, as well as the R.S.A., R.P., and with the U.A. For many years she has successfully taught portrait-painting at Swindon College of Art.

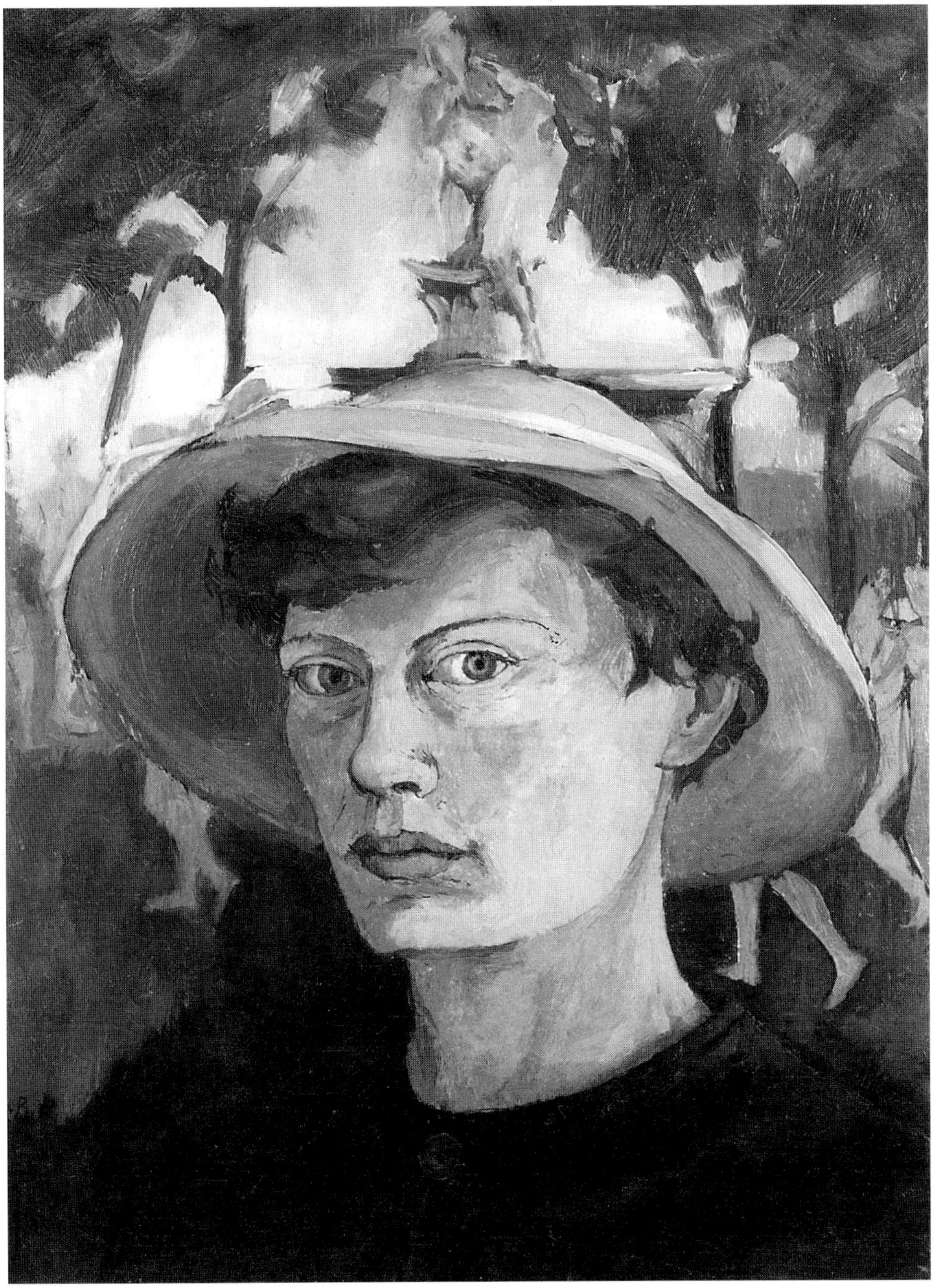

ANNE BUCHANAN-CROSBY. *Self Portrait*, 1950. Oil on panel, 15¾in x 12in. Private collection.

BUCHANAN-CROSBY, *Finella Anne* (*née* Buchanan) (b.1929)
A student at Camberwell from 1949-53, where her main influences were Dodgson*, Matthews*, Pitchforth*, and Rogers*. She exhibited many times with the L.G. and in the early 1970s had a one-woman exhibition at the Artists International Gallery (A.I.A.) and has also been included in open exhibitions at the Hayward Gallery. She has shown internationally, particularly in Washington D.C. and was featured more recently in an Arts Council Travelling Exhibition entitled 'Looking at Paintings'. She divides her time between New York and London.

BUCKLAND-WRIGHT, *John* L.G., S.W.E. (1897-1954)
After a distinguished career in the First World War when he was awarded the Croix de

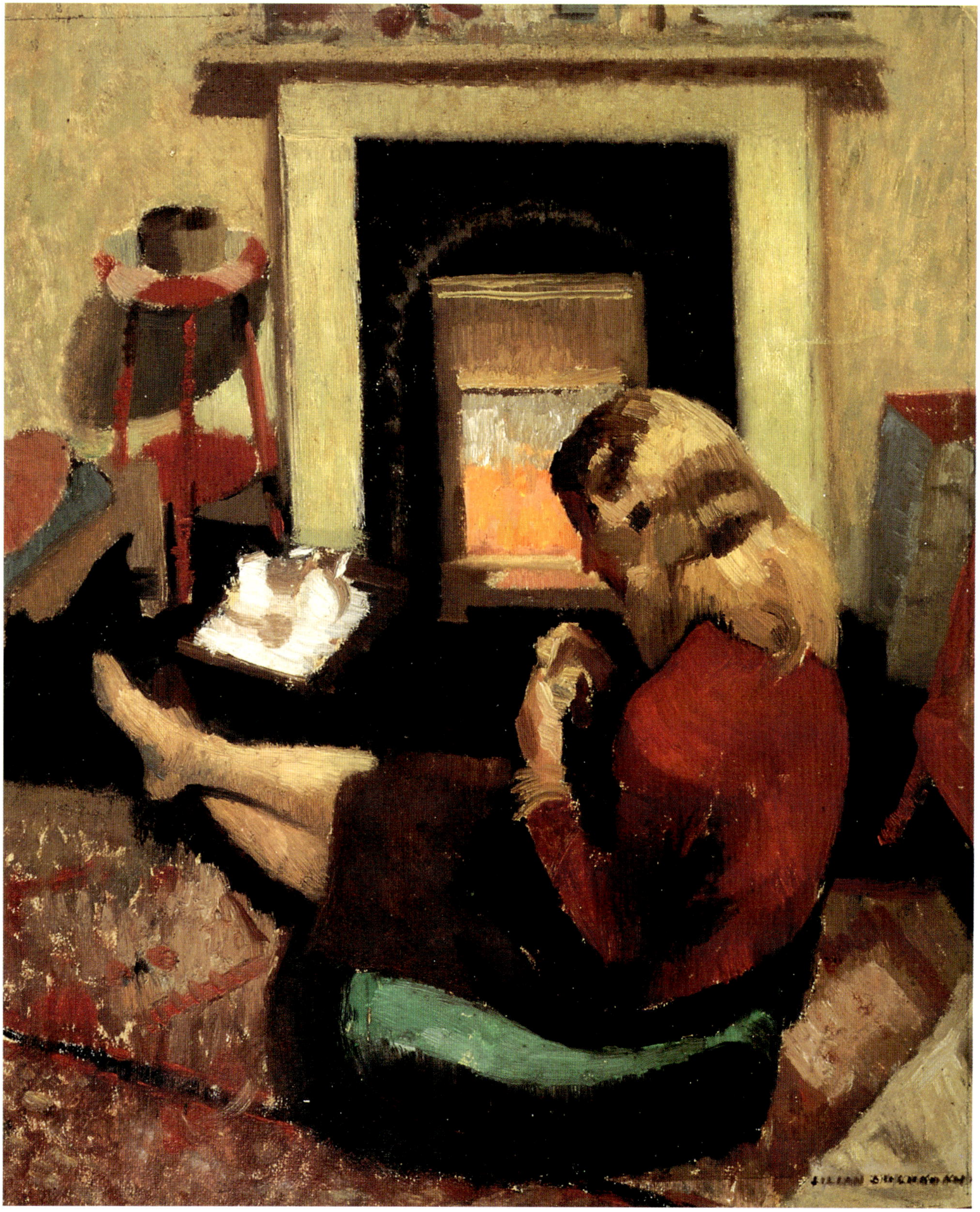
LILIAN BUCHANAN. *The Darn*, 1947. Oil on board, 17in x 13in. Private collection.

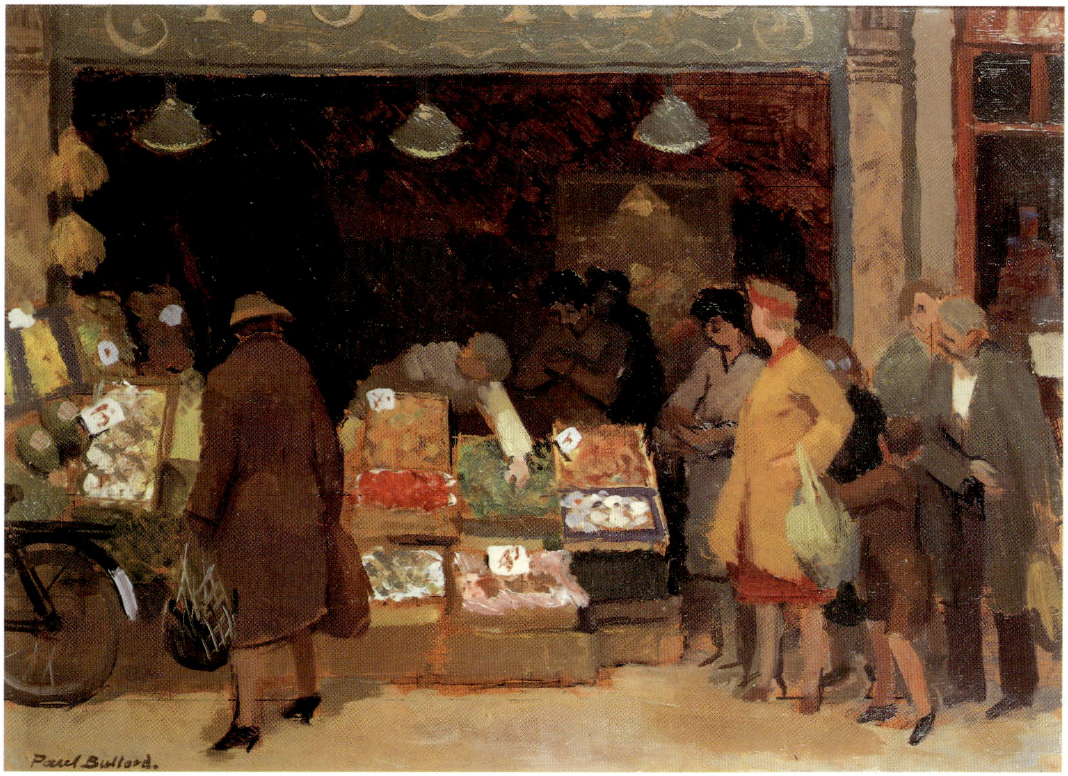

PAUL BULLARD. *The Greengrocer's*, 1947. Oil on board, 12in x 16in. Private collection.

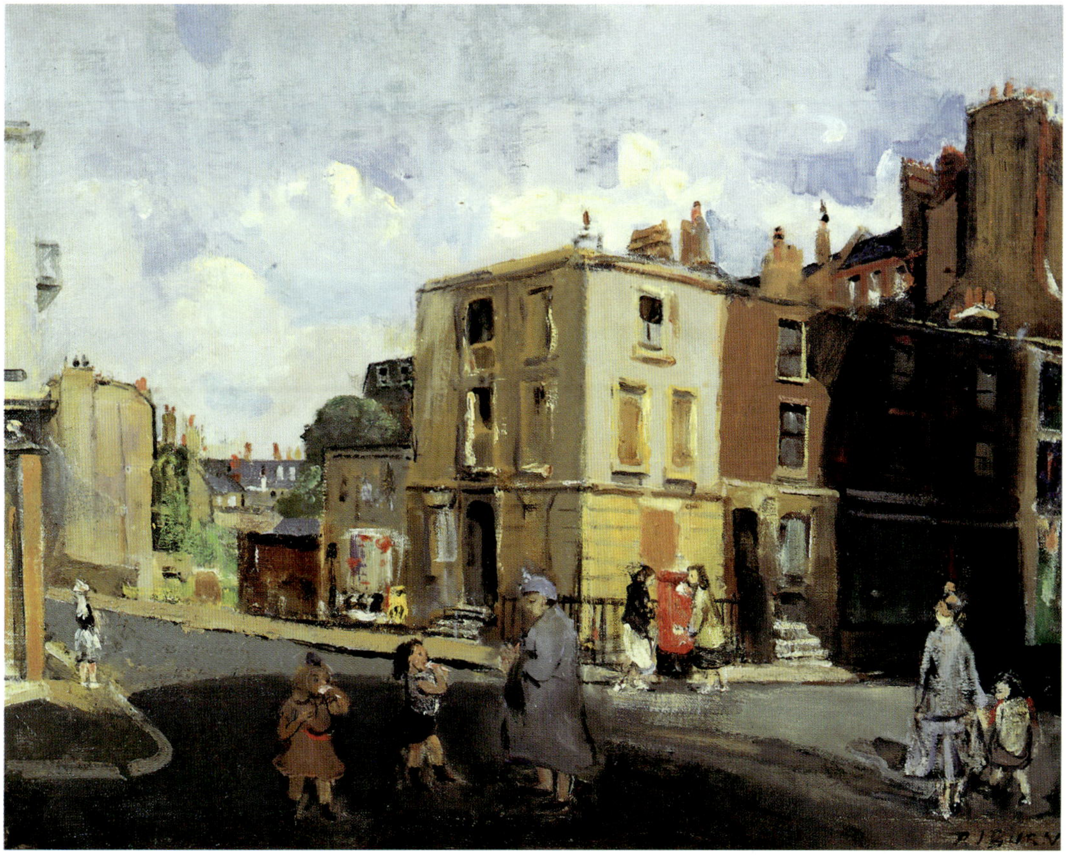

RODNEY BURN. *A Chelsea Street*, 1950. Oil on canvas, 24in x 30in. Courtesy of the Cheltenham & Gloucester Building Society.

Guerre, he studied History at Oxford, followed by a short spell at London University studying Architecture. During the mid-1920s he taught himself wood-engraving, living for a time in Belgium and gaining a reputation as a print maker and book illustrator. He joined Hayter's Paris studio 'Atelier 17', where he became a Director in the early 1930s. Living and working in Paris, he met many famous artists, including Brancusi, Matisse, Miró and Picasso. By the mid-1930s his work became known to the British public when he began to illustrate for the Golden Cockerel Press. During the Second World War he worked in England for the Camouflage Unit. Shortly after the end of the war, in 1948, he joined the staff at Camberwell where he stayed until 1953, when he joined the Slade School of Fine Art at the recommendation of John Piper.

BULLARD, *Paul* A.R.C.A. (b.1918)
He first studied before the war at Clapham School of Art, where his fellow students included Christopher Chamberlain* and James Palmer*, both of whom later taught with him at Camberwell. In 1938 he won a Scholarship to the R.C.A., but the onset of war interrupted his studies. During six years of military service he was taken prisoner in Libya but managed to escape in Italy fifteen months later. He resumed his studies at the R..C.A. in 1946, gaining his Associateship soon after. His teachers were Charles Mahoney and Vivian Pitchforth*, who was later to become a colleague at Camberwell. He has exhibited his work regularly at the R.A., since the immediate post-war years. After teaching at several London art schools, numbering Alan Reynolds amongst his pupils, he joined the staff at Camberwell in 1958, where he was head of the Foundation Department for nearly twenty years. His work is in the permanent collection of the Imperial War Museum. Since retiring he has lived in Suffolk and in 1992 held a solo exhibition at the Louis C. Morton Gallery in Mexico City.

BULLOCK, *Phoebe* (*née* Whitehead) N.D.D. (b.1935-c.1990)
During the four year period from 1953 spent at Camberwell, she was taught and influenced most by Brason*, Christopher Chamberlain*, Eurich*, R. D. Lee*, Matthews* and Gilbert Spencer*. After leaving Camberwell, she lived for a while in Greece and on her return to England taught in schools and at Adult Art Education centres. In recent years, after returning to London, she began Print Making at Sir John Cass School of Art. Her work has been shown extensively and she had one-woman exhibitions in Bristol during the mid-1970s and has shown in mixed exhibitions, including the Festival Gallery (Bath) and the Bristol Guild Gallery.

BURN *Rodney Joseph* R.A., N.E.A.C., R.S.M.A. (1899-1984)
He studied at the Slade School of Fine Art from 1918-22, winning several major prizes including the Summer Composition for his painting 'The Beach'. He began exhibiting at the N.E.A.C. during the mid-1920s, and became a tutor at the R.C.A. between 1929-31. He had a three year period in Boston (U.S.A.) teaching at the School of the Museum of Fine Arts between 1931-34. He joined the staff at Camberwell on a part-time basis during the late 1940s, where he remained for many years teaching Life Drawing before eventually joining the staff of the Slade School of Fine Art towards the end of the 1950s. In 1946 he joined the Faculty of Painting in the British School at Rome. In 1954 he was elected an Associate of the R.A., becoming a full Member by 1962. He is represented in several public collections, including the Tate Gallery, B.M., Brighton Museum & Art Gallery and Bristol Museum & Art Gallery. His work was also purchased by the Chantrey Bequest and the Contemporary Arts Society. His, wife, Dorothy Sharwood-Smith, also taught sculpture at Camberwell for many years.

BUTLER, *Caroline Anne see* CARY, *Caroline Anne*

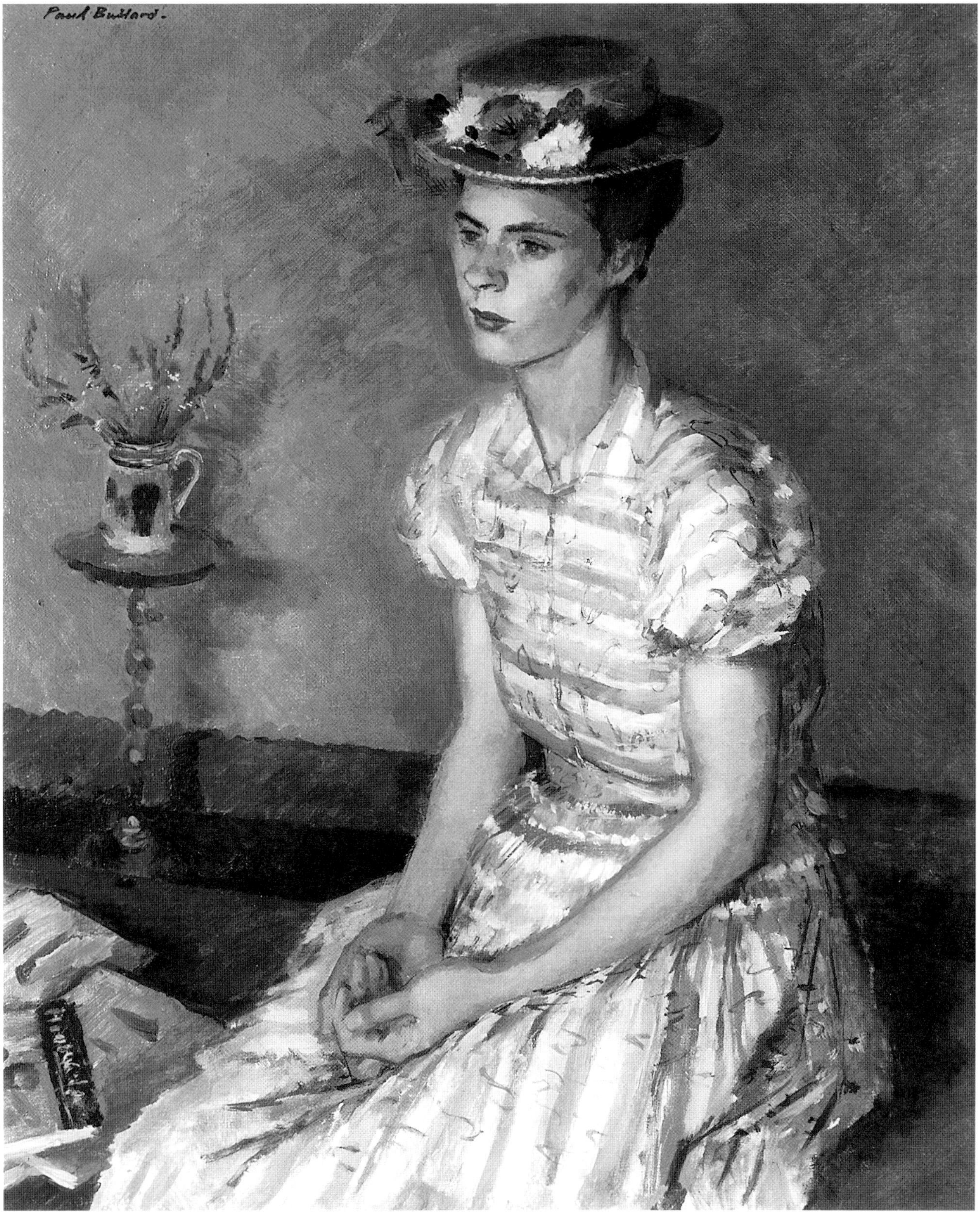

PAUL BULLARD. *The New Look* (the Artist's wife), 1947. Oil on canvas, 24in x 20in. Private collection.

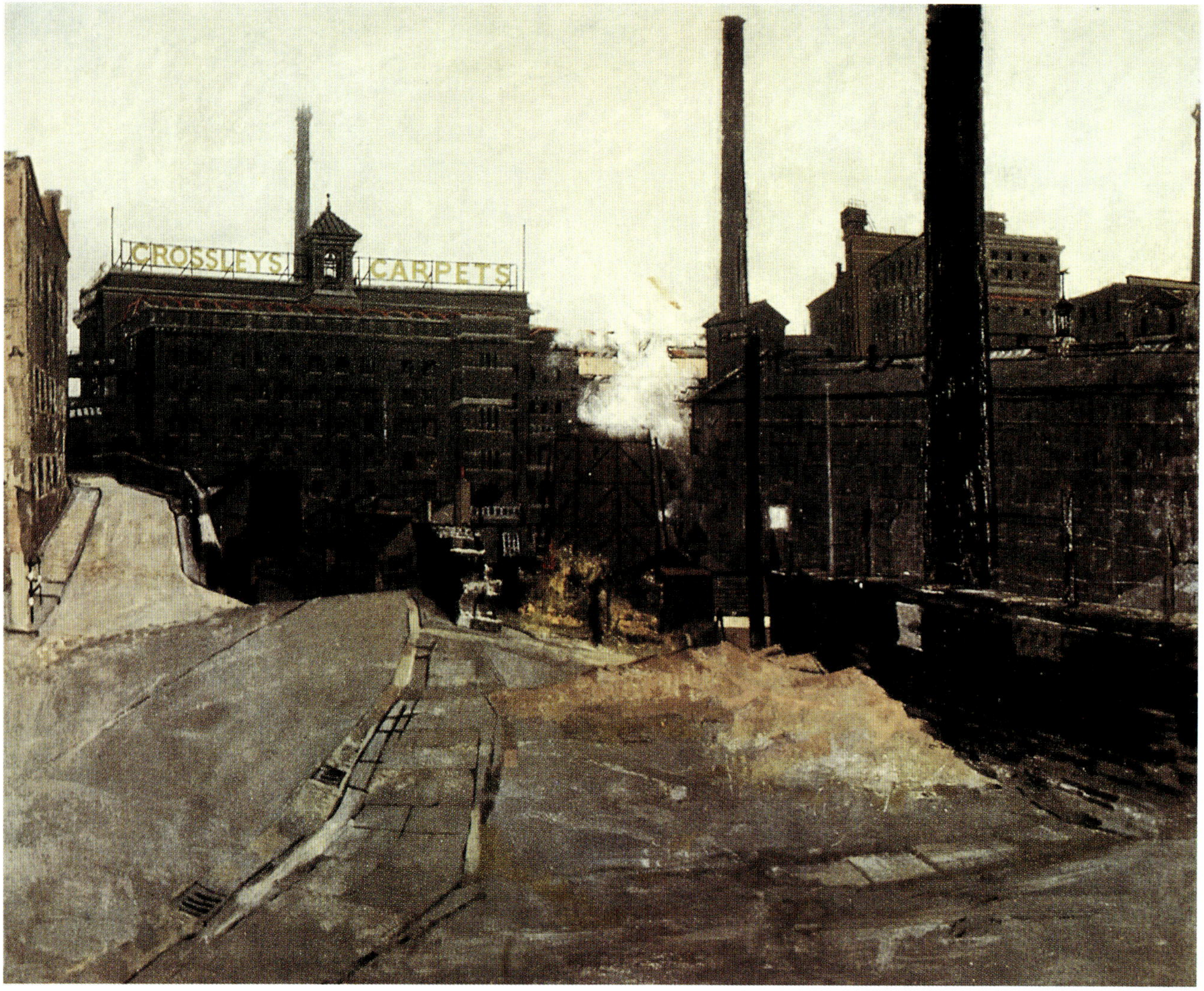

CHRISTOPHER CHAMBERLAIN. *Crossley's Carpet Factory, Halifax*, 1954.
Oil on canvas, 36in x 48in. Private collection.

C

CAIGER-SMITH, *Alan* (b.1930)
A painting and drawing student at Camberwell from 1947-48, where he was taught by Pasmore* and Seabrooke*. During the mid-1950s he attended the Central School of Arts & Crafts, where he studied Ceramics and he has since become a potter of international repute. He has held many exhibitions, both in the U.K. and overseas, as a well-known ceramicist.

CALVER, *Jennifer see* PROCTOR, *Jennifer*

CAMP, Jeffrey Bruce R.A., L.G. (b.1923)
Studied at Lowestoft and Ipswich Schools of Art, and the Edinburgh College of Art, where he gained a D.F.A., his main teacher and influence was Sir William Gillies R.A., R.S.A. He has had several one-man and group exhibitions, amongst which are Galerie de Seine, Beaux Arts Gallery, The New Art Centre, Bradford City Art Gallery, Browse & Darby, and the Hayward Gallery Annual Exhibitions. His work has been shown extensively abroad with the British Council Touring Exhibitions and through Nigel Greenwood Gallery (London). Currently he lectures at the Slade School. He taught at Camberwell on a part-time basis during the late 1950s. He married the artist Laetitia Yhap*.

CAMPBELL, *Panama* (*née* Hegarty) (b.1935)
Born in Panama, her early life was spent in Central America, Mexico and the U.S.A. She became a student at Camberwell in 1950 and remained there for the next five years before obtaining her N.D.D. Her main teachers at Camberwell were Bloch*, Frith* and Pitchforth*. In 1955 she attended the Slade School of Fine Art for two years before obtaining her Diploma. She has had numerous exhibitions, including the East London Gallery in 1974, the South London Art Gallery in 1977 and more recently the William Morris Gallery in 1987. She has now developed a keen interest in crafts associated with stained glass and is currently producing two and three dimensional works in this material. Since 1976 she has taught Art & Stained Glass in various art schools.

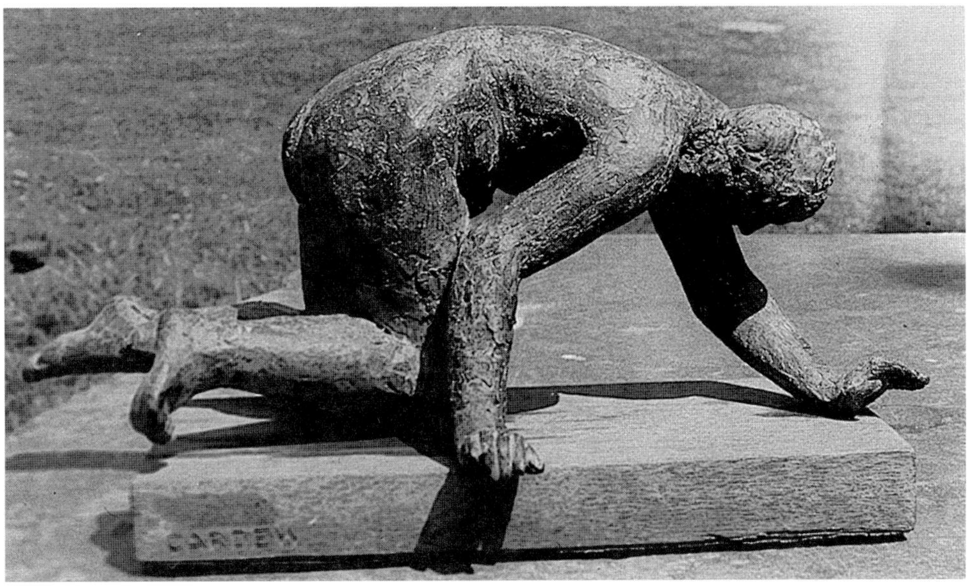

SETH CARDEW. *Jutta,* 1959. Bronze, 5in x 9in. Artist's collection. Photo courtesy of Reg Watkiss.

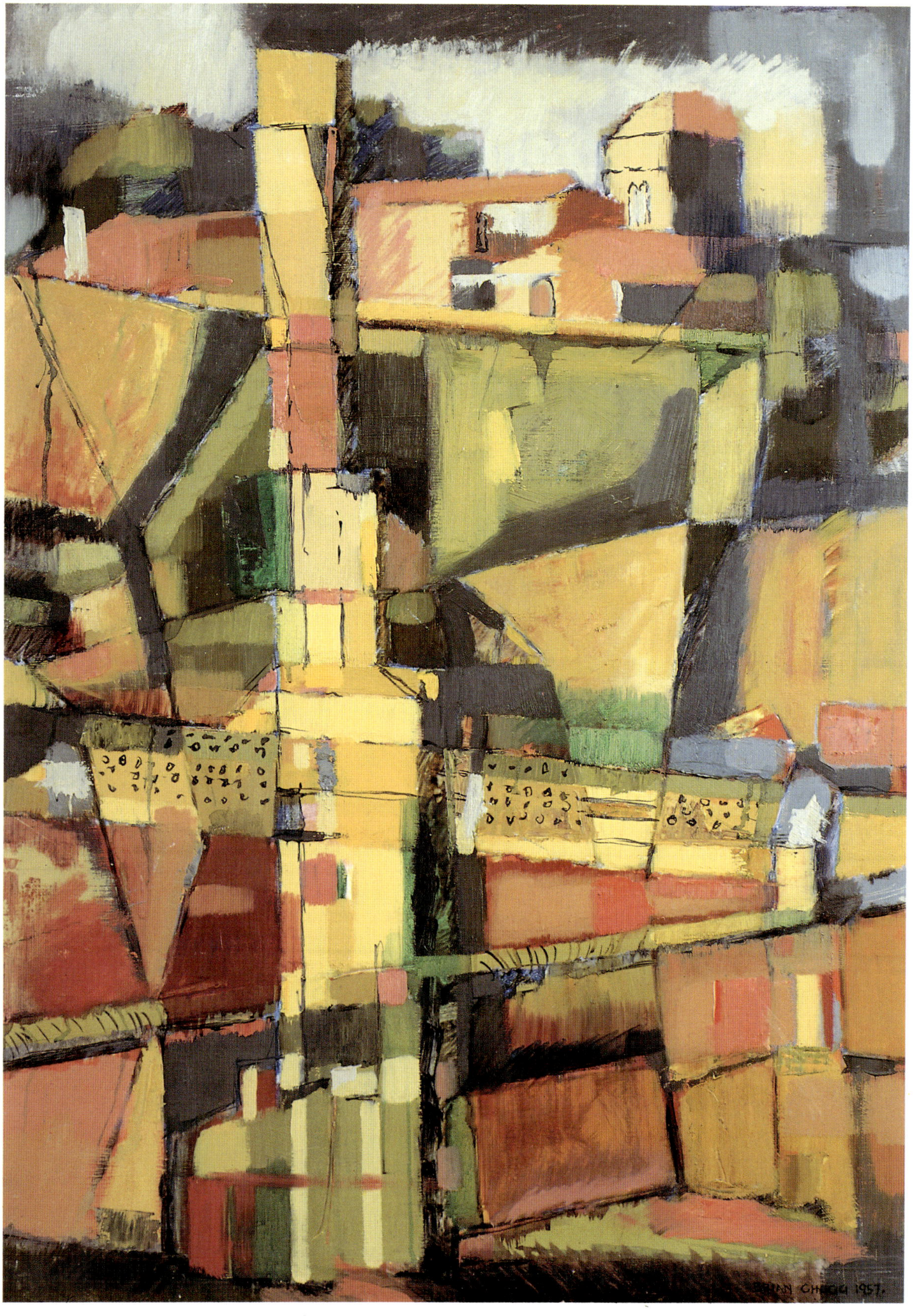

BRIAN CHUGG. *Landscape with Monolith, Provence.* Oil on board, 28in x 20in. Courtesy of Eve Phillips.

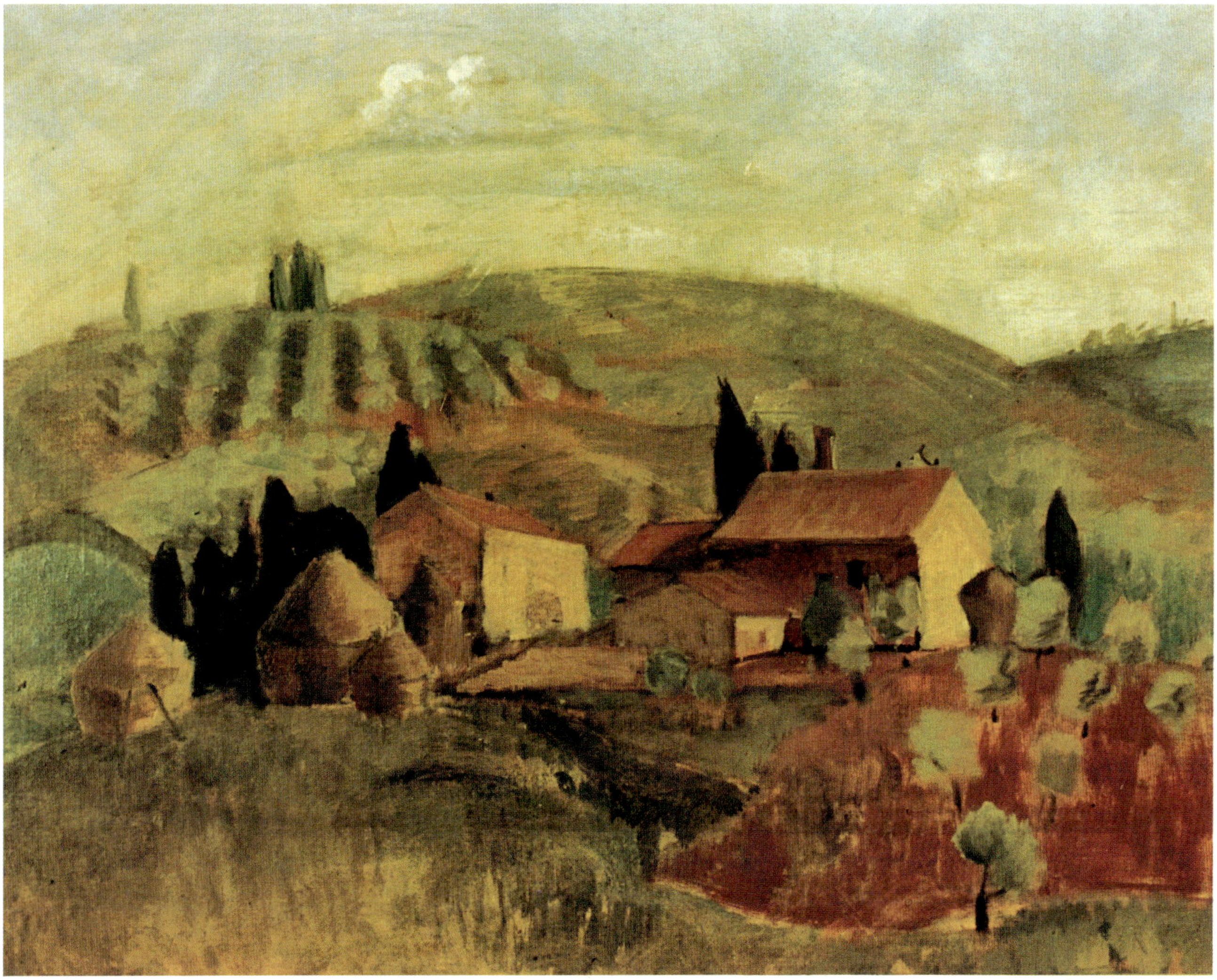

PENELOPE COLMAN. *Tuscan Landscape*, 1949. Oil on board, 14in x 17in. Courtesy of Juliet Pilkington.

CARDEW, *Seth Christopher Mason* (b.1934)
A sculpture student from 1957-61, he was taught and most influenced by Vogel*. After leaving Camberwell he spent the next ten years in the film industry working as a sculptor and model maker with MGM at Pinewood and Shepperton. During the 1970s he also taught sculpture at various schools in London. By 1974 he had started the Wenford Bridge Pottery in Cornwall, where he is still based. During his student years he showed his work at the R.A. Summer Exhibitions and more recently he has shown his pottery at various ceramic exhibitions in England and America.

CARMICHAEL, *Sandy see* FAWKES, *Sandy*

CARTER, *Bernard Arthur Ruston* (b.1909)
Known as Sam Carter, he originally studied Modern Languages at Cambridge, Grenoble and Innsbruck before commencing Art studies at the Central School in 1932. He exhibited regularly with the Euston Road Group before the War, and taught at Camberwell from 1944-49. He left and joined the staff at the Slade, where he taught Perspective and eventually became Professor of Perspective at the R.A. Schools in 1975 until his retirement in 1983.

CARY, *Caroline Anne* (*née* Butler) (b.circa 1940)
Trained at Camberwell School of Art 1958-59 and later at Chelsea School of Art. She

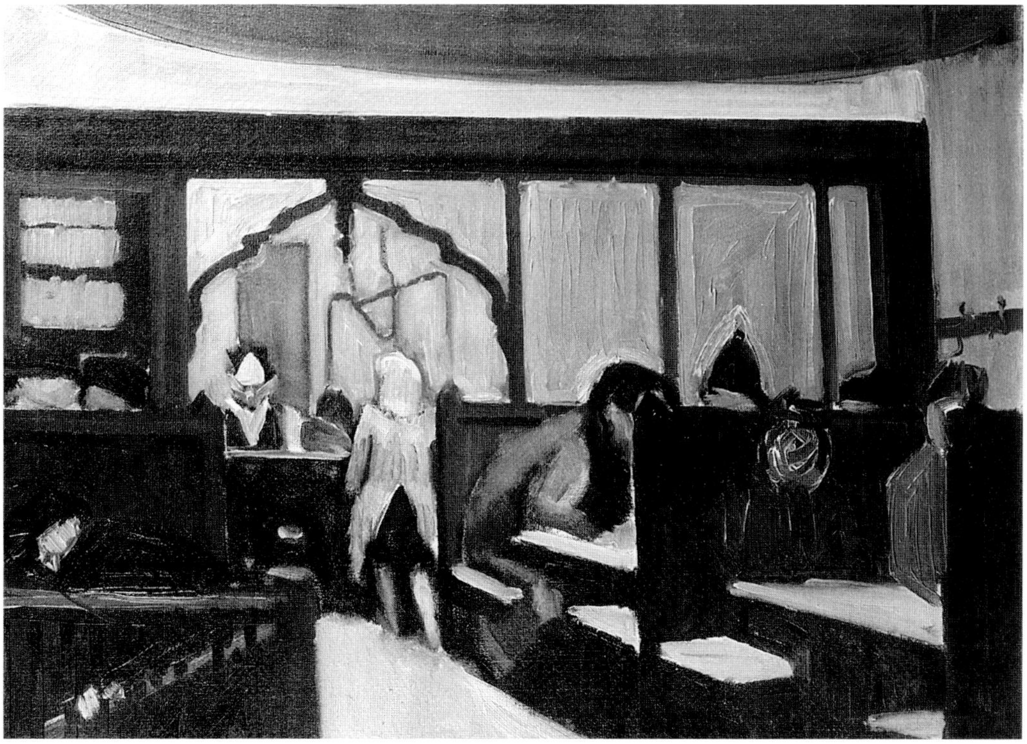

B. A. R. (SAM) CARTER. *Winchester Dining Rooms.* Oil on canvas, 18in x 24in. Private collection.

ceased painting professionally for many years in order to look after her family. She commenced exhibiting professionally during the early 1970s and has shown in group exhibitions at the Mall Galleries, Clarges Gallery, Jonathan Poole Gallery and at Austin/Desmond Fine Art, Exeter. Her one-woman shows have been held at the Loggia Gallery, Century Gallery (Henley-on-Thames) and at other galleries at home and abroad including Nairobi, Kenya. Her most recent one-woman exhibition was at the Sue Rankin Gallery, London, 1992.

CASH, *Christopher* (1919-1982)
Educated at Stowe School, he spent the years 1938-39 at Reading University in the Art Department. After the war years in the Far East as a decoder, he joined Camberwell in 1946 as a mature student. In 1950, he went to Bedales School as Art Master, a position he was to hold until 1978. We have been unable to find any instances of his work having been exhibited and none of his early work seems to exist.

CHAMBERLAIN, *George Christopher* A.R.C.A. (1918-84)
Attended Clapham School of Art 1934-38 when he joined the R.C.A. before the war interrupted his studies. After the war, at the beginning of 1946, he continued his studies, receiving his Associateship from the R.C.A. in 1947. He first taught at Camberwell during 1948 on a part-time basis, holding a similar position at Bromley College of Art for a number of years. In 1972 he became a full-time Senior Lecturer at Camberwell. He had a painting purchased by the Chantrey Bequest for the Tate Gallery in 1954 and his work is in many public collections, including Southampton Art Gallery; and the National Gallery of South Australia. He had a one-man exhibition in 1954 at the Trafford Gallery, London.

CHAPMAN, *June Dianne* (b.1939)
A student at Camberwell from 1955-56, her main teacher was Christopher Chamberlain*. She has shown her work in numerous group exhibitions, including the R.B.A., R.O.I., the U.A. and at the Blackheath Gallery. She abandoned painting for many years and only recently recommenced as a full-time freelance artist.

CHARLESWORTH, *Geoffrey Terence* (b.1930)
He began his art studies in his native South Africa where, from 1948-51, he attended the Durban School of Art, winning the Emma Smith's Scholarship for Overseas Study, when from 1951-52 he attended Camberwell. On his return from studying abroad he became a full-time professional painter in Durban, painting mainly landscapes and commissioned portraits. He has exhibited extensively in South Africa and his work is included in the collection of Durban Art Gallery.

CHRISTIE, *Eleanor Graham* (*née* Munro) (b.1929)
She was a student in the Sculpture School under Vogel* from 1959-63, having already had some art tuition at Glasgow School of Art during the mid-1950s. She has held numerous teaching posts in the London area and, with her late husband, Fife Christie, had a joint exhibition at the Woodlands Gallery (Blackheath) in 1979.

CHUGG, *Brian John* (b.1926)
Studied art at Bideford, Devon, from 1946-49 before joining Camberwell, where he was to remain for twelve months. Having decided to make a career in teaching, he attended the University of London (Institute of Education) before returning to his native Devon where, from 1953 until 1979, he was an Art Lecturer. In 1953 he held a retrospective exhibition in Barnstaple and he has also exhibited widely, including the R.B.A., Piccadilly Gallery, Leicester Gallery and various other London venues. He is the author of *Victorian and Edwardian Devon from Old Photographs* (1975) and *Devon: A Thematic Study* (1980). He was for many years a contributor to 'Country Diary' in the *Guardian.*

CLARE, *Joan* (b.1925)
During the years 1942-45 she studied art at the Witwatersrand Technical Art School under Maurice van Essche (1906-1977). Arriving in London during the post-war years, she attended Regent Street Polytechnic and Camberwell 1948-49, where she studied under Pasmore* and Buckland-Wright*. She had further part-time tuition at the Anglo-French Art School. During the early 1950s she exhibited her work with the Young Contemporaries and showed in group exhibitions in New Zealand. Returning to South Africa in 1952, she taught for eight years at the Transvaal Teachers Training College and for a further two years at a College in Johannesburg. She participated in numerous group exhibitions, but only held two solo exhibitions during a ten year period. Towards the end of the 1970s she attended the University of Pretoria, where she studied Landscape Architecture. Her other group exhibitions include the Venice Biennale (1956), São Paulo Biennale (1966), and her work is in the public collections of the Pretoria Arts Museum and the University of Witwatersrand Galleries.

CLARKE, *Anna Maria* (*née* Potworowska) (b.1936)
The daughter of the Polish artist Peter Potworowski (1889-1962), she arrived in England as a refugee in 1944 by way of Sweden. She attended Camberwell from 1956-59, where she studied Textile Design and was greatly influenced by Joe Dixon. Following a further two years at the R.C.A, she worked in the Textile Design studio of Liberty's in London, until 1964. She has also lectured in printed textiles at Hornsey College of Art, Middlesex Polytechnic and the Central School of Arts and Crafts until the early 1980s.

CLARKE, *John George* (b.1913)
During the early 1950s whilst studying at Camberwell he was taught by Frith* and Nuttall-Smith*. He appears not to have shown his work anywhere, with the exception of a group exhibition involving graphic artists at the Mall Galleries in the early 1970s.

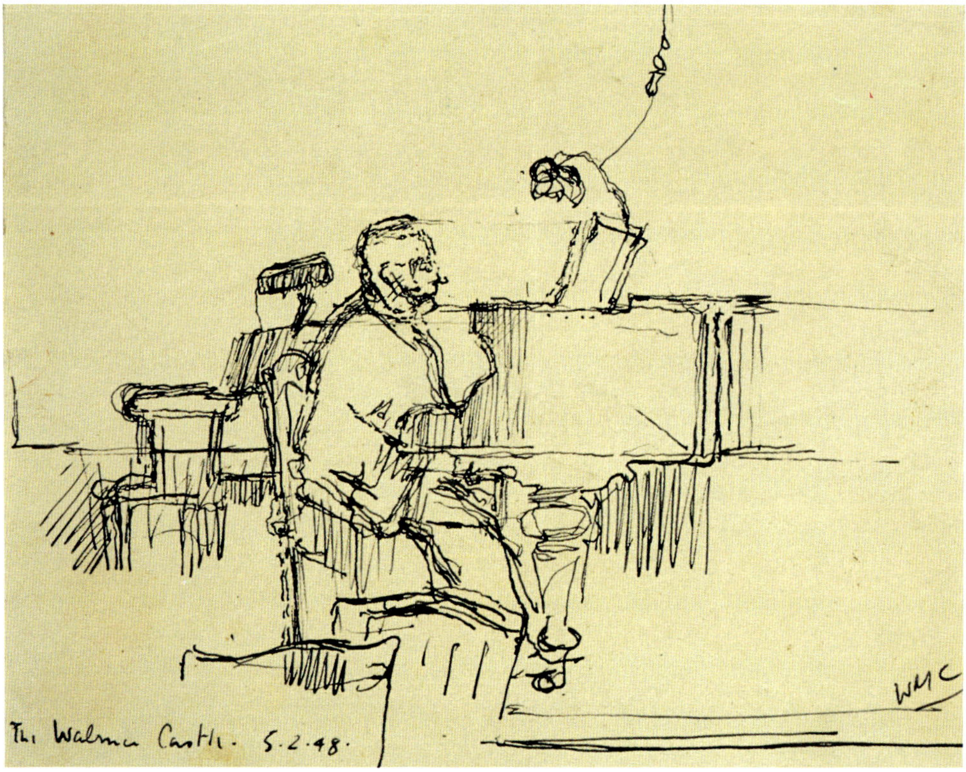

WILLIAM COLDSTREAM. *The Piano Player, Walmer Castle Pub*, 1948. Ink, 5in x 7in. Private collection.

CLIPSON, *Michael Clark* N.D.D., A.T.C. (b.1935)
He studied at Camberwell 1952-56, where he was taught and influenced by Dixon* and Michael Rothenstein*. After completing his National Service, he spent two years at Brighton College of Art studying for teacher training. He has spent all his working life as an art teacher and is currently Head of Art at the Bluecoat School in Oldham.

COHEN, *Harold* (b.1928)
Following National Service in the R.A.F., where he did a little spare-time painting, he joined the Slade School of Fine Art in 1948. After four years of study he was awarded the Abbey Travelling Scholarship, enabling him to visit Italy for six months. On his return in 1952, he was appointed as Lecturer in Art History at Camberwell, a position he was to hold for the next two years. Simultaneously, he was to follow his passion for mathematics by teaching it at a Preparatory School. In 1959 he resided in New York, thanks to a Harkness Commonwealth Fellowship, and travelled extensively throughout the U.S.A. On his return to England in 1961, he taught at St. Martin's School of Art, and then for three years at the Slade School of Fine Art. He is currently living and working in California where, with the aid of computers, he is exploring new fields in art. He has had numerous one-man exhibitions, including the Ashmolean Museum (Oxford), Gimpel Fils and the Whitechapel Art Gallery. His group exhibitions have included 'Eleven British Painters', (I.C.A.), 'Dimensions' (O'Hana Gallery), Auckland City Art Gallery, The Art Gallery of New South Wales, John Moores Exhibition (Liverpool), Musée de l'Art Moderne (Paris), the Carnegie Institute, The Dallas Museum of Contemporary Arts, Tokyo Metropolitan Art Gallery and The Tate Gallery. His work is in many public collections, including the Art Gallery of Toronto, Arts Council of Great Britain, The British Council, The Gulbenkian Foundation, The Tate Gallery and The Peter Stuyvesant Foundation.

COLDSTREAM, *William Menzies* Kt., C.B.E. (1908-1987)
In 1926 he attended the Slade School of Fine Art for three years under the tuition of

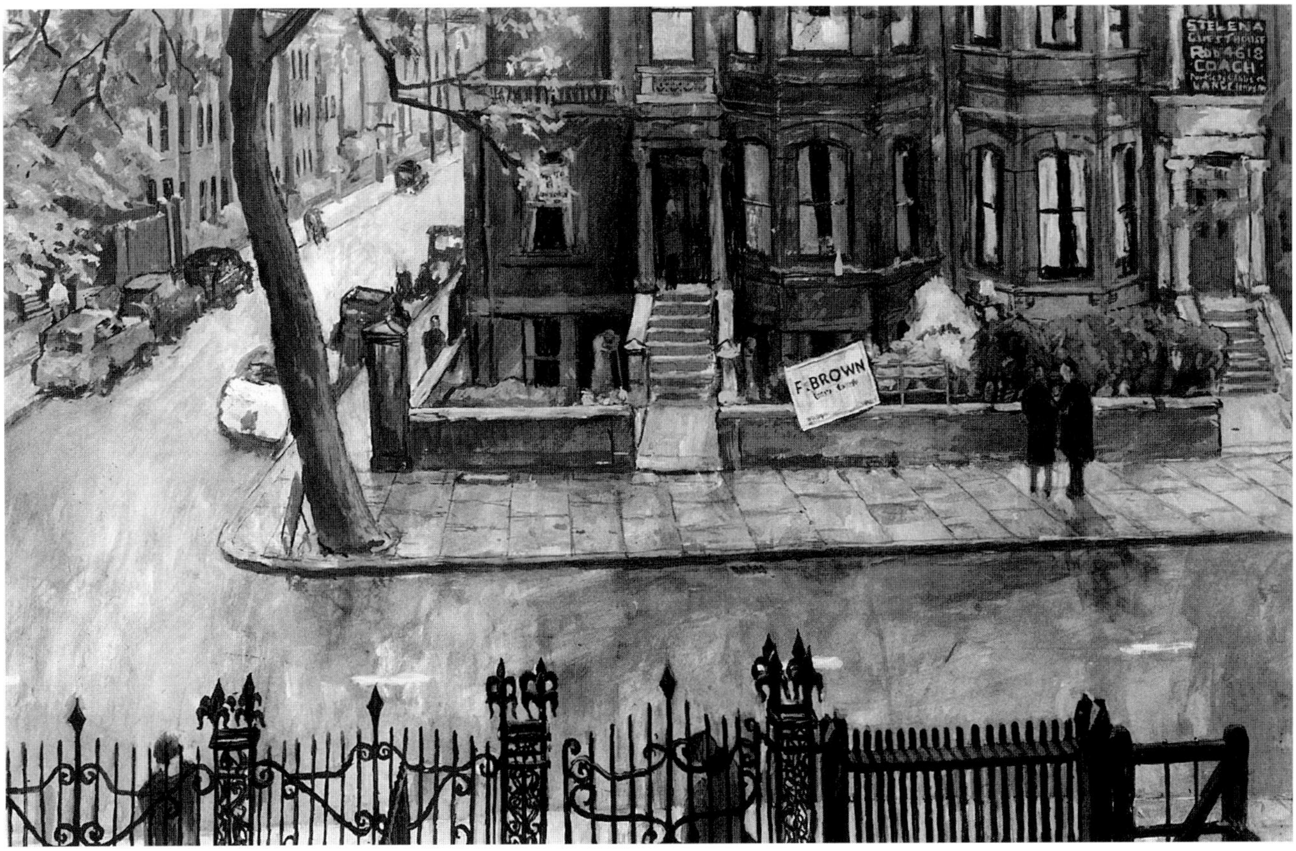

FRANK COLLINS. *A View from Camberwell Art School,* 1955. Gouache, 14½in x 21¾in. Private collection.

Henry Tonks. In 1931 he joined the L.A.A. and became a member of the L.G. in 1933. The following year, uncertain about his own work, he abandoned painting altogether and joined the G.P.O. Film Unit under the leadership of John Grierson, making documentary films including *The King's Stamp* and *Coal Face*, on which he worked with W. H. Auden. In 1937, under the patronage of Sir Kenneth Clark, he resumed full-time painting and with his friends – Claude Rogers* and Victor Pasmore* – started a School of Drawing and Painting, later to become known as the Euston Road School, a title which was to adhere to the work of its teachers and pupils. It was to close as soon as war began and Coldstream's career was interrupted when he joined the Royal Artillery in 1940. Three years later he was appointed an Official War Artist, working first in Cairo and later in Italy. On his return to England in 1945 he went to teach at Camberwell School of Art and Crafts, again joining forces with his Euston Road colleagues. The influence that Coldstream had on the students was paramount. This lives on in the work of many of the pupils who came under his instruction. By 1949 he had been appointed Slade Professor at University College London, a position he was to hold until his retirement in 1975. His work was shown internationally as early as 1938 in the World's Fair in New York and a retrospective exhibition organised by his pupil friend and colleague, Philip Matthews*, was held at the South London Art Gallery in 1962. His work is represented in the collections of the Tate Gallery, National Gallery of Canada, National Museum of Wales, the Ashmolean Museum, the Imperial War Museum, the Arts Council of Great Britain, and Bristol Art Gallery.

COLLINGWOOD, *Peter Dodgson* O.B.E. (b.1922)

Currently one of the country's leading authorities on textiles, he studied under Ethel Mairet, Barbara Sawyer* and Alistair Morton during the late 1940s and early 1950s. He first taught at Hammersmith School of Art before joining the staff at Camberwell about 1958. As well as running his own workshop he has also taught at the Central School of Arts & Crafts and Farnham College of Art. His solo exhibitions have included such venues as the V. & A., Roland, Browse & Delbanco, Textile Museum, Washington, U.S.A. and the Crafts Council Gallery, London.

COLLINS, *Frank* A.R.C.A., N.D.D. (b.1938)
Studied at Camberwell 1954-58. During this time he was awarded a French Government Scholarship and he studied etching with S. W. Hayter at 'Atelier 17' in Paris during the late 1950s. He continued his studies at the R.C.A. 1960-63 and was awarded his Associateship in 1963. He was awarded an Arts Council prize for painting in 1974. He has travelled widely around the world and has held one-man exhibitions at the A.I.A. Gallery, Whitechapel Art Gallery, and the City of London Polytechnic Gallery. His group exhibitions include the L.G., Young Contemporaries, John Moores, and the Barbican Centre (London). His work is represented in public collections at the R.C.A. and the Camberwell School of Art and in many private collections around the world. He currently teaches at the Sir John Cass Faculty of Arts where he is Senior Lecturer and Course Organiser for Foundation Art and Design. He has written many articles on art, including a series of Master Classes on the use of Acrylics for the *Artist* magazine, where his work is illustrated.

COLMAN, *Penelope* (b.1927)
She was a student at Camberwell 1946-48, where Burn* and Johnstone* affected her early career. In 1949 she left Camberwell for a three year spell at the Central School of Arts & Crafts, spending a great deal of her time in the Theatrical Design department. She has exhibited widely, including Women's International Art Club and Galerie de Seine. During the 1950s she worked in theatre design and for twenty years, until the beginning of the 1980s, she stopped painting completely. However, during the last few years she has begun to exhibit again at galleries in Suffolk, Norfolk and London.

COMYNS CARR, *Julian Gustav* (b.1932)
Now known as Julian Pemberton, he was a student at Camberwell from 1949-53, where his teachers and main influences were Bloch* and Salaman*. Almost immediately after leaving Camberwell, he went into commercial television and by the early 1960s was running his own scenery business. His biggest painting to date has been one of 530ft. in length and 30ft. high for the British Pavilion in Tokyo. He is still involved in television.

COOK, *Rosemary Ann* (*née* Reckitt) (b.1934)
Studied at Camberwell 1952-54, where she was taught by Brason*, Dixon* and Pitchforth*. She worked as a picture editor with Bodley Head for six years, where she was involved with the History of the First and Second World Wars.

COOKE, *Jean Esme Oregon* RA (b.1927)
Born in London, Jean Cooke first studied illustration and textile design at Central School of Arts and Crafts, 1943-45. She attended Camberwell 1946-48, where she studied painting and sculpture. She also attended Goldsmiths' College 1949-50, before setting up a pottery workshop in Sussex. In 1953 she met and married John Bratby (1928-1992) and continued her studies at the Royal College of Art. She has held solo exhibitions since the mid-1960s at such venues as Leicester Galleries, Bear Lane Gallery (Oxford), Ash Barn Gallery (Farnham) and New Grafton Gallery. She has also shown in group exhibitions at the Tate Gallery, Agnews, R.B.A., L.G. and the Royal Academy, of which she was elected an Associate in 1965 and a full Member in 1972.

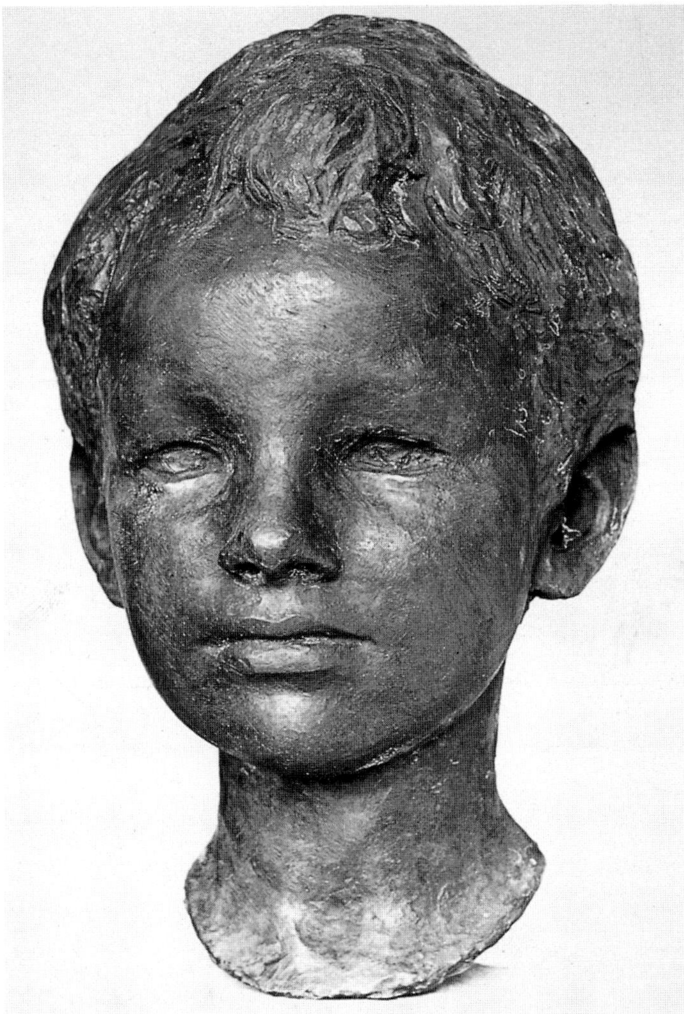

RICHARD COWDY. *Portrait of a Child.* Bronze, 10in high. Artist's collection.

COPE, *Lesley Yvonne* (*née* De Villiers) (1921-1988)
Much influenced by the Euston Road teachers, she first went to Camberwell in 1945. She showed her work only in student exhibitions in this country but since the early 1950s, when she took up residence in South Africa, she held numerous one-woman exhibitions in Cape Town, Port Elizabeth, Johannesburg and Durban. She married the writer Jack Cope, and was also a prolific book illustrator, working with the author Sue Hart on her children's and conservation books, one of the more recent being *Secret of the Sycamore Tree*, 1983, Johannesburg.

COWDY, *Richard Davenport* (b.1937)
He entered Camberwell as a seventeen year old, where he studied sculpture with Vogel* and Sheppard*. By 1958 he had joined the staff and was to teach there for a further three years. He has exhibited at the R.A., L.G. and at the Orangery, Holland Park. He worked at the Morris Singer Bronze Foundry for two years prior to establishing his own small foundry and studio with the help of his ex-Camberwell colleague, Nigel Konstam*.

COX, *Kenelm* (1927-1968)
His art studies began during the immediate post-war years at the R.W.A. in Bristol. In 1950 he began his studies at Camberwell and for the next three years was much influenced by Rogers*. During the early 1960s he held various teaching posts in

ANNE CREWS. *Wimbledon Fair Ground*, 1952. Oil on panel, 7½in x 9¾in.
Artist's collection.

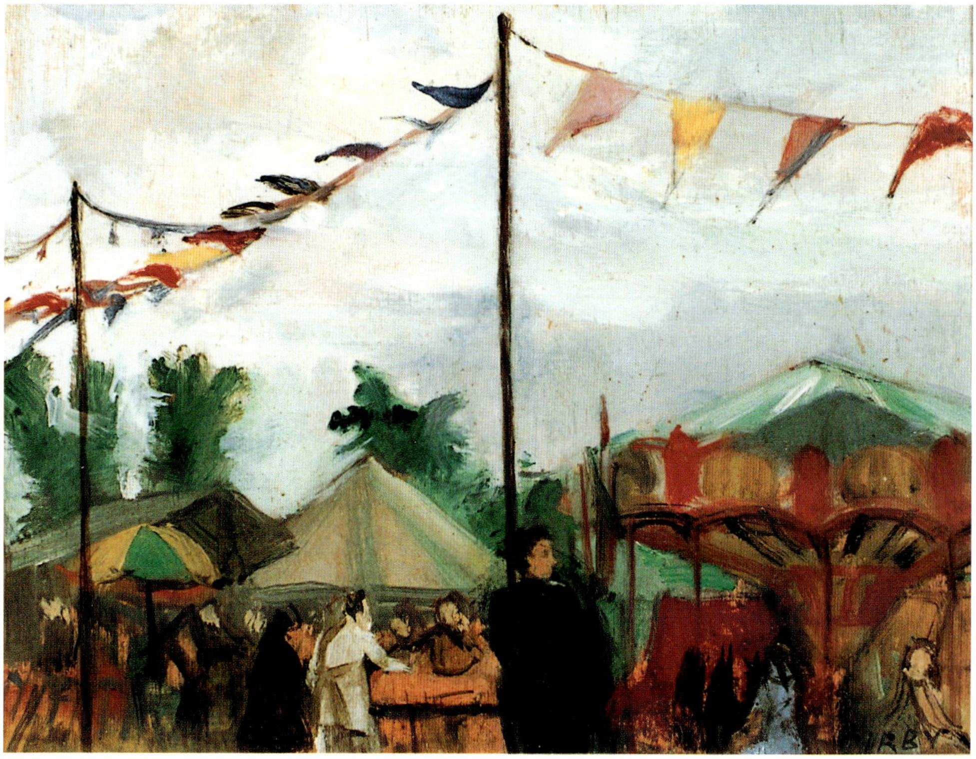

both Gloucestershire and Oxfordshire and in 1965 he exhibited at the I.C.A. in 'Between Poetry and Painting'. In the remaining few years of his short life, he continued to exhibit in various group shows including the Midlands Group (Nottingham), Arnolfini (Bristol), and in 1968 his only one-man show was held at the Lisson Gallery. Little else is known of his career as an artist but thanks to research by Mr. Richard Sladden and the Librarian of the Epsom School of Art & Design, and to information supplied by the Tate Gallery Library, it is apparent that Cox was also known for his involvement in cybernetics and computer related arts and he is mentioned in an article published in *Studio International* magazine entitled 'Cybernetic Serendipity' (1968).

CRAMPTON, *Christine Winifred see* MORLEY, *Christine Winifred*

CREWS, *Anne Pauline* (*née* Irby) (b.1927)
Following a period at Maidenhead School of Art, she attended the Central School, where she studied theatre design. At the end of the Second World War she worked at Pinewood Film Studios as a set designer and also as a researcher in the theatre. She first attended Camberwell School of Art in 1949 where she furthered her studies under Claude Rogers* and Richard Eurich*. In 1950, after receiving a major county award, she was able to continue her studies until the end of 1951. During this time, she exhibited with the L.G. before marrying an ophthalmic surgeon and moving to Birmingham, where she now resides. She has also exhibited at the Ikon Gallery, Arts Faculty of Birmingham University, Royal Society of Birmingham Artists and the R.A. An accomplished printmaker, she has studied in Cornwall with Bryan Ingham and has worked seriously as a printmaker since the early 1980s. In 1993 she helped to establish the Birmingham Print Workshop.

CROSS, *Roy* (b.1924)
He attended Camberwell briefly between 1952-53, since then he has become an important historical marine and aviation painter, who has exhibited at galleries in the U.K., Sweden and the U.S.A. He has also worked as a freelance illustrator and until the early 1970s as a commercial artist. A member of the R.S.M.A. and the Society of Aviation Artists, his work shows no obvious signs of Camberwell influence.

D

DANIEL, *Valerie* (*née* Bennett) (b.1926)
Awarded a Slade scholarship in 1946, she taught Design and the History of Costume at Camberwell between 1949-54. She has held one-woman exhibitions in London and Suffolk and has exhibited widely in mixed exhibitions at the R.A., Pallas Gallery and in Ireland and Canada.

DANIELS, *Leonard James* R.C.A. (b.1909)
Began art studies at the R.C.A. c.1929, winning the Royal College Portrait Prize in 1932. He exhibited at the Goupil Gallery several times during the mid-1930s and at the Redfern Gallery in 1939. He was commissioned by the War Artists' Advisory

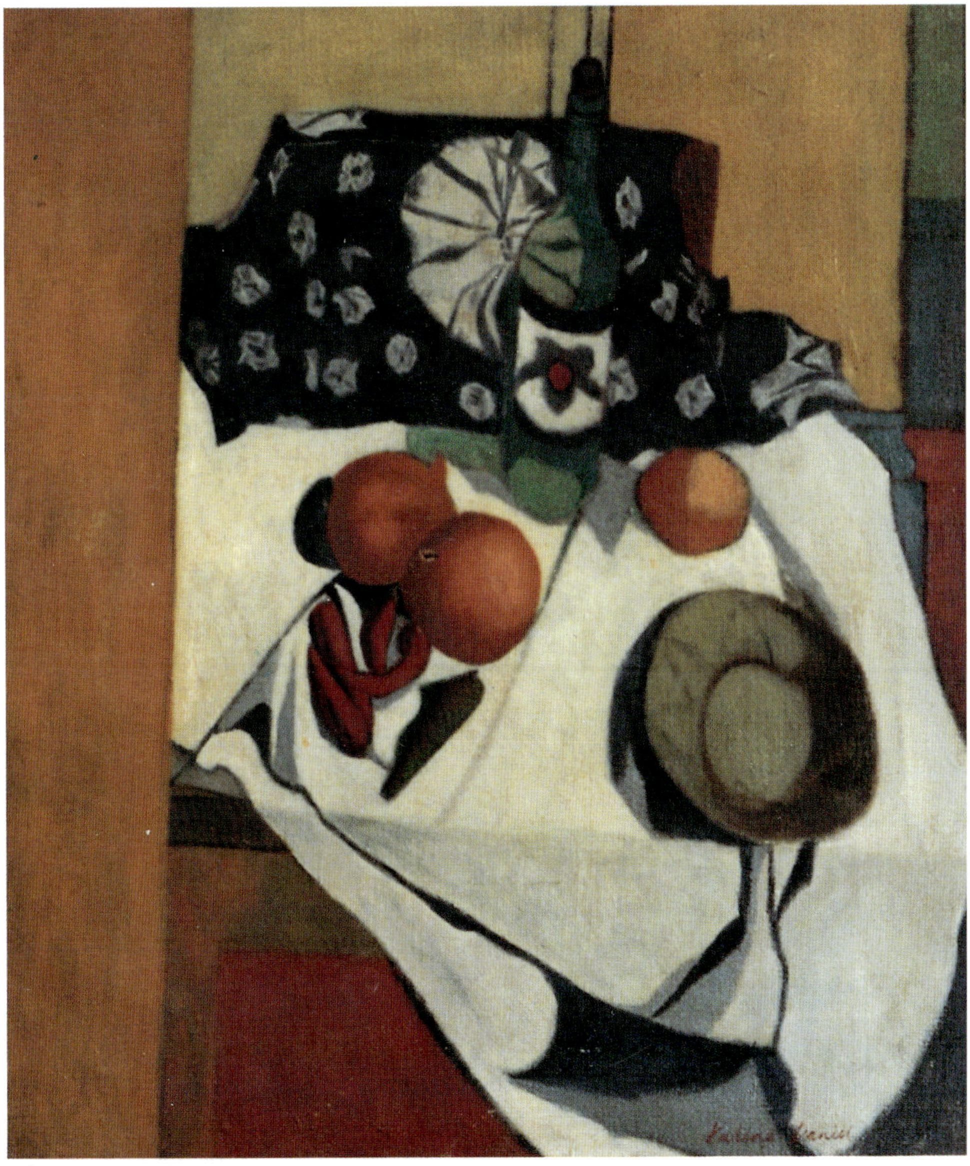

VALERIE DANIEL. *Still Life.* Oil on canvas, 40in x 30in. Artist's collection.

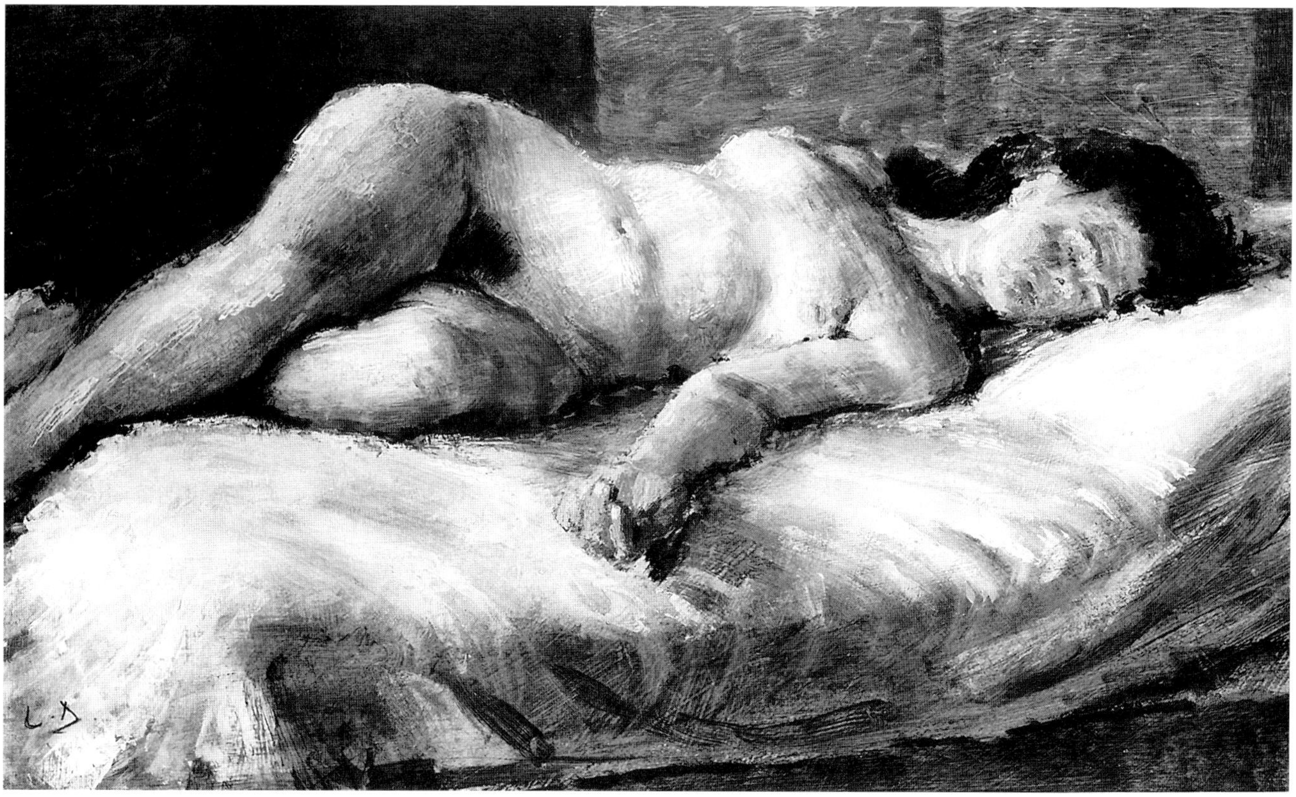

LEONARD DANIELS. *Reclining Nude*, c. 1947. Oil on board, 11in x 17in. Private collection.

Committee and his work is represented in the Imperial War Museum. After the war he showed in Leeds in group exhibitions before becoming the Principal of Camberwell in 1948 until his retirement in 1975. He had a sabbatical leave in 1972, working extensively in the South of France.

DAWSON, *Peter Norman* A.R.C.A., L.G. (1904-1960)
He won a scholarship to the R.C.A. in the years following the First World War, having previously attended both Glasgow School of Art and St. John's Wood School of Art. In 1924 he received his Associateship, winning prizes at the R.C.A., which included a travelling scholarship in Decorative Painting, and he was also a Rome Scholarship finalist in 1925. Whilst at the College he studied, amongst other things, Etching and Engraving under Sir Frank Short, R.A., and he furthered his studies in Paris, Rome and Florence. During the years preceding the Second World War, he showed extensively at the N.E.A.C., Redfern Gallery, Goupil Gallery, Whitechapel Art Gallery, the Bradford Art Gallery and with the L.G., of which he was elected a Member in 1934. He was also associated with the first British Surrealist Exhibition during the 1935-36 period, and exhibited his Surrealist work with Yves Tanguy. He taught at Camberwell some ten years later and the records there show that he lectured in Industrial Design, Commercial Art and also taught Life Drawing. He was appointed as Principal of Winchester School of Art & Crafts in 1946, where he remained until 1952. His work is in the permanent collection of the Museum of Modern Art (New York). After leaving Winchester, he seems to have disappeared and it is probable that his last teaching post was in Secondary Education in London.

DEANE, *Sheila* *see* FORGE, Sheila

DE MAUNY, *François Gustave Lawrence* (b.1924)
Born in New Zealand, he first studied art in Wellington and, following a brief career in advertising, he arrived in London in 1946. He enrolled at Camberwell soon after and was to remain there for the next seven years, as a student firstly, and later as a

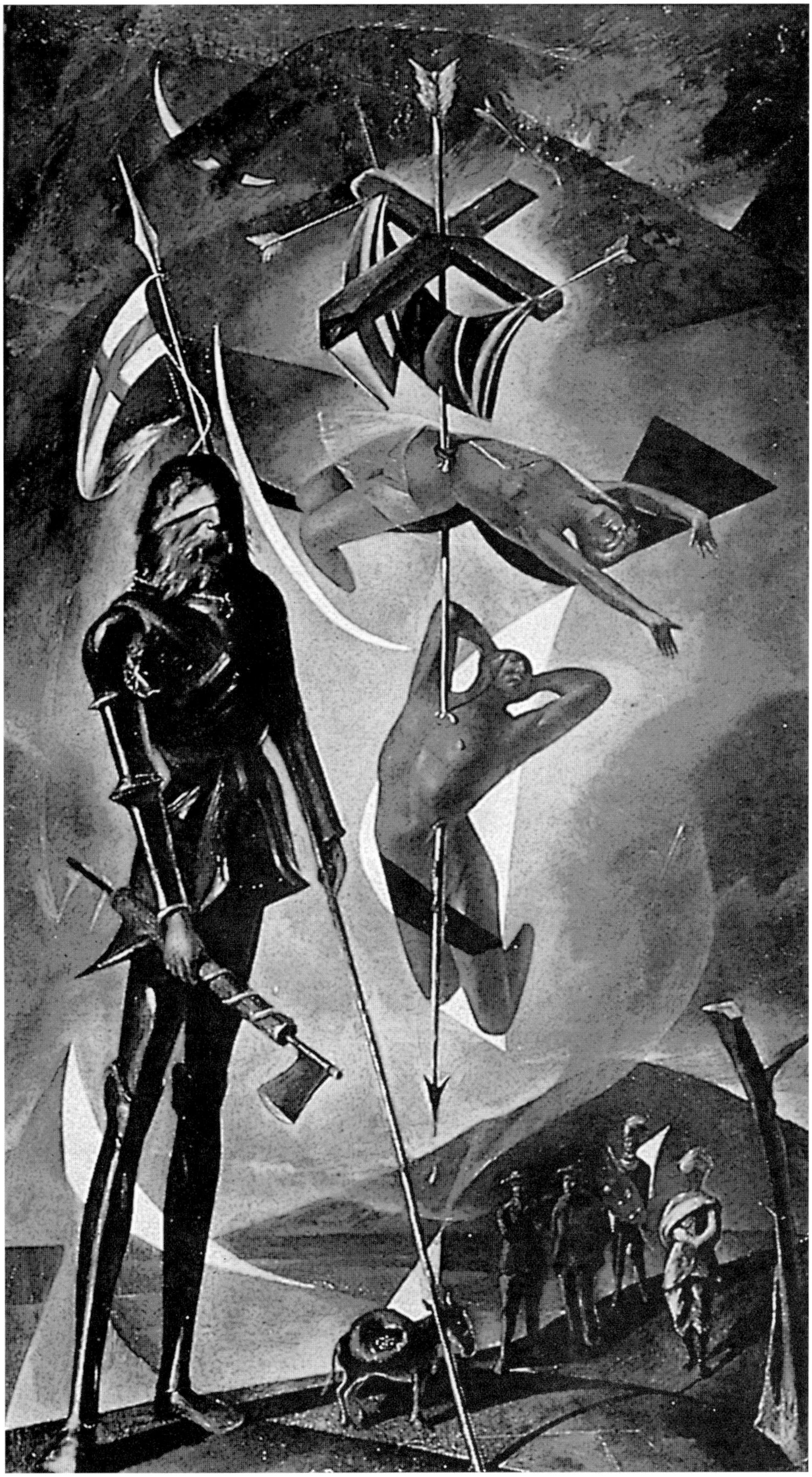

NORMAN DAWSON.
Untitled. Present whereabouts unknown.

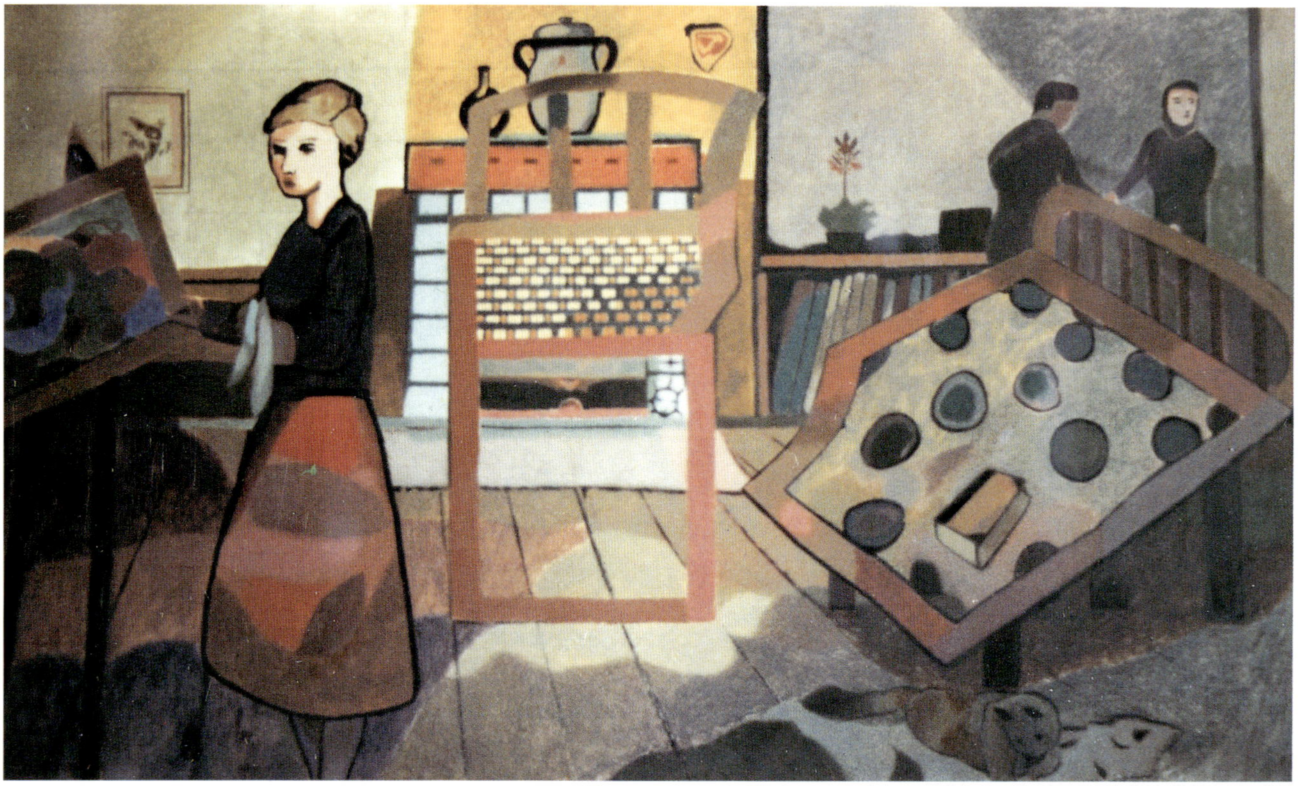

JOHN DODGSON. *Title unknown*, c.1945. Oil on canvas. Private collection.

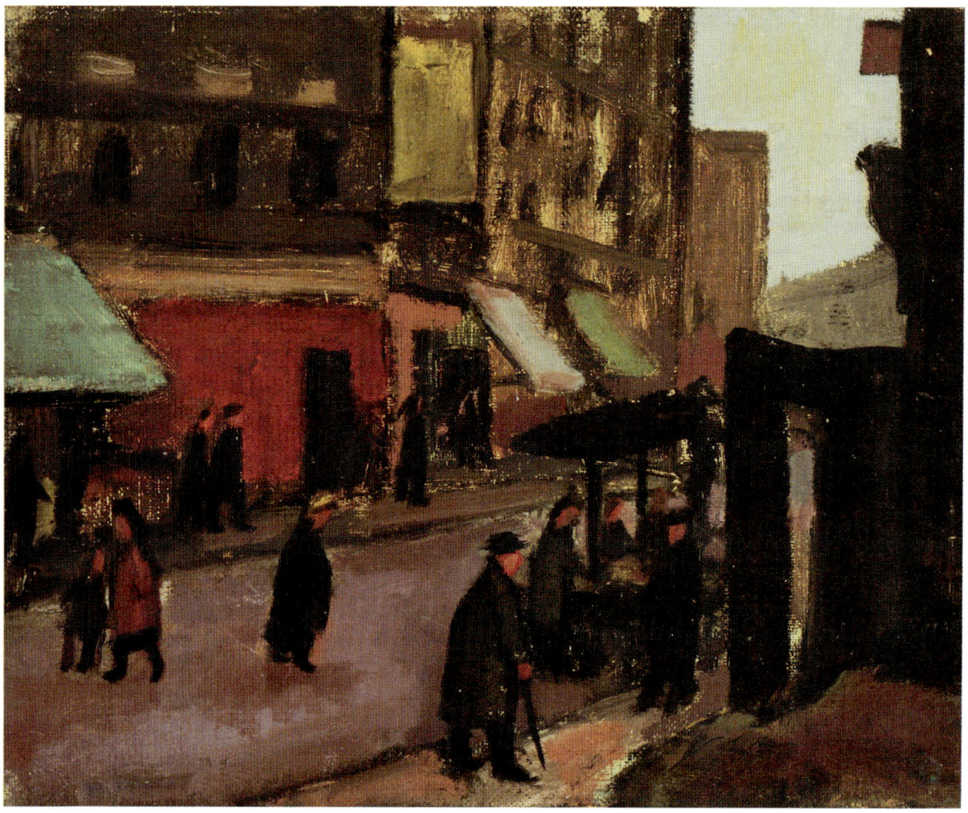

ERIC DOITCH. *Street Market, Camberwell*, c.1946. Oil on board, 10in x 12in. Private collection.

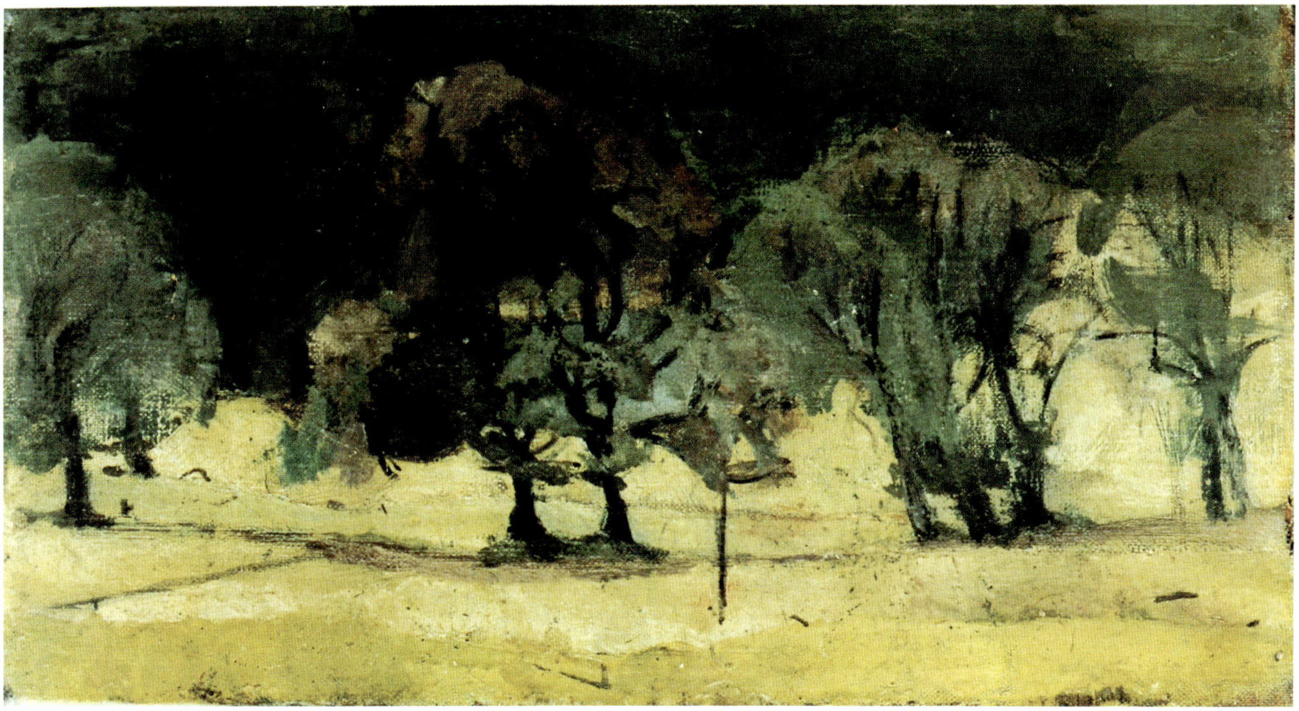

NATALIE DOWER. *Penicuik – The Low Pond.* Oil on canvas, 7¾in x 14in. Courtesy of Lucy Dynevor.

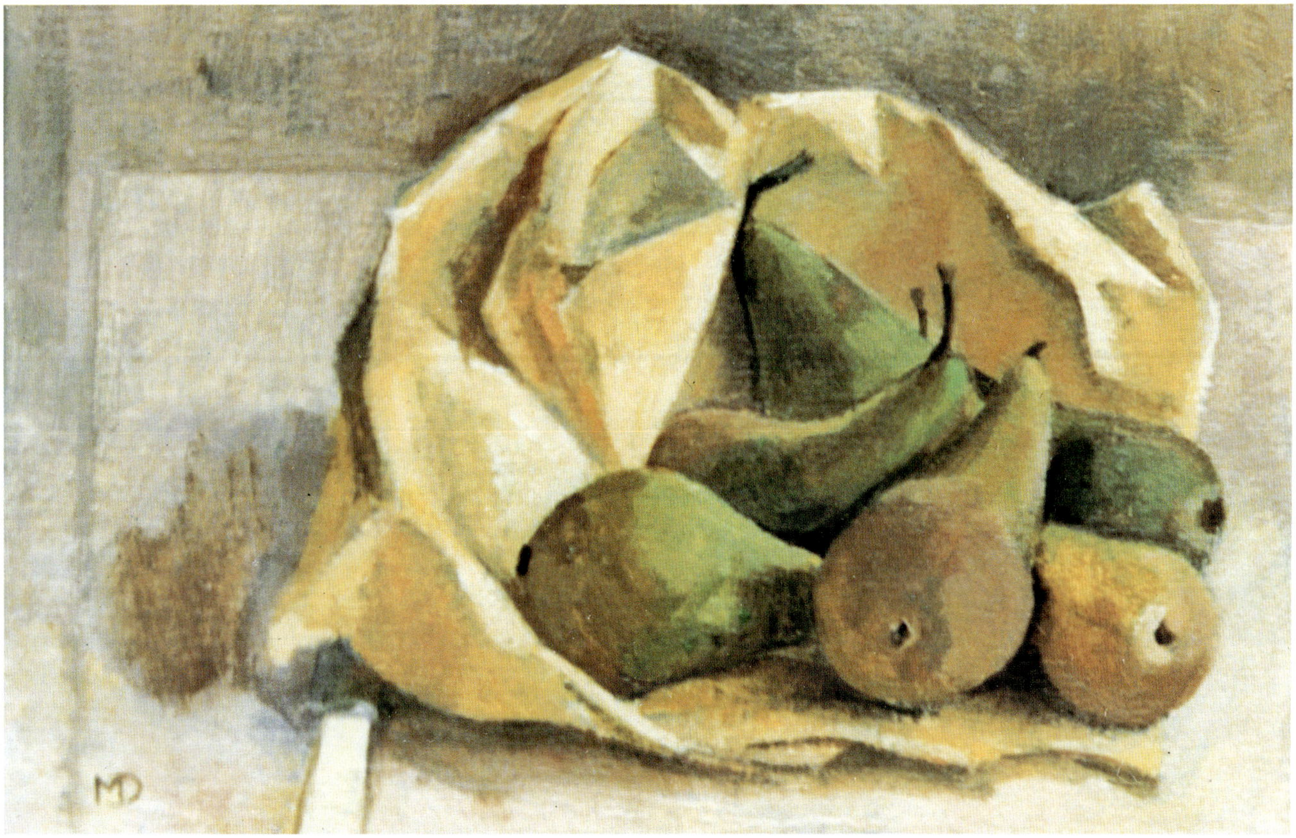

MARIANNE DOWNING. *Still Life with Pears*, 1945. Oil on canvas, 10in x 14in. Artist's collection.

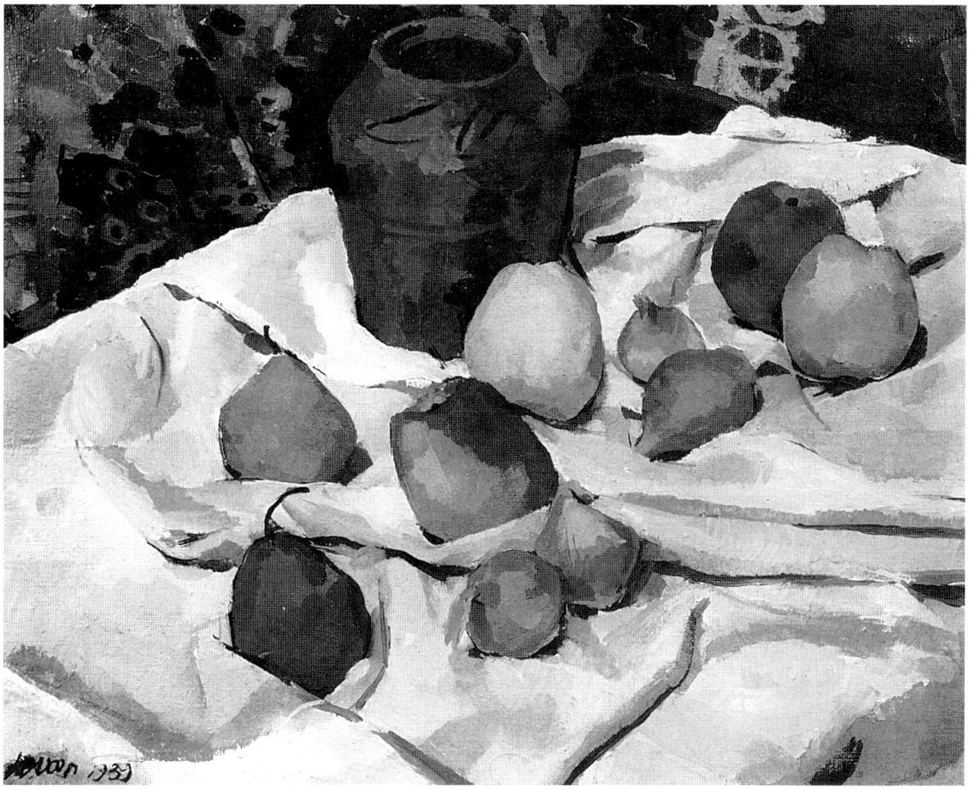

JOE DIXON. *Still Life with Fruit*, c.1939. Oil on canvas laid on board, 15½in x 19½in. Private collection.

teacher in the Junior School. He has exhibited both in France and in Cornwall where he has lived for some time. He has also followed a career in industry as a graphic designer.

DENNING, *Sheila* (b.1920)
Following a year at Heatherley's, she furthered her studies at Camberwell between 1947-51 under Bloch*, La Dell* and Pasmore*. She has shown her work in mixed exhibitions, including the R.A., R.B.A., S.W.A., R.P. and the S.G.A., and also a one-woman show at the Clarendon Gallery (London) in 1985. She taught for many years in the Adult Education Department of Chichester College of Technology. She has work in private collections in Great Britain, U.S.A. and in Spain.

DENNISTON, *Patricia Amy see* MARTIN, Patricia Amy

DE VILLIERS, *Lesley Yvonne see* COPE, *Lesley Yvonne*

DINWOODIE, *Gloria Helen Dougall see* LASER, *Gloria Helen Dougall*

DIXON, *Joseph* A.R.C.A. (1915-1991)
In 1935, following his art examination success in Lancashire, he was awarded a Royal Exhibition scholarship and for the next four years attended the R.C.A. He was mainly in the Mural Painting Department and in 1938 he was awarded a Fellowship with a Distinction and granted a Post-Graduate Award. In his final year, he was awarded a Travelling Scholarship which was not taken up until 1948. He travelled throughout Europe, spending most of his time in Florence and Rome and his love of Italy remained with him for the rest of his life. On his return to England in 1949, he took up teaching and joined Camberwell, where he remained for the next thirty years, holding various positions including Senior Lecturer, Head of Department and eventually Vice-Principal. He exhibited firstly in the mid-1930s in his native north-east Lancashire, and since 1950 on a regular basis at the R.A. He also showed at the R.W.A. and more recently in the Spirit of London exhibitions at the Hayward Gallery.

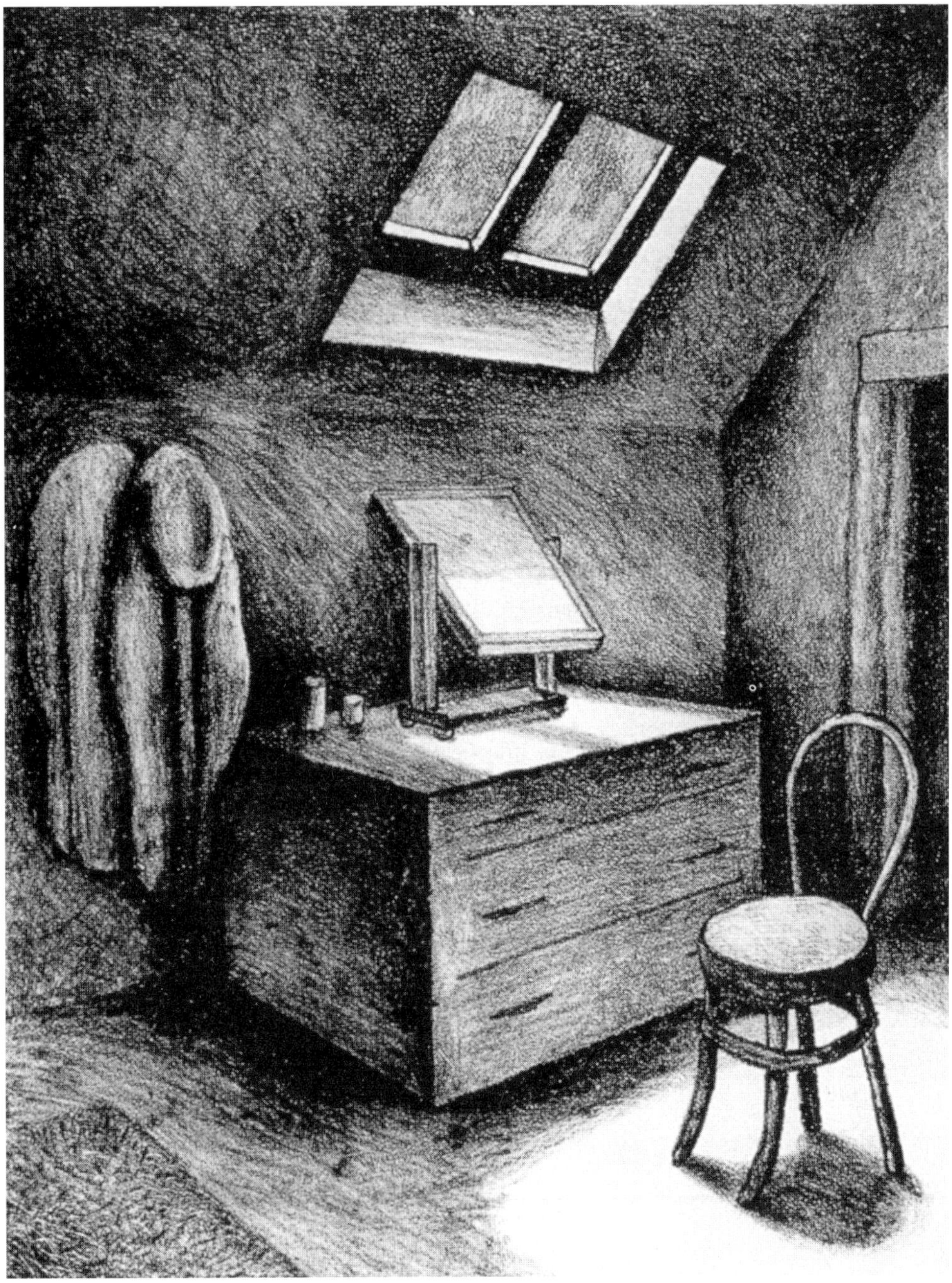

SHEILA DENNING. *The Attic in Moonlight*, 1949. Lithograph, 9½in x 7¼in. Artist's collection.

DODGSON, *John Arthur* P.L.G. (1890-1969)
Studied at the Slade School of Fine Art under Henry Tonks 1913-15. Shortly after the First World War, he was for a brief period Assistant Director of the National Gallery under Sir Charles Holmes. His first exhibition was in 1928 at the Claridge Gallery, Brook Street, London. He was exhibiting regularly with the L.A.A. in the early 1930s and held a joint exhibition with Claude Rogers at their premises in the Cooling Galleries in 1933 and was an early exhibitor with the Euston Road Group. He joined the staff at Camberwell under the Principalship of William Johnstone* during the early 1940s and remained there until 1951, before joining Chelsea School of Art, where he stayed for a period of eight years. He was a regular exhibitor during this period with the L.G. and became their President from 1950-52. He held a one-man

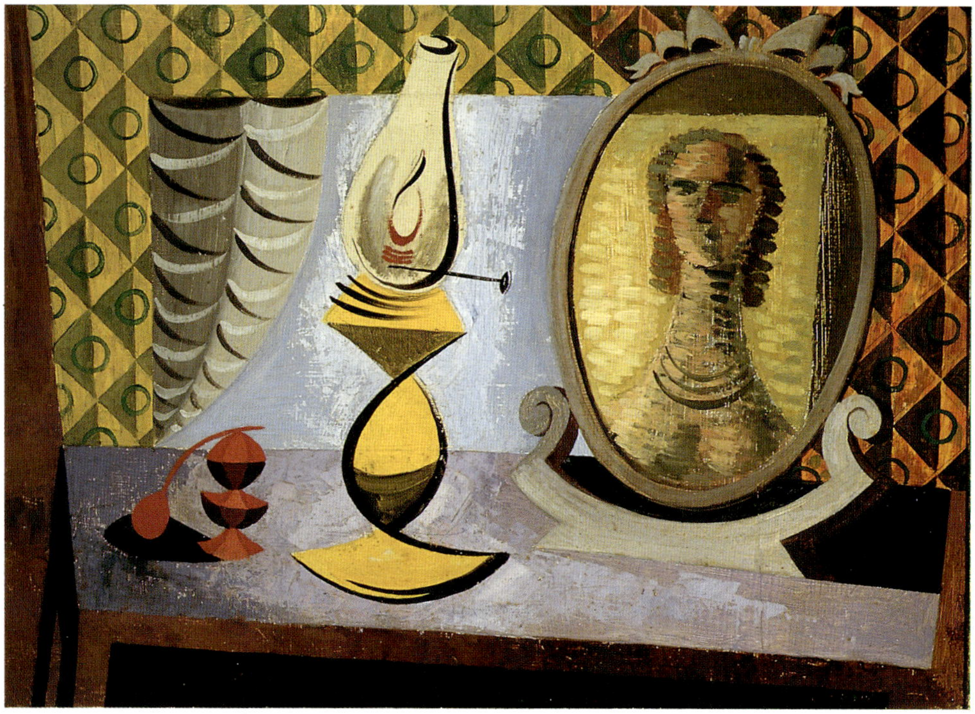

JACOB DREW. *The Oil Lamp*, 1946. Oil on panel, 18in x 24in. Private collection.

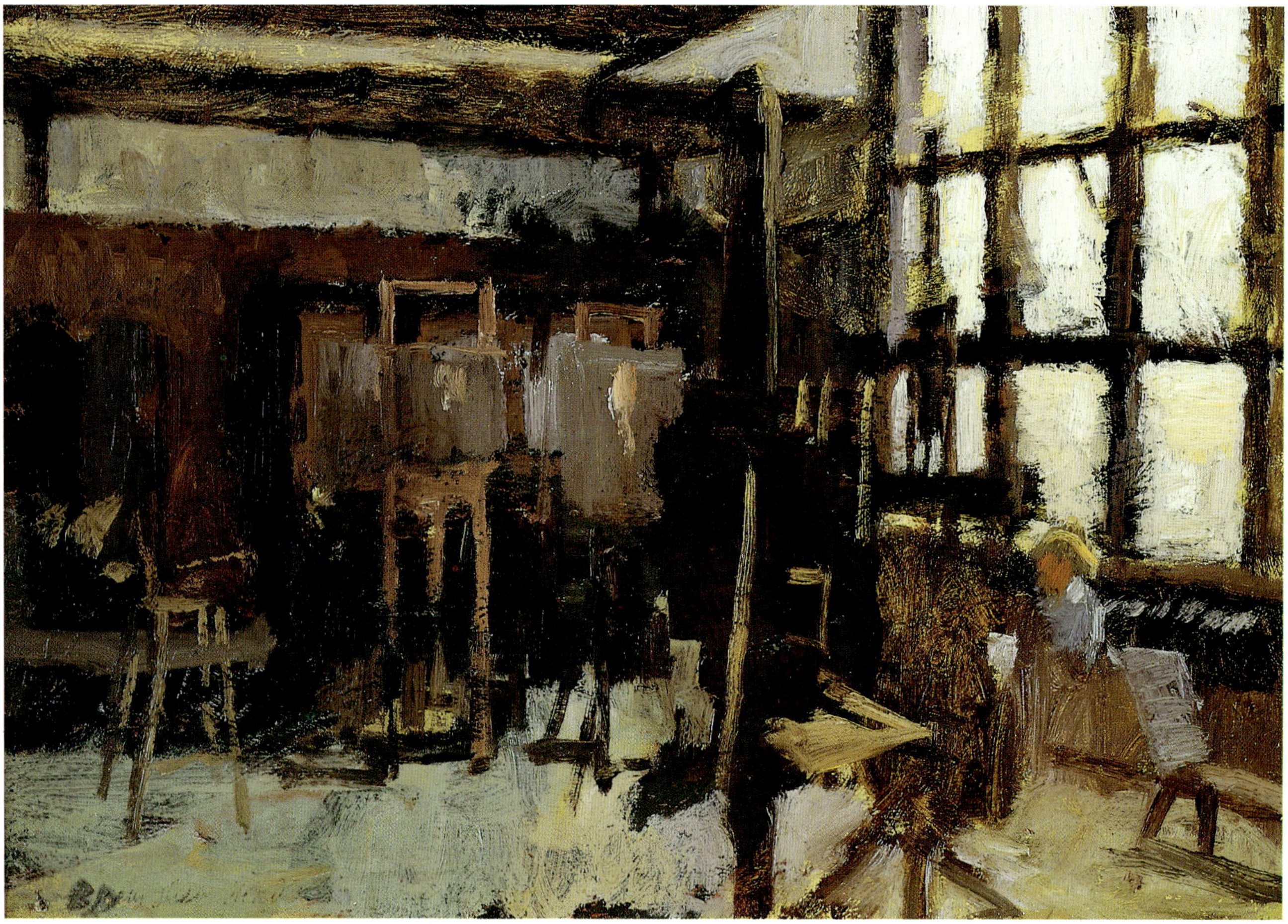

BERNARD DUNSTAN. *The Life Room*, 1950. Oil on board, 12in x 8in. Courtesy of Belgrave Gallery.

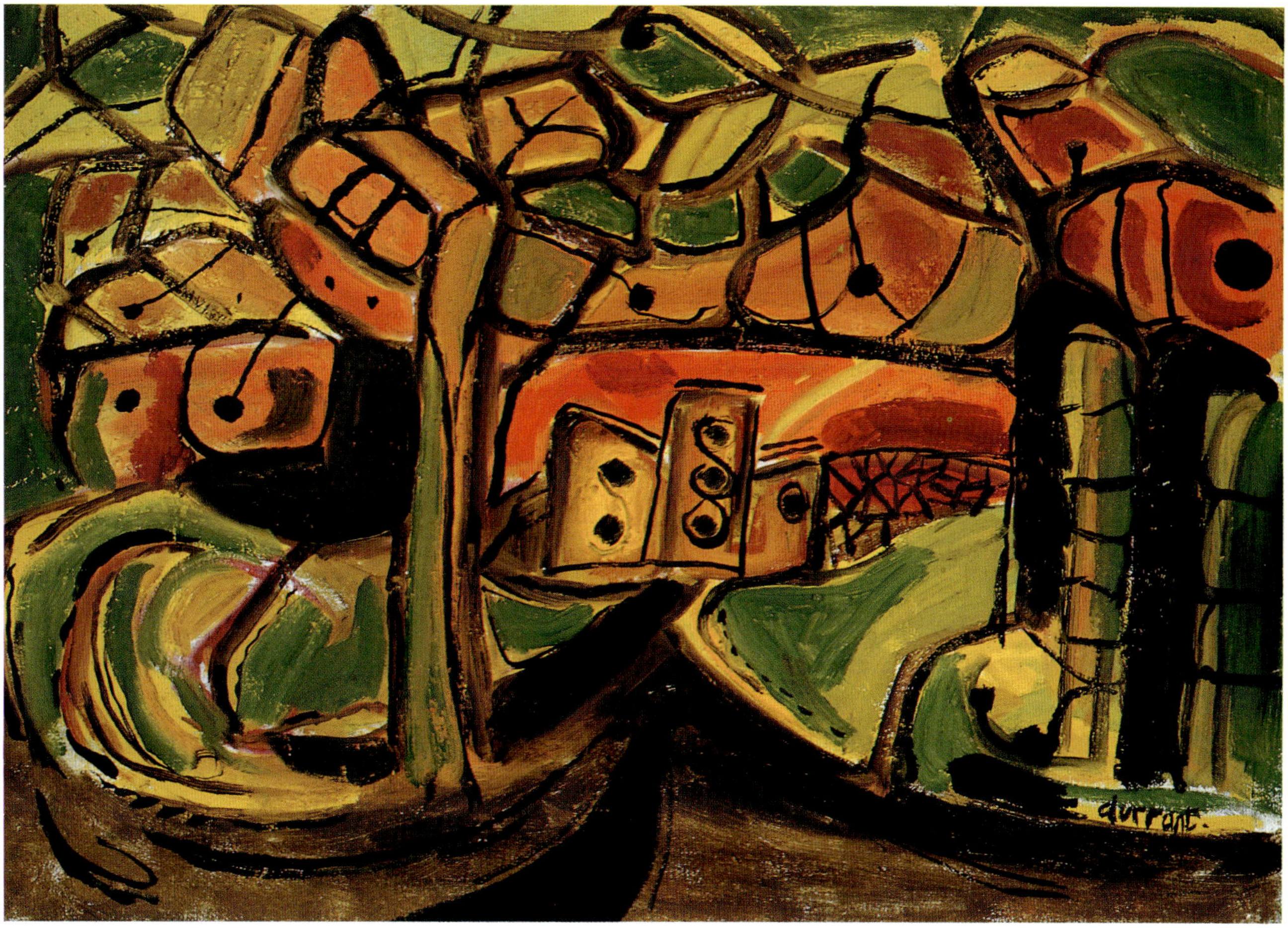

ROY TURNER DURRANT. *Landscape, Evening,* 1949. Oil on canvas, 16in x 22in. Private collection.

exhibition at the Beaux Arts Gallery a year after moving to Suffolk in 1958. Unfortunately his studio was burnt to the ground in 1964, and the vast majority of his work was lost for ever. His retrospective exhibition was held at the South London Art Gallery in 1971.

DOITCH, *Eric* A.R.C.A. (b.1923)
Born in Vienna, he came to England in 1939 as a refugee from Nazism. He was a student at Camberwell from 1946-49, where Gowing*, Pasmore* and Rogers* taught and influenced him. In 1951 he won a three year scholarship to the R.C.A., gaining his Diploma in 1954. He returned to Camberwell in 1960 as a teacher, a position he was to hold for the next four years. His work has been shown widely in Europe and the U.S.A., and in 1962 he held a one-man exhibition at Staatsdurckerei (Vienna). In 1971 his work was shown with that of his wife, Mary Fitzpayne, at the South London Art Gallery. In 1983 his work was shown in the Usher Art Gallery (Lincoln). He is currently teaching part-time at Chelsea School of Art.

DOWER, *Natalie* (b.1931)
She first began to study art at St. Martin's, which she attended from 1948-49. She then became a pupil at Camberwell, where she remained until 1952 before joining the Slade School of Fine Art for a two year period. Her main teachers and influences at Camberwell were Dodgson*, Kenneth Martin* and Salaman*. During the mid-1960s and early 1970s she taught at the American School in Tangier, Morocco and, since 1973, she has worked mainly in Portugal. Her work has been shown extensively and her group exhibitions have included the Hayward Annual, Curwen Gallery, Scottish Gallery (Edinburgh), Henri Gallery (Washington D.C.) and her

one-woman shows include Air Gallery (London 1983), Gummesons Könstgalleri (Stockholm, 1986) and Curwen Gallery (London 1987). Her work has been purchased by the Arts Council of Great Britain.

DOWLING, *Jean Elizabeth Moore* (*née* Surridge) (b.1929)
A post-war student at Camberwell from 1945-49. Her exhibiting career has included shows at the Crawford Municipal Art Gallery (Cork) and various group exhibitions in the London area. She is particularly involved with the painting of icons and has taught Icon painting and Lithography for a number of years in London.

DOWNING, *Marianne* (*née* Katz) (b.1921)
She was at Camberwell between 1943-48, where she was influenced by Carter*, Minton*, Pasmore* and Pitchforth*. She exhibited widely in the immediate post-war years, particularly with the L.G. Her first one-woman exhibition was held in Bonn, West Germany in 1986.

DRESCHA, *Trata Maria see* MAHONEY, *Trata Maria*

DREW, *Graham* (1918-1986)
Educated at Stowe School and later Caius College, Cambridge, where he briefly studied Medicine and Architecture. During the war he was a Brigade Major, executing portraits of most of the Officers of the Royal Army Corps, whose history was published after the war. He attended Camberwell School of Art as a student from 1946-48 and spent his life teaching at Bromley Grammar School in the mid-1950s, joining Winchester College where he was art master from 1958 until his retirement in 1980.

DREW, *Jacob* (b.1909)
Attended Stoke-on-Trent School of Art 1926-29 before winning a Scholarship to the R.C.A. from 1929-33. For some years after the war he was a decorator of pottery and glass. He joined the staff at Camberwell in 1946, where he was to remain for three years before becoming Principal of Willesden School of Art and subsequently Principal of Ealing School of Art from 1959 until his retirement in 1972.

DREW, *Jean* (b.1904)
Originally trained in the Design School at the R.C.A. 1929-32, after spending two years at Northampton School of Art. She then followed a career in textile design and for many years successfully sold hand-printed fabrics through major outlets such as Heals and Fortnum & Mason in London. She was offered and accepted a place teaching Textile Design at Camberwell in the immediate post-war years and was to remain there until her retirement during the 1960s, since when she has followed a career as a landscape and flower painter at her home in Wales. She married the painter Jacob Drew*.

DUNBAR, *Peter* (1929-1983)
He was a student at Camberwell for only a short period between 1946-47, during which time he was influenced by his teachers Gowing* and Minton*. His work was exhibited in the late 1940s with the 'Young Contemporaries'. He held a three-man exhibition at the St. George's Gallery with Bobby Hunt* and Owen Wood*, his two closest friends from Camberwell days. His work was shown by Michael Parkin in 'Artists of the Colony Club'. For many years he was the Art Editor of the *Financial Times*, then the *Economist.*

DUNN, *Lorna Gertrude Hayes* N.D.D. (b.1920)
Following war service with the W.R.N.S. in 1946 she enrolled as a student at

Camberwell where, for the next four years, she studied under and was most influenced by Hermes*, Minton* and Townsend*. Her work was exhibited in the late 1940s and early 1950s with the L.G. and the R.W.A. After leaving Camberwell she continued her studies at Hammersmith School of Art, taking Lithography with Alistair Grant and Drawing with Ruskin Spear and Carel Weight. Since then she has held several teaching posts in London, Essex and East Anglia and has shown her work in numerous mixed exhibitions.

DUNSTAN, *Bernard* R.A. R.W.A., N.E.A.C. (b.1920)
He first studied at the Byam Shaw School of Art under Ernest Jackson and in 1939 joined the Slade School of Fine Art, where he remained for two years. At the end of the war, he was elected a Member of the N.E.A.C. and began teaching at the West of England Art School in Bristol. In 1950 he returned to London, where he began teaching at Camberwell, a position he was to hold until the mid-1960s. He has also held many other teaching positions at Byam Shaw School of Art, Ravensbourne Art College and at the City and Guilds London Art School. His work has been exhibited widely and he has had very many successful one-man exhibitions at Agnews, Roland Browse & Delbanco and the Stremmel Galleries (Reno, Nevada). He has also published many books on painting techniques, amongst them *Painting Methods of the Impressionists*, 1976. His work is represented in many public and private collections.

DURRANT, *Roy Turner* N.D.D., F.R.S.A., F.F.P.S., N.E.A.C. (b.1925)
A student at Camberwell from 1948-52, his main teachers were Buckland-Wright*, Minton*, Michael Rothenstein* and Salaman*. During his time at Camberwell and in the early 1950s he had one-man exhibitions at Beaux Arts Gallery, A.I.A. Gallery and Roland Browse & Delbanco. Other one-man and group exhibitions have included the R.A, N.E.A.C., R.I., Grabowski Gallery, and Loggia Gallery in London. His work, besides being in the private collection of the Prince of Wales, can be found in numerous public galleries, including Graves Art Gallery (Sheffield), Usher Gallery (Lincoln), Imperial War Museum, City of Bradford Art Gallery, Southampton Art Gallery, Carlisle Art Gallery, Kettle's Yard Collection (Cambridge University), Castle Museum (Norwich), Western Australia Art Gallery (Perth), Beecroft Gallery (Westcliff-on-Sea, Essex), Museum of Modern Art (Rio de Janeiro), Royal Air Force Museum (Hendon), Worthing Art Gallery, Hove Museum & Art Gallery and the University of Adelaide (Australia). In 1960, Scorpion Press published his book of poems entitled *A Rag Book of Love*. A major retrospective was held at Belgrave Gallery in 1991.

EAGLETON, *Godfrey Paul* N.D.D. (b.1935)
He joined Camberwell as a student in 1948, where he remained until 1955. His main teachers and influences were Bloch*, Dixon* and Pitchforth*. Following two years' National Service he went to the Slade School of Fine Art until 1959, when he obtained a First Class Honours Degree in Art History. The following year, 1960, he joined the staff at Camberwell where, for seven years, he was a part-time lecturer. His earliest exhibitions were at Foyles Art Gallery, where historical and plant drawings were shown by him as a young teenager. Other exhibitions followed, including Greenwich Art Gallery, South London Art Gallery, John Moores Exhibition (Liverpool), the L.G. and in the 1980s exhibitions of Drawings and Etchings at the London College of Fashion.

EATWELL, *Brian Sydney* N.D.D. (b.1939)
Student at Camberwell 1956-60, where he was taught by Dixon*, Eyton*, Fry*, Salaman* and Symons* He gained his N.D.D. in 1960, shortly before joining The Old Vic as a theatre designer. Like his friend and colleague, Leo Austin, he is now a freelance production designer working all over the world in films and television. He is currently based in Los Angeles.

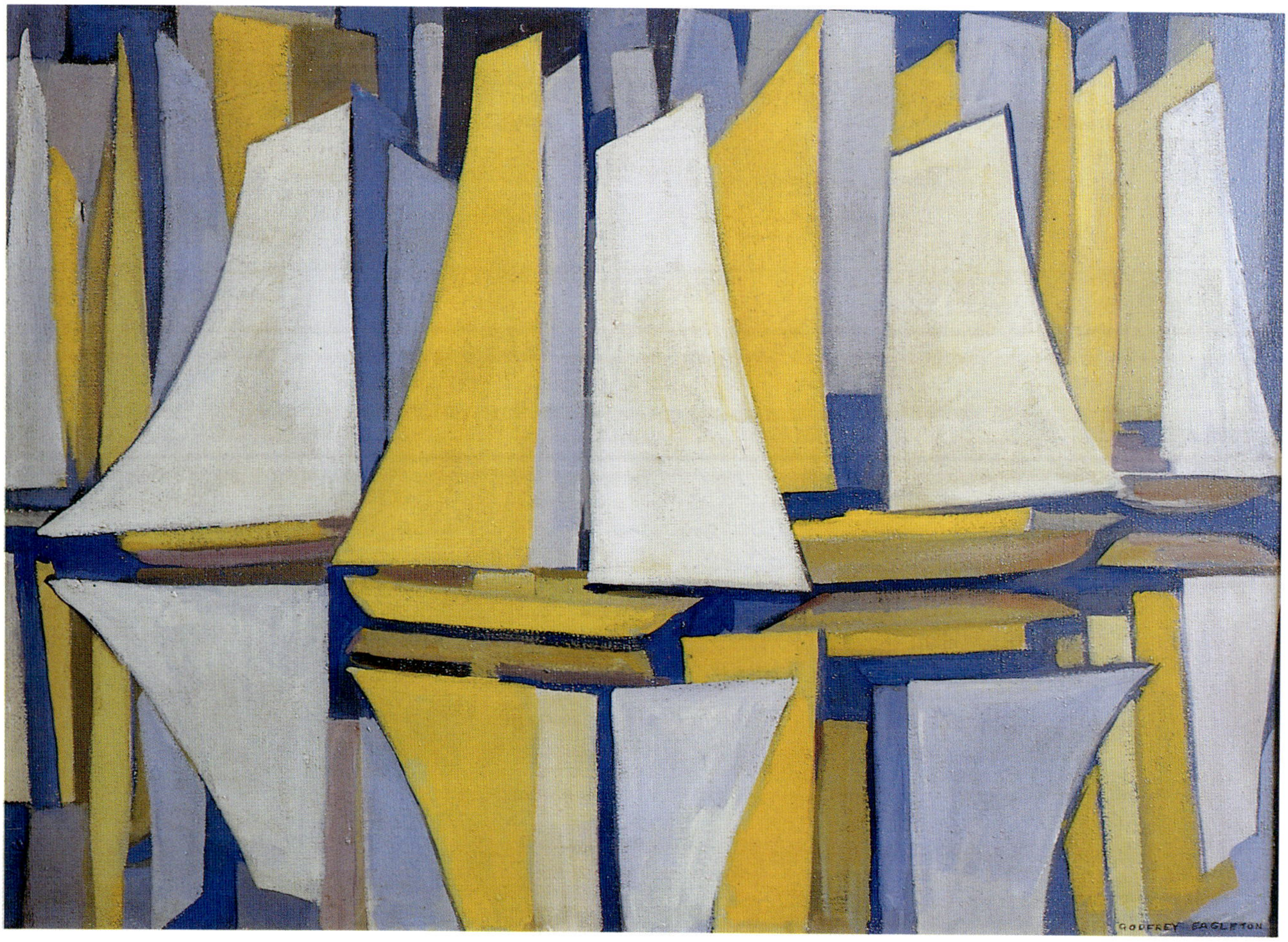

PAUL EAGLETON. *Sails.* Oil on canvas, 23in x 31in. Courtesy of Eve Phillips.

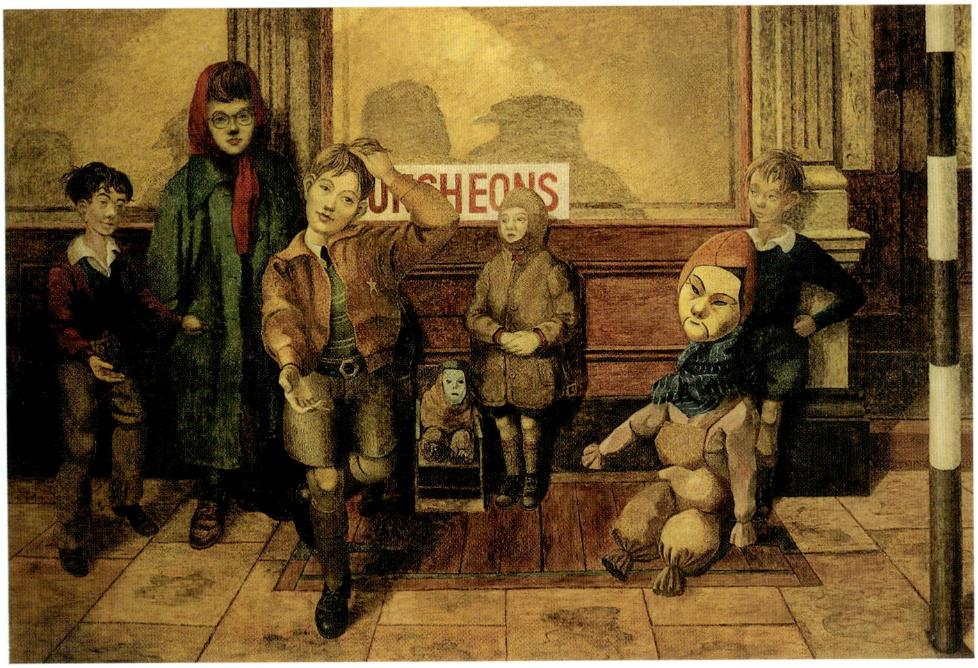

HAROLD ELDRIDGE. *Penny for the Guy*, 1954. Oil on board, 45in x 65in. Courtesy of Mercantile & General Re-insurance Co. plc.

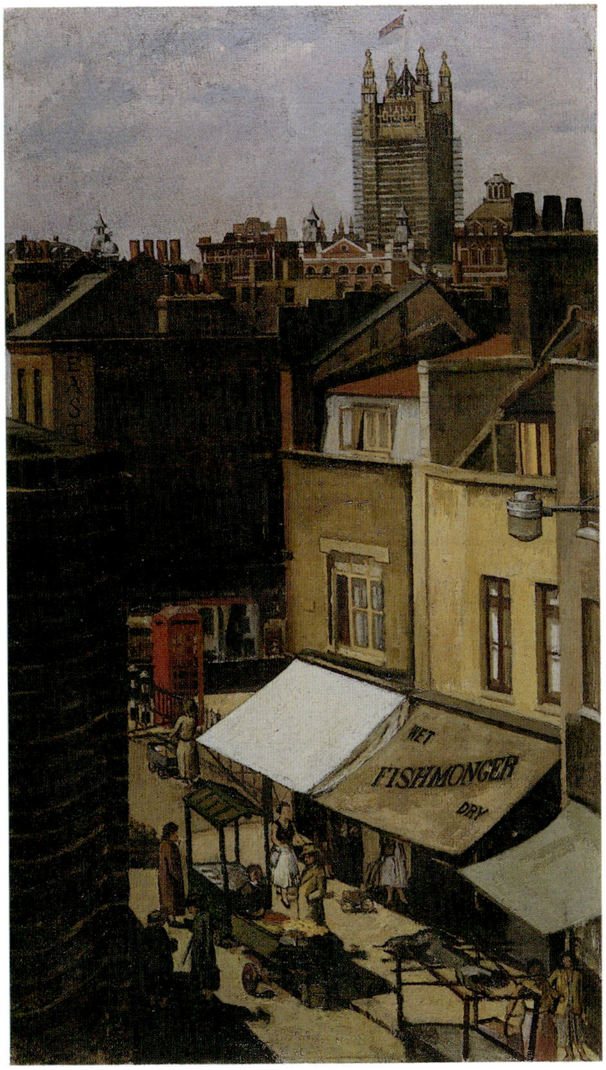

TOM EPSLEY. *Lower Marsh*, 1950. Oil on canvas, 32in x 18in. (Painted from the roof of No. 22A, Lower Marsh, London SE1.) Artist's collection.

ECHALAZ, *Daphne Auriol see* AYRES, *Daphne Auriol*

ECHALAZ, *Opal St. Clair see* HOWARD, *Opal St. Clair*

EINZIG, *Susan* (b.1922)
Following her education at the Breuer School of Design in Berlin in the immediate pre-war years, she came to London and studied at the Central School of Arts and Crafts from 1939-42. She joined the staff of Camberwell in 1946 where she stayed for four years and, together with her friend and colleague, John Minton*, exercised enormous influence over those pupils who came under her tuition for Drawing and Illustration. Further lecturing posts at St. Martins 1948-1951, Beckenham and Chelsea School of Art have helped to make her name as a leading illustrator and teacher. Amongst the books she has illustrated, *Sappho* by Alphonse Daudet, *Mozart on the Way to Prague* by Eduard Mörike, *Ripening Seed* and *My Mother's House* by Colette, *Jane Eyre* by Charlotte Brontë and *Wuthering Heights* by Emily Brontë are some of the better known.

EISENMAYER, *Ernst* (b.1920)
A refugee from Nazism, he came to England in 1939. Originally trained as a jeweller, he did not become a student at Camberwell until 1946, where he was to remain for the next three years. His original studies were entirely centred around painting and during the immediate post-war years he exhibited regularly in group exhibitions including the A.I.A., R.A., R.S.A., R.B.A., L.G. and Roland Browse & Delbanco. By the mid-1960s he had turned to sculpture full-time and is now known internationally. He has had numerous one-man exhibitions, including the Ben Uri Gallery (London), Callard Gallery (Chicago), Vienna Secession Gallery, Gallery Welz (Salzburg), and the Sheldon Swope Museum & Art Gallery (Indiana). His commissions have included the Steel and Bronze Sculpture for the British Pavilion at EXPO '70 (Tokyo) and the Sculptured Trophy for the John Players Classic Golf Tournament. Since 1975 he has lived and worked in Italy near Carrara, as he feels that the availability of marble and other facilities are more conducive to his work. Part of his year is spent in Holland, where he is an active member of the Amsterdam Sculptors' Group.

ELDRIDGE, *Harold Percy* A.R.C.A. (b.1923)
He first went to Camberwell School of Art in 1938 but was forced to abandon his studies because of the War. In 1942 he became an evening student, where he was greatly influenced by Minton* and Pasmore.* He remained at Camberwell until 1947, where for the last two years he became an evening teacher alongside his friend Pitchforth*. He was awarded a scholarship to the R.C.A. in 1947 and in 1950 he won the Gilbert Murray Prize for Painting from the R.A. Schools. He has exhibited at the R.A, the R.B.A. and the L.G. and spent his early career painting murals. For many years he taught art in the West Midlands and since his retirement he now restores early pianos and makes harpsichords.

ESPLEY, *Tom* (b.1931)
Educated at Bryanston School, he studied at Camberwell School of Art 1949-51 before winning a scholarship to the Slade School of Fine Art. He won the Sir Andrew Taylor Drawing Prize in 1954 and during his National Service in the R.A.F. took up photography. Between 1957-63 he worked in the Special Effects Department at Metro-Goldwyn Mayer. He has held one-man exhibitions at Green and Abbott, Belgrave Gallery (1978) Amwell Gallery, Menuhin School (1982) and the Alliance Building Society (1985) and has exhibited in group shows including the R.A., New Grafton Gallery, Browse & Darby, Camden Art Centre, Hayward Annual,

South London Art Gallery and, during the late 1970s, in Tokyo. His works are in the collections of British Rail, Chase-Manhattan Bank, and Camden Council. He is currently lecturing part-time at Camberwell.

EURICH, *Richard Ernst* O.B.E., R.A., N.E.A.C. (1903-1992)
Bradford born, he studied at Bradford School of Art and the Slade School 1924-27, where his greatest influence was Henry Tonks. He was befriended by Sir Edward Marsh and through his encouragement held his first one-man show at the Goupil Gallery in 1929. He was appointed Official War Artist 1940-45 and taught at Camberwell on a part-time basis from 1949-68. He has exhibited widely at the R.A., where he was made an Associate in 1942 and a Member in 1953, the N.E.A.C., the L.G., the Redfern Gallery, the Pittsburgh International Exhibitions and the Fine Art Society. His work is in museums, including the Tate Gallery, the Chantrey Bequest, the Contemporary Arts Society, the Imperial War Museum, the National Maritime Museum and in Australia and Canada.

EVANS, *Bernard* (b.1929)
His first official art training was at Liverpool College of Art where, in the immediate post-war years, he studied for two years before becoming a student at Camberwell from 1951-54, where he was taught and most influenced by Bloch*. After leaving Camberwell, he held numerous teaching posts in various art establishments and colleges of education before retiring and since 1977, has been the organiser of a Summer Painting School in Cornwall. He has had numerous one-man and group exhibitions including the Newlyn Orion Gallery, Penwith Group, R.S.M.A. and the Nottingham and Midland Group of Artists.

EYTON, *Anthony* R.A., A.R.W.S., R.W.A., L.G., N.D.D. (b.1923)
He first encountered William Coldstream* whilst being educated at Canford School, where he received his basic art grounding. In 1941 he spent one term at Reading University in the Department of Fine Art, where Professor Anthony Betts encouraged him to paint from drawings. His war service was spent in the Army and after the war he spent two years in Egypt, where he painted spasmodically. He attended Camberwell School of Art from 1947-51, where Dodgson*, Rogers* and Coldstream* had a great influence on him, and where he was awarded an Abbey Major Scholarship by the British School at Rome. He was subsequently to spend two years, from 1951, in the company of Anthony Fry* (the Rome Scholarship winner) in Italy. During this period he began to exhibit with the L.G. for the first time, and on his return from Italy he showed at the R.A. during the mid-1950s. He began teaching at Camberwell in 1955 and continued to do so on a part-time basis until the 1980s. He has held numerous one-man shows, the first being at St. George's Gallery in 1955 and at Galerie de Seine, The New Art Centre, Boswell's Gallery (Ontario Canada) and Browse & Darby. He was elected an Associate of the R.A. in 1976 and a full Member in 1987. He has travelled the world extensively and has held teaching appointments in Canada. His work is in the permanent collection of the Tate Gallery and in 1983 the Imperial War Museum had an exhibition of his paintings.

RICHARD EURICH.
Mummers, exh. R.A. 1952.
Oil on canvas, 40in x 40in.
Hove Art Gallery Collection.

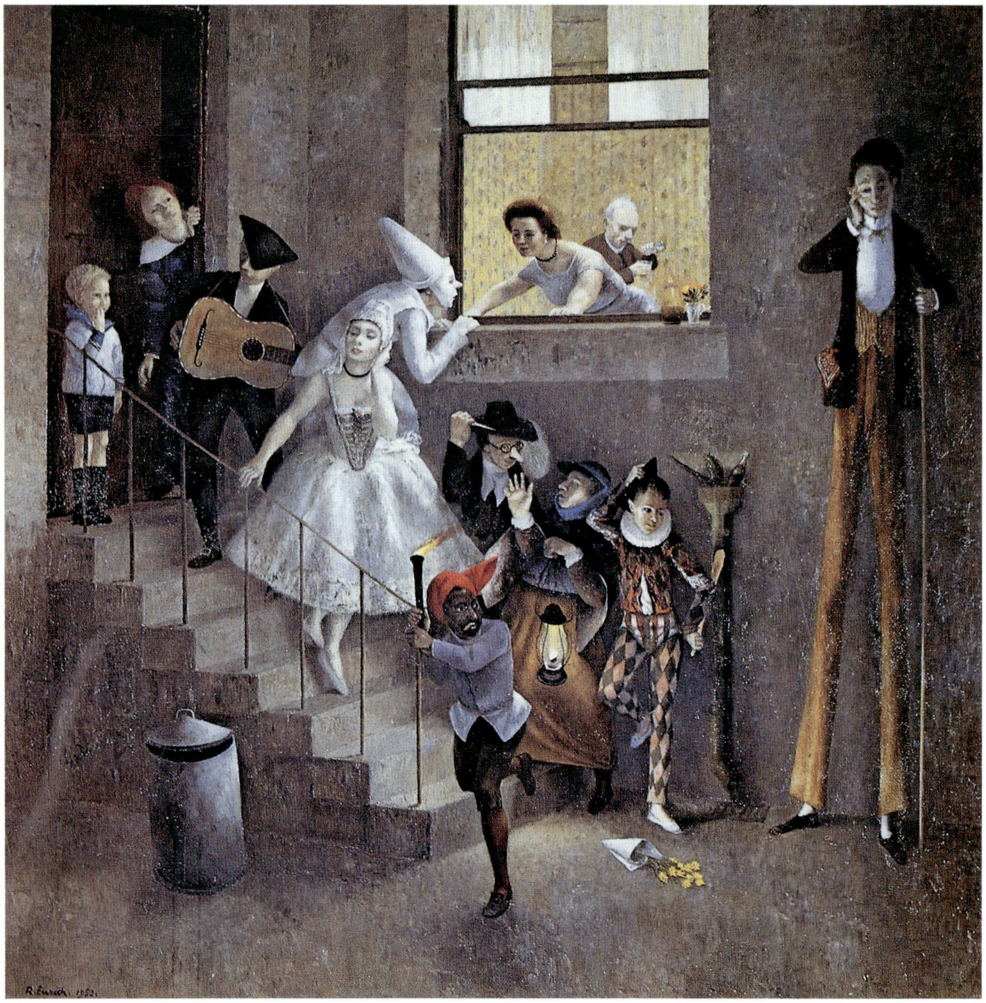

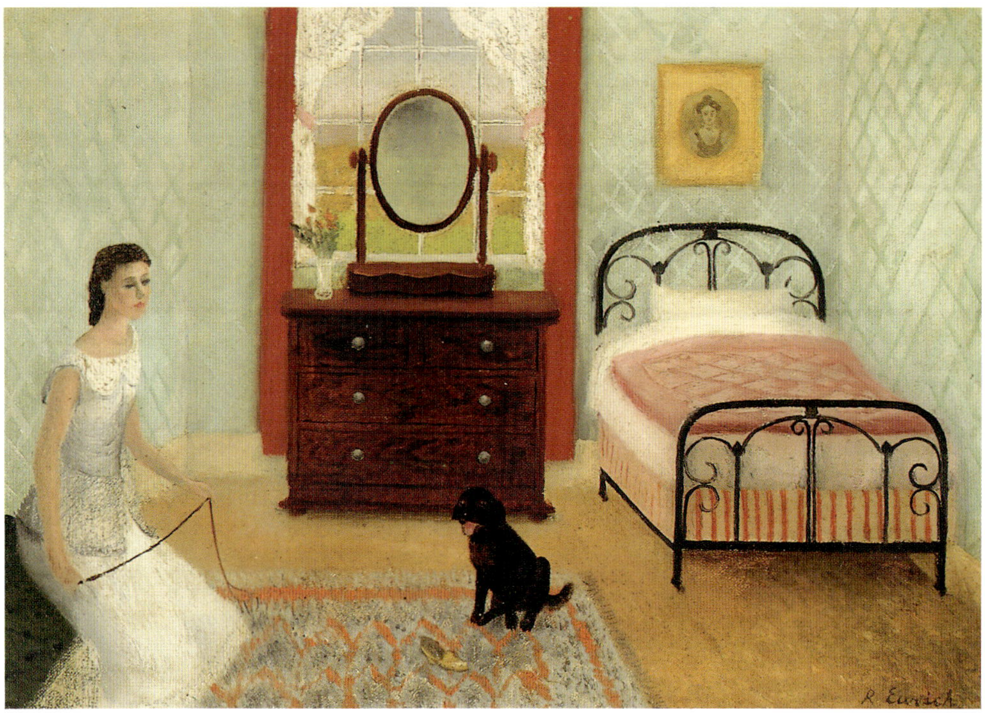

RICHARD EURICH. *The Bedroom*, 1945. Oil on board, 10in x 14in. Private collection.

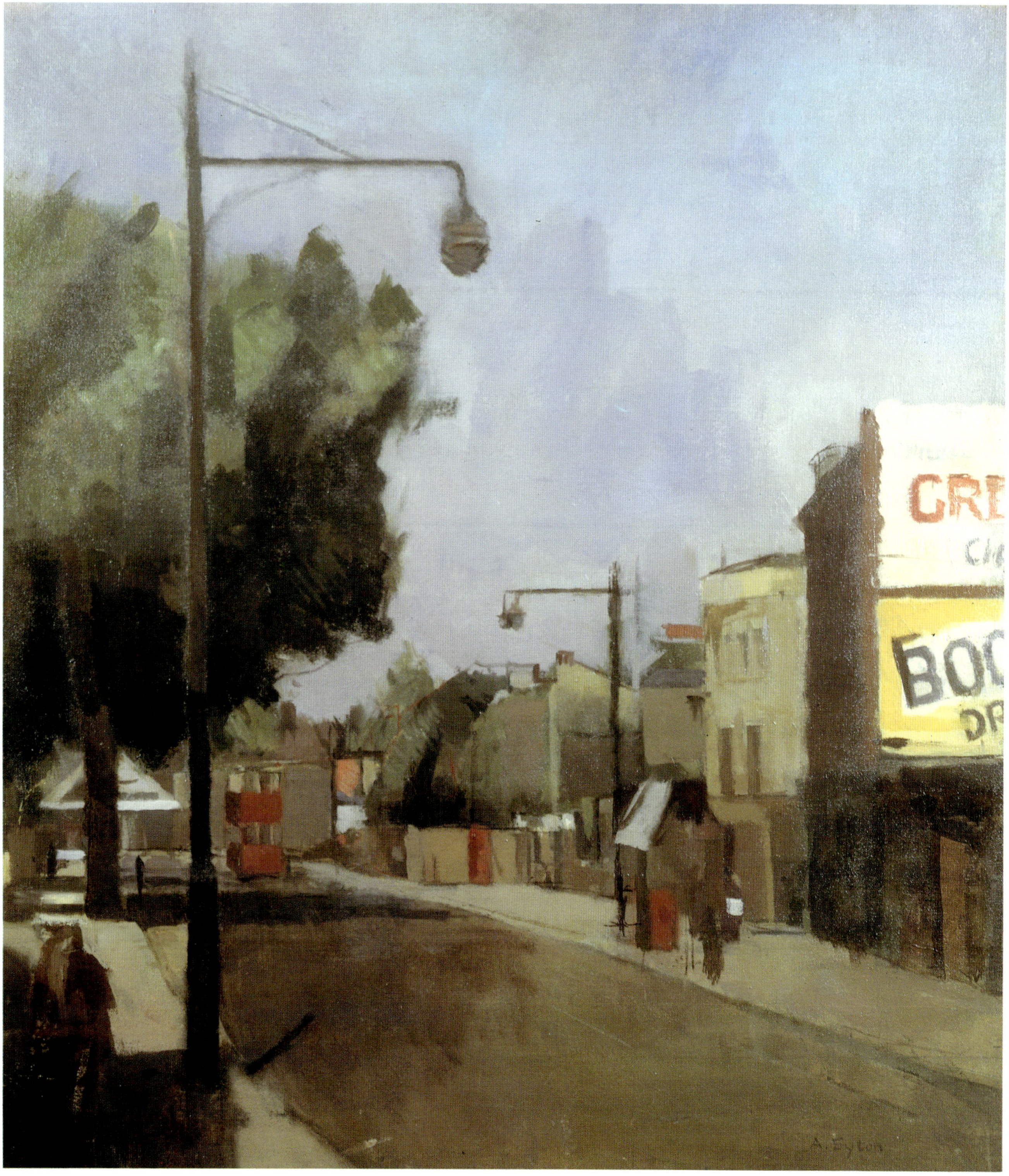

ANTHONY EYTON. *Peckham Road, Camberwell.* Oil on canvas, 29½in x 25in. Private collection.

F

FANTONI, *Barry Ernest* (b.1940)
A student at Camberwell 1953-58, where he was mainly influenced by R. D. Lee* and Myers*. After leaving Camberwell he was appointed cartoonist to *The Listener.* He has been associated with satirical humour through his cartoons and writings with such magazines as *Punch* and *Private Eye* and contributed a daily cartoon to *The Times* during the 1980s. He is a jazz musician of no mean achievement and a regular broadcaster on Radio 4 with *Chinese Horoscopes.* He has shown in several one-man and mixed exhibitions, including Woodstock Gallery (London), Brunel University, New Grafton Gallery, R.A., Bradford Print Biennale, Browse & Darby and the Gillian Jason Gallery. He has illustrated and written numerous publications and is a past Chairman of the Chelsea Arts Club.

FARRINGTON, *Pauline Joy see* ROMP, *Pauline Joy*

FAWKES, *Walter* (b.1924)
Born in Vancouver, Canada, he came to England as a child in 1931, enrolling at Sidcup Art School, Kent, in 1938. Financial difficulties forced him to abandon his studies and look for paid work, which he found during the early war years painting camouflage in a factory in Woolwich. Towards the end of the war, whilst working as a graphic artist for the *Daily Mail,* he became, due to his musical prowess on the clarinet, a founder member of the George Webb Dixieland Band. Shortly after the war, the Band was to acquire a new trumpeter in the form of Old Etonian, ex-Guards Officer, Humphrey Lyttleton*, who was at the time an art student at Camberwell. Through Lyttleton, Fawkes was introduced to Camberwell and the work of John Minton*, who taught him illustration, for one day per week. He is arguably better known as the cartoonist 'TROG'.

FAWKES, *Sandy* (*née* Carmichael) (b.1930)
She studied at Camberwell 1946-48. She married the artist Wally Fawkes* (Trog) and is also a journalist.

FENN, *Constance* (b.1933)
Student at Camberwell 1948-50, and later taught there during 1959-60. Her main influences were Edward Ardizzone*, Christopher Chamberlain*, Coldstream* and Einzig*. Whilst at Camberwell, she was awarded the Edwin Austen Abbey Major Scholarship to Rome and won a further scholarship to the R.C.A. She has exhibited widely, including the R.A., N.E.A.C. and in France. She held a one-woman show at the Zaydler Gallery in 1971.

FENTON, *Phyllis see* HARRIS, *Phyllis*

FIDO, *Kay* (b.1935)
She was both a student and teacher of sculpture at Camberwell, first enrolling as a junior in 1948. By 1956 she was on the staff, where she remained as a teacher of sculpture for the next seven years. She has spent much time in art education, holding teaching positions in Guildford, Cardiff, Belfast and at Goldsmith's College (London). She has exhibited on numerous occasions from the mid-1950s at the A.I.A. Gallery, R.A., L.G., John Moores (Liverpool), South London Art Gallery, Camden Arts Centre, Wolverhampton Art Gallery, Edinburgh Art Gallery, Geffrye Museum (London), Arts Council Gallery (Belfast), Municipal Gallery of Modern Art (Dublin), Leeds University, Courtauld Institute (London) and Hayward Annual Exhibition. Examples of her work are to be found in the public collections of the G.L.C, Contemporary Arts Society, and Harlow New Town.

FORGE, *Andrew Murray* P.L.G. (b.1923)
Studied at Camberwell 1947-49. His main influences were Coldstream*, Dodgson*, Kenneth Martin* and Pasmore*. He exhibited with the London Group during the late 1950s, becoming their President from 1965-71. He is a Trustee of the Tate Gallery and held a similar position during the 1960s with the National Gallery. His work is in the collection of The Arts Council of Great Britain, The Ministry of Works and the Tate Gallery, and he has written books on Klee, Soutine, and Rauschenberg. He is currently Dean of the Yale School of Art, Newhaven, Connecticut, U.S.A.

FORGE, *Sheila* (*née* Deane) N.D.D. (b.1926)
Student at Camberwell 1947-49. Her main influences were Dodgson* and Kenneth Martin*. Her work was never shown, other than in student exhibitions. She married the artist Andrew Forge*.

FORSEY, *Pamela* N.D.D. (b.1934)
She was a student at Camberwell in 1947 in the Junior School and remained at the school for seven years. During this period she was most influenced by Dunstan*, Frith* and Gilbert Spencer*. In 1954 she left England for South Africa where she has since remained, teaching at various art schools in Natal. She has also opened her own art gallery where she sells her work on a regular basis.

FORTNUM, *John* (b.1935)
In 1959 he entered Camberwell School of Art where most of his time was spent in the Sculpture School, under instruction from Vogel*. In 1962 he won the Anna Berry Sculpture Award and after leaving Camberwell in the mid-1960s he became Assistant to Freda Brilliant and Phillip King. He has also lectured in Ceramics, Sculpture and Three Dimensional Design. His one-man exhibitions have included the New Grafton Gallery, Greenwich Theatre Gallery and galleries in Oslo, Norway. In 1989 he held a solo exhibition of sculptures, ceramics, drawings, paintings and photographs at the Edith Grove Gallery, Chelsea, London. He has also shown pastel drawings in the open exhibitions at the Whitechapel Art Gallery and Summer Exhibition at the R.A. on several occasions.

FOSTER, *Heather Gay* (b.1929)
She attended Camberwell from 1948-51, where her teachers included Rogers* and Salaman*. In 1952 she studied at London University where she was awarded her Art Teachers Diploma. Her career as a teacher has included the teaching of painting, pottery and textiles at a variety of art colleges in England and Nigeria. She has exhibited extensively throughout the U.K. with the Print Makers Council and has shown at the Festival Hall, London, Bankside Gallery, London, R.W.A. and the Society of Scottish Arts, Edinburgh. She has executed several murals and examples of her work can be seen at Scarborough Art Gallery.

FREEMAN, *Barbara Dorothy* (*née* Price) (b.1937)
She first studied at St. Martin's School of Art from 1955-58, before joining the Sculpture School at Camberwell under Vogel*. She left Camberwell in 1960 to complete her studies at Hammersmith College of Art, where she obtained her N.D.D. in 1962. She has exhibited not only sculpture but drawings, constructions, paintings and prints at various venues, including the Jefferson Place Gallery (Washington D.C.), University of Leeds, University of Bradford, Bradford Museum & Art Gallery, Wolfson College (Oxford) and at galleries in Zagreb (Yugoslavia), Budapest (Hungary), Imperial College (London) and at numerous galleries in Ireland. Her work is in private collections in Great Britain, U.S.A, Ireland,

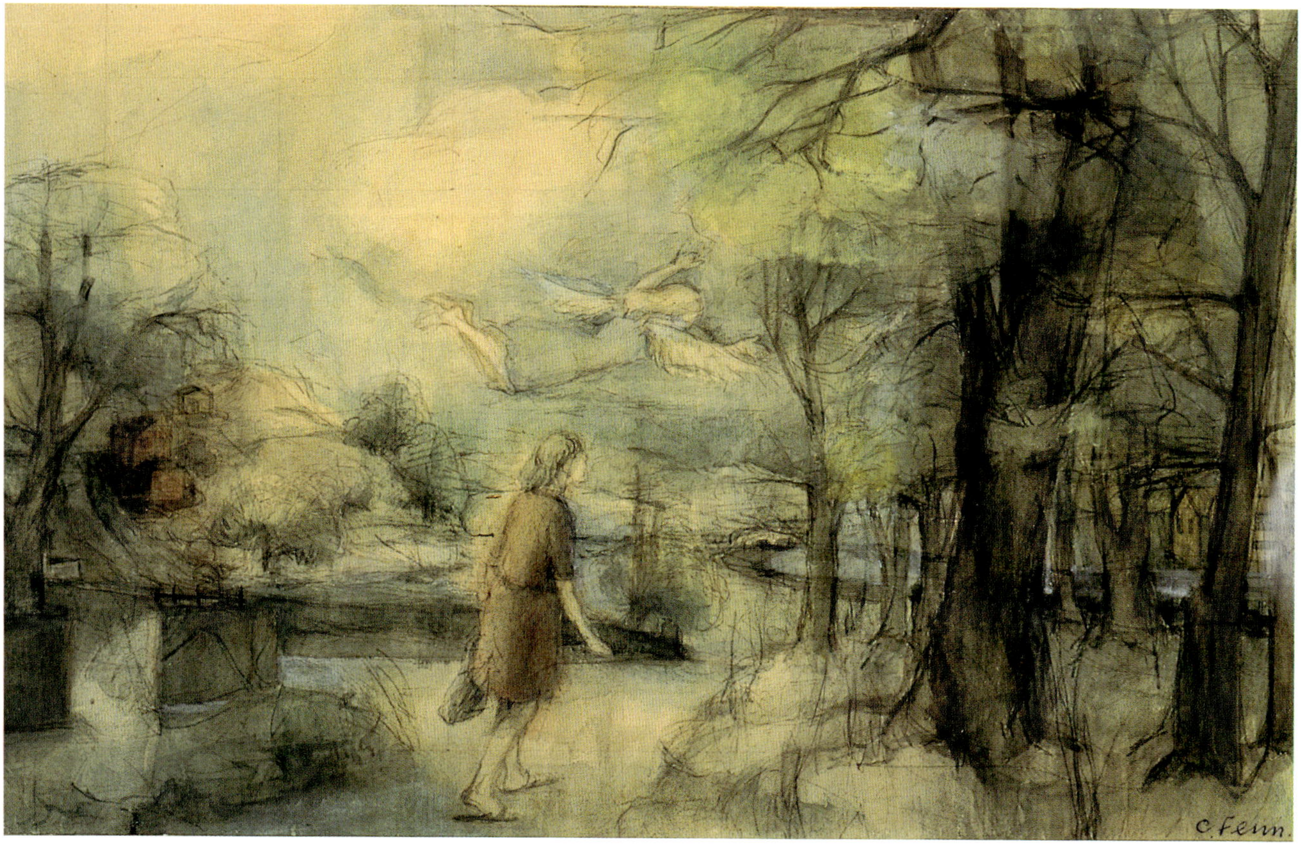

CONSTANCE FENN. *Tobias and the Angel*, 1947. Watercolour, 10in x 16in. Private collection.

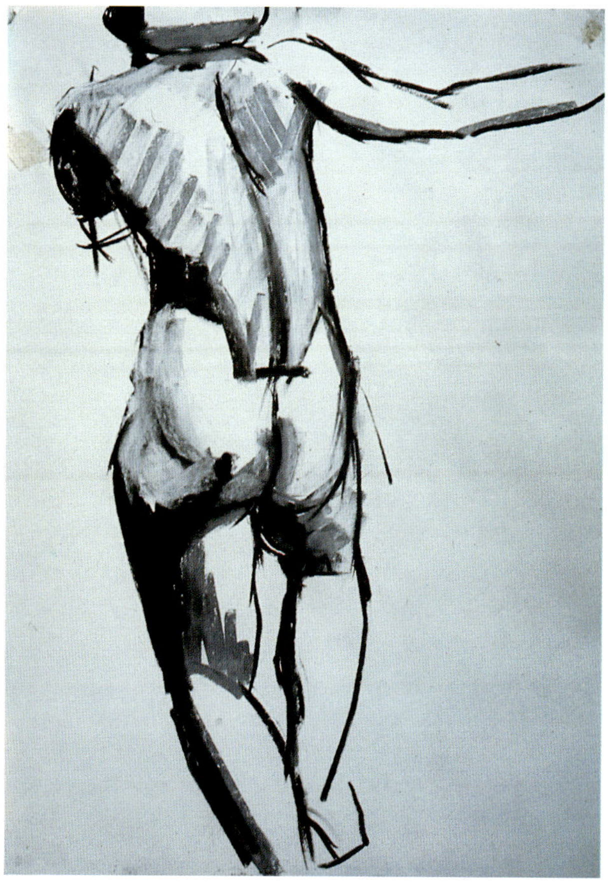

JOHN FORTNUM. *Dancing Nude,* 1958. Pastel, 24in x 18in. Artist's collection.

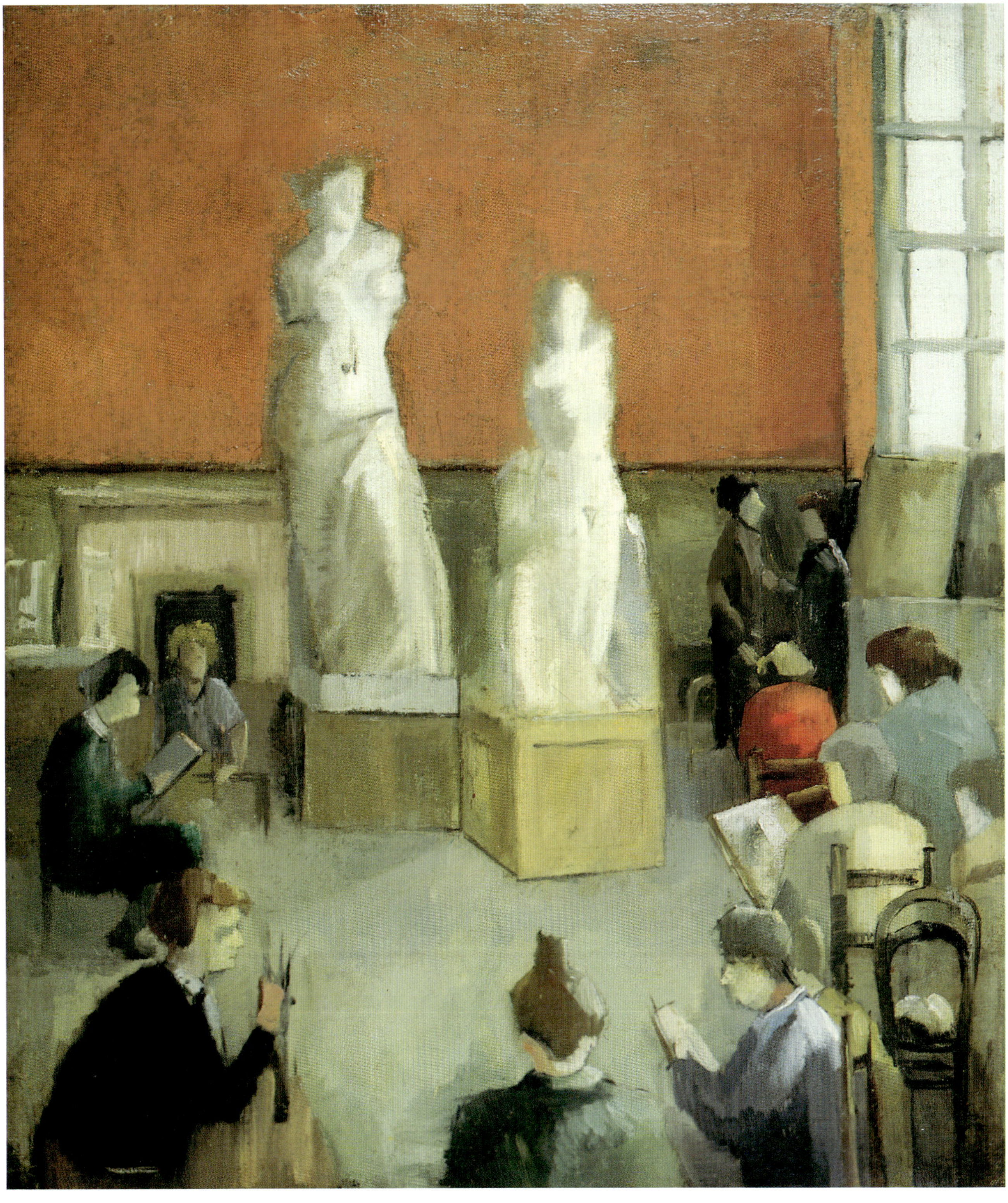

ANTHONY FRY. *Students with the Antique*, 1948. Oil on canvas, 24in x 20in. Private collection.

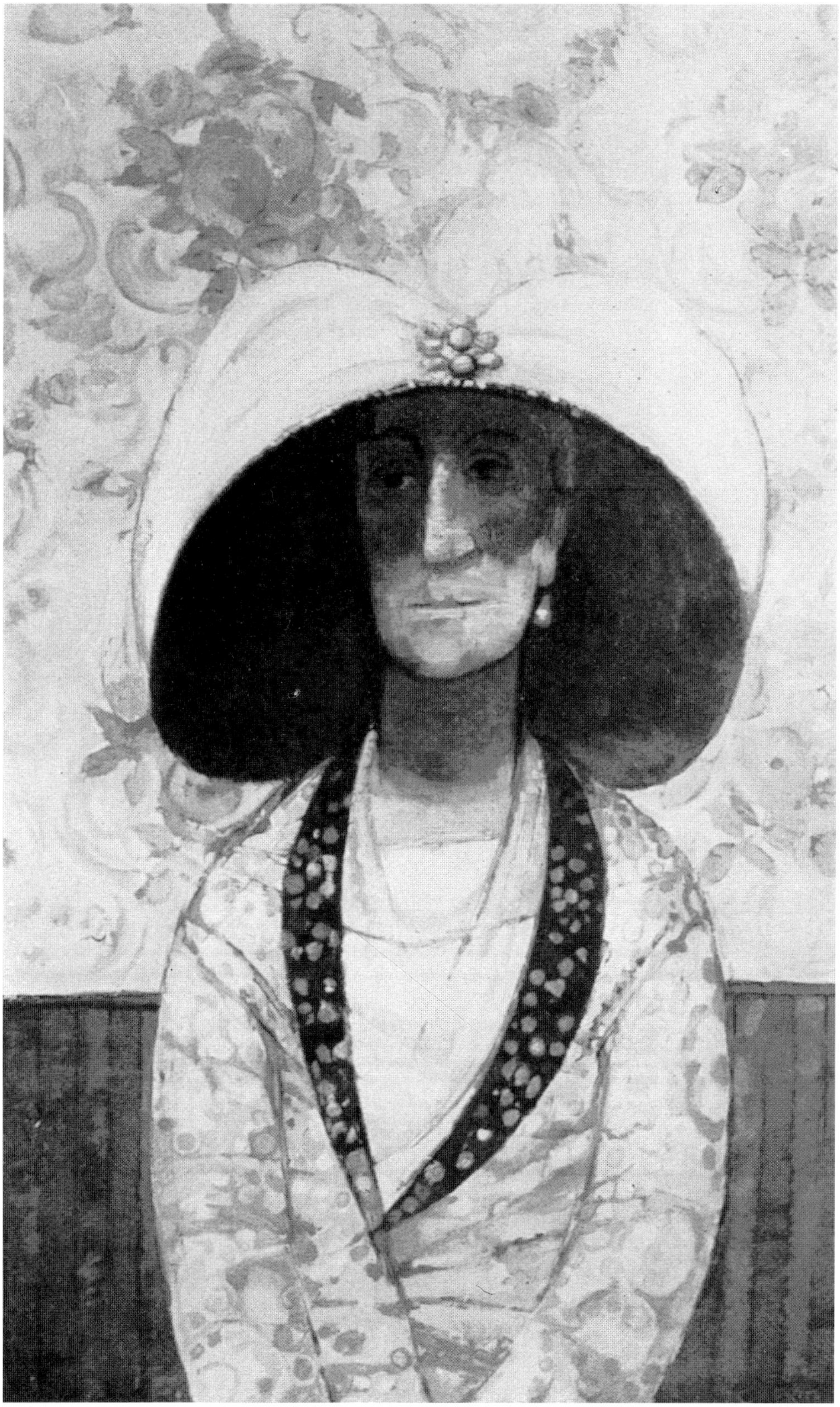

CLIFFORD FRITH. *The Pearly Queen.* Oil, 30in x 21in. Courtesy of Mr and Mrs Adrian Thomas.

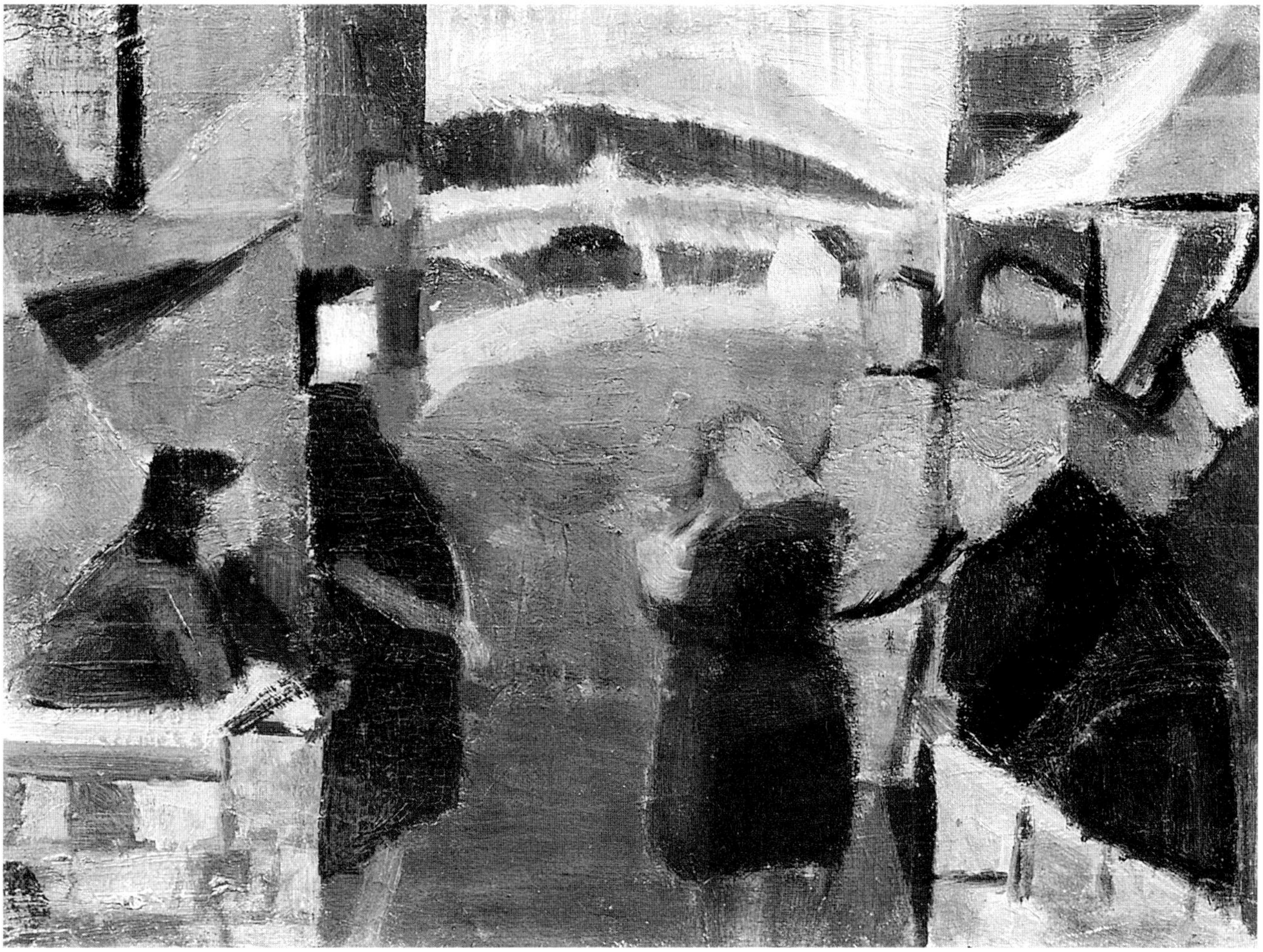

TERRY FROST. *Downalong, St Ives*, c. 1949. Oil on panel, 9¼in x 12in. Courtesy of Belgrave Gallery.

Yugoslavia, Hungary and Kuwait as well as the National Museums of Yugoslavia and Hungary, the University of Bradford, Leeds City Council and the Contemporary Art Society of Ireland.

FRITH, *Clifford* (b.1924)
He first studied at Camberwell before the war in 1938. He continued his studies at St. Martin's School of Art during the early years of the war. By 1942 he had joined the staff at Camberwell and continued to teach there and at Goldsmiths' College of Art until 1959. He left England for Nigeria and became Head of Fine Art at the Ahmadu Bello University, where he remained until 1962. On his return to England he was appointed Head of Fine Art at Croydon. In 1972 he emigrated to Australia where he is currently Senior Lecturer at the South Australian School of Art (Adelaide). His work has been exhibited at Wildenstein Gallery, South London Art Gallery, the Redfern Gallery, Tasmanian Museum & Art Gallery and he has had many other one-man exhibitions in Canada and Australia. His work is in many public and private collections, including The Tate Gallery, The Contemporary Art Society, The Australian National Gallery and The Art Gallery of South Australia.

FROST, *Terence Ernest Manitou* L.G., R.A. (b.1915)
Whilst a P.O.W. in 1943 he met Adrian Heath (1920-1992), who encouraged him to paint in oils – prior to this he had only done a few caricature drawings and little serious oil painting. In 1945 his application for a grant was rejected and he was unable to attend Camberwell School of Art so he took up employment with an

electrical wholesaler. By 1946, because of ill-health, he moved to Cornwall where he attended the St. Ives School of Painting run by Leonard Fuller. He moved into a caravan in Carbis Bay and his neighbours at the time were Ben Nicholson and Barbara Hepworth. Finally, in 1947, he succeeded in joining Camberwell School of Art as a student with a training grant for ex-service personnel. He remained there until 1950, when he returned to St. Ives. During his time at Camberwell he came under the influence of Kenneth Martin* and Pasmore*. He is now known as an abstract artist of international repute and has exhibited in major cities throughout the world. In 1954 he was awarded the Gregory Fellowship in Painting at Leeds University for a two year period. A Painting Fellowship at Newcastle University followed in 1964 and he has taught and lectured in Canada and America. He has held one-man exhibitions at the Leicester Galleries, Waddington Galleries, The Laing Gallery (Newcastle-upon-Tyne), Museum of Modern Art (Oxford), I.C.A., and galleries in New York, California, Vancouver, Auckland, Paris and Tokyo. The Arts Council held a retrospective exhibition of his work in 1977. He was elected a Member of the R.A. in 1992.

FRY, *Anthony* L.G., R.W.A. (b.1927)
He was educated at Bryanston School and then began to study at Edinburgh College of Art. In 1949 he joined Camberwell as a student and was most influenced by Coldstream* and Rogers*. In 1950 he won the Rome Scholarship, spending two years in Italy with his friend and fellow pupil Anthony Eyton*. By 1954 he had joined the L.G., of which he later became President. During the period 1953-59 he taught at the Bath Academy of Art and from 1956-60 he was a visiting lecturer at Camberwell. His first one-man exhibition was held at St. George's Gallery in 1955 and since then he has had many more at Browse & Darby. During the early 1960s he spent two years in America, having been awarded the Harkness Fellowship. His work is in many public collections, including the Tate Gallery, Arts Council of Great Britain, Graves Art Gallery (Sheffield), Stuyvesant Foundation and the Contemporary Arts Society. He was married to the artist Barbara Harris*.

FRY, *Nora see* LAVRIN, *Nora*

FUCHS, *Annette* (1939-1992)
Born in Knutsford, Cheshire, she trained at the Royal Salford Technical College School of Art, and attended Camberwell School of Art in 1956. Her greatest influence was undoubtedly Lucie Rie*, whom she met during her studies at the School. To gain practical experience she worked at the Briglin Pottery before joining her sister in a joint studio in London. In 1965 she set up her own pottery near Henley-on-Thames, Oxfordshire, which she ran until her premature death at the age of fifty-two. She worked in earthenware, stoneware and porcelain, throwing individual pieces and domestic ware with a wide range of subtle glazes. Her major exhibitions included shows with the Craftsmen Potters Shop, Seibu Stores Tokyo, Boadicea London, Pennsylvania State University Museum, Barclaycraft Brighton, Terrace Gallery Worthing, Courtyard Gallery Cheltenham and at the Sainsbury Centre Norwich in 'Lucie Rie, Hans Coper and their Pupils'.

G

GARBETT, *David* N.D.D. (b.1928)
He was a student at Camberwell between 1949-50. His principal teachers and influences were Bloch* and Vogel*. He has never shown his work professionally and has been in teaching most of his life. He taught at Goldsmiths' College until 1982.

GARRETT, *Albert Charles* R.O.I., F.R.S.A., P.S.W.E. (1915-1983)
Following war service in the Army, he joined Camberwell School of Art, where he studied wood engraving under Hermes* and Buckland-Wright* from 1947-49. From 1949-50 he continued his studies at the Anglo-French Art Centre in St. Johns Wood, again under his friend and teacher Buckland-Wright. He was to spend a further twelve months (1950-51) perfecting his wood engraving techniques at the Slade School of Fine Art and by the late 1950s was elected a member of the S.W.E., becoming its Secretary in 1965 and its President two years later. In 1963 he was appointed lecturer at the Polytechnic of North London, where he remained for much of his career. His one-man exhibitions included Gallery One (London), Mall Galleries, Loggia Gallery and galleries in Canada and Paris. He also exhibited regularly at the S.W.E., R.O.I., F.P.S and at the R.E. His works are to be found in the collections of the B.M., Tate Gallery, V. & A., Ashmolean Museum and the Art Galleries of Derby, Portsmouth and Hull. He wrote what is arguably the definitive work on his favoured medium – *A History of British Wood Engraving* (Midas Books, 1978) as well as books on the engravings and drawings of Iain Macnab of Barachastlain.

GAULT, *George* N.D.D. (b.1916)
Student at Camberwell 1947-51. His main influences were Coldstream*, Kenneth Martin*, Matthews*, Pasmore* and Townsend*. He has exhibited on numerous occasions at the R.A., Paris Salon (Silver Medal Winner 1954), the L.G., R.B.A., N.E.A.C., the R.P. and Roland Browse & Delbanco. He has taught for many years in adult art education in South London, where he now lives.

GAUSSEN MARKS, *Elena* (*née* Gaussen) (b.1942)
Student at Camberwell 1958-60. Her main influences were Eyton*, Hoyland*, and Matthews*. She has exhibited several times at the R.A. and in 1991 held a successful exhibition at Spinks Gallery, St. James's, London. For many years she shared a studio with Robert Buhler, R.A.(1916-1989) by whom she was greatly influenced.

GEORGE, *Patrick* N.D.D. (b.1923)
Educated at the Downs School at Colwall near Malvern, where the Art Master was Maurice Feild. During his time there Coldstream* visited the school to paint his friend W. H. Auden, who was the English Master. In 1939 he attended Edinburgh College of Art where he came under the influence of Sir William Gillies R.A., R.S.A. (1898-1973). Having spent the war years in the Navy, he arrived in 1946 at Camberwell School of Art, where his main influences were again Coldstream, Gowing*, Monnington*, Pasmore* and Rogers*. He left Camberwell in 1949, following William Coldstream to the Slade School of Fine Art. He has exhibited with the L.G. and has had one-man exhibitions at Gainsborough's House in Sudbury and at the Serpentine Gallery in London in 1980. Like his friends and mentors, Coldstream and Gowing, he became Professor of Fine Art, Slade School, University College London.

GODFREY, *Ian* (1942-1992)
Born in Ely, he joined Camberwell as a painting student in 1957. Fascinated by the concepts of pottery, he soon switched to the ceramics department, where his

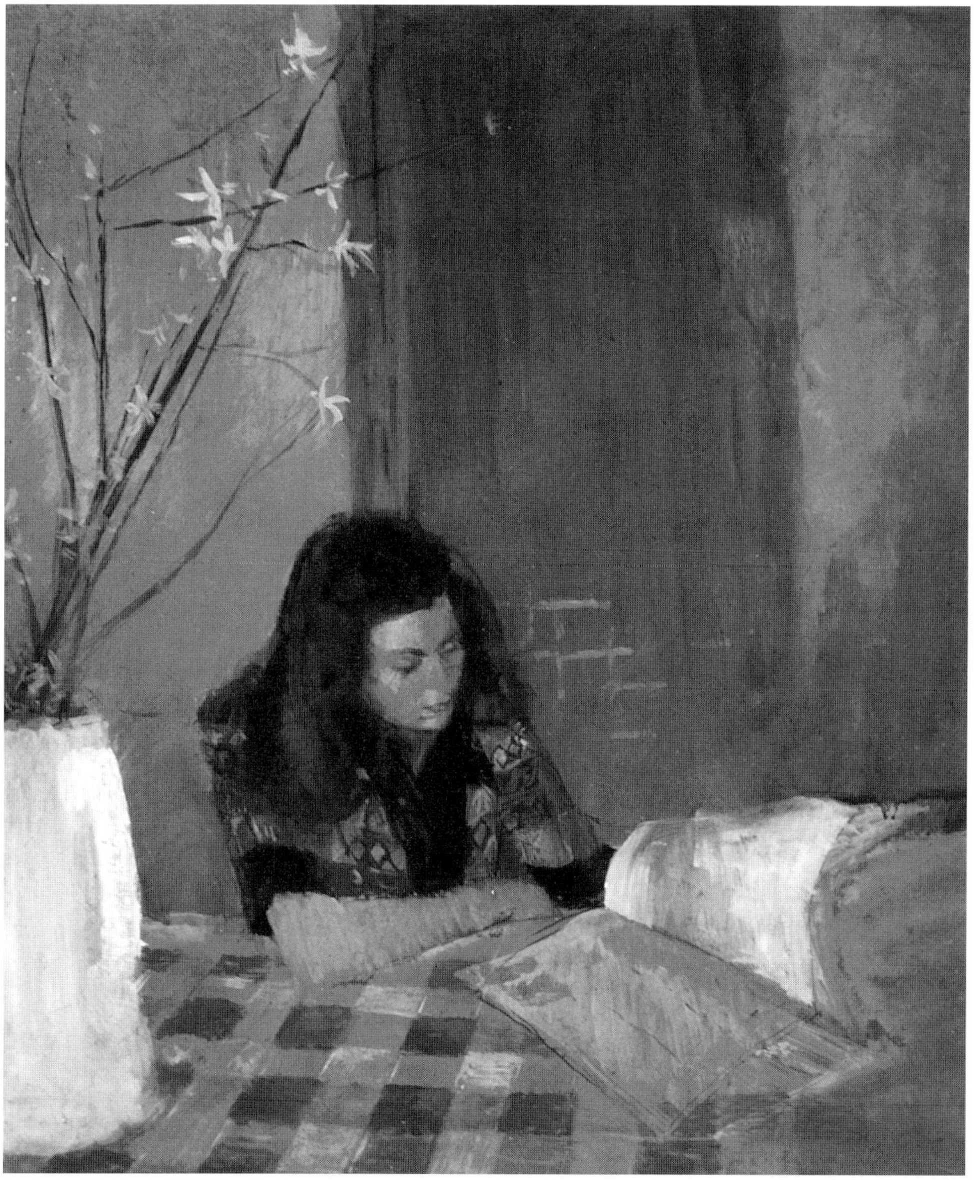

GEORGE GAULT. *The Reader*, 1948. Oil on canvas, 30in x 24in. Artist's collection.

teachers included Ian Auld*, Dick Kendall*, Lucie Rie* and Hans Coper (1920-1981). There followed part-time teaching at Camberwell and within five years he had started his own pottery workshop in an Islington basement. During the period 1967-68 he was awarded a Fellowship at the R.C.A. He began showing at the Primavera Gallery in London during the early 1960s and also in group shows across Europe. In 1974 he was awarded a gold medal at the Faenza International Exhibition and a year later moved to Denmark where, for the next five years, he made domestic pottery ware in Jutland. He returned to England in 1980 and ran a workshop in Highgate, London, until his death. Examples of his pottery can be seen in many public collections including Aberdeen Art Gallery, Glasgow Museum and Art Gallery, Paisley Museum and Art Gallery, Cleveland (Ohio) Museum of Art and the V. & A.

GOLDBERG, *Woolf* A.R.C.A. (b.1920)

As a fifteen-year old he attended the Sir John Cass School of Art in London's East End, winning a scholarship to the R.C.A. in 1939. The outbreak of war prevented his attending and he eventually became a student during its evacuation to Ambleside. During his years at the R.C.A. he won a silver medal for Distinction in Painting, gaining his diploma in 1947. He joined the staff at Camberwell School of Art, where

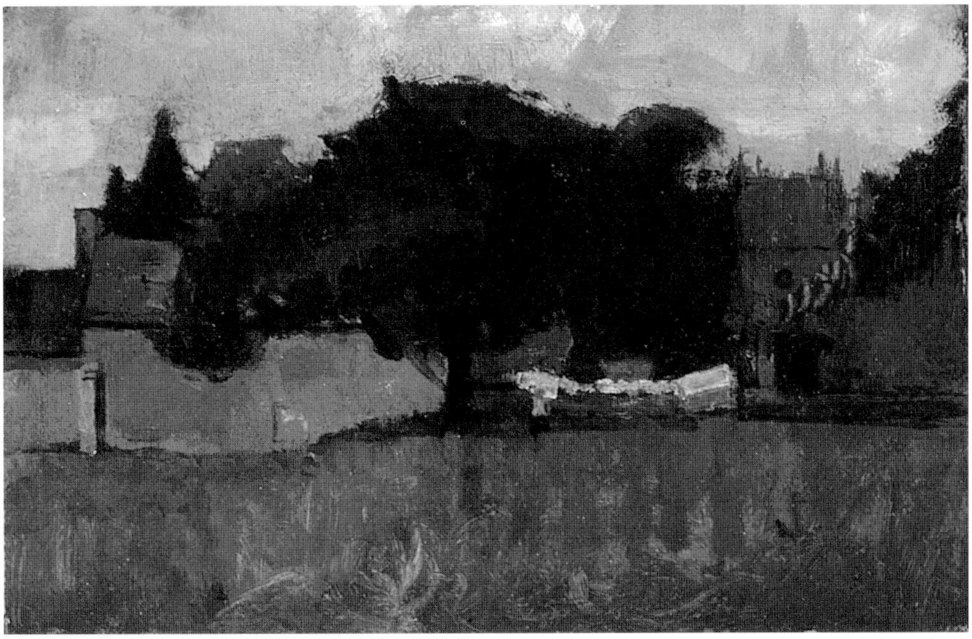

PATRICK GEORGE. *Church, Enstone, Oxfordshire*, 1950. Oil on panel, 8in x 11in. Author's collection.

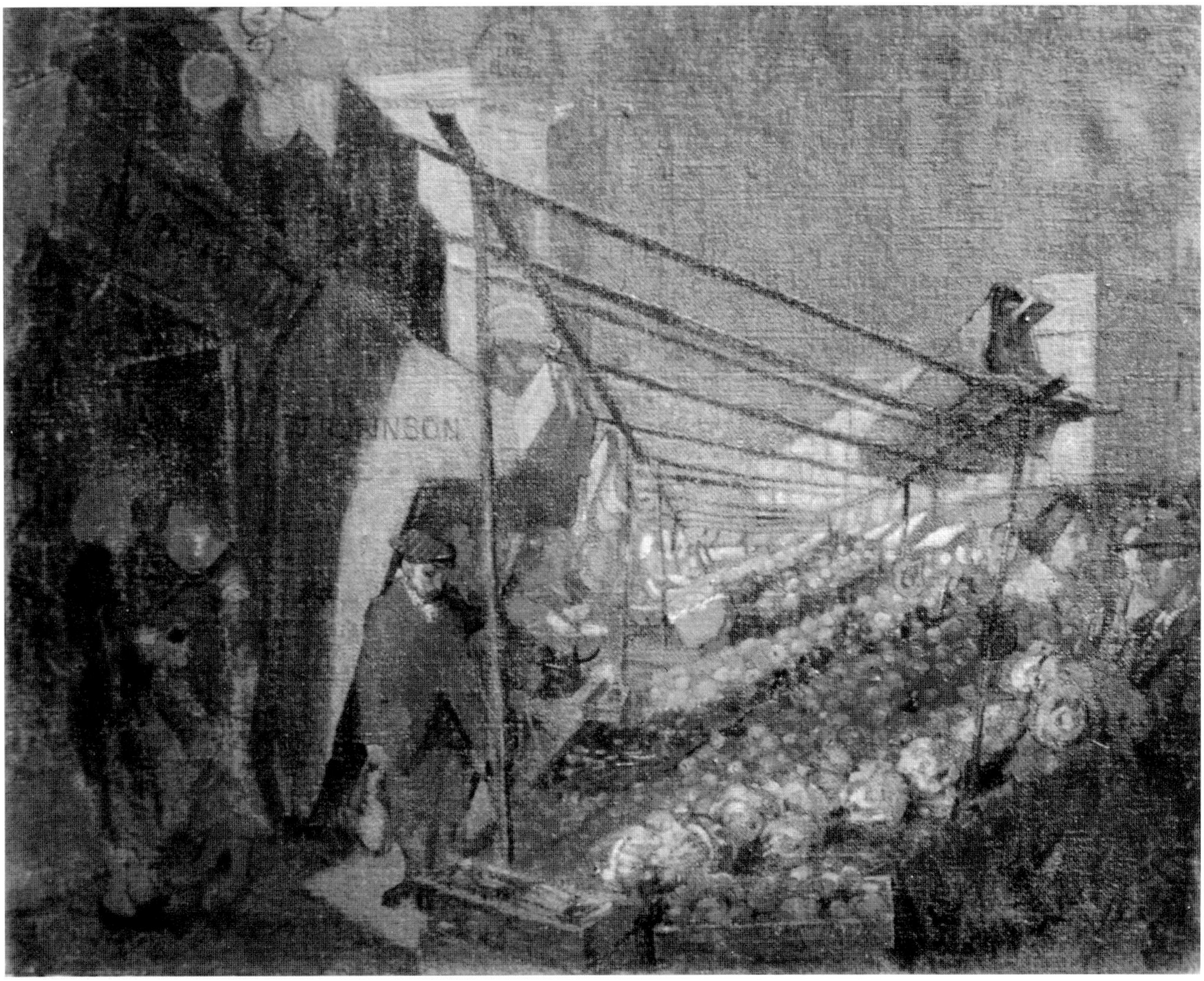

WOOLF GOLDBERG. *Hackney Market*, 1948. Oil on canvas, 25in x 30in. Artist's collection.

ALASTAIR GORDON.
Kenyan Girl, 1949. Oil on board, 18in x 15in.

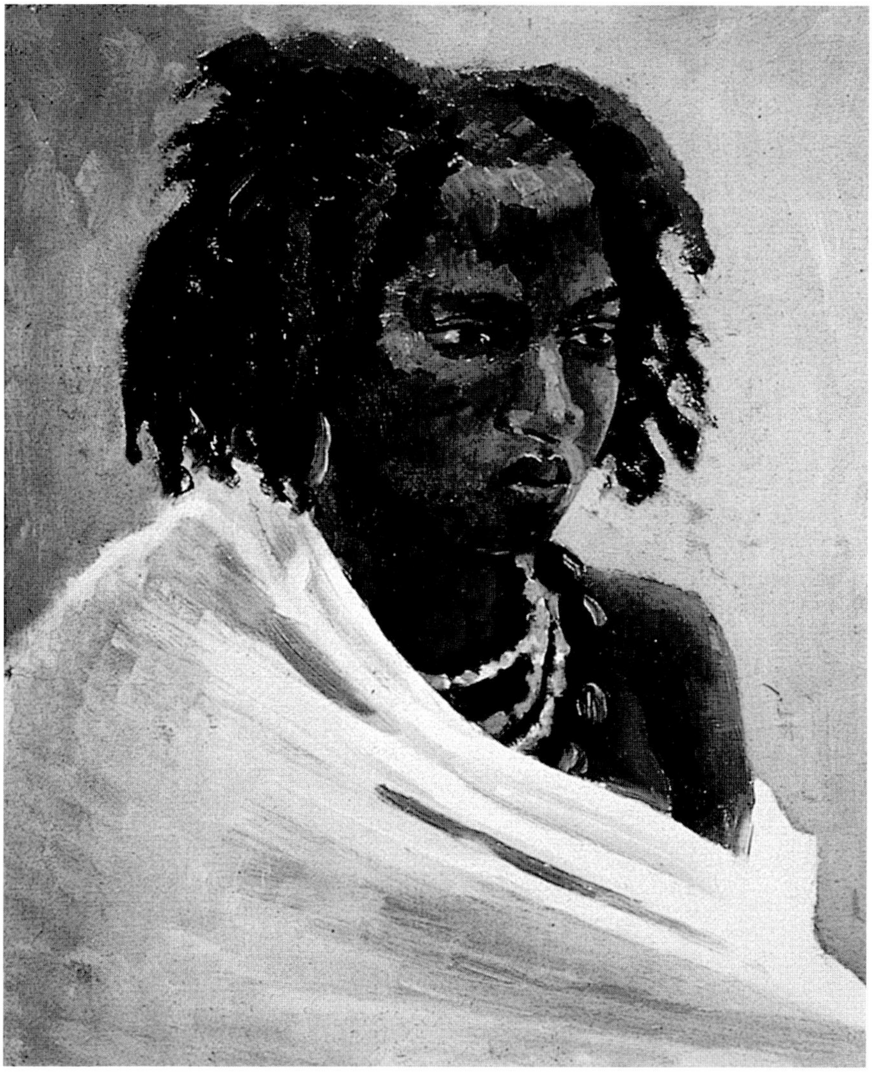

he not only taught Drawing and Painting but initiated a marionette theatre where he produced and directed student shows for the public in the adjoining Pasmore Edwards Gallery. He stayed at Camberwell until 1956 when he variously followed careers in film, television and art teaching. He has exhibited at the N.E.A.C. and at the R.A. Summer Exhibitions.

GOLDSBROUGH, *Robin* (b.1925)
Following war service in the Navy, he joined Camberwell in 1948, where his main teachers were Carter*, Coldstream* and Rogers*. By 1950 he had entered the Slade School of Fine Art, where he was to remain for the next three years. Most of his career has been spent in teaching and for a time, he was the Art Master at St. Pauls School in London. He appears to have shown his work very little.

GORDON, *Alastair Ninian John* (The Marquess of Aberdeen) (b.1920)
Student at Camberwell 1946-48. His main influences were Coldstream*, Dodgson*, Gowing*, Monnington* and Seabrooke*. He has held several joint exhibitions with his wife – Anne Gordon* – in New York, Sydney and London and has had one-man shows in London at regular intervals since the mid-1970s. He has been awarded silver medals for his botanical paintings, in which he now specialises, by the Royal Horticultural Society. He was the Chairman of the Dover Arts Club from 1965-75.

GORDON, *Anne* (*née* Barry) (The Marchioness of Aberdeen) (b.1924)
A student at Camberwell 1946-48, her teachers were Coldstream*, Monnington* and

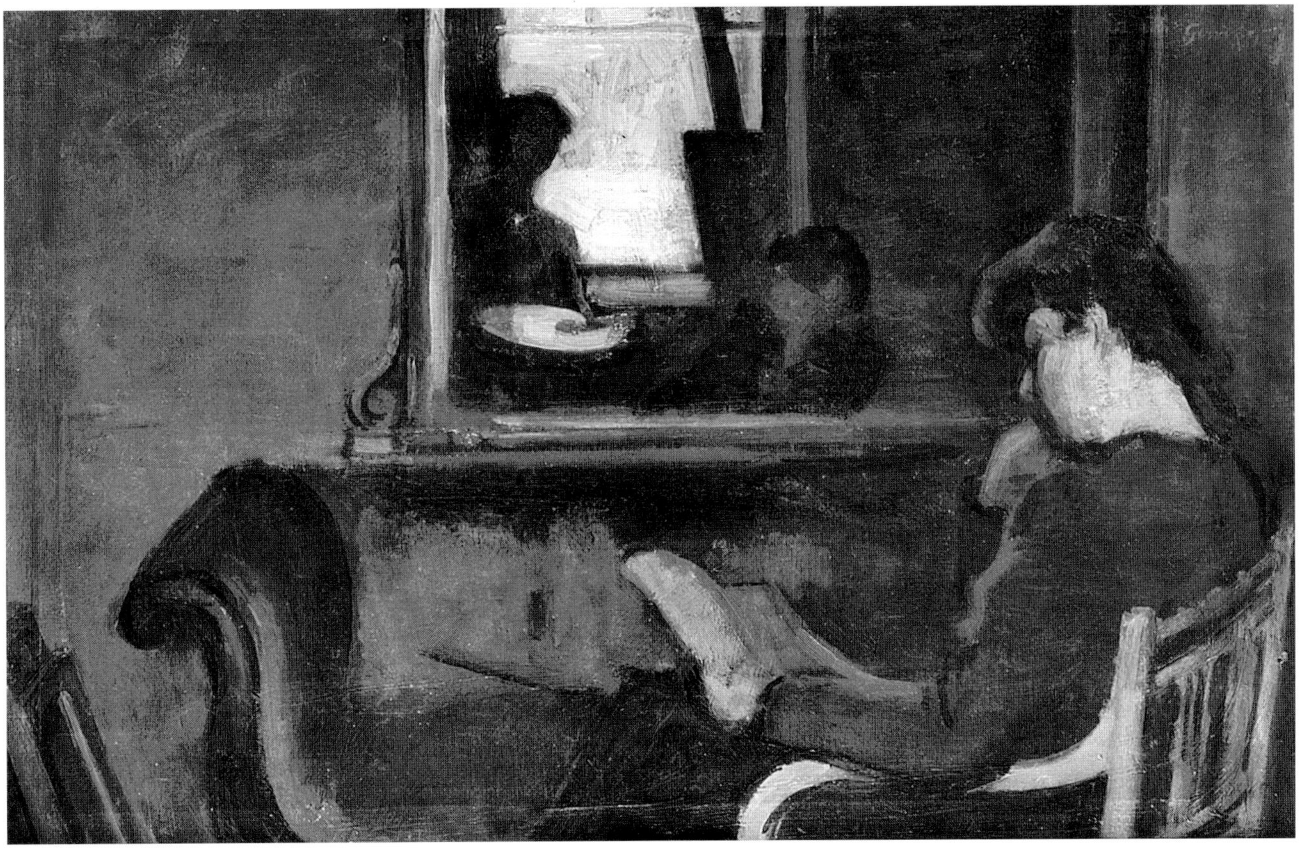

LAURENCE GOWING. *The Painting Room*, 1945. Oil on canvas, 15in x 24in. Private collection.

Seabrooke*. She later turned to ceramics and has held joint exhibitions with her husband, Alastair Gordon*, in New York, Sydney and London. She has held several one-woman shows in London since the mid-1960s. She is highly regarded as a ceramicist and her work is in private collections, including those of Charles Ryskamp, the Director of the Frick Museum (New York), and many other luminaries in the porcelain world.

GOWING, *Lawrence Burnett* C.B.E., R.A., Kt. (1918-1991)
He was educated at the Downs School, Colwall, near Malvern, where he was first taught to paint by Maurice Feild. In 1938 he studied at the Euston Road School, having been introduced to Coldstream* by their mutual friend W. H. Auden in 1936. He taught at Camberwell School of Art 1943-47, where some of his most poignant paintings were executed. He was appointed Professor of Fine Art at Durham University and Principal of Newcastle School of Art the following year, a position he was to hold for the next decade. In 1959 he was appointed Principal of Chelsea School of Art, and in 1961 was made a Trustee of the Tate Gallery. After Coldstream's retirement from the Slade in 1975, Gowing took over as Professor of Fine Art. It was during his ten-year stay at the Slade that he was elected an Associate of the R.A. and in 1982 was created a Knight. He had many solo and mixed exhibitions, including shows at the Leicester Galleries, Marlborough Fine Art, Waddington Galleries and the Serpentine Gallery (London). He wrote many books on famous artists, including Vermeer, Cézanne, Turner, Matisse, Hogarth and Lucian Freud. Coming to national prominence during the 1980s with a series of television films for the B.B.C., his ability to describe an artist's work, and to relate it to the times in which he lived, captivated the millions who watched him regularly.

GRIBBLE, *Kenneth James* (b.1925)
His first introduction to art was received at Harrow School of Art during the war years of 1943-44. At the end of the war he became a student at Camberwell, where he was to remain until 1947. Here he was most influenced by Minton*, Pasmore*

KEN GRIBBLE. *Grandetown, Middlesbrough.* Oil on canvas, 12in x 14in.
Courtesy of Holmes Fairbrass.

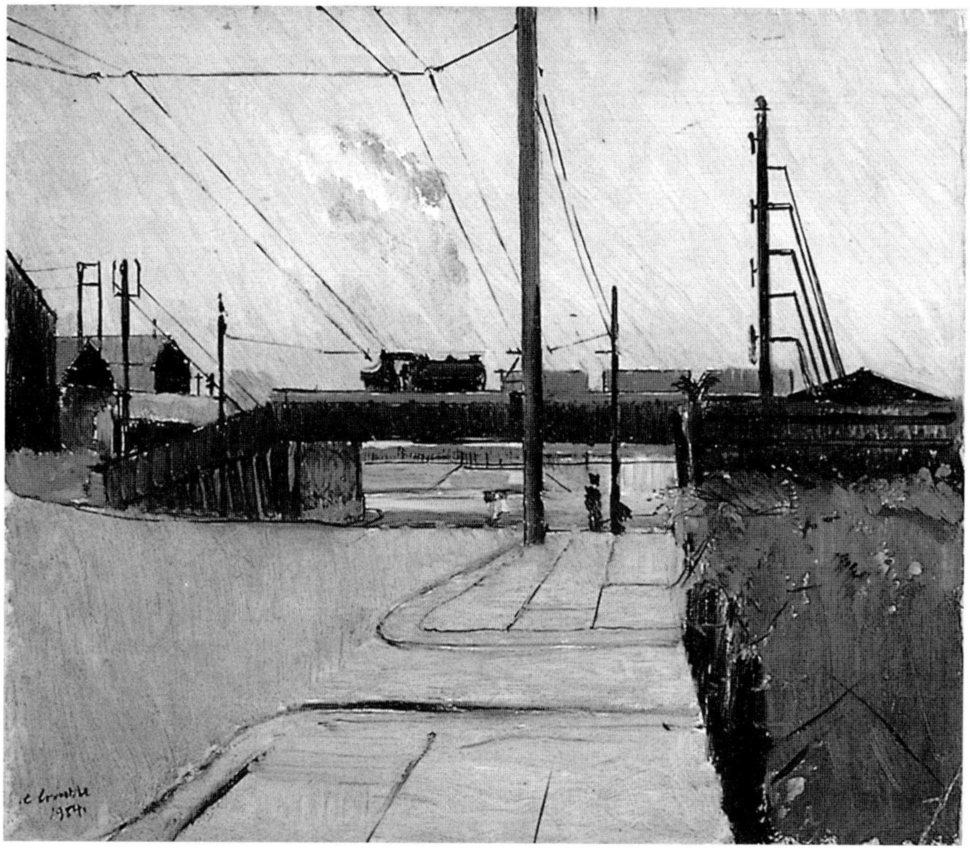

and Rogers*. At the same time, he attended part-time evening classes where he came under the instruction of David Bomberg (1890-1957). A prolific student and prize winner at Camberwell, he showed his work regularly at the Young Contemporaries and numerous student exhibitions. In 1947 he joined the Slade School of Art, where he was to remain for the next three years before joining the staff of the Central School of Art where he taught Lithography alongside his former teacher from Camberwell, John Minton. By 1956 he had been appointed Principal at the Ashton-under-Lyne School of Art and, four years later, he became the Principal of Lincoln School of Art. His other principalships have included Taunton College of Art and Maidstone College of Art, from where he retired in 1984. His other exhibitions have included one-man shows at the Teeside School of Art and at Taunton's Brewhouse Theatre. He is a member of the Manchester Academy of Fine Art, where he has exhibited on numerous occasions, as well as at the R.W.A. and the R.A. Summer Exhibitions. He has also shown his work at the R.B.A., Beaux Arts Gallery, Walker Art Gallery and the Leeds Art Gallery. His work is in the permanent collection of Manchester City Art Gallery, Salford City Art Gallery, Rochdale Art Gallery, The Usher Gallery (Lincoln) and numerous private collections at home and abroad.

GUYATT, *Richard Gerald Talbot* C.B.E. (b. 1914)
A designer and teacher, he studied with Bernard Meninsky (1891-1950) and Mark Gertler (1891-1939) as an evening student at Westminster School of Art from 1933-36. His early career included poster designs for Shell-Mex and B.P. Following war service as a camouflage officer, he joined the staff of Camberwell as a part-time teacher of typography in 1946. In 1948 he was appointed Professor of Graphic Arts at the R.C.A. and remained there until his retirement in 1981, during the last three years he was Rector. His major commissions include Wedgwood commemorative mugs for the Coronation, 1953, designs for the Royal Silver Wedding, 1973 and for the commemorative crown piece for the Queen Mother's eightieth birthday. He was awarded the C.B.E. in 1969.

H

HADDON, *Pamela Margaret* (b.1921)
A student at Camberwell School of Art 1946-51, mainly taught by Kenneth Martin* and Minton*. She exhibited in a group exhibition in Oxford in 1945, other than that she appears not to have shown her work at all.

HAIG, *The Earl George Alexander Eugene Douglas* O.B.E., D.L., M.A., F.R.S.A., A.R.S.A. (b.1918)
Whilst a P.O.W. he began to take an interest in art and in 1945 he attended Camberwell, where he was most influenced by Coldstream*, Gowing*, William Johnstone*, Pasmore* and Rogers*. During his vacation periods, he painted with Paul Maze (1887-1979) and some of his work from this period shows this influence. He has held numerous one-man exhibitions from 1945 until the present and these include the Scottish Gallery (Edinburgh), The Redfern Gallery, Leicester Galleries, O'Hana Gallery, Richard Demarco Gallery (Edinburgh), Clarges Gallery and Gallery 10. His group exhibitions have been on an international scale in Poland, Wales, Canada, Dublin and New York and he has also exhibited in mixed exhibitions at the Ashmolean Museum (Oxford) and the John Moores (Liverpool). His work is in the private collections of the Queen, the Queen Mother, the Duke of Edinburgh, Scottish National Gallery of Modern Art, The Arts Council of Great Britain, The Scottish Arts Council, Ministry of Works, British Railways, Edinburgh University, Abbot Hall Gallery (Kendal), The Imperial War Museum, the Cheltenham and Gloucester Building Society and many others throughout the world.

HALL, *James Oliver* (b.1916)
A New Zealand-born sculptor and a potter. He first studied at Dunedin School of Art, New Zealand, 1938-39. He came to London in 1946 and spent three years at the Slade, studying under Fred McWilliam and gaining a Diploma in Fine Art in 1949. That same year he enrolled at Camberwell, where he joined the pottery and ceramic classes under Jacob Drew* and Richard Kendall*. He has since lived in South Africa, teaching sculpture at the Natal Technical College, and has participated in group exhibitions in Durban and in London. Examples of his work can be seen at Hanley Art Gallery, Stoke-on-Trent and his public commissions include ceramics for the Holy Trinity Church, Durban and a fibreglass sculpture for the Ocean Terminal, also in Durban.

HALLIWELL, *Albert Edward* A.R.C.A., F.R.S.A., A.S.I.A.D (1905-1986)
He attended Southport School of Art 1920-23, where his exceptional talent as a graphic artist won him a scholarship to the R.C.A., where he stayed until 1926. As a freelance artist, he produced memorable posters for the London Underground, Southern Railway and the emergent airport authorities during the late 1920s. He joined the staff at Camberwell as early as 1927 and, for the three years from 1945 until he left in 1948, he not only organised courses for demobilised servicemen but was for a time Vice-Principal under William Johnstone*. In 1948 he moved to the Central School where he stayed until his retirement in 1970. He is known chiefly for his experiments which explored connections between graphic creativity and industrial design education.

HAMLYN, *Edward William* (b.1941)
Following a year at Woolwich Polytechnic School of Art in 1956, he became a full-time painting student at Camberwell where he was influenced by Auerbach*, Medley* and Uglow*. In 1960 he won a scholarship to the R.C.A. where, during the next three years, whilst furthering his studies, he was to win the David Murray Landscape Painting Prize. He has held various teaching posts and shown his work occasionally in group exhibitions, including a two-man exhibition at the Welsh Arts

THE EARL HAIG. *Jockeys*, c.1949. Oil on canvas, 15½in x 11in. Private collection.

Council Gallery, Cardiff in 1983. In 1975 he moved to South Yorkshire where, with his wife Jane, he set up a pottery from where he continues to paint.

HAMP, *Katherine Frances see* MARTIN, *Katherine Frances*

HARDIMENT, *Melville Hubert Ernest* (b.1915)
First introduced to painting by his friend Sven Berlin (b.1911) in 1945, he was originally classed as a 'primitive'. Shortly after, he met Wyndham Lewis (1882-1957) who encouraged him to attend Camberwell to further his artistic career. He enrolled

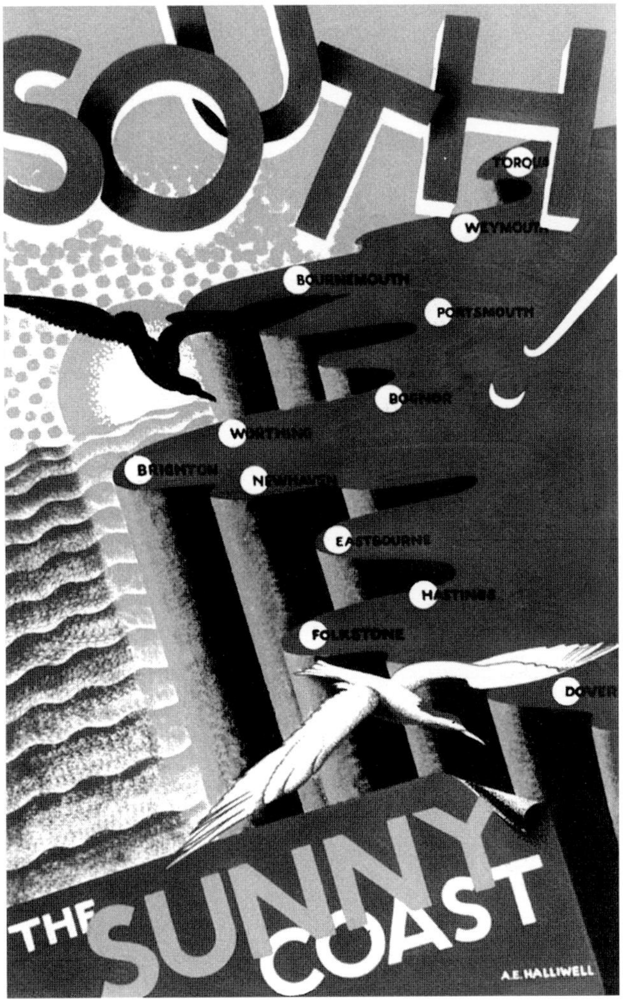

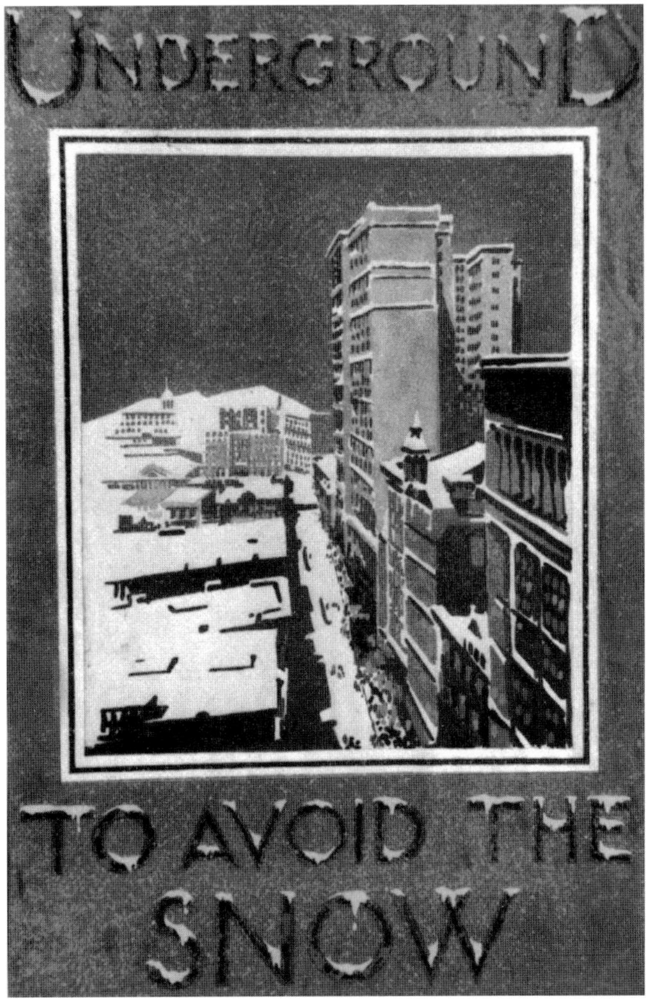

ARTHUR HALLIWELL. Travel posters. Gouache, 13½in x 22½in. Courtesy of National Arts Education Archive.

in 1946 for a two-year period, where he was almost entirely influenced by Pasmore*. He exhibited with the L.G. during the late 1940s and in the early 1950s showed drawings at the Beaux Arts Gallery, London and at the Galerie Rue Paradis, Marseilles in 1954. He has also written, illustrated and published many poems, the latest being a book of war poems and drawings *Remembering the Huns*, published in 1993 by Migrant Press.

HARPLEY, *Sydney Charles* (1927-1992)
He studied at Hammersmith College of Art 1950-53 and at the R.C.A. until 1956 under John Skeaping (1901-1980). He taught Sculpture and Drawing at Camberwell during the 1950s. He exhibited at the R.A. from 1954, when he showed the first of his 'Seated Girl' bronzes, by which he was to become widely known. He was elected an Associate of the R.A. in 1974 and a full Member in 1981. His portrait busts include Edward Heath and Lee Kwan Yew, the Prime Minister of Singapore. His works are in collections and museums world-wide, including the National Gallery of New Zealand, National Gallery of Cape Town, Paul Mellon Foundation (U.S.A.) and the late Princess Grace of Monaco. He held two successful one-man exhibitions at the Chris Beetles Gallery, London, in 1987 and 1990.

HARRIS, *Barbara* (1925-1968)
A gifted student at Camberwell from 1947-50, she came directly under the influence of Coldstream,* Rogers* and the general traditions of Euston Road. She was not a prolific artist and did not show her work in any exhibitions. In 1950 she

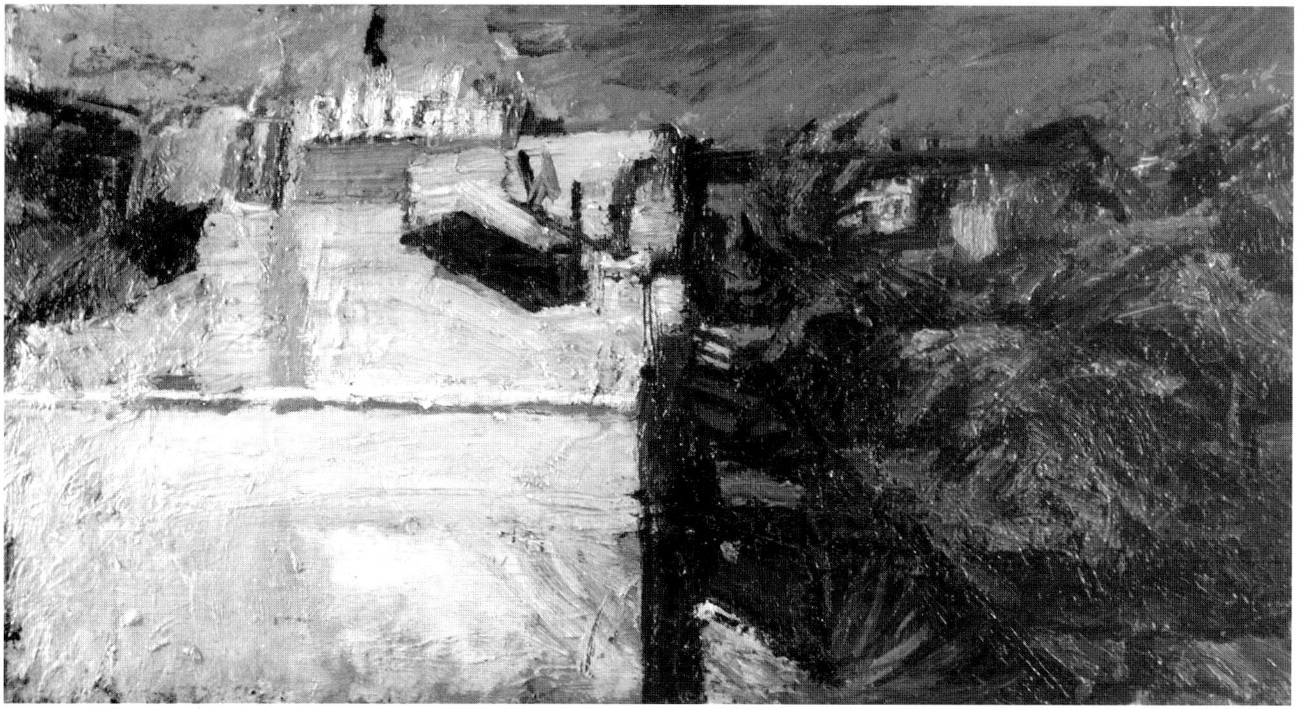

EDWARD HAMLYN. *Yellow House*, 1960. Oil on board, 39in x 22in. Artist's collection.

accompanied her husband, Anthony Fry*, to Rome for two years. She taught art for a while at a school in Kings Lynn.

HARRIS, *Donald* (b.1925)
He first attended Johannesburg Technical College in his native South Africa during the war years of 1942-45, where his teachers included Maurice Van Essche (1906-1977) and Eric Byrd (b.1905). He arrived in the U.K. in 1949 and spent the next three years at Camberwell School of Art, where his teachers and influences included Eurich*, Masterman*, Matthews* and Pitchforth*. The majority of his working life has been spent in art education at various comprehensive schools in the London area. Not only is he known as a painter, but also as a printmaker, having taken etching courses at Goldsmiths' in the mid-1950s under the tuition of Paul Drury (1903-1987). Since returning to the practice of etching in the early 1970s, he has been a regular exhibitor at the R.E. and at the N.E.A.C. He has also shown his work at the R.A., the Mall Gallery and has held one-man exhibitions at the Gallery on the Heath (Blackheath) and the Medici Gallery (South Kensington). His prints and paintings are in collections in the U.K., South Africa, Australia, New Zealand, Germany, France, U.S.A. and Canada, his work having been shown publicly in all of these countries. He has served as both Secretary and Chairman of the Greenwich Printmakers' Association.

HARRIS, *Phyllis* (*née* Fenton) (b.1925)
Studied at Brighton School of Art and Reading University during the war years, before attending Camberwell 1944-49 where she was influenced by the work and teaching of Minton* and La Dell*. Family commitments prevented her from following her artistic career for many years and it was not until the early 1970s that she began exhibiting professionally and has since become a member of the S.W.A., where she has shown regularly since the mid-1970s.

HAYLETT *Louise* (*née* Hencke) (b.1934)
She was a student at Camberwell 1950-55, where she studied both Painting and Sculpture, under Bloch*, Salaman* and Vogel*. Her early exhibitions included 'Looking Forward' arranged by John Berger and 'Painting and Sculpture at

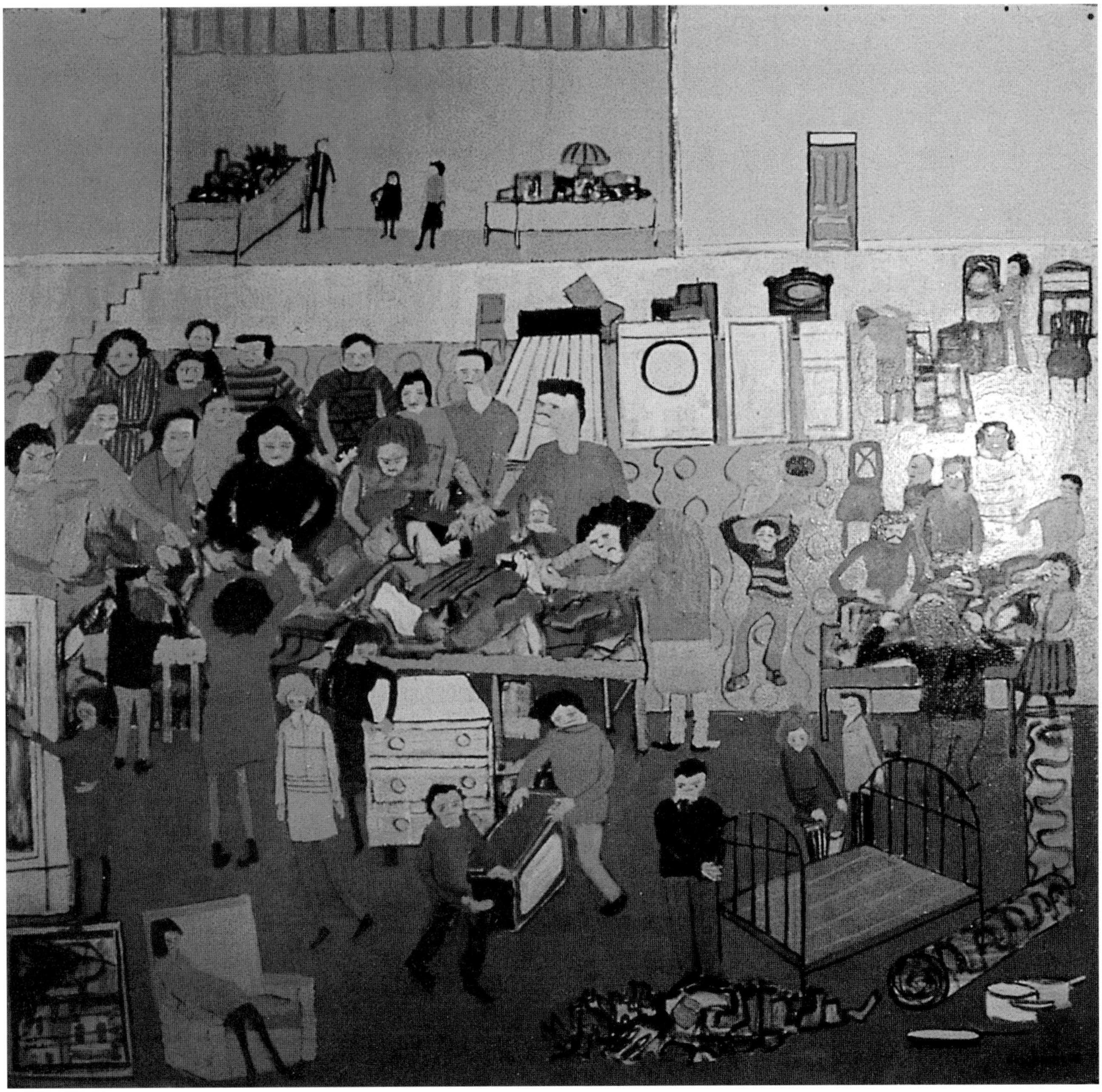

MELVILLE HARDIMENT. *Jumble Sale.* Oil on board, 40in x 40in. Artist's collection.

Camberwell Art School' held at The South London Art Gallery in 1957. Since leaving Camberwell she has attended Goldsmiths' College where she has recently been awarded an advanced Dip. A.D. She has held one-woman and group exhibitions at various venues in London, including Covent Garden, Greenwich and at the B.M.'s Department of Ethnography.

HAYWARD, *Rosamond Florence* (*née* Brown) (b.1930)
At the age of seventeen she enrolled as a student at Camberwell, where she eventually specialised in pottery. Her teachers included Norah Bradon* and Dorothy Wilmott. After several years of being unable to follow her artistic career due to family commitments she has recently started to paint.

HEGERTY, *Panama see* CAMPBELL, *Panama*

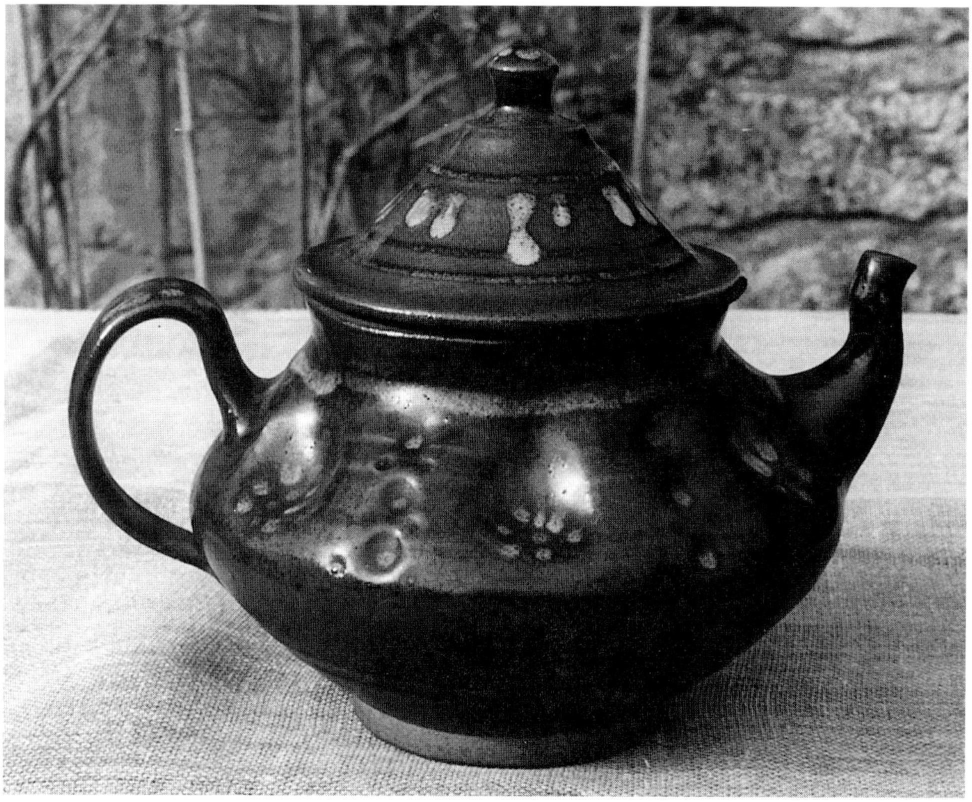

ROSAMOND HAYWARD. Teapot decorated with Tenmoku glaze, 1952. Stoneware, 6½in high.
Artist's collection.

HENRY, *Dennis* (b.1919)
Following active war service in which he was a P.O.W. for six years, he joined Camberwell in 1946. During his four years as a student he was taught by Coldstream*, Pasmore* and Rogers*. He exhibited at the R.B.A., A.I.A., N.E.A.C. and at the R.A. He is known to have emigrated to Ontario, Canada in 1953 where he was active as a teacher and exhibitor in his local community.

HEPHER, *David* (b.1935)
Studied at Camberwell from 1955-58, where he was influenced by Eurich*, Matthews*, Salaman* and Gilbert Spencer*. In 1959 he had a two-year period at the Slade School of Fine Art, where he was further influenced by Coldstream*. He returned to Camberwell in the early 1960s, where he taught on a part-time basis for twenty years. He has held numerous one-man exhibitions at venues including The Serpentine Gallery, Angela Flowers, Mappin Art Gallery Sheffield, Whitechapel Art Gallery and The Hayward. Since 1961, when he first exhibited in the 'Young Contemporaries' David Hepher has continued to show on a national and international scale in group exhibitions in such places as Cologne, Paris, Verona, Edinburgh, New York and Tokyo, where he won the first prize in the '1st International Tokyo Biennale'. His work is in public collections including the Arts Council of Great Britain, Bradford Art Gallery, Brighton Art Gallery, the Contemporary Art Society, the Tate Gallery, University College London and the V & A. He is currently teaching at Chelsea School of Art.

HEPWORTH, *Elizabeth Barbara* (b.1904)
The daughter of a pioneer of cinematography – Cecil Hepworth – she played in her father's films and, when only eight months old, she was the 'star' of one of the early silent films, *Rescued by Rover*. During the late 1920s and early 1930s she was employed at the Hogarth Press, where her employers and friends were Leonard and Virginia Woolf and the Bloomsbury Set. It was not until immediately after the end of

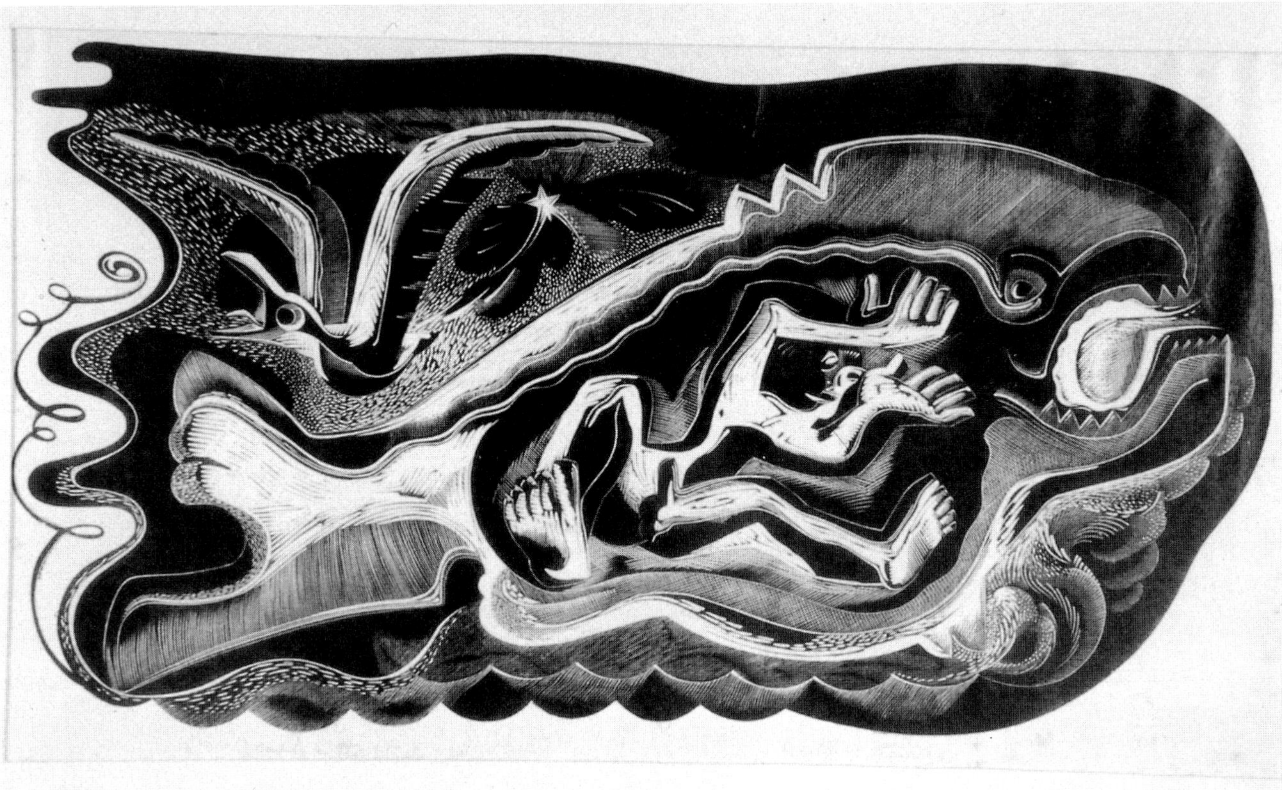

GERTRUDE HERMES. *Jonah and the Whale.* Wood engraving, 8½in x 15in. Courtesy of Hilary Chapman.

the war that she attended Camberwell as a student and was then influenced greatly by Rogers* and Pasmore*. In those years, and more recently, she has shown her work extensively in the R.A., the Leicester Galleries, N.E.A.C. and with the L.G. She has also held numerous art teaching posts in further education. Her work is in the collections of St. Pancras Borough Council and Hertfordshire County Council.

HERMES, *Gertrude Anna Bertha* R.A., R.E., L.G., S.W.E. (1901-1983)
She first studied art at Beckenham Art School in the years immediately preceding the First World War. From 1921-25 she studied at the Leon Underwood School of Painting and Sculpture with her friends and fellow students Henry Moore (1898-1986), Raymond Coxon (b.1896), Eileen Agar (1899-1991) and Vivian Pitchforth*. During the mid-1930s she began exhibiting at the R.A. and in 1935 was elected a member of the L.G. Soon after her appointment to the staff at Camberwell as an Assistant Instructor in the Life Drawing Class, she cut a small woodblock which appeared on the school prospectus. As the war intensified, for the protection of her children and at the invitation of relatives, she spent the next five years in Canada, returning to London in 1945 to teach Engraving and Printing, again at Camberwell, where she remained until 1947. She also taught at St. Martin's, the Central School and at the R.A. Schools. She was elected an Associate of the R.A. in 1963, becoming the first female wood engraver to do so, and a Member in 1971. She was married to the artist Blair Hughes-Stanton (1902-1981), with whom she collaborated on wood engravings for various print houses, including Cresset and Golden Cockerel, during the late 1920s and early 1930s. She also turned her hand to sculpture and carving, and was responsible for the mosaic floor and door furniture at the Shakespeare Memorial Theatre at Stratford-on-Avon. Examples of her work are to be found in the B.M., V & A, Tate Gallery, National Portrait Gallery and the Arts Council Collection, amongst many others.

HIGSON, *Josephine Elspeth see* SCANNELL, *Josephine Elspeth*

HIRST, *Barry Elliot* (b.1934)
Born in Padstow, Cornwall, he studied at Camberwell between 1950-52 and again from 1954-56 when he eventually taught for a short period in the Saturday drawing classes with Dixon*. During this period, his main teachers and influences were R. D. Lee*, Matthews* and Pitchforth*. In 1956 he was awarded the David Murray Scholarship during a two year period at the Slade. In 1958 he spent two years as a freelance designer with film companies in Paris, and from 1959-80 he wrote many articles and critical reviews for various art and crafts magazines and periodicals. He also taught at various art schools, including Heatherley's and Chelsea, before taking up his current position at Sunderland Polytechnic. In 1986 he was appointed Head of the School of Art and two years later became Dean of the Faculty of Art and Design. He has had one-man exhibitions at the Hanover Gallery, Stone Gallery (Newcastle-upon-Tyne) and in Australia, New York, Glasgow and Edinburgh. His most recent exhibition was held at the Mercury Gallery in London's Cork Street in 1994. His group exhibitions have been numerous, including Galerie de Seine, Anderson-Meyer (Paris), Arts Council Exhibition in Belfast, 'Hirst, Mundy, Wragg' and at locations abroad including Sydney, New York, and Washington. Hirst's work is in permanent collections around the world, including the Contemporary Arts Society, British Council, Tyne and Wear Museums, São Paulo Museum (Brazil), Museum of Modern Art (Tel Aviv) and The Duchess of Kent.

HODGKIN, *Howard* Kt., C.B.E. (b.1932)
He became a pupil at Camberwell in 1949, where he was to stay for nearly two years before entering the Bath Academy of Art to further his studies until 1954. His first teaching post was at Charterhouse School, but by 1956 he had returned to Corsham, where he was to remain on the staff until the mid-1960s. His other teaching posts have included occasional visits to the Slade School of Fine Art and the Chelsea School of Art. His work has been shown internationally and his major one-man exhibitions include Arthur Tooth & Sons, Kasmin Gallery, Arnolfini Gallery, Dartington Hall, Gallery Müller (Cologne), Waddington Galleries, Kornblee Gallery (New York), Museum of Modern Art (Oxford), Bernard Jacobson (New York), Knoedler Gallery (New York) and the Tate Gallery. In 1977 he was awarded a C.B.E. for services to art and since 1978 he has been a Trustee of the National Gallery. He won the Turner Prize in 1985, having been a contender the previous year, and in 1986 he was awarded first prize in the Bradford Print Biennale. His works are in major public collections throughout the world, including the Arts Council of Great Britain, the Contemporary Arts Society, São Paulo Museum (Brazil), Oldham Art Gallery, Tate Gallery, V. & A., Bristol City Art Gallery, National Gallery of South Australia, Museum of Modern Art (Edinburgh), Southampton Art Gallery, Museum of Modern Art (New York) and the Whitworth Art Gallery (Manchester). He was given a Knighthood in 1992.

HOLLWEG, *Alexander* (b.1936)
Following National Service and a degree in Modern Languages at Oxford University, he joined Camberwell School of Art in 1960, where he was to remain for three years. His teachers included Medley* and Matthews*. A prolific exhibitor in the U.K., Europe and the U.S.A., he has shown in a variety of galleries, including the Whitechapel Art Gallery, where he held his first one-man exhibition in 1971, Camden Arts Centre, Kornblee Gallery (New York) and the Oklahoma Art Centre. He has illustrated several publications, including *Brick Wall* published by Bernard Jacobson, 1974. He has been a visiting lecturer at Bristol Polytechnic, Slade School, Boston Museum School and Massachusetts Institute of Art. Latterly, he has also designed stained glass windows for churches, including the church at Corsock in Scotland.

HOLT, *Jeremy* (1931-1965)
Little information is known about this young painter who studied at Camberwell during the immediate post-war years. He made quite a reputation for himself as a portrait painter in the U.K., as well as in America and Canada. He is also known to have studied at the Chelsea School of Art and a posthumous solo exhibition was held at the New Grafton Gallery in 1977.

HOPSON, *Phoebe see* ATKINS, *Phoebe*

HOWARD, *Charles* (1899-1978)
Born in New Jersey, U.S.A., one of five children, his early years were spent in California where he graduated from the University. He spent three years in the early 1920s travelling in Europe and his time in Italy inspired him to take up painting as a career. On his return to the U.S. he worked as a mural painter and by 1926 had held his first one-man exhibition in New York. By 1933 he had again travelled to Europe and this time he took up residence in London. In 1935 he held a one-man exhibition at the Bloomsbury Gallery and during the period 1936-38 was involved with the Surrealist Group in London. The U.S. Government ordered his return in 1940 and he remained in San Francisco, being involved in the war effort. In 1946 he returned to England and had various exhibitions, including the Hanover Gallery and the Whitechapel Art Gallery, where a major retrospective was held in June 1956. He was invited to join the staff at Camberwell in 1958 at the suggestion of his friend Robert Medley*, who was then Head of Painting. He remained there on a part-time basis for several years.

HOWARD, *Opal St. Clair* (*née* Echalaz) (b.1921)
Studied at Camberwell 1946-49, where she was strongly influenced by Rogers*, La Dell* and Minton*. She exhibited widely at exhibitions, including the Young Contemporaries, the R.A., the L.G. and the N.E.A.C., and more recently at a mixed exhibition at the Caplan Gallery, Sheffield in 1979.

HOYLAND, *Francis Somervell* (b.1930)
He was educated at the Downs School, Colwall, near Malvern, where his first introduction to art was under Maurice Feild. He became a student at Camberwell in 1947 where he stayed until 1950. He was greatly influenced by Coldstream*, Dodgson* and Rogers* and also his close friend and contemporary, Patrick George*. He then spent a short time at the Slade School of Fine Art. He was an Abbey Minor Scholar in 1951 and from 1955-59 he taught at Bristol School of Art. He held exhibitions at the Galerie de Seine and the Beaux Arts Gallery in the late 1950s and early '60s. He has appeared on television many times on 'Painting of the Month' and 'The Art Game'. In 1969 he illustrated *The Oxford Old Testament.* He has written many books, including *A Painter's Diary* in 1967; and *Alive to Paint* in the same year. He was Art Critic for *The Listener* from 1966-68 and held a retrospective exhibition at South London Art Gallery in 1969. He commenced teaching at Camberwell in the late 1950s and continues to do so into the 1990s.

HUGHES, *Jane Seymour* (*née* Sewell) (b.1930)
Studied at Camberwell 1948-52, where she was strongly influenced by Carter*, Coldstream*, Dodgson*, Pitchforth* and Rogers*. She exhibited at various Camberwell student exhibitions held at the Walmer Castle public house, and in the early 1950s with the L.G. She is married to the sculptor, Ken Hughes.

HUISH *Barbara Anne* (*née* Kemp) (b.1942)
A student at Camberwell from 1955-62, her teachers and influences included Sidney

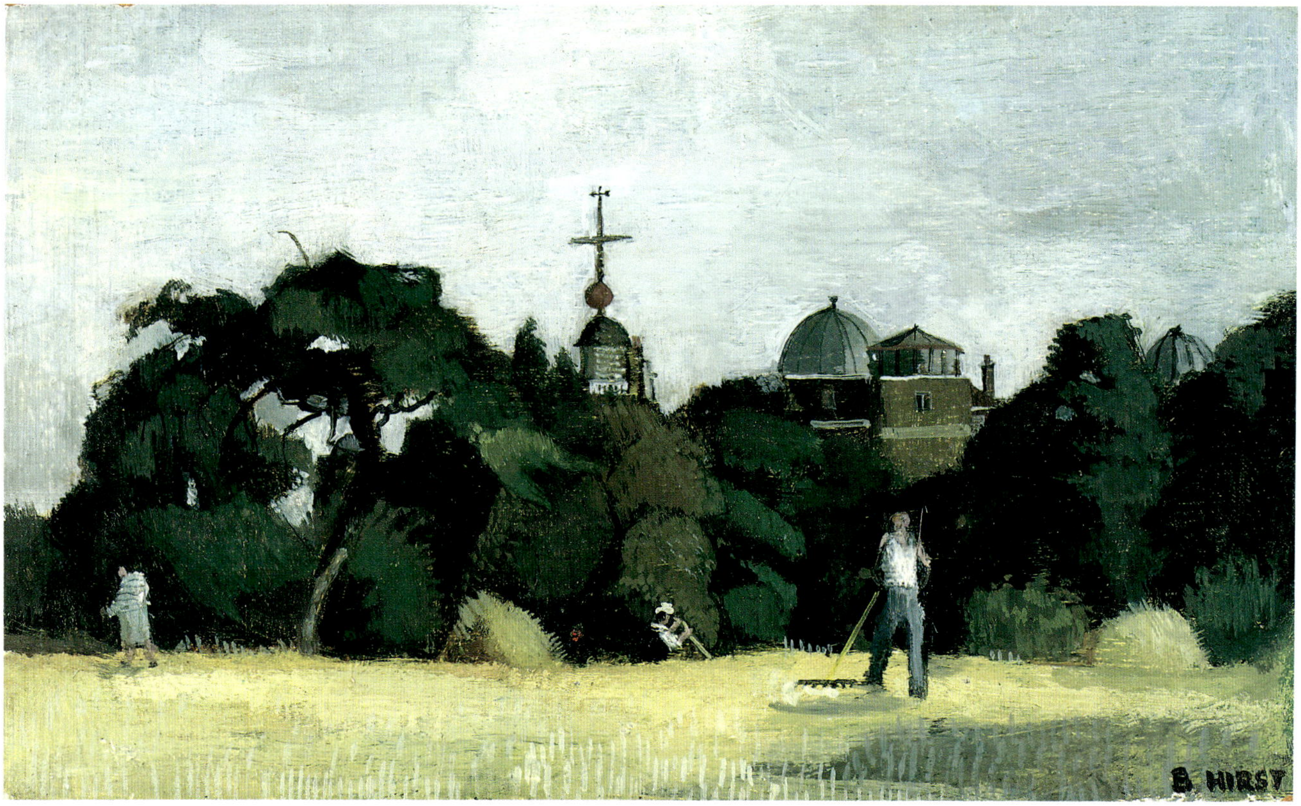

BARRY HIRST. *Towards Greenwich*, 1953. Oil on panel, 7in x 12in. Private collection.

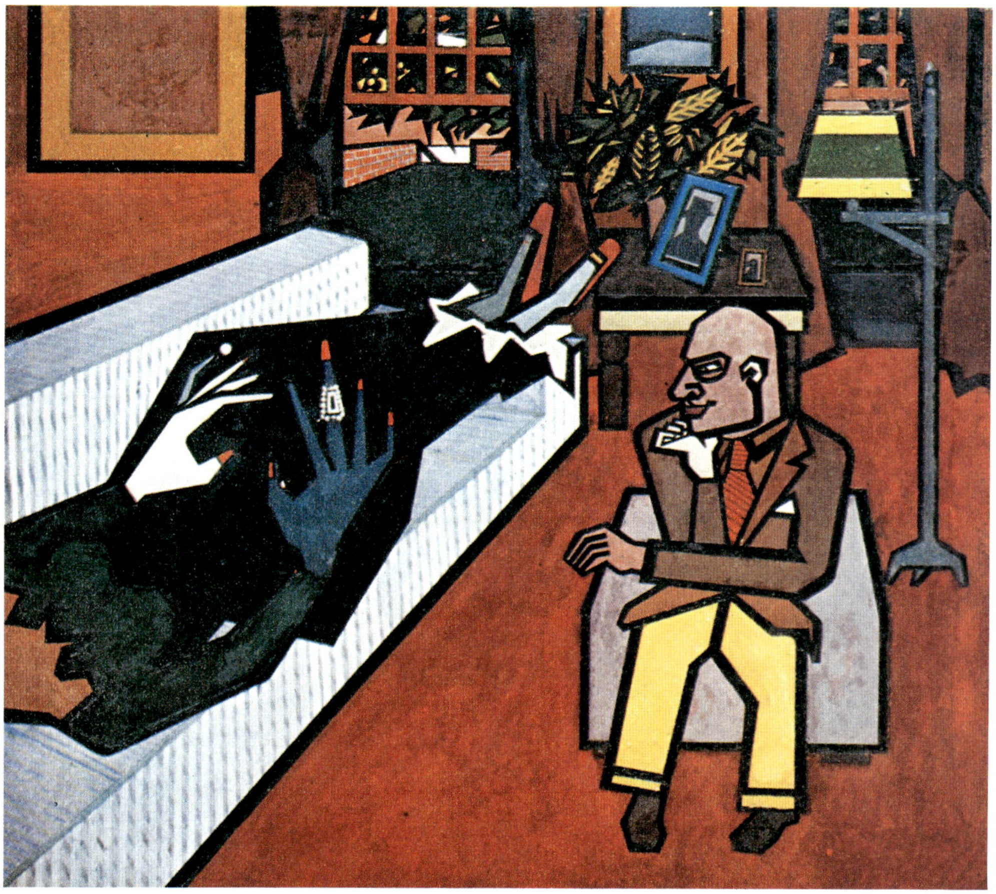

HOWARD HODGKIN. *Memoirs*, 1949. Gouache on board, 10in x 8½in. Private collection.

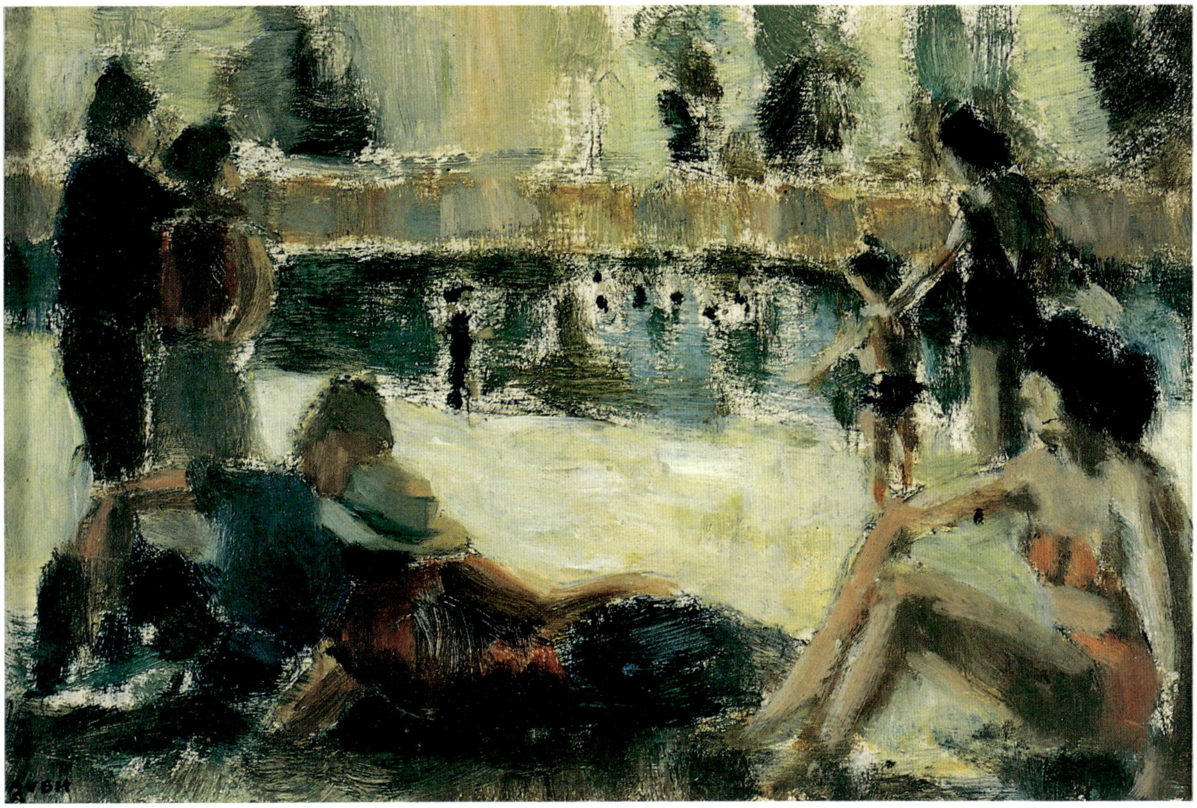

ALEXANDER HOLLWEG. *The Bathing Party.* Oil on board, 7in x 10in. Private collection.

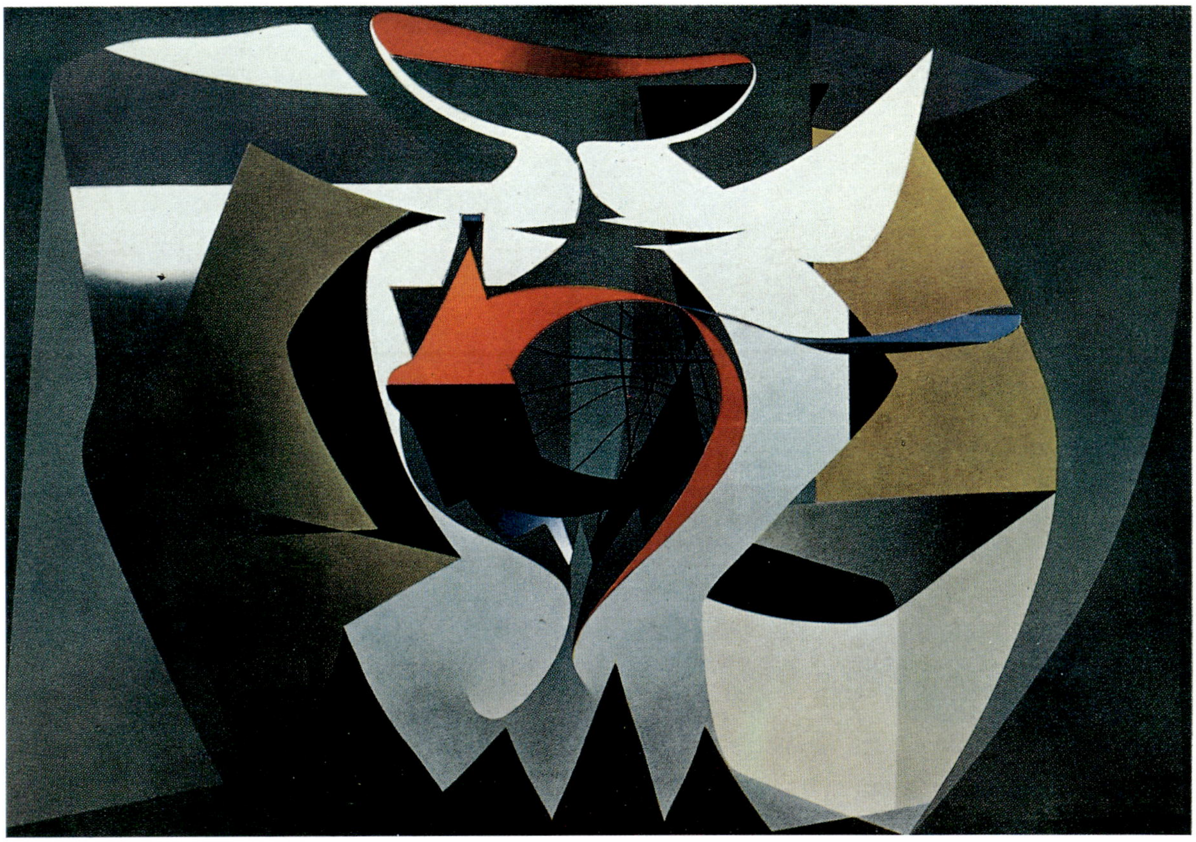

CHARLES HOWARD. *Night Painting*, 1955. Oil, 40in x 57in. Private collection.

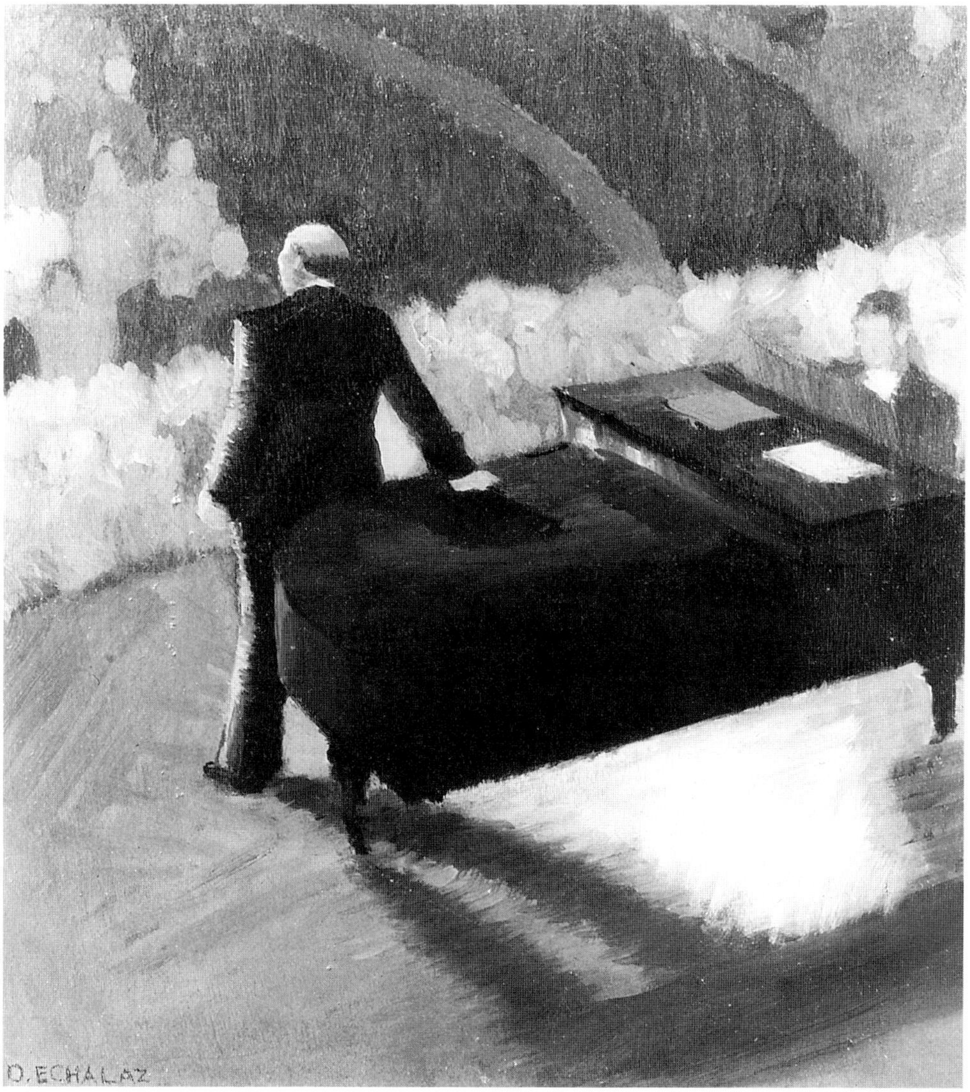

OPAL HOWARD (*née* Echalaz). *Gigli's Last Concert, Albert Hall*, c. 1949. Oil on panel, 12½in x 11in. Private collection.

Bendall*, Vernon Shearer* and Joe Dixon*. During her time there she studied mainly Illuminating, Lettering and Lithography. She has shown her work in various mixed exhibitions and recently held a one-woman show of Watercolours and Batiks at Eltham (London). She has held numerous teaching posts, including visiting lecturer at Camberwell from 1982-87.

HUISH, *William* (1942-1982)
Like his wife, Barbara*, he was a student at Camberwell from 1955-62, where his influences included Bullard*, Dixon* and R. D. Lee*. He shared various exhibitions with his wife, as well as numerous group shows from the early 1960s until the late 1970s. He continued his art career as a teacher until his untimely death at the age of forty.

HUME, *David Harry* (b.1930)
Studied at Camberwell from 1949-51, where he was influenced by Dodgson*, Rogers*, and Salaman* as well as his fellow students, Patrick George* and Francis Hoyland*. He abandoned painting rather early in his career and now works for Independent Television.

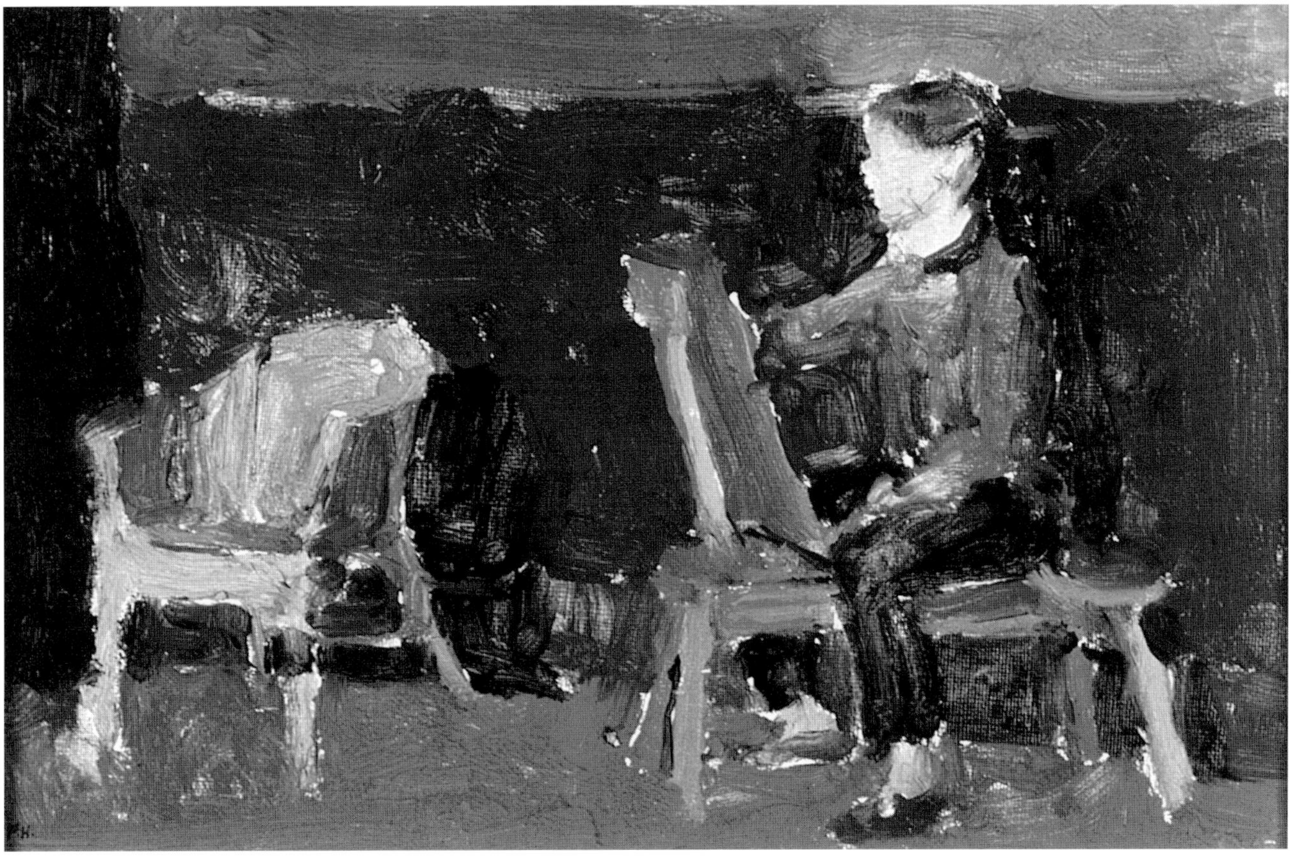

FRANCIS HOYLAND. *Sketch of a Child*, c.1953. Oil on board, 7in x 11in. Private collection.

HUNT, *Gerald* (b.1927)
Studied at Camberwell School of Art 1953-55 and has taught there on a part-time basis since 1960. He won a scholarship to the Slade School of Fine Art in 1956 and was greatly influenced by Coldstream* and Rogers*. Towards the end of his time at the Slade, in 1959, he abandoned working from nature and was painting in line with abstract expressionism. He has had one-man and mixed exhibitions at the L.G., Young Contemporaries, John Moores, Camden Art Centre, Aberdeen Art Gallery, Kettle's Yard (Cambridge) and the South London Art Gallery. He has also exhibited in the U.S.A.

HUNT, *Robert Sydney* (b.1929)
He was a student at Camberwell from 1943-47, during which time he was greatly influenced by Minton* (who was later to become a close friend and for a time his employer and landlord) and Vaughan*. He has exhibited widely, including the L.G. during the late 1940s and early '50s. In 1949 he also exhibited at the I.C.A., and held a three-man exhibition at the St. George's Gallery with Peter Dunbar* and Owen Wood* in 1956. His varied career has included a job at Soho's famous Colony Club as a cloakroom attendant. He has lectured extensively on illustration and between 1966-72 he was the Picture Director for the British Printing Corporation. He also exhibited in 'Artists at the Colony Club' held at the Parkin Gallery in 1983. He is currently the in-house artist with the *New Statesman* and the Art Consultant to Orbis Publishing,

HURDLE, *Robert Henry* (b.1918)
He was a student at Camberwell between 1946-48, where his teachers were Kenneth Martin*, Rogers* and Townsend*, but he was also greatly influenced by Coldstream* and Pasmore*. During his student years, he showed at the A.I.A. Students' Group, the R.A., and the L.G., where he continued to exhibit regularly

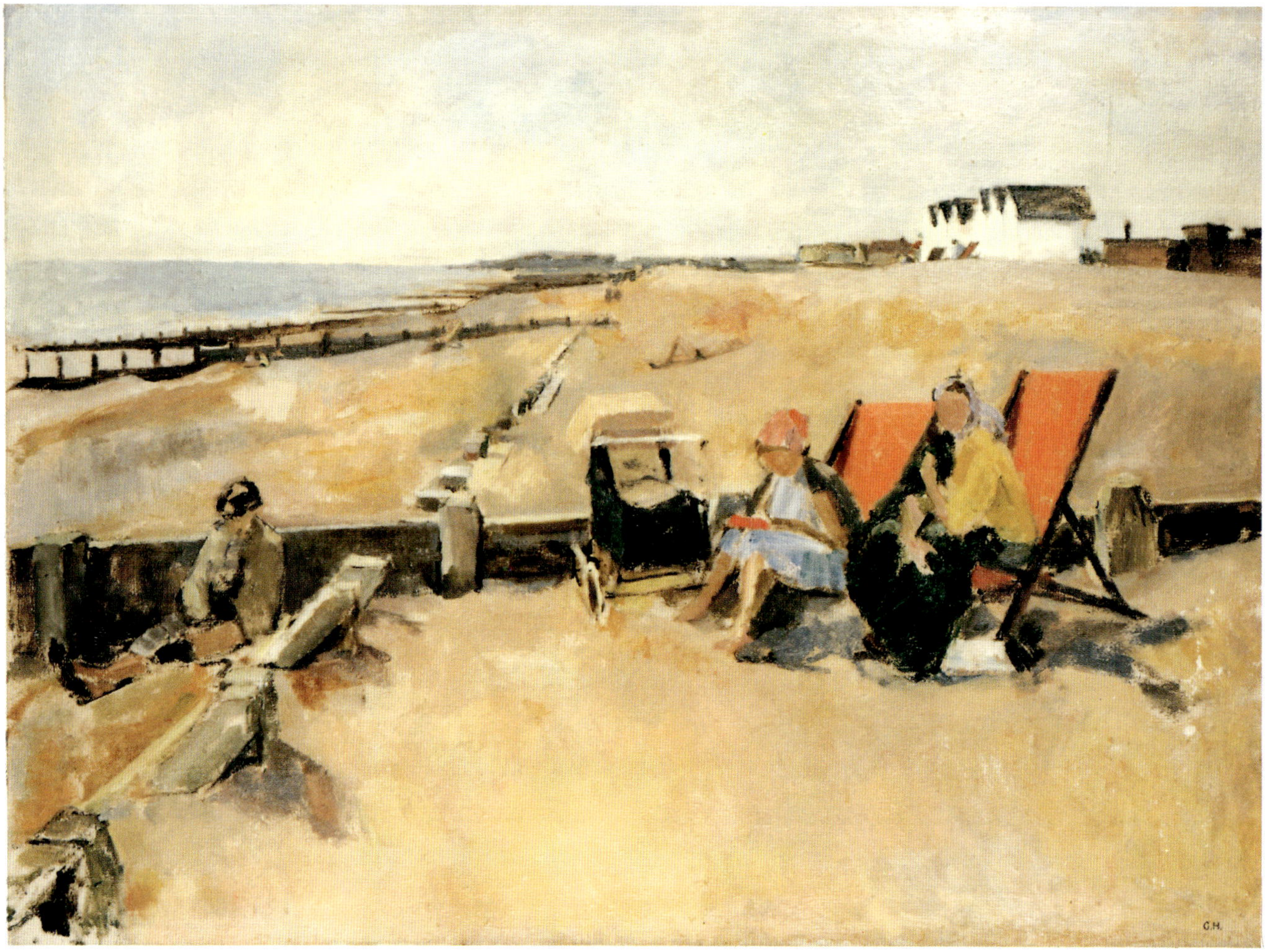

GERALD HUNT. *Worthing Beach*, 1956. Oil on canvas, 36in x 48in. Private collection.

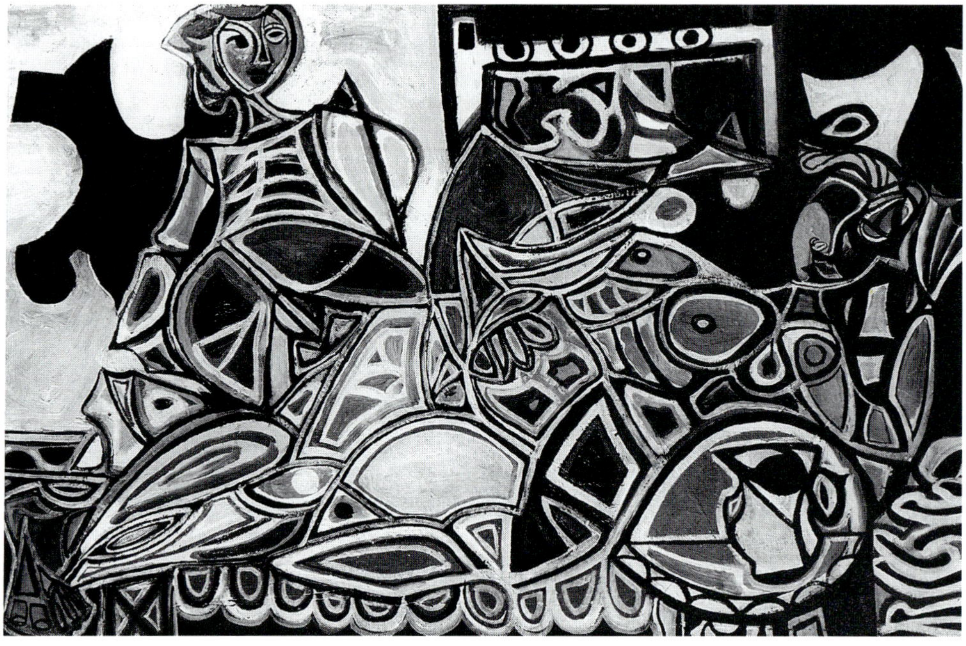

ROBERT HUNT. *Two Women*, 1950. Oil on canvas, 20in x 30in. Private collection.

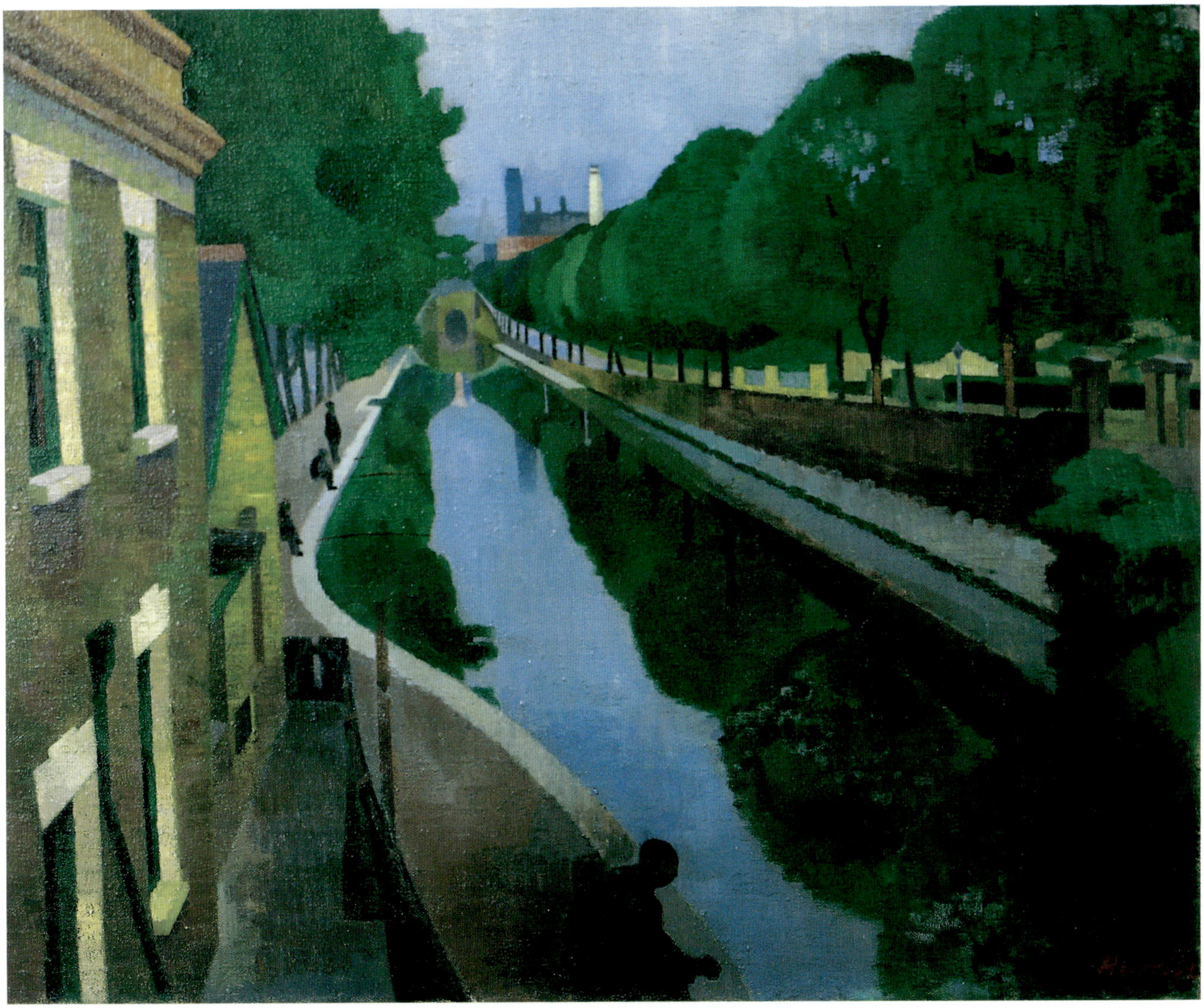

ROBERT HURDLE. *Canal , Maida Vale*, 1945. Oil on canvas, 20in x 24in. Private collection.

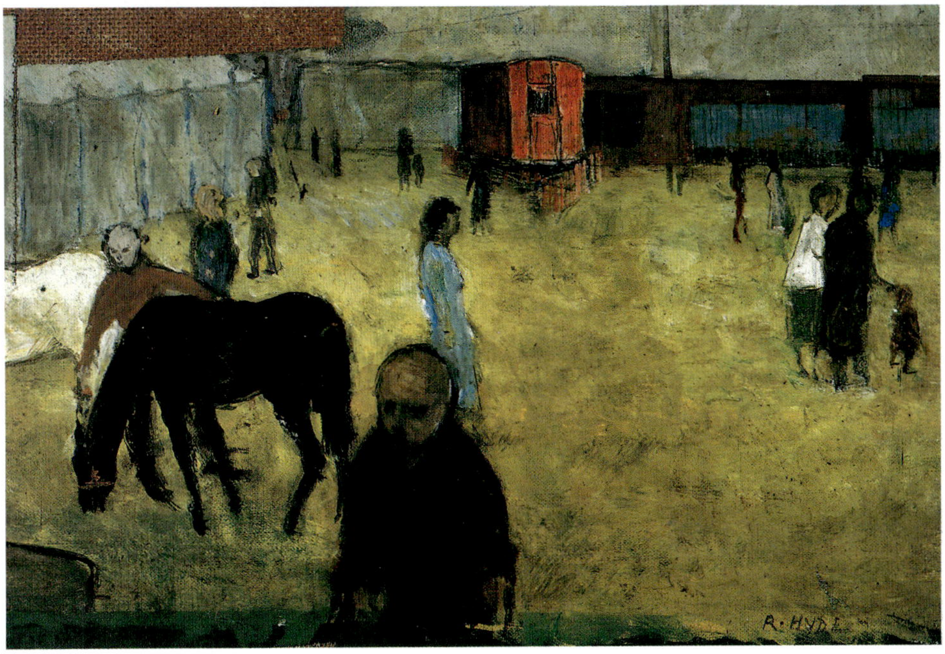

RICHARD HYDE. *Fairground Workers.* Oil on board, 11½in x 8in. Collection of the late Richard Eurich.

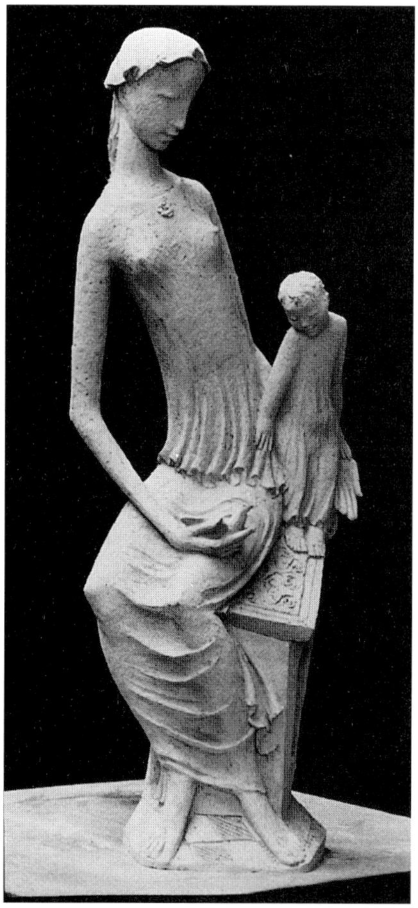

T. B. HUXLEY-JONES. *Mother and Child*, c.1955. Stoneware, lifesize. Present whereabouts unknown.

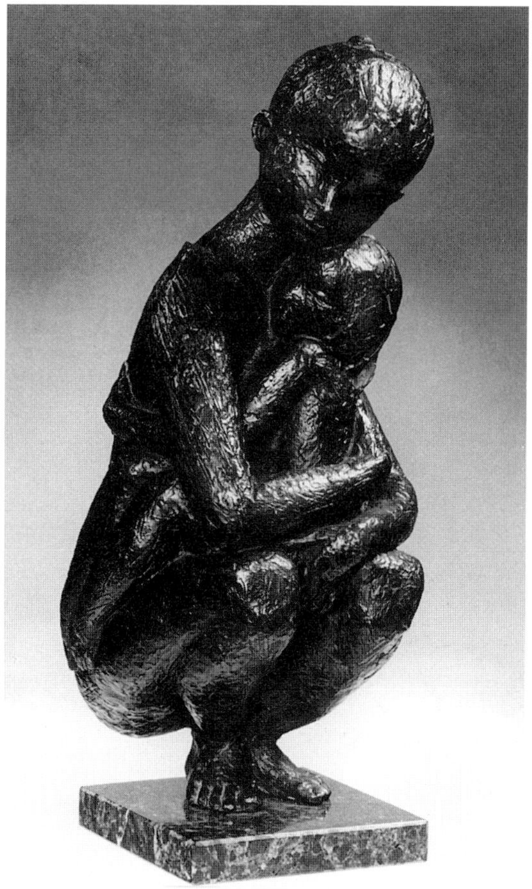

T. B. HUXLEY-JONES. *Tenderness.* Bronze, 13½in high. Collection Wenlock Fine Art.

until 1958. He now lives in Bristol where he taught at the R.W.A. Schools, taking over from Bernard Dunstan* in the early 1950s.

HUXLEY-JONES, *Thomas Bayliss* F.R.B.S., R.B.S.A., A.R.C.A. (1908-1969)
Born in Grahamstown, South Africa he came to England at the age of four years. He studied sculpture at Wolverhampton under Robert Jackson Emerson (1878-1944), before winning a scholarship to the R.C.A. in 1930. Here he studied under Henry Moore (1898-1986) and won a Travelling Scholarship in 1933 followed by the coveted Prix de Rome the following year. He chose however to resign these awards in favour of a teaching post at Glasgow School of Art. He later became Head of Sculpture at Gray's College, Aberdeen and after the war returned to England where, in 1949, he joined the staff at Camberwell. He taught there on a part-time basis for nearly ten years. He was a regular exhibitor at the R.A. and R.S.A., and he also showed at Birmingham, Liverpool and at the Glasgow Institute. He worked in a variety of media, including stone, ciment fondu, bronze and ivory, and his commissions included the Helios Statue in the B.B.C. at White City. Examples of his work were purchased by the art galleries of Wolverhampton, Aberdeen and Glasgow and are in collections in South Africa and America. He was married to the sculptor Gwynneth Holt (b.1909).

HYDE, *Richard* (b.1936)
He first joined Camberwell at the age of thirteen in 1949, where he was to remain until 1956. His main teachers were Brason* and Christopher Chamberlain*. Following his National Service, he continued his studies at the Slade School of Fine Art 1958-60. He is believed to be living and working in Cornwall.

I

INGHAM CLARK, *Prudence* (*née* Makower) (b.1928)
A student at Camberwell from 1946-49, her teachers included Coldstream*, Minton* and Pasmore*. She has followed a career as a textile designer for many years.

INLANDER, *Heinz Kurt* (1925-1983)
Born in Vienna, he came to England in 1938; his family leaving Austria in the aftermath of the Anschluss. Immediately after the war he studied at Camberwell until 1949, spending the next three years at the Slade School of Fine Art. In 1952 he won the Prix de Rome that was to lead to a lasting passion for Italy until the end of his life. During the mid-1950s he was to spend two years as Art Adviser to the British School at Rome. He returned to Camberwell as a Lecturer in Painting in 1957, a position he was to hold for the next twelve years. He exhibited both nationally and internationally at the Leicester Galleries, Tate Gallery, British Arts Council, John Moores, Roland Browse & Delbanco and in Rome, New York, Zurich, Calgary, and Vienna. His work is in numerous public collections, including Aberdeen Art Gallery, National Gallery of South Australia, Belfast Museum, Scottish National Gallery of Modern Art, Tate Gallery, the Arts Council of Great Britain, the Contemporary Art Society, the National Gallery of Victoria, the Nuffield Foundation, the Arts Council of Northern Ireland, the Graves Art Gallery, and in numerous private collections in Europe and the U.S.A. He married the artist Antonia O'Brien.

IRBY, *Anne Pauline see* CREWS, *Anne Pauline*

J

JAMES, *Owen Mervyn* A.R.O.I., S.G.A. (b.1934)
He first studied art at Lydney School of Art from 1951-53, before spending two years at Camberwell, where he studied Sculpture under Vogel*. He has shown his work extensively, including Summer Exhibitions at the R.A., R.B.A., N.E.A.C., S.G.A. and the R.O.I. His work is in numerous private and public collections, including the Municipal Galleries of Derby, Lincoln, Rotherham, Darlington, Cheltenham, Wakefield and Wolverhampton.

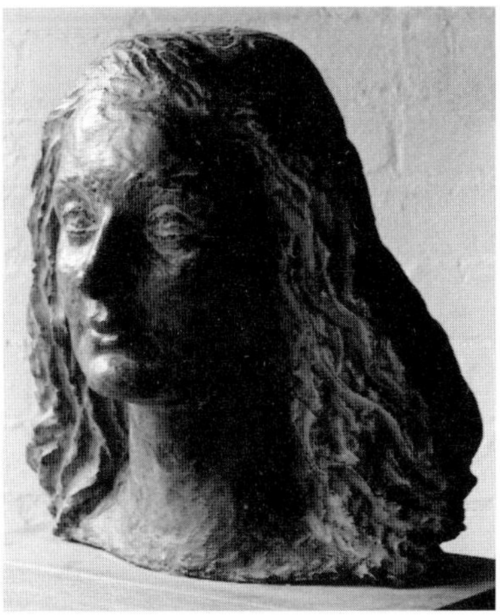

OWEN JAMES. *Zoë*, 1954. Plaster, 15in high. Artist's collection.

JARVIS, *Donald* (b. 1936)
Painter, designer, poet and mathematician. He attended Camberwell from 1952-56 before transferring to the Central School for a further three years' study, obtaining his N.D.D. in 1959. He exhibited with his fellow students at the Walmer Castle pub and in 1954 won the school painting prize. He also showed at the neighbouring South London Art Gallery. His paintings developed towards geometrical abstraction and later he obtained a B.Sc and then an M.Sc in mathematics from London University. His poetry led to his interest in artists' books and mail-art and he currently sells more work outside than inside the U.K. He runs his own company, Aard Press, from his London home and is Chairman of the Small Press Group of Britain.

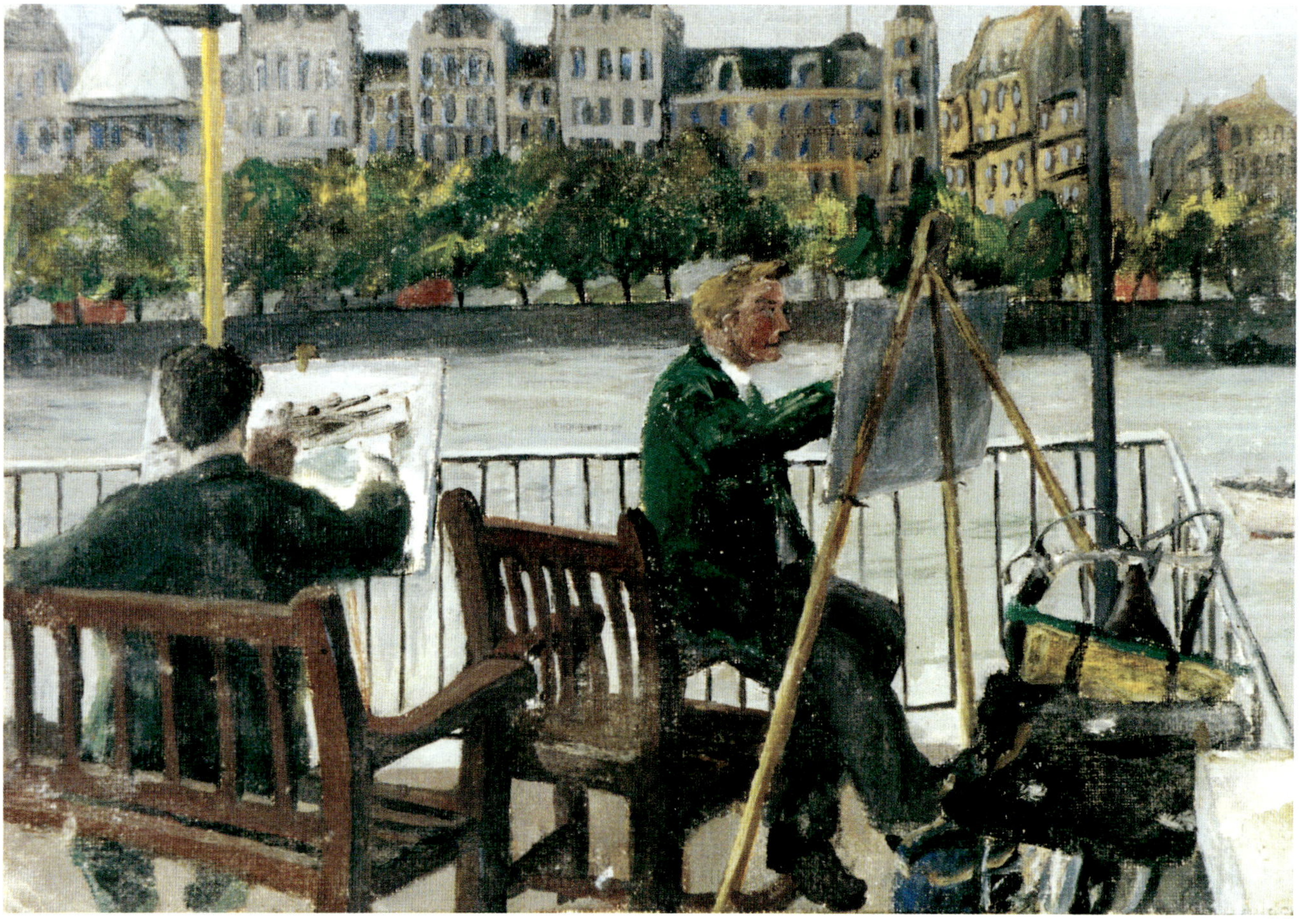

DONALD JARVIS. *South Bank Whitsun*, 1955. Oil on board, 11in x 15in. Artist's collection.

JENKIN, *Ian Evers Tregarthen* O.B.E., M.A. (b.1920)
He studied at Camberwell from 1947-49, where he was influenced by Carter*, Coldstream*, Pitchforth* and Salaman*. In 1949 he was appointed Secretary and Tutor at the Slade School of Fine Art, a position he held until 1975 when, on the retirement of Leonard Daniels*, he was appointed Principal at Camberwell. He retired in 1985, whereupon he was immediately appointed the Curator at the R.A. He has painted very little and has only exhibited on rare occasions with the London Portrait Society in 1938 and at the Upper Grosvenor Gallery in 1968. He has been enormously involved in art education and some of his activities have included Vice-Chairmanship of the Arts Council of Great Britain, Chairman of the British School at Rome, Faculty of Painting, and Governorships of West Surrey College of Art & Design, Wimbledon School of Art and Loughborough College of Art. He is also a Trustee of the Stanley Spencer Gallery at Cookham and he was appointed as the first Director of the newly formed Open College of Arts.

JOHNSON, *Dorothy see* BEVAN, *Dorothy*

JOHNSTONE *William* O.B.E. (1897-1981)
He studied at Edinburgh College of Art from 1919-23 and at the R.S.A. schools during the next two years. In the mid-1920s he spent two years in Paris studying under André L'Hôte and at Colarossi's. The majority of his artistic life was spent as an educator, teaching at such places as Regent Street Polytechnic, and he was first appointed as a Principal in 1936 at Hackney School of Art. Two years later, in 1938, he was appointed Principal of Camberwell. It was while there, and later at the Central School where he became Principal in 1947, that he became the driving force

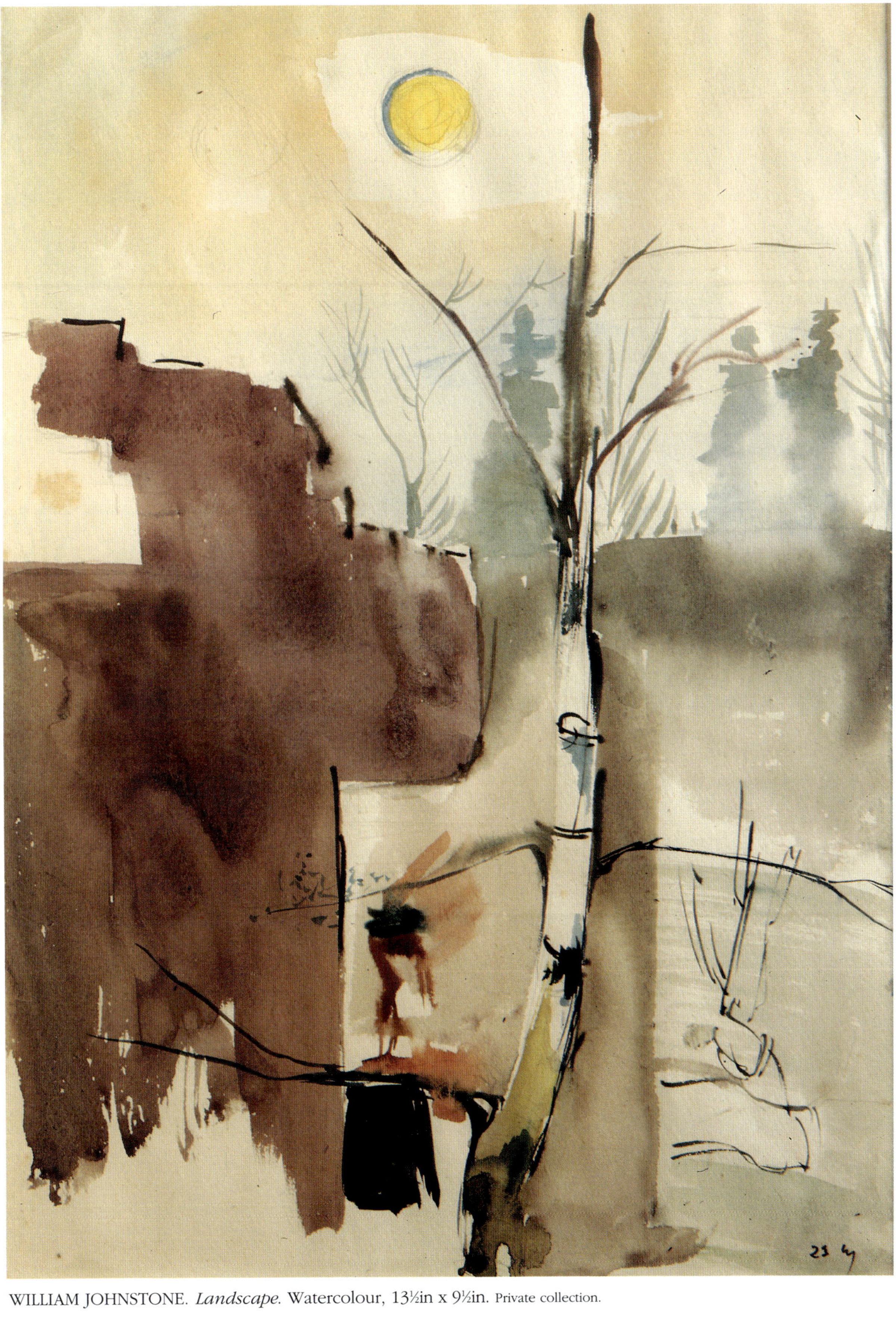

WILLIAM JOHNSTONE. *Landscape.* Watercolour, 13½in x 9½in. Private collection.

in the encouragement of artists and designers of distinction to take up positions as teachers in order to pass on their experiences to art students. However, by the time the 1960s had arrived, Johnstone was so disillusioned with the bureaucracy that was creeping into the world of art education that he gave up his career as a teacher and returned to his native Scotland, where he took up the combined roles of gentleman farmer and artist. His work was exhibited widely in one-man exhibitions such as the Wertheim Gallery, Aitken Dott & Son (Edinburgh), Gimpel Fils, Reid & Lefevre and the Stone Gallery (Newcastle). His group exhibitions were equally as numerous and included Le Salon des Beaux Arts (Paris), Mayor Gallery, Whitechapel Art Gallery, Hanover Gallery, Leicester Galleries, The International Exhibition at the British Embassy (Brussels), Contemporary Scottish Painters (Wales). His work is in public and private collections throughout the world and the Scottish Arts Council held a retrospective in 1970. He was also an author, his books *Creative Art in England* (1936) and *Child Art to Man Art* (1940) were at the time important landmarks in art education publishing. His autobiography *Points in Time* (Barrie & Jenkins, 1980) makes interesting reading for students of modern British Art. A sale of the remains of his studio contents was held by Christie's at their Glasgow salerooms in April 1990. The success of this auction brought Johnstone's work to the attention of a wider public and established him as arguably Scotland's leading 20th century abstract artist.

JUPP, *Mo* (b.1938)
Born in London, were he now lives, he trained at Camberwell under Hans Coper, Lucie Rie* Ian Auld* and Bryan Newman* during the later 1950s and at the R.C.A. He has worked from various studios in the Gloucestershire area, including a 15th century farmhouse and manor house, and he still teaches pottery courses at Bristol Polytechnic, Bath Academy of Art, Middlesex Polytechnic and Harrow. He makes sculptured ceramics and works with any materials that can be fired, using a variety of methods. His latest works, still on the theme of women, are slender figures and torsoes. Major exhibitions include Primavera, London and Cambridge; 1st Triennale of Ceramics, Belgrade; Arts Council shows in Japan and U.S.A.; Oxford Gallery; British Crafts Centre/Contemporary Applied Arts; V. & A.; Westminster Gallery, Boston and Aberystwyth Arts Centre.

K

KATZ, *Marianne see* DOWNING, *Marianne*

KAYE, *Margaret* A.R.C.A. (b.1912)
Studied at Croydon School of Art, then in the late 1930s at the R.C.A, where she concentrated on stained glass and needlework. From 1947-76 she was a part-time teacher at Camberwell in both Foundation and Textiles. She has held full-time teaching posts at the Birmingham College of Art and she has also taught at St. Martin's School of Art. Since 1949 she has exhibited at such venues as Roland Browse & Delbanco, and her work has also been seen in the R.A. and at various craft shows in Britain, Europe, the U.S.A. and Canada. Her work is in various public collections, including the V. & A., Contemporary Arts Society, and Manchester Art Gallery. She has also worked extensively in collage and embroidery, designing many frontals and copes. Examples of these can be seen at Winchester Cathedral and in other major places of worship around the country.

KELLY *Jennifer* (*née* Somerville) (b.1930)
She spent two years from 1947 as a student at Camberwell where B. A. R. Carter* taught her and influenced her most. By 1949 she had left Camberwell and continued her studies under Coldstream* at the Slade School of Fine Art. She was not prolific and all her early work from this period has been destroyed. Due to family commitments she has only recently recommenced painting and in the early 1970s had a one-woman exhibition at the Glynn Vivian Art Gallery, Swansea. During her time at Camberwell she kept a diary, extracts of which are reproduced in this book.

KEMP, *Barbara Anne see* HUISH, *Barbara Anne*

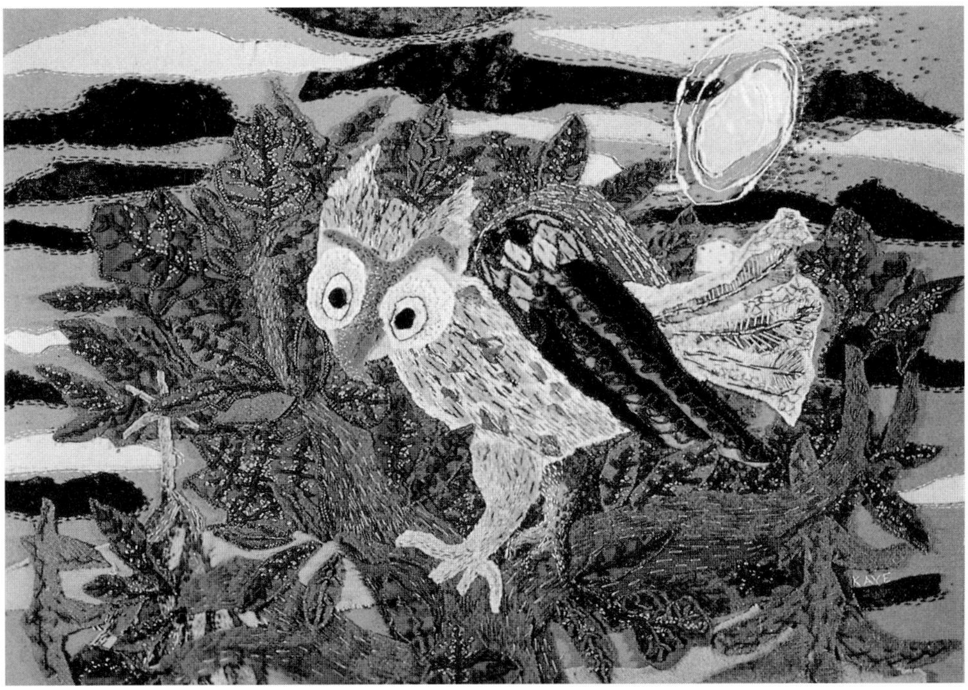

MARGARET KAYE. *Owl by Moonlight*, 1947. Fabric collage with threads, 24in x 30in. Artist's collection.

MARGARET KERR.
Stoneware pot with iron slip incised decoration and Tenmoku glaze, 1952. 9½in high. Artist's collection.

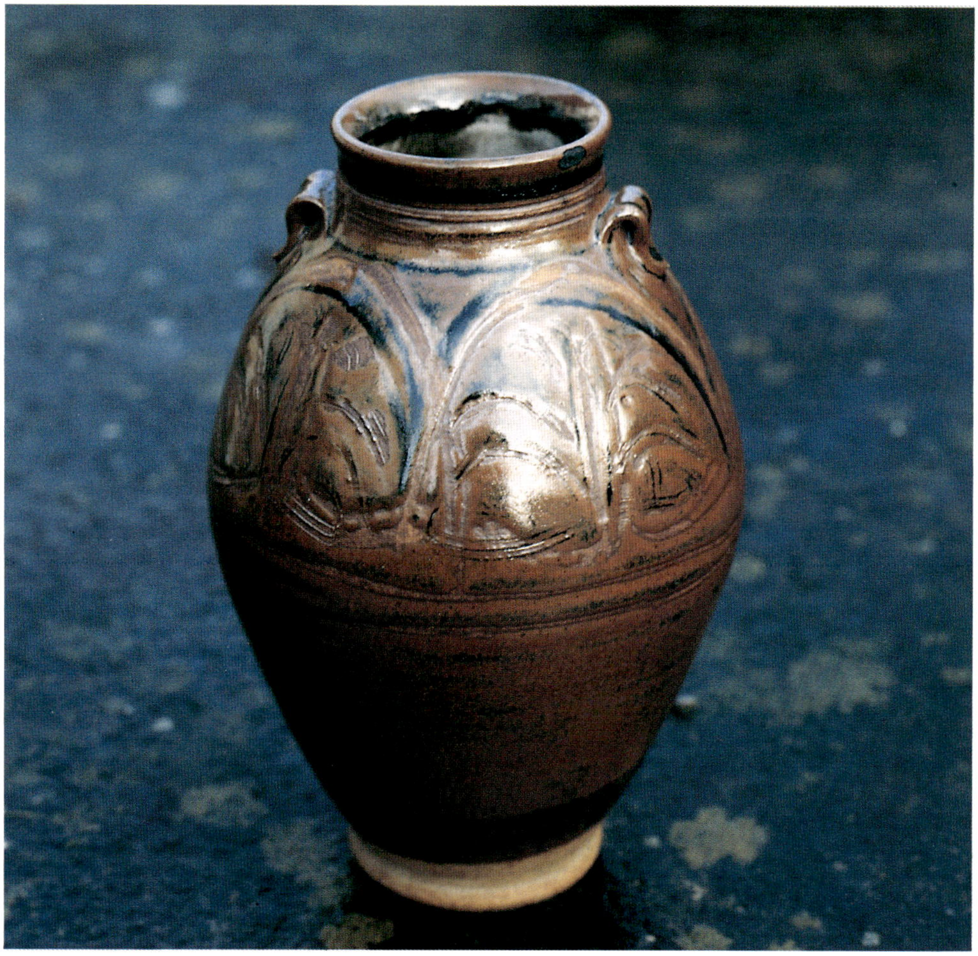

KENDALL, *Richard Houghton* (1917-1974)
As a student at the Slade School of Fine Art during 1936-40, his career at that time seemed destined to be that of an artist, however, at the end of the war he spent two years working with Bernard Leach at his pottery in St. Ives and in 1946 he joined the staff at Camberwell where he remained until 1971 – the majority of his time being spent as the Head of the Ceramic Department, working alongside such colleagues as Lucy Rie* and Hans Coper. His premature death from multiple sclerosis deprived British studio pottery of one of its finest practitioners and most respected teachers.

KERLANDER, *Judith* (*née* Radenhurst) (b.1941)
She joined Camberwell in 1960, where she won a Major County Award before acquiring her N.D.D. in sculpture four years later. Her sculpture has been shown at several exhibitions, including the R.A. and the Royal Glasgow Institute of Fine Arts. By the end of the 1960s she began working at Shepperton Film Studios where, amongst others, she was engaged in working on *Anne of a Thousand Days* and *Cromwell.* She continued to show her sculpture regularly but by the mid-1970s had turned to painting, when her work was shown in a mixed exhibition at the Whitechapel Art Gallery. She has lately turned to silk-screen printing and has been involved in the design of textiles and the printing of fabrics. She has also continued in the fashion world as a millinery designer and her work has been used by many couturiers, including Norman Hartnell, Sarah Spencer and Benny Ong.

KERR, *Margaret Williams* (b.1920)
She arrived at Camberwell as a mature thirty-year old student, having already studied part-time at Hereford Art School where her interests lay in pottery. There were, however, no kilns available so it was not until she arrived at Camberwell that

she was able to get to grips with her chosen subject. She was already a qualified teacher, having spent three years in teacher training at the Froebel Institute. Since leaving Camberwell, she has taught in Deptford and Goldsmiths' College in their Ceramics Department, where she was involved in the post-graduate Diploma course. During the early 1970s she attended Cardiff University, where she took a Diploma in art education. Since retiring in 1981 she has lived in Wiltshire.

KESSEL, *Mary* (1914-1977)
She first studied at Clapham School of Art from 1935-37 and further studied at the Central School of Arts & Crafts from 1937-39. During the early years of the war, she was commissioned to paint a mural entitled 'Judith and Holofernes' at Westminster Hospital. She was appointed an Official War Artist and during 1945 she visited Belsen and other concentration camps to make drawings of refugees, which are now in the collection of the Imperial War Museum. Her first one-woman exhibition was held at the Leicester Galleries in 1950 and, shortly after, she began lecturing in Jewellery Design at the Central School of Arts & Crafts. She joined the staff at Camberwell in 1955 and remained there until 1960. Equally well-known as an illustrator, she was commissioned by Osbert Sitwell to illustrate *Mrs. Kimber* in 1937. Her work is in many public and private collections, including the Tate Gallery, the Contemporary Arts Society, The Arts Council, National Gallery of Victoria (Australia), The Ministry of Works and the collection of the late Lord Clark. She was married to the artist and poster designer, Tom Eckersley.

KNIGHT, *David* (1923-1982)
A student at Wimbledon School of Art 1940-42, he pursued a career as a graphic designer for many years, illustrating such publications as *Radio Times*, *Lilliput* and various posters for the G.P.O. He taught illustration at Camberwell School of Art from 1955-60 and it is not known if he exhibited his work on a professional basis.

KNOWLAND, *Dennis George* N.D.D. (1918-1985)
When he was sixteen years of age, he met and was befriended by R .O. Dunlop, R.A. (1894-1973), who quickened an already growing interest in art. During the mid-1930s he spent a year at Chelsea School of Art, where his teachers were Graham Sutherland (1903-1980) and Robert Medley*. During this time he was awarded a prize for landscape painting. He first showed with the L.G. in 1938 and at the outbreak of war he was earning his living in the world of advertising. Shortly after he was to illustrate a book entitled *Bevis at Home* by Richard Jefferies, published by Dent in 1940. During the beginning of the war, whilst stationed in Scotland, he met Anne Redpath (1895-1965) who was kind enough to lend him a studio during his leave, where he again took up painting. As the war ended, he was determined to continue painting and a Government grant enabled him to spend three years at Camberwell, where he came under the influence of Coldstream*, Gowing* and Rogers*. After leaving Camberwell, until 1972, he spent most of his time as an examiner and teacher in Oxfordshire, being associated with such places as Charterhouse, the Ruskin School and St. Clare's Hall. He retired from his teaching and examining work in the early 1970s and continued to paint and travel until his death. He exhibited widely, not only in the U.K. but in Germany, Cape Town, and Johannesburg. His memorial exhibition was held at the Central Library, Westgate, Oxford in 1987.

KNOX, *George* (b.1922)
Currently Professor Emeritus of Art History at the Department of Fine Arts, University of British Columbia, Canada, he was, between 1950-52, a visiting lecturer at Camberwell. He has also taught Art History at the Slade, Durham University and

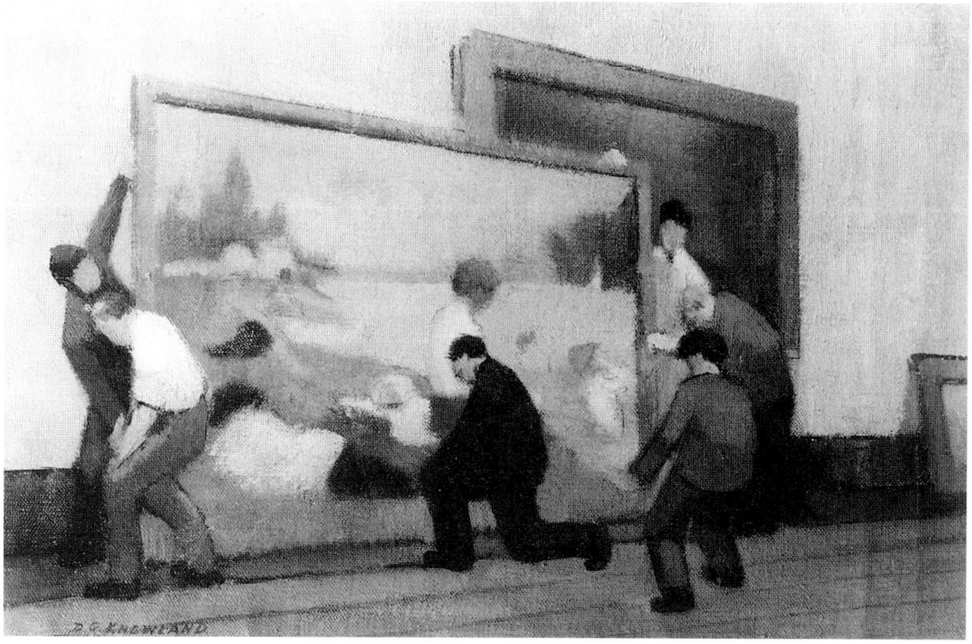

DENNIS KNOWLAND.
Moving the Seurat, 1948.
Oil on canvas, 8in x 11½in.
Photograph courtesy of Belgrave Gallery.

Portsmouth College of Art, before emigrating to Canada in 1970. An expert on Italian 18th century art, he has written and compiled many books and catalogues on the subject and organised numerous exhibitions in the U.K. and North America. His most recent publication is *Antonio Pellegrini (1675-1741)* published by the Clarendon Press, Oxford, 1993.

KONSTAM, *Nigel* (b.1932)
Educated in both the U.S.A. and at Radley College, Berkshire, he attended St. Martin's School of Art during the early 1950s. He was a student at Camberwell from 1955-57, when he became a part-time member of staff teaching on Saturday mornings. His teachers and greatest influences were R. D. Lee* and Karel Vogel*. His sculpture has been shown widely, including the N.E.A.C., R.A., L.G., Bradford Biennale, Leicester Galleries, O'Hanna Gallery, John Moores Exhibition (1959) and the Kreisler Gallery (Madrid). He has also taught sculpture at Wimbledon Art School from 1963-67 and has lectured at numerous art establishments, including the R.C.A., Slade School of Fine Art, the R.A. Schools, Leicester Polytechnic and Chelsea School of Art. From 1982 to date, he has been the Director of the Verrocchio Arts Centre (Siena, Italy) and was the Founder of the Artists' Historical Society. His work is in the collections of Leicester Education Authority, Bolton Museum, B.M. and in numerous private collections in England and Europe. His portrait busts include the King and Queen of Spain and Otto Klemperer. *Burlington* magazine published in February 1977 an article written by Konstam on Rembrandt's use of models and mirrors, on which he is an authority. In 1984 he wrote *Sculpture – the Art and the Practice,* published by Collins.

KOPPEL, *Heinz* (1919-1980)
Born in Berlin, his art training began in 1933 when he attended the Prague Academy of Fine Arts. He attended Martin Bloch's* own Painting School in the years immediately preceding the Second World War when Bloch had settled in London. By the middle war years, Koppel had moved to Wales, where he was to spend the majority of his remaining years. In 1949 he married Renate Fischl, a former pupil of Cedric Morris and Camberwell Art School. He joined the staff at Camberwell in 1960 where he remained for four years until he became Senior Lecturer in Painting at Liverpool Polytechnic. His group exhibitions have included a two-man show with Kurt Schwitters (1887-1948). His one-man exhibitions have included Glynn Vivian Art Gallery (Swansea), Beaux Arts Gallery and Oriel Gallery (Cardiff). He was a founder member of the 56 Group in Wales.

L

LA DELL, *Thomas Edwin* A.R.A., R.B.A., F.R.C.A. (1914-1970)
A student at Sheffield School of Art from 1933-35, he won a scholarship to the R.C.A. where he was to study Painting and Print-Making until 1938, when he gained his Diploma. He exhibited his work extensively at the R.A., R.B.A., L.G. and the N.E.A.C. Shortly after the war, during which he had worked in camouflage at Leamington Spa, he joined the staff at Camberwell where he taught Lithography from 1946-49. By the early 1950s he had joined the staff at the R.C.A. where he was Senior Tutor and Head of the Print-Making Department. His works are in the collections of the British Council, Sheffield Museum & Art Gallery and Maidstone Museum & Art Gallery.

LANGLEY, *Winifred Norah* (1906-1991)
She joined Camberwell as a mature student at the beginning of 1946 and stayed for nearly four years, during which time she was most influenced by Coldstream* and Monnington*. During the mid-1950s, she attended Brighton College of Art where she studied Etching, Engraving and Print-Making. She exhibited widely from 1946 and has shown her work at venues which include Leicester Galleries, Redfern Gallery and Wertheim Gallery. She also exhibited several times with the L.G.

LASER, *Gloria Helen Dougall* (*née* Dinwoodie) (b.1923)
After four years at art school in Johannesburg 1944-47, she came to Camberwell where she was to spend the next two years studying under Buckland-Wright*,

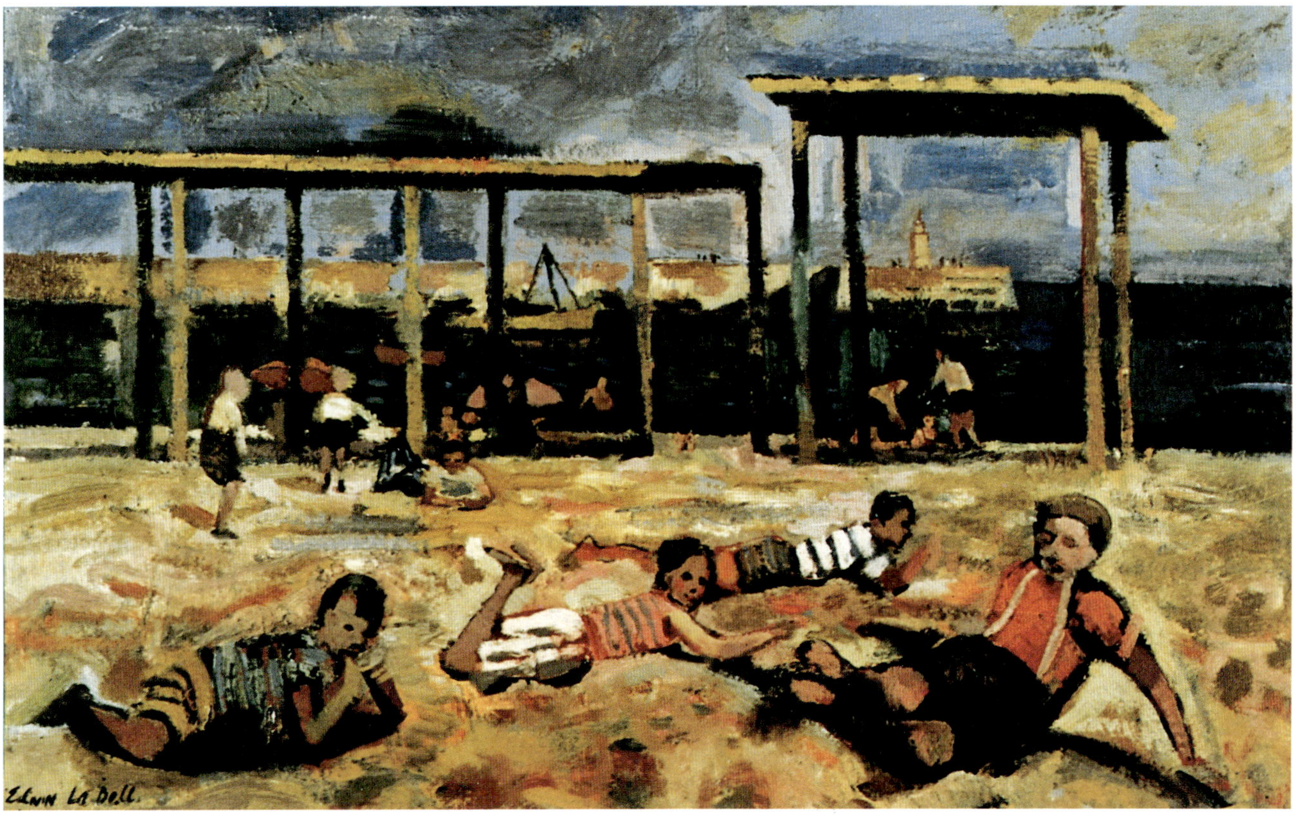

EDWIN LA DELL. *Blaines Beach.* Oil on canvas, 19in x 30in. Courtesy of Cheltenham & Gloucester Building Society.

Coldstream*, Pasmore* and Rogers*. During her brief time in England she showed with the Young Contemporaries and at various art school exhibitions in and around the capital. On her return to South Africa she took many teaching posts and continued to show her work, which included ceramic sculpture.

LAUGHTON, *Bruce Kyle Blake* Ph.D. (b.1928)
He had two periods as a student at Camberwell, 1945-46 and again in 1949-50, having read English at Oxford University in the interim period. He was strongly influenced during his student years by Coldstream*, Gowing*, Pasmore* and Rogers*. After leaving Camberwell, he studied part-time at the Slade School of Fine Art. He has been an occasional exhibitor with the London Group and had a one-man exhibition at the Woodbridge Art Gallery, Suffolk, in 1966. He is the author of the standard work on Philip Wilson Steer (1971) and more recently *The Euston Road School* (1986). He is currently Head of the Department of Art at Queen's University, Ontario, Canada. He married the artist Mary Orde Shields*.

LAUGHTON *Mary Orde* (*née* Shields) (b.1928)
She studied at Camberwell 1946-49, where she was influenced and taught by Carter*, Coldstream*, Gowing* and Monnington*. She has exhibited regularly at the R.W.A. and in the R.A. Summer Exhibitions and, in 1965, had a one-woman exhibition in Hadleigh, Suffolk. She also participated in a group exhibition in the South London Art Gallery in 1979. She married the artist and writer Bruce Laughton*.

LAVRIN *Nora* (*née* Fry) (1897-1985)
She trained at Liverpool School of Art and at the R.C.A., where she was a pupil of Robert Austin (1895-1973) in the Engraving School. During the Second World War she produced drawings of people at work on behalf of the Ministry of Information, however, her main occupation for many years was that of an illustrator of children's books and, in collaboration with Molly Thorp, she wrote and illustrated a children's adventure story called *The Hop Dog,* based on observations of hop-picking in Kent. This was subsequently made into a film by the Children's Film Foundation. She taught 'Picture-Making', a form of composition, at Camberwell on a part-time basis during the years immediately after the Second World War. Her exhibiting career embraced the R.A., R.H.A. and the Walker Art Gallery (Liverpool).

LAZARD, *William Robert* (b. 1936)
He attended Camberwell as a student in the Junior School from 1949-52, moving to the Senior School for a further four-year period of study. His exhibitions include group shows with the Young Contemporaries and a solo exhibition at Stockwell College in 1978. By 1959 he was assisting John Skeaping (1901-1980) in the Sculpture Department at the R.C.A., where he spent two years. Although he studied painting at the School, his early friendship with Ivor Abrahams* (they shared lodgings until the early 1960s) gave him an above average insight into sculpture. This, coupled with his experiences assisting Skeaping, has latterly afforded him commissions in both media. He has also taught for many years and spent nearly two decades as the head of a design faculty in Kent.

LEE, *Richard Dale* (b.1923)
Born in Rhodesia, he served for four and a half years in the Navy during the Second World War and in 1948 became a student for two years at Camberwell. His main influences were Coldstream*, Dodgson*, Monnington*, Pasmore* and Rogers*. In 1951 he won an Abbey Major Scholarship and spent one year in Rome. Before he left Camberwell for this brief period, however, he had already begun teaching in the Junior School. He remained on the staff at Camberwell until his retirement in

1982. He also taught for a brief spell at Maidstone College of Art. His one-man exhibitions have included Galerie de Seine, Duke Street Gallery (Hadleigh), the New Grafton Gallery, 'Dick Lee's Practical Dada' at Gillian Jason Gallery (London) and Cadogan Contemporary (London). His group exhibitions have included the R.A., L.G., John Moores, R.W.A. and 'Vanishing London' at the New Grafton Gallery. His works have been purchased by the Arts Council, the R.A., Southampton Art Gallery, Devon County Council and Reading Museum.

LEE, *Terry Glyn* D.F.A. (b.1932)
He studied firstly at Sheffield College of Art and then for three years from 1955 at the Slade School of Fine Art under Coldstream*. Shortly after leaving the Slade, he joined the staff at Camberwell and taught there until 1961. He returned to his native Sheffield, becoming Head of Painting at his old art school until 1984. His work is in many public collections, including Liverpool Art Gallery, Ferens Art Gallery (Hull), Coventry Art Gallery, Oldham Art Gallery and the Arts Council of Great Britain.

LEIBMAN, *Ruth* (b.1927)
Born in Glasgow, she left shortly after with her parents for South Africa and was to spend all her youth in Johannesburg where, from 1944-47, she was a full-time art student at Johannesburg College of Art. For eight months after qualifying, she was to teach students Art and Art History in Johannesburg before leaving for London in 1948. For the first three years in England, she taught and also painted several commissions. By the early 1950s she decided to return to art school to further her painting studies and, in 1951, she became a full-time student at Camberwell where her teachers included Dunstan* and Pitchforth*. During this period, she exhibited at the major London exhibitions including the N.E.A.C., R.B.A., R.O.I. and the R.A. Summer Exhibitions. Since then she has taught in various art schools in London and started her own Painting and Drawing School, known as 'Centre One'. More recently she has written a teaching manual which is also accompanied by a video showing her various techniques and is also writing for various art magazines, including *The Leisure Painter*. She held a solo exhibition at the Addison-Ross Gallery, London, in 1993.

LEVACK, *David William McLeod* (b.1924)
Studied at Camberwell 1947-51 and later became a member of staff, teaching there from 1957-73. As a student he was influenced by Dodgson* and Salaman*. He exhibited with the L.G. in the early 1950s and has shown at the Whitechapel Art Gallery and the South London Art Gallery.

LEWIS-EVANS, *Adrian* (b. 1927)
After an engineering apprenticeship he was introduced to pottery by Heber Matthews and in the early 1950s set up his own studio in Kent. Deciding to widen his knowledge, he became a student at Camberwell in 1952. Here he was taught by Norah Bradon* who was and has remained a strong influence on his work. Rarely exhibiting his work, he prefers to sell from his successful studio at his home in Dorset, where he makes mainly stoneware.

LIDZEY, *John* (b.1935)
Studied part-time at Camberwell 1952-55, and also at Hornsey College of Art, 1957-59. He has worked as a typographical and graphic designer, teaching typographic design at Camberwell from 1967-83. He later founded and ran a graphic design course at Southwark College, 1983-88. By the late 1980s he had resigned his teaching posts to paint full-time and was successful in winning the Daler-Rowney Award at the R.W.S. exhibition in 1990.

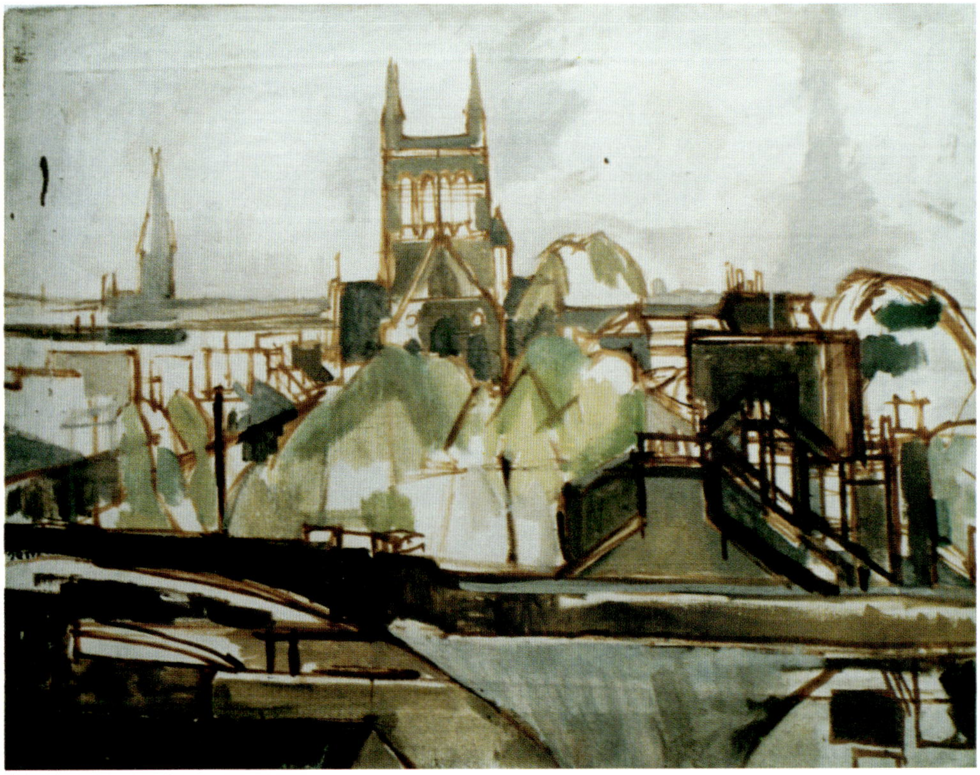

WILLIAM LAZARD. *Camberwell Rooftops*, c.1955. Oil on canvas, 28in x 36in. Artist's collection.

LIEDTKE, *Barbara Anne see* SHAPIRO, *Barbara Anne*

LIVERTON, *Thomas Alfred* R.B.A., A.R.C.A. (1907-1973)
The son of a potter, he studied firstly at Ravensbourne and later at the R.C.A., obtaining his diploma in 1931. He held numerous teaching posts at St. Martin's School of Art and the London College of Printing. He was on the staff of Camberwell from 1956-59 and regularly exhibited his work at the R.A., the N.E.A.C. and the R.B.A., of which he was elected a Member in 1964. He occasionally wrote articles on the techniques of watercolour painting, and his work is in the collections of numerous museums and art galleries. He had two one-man shows in the 1950s in New York.

LOVELY, *Patrick Anthony* N.D.D. (b.1938)
Studied at Camberwell 1952-59. The artist maintains that he had no single influence amongst his teachers or colleagues but that art books were his main source of inspiration. He has exhibited in many group shows, in particular the Young Contemporaries, the Guggenheim Collection and at exhibitions at the Piccadilly Gallery and Morley College Gallery. He was a prizewinner at the Spirit of London Exhibition in 1984. He is currently living in the South of France.

LUGG, *Jack* (b.1924)
He studied art at Natal Technical Art School under Walter Battiss (1906-1982) in the years immediately after the Second World War. After winning the Emma Smith Travelling Scholarship he became a student at Camberwell from 1948-50, where his main teachers were Gilbert Spencer* and Bloch*. Whilst in England he showed his work at group exhibitions in London University and Whitechapel Art Gallery. Returning to his native South Africa in the mid-1950s, he was appointed Head of the East London Technical Art School at the age of twenty-nine. He has executed murals for, amongst others, Philips S.A., and he has exhibited his work extensively in South Africa, U.S.A and Europe. His work is in public collections including Ann

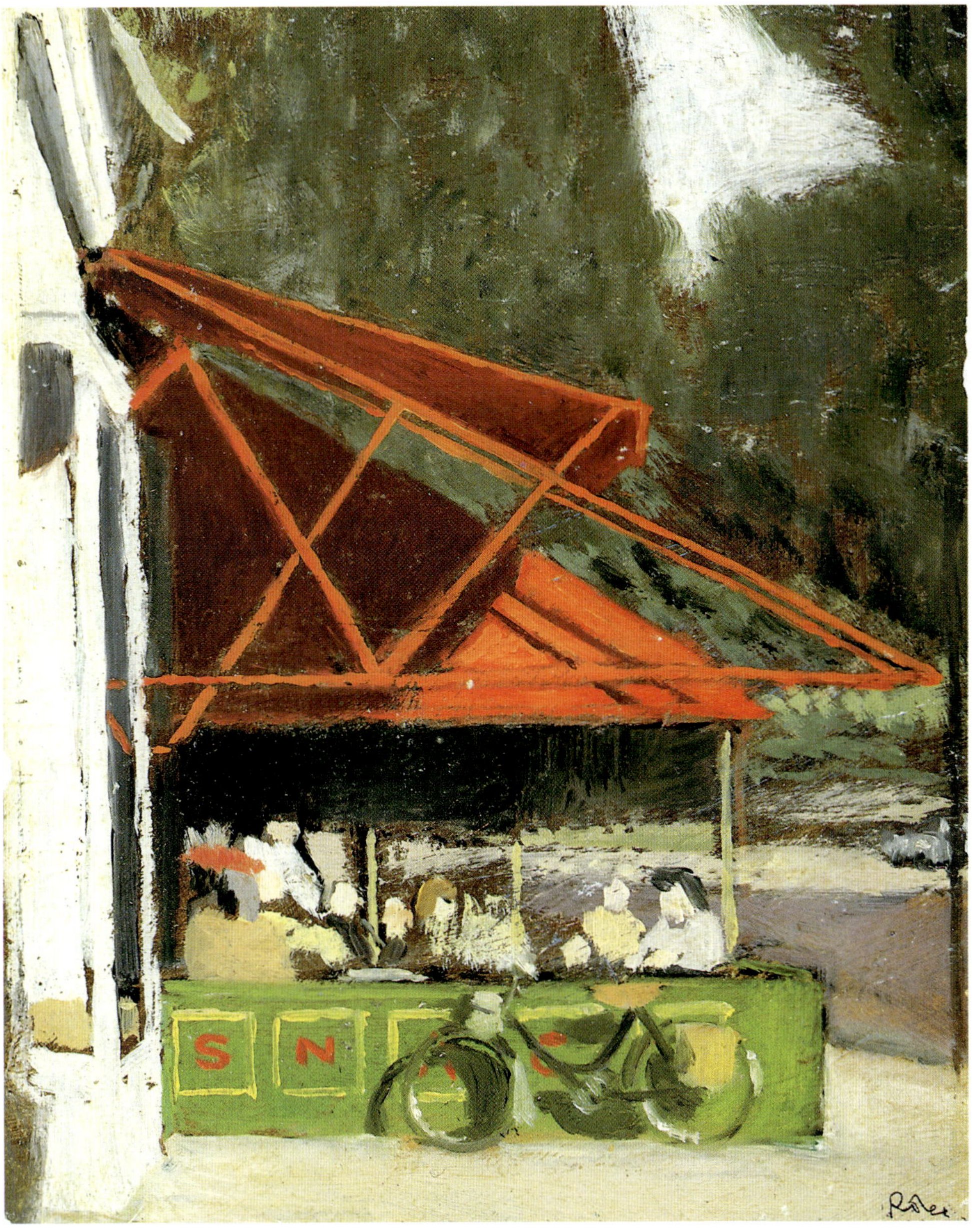

R. D. LEE. *Parisian Cafe*, c.1950. Oil on board, 7½in x 5½in. Author's collection.

Bryant Gallery (East London), Queenstown Art Gallery, Hester Rupert Art Gallery (Graaf-Reinet) and the Boston Gallery of Modern Art (U.S.A.).

LYTTLETON, *Humphrey Richard Adeane* (b.1921)
He was a student very briefly at Camberwell between 1946-47 where his sole influence was Minton.* Lyttleton himself, however, was an enormous influence, because of his music, on many of his fellow students. He initially emerged as a bright young trumpeter with George Webb's Dixielanders, playing regularly at the 'Red Barn' in Barnehurst, Kent, the Mecca for post-war jazz enthusiasts who numbered many Camberwell students of the day. Shortly after leaving Camberwell, he formed his own band and soon established himself as the country's leading jazz trumpeter. From 1949-53 he worked as a cartoonist with the *Daily Mail.* His contribution to the British jazz scene is incalculable. In more recent years he has taken on a second career as a quiz master for the B.B.C.

M

MACDONALD, *Erica* N.D.D. (b.1927)
She studied at Camberwell 1943-47, where she was instructed by Ayrton*, Minton*, Pasmore* and Rogers*. During the 1940s and 1950s she showed her work extensively at the A.I.A. and the I.C.A. It was also during this period that she furthered her studies at St. Martin's School of Art, gaining First Class Honours in her N.D.D. in 1957. She has also shown her work both in the R.A. and R.S.A., and during the 1970s at the R.P. She has also been a freelance illustrator and has taught art for many years.

MACDONALD, *Richard* R.W.A., A.R.C.A. (1919-1993)
Following a period of study from 1935-38 at the West of England College of Art in Bristol, he won a scholarship to the R.C.A., where his main influence was Gilbert Spencer*. Following war service as an Officer in the Royal Navy, he returned to the R.C.A. to complete his studies and by 1948 was appointed Head of the School of Painting at Leeds College of Art, where he remained for the next three years. In 1951 he was appointed to the staff at Camberwell, where he taught Drawing and Painting, a position he was to hold until 1955. During his career as an artist, he exhibited at the R.A. from as early as 1948 and several of his exhibits were reproduced in the *Royal Academy Illustrated*. In 1950 he was also elected a Member of the R.W.A. and in 1981 a joint exhibition of his work with other selected members took place. His first solo exhibition was held at Wildenstein Gallery in 1953, a second followed at Maltzahn Gallery, London, in 1971. By the middle of the 1950s his association with the film world had begun, when in 1954 he gained work as a sketch artist with the film director Joseph Losey on the film *The Sleeping Tiger*. Thereafter he worked with Losey as an art director and production designer, some of the better-known films being *Blind Date* 1959; *Eva* 1961; *The Servant* 1963; *Modesty Blaise* 1966; *Far from the Madding Crowd* 1966 and more recently *Plenty* and *Russia House* during the 1980s. His collaborations with Ken Russell, the British film director, included *Altered States* and he also executed the stage designs for Russell's production of the opera *Madam Butterfly*, seen at the 1983 Spoleto Festival and three years later at the Melbourne Opera House. His final film, *The Firm*, starring Tom Cruise and written and directed by Sydney Pollack, was a box

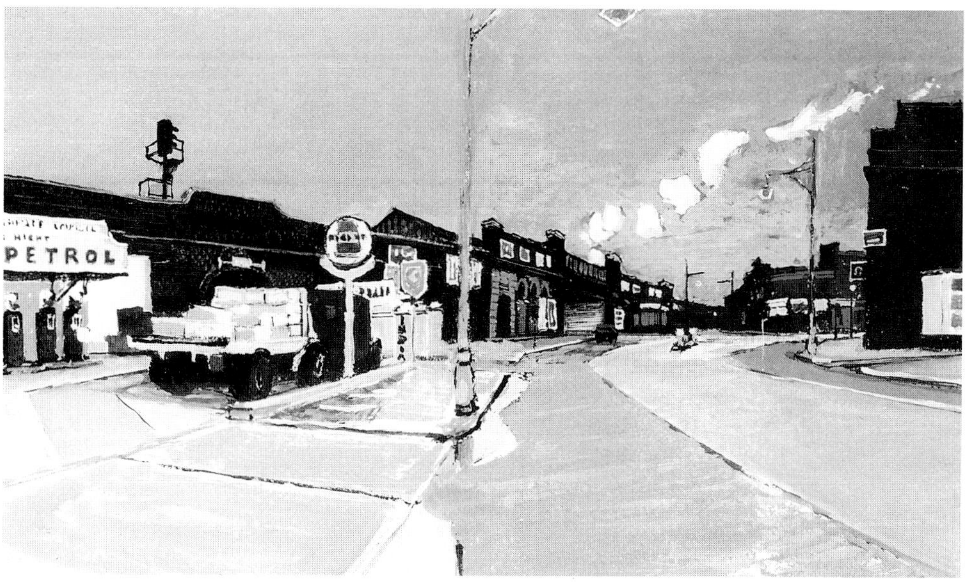

RICHARD MACDONALD. *Street Scene near King's Cross.* Oil on card, 6¾in x 11in. Private collection.

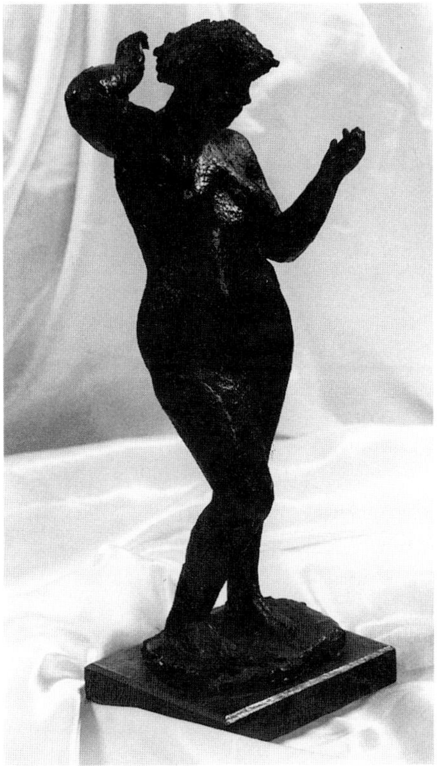

RAPHAEL MAKLOUF. *Female Nude.* Bronze, 12in high. Private collection.

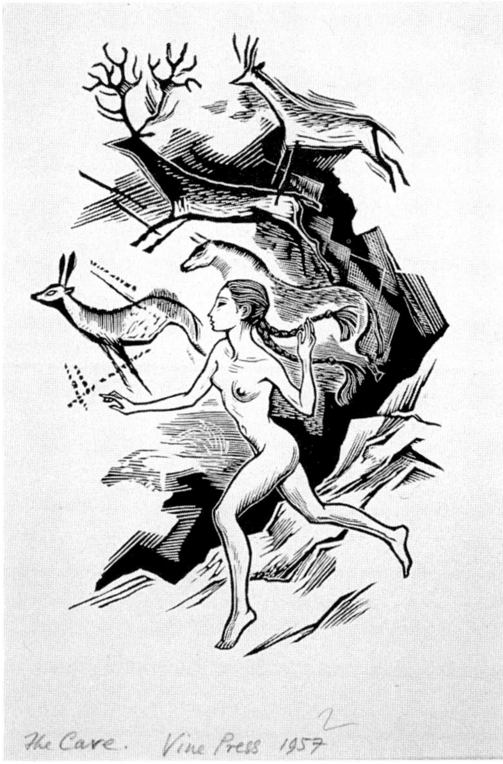

FRANK MARTIN. *The Cave-Vine Press*, 1957. Wood engraving, 8in x 5in. Artist's collection.

office hit. He lived and worked in Los Angeles for many years and a posthumous exhibition of his American paintings was held at the Couturier Gallery in his adopted city a few weeks after his death.

MACINNES, *Colin* (1914-1976)
Descended from a long line of artistically well-known forebears – his mother was a cousin of Stanley Baldwin and Rudyard Kipling and MacInnes himself was a grandson of Sir Edward Coley Burne-Jones (1833-1898). His early years were spent in the company of his mother, the well-known novelist Angela Thirkell, his parents having divorced when he was extremely young. He was educated in Australia until 1929, returning to England the following year. The next six years or so were spent in various occupations on the Continent but by 1936, wishing to attend the Slade School of Fine Art, he returned to England. By 1938 he was a member of the Euston Road School where his fellow student and close friend, Graham Bell (1910-1943), encouraged him with his painting. His war years were spent in Military Intelligence, where his ability as a linguist was often used. By 1946 he had joined the staff at Camberwell, where for nearly two years he lectured on the History of Art and Methods and Materials of Painting. He showed his work at this time at the Anglo-French Art Centre and also spent occasional periods studying in Paris with André L'Hôte (1885-1962). He is equally as well-known for his ability as a writer and for a while, during the late 1940s, he was Art Critic for the *Observer* newspaper and wrote many novels, his first being *To the Victors the Spoils* in 1950. His other novels included *June in her Spring*, *City of Spades*, and *Absolute Beginners*, which eventually became a West End musical. A multi-talented man, he was once described by Bernard Levin as "one of the most penetrating, sensible, balanced, yet passionate observers of England...for centuries".
(The Author is indebted to Kenneth Gribble who assisted with this information).

MACLAREN, *Andrew* N.D.D., A.R.C.A. (b.1941)
He attended Camberwell from 1955-61, during which time he attained his N.D.D.

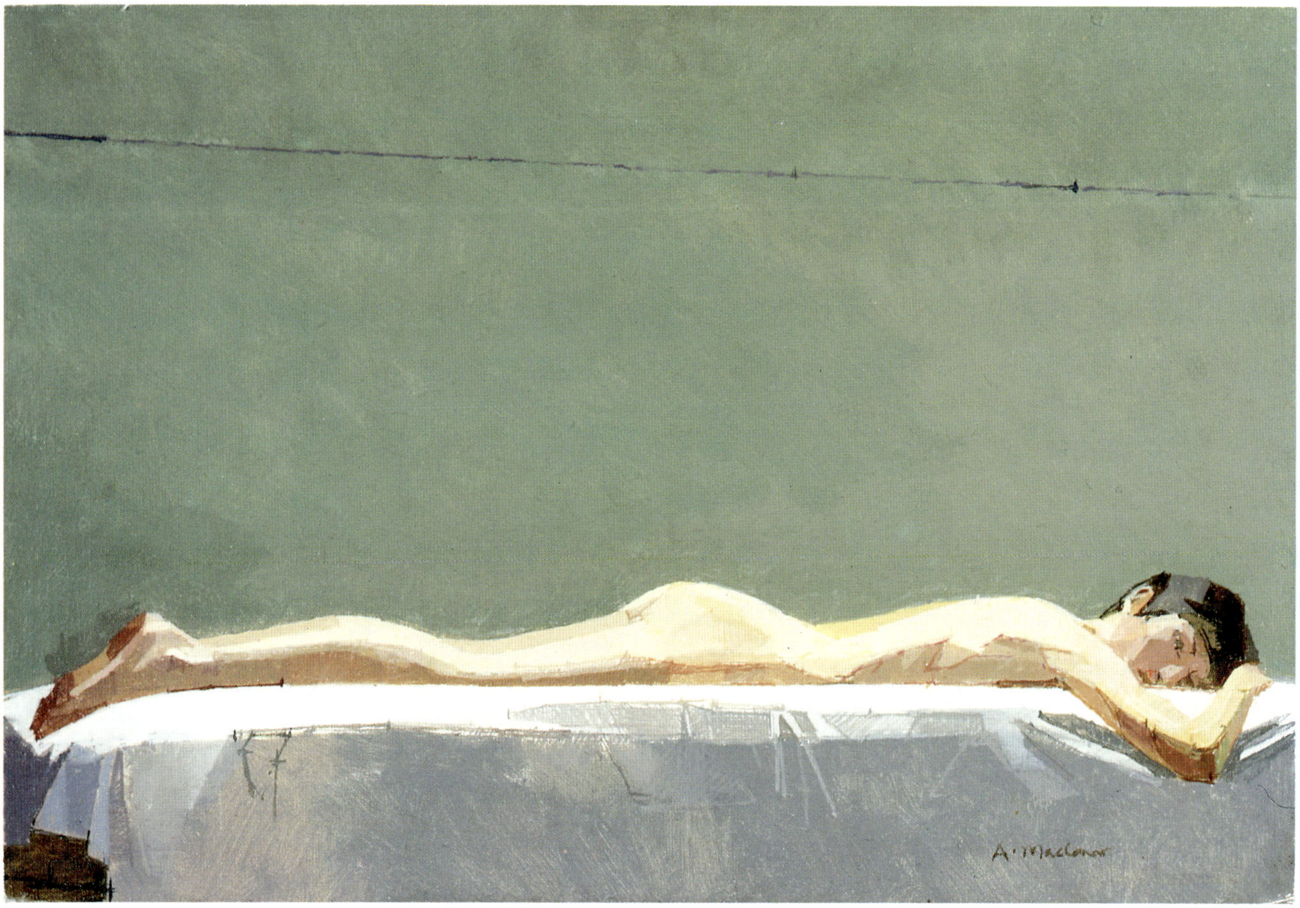

ANDREW MACLAREN. *Nude*, 1958. Oil on board, 11in x 16in. Private collection.

specialising in painting. His main teachers during this period were Eyton*, Matthews*, Medley*, Symons* and Uglow*. In 1961 he commenced at the R.C.A., graduating three years later with a First Class Degree and a Silver Medal, winning an Abbey Major Scholarship. On his return from Rome, he was appointed to the Department of Fine Art at Newcastle University and in 1980, on the retirement of Professor Kenneth Rowntree (b.1915), he became the Head of the Painting School. During the 1960s he exhibited with the L.G. and he has had one-man shows at Lincoln Art Gallery, Hatton Gallery (Newcastle), Linton Court Gallery (Settle) and the Art Gallery of Preston Polytechnic.

MADERSON, *Arthur Karel* (b.1942)
He began his art studies at Camberwell in 1960 where he was to remain for the next four years, studying under Howard*, Auerbach* and Medley*. By the early 1970s he was employed as an art therapist with psychiatric patients, including brain injured children, but by the early 1980s had become a full-time painter and has exhibited since then at The Gallery (Street), Cleveland Gallery (Bath), R.W.A., Southgate Gallery (Moreton in Marsh), Alpine Gallery (London), and the R.A. He now lives and works in Ireland.

MAHONEY, *Trata Maria* (*née* Drescha) (b.1928)
A student at Camberwell from 1946-48, where she was taught by Victor Pasmore*. She won a scholarship to the R.A. Schools where she specialised in mosaics, which she has since made her career. She works in her maiden name of Drescha.

MAKLOUF, *Raphael David* N.D.D. (b.1937)
He began his studies at Camberwell in 1953 and remained there for a period of fifteen years as both student and teacher. He was most influenced by Karel Vogel*, who taught him sculpture. His most important commission was the new effigy of

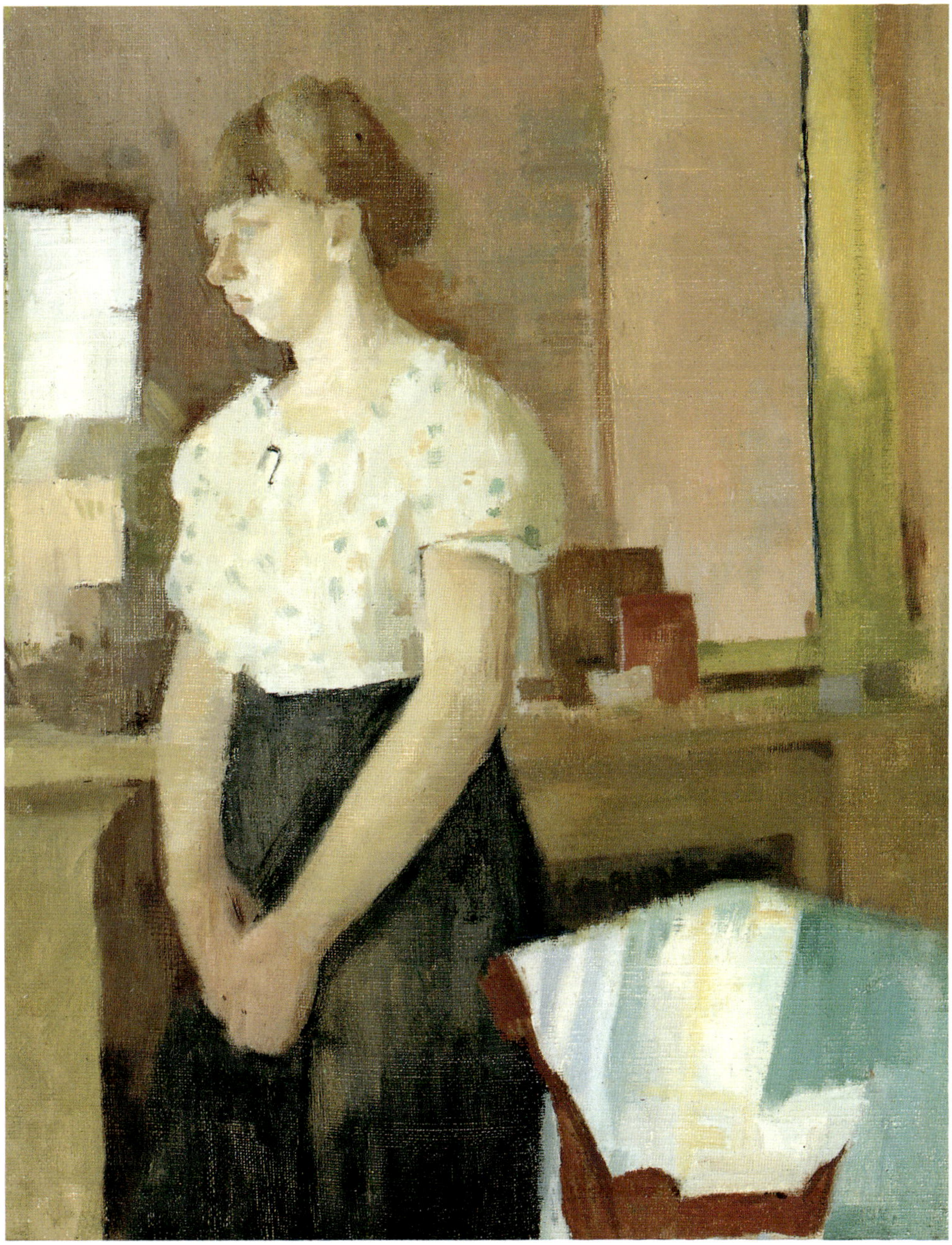

PHILIP MATTHEWS. *Portrait of Sandy Carmichael*, c.1947. Oil on canvas, 14in x 10in. Private collection.

the Queen to be found on all U.K. coinage from 1985. He has exhibited his work extensively including the R.A. Summer exhibitions. His work is in numerous public collections, including the Tower of London, which houses his statue of Sir Thomas More, and in Carnegie Hall (New York).

MAKOWER, *Prudence see* INGHAM CLARK, *Prudence*

MANN, *Sargy* (b.1937)
Following a technical training at Oxford Technical College he became a student at Camberwell in 1960 where, during the next four years, he was taught and influenced by Auerbach*, Hoyland*, Lee* and Uglow*. He has shown his work extensively, his first one-man exhibition being at the Salisbury Festival of Arts in 1973. His group exhibitions have included the L.G. at the Whitechapel Art Gallery, Second International Drawing Biennale (2nd Prize Winner), Hayward Annual, The Spirit of London 1983 (2nd Prize) and again in 1985 (1st Prize), R.A. Summer exhibitions and the Arts Council Touring Exhibition (The Experience of Landscape).

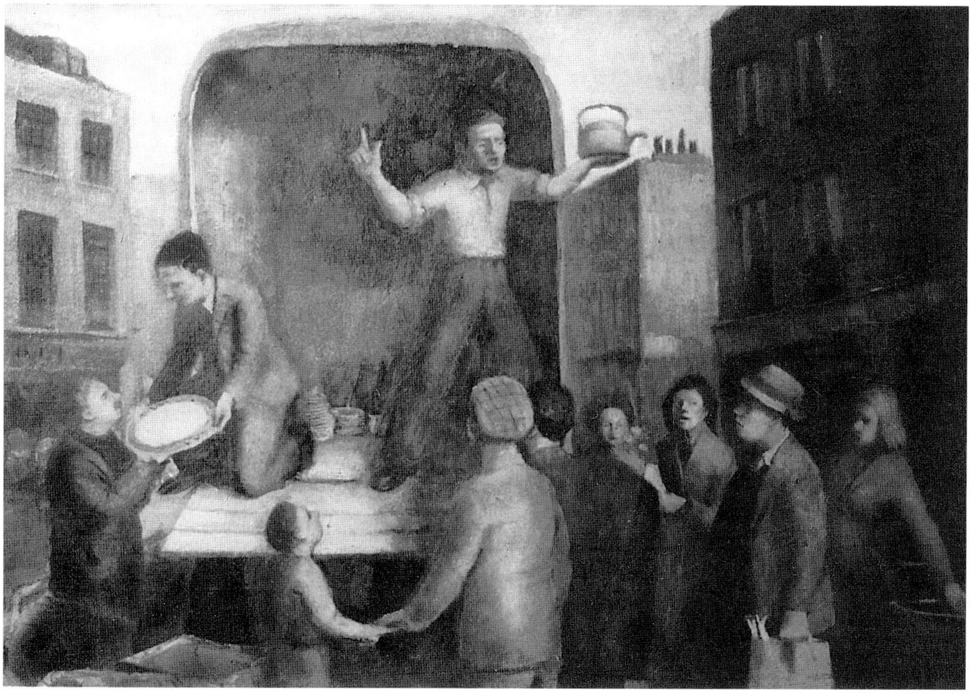

MICHAEL MARKHAM. *The Auction.* Oil on board, 21in x 28in. Courtesy of John Denham Gallery, London.

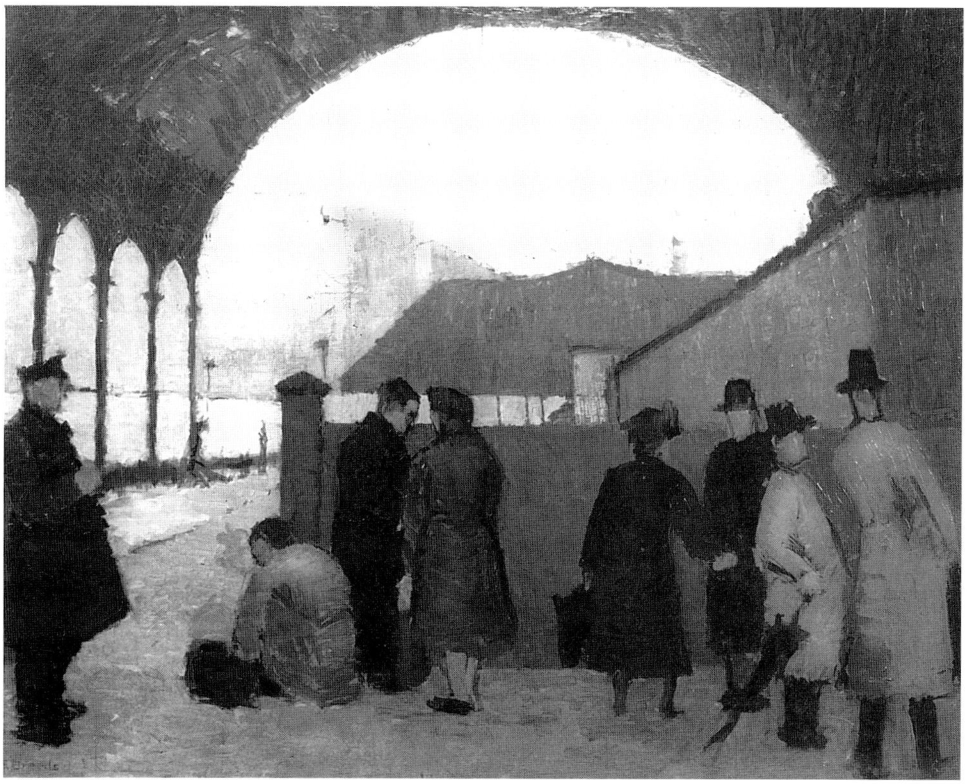

ELIZABETH MASSEY (*née* Breeds). *The Station,* 1946. Oil on panel, 16in x 20in. Private collection.

His selected writings include *Drawings by Bonnard,* for the Arts Council of Great Britain (1984). His work is in the public collections of the Contemporary Arts Society, The Arts Council of Great Britain and in private collections including the late Sir John Betjeman, the late Cecil Beeton, Iris Murdoch, Kingsley Amis, Sir Robin Day and the Sultan of Oman. By the end of the 1960s he had been appointed to the staff at Camberwell.

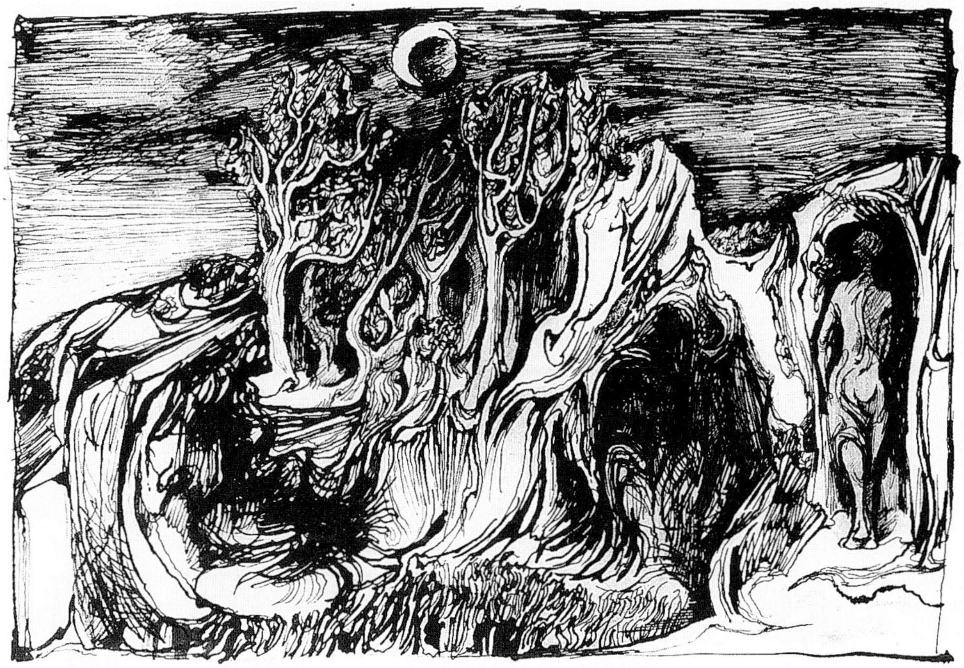

JOHN MINTON. *Landscape with Figures.* Pen and ink, 6½in x 9¼in. Private collection.

MARKHAM, *Michael Adrian* (1921-1984)
He first attended Malvern College of Art during the early years of the Second World War, where his main teacher was Victor Moody (1896-1990). Following his National Service he attended St. Martin's School of Art and by 1946 studied on a part-time basis at Camberwell, where he was taught predominantly by Victor Pasmore*. He showed his work extensively at various group exhibitions including the R.A., N.E.A.C. and the R.B.A. For many years he held teaching posts in London and the Home Counties.

MARKS, *Gerald* (b.1921)
Between 1938-41 he attended the Central School of Arts and Crafts where Morris Kestleman (b.1905), Bernard Meninsky (1891-1950), William Roberts (1895-1980) and Vivian Pitchforth* were his teachers. However the war interrupted his studies and these were not resumed until 1946. He was a Member of the Central Committee of the A.I.A. from 1946-57. He held numerous teaching posts, being a lecturer at Camberwell from 1949-61. His work has been shown in many group exhibitions from as early as 1939 where it was first shown at the New Burlington Galleries. Other exhibitions have included the A.I.A., L.G., Piccadilly Gallery, Redfern Gallery, Leicester Galleries (Artists of Fame and Promise) and the Ben Uri Gallery. He held a one-man show at the Drian Gallery in 1962. His work is in the collection of the Arts Council of Great Britain.

MARTIN, *Frank* M.A., R.E., M.S.I.A.D. (b.1921)
After attending Oxford University and obtaining his M.A. in History, Martin studied at St. Martin's School of Art under Gertrude Hermes*. Following war service he became a freelance illustrator and wood engraver and was elected a member of the S.W.E. in 1952. The following year he joined the staff at Camberwell, where he taught not only wood engraving but etching and illustration for a period of twenty-seven years, during the last four of which he was Head of the Department of Graphic Arts. He exhibited his work regularly at the R.E. He has shown his work not only in the U.K. but in the U.S.A., Germany and New Zealand.

MARTIN, *Katherine Frances* (*née* Hamp) (1926-1967)
Student at Camberwell 1947-49. She was encouraged by Pitchforth*, having known him during his brief stay in South Africa immediately after the war. She journeyed with her friend Patricia Denniston*, at Pitchforth's instigation, to take up art in

England. She died very young, before having had time to express herself fully through her art.

MARTIN, *Kenneth* O.B.E., L.G., A.R.C.A. (London) (1905-1984)
He studied at Sheffield School of Art in 1921-23 before entering the R.C.A. in 1929, gaining his Diploma three years later. He exhibited continually with the L.G. from 1936, becoming a Member in 1949. He taught at Camberwell during the late 1940s and whilst there began to paint abstract works. He and his wife Mary Balmford, L.G., A.R.C.A. (1907-1969) became the core of British abstract art that was then described as geometric. During the 1950s and '60s he was most associated with 'Screw Mobiles' which twisted and turned in space, creating different forms with each movement. He had numerous one-man exhibitions including 'Essays in Movement' at the I.C.A., The Axiom Gallery, The Arts Council of Great Britain and Waddington Galleries. His mixed exhibitions included British Abstract Art at the A.I.A. Gallery, 'This is Tomorrow' at Whitechapel Art Gallery, and at numerous other venues, including O'Hanna Gallery, Stedelijk Museum (Amsterdam), Drian Galleries, Galerie Dautzenberg (Paris), The Arts Council, Grabowski Gallery, Tate Gallery, Redfern Gallery, The Museum of Tel Aviv, Scottish Arts Council, Hayward Gallery, Annely Juda Gallery, Arthur Tooth & Sons and the Serpentine Gallery.

MARTIN, *Patricia Amy* (*née* Denniston) (b.1923)
With her friend Katherine Hamp* she was at Camberwell from 1946-48, having known Pitchforth* during his stay in South Africa. She was greatly influenced by Monnington* and Townsend*. She is currently living in Ontario, Canada.

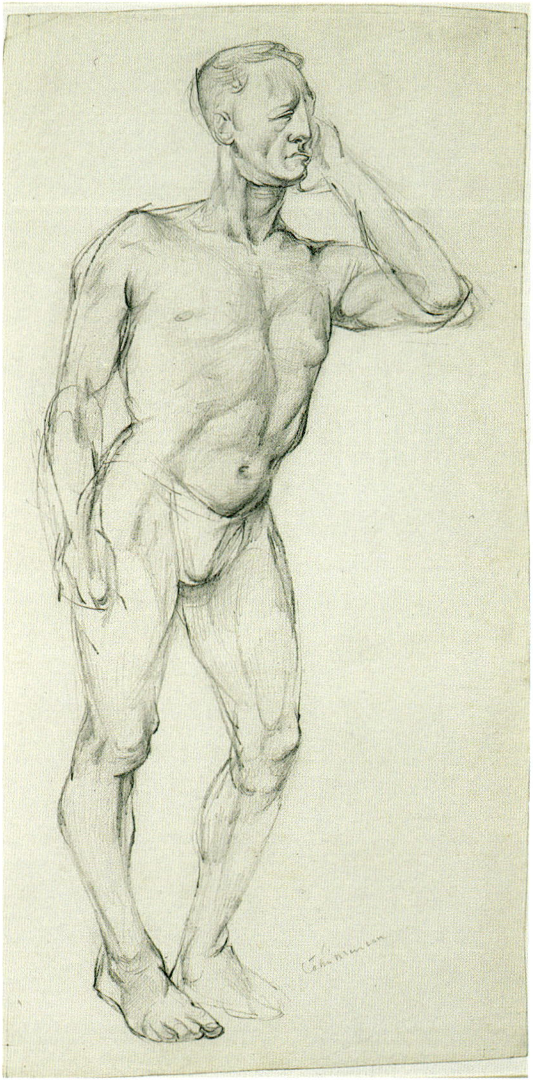

JOHN MINTON. *Life Study.* Pencil, 14in x 7in. Author's collection.

MASSEY, *Elizabeth Joan* (*née* Breeds) (b.1922)
She was a student at Camberwell 1946-50, where her teachers and influences were Coldstream*, Pasmore* and Rogers*. She has exhibited her work at the R.A. and with the L.G.

MASTERMAN, (Dodie) *Rhoda Helen* (b.1918)
Whilst at boarding school she attended Leicester School of Art on a part-time basis and soon after won a scholarship to the Slade School of Fine Art where she attended from 1934-39. Besides studying painting, she was taught Stage Design by Vladimir Polunin (1880-1957). During the war, she served in the W.V.S. and was also during this period a model for *Vogue* magazine. In 1945 she joined the staff at Camberwell as a Lecturer in Drawing and Illustration. She was to remain there for the next twenty years. She is well-known as a book illustrator and has illustrated many works, including *Little Women* (Louisa M. Alcott), *A Portrait of the Artist as a Young Man* (James Joyce), *The Virgin and the Gypsy* (D. H. Lawrence), *A Hero of our Time* (Mikhail Lermontov), *Cakes and Ale* (W. Somerset Maugham) and *Anna Karenina* (Leo Tolstoy). Her work has been reproduced in many periodicals, including the *Radio Times* and *Vogue*. She has exhibited extensively at venues, including the N.E.A.C., Leicester Galleries, the Folio Society and in various Arts Council Travelling Exhibitions.

MATTHEWS, *Harold Philip* (1916-1984)
Born in Belfast, he first studied at Maidenhead School of Art in the years preceding

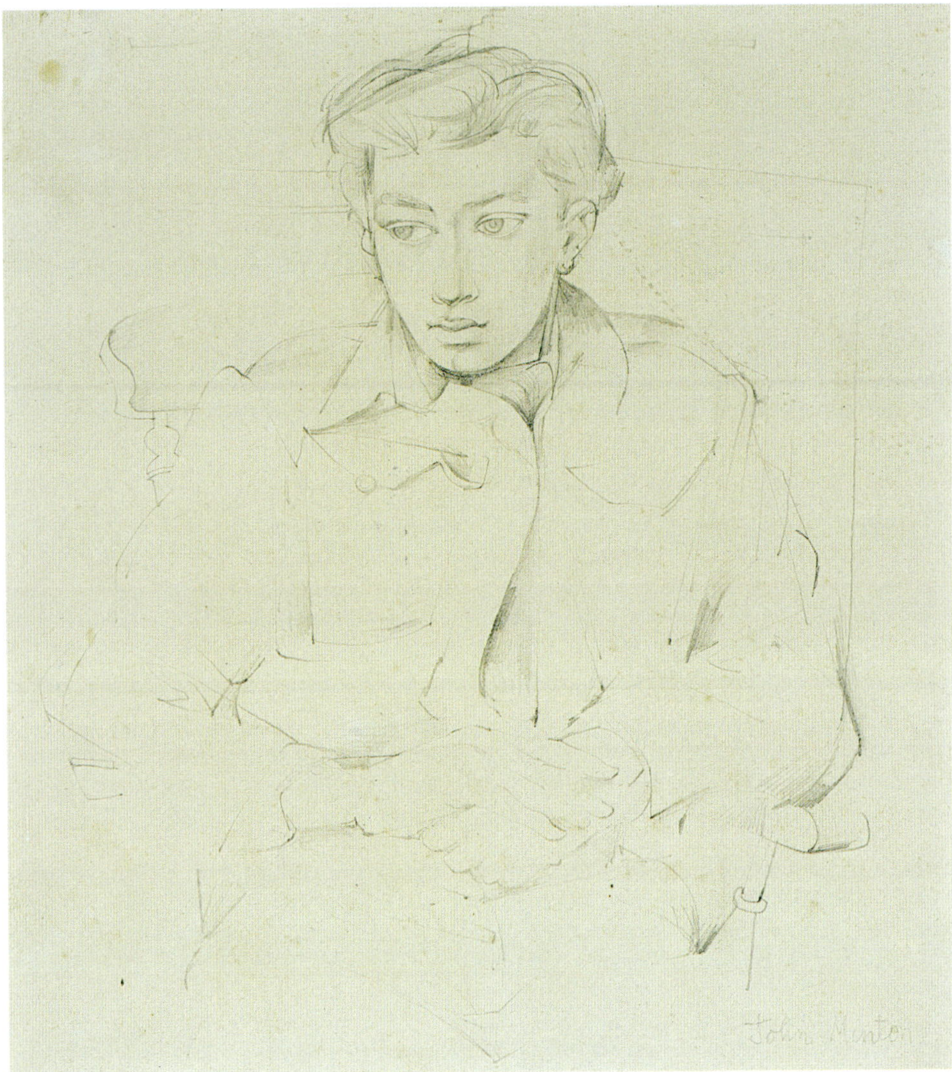

JOHN MINTON. *The Boy*, 1945 (portrait of Robert Hunt). Pencil on paper.
Present whereabouts unknown.

the Second World War. He painted at the Euston Road School at the beginning of 1939 and received private study from Coldstream* and Pasmore*, whom he was later to join on the staff at Camberwell in 1946, where he remained until his retirement in 1981. In 1964 he was appointed Head of the Fine Art Department. He exhibited often at the R.A., R.W.A., Leicester Galleries, Wildenstein and was included in the travelling exhibition 'Euston Road and Others' in 1948. His works are in the permanent collections of the Arts Council, Ministry of Works and the South London Art Gallery.

McCULLOCH, *Joseph Ridley Ratcliffe* A.R.W.S., N.S., A.R.C.A. (1893-1961)
Following an initial period of study at Leeds College of Art, he came to London and studied at the R.C.A., where he was awarded his Diploma in 1921. Shortly after he became Painting Master at Ipswich School of Art, where he remained until 1925. He also held teaching posts at Goldsmiths' College during the war years and in 1949 he joined the staff at Camberwell where he remained for two years. He exhibited his work extensively at the R.A., N.E.A.C. and the R.W.S.

MEDD, *Scott* (1911-1984)
Born in Ontario, Canada, it was not until the early 1930s, after working in a bank, that his exceptional talent as an artist was recognised by a local teacher who advised him to apply for study at the R.A. Schools in England. He arrived in England in 1932, was duly accepted and distinguished himself as a diligent student, winning

the Landseer Prize three times. In 1936 he was awarded the Edwin Abbey Fellowship. During the Second World War he served in the Royal Artillery. In 1946 he returned to Canada, where he stayed for two years. On his return in 1948 he joined the staff at Camberwell where he taught for six years. He was by now very friendly with Monnington* and the two of them worked together on a large mural decoration for the Council House in Bristol in 1954. Four years later a second commission followed for the ceiling of the Chapel at Exeter University. In 1960 Medd was appointed Resident Adviser to painting students at the British School at Rome, a position he was to hold for the next seven years. In 1963 he was commissioned to replace the decorations in the Dome of Castle Howard, Yorkshire, the original having been executed by the 18th century Italian master, Pellegrini, but alas destroyed by fire in 1940. As well as his mural painting he was most prolific as a landscape, portrait and architectural painter, particularly in watercolours. His work was exhibited in many group exhibitions, including the R.B.A., the N.E.A.C., the R.P., the R.W.A. and the R.O.I.

MEDLEY, *Robert* C.B.E., R.A., L.G. (1905-1994)
In 1921 Medley enrolled at the Byam Shaw School of Art on the recommendation of his mother, who herself had studied there under its then Principal – F. E. Jackson R.A. (1872-1945). During this period he also had a brief spell at the R.A. Schools, being much impressed by the work of Sir George Clausen R.A. (1852-1944). Two years later, in 1923, he gained entrance to the Slade School of Fine Art but quickly became disillusioned by the teaching methods that prevailed there. During the late 1920s he lived in Paris for two years where he was influenced by Jean Marchand (1883-1940). By 1930 he had become a member of the L.G. and also of the L.A.A. which had been formed by Maynard Keynes and Samuel Courtauld as an artists' co-operative. His first one-man exhibition was held in 1931 at the Cooling Galleries and the following year he began to teach at the Chelsea School of Art. In 1936 he participated in the first 'Surrealist Exhibition' at the New Burlington Galleries. Following service as a War Artist he held exhibitions at Reid & Lefevre Gallery and in 1949 he returned to the Slade School of Fine Art, teaching in the Department of Theatre Design. He left in 1958 to become the Head of the Department of Fine Art at Camberwell, a position he held until 1965. During this period he also served on the Faculty of Painting at the British School at Rome and in 1967 he became its Chairman. His work is in numerous public and private collections, including the Contemporary Arts Society. A major retrospective exhibition was held at the Whitechapel Art Gallery in 1963. He was appointed C.B.E. in 1982 and made a Member of the R.A. in 1986.

MENDEZ, *Theodore Ronald Pereira* (b.1934)
He was a student for five years from 1950 at Camberwell where he was greatly influenced by Bloch,* Christopher Chamberlain*, Pitchforth* and Michael Rothenstein*. In 1958 he began part-time teaching at Camberwell and by the early 1960s was a full-time Lecturer. By 1975 he had been appointed as Head of the Department of Textiles, a position which he held until his retirement in 1984. His work has been shown in group exhibitions including the V & A, the Redfern Gallery, Bear Lane Gallery (Oxford), Arnolfini Gallery (Bristol), South London Art Gallery, the Ulster Museum (Belfast) and the John Moores Exhibitions.

MIERS, *Elise* (b.circa 1918)
First began to study painting in France before the war under M. Lietar. Student at Camberwell 1947-51. Her main influence was Pasmore* when he began to do abstract painting during the late 1940s. She became friendly with and was

influenced by Anthony Fry*. Subsequently she attended the Slade School of Art for four years part-time, studying Stage Design. She had one-woman exhibitions in London at the Kensington Art Gallery and at the Galerie de Seine, 1957. She has also exhibited several times with the L.G., R.B.A., A.I.A. and at the Leicester Galleries.

MILLAR, *William* N.D.D. (b.1914)
Before the war Jock Millar, as he is known, attended Glasgow School of Art and in 1945 for three years he attended Camberwell, where his fellow Scotsman and Principal of the School, William Johnstone*, exerted the most influence on his career. During the 1950s and 1960s he concentrated mainly on mural painting and his most important works can be seen at the Carron Ironworks in Scotland, the British Rail Experimental Centre at Derby, and the Hotel Altair, Palma, Majorca. He also taught during this period at the Central School of Arts & Crafts on a part-time basis from 1952-69 in both the Department of Mural Painting and in the Department of Industrial Design. In 1969 he spent four years in Nigeria where he was the Art Director for the Kano Educational Development Centre. For many years now he has lived in Spain and during this period he has had extensive exhibitions, including Caja Provincial, Granada; Galeria Ribalta, Valencia; Madrid (courtesy of the National Westminster Bank) and Galeria Argar, Almeria.

MILLER, *Anthony George Frederick* (b. 1935)
Although born in England, he spent most of the first ten years of his life in Borneo, where he and his family were interned by the Japanese during the Second World War. During the early 1950s he spent two years at an Arts & Crafts School in Manchester. He enrolled at Camberwell in 1952, where for the next two years he was taught, amongst other subjects, furniture design and cabinet-making. In 1954 he joined the Central School, where he was to spend the next three years studying furniture design. He received a diploma from the R.C.A. in 1960 and has subsequently designed furniture for Heals before joining the architects' department at Southend-on-Sea, Essex. He has also worked in private architectural practices designing interiors and exteriors of buildings. His early tuition in painting never left him and he continues to paint occasionally.

MILMAN, *Michael Horsley* (1923-1992)
Known as Michael Horsley during his student days at Camberwell (1948-49). During his war service in the R.A.F. and the Camouflage Unit, he did some initial painting and design. His first painting was exhibited at the University of Toronto in 1942 and, following his discharge from the R.A.F., he took up interior design and display. His first serious study of painting was in the immediate post-war years under Sir Francis Rose and, following several private lessons from Augustus John (1878-1961) whilst living in Chelsea, he decided to become a full-time art student. His first exhibit in the R.A. was in 1947. Following his tuition at Camberwell under Minton* and Pasmore*, he was an Official War Artist to the United Nations in Korea during the early 1950s. After the Korean War he stayed in the Far East, remaining in Japan until 1955 as an Industrial Design Consultant to, amongst other organisations, the Chamber of Commerce in Tokyo. He was also involved in styling some of the very early Nissan and Toyota vehicles long before Italian designers were imported to Japan. During the early 1960s he spent some considerable time in Provence and was much influenced by the landscape that had years earlier inspired Van Gogh. He spent many years living in Canada and the U.S.A., where he painted and exhibited his work. By 1973, however, he had returned to England where he continued to paint and sell his work directly from his own studio gallery.

GERI MORGAN. *Marion.*
Oil on canvas, 36in x 24in.
Artist's collection.

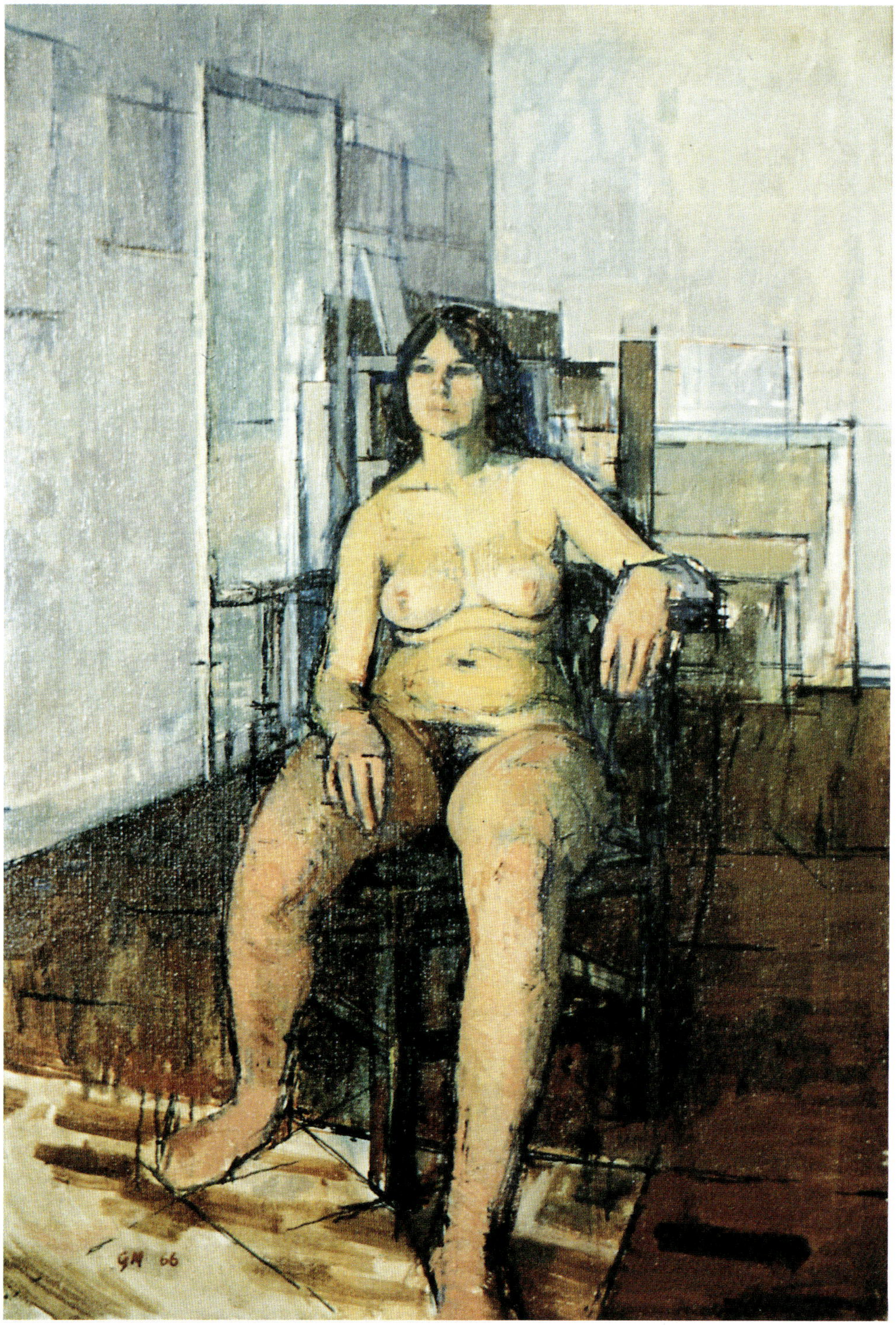

MINTON, *Francis John* R.B.A., L.G. (1917-1957)
He first studied at St. John's Wood Art School under Kenneth Martin* from 1936-38. This was followed by a brief spell, immediately before the war, in Paris at Colarossi's. As a conscientious objector, he served in the Pioneer Corps until he was appointed to the staff at Camberwell in 1943. During his four years teaching illustration, composition and perspective, he exerted an enormous influence over his pupils. During this period, in 1945, his first one-man show was held at the Redfern Gallery. He continued to exhibit widely, including the R.A., the R.B.A. and the L.G., where he was elected a Member in 1949. He travelled widely throughout

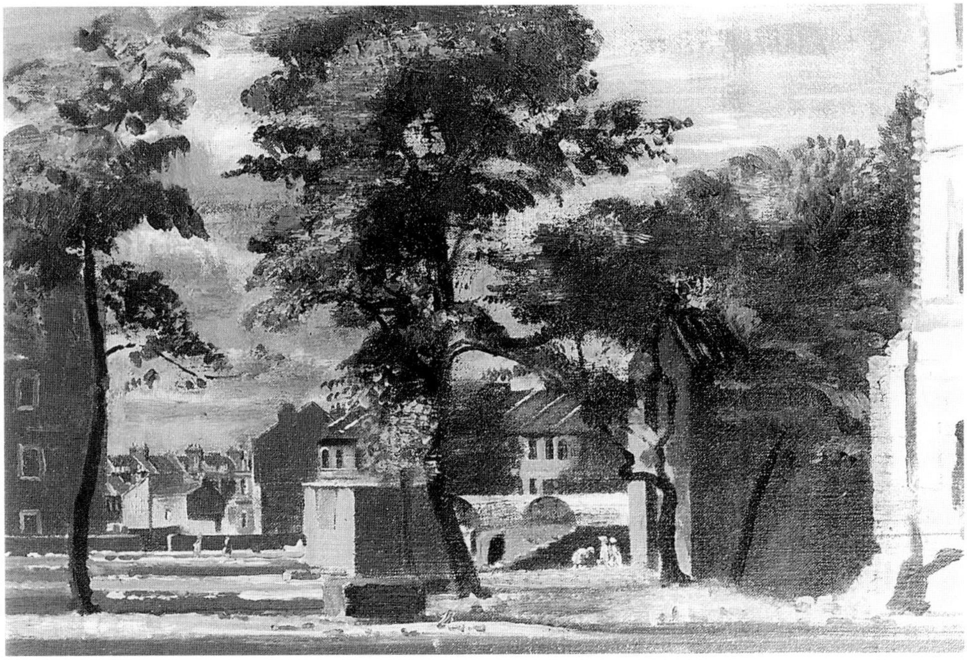

THOMAS MONNINGTON. *Camberwell from the Art School.* Oil on canvas, 11in x 14½in. Photograph courtesy of Belgrave Gallery.

Europe, the West Indies and North Africa. William Johnstone* persuaded Minton to join him at the Central School of Arts & Crafts where Minton remained until 1948 before joining the staff at the R.C.A., where he taught continually until shortly before his death at the beginning of 1957. During his lifetime he became well-known for his book illustrations and during the early 1950s, amongst other things, he illustrated Elizabeth David's *A Book of Mediterranean Food* and *French Country Cooking*. His style was much imitated by pupils in post-war British art and, more recently, his work has found favour as one of the Neo-Romantic artists.

MONK, *Geoffrey* (b.1911)
His art education began at Chelsea, where he was a student between 1927-29 before gaining a scholarship to the R.C.A where he remained until 1933. His first experience as a teacher was at Chelsea Art School, a post he was to hold until the outbreak of the Second World War. At the end of the war, he returned to his teaching at Chelsea and during this period he also taught at Guildford and St. Martin's Schools of Art. In 1949 he was appointed Head of Department of Design and Crafts at Camberwell. By the early 1950s he was appointed Vice-Principal, a position he was to hold until his retirement in 1975.

MONNINGTON, *Walter Thomas* P.R.A. (1902-1976)
In 1918 he entered the Slade School of Fine Art where he studied under Fred Brown (1851-1941), Henry Tonks (1862-1937), W. W. Russell (1867-1949) and Philip Wilson Steer (1860-1942), Tonks having perhaps the greatest influence on his future career. In 1922 he won the Scholarship in Decorative Painting from the British School at Rome for a three year period. He met and married the first woman to win the Rome Scholarship, Winifred Knights (1899-1947). During the late 1920s and early '30s he began teaching on a part-time basis at the R.C.A. In the years preceding the Second World War, Monnington was engaged in numerous commissions, including several murals for the Bank of England. During this period he was elected an Associate of the R.A., despite the fact that he had never exhibited there. Before he was thirty years of age he had already begun teaching in the R.A. Schools. He also executed many portrait commissions during this period, including the playwright Sir James Barrie and Stanley Baldwin, the latter being exhibited in the R.A. in 1934. By the time the Second World War had commenced, Monnington had become a full Member of the R.A. at the remarkable age of thirty-six. His war years were spent with the Ministry of Camouflage until 1943, when he became an Official War Artist with the R.A.F. In 1947 he joined the staff at Camberwell, where

he remained for three years before joining his friend Coldstream* at the Slade School of Fine Art. He was appointed President of the R.A. in 1966, a post he held until his death ten years later. His work is represented in public collections throughout the world.

MORGAN, *Geri* (b.1926)
Student at Camberwell 1948-51, during which time he was taught by Coldstream*, Pasmore*, Rogers* and Salaman*. In 1950 he won the David Murray Landscape Scholarship and exhibited regularly during the fifties and sixties with the L.G. and at the R.A. He has had two one-man shows, both in 1969, one of paintings in the Galerie Sept in Mons (Belgium) and the second of prints at the Bear Gallery in Sheffield. He has exhibited every year at the R.A. since 1965. Geri Morgan has been a teacher for a number of years, returning to Camberwell to teach Painting and Drawing in the Foundation Course from 1963-70. He is currently the Principal of the Byam Shaw School of Art.

MORGAN, *Glyn* (b.1926)
His initial training was at Cardiff School of Art and he attended Camberwell briefly during 1947, where he was mainly influenced by La Dell* and Minton*. Shortly after leaving he made his first visit to East Anglia and Cedric Morris's Art School where he attended every summer, well into the 1980s. He has exhibited widely in Wales, London, Greece and has had one-man exhibitions at the Drian Gallery, the Minories (Colchester), Richard Demarco Gallery (Edinburgh), University of Sussex, Welsh Arts Council and his work is in collections around the world including Auckland Art Gallery, Brisbane Art Gallery, the Contemporary Arts Society for Wales, the Welsh Arts Council and in private collections in Britain and the U.S.A. In 1995 'A Fifty Year Retrospective' exhibition was held at the Simon Carter Gallery, Woodbridge, Suffolk.

MORLEY, *Christine Winifred* (*née* Crampton) (b.1938)
Following an initial art training begun at Sidcup School of Art, her formative art training at Camberwell, under the tuition of Salaman* and Christopher Chamberlain*, was during the period 1955-58. Her exhibiting during these years was confined to student shows at the Walmer Castle public house. She has spent most of her career in art education, having obtained A.T.C. at Sussex University in 1967 and a B.A. (Hons.) in History of Art from London's Courtauld Institute in 1990. Her many teaching posts include Scarborough School of Art, Farnham (West Surrey) College of Art and Design and Ravensbourne College of Art and Design. She has also contributed entries on Italian Art for Everyman's *Encyclopaedia* and more recently, after obtaining an M.A. in History of Design, has given lectures at the V. & A. and Royal College of Art.

MORLEY, *Malcolm* (b.1931)
As a teenager he spent a year in Borstal followed by three years in prison, where he first became interested in painting. He furthered his ambitions by becoming a student at Camberwell from 1952-53 where he used his step-father's name of Evans; before going on to the R.C.A. until 1957. His work of the late 1950s was completely abstract, but he first gained recognition as a 'pop-artist' when he coined the word 'Superrealist' to describe his work. During the period prior to his departure to the U.S.A., he worked in the studio of Peter Lanyon (1918-1964) in St. Ives. He has exhibited his work extensively including The Guggenheim Museum (New York), Atkins Museum (Kansas City), Contemporary Arts Museum (Houston, Texas), Witney Museum of American Art (New York), Princeton University (New York),

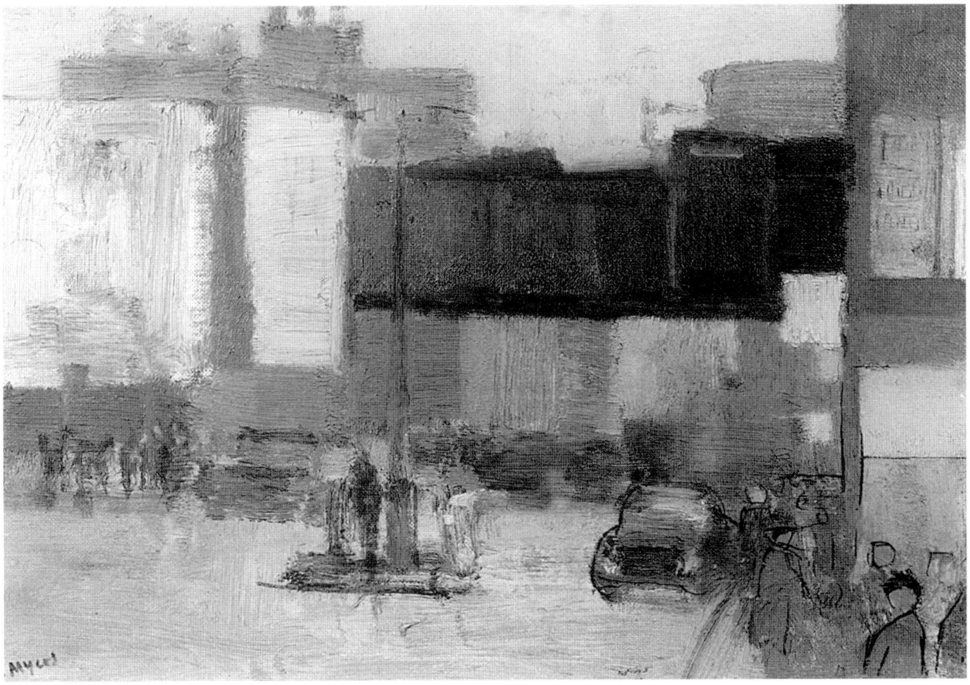

BERNARD MYERS. *Stratford, East London.* Oil on board, 10in x 14in. Private collection.

Stadtische Kunsthalle (Düsseldorf), Museum of Contemporary Art (Chicago), Galerie Ostergren (Malmø, Sweden), British Painting 1952-1977 (R.A., London), A New Spirit in Painting (R.A., London), Museum of Modern Art (New York) and numerous group exhibitions at Xavier Fourcad (New York). His one-man exhibitions have included a major retrospective at the Whitechapel Art Gallery in 1983, which travelled extensively in both Europe and the U.S.A. In 1984 he was the first winner of the prestigious Turner Prize at the Tate Gallery (London).

MUNDY, *Henry* (b.1919)
Having first studied at the Laird School of Art in Birkenhead, he attended Camberwell from 1946-50. In 1961 he was awarded the William Frew Prize at the Carnegie Institute in Pittsburgh (U.S.A.) and in the same year he won First Prize at the John Moores Exhibition. He taught at St. Martin's School of Art and the Bath Academy of Art for many years, and his one-man exhibitions include Gallery One (London), Hanover Gallery, Stone Gallery (Newcastle-upon-Tyne), and Kasmin Gallery. His group exhibitions include the Carnegie Institute, the Guggenheim Museum (New York), Hayward Gallery, and 'British Painting 1952-1977' at the R.A. His work is in numerous public collections, including the Art Gallery of Victoria (Melbourne), Arts Council of Great Britain, Bristol City Museum & Art Gallery, the British Council, Brooklyn Museum (New York), Contemporary Arts Society, National Gallery of Canada, San Francisco Museum of Art and the Tate Gallery. He married the artist Gillian Ayres*.

MUNRO, *Eleanor Graham see* CHRISTIE, *Eleanor Graham*

MYERS, *Bernard L.* N.D.D., A.R.C.A., Hon. F.R.C.A., Hon. Prof. R.C.A. (b.1925)
He first studied at St. Martin's School of Art from 1947-49, followed by a two year period at Camberwell, during which time he was greatly influenced by Bloch*, Dixon* and Salaman*. He studied at the R.C.A. from 1951-54 and has exhibited widely, including the L.G., R.A. Summer Exhibitions and has held regular one-man shows at the New Art Centre. He has taught at numerous London art schools, including Camberwell between 1954-58 part-time in the Junior Art School. From 1968-72 he was a visiting Professor at the Indian Institute of Technology in New Delhi. His work is in permanent collections of the Arts Council of Great Britain, Carlisle City Art Gallery, the Contemporary Arts Society, Graves Art Gallery (Sheffield) the National Maritime Museum (Greenwich) and the Tate Gallery.

N

NEGUS, *Richard* (b.circa 1922)
Following war service with the Royal Marines, he enrolled as a student at Camberwell in 1945 and was to remain there for the next two years, studying illustration under Minton* and del Renzio*. He worked with Hugh Casson (b.1910) on the Festival of Britain staff from 1947-51 and also lectured at the Central School of Art and Hornsey College of Art. He has been a design consultant for British Airways, the National Theatre, English Heritage and the Science Museum, amongst others. During the 1980s he was for many years a member of the Design Council. He is the only known former Camberwell student to become a Governor of the School (1967-78).

NEWMAN, *Bryan* (b. 1935)
He trained at Camberwell School of Art from 1951-56 and was taught by Dick Kendall* and Hugh Purdy. He was subsequently a technical assistant in the Pottery Department from 1958-59 and also taught there on a part-time basis until 1966. Newman also taught at Harrow School of Art and at Bath Academy of Art before starting his own pottery in Somerset in 1973. He makes a range of thrown domestic stoneware and also distinctive sculptural pieces which are assembled from thrown and slabbed units into intricate forms, boats, buildings and bridges. He has travelled widely overseas, giving pottery workshop demonstrations and visiting countries where pottery remains part of the folk tradition. He has shown in numerous group ceramic exhibitions which include Primavera 1964, Peter Dingley, Stratford-on-Avon, Craftsmen Potters Association and at overseas exhibitions in Munich, Hamburg, Geneva, Copenhagen, Tokyo, San Francisco, Sydney and Melbourne. Examples of his work are represented in the collections of the V & A and Inner London Education Authority.

NICHOLSON, *William Michael* (b.1916)
Sculptor, born in Nottinghamshire, who eventually made his home in Australia. From 1933 he spent three years at Sandhurst as a military cadet. His artistic training began in 1938 when he studied for nearly two years at the City and Guilds School of Arts and Crafts, London. He served in France and Burma during the Second World War, attaining the rank of Major before continuing his studies at Camberwell, 1947-48. Here his studies brought him into contact with Karel Vogel* under whom he began his sculpting career. After leaving Camberwell he was appointed to the staff of the Central School before travelling to the Antipodes. He has held various appointments in New Zealand and Australia, including that of Senior Tutor at the School of Architecture at the University of New South Wales, Sydney. His commissions have included many decorative works for large offices in Sydney and he was for some years President of the Society of Sculptors and Associates, Sydney, Australia. His work has been exhibited at the National Gallery of Victoria and is also represented in the collections of Auckland City Art Gallery, New Zealand and in the Art Gallery of New South Wales.

NOTT, *Andrew* (b. 1946)
Born in Sydney, Australia, he studied at Camberwell, living in London between 1959-63, attending the School as a junior at the age of fourteen. He returned to Australia in the mid-1960s and since 1969 he has had several solo exhibitions in his native country and in America. He travelled to Europe and New York City after he won the Flotta Lauro Scholarship in 1970, and is represented in the National Gallery, Canberra and the Art Gallery of New South Wales.

NOYES, *Margot Frederica* N.D.D. (b 1939)
She was a student at Camberwell 1956-60, where her main teachers and influences

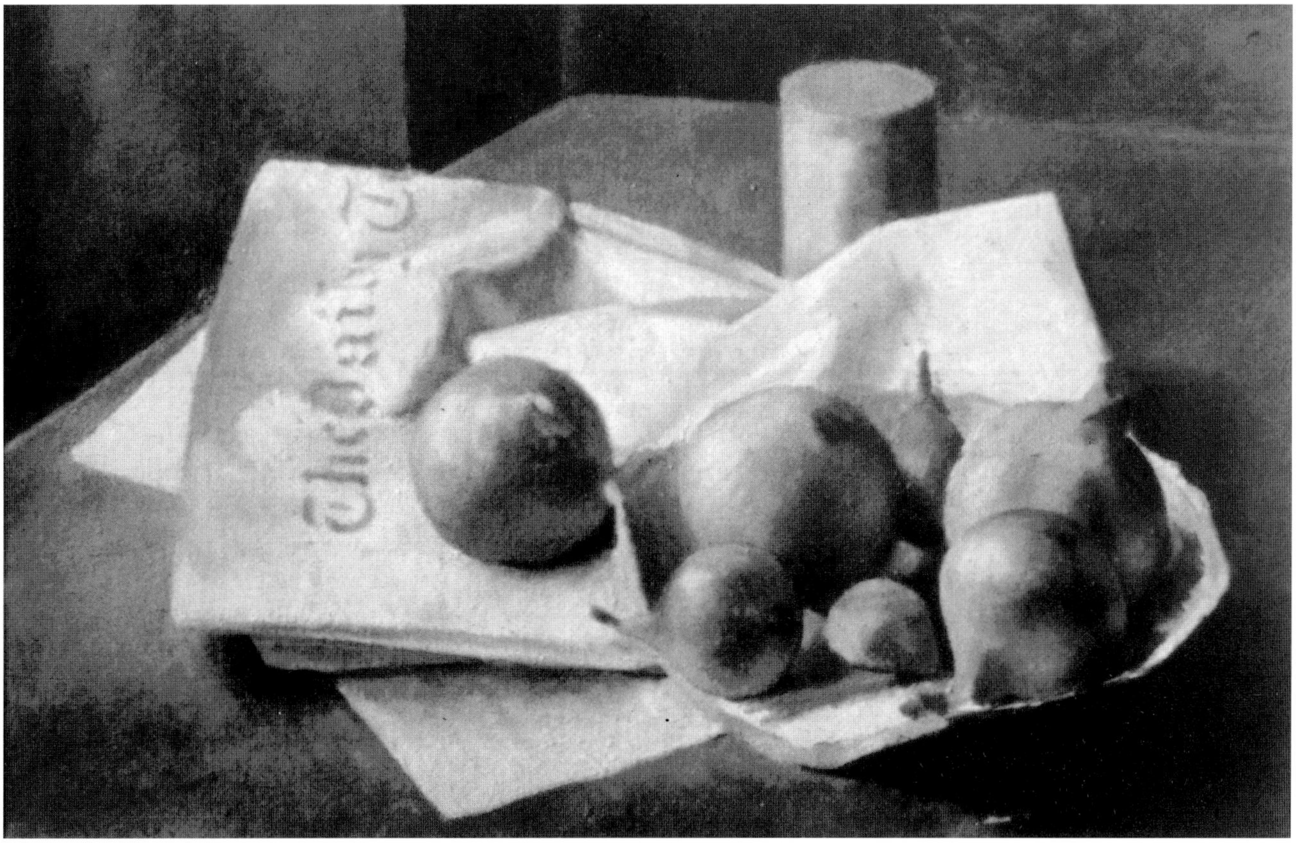

RALPH NUTTALL-SMITH. *Still Life with Onions.* Oil on canvas, 12in x 18in. Private collection.

were Eyton*, Dixon*, Fry*, R. D. Lee* and Symons*. She has shown her work in group exhibitions, including the Edinburgh Festival, the Piccadilly Gallery, the Bath Festival, the Solomon Gallery, the Royal Society of Oil Painters and several R.A. Summer Shows. Her one-woman exhibitions include Bead's Gallery (Aldeburgh), Keswick Hall (Norwich), and Upper Street Gallery (Islington). She married the artist Leo Austin*.

NUTTALL-SMITH, *Ralph* (1898-1988)
His art studies began in 1920 at the Slade School of Fine Art under Brown (1851-1941), Steer (1860-1942) and Tonks (1862-1937). He taught sculpture at the Slade School during the immediate post-war years and in 1949 he joined the staff at Camberwell to teach painting and drawing, a position he was to hold until the mid-1960s. He exhibited in numerous group exhibitions, including the R.A., L.G., N.E.A.C. and in 1971 had a retrospective exhibition at the Minories, Colchester. As Secretary to the Euston Road Group, he exhibited with them in their early years before the Second World War.

O

OSBORNE, *Dennis Henry* (b.1919)

Following war service and three years as a P.O.W., along with many other students he enrolled at Camberwell in 1946, where he was to study art for the next four years. In 1953 he emigrated to Canada, where he taught and practised art until he returned to England in 1960. A prolific exhibitor, he has shown at the N.E.A.C., R.A., R.H.A. and at many exhibitions in Canada. His work is represented in the permanent collections of Hamilton Art Gallery (Ontario), Toronto Art Gallery (Ontario) and Lisburn Museum (Northern Ireland). He is currently living in Northern Ireland and is a member of the Royal Ulster Academy. He married the painter Jean Osborne*.

OSBORNE, *Jean* (*née* Miekle) (1926-1965)

Born in Larne, Northern Ireland, she was originally taught art by Paul Nietsche (1885-1950) who had left his native Russia during the mid-1920s. She attended Camberwell from 1948-50, where she was much influenced by the teaching of John Minton*. She exhibited with the L.G., R.W.S., The Young Contemporaries and at the A.I.A. Gallery in London. With her husband Dennis, she emigrated to Canada and continued to exhibit widely throughout the North American continent. A few years after her return to England, she died and was honoured by a retrospective exhibition by the Arts Council of Northern Ireland in 1967.

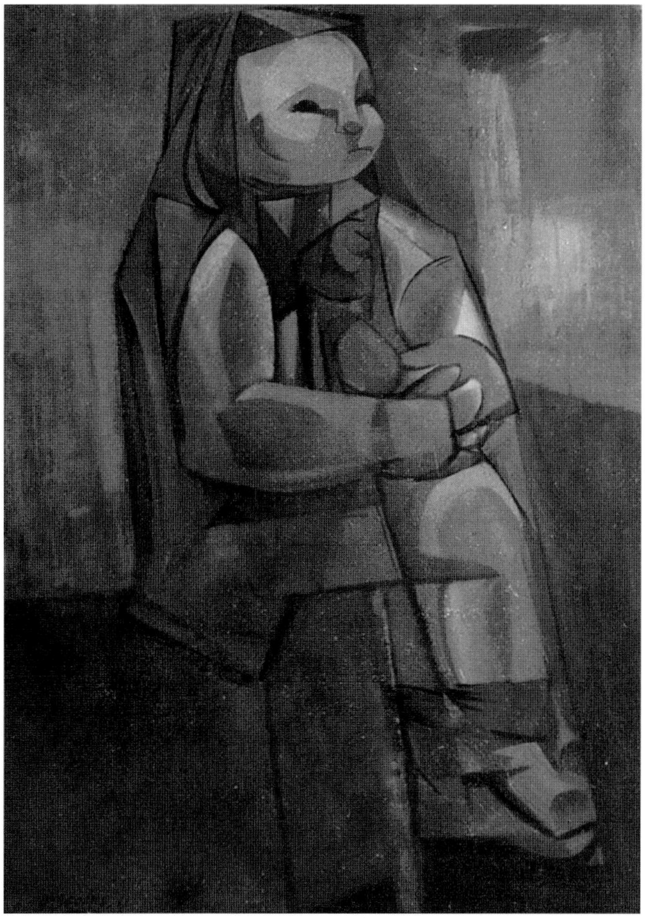

DENNIS OSBORNE. *Seated Child.* Oil on board, 35in x 24in. Courtesy of Eve Phillips.

P

PALMER, *James Francis* A.R.C.A. (b.1917)
He first studied at Clapham School of Art 1934-38, followed by a two year period at the R.C.A. At the end of the war he began teaching and has since taught at Ravensbourne, Canterbury College of Art and during the early 1950s had a three year period at Camberwell as a member of staff. He has exhibited regularly, including such venues as John Moores (Liverpool), the L.G., The N.E.A.C., Leicester Galleries and on a regular basis at the R.A. Summer Exhibitions during the last forty years.

PARROTT, *Denis William* N.D.D., A.T.C., F.R.S.A., F.S.A.E. (b.1931)
He first studied at Batley School of Art from 1948-51 before attending Camberwell for a two year period. His main influences were Bloch*, Eurich*, Pitchforth* and Spencer*. He returned to his native Yorkshire in 1957 where he had a further period of study at Leeds College of Art. He has exhibited at various locations, including the R.A., the University of Leicester, Le Salon de Nations at the Paris International Contemporary Arts Centre and has held a one-man exhibition at the Sir Alfred East Gallery in Kettering, Northamptonshire. He was a Fulbright Scholar living and working in America during the early 1970s. His work is in collections in the U.K., U.S.A., South Africa, Germany and France.

PASMORE, *Edwin John Victor* C.H., C.B.E., R.A., L.G. (b.1908)
He first began to paint at Harrow School in 1923. In 1927, following the death of his father, he was forced to earn a living and so took a position as a clerk in the Health Department of the L.C.C. He continued his art studies by attending evening classes at the Central School of Art under the tuition of A. S. Hartrick (1864-1950). In 1932 he joined the L.A.A. where, during the next two years, he became very friendly with William Coldstream* and Claude Rogers*. By 1934 he had been elected a Member of the L.G. and exhibited regularly with them, showing sensitive Fauve-like paintings. By this time he had begun some experimentation into Abstraction but, dissatisfied, destroyed them, turning more to the Camden Town Group for his influences. In 1937 he joined his friends Coldstream and Rogers in setting up the School of Drawing and Painting which soon became known as the Euston Road School when it moved premises to Euston Road from its original location in Fitzroy Street. He joined the staff at Camberwell on the recommendation of Sir Kenneth Clark at the end of 1942 where he was soon joined, after the cessation of hostilities, by some of his former colleagues from the Euston Road Group. In 1947 he again turned to abstract art, at which he still works today. He left Camberwell in 1949 to join the Central School of Arts & Crafts where he introduced a Basic Form course. His other teaching posts include Master of Painting at Durham University (1954-61), and Consulting Director of Urban Design for the South West Housing Area of Peterlee New Town where he designed the Pavilion. In the early 1950s he joined the Penwith Society in St. Ives, but only remained a member until 1953. By the early 1960s his work was being shown in numerous international exhibitions and by 1961 he had ceased to teach and began painting full-time. His one-man exhibitions include Musée des Arts Décoratifs (Paris), Stedelijk Museum (Amsterdam), Palais des Beaux Arts (Brussels), Tate Gallery, Cartwright Hall (Bradford), Marlborough Galleries. His work is in the permanent collections of the Tate Gallery and in public collections in Canada, Holland, Australia, Italy, Austria, Switzerland, France and the U.S.A. In 1966 he purchased a house in Malta, where he now spends most of his time.

PATTERSON, *Rachel Caridwen* (*née* Richards) (b. 1932)
Raised in an artistic environment, the daughter of Ceri and Frances Richards*, she enrolled at Camberwell in 1950. During the next four years she studied illustration,

lithography and wood engraving under Ardizzone*, Rothenstein* and Frank Martin*. It was not until the 1980s that she began to exhibit at such venues as the Hammersmith Art Society and the S.W.A. and in 1992 she held a two-person show with her former Camberwell colleague, Joyce Arimatsu*.

PEAKE, *Mervyn Lawrence* (1911-1968)
Born in China, he did not arrive in England until he was twelve years old. Following a brief period at Croydon School of Art, in the early 1930s he attended the R.A. Schools, winning the Arthur Hacker Prize. His first teaching post was at the Westminster School of Art from 1935-38, where he taught Life Drawing, counting the young John Minton* as a pupil. He was invalided out of the war in 1943 and at this time, whilst concentrating on his writing and illustrating, held a part-time teaching post at Camberwell. In 1950 he joined the staff at the Central School of Arts & Crafts where he taught part-time for the next ten years. By the mid-1950s, however, the signs of Parkinson's disease began to appear and he gradually became more incapacitated, spending the last four years of his life in hospital. He is known predominantly as an illustrator, and amongst the innumerable books that he has illustrated are *Doctor Jekyll and Mr. Hyde* and *Treasure Island* (Robert Louis Stevenson), *Droll Stories* (Honoré de Balzac), *The Rime of the Ancient Mariner* (Samuel Taylor Coleridge) and *All This and Bevin Too* (Quentin Crisp).

PELL, *Cynthia Wendy* (1933-1977)
She was a student at Camberwell 1950-55, where she was influenced by Martin Bloch*. Her work was shown in the mid-1950s at the Beaux Arts Gallery and at the same time in various galleries in Paris. Very few of her paintings survive but a work of hers was shown in 'The Forgotten Fifties' at Camden Arts Centre, August 1984. She was married to the artist Ronald Weldon*.

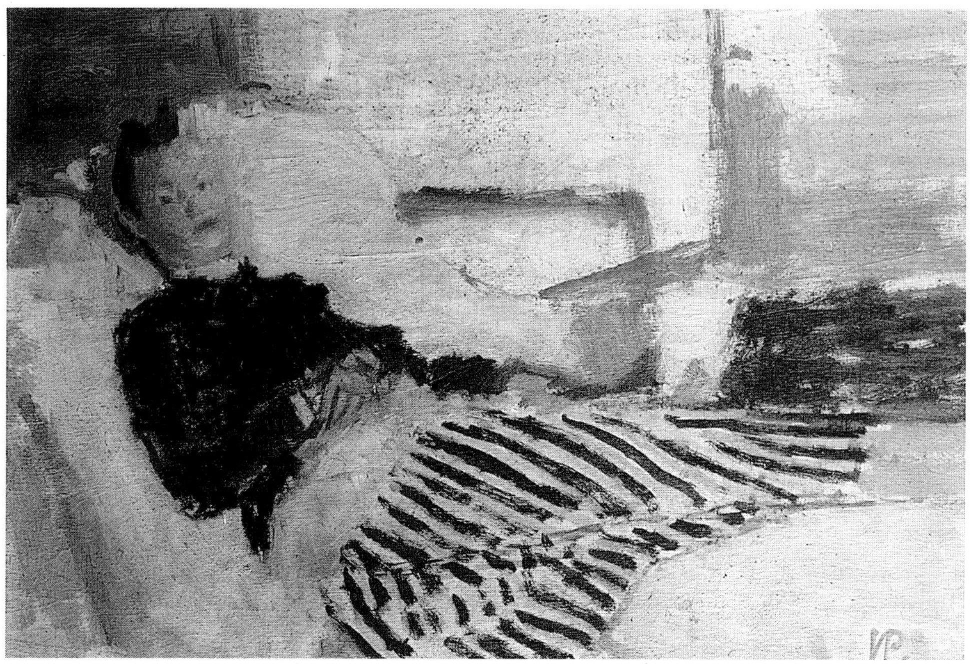

VICTOR PASMORE. *Study of Dodie Masterman.* Oil on panel, 10in x 14in. Private collection.

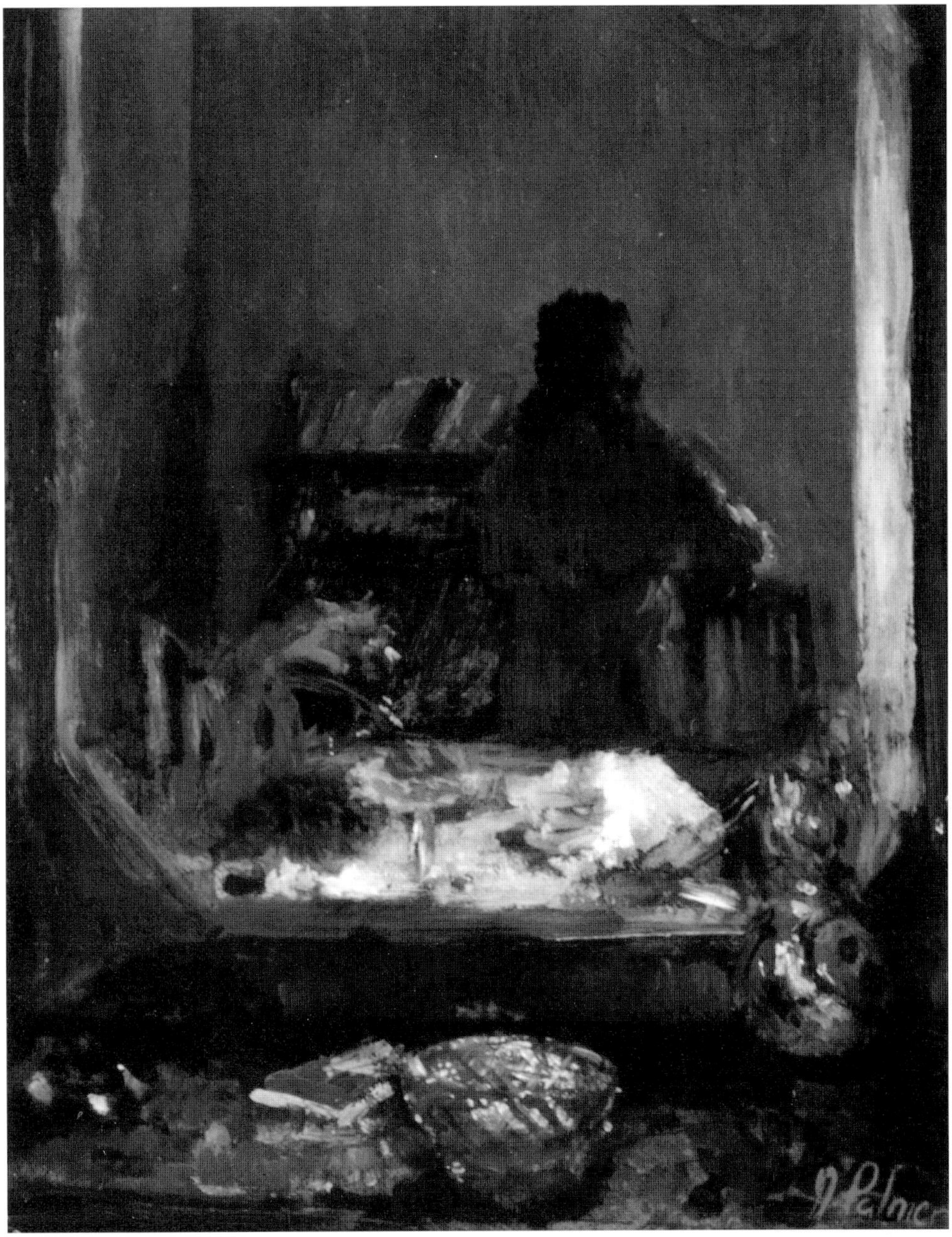

JAMES PALMER. *Interior with Mirror*, 1947. Oil on panel, 12in x 21in. Private collection.

PEMBERTON, *Christopher Henry* (b.1923)
He was a student at Camberwell 1948-49. and was influenced by Coldstream* and Rogers*. During the 1950s he began exhibiting his work at the R.A. and John Moores (Liverpool). He has also had one-man exhibitions at Bury St. Edmunds Art Gallery, Woodlands Art Gallery (Blackheath), in Cyprus and at Cadogan Contemporary. From the mid-1950s until his retirement in 1985 he taught Drawing and Painting at Camberwell and was, for the last three years of his career, Head of Foundation Studies.

PEMBERTON, *Julian see* COMYNS CARR, *Julian*

PERIES, *Leela Ranjini Merl* (*née* Dias Bandaranayake) (b.1939)
Her initial art training began in the mid-1950s under Harry Pieris who was the founder member of the '43 Art Group in Colombo, Ceylon. During 1959 she became a full-time sculpture student studying under Vogel* at Camberwell. On her return

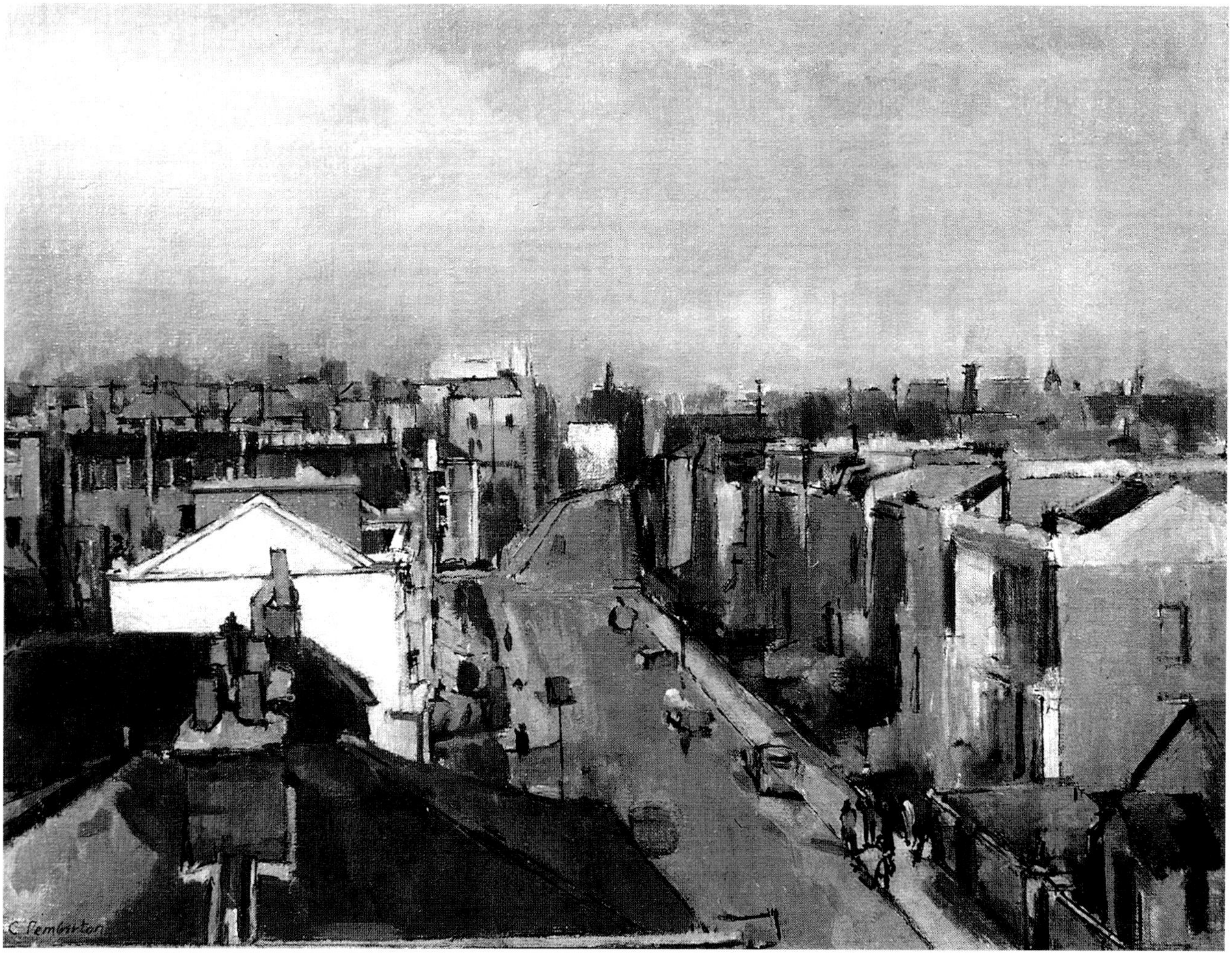

CHRISTOPHER PEMBERTON. *Street Scene, Chelsea*, 1950. Oil on canvas, laid on board, 13½in x 17¾in. Private collection.

home to Ceylon (Sri Lanka) in 1960, her first major commission was a life-size bronze of Reverend Sorata Thero – the Vice-Chancellor of Vidyodaya University. Since then other important commissions have followed, including a bronze bust of His Excellency J.R. Jayewardene – the President of Sri Lanka, followed by a bronze head of The Honourable R. Premadasa – the Prime Minister of Sri Lanka. Without doubt Leela Peries is the most important sculptor in the Indian sub-continent.

PIER, *Celia* (b.1919)
Lily Pier attended Camberwell in the immediate pre-war years of 1938-39, but during the war worked as a librarian and telex operator. She returned to Camberwell in 1947, where she continued her art studies for a further four years. Her work was particularly influenced by Bloch* and Salaman*. She has had numerous one-woman exhibitions including shows at the Walmer Castle in 1957, the Ben-Uri Art Gallery in 1958, and the St. Martin's Gallery in 1963. She also showed her work regularly with the South London Group and in various group exhibitions at the Beaux Arts Gallery, and the Arts Exhibitions Bureau touring shows.

PINSENT, *Christopher Roy* Bt. (b.1922)
Studied at Camberwell 1946-48, where his main influences were Gowing*, Kenneth Martin* and Pasmore*. He showed his work in group exhibitions including 'Euston Road and Others' in the late 1940s and at the same time he also showed at the N.E.A.C.

He became a member of the staff at Camberwell where he lectured from 1962-86.

PIPER, *Denis John* (1928-1987)
A student at St. Martin's School of Art in 1941, he continued his studies at Camberwell until 1946; following a break for National Service, he returned in 1948 for a further three years. His main influences were Bloch* and Minton*, and his exhibitions included 'Artists of Fame & Promise' at the Leicester Galleries, and various graphic art shows in London. He painted very little after leaving Camberwell and worked entirely in publishing for the remainder of his life. He was the first Art Director of the internationally renowned *Women's Wear Daily* newspaper and was also the Art Director of the *Economist* newspaper. He taught graphics in the late 1950s and early '60s at both Croydon and St. Martin's College of Art. He also designed record covers and book-jackets for Penguin Books.

PITCHFORTH *Roland Vivian* R.A., R.W.S., L.G., A.R.C.A. (1895-1982)
Born in Wakefield, he attended Leeds College of Art with Henry Moore (1898-1986), Barbara Hepworth (1898-1978) and Raymond Coxon (b.1896) between 1914-15, and again after Military Service during the First World War between 1919-20. He won a Scholarship to the R.C.A. where he studied under Sir William Rothenstein (1872-1945) between 1921-25. Shortly after leaving the R.C.A., one of his first teaching appointments in 1926 was at Camberwell School of Art. He was a teacher of the highest quality and taught at several London art schools, including St. Martin's, Chelsea, Sir John Cass and the R.C.A. He was able to demonstrate with inspiring drawings whilst continually giving a running commentary. His deafness, in some perverse way, helped to concentrate his thoughts during the life classes and all who came under his tuition had the highest regard for him as an artist, a teacher and a man. He exhibited widely, holding his first one-man show in 1928 at the L.A.A., and became a Member of the L.G. the following year, after many exhibitions with them. He first exhibited at the R.A. in 1922 and was elected an Associate in 1942, becoming a full Member in 1953. During the Second World War he was appointed an Official War Artist with the Admiralty and travelled extensively around Ceylon (Sri Lanka) and Burma. In the immediate post-war years, he took up residence in Durban, South Africa, and whilst there was instrumental in sending students to Camberwell. He returned to England in 1947 and continued his teaching until the mid-1960s, spending the majority of his time at Camberwell and St. Martin's where he taught life drawing. His work is represented in many private and public collections, including the Tate Gallery, Imperial War Museum and the V. & A.

PLANT, *Geoffrey* (b.1930)
Following two years National Service in the R.A.F. he became a student at Camberwell in 1951, having been awarded a scholarship from Halifax School of Art which he previously attended. His main teachers included Bloch* and Eurich*. His one-man exhibitions have included shows at the University of Hull and Doncaster Art Gallery, his group exhibitions have included 'Modern Art in Yorkshire' at the Wakefield Art Gallery and with the Yorkshire Artists on various occasions at the Leeds City Art Gallery. He has also shown with the N.E.A.C and at Harrogate Art Gallery. He has held numerous teaching posts since the mid-1950s in and around the Yorkshire area and has also accepted private commissions for murals in the county. His work is in the permanent collection of Leeds City Art Gallery.

PLANT, *John* A.R.C.A. (b.1916)
His original studies began at Sheffield School of Art, followed by the R.A. in the years preceding the Second World War. Following war service with the R.A.F. he

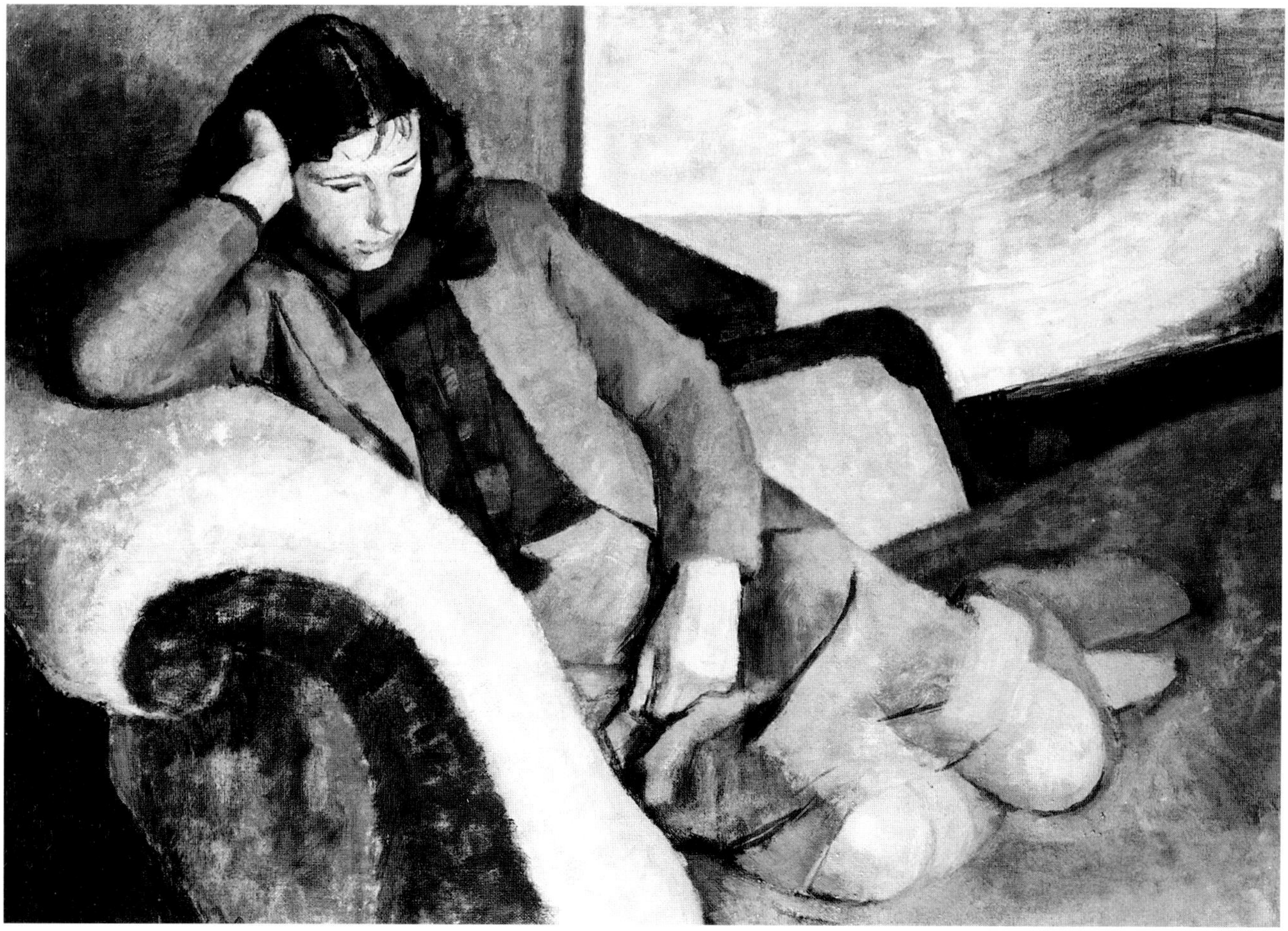

CHRISTOPHER PINSENT. *Portrait of Jo Higson*, 1947. Oil on canvas, 22in x 30in. Private collection.

was for five years a lecturer at Camberwell, where he taught Graphic Design. However, in the late 1940s, he began a career as an illustrator in the world of advertising.

PLUMMER, *Jean Mary see* BARHAM, *Jean Mary*

POTWOROWSKA, *Anna Maria see* CLARKE, *Anna Maria*

POULTNEY, *Tony* (b.1938)
A painter, he studied at Camberwell School of Arts and Crafts 1951-58, studying music during the same period. He has since travelled round the world playing music and working as an artist. He has been commissioned to paint murals in Yokohama and San Francisco. His first solo exhibition was held at the Woodstock Gallery, London, 1968.

PRESCOTT *Valerie* (*née* Bond) (b.1923)
She was at the R.C.A. in the immediate post-war years, joining the staff at Camberwell in 1951, remaining there for only twelve months teaching pottery. She has shown her work in group exhibitions during the late 1940s and early '50s, including the R.B.A. and at the Festival of Britain. More recently, her work has been shown at the Stonegate Gallery (York) and in 1987 she held a one-woman exhibition in Lyme Regis.

PRICE, *Barbara Dorothy see* FREEMAN, *Barbara Dorothy*

PROCTOR, *Jennifer* (*née* Calver) (b.1931)
A student at Camberwell from 1948-53, she was taught and became influenced by

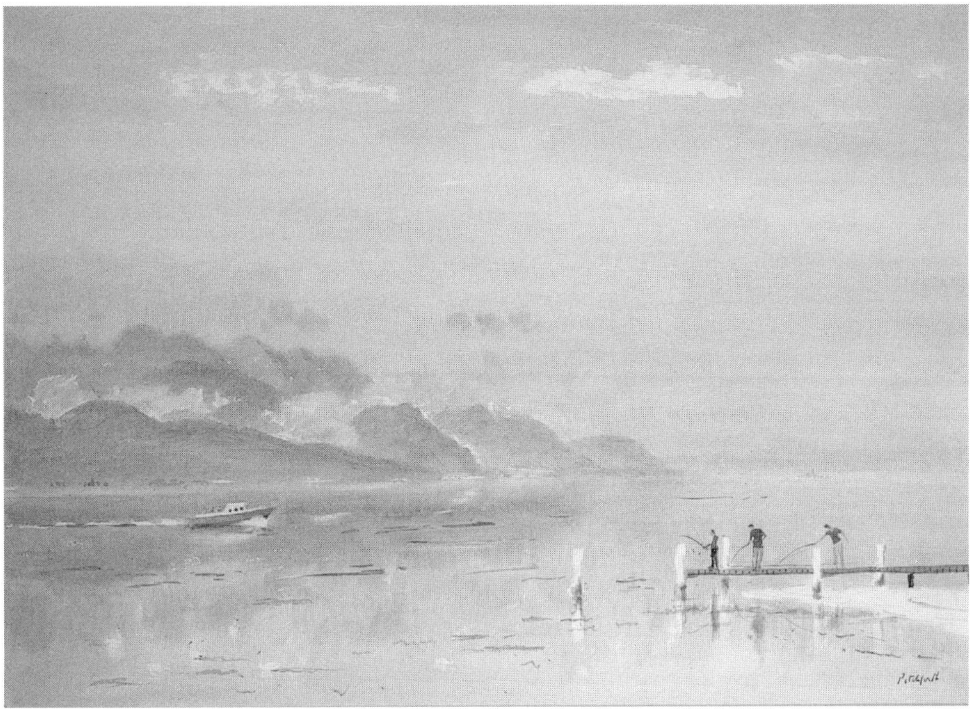

R. V. PITCHFORTH. *Lake Geneva.* Watercolour, 16in x 23in. Private collection.

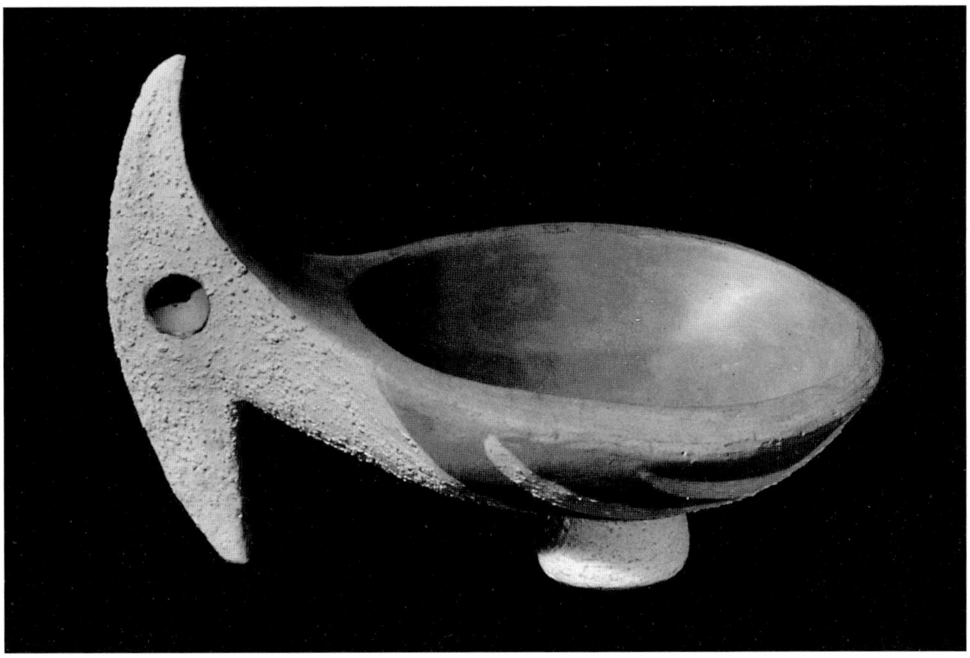

VALERIE PRESCOTT. Bird bowl, 1950. Slip decorated terracotta. Artist's collection.

Bloch*, Buckland-Wright* and Eurich*. Although only studying sculpture very briefly, she also found Vogel* to be a great encouragement in her five years at Camberwell. After leaving Camberwell, she spent a period of time in Cornwall and held various positions, including that of art teacher. In the late 1950s she married an Army Officer and spent many years in different locations around the world. By the end of the 1960s her painting had ceased due to family commitments but she did exhibit in various group exhibitions in the South of England, and with the R.S.A.

Q

QUINN, *Thomas William* (b.1918)
He was a student at Camberwell 1946-48, where he was influenced by Einzig*, Minton* and del Renzio*. He has had one-man exhibitions at the Alpine Gallery and at Century Gallery, Henley-on-Thames.

R

RABIN, *Samuel* (1903-1991)
Born Samuel Rabinovitch in Manchester, he was the son of Jewish immigrant parents from Russia. By 1914 he had won a scholarship to Manchester School of Art and still holds the distinction of being their youngest ever pupil. He was taught by Adolphe Valette (1876-1942) and his fellow students included L. S. Lowry R.A. (1887-1976) and James Fitton R.A. (1889-1982). In 1921 he attended the Slade School of Fine Art for three years where he was taught drawing by Henry Tonks (1862-1937). In the mid-1920s he spent a year in Paris and on his return he began to attract attention as a sculptor and subsequently worked with Henry Moore (1898-1986) and Eric Gill (1882-1940) on decorations for the London Underground Headquarters. He had been an incredible athlete in his youth, and in 1928 he won a Bronze Medal for Wrestling in the Amsterdam Olympics. This stood him in good stead, because he was unable to find a teaching post and in order to finance his art he began to wrestle professionally throughout the early 1930s. During this period, besides exhibiting with his friend Lowry, he actually starred in a Korda film *The Private Life of Henry VIII*, playing the part of a champion wrestler. A second film, *The Scarlet Pimpernel*, followed soon after, in which he played Mendoza, a famous prize-fighter. Alongside his many activities he was blessed with an extraordinarily fine singing voice and, during the war years, he toured army camps in Britain and Germany entertaining the troops. It is quite possible he could have taken a career as an opera singer but instead he decided to concentrate on his drawing. In 1949 he joined the staff at Goldsmiths' College of Art, where his pupils included Bridget Riley (b.1931), Mary Quant (b.1934) and Tom Keating (1918-1984). He remained on the staff at Goldsmiths' until 1965. During this period he became a visiting lecturer at Camberwell where he also taught Life Drawing. His work has been exhibited in numerous exhibitions, including such venues as Wildenstein, Whitechapel Art Gallery, Carlisle Art Gallery, Leicester Galleries, British Museum, Belgrave Gallery and the Cartwright Hall Art Gallery (Bradford). A major retrospective exhibition was held at the Dulwich Art Gallery in 1985.

RADENHURST, *Judith see* KERLANDER, *Judith*

RAINER, *George William* (b.1923)
Born in Macao, South China, he served in the Australian Army 1942-46. He came to England in 1948 and following a short spell in a stained glass studio he enrolled at Camberwell in 1949. He spent two years studying ceramics under Richard Kendall* and Norah Bradon* and in 1952 he commenced teaching the first pottery courses at

Shrewsbury School of Art. In 1961 he was appointed to the staff of the West of England College of Art (later to become Bristol Polytechnic) where he eventually became Head of the Ceramics Department. He has exhibited paintings with the L.G. and at the R.W.A. and has held solo ceramic exhibitions at Primavera, Cambridge in 1971 and at the Bohum Gallery, Henley-on-Thames in 1981. He has participated in group exhibitions in Tokyo, America and Italy and has exhibited regularly at the Craftsmen Potters Association shows in this country.

RAVERA, *John Eli* P.R.B.S. (b.1941)
Known predominantly as a sculptor, he joined the Junior School at Camberwell in 1954 and was to remain there for nearly eight years. His main teacher during this time was Vogel*. He was at one time an Assistant Sculptor to F. Mancini and A. Nemon. He has had numerous exhibitions at galleries in the U.K. and abroad and he has commissioned work at the Academy of Arts in Hong Kong. He has been the Treasurer for the R.B.S. and more recently their President.

RAYBOULD, *Terry* (b.1940)
A student at Camberwell from 1958-62, he was much influenced by R. D. Lee*, Eyton*, Symons* and Uglow.* During his time there he won numerous Summer Composition prizes, winning the First Prize in the Ana Berry Award during his last term. On completion of his studies he was invited back as a part-time teacher at Camberwell, a post which he was to hold until 1975. He has also taught in the Fine Art Department at Farnham Art College and since 1977 he has been Head of Art at Northampton School for Boys. His work has been shown in many group exhibitions, including Young Contemporaries, L.G., New Grafton Gallery and in 'Together Again' at the South London Art Gallery. He has also held one-man shows at Woburn Abbey, Leicester University and the Four Seasons Gallery.

RECKITT, *Rosemary Ann see* COOK, *Rosemary Ann*

REES, *Brian Harland* (b.1930)
He first studied art at Swansea from 1947-49, before furthering his studies at Camberwell 1950-52, where he was influenced by Ardizzone* and Rothenstein*. He returned to Swansea School of Art where for a brief period he taught before freelancing. In the late 1950s, having been awarded a scholarship by the Steel Company of Wales, he spent two years studying book production and printing at the Central School of Art. Most of his working career since then has been involved in graphic work for book publishers, including J. M. Dent and the Woburn Press. He has exhibited in numerous group exhibitions, including the Welsh Arts Council, Young Contemporaries, and James Howell (Cardiff). His commissions have included a book jacket for *Under Milk Wood* (Dylan Thomas) for J. M. Dent, and graphic work for British Rail, Shell, *Daily Telegraph* and many advertising agencies.

REID, *Louise* (*née* Young) (b.1926)
Born in South Africa, she began studying Fine Arts at Pietermaritzburg University in 1944 and before leaving had a further year's study under Mary Vaughan-Williams A.R.C.A. (b.1913). She attended Camberwell in 1946 for three years and found the students with whom she was working most influential, especially Anthony Eyton* and Anthony Fry*. During these years in London she exhibited with the L.G. and in the Young Contemporaries exhibitions. Before returning to her native South Africa in 1958, she taught art at a school near High Wycombe. Although her young family demanded much of her time she continued to draw and paint and even taught in Natal for a three year period. She continues to paint and exhibit in South Africa and is planning a one-woman exhibition in Durban.

del RENZIO, *Toni* (b.1915)

His early influences were De Chirico (1888-1978), Dali (1904-1989) and André Masson (1896-1987), resulting during the late 1930s and early '40s in his producing some outstanding Surreal paintings. In 1942 he published *Arson*, which was the only organised attempt in Europe at the time to give a clear focus to Surrealism. He had the full support of Conroy Maddox (b.1912), Eileen Agar (1899-1991), Edith Rimmington (1902-1986) and others. He joined the staff at Camberwell during 1944 for a two year period where he taught Design. During this period, although predominantly surrounded by the Euston Road Group members, he felt more in sympathy with John Minton*. His work has recently been shown in 'Surrealism in England 1936 and After', at Canterbury College of Art 1986; and 'Surrealism in Britain in the Thirties' at Leeds City Art Gallery 1986. He was married to the Surrealist painter and poet Ithell Colquhoun (1906-1988).

RICHARDS, *Frances* (1901-1985)

Born in the Potteries, whilst still in her teens she became a designer for the Paragon China Company. From Burslem School of Art she won a Scholarship to the R.C.A. 1924-27, where she quickly gained recognition as a student of outstanding ability. During the 1930s she was commissioned by T. S. Eliot to work on lithographic illustrations for *The Book of Revelations* which was published by Faber & Faber. During her years at the R.C.A. she met the artist Ceri Richards (1903-1971) whom she married in 1929. She joined the staff at Camberwell during the 1930s and she was to remain there as a teacher in the Textile Department for nearly thirty years. During this period, she also held a similar position at Chelsea School of Art. During the 1940s and 1950s she created some wonderful embroidery designs and held exhibitions of these works at the Redfern Gallery. She also showed her work during the 1950s and '60s at both the Hanover Gallery and the Leicester Galleries. Her work is represented in numerous public collections, including the V. & A., the Tate Gallery, the National Museum of Wales and the Stoke-on-Trent City Museum.

RICHARDS, *Gordon Dennis* (b.1926)

He first attended Camberwell in 1942-44 and after a two year spell in the Navy he resumed his studies in 1946, attending the Saturday morning classes that were so popular under the instruction of Pasmore*. Richards' other main teachers were Ayrton*, Minton* and Vaughan* and his early work can be seen to contain their influence. During the two years prior to 1951, he became a part-time studio assistant to Pasmore in Chiswick for the then princely sum of a shilling a day. He must have been successful because before long his services were in demand by Pasmore's colleagues Gowing* and Rodrigo Moynihan (1910-1990). 'Rik', as he is known to his friends, exhibited his work only on rare occasions with the L.G. and the Young Contemporaries. During the mid-1950s he spent two years living and working in Cornwall and as a friend and neighbour was much influenced by Sven Berlin (b.1911). From his days at Camberwell, he was friendly with Minton and on numerous occasions assisted him with stage designs. It has been in the theatre that Richards has spent most of his working life as a stage-hand and an occasional designer and scene painter. He began teaching Perspective and Drawing at the London College of Furniture in the early 1980s.

RICHARDS, *Rachel Caridwen see* PATTERSON, *Rachel Caridwen*

RIE *Lucie* (*née* Gomperz) O.B.E., C.B.E. (b.1902)

Born in Vienna, she first began her studies at the age of twenty at the Künstgewerbeschule as a student of Michael Powolny, exhibiting her first pots a

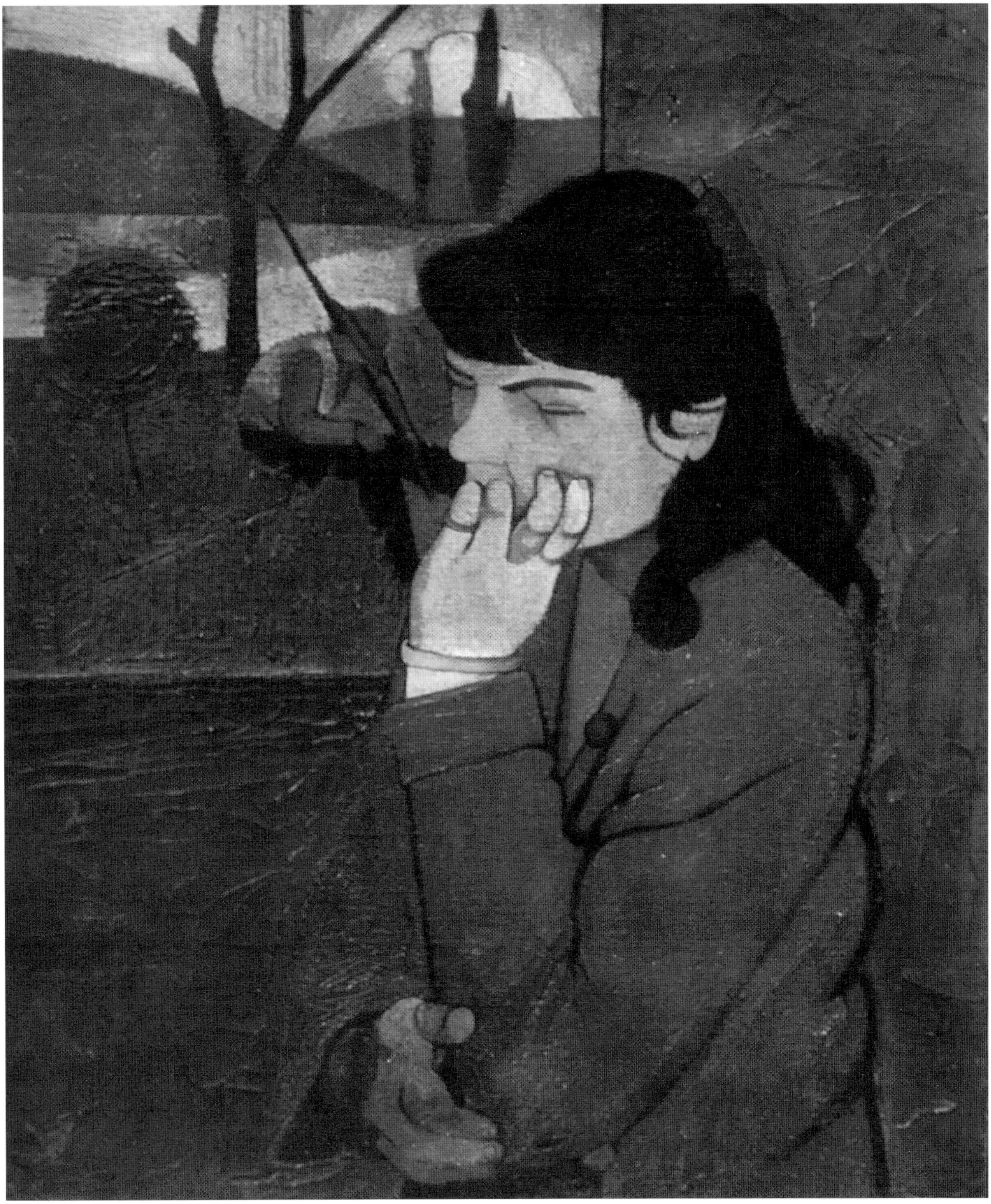

GORDON RICHARDS. *Portrait of a Thoughtful Girl*, 1948. Oil on canvas, 24in x 20in.
Artist's collection.

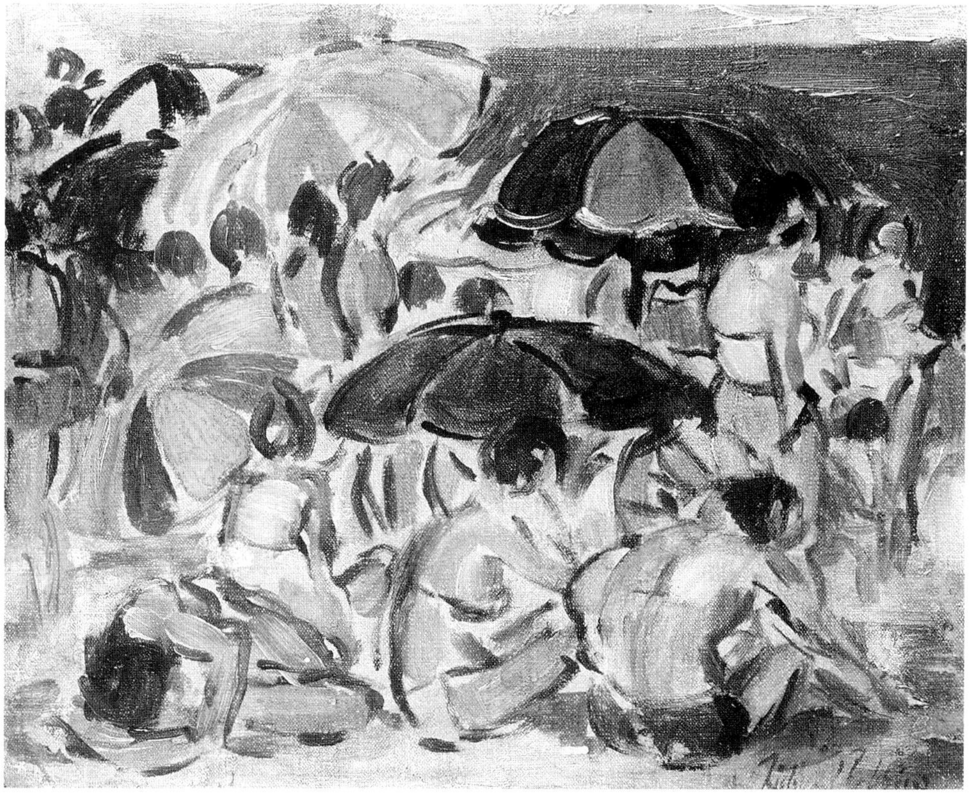

RICHARD ROBBINS. *Beach Scene.* Oil on canvas, 10in x 12in. Private collection.

year later in Brussels. By the late 1920s and early '30s she was exhibiting on an international scale, winning Gold Medals in Brussels and Milan. In 1938 she arrived in England and during the war years spent her time with the Home Guard and working in a Soho button factory with fellow refugees Hans Coper* and Jupp Dernbach (1908-1990). By 1946 she had joined forces with Coper in the Albion Mews Pottery and during the next four decades became a potter of national and international repute; her work being purchased by major public collections throughout the world. At the suggestion of Bernard Leach, whose son-in-law, Richard Kendall*, was already teaching at Camberwell, she joined the staff there in 1959. Within twelve months, Hans Coper had joined her on the staff where he taught Industrial Ceramics. However, Lucie Rie was not a good teacher, finding it difficult to encourage unmotivated students. In 1968 she was awarded an O.B.E. and the following year, an Honorary Doctorate by the R.C.A., where she also occasionally taught. In 1981 she was awarded a C.B.E. and in her late eighties was still working long hours in her Albion Mews studio.

RIPLEY, *Maureen* N.D.D. (*née* Webb) (b.1924)
She was a student at Camberwell 1946-49, where her main influences were Ardizzone*, Minton* and Rothenstein*. Her group exhibitions include Campbell & Franks and the Curwen Gallery and in 1984 she had a one-woman show at the Omnibus Workspace. She married the artist Geri Morgan*.

ROBBINS, *Richard* (b.1927)
Following a degree from Oxford University he attended the Slade School of Fine Art for six years on a part-time basis, immediately after the war. His uncle, Clive Gardiner (1891-1960), the Principal of Goldsmiths', encouraged him throughout this period. Robbins eventually joined the staff at Camberwell in 1958, where he remained for approximately seven years. His work was exhibited in a group exhibition at Wildenstein in 1960, and more recently, in 1989, he held a one-man show at the Phoenix Gallery (Lavenham).

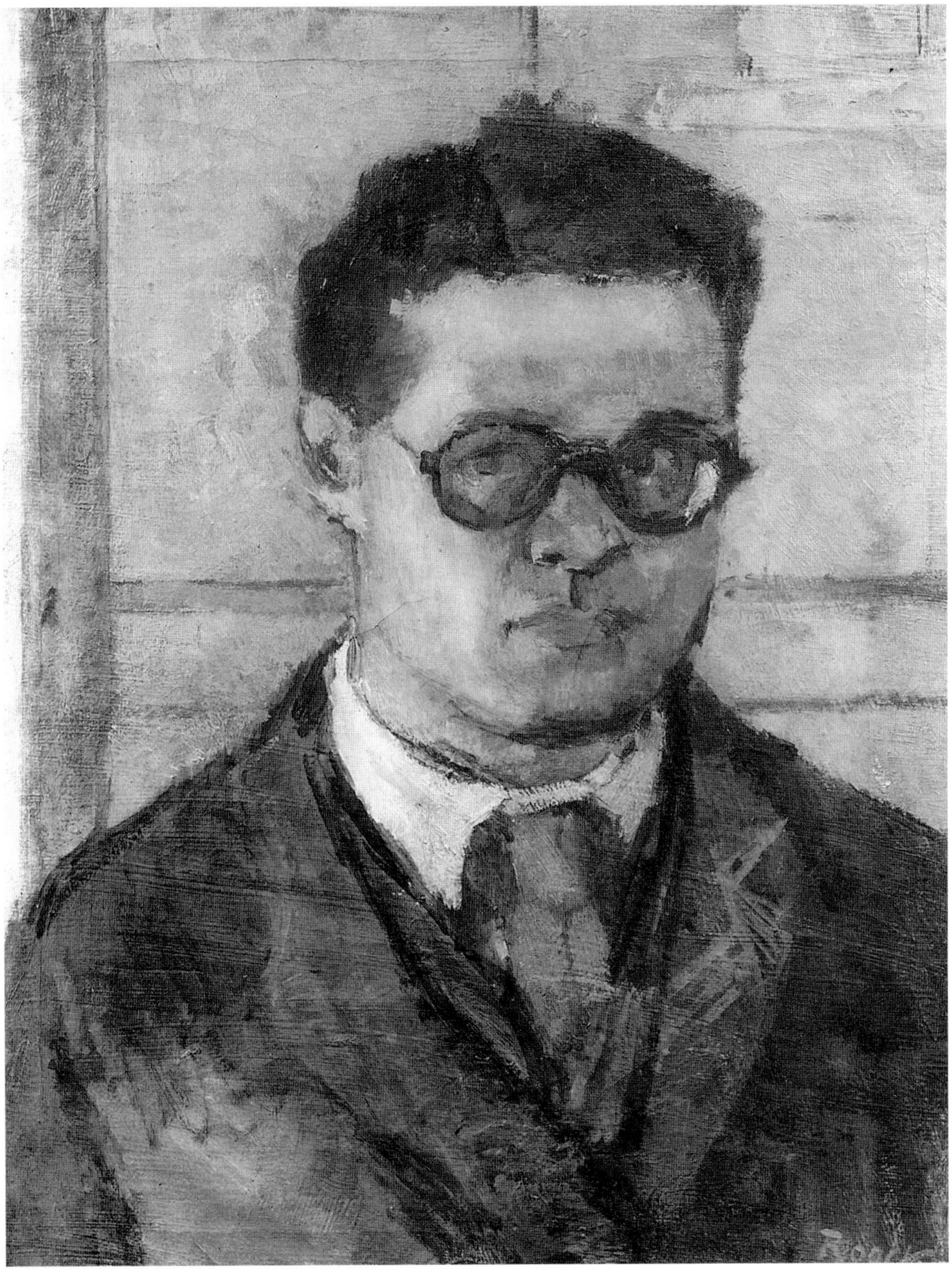

CLAUDE ROGERS. *Self Portrait*, 1943. Oil on canvas, 18in x 14in. Private collection.

ROGERS, *Claude Maurice* O.B.E., P.L.G., N.E.A.C. (1907-1979)
Although born in London, he spent a good part of the first seven years of his life in Argentina. In 1925 he won a scholarship to the Slade School of Fine Art where he was to meet, for the first time, Coldstream*, Rodrigo Moynihan (1910-1990), Geoffrey Tibble (1909-1952) and William Townsend*. His main influences and teachers during his three years at the Slade were Tonks (1862-1937) and Steer (1860-1942). He first exhibited with the L.G. in 1930 and by 1933 he was exhibiting regularly with the L.A.A. His first teaching appointment came in 1935 at Raynes Park. In 1937 he was a founder member of the School of Drawing & Painting at 316 Euston Road with his friends William Coldstream and Victor Pasmore*. This was later to be called the Euston Road Group. In 1940 he had his first one-man show at the Leicester Galleries and after being invalided out of the Army he became a

lecturer at Camberwell in 1945; a position he was to hold until the early 1950s. Between 1948-63 he lectured regularly at the Slade School where by now his old friend William Coldstream was Principal. In 1952 he was appointed President of the L.G., a position he held for thirteen years. He was awarded the O.B.E. for his services to art in 1959 and in 1963 he was appointed Professor of Fine Art at the University of Reading, a position he held until his retirement in 1972 when he was created Professor Emeritus. His work is in private and public collections, including the Arts Council of Great Britain, the Ashmolean Museum, Bradford City Art Gallery, Fitzwilliam Museum, The Earl Haig, Laing Art Gallery (Newcastle), the R.W.A., Sheffield City Art Gallery, the Slade School, University College (London), Southampton City Art Gallery, Tate Gallery and Trinity College (Cambridge). A touring retrospective exhibition was held in 1973 and again in conjunction with the Ben Uri Gallery in 1992/3. An exhibition of his works on paper was held at the Belgrave Gallery, Hampstead, in 1995.

ROMP, *Howard John* (b.1939)
He studied at Camberwell 1956-61, where his main teachers and influences were Dixon*, Eyton*, Fry* and Charles Howard*. Before leaving he was appointed to the staff and taught during his post-graduate year. He has had numerous one-man and mixed exhibitions, including 'Pictures for Schools' at the R.C.A., The Towner Art Gallery (Eastbourne), and 'Evidence of Performance Art' at the Slade School of Fine Art. Since the late 1960s he has been heavily involved as a freelance theatre designer. He married the artist Pauline Romp*.

ROMP, *Pauline Joy* (*née* Farrington) (b.1940)
She studied at Camberwell 1957-61 where her teachers and influences were Eurich*, Eyton*, Fry* and Medley*. She has shown her work in numerous group exhibitions, including the Edinburgh Festival, The Towner Art Gallery (Eastbourne), and the University of Surrey.

ROSE, *Francis Cyril Stanley* Bt. (1909-1979)
In the early 1920s he commenced his artistic studies with private tuition under Henry Tonks (1862-1937), followed by further studies in Paris with Francis Picabia (1878-1953) and, during this time, he became friendly with the avant-garde of the day including Jean Cocteau, Gertrude Stein and Picasso. He exhibited his work internationally including Petit Palais (Paris), The Mayor Gallery (London) and the Art Club (Chicago). He also designed extensively for the ballet including productions for Serge Lifar. He continued to show regularly in London and Paris throughout most of his life, and in 1966 had a major retrospective exhibition at the South London Art Gallery. In 1957 he joined the staff at Camberwell where he remained for a decade, teaching Painting and Illustration. He wrote many books, including his autobiography *Saying Life* in 1961.

ROSOMAN, *Leonard Henry* O.B.E., R.A. (b.1913)
From 1930-35 he studied at King Edward VII School of Art at the University of Durham under E. O'Rorke Dickey (1894-1977). In the same year he joined the R.A. Schools where he spent twelve months before completing his studies at the Central School of Arts & Crafts, studying under Bernard Meninsky. During this period he was also greatly influenced by Samuel Palmer (1805-1881) and Graham Sutherland (1903-1980). One of his earliest teaching posts, 1938-39, was at the now defunct Reimann School of Art in London, which concentrated heavily on art and design in industry. At the outbreak of war he painted many pictures relating to the Civil Defence and was a Fireman Artist until being appointed an Official War Artist to the

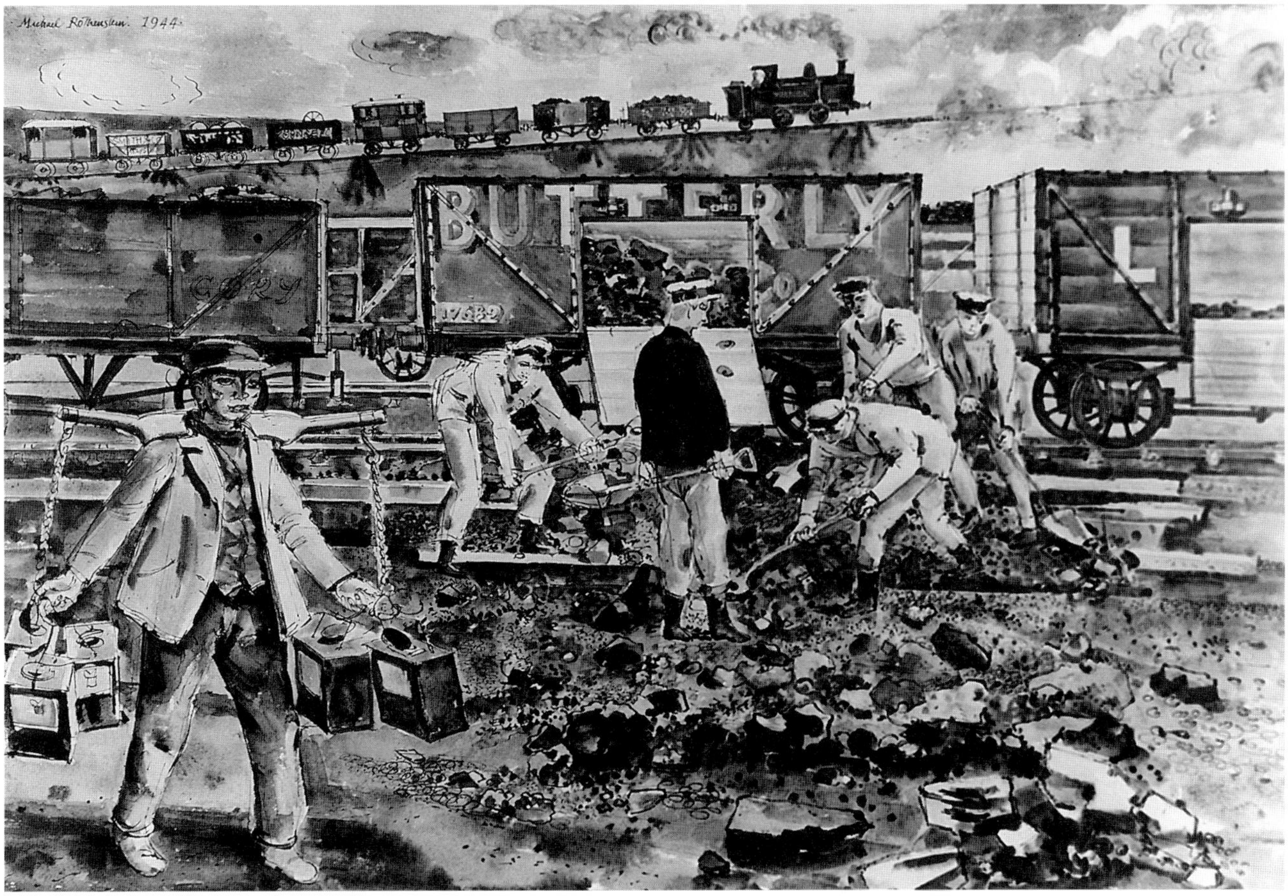

MICHAEL ROTHENSTEIN. *Unloading the Coal*, exh. Leicester Galleries 1944. Watercolour and ink on paper. Private collection.

Admiralty in 1943. The Imperial War Museum held 'A Ware Retrospective' exhibition of his work in 1989. He joined the staff at Camberwell in 1946, where he remained for two years. His first one-man exhibition was held in 1946 at the St. George's Gallery. In 1948 he joined the staff at Edinburgh College of Art, where he stayed for eight years until returning to London in 1956. He joined the staff at the R.C.A., a position he held for the next twenty years. His mural paintings, an important exhibit at the Festival of Britain in 1951, received much critical acclaim. He has exhibited throughout his career, including shows at Roland, Browse & Delbanco, The Fine Art Society, Oldham Art Gallery, The Lincoln Centre (New York), The New York State University and the Touchstone Gallery (New York). His work is represented in public and private collections throughout the world. He was elected an Associate of the R.A. in 1960 and a full Member nine years later. He was awarded an O.B.E. for his services to art in 1981.

ROTHENSTEIN, *Michael* R.A. (1908-1993)
Son of Sir William Rothenstein R.A. (1872-1945), and the brother of Sir John Rothenstein, he first studied at Chelsea Polytechnic followed by a three year period at the Central School of Arts and Crafts 1924-27. His first one-man show was held at Matthiesen Gallery in 1938. He joined the staff at Camberwell, succeeding Minton*, in 1948 where he remained for ten years, being involved in Print Making and Graphics. He held numerous one-man exhibitions in Canada, Norway, Sweden and in London at the I.C.A., Grabowski Gallery, Angela Flowers and the Redfern Gallery. His group exhibitions have also been on an international basis, including Poland, Switzerland, Spain, Canada, Italy, Yugoslavia, Norway, Germany, South America, U.S.A, Finland and the U.K. Undoubtedly one of this country's most important printmakers, examples of his work are to be found in public and private

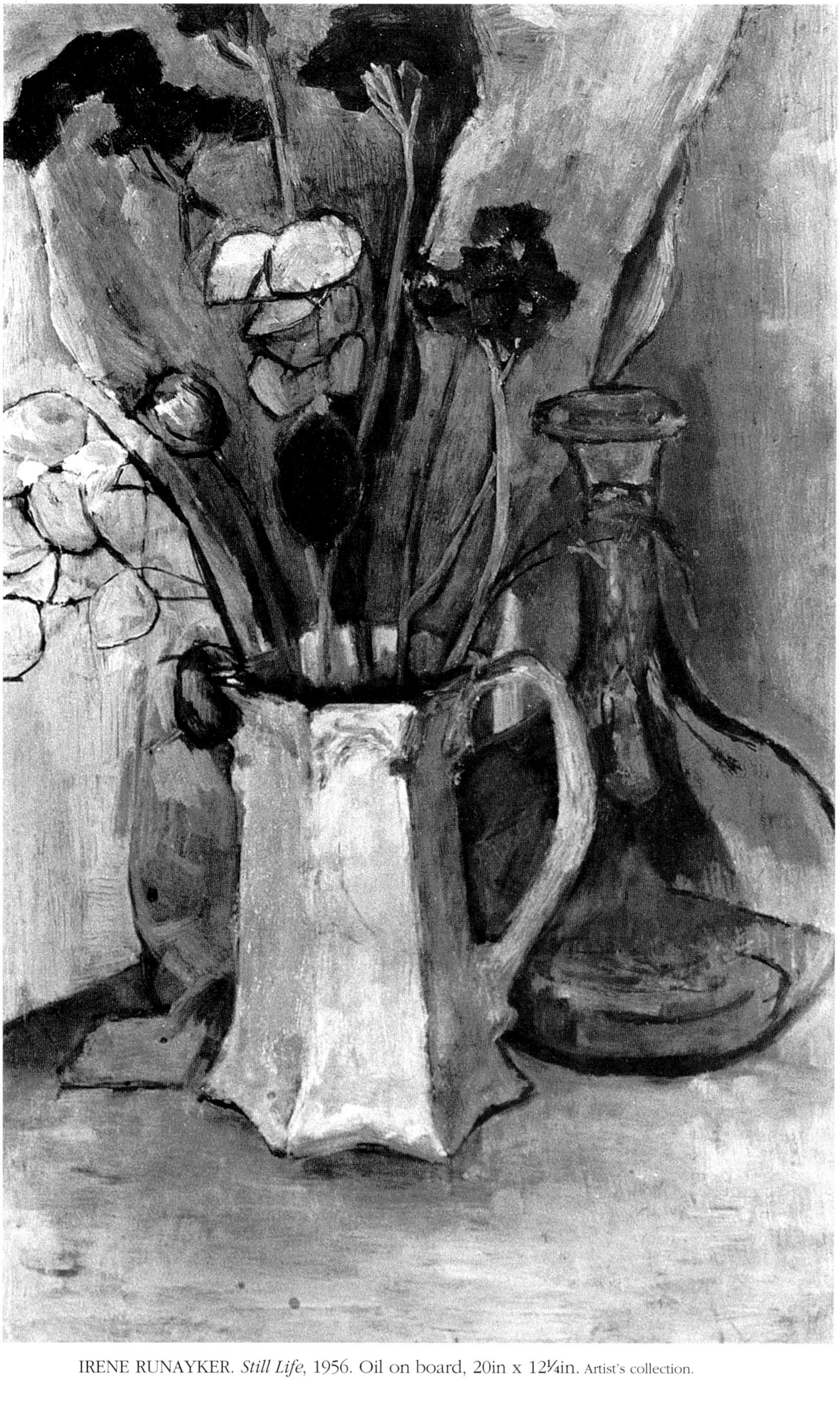

IRENE RUNAYKER. *Still Life*, 1956. Oil on board, 20in x 12¼in. Artist's collection.

collections around the world. These include the Museum of Modern Art (New York), Tate Gallery, V & A, B.M., the Printroom of the Library of Congress (Washington D.C.), Brussels Museum of Fine Art, The National Gallery of Australia, The Arts Council of Great Britain, The Dallas Museum of Fine Art, The Albright Knox Gallery (Buffalo, New York), City Art Gallery (Manchester) and The Smithsonian Institute (Washington D.C.). He was elected A.R.A. in 1977 and a full Member five years later. A *catalogue raisonné* of his prints was published by Scholar Press in 1993, a few weeks before his death, and coincided with a final exhibition of his work at Flowers East Gallery, London.

ROUX, *Jacobus François* (b.1927)
Painter who was born at Fort Victoria, Rhodesia, (now Masvingo, Zimbabwe). In 1943 he spent two years at Stellenbosch Technical College in South Africa studying under Siegfried Hahn. In 1946 he enrolled at Camberwell, spending nearly two years painting and drawing under Rogers* and Coldstream*. He furthered his studies by spending four years at the R.C.A., where his teachers included Philip Connard (1876-1958) and Bernard Fleetwood Walker (1893-1963). He returned to Rhodesia but in 1967 relocated to Cape Town, where he has worked since and taught art privately. He is a member of the South African Association of Arts and has held several solo exhibitions in Rhodesia and his adopted South Africa. He has also taken part in several group exhibitions in England including the Young Contemporaries at the Mall Galleries. His public commissions include several portraits of South African politicians and his work can be seen in the National Gallery in Cape Town.

RUBENS, *Godfrey Stephen* (b.1925)
He was a student at Camberwell 1949-53, where he came into close contact with and was much influenced by Bloch* and Frith*. He has never shown his work, apart from exhibiting in his own studio when he lived in London. In 1972 he was awarded the University of London Leon Fellowship. He has lived for some time in France and he married the artist Panama Hegarty*.

RUHEMANN, *Helmut Moritz* (1891-1973)
Born in Germany, he was taught and influenced by Max Liebermann (1847-1935) and Maurice Denis (1870-1943). From 1911-28 he worked as an artist and a freelance restorer in Berlin and was also, prior to his emigration to England in 1933, the Curator and Chief Picture Restorer for the National Gallery of Germany in Berlin. Soon after his arrival in England, he took the position as a restorer at the National Gallery, London, and his abilities soon became widely known through his important lectures and writings on the restoration and conservation of paintings. He taught techniques of painting at Camberwell for many years during the 1950s.

RUNAYKER, *Irene Rosalind* (b.1937)
Born in London, she spent four years at Camberwell from 1954-58. She then studied for two years at the Central School of Art, where she studied drawing with Merlyn Evans (1910-1973). She taught with the Inner London Education Authority for many years and has exhibited in Galleries at Loch Fyne in Scotland and more recently at the Museum of Modern Art at Gelsenkirchen, Germany. She has also shown at the Morley College Gallery, the Shaw Theatre and at the Orangery in Holland Park. Her work is in the collection of the London Borough of Camden, as well as private collections around the world.

S

SALAMAN, *Michael Jonathan* (1911-1987)
He studied at the Slade School of Fine Art 1928-30 and later at the Ruskin School of Art 1930-31, followed by a short period at the Académie Ranson in Paris. He exhibited regularly at the R.A., with the L.G. and at the Leicester Galleries. A retrospective exhibition of his work was held at the Morley Gallery in 1975. He was first appointed to the staff at Camberwell about 1950 and for the last thirty years of his life taught at several London art schools, including the R.A. and Chelsea. His work is represented in many private and public collections, including the V & A and the South London Art Gallery.

SASH, *Cecily* B.A. (HONS), M.A. (b.1925)
Born in Delmas, Transvaal, South Africa, Sash first studied art at Witwatersrand Technical College in Johannesburg under Maurice van Essche (1906-1977) between 1943-46. In 1948 she first visited England, where she studied at both Chelsea Polytechnic and Camberwell School of Arts, and her only influence was Victor Pasmore*. She returned to South Africa in 1952 for a two year period studying part-time for her Bachelor of Arts at the University of Witwatersrand. She has exhibited her work on an international scale and her group exhibitions have included The South African Academy, The Van Riebeeck Festival, The First and Second South African Quadrennial Exhibition, The São Paulo Biennale, The Grosvenor Gallery (London) and The Venice Biennale. Her one-woman exhibitions have included the South African Association of Arts (Johannesburg), The Lidchi Galleries (Johannesburg and Durban) and the Victoria Art Gallery (Bath). Her work is included in the public collections of the South African National Gallery, The Durban Art Gallery, the University of Natal, King George VI Gallery (Pretoria) and the William Humphreys Gallery (Kimberley).

SAUNDERS, *Peter* (b.1940)
He was a student at Camberwell 1957-61, where he was taught and influenced by R. D. Lee*. He won a Scholarship to the Slade School of Fine Art where he remained until 1964, winning the Slade School Painting Prize in 1963. He joined the staff at Norwich School of Art in 1964 where he remained until 1981. The following year he became a member of staff at the Sir John Cass Faculty of Arts and is still a visiting lecturer there and at the Ruskin School of Painting & Drawing (Oxford), and Newcastle-upon-Tyne University. His work has been shown extensively in group exhibitions including Morley College Gallery, the Castle Museum (Norwich), the Fitzwilliam Museum (Cambridge), Camden Arts Centre, Graves Art Gallery (Sheffield), the R.A., the N.E.A.C., the L.G., the Penwith Gallery (St. Ives), Whitechapel Art Gallery, Museum of Modern Art (Oxford), Leeds City Art Gallery and Wolverhampton Art Gallery. In 1980 he won first prize in the Spirit of London Exhibition at the Festival Hall. He has also had two solo shows during the 1980s at the Air Gallery and at Corpus Christi College (Oxford). His work is in numerous public and private collections, including the Arts Council of Great Britain. His most recent solo exhibition was at the Cadogan Contemporary Gallery in 1990.

SAWYER, *Barbara Joan* (1919-1982)
One of Camberwell's most influential teachers of textiles, she studied at Birmingham College of Art 1937-43. After leaving Birmingham she began her teaching career at Hastings School of Art before moving to Hull in 1945. She joined the staff at Camberwell in 1950, where she was to remain until a short time before her death. In the early 1970s she was also appointed an Associate Lecturer to the Department of Textiles at Camberwell and gave advice and recommendations on the core curriculum for Woven Textiles to the two Heads of Department, Joseph

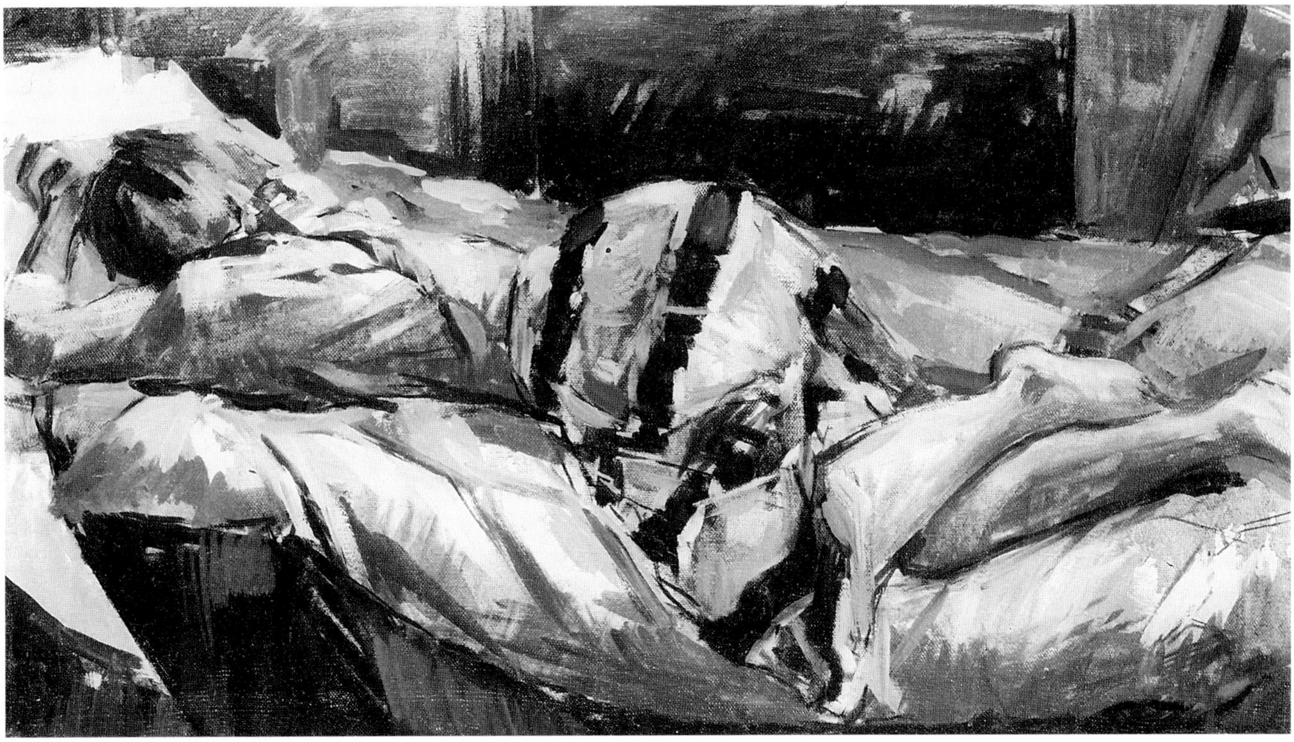

PETER SAUNDERS. *Girl Resting*. Oil on canvas, 12in x 20in. Private collection.

Dixon* and Theo Mendez* who succeeded him. Barbara Sawyer primarily wove mats and wall-hangings, selling them through such prestigious outlets as Heals and Primavera, London. Her work was exhibited around the world through the British Council, Design Centre and the Crafts Council, London. She also showed at the V & A, who hold examples of her work in their permanent collection.

(The author is indebted to Holburne Museum and Crafts Study Centre, Bath, for supplying information from their archive.)

SCALES, *Terence* (b.1932)

He was a student at Camberwell 1946-52, during which time he was most influenced by Bloch*. He has exhibited his work widely, including the I.C.A., Morley Gallery, Ikon Gallery (Birmingham), Whitechapel Open Exhibition, Camden Arts Centre, Campbell & Franks, 'Spirit of London' at the Royal Festival Hall, R.A. Summer Exhibitions and the Rheinikendorf Gallery (Berlin). In 1960 he joined the staff at Camberwell as a visiting lecturer, where he has since remained. He has also taught at the Byam Shaw School of Fine Art for many years.

SCANNELL, *Josephine Elspeth* N.D.D. (*née* Higson) (b.1925)

She was at Camberwell 1946-48, where she was influenced by Coldstream*, Gowing* and Rogers*. She exhibited her work extensively during the late 1940s and early '50s at the L.G. and the Leeds & Bradford Arts Society. She taught at Leeds School of Art for several years during the 1950s but unfortunately most of her work from this period was lost when her studio caught fire. She has recently begun painting again and her work has been hung in the R.A.

SCOTT, *Gordon Noel* A.R.C.A. (b.1914)

He studied art at the R.C.A. between 1934-38 under Gilbert Spencer*, Alan Sorrell (1904-1977) and Charles Mahoney (1903-1968). In 1938 he was awarded a Travelling Scholarship by the R.C.A. for painting. After the war in 1946 he joined the staff at Camberwell, where he remained until his retirement in 1980. He has exhibited his work at the R.A., the L.G., the Mall Galleries, Russell-Cotes Art Gallery and Museum, Bournemouth and during the late 1940s at the Cooling Gallery. He has also shown his work on occasions at the R.P.

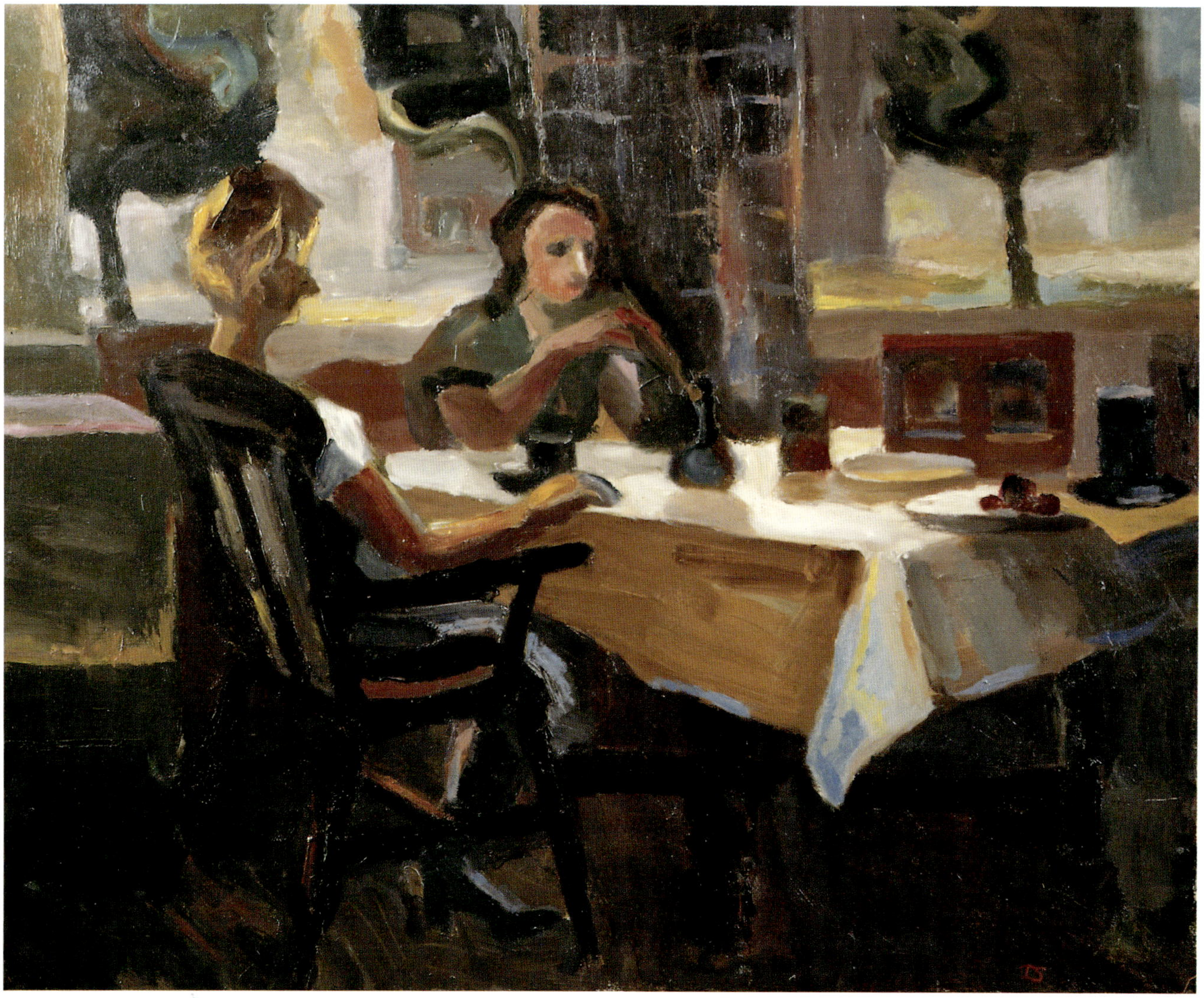

TERENCE SCALES. *Conversation Piece – Prefab interior, Bermondsey*, 1960. Oil on canvas, 25in x 30in. Courtesy of Mr and Mrs James Mair.

SCOTT, *Hilda Elizabeth* (b.1927)
During the war as an evacuee she first began her art studies at the Northampton School of Art. By 1943, on her return to London, she became a student at Camberwell where for the next two years she was greatly influenced by Ayrton*, Minton* and Pasmore*. By the end of the 1940s she was exhibiting frequently with the L.G. and at this time she also began teaching at the West of England College of Art at Bristol. She was also exhibiting at the R.W.A. before the onset of her family caused her to all but abandon her artistic career. However, in more recent years she has recommenced painting. She is married to the artist and sculptor, Richard Sladden.

SEABROOKE, *Elliott* L.G. (1886-1950)
He attended the Slade School of Fine Art from 1906-11 and, during this period, was greatly influenced by Roger Fry's first Post-Impressionist Exhibition at the Grafton Galleries in 1910. He first exhibited his work as early as 1911 at the N.E.A.C. alongside his friends and contemporaries Mark Gertler (1891-1939) and William Roberts (1895-1980). The following year he held his first one-man exhibition at the Carfax Gallery. During the First World War, he was appointed an Official War Artist on the Italian Front. He was one of the first members of the L.G. during its formative years, immediately after the First World War. By the 1940s, his work had gradually

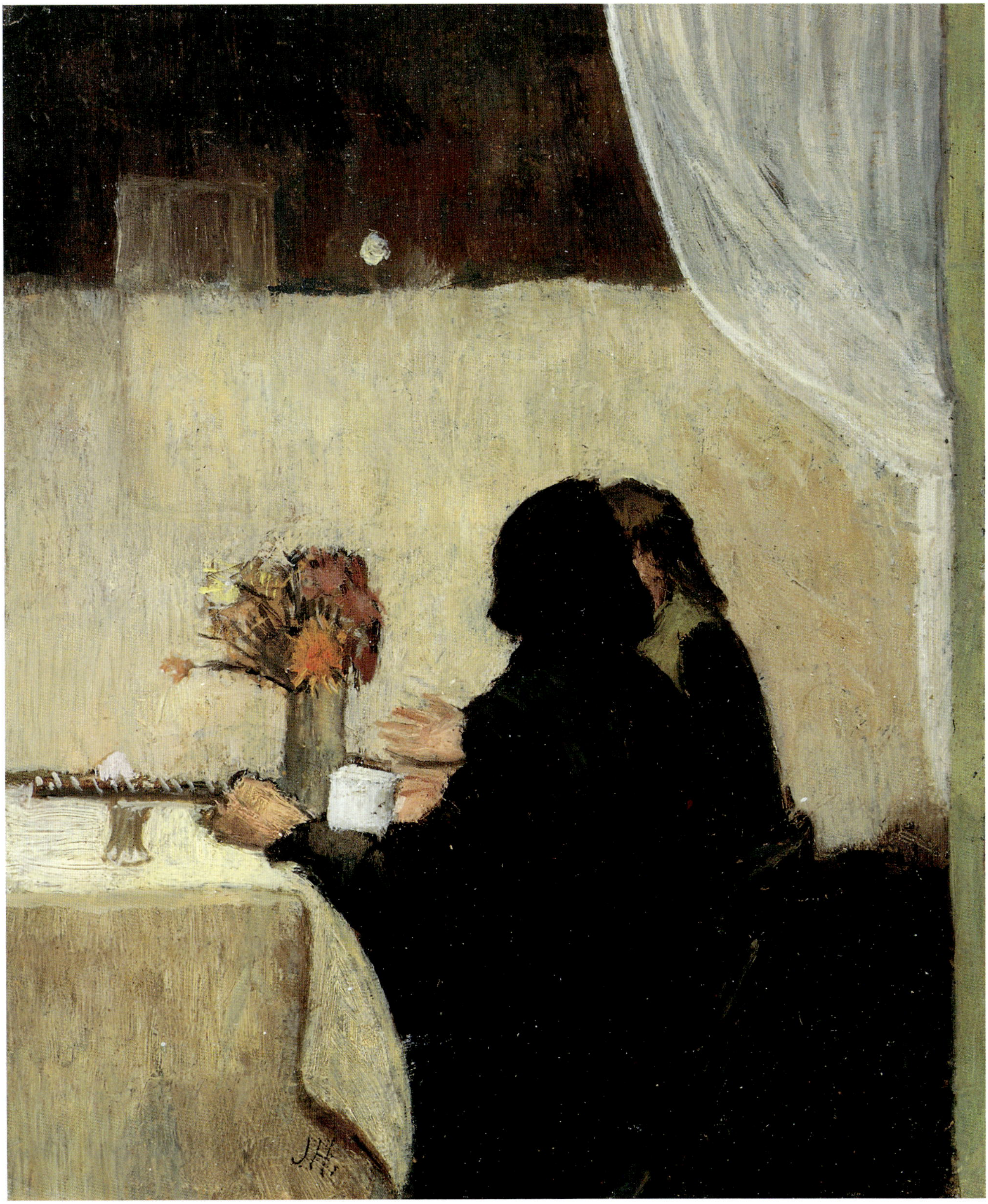

JO SCANNELL (*née* Higson). *The Cafe.* Oil on board, 6in x 5in. Private collection.

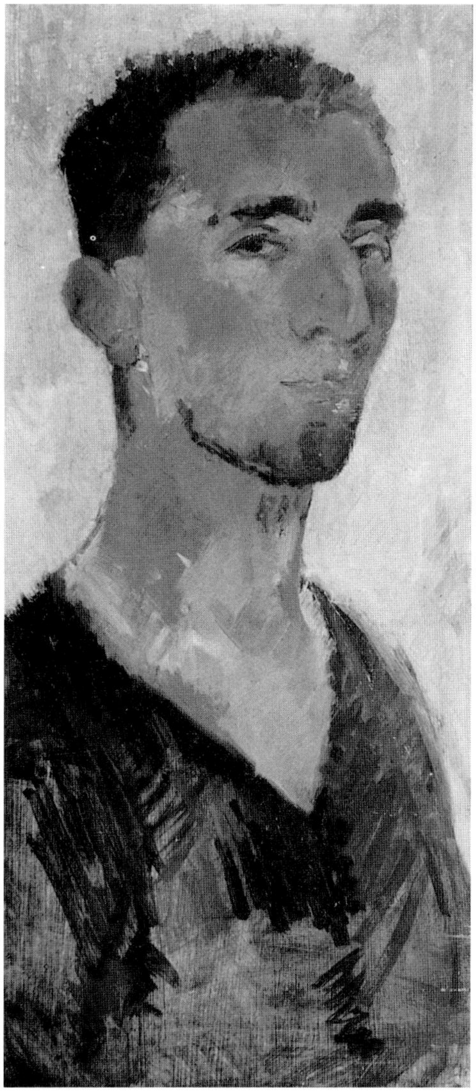

HERMON SHAPIRO. *Self Portrait.* Oil on board, 27in x 12in. Artist's collection.

changed from a technique originally developed from Cézanne through to a Pointillist technique, eventually becoming more and more abstract. He was elected as President of the L.G. in 1943, a position he held for the next five years. He joined the staff at Camberwell as a visiting lecturer in 1946 and was to remain there for almost the rest of his life. In 1949 he was commissioned for an exhibition by the Leicester Galleries and in March 1950, whilst in the South of France painting for this exhibition, he died suddenly. His memorial exhibition was held the following year at the Leicester Galleries and retrospectives were held at the Matthiesen Gallery and Leeds City Art Gallery during the 1950s and '60s. His work is represented in public collections, including the Tate Gallery.

SEWELL, *Jane Seymour see* HUGHES, *Jane Seymour*

SHAPIRO, *Barbara Anne* (*née* Liedtke) (1927-1969)
As a student for four years from 1950 she was taught and greatly influenced by Ardizzone*, Bloch* and Buckland-Wright* She only painted for a brief period after leaving Camberwell. She married the artist Hermon Shapiro*.

SHAPIRO, *Hermon* N.D.D. (b.1933)
He was a student from 1946-54, where he was taught and greatly influenced by Bloch*, Minton* and Vaughan*. By the mid-1950s he had begun a career as an art teacher in local schools in South Wales and during the early 1960s he lectured at Cardiff College of Art. He has shown his work widely, including Young Welsh Artists (1959), the Royal Cambrian Academy, R.W.A., Contemporary Arts Society for Wales, Piccadilly Gallery, London; and the Howard Roberts Gallery (Cardiff). His work is in the permanent collections of the Welsh Arts Council, National Museum of Wales and various Educational Authorities in England and Wales, as well as private collections in the U.K. and Europe.

SHEARER, *Vernon Brodie* (1916-1987)
He first studied at Blackburn School of Art, before winning a scholarship to the R.C.A. in the years immediately following the Second World War. He was chosen to paint murals for the Festival of Britain in 1951 and became well-known in the fields of book-binding, calligraphy and printing. He joined the staff at Camberwell in 1947 to teach Lettering and Illuminating and in 1964 was appointed Head of Graphic Design, a position he was to hold for the next twelve years.

SHEPPARD, *Christina Clare* (b.1932)
The daughter of Sydney Sheppard*, she studied illustration at Camberwell from 1951-53. Her teachers at this time included Ardizzone* and Buckland Wright*, who were her greatest influences during her early years. She was a freelance children's book illustrator for the publishers Faber & Faber and designed pottery before establishing her own ceramic tile business in 1964. In 1985 she moved to Spain where she began to paint in oils, returning to England in 1990. She has exhibited her work at the Design Centre, the Craftsmen Potters' Association and recently in her exhibition '1000 Years of Tiles' organised by the Arts Council as a travelling exhibition. Examples of her work are in the permanent colleciton of the V. & A.

SHEPPARD, *Stephen Horace James* (1922-1985)
Following war service he commenced his studies at L'Ecole des Beaux Arts in Paris

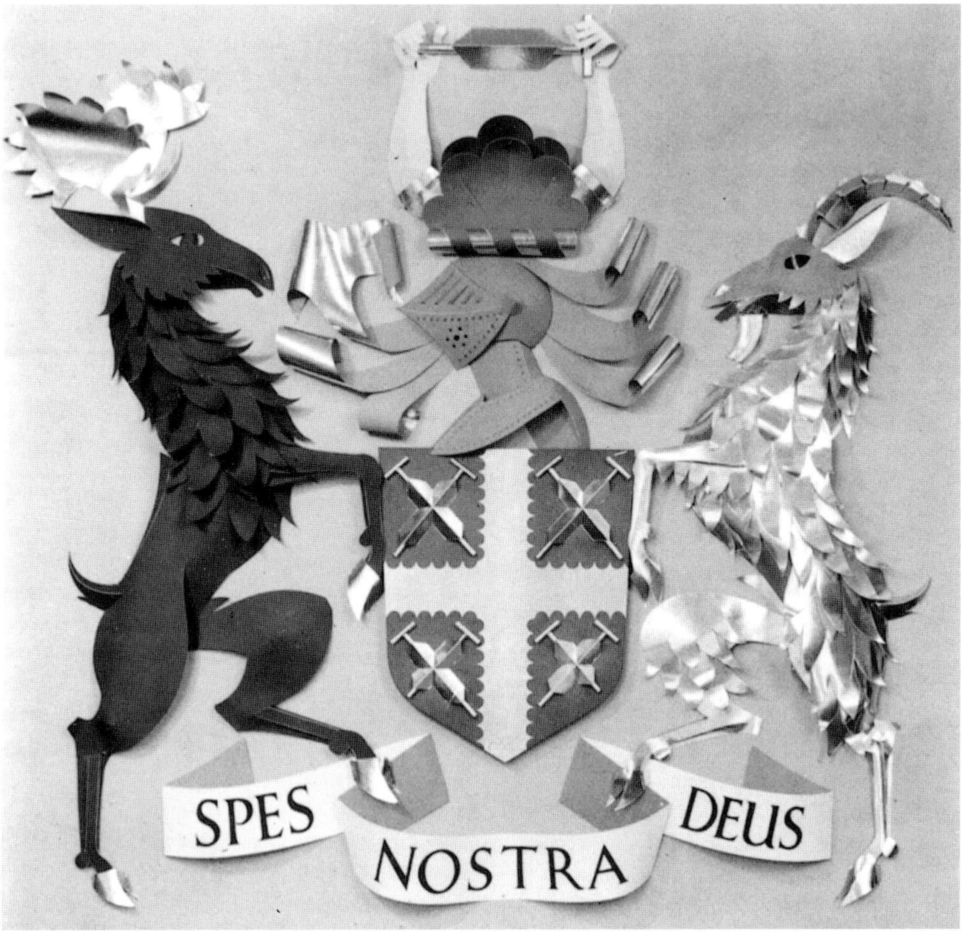

VERNON SHEARER. Arms of the Curriers' Company. Paper, card, silver and gold foil.

from 1946-48. He returned to England and furthered his studies at Camberwell, where he remained until 1952. He had one-man exhibitions at galleries in Kent where he lived and in France, a country that he made his second home, at Galerie Gigondas and Galerie M. L. (Paris). He also exhibited in a number of leading exhibitions including the L.G., John Moores and the New Grafton Gallery. He was commissioned to paint a large mural at Queen Elizabeth Hospital, Woolwich, in 1980.

SHEPPARD, *Sydney Herbert* (1905-1991)
Born in Cairo, the son of a railway engineer, he was educated at Marlborough and then at the Slade School, where he studied painting under Henry Tonks (1862-1937) during the late 1920s. He left England to further his studies in France at the Atelier of André L'Hôte (1885-1962), where he was also befriended by the sculptor Aristide Maillol (1861-1944), who in no small degree was influential in raising Sheppard's awareness of sculpture. During the 1930s he was studio assistant to Frank Dobson (1886-1963) and after the war, in 1946, he joined the staff at Camberwell. By 1951 he had become a full-time lecturer, working alongside Karel Vogel* for many years. Most of his sculpture work was commissioned but he continued to paint all his adult life. He only rarely showed his painting at the L.G. during the 1930s, but a retrospective exhibition of his paintings was held at the Sally Hunter Gallery, London in 1994.

SHIELDS, *Mary Orde see* LAUGHTON, *Mary Orde*

SIDONIO, *Betty Elizabeth* (b.circa 1928)
She was a student at Camberwell from 1946-49 and was strongly influenced by the Euston Road painters. She did not begin exhibiting until the late 1970s and since then has shown her work with Campbell and Franks and at the Woodland Art Gallery (Blackheath). Her work has also been shown extensively abroad, including Yugoslavia, Germany and Italy.

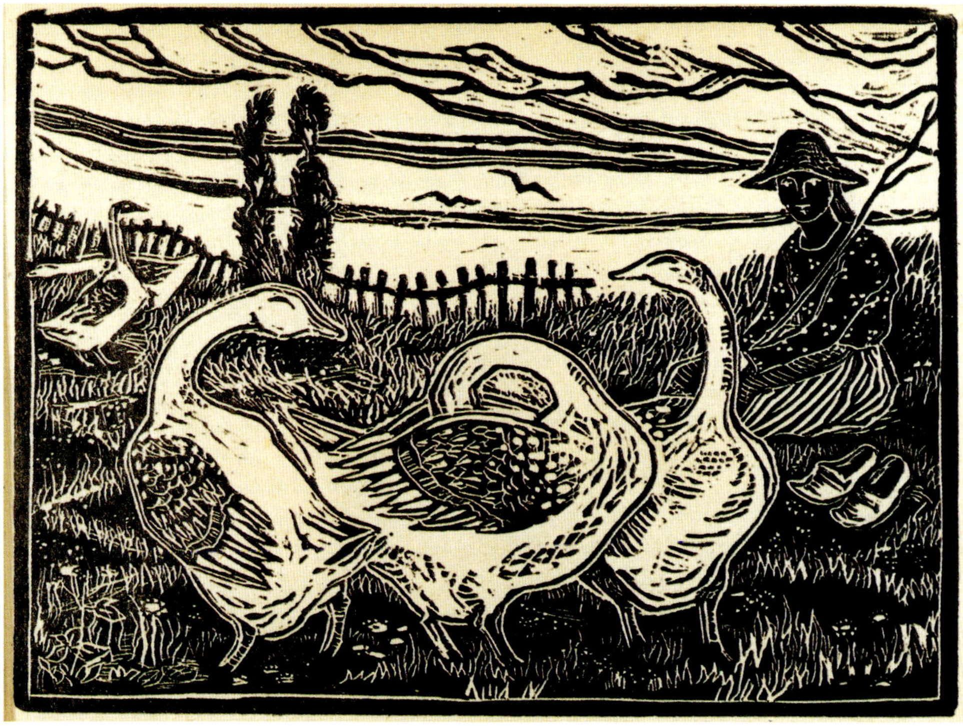

CHRISTINA SHEPPARD. Wood engraving, 3in x 4in. Artist's collection.

SMEDLEY, *Geoffrey* (b.1927)
His art education began when he joined Camberwell in 1948, where he remained for the next four years. In 1952 he won a scholarship to the Slade School of Fine Art, where he completed his art education in 1956. He began showing his work seriously in 1957 and held numerous one-man exhibitions in Portsmouth, Southampton and Worthing City Art Galleries during this period. He has also shown his work in numerous A.I.A. exhibitions and at Cardiff City Art Gallery, Grosvenor Gallery, the Arts Council of Great Britain, Arnolfini Gallery (Bristol), Reading Art Gallery and the R.A. Summer Exhibitions. In 1964 he was appointed Head of Sculpture at Portsmouth Polytechnic, where he remained until the late 1970s when he was appointed Professor of Sculpture at the University of British Columbia, Vancouver, Canada. He has participated in numerous exhibitions in Canada, including the Royal Canadian Academy Exhibition and his first one-man exhibition was held in Vancouver Art Gallery in 1982. He is now a Canadian citizen and spends his time lecturing, writing and painting.

SMITH, *Denis Kennedy* (b.1923)
He was a student at Camberwell 1952-56, having previously had some art lessons under Carel Weight (b.1908) and Henry Carr (1894-1970) at Beckenham School of Art. At Camberwell he was most inspired by Frith*, who was to become a close friend. He showed his work quite regularly at the Guildhall Exhibitions and, during the 1960s and 1970s, occasionally at various galleries in the north Kent and Medway regions.

SNOWDEN, *Michael Alan* R.S.A. (b.1930)
He began his studies at Camberwell in 1953, where Bloch* and Vogel* were his main teachers and influences. He was to remain there until 1962, by which time he had spent six years teaching in the Sculpture School. In 1964 he joined the staff of Edinburgh College of Art where to date he still teaches sculpture. His one-man exhibitions include the Leicester Galleries, Bruton Gallery (Somerset) and the English Speaking Union (Edinburgh). His public commissions include work for Southwark Cathedral, Livingston New Town (West Lothian) and the Royal Bank of Scotland Fountain for the Glasgow Garden Festival of 1987-88.

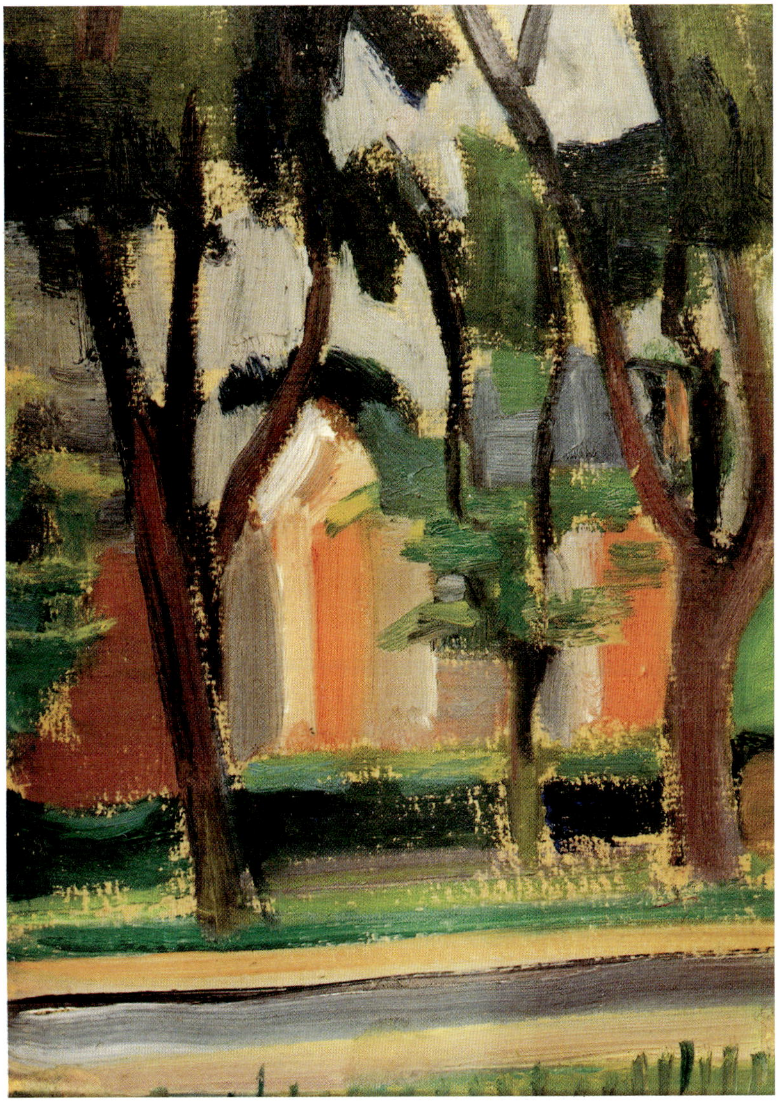

SYDNEY SHEPPARD. *Bois de Boulogne.* Oil on board, 8¼in x 6in. Courtesy of Christina Sheppard.

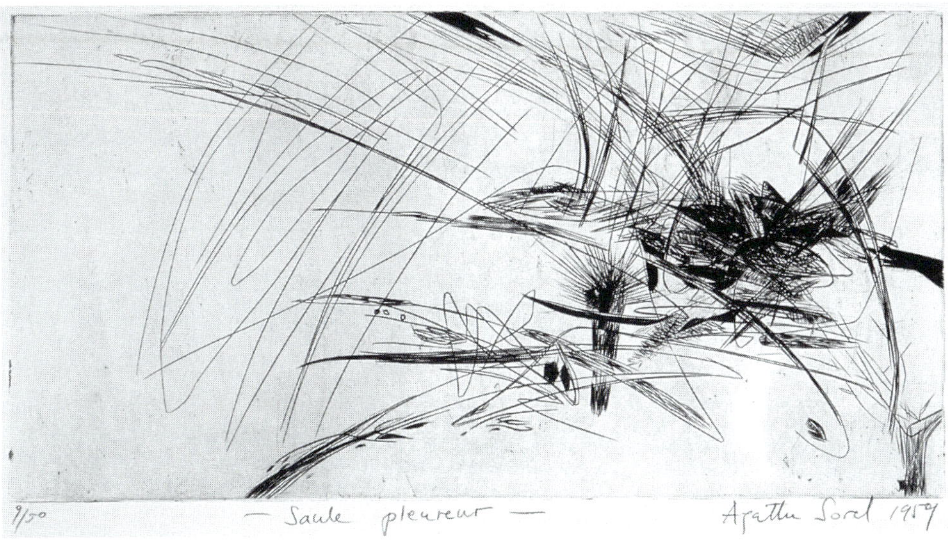

AGATHE SOREL. *Saule Pleurer,* 1959. Line engraving, 7½in x 14in. Artist's collection.

SOMERVILLE, *Jennifer see* KELLY, *Jennifer*

SOREL, *Agathe* (b.1935)
She came to England from her native Hungary in 1956, having already attended the Academy of Fine Arts in Budapest. She spent two years at Camberwell under the tuition of Michael Rothenstein*, Frank Martin* and, for a short period, Robert Medley*. In 1958 she spent two years in Paris as a student of Stanley Hayter (1901-1988) at 'Atelier 17', having won a Gulbenkian Scholarship. She was also awarded a Churchill Fellowship in 1966-67 enabling her to work and travel in the U.S.A. and Mexico. She was a founder member of the Printmakers' Council and its Chairwoman from 1981-83. She has held numerous one-woman shows, including the Curwen Gallery (London), Arleigh Gallery (San Francisco), Ben Uri Gallery (London), Old Jaffa Gallery (Tel Aviv), de Vorzon Gallery (Los Angeles) and her work is in public collections throughout the world, including the Tate Gallery, V & A, Arts Council of Great Britain, B.M., R.C.A., South London Art Gallery, New York Public Library, Museum of Fine Art (Philadelphia), Smithsonian Institute (Washington D.C.), Boston Museum of Fine Arts and the Los Angeles Museum of Art. She is currently a visiting lecturer at Camberwell School of Arts & Crafts.

SOUTH, *Lesley* (b.1931)
At the age of fifteen she became a sculpture student at Portsmouth College of Art, where she remained for five years, later spending a year at Bournemouth where she studied art teacher training. She joined Camberwell as a post-graduate sculpture student in 1952. Within a little over a year her great friend and mentor, Karel Vogel*, had appointed her as a teacher, her particular forté being stone and wood-carving. She rarely exhibits because most of her work is for local authorities and private commissions. However, she has shown at the R.A. during the 1950s. Since leaving Camberwell she has taught occasionally at art schools which include Bristol and Cheltenham. She married the sculptor, Peter Strong*.

SOUTHALL, *Derek* (b.1930)
He studied at Camberwell 1949-51, where his main influences were Bloch* and Eurich*. In 1954 he spent a semester in Berlin with Bloch's friend and colleague Karl Schmidt-Rottluff (1884-1976). His group exhibitions have included the Museum of Modern Art (Oxford), Axiom Gallery (London), Arts Council of Great Britain, Rowan Gallery (London), Museum of Modern Art (Oxford), The Herbert Art Gallery (Coventry), the University of Warwick, The Columbia Museum of Art (Ohio), Newcastle Polytechnic Gallery, Arnolfini Gallery (Bristol), and Nicola Jacobs Gallery (London). A film of his work has been made by B.B.C. Television and he has written a suite of poems, *Small Writings*, which is now housed in the British Collection at Yale University. His work is in private and public collections, including the Tate Gallery, The Contemporary Arts Society, Arts Council of Great Britain, The Herbert Art Gallery (Coventry), New York University, I.C.A. (London), the Contemporary Arts Society of Wales, Museum of Modern Art (Oxford) and the Victoria Museum (Bath). He held a solo exhibition at the Victoria Museum, Bath at the begining of 1993.

SPENCER, *Gilbert* R.A., R.W.S., N.E.A.C., I.S. (1892-1979)
The younger brother of Sir Stanley Spencer, R.A. (1891-1959), he first studied at Camberwell as a pupil 1910-11. He later went to the R.C.A. and completed his art training at the Slade School of Fine Art under Brown (1851-1941) and Tonks (1862-1937) in the years immediately following the First World War. He was appointed a member of the N.E.A.C. in 1919 and in 1923 had his first one-man show at the

Goupil Gallery. Three years later he was to again exhibit at the Goupil Gallery, together with Mark Gertler (1891-1939) and John Nash (1893-1977). During the late 1920s his abilities as an illustrator became widely known by his work for *Three Things* by W. B. Yeats. He was appointed Professor of Painting at the R.C.A. in 1932, a position which he was to hold for the next sixteen years. In 1948 he went to Glasgow School of Art and he joined the staff at Camberwell in 1950 as Head of the Painting Department until his retirement in 1957. His work is represented in private and public collections, including the Chantrey Bequest, Reading Museum & Art Gallery, Tate Gallery, Imperial War Museum and Leeds City Art Galleries. His autobiography, *Memoirs of a Painter*, was published by Chatto & Windus in 1974. A retrospective exhibition was held at the Fine Arts Society (London) in 1974.

SPENCER, *John Edward* N.D.D. (b.1928)
After a twelve month period at the Regent Street Polytechnic studying sculpture, he became a full-time painting student at Camberwell in 1949, where his teachers and influences were Ardizzone*, Eurich*, and Symons*. He exhibited in numerous group exhibitions during the early and mid-1950s, including the South London Art Gallery, L.G., R.A., New Burlington Galleries and the Whitechapel Art Gallery. His first one-man exhibition was at the Portal Gallery in March 1964, which contained original icons fashioned from antique iron locks involving a combination of painting, wood-carving and metalwork. In 1965 he moved to Mexico, where he now resides and works.

SPOTTISWOOD, *Elspeth* (b.1926)
Educated in Scotland, she joined Camberwell School of Art in 1946 where she remained for the following two years. By her own admission, she took no active part in the life of the School and was extremely shy, even to the point of embarrassment when Pasmore* and Johnstone* would attempt to look at a drawing. By 1948 she had left Camberwell and for twelve months attended the Anglo-French Art School in St. John's Wood. Her teachers included Minton*, and Eduardo Paolozzi (b.1924). It was also during this time that her first encounter with Cornwall and St. Ives took place. In the ensuing years, she frequently visited Cornwall, spending longer and longer periods there. By the early 1950s, after she had left the Anglo-French Art School, she met by chance Oskar Kokoschka (1886-1980), who greatly influenced her thinking artistically. By the mid-1950s she had met and befriended the late Patrick Hayman (1915-1987), an artist who was already by then living in Cornwall and she was instrumental in contributing many articles to the magazine he edited – *The Painter and Sculptor*. She eventually settled in Cornwall by the end of the 1950s and was to remain there for nearly thirty years. She has exhibited her work widely and has taken part in both group exhibitions and one-woman shows at the Sail Loft Gallery, Woodstock Gallery, Dartington Hall; Falmouth Art Gallery and her work is represented in the collection of the Cornish County Authorities.

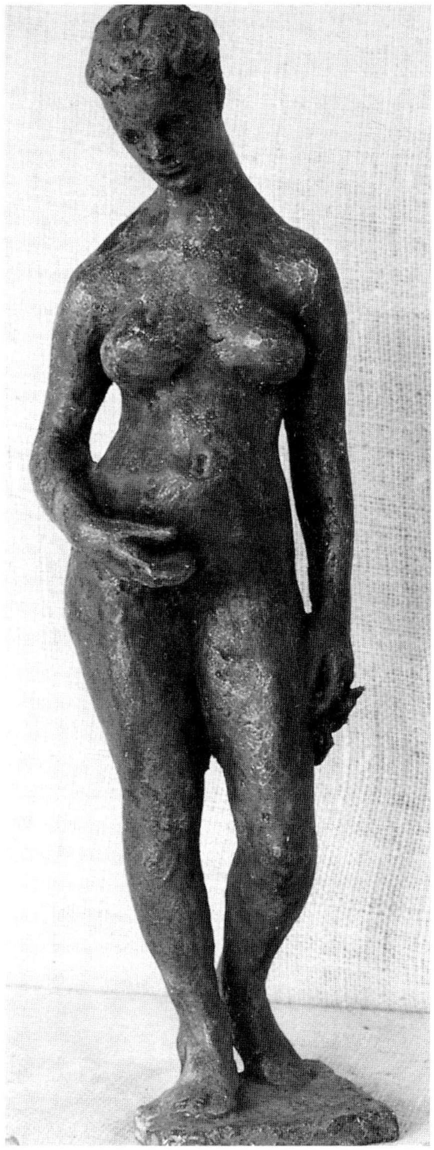

LESLEY SOUTH. *Helena*, 1954. Bronze, 11in high.
Private collection.

SPRING, *Jerome Charles* (b.1929)
Although commencing his art studies as a painter, he soon changed direction and was taught by Dennis Young, the furniture designer. Spring had two periods of study at Camberwell, 1945-47 and following his National Service in 1949-52. He then continued his studies at the R.C.A. and has followed a career in designing for industry and commerce from 1956. He has also taught in adult education from the

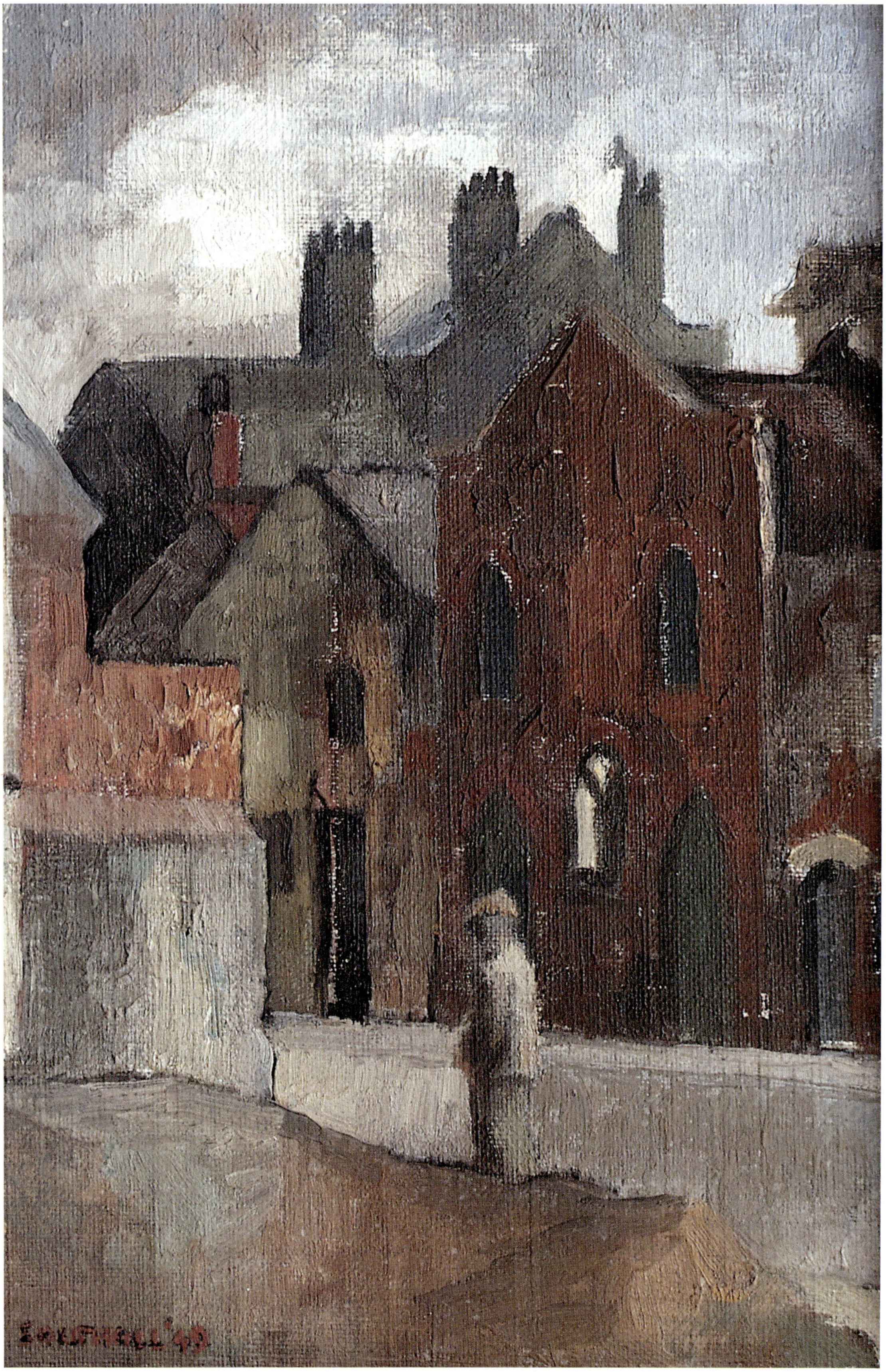

DEREK SOUTHALL. *A London Street*, 1949. Oil on board, 11in x 7in. Artist's collection.

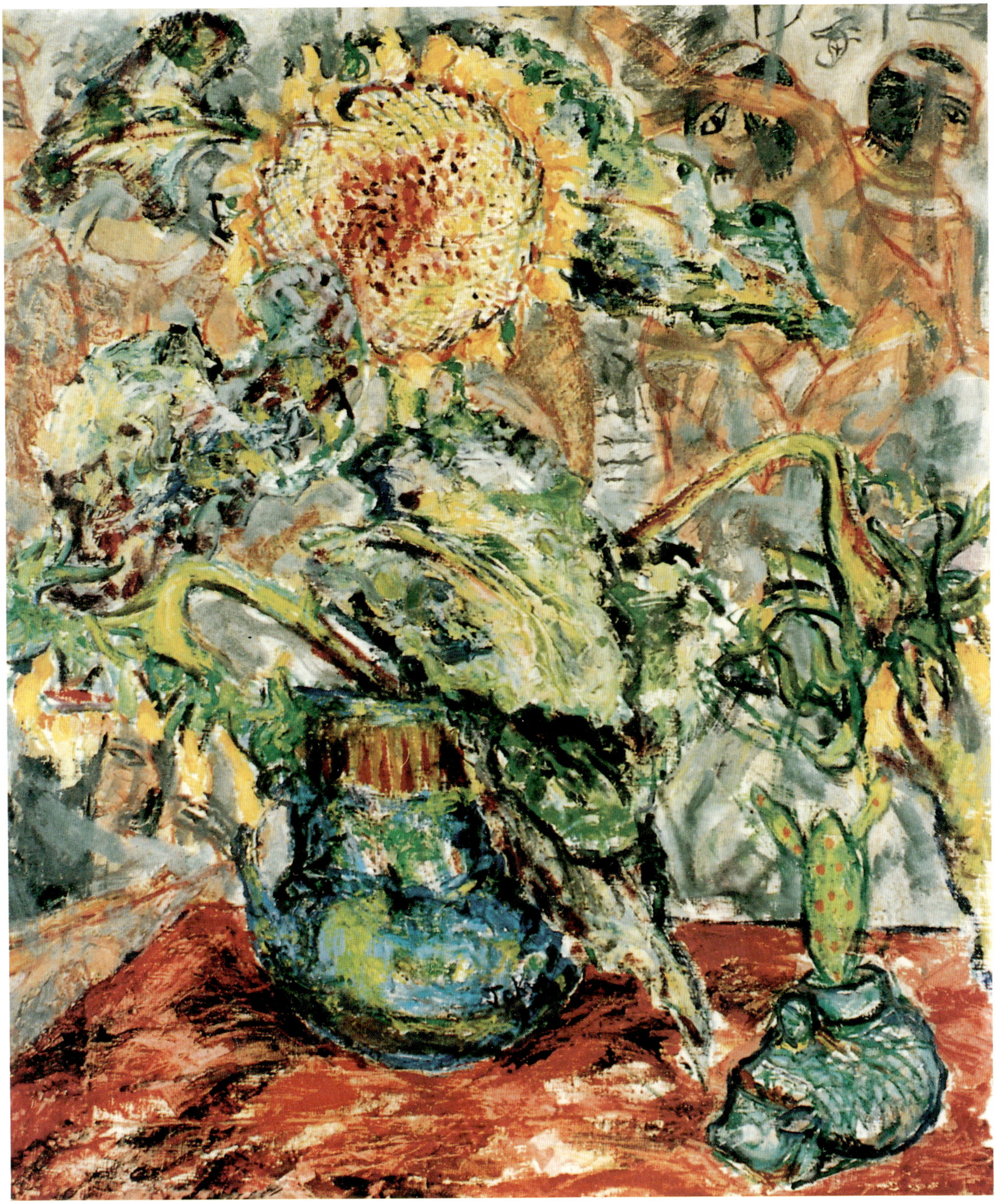

JOHN SPENCER. *Still Life with Cactus*, 1951. Oil on canvas, 29in x 24in. Courtesy of Anne Crews.

early 1970s and more recently has recommenced painting. According to his peers, he was the leading light in the production of revues for student parties.

STEEMSONNE, *Gloria Jean* (b.1944)
She enrolled at Camberwell in 1960 and was to remain there for the next four years. Her personal tutors included Fry* and Salaman* during this period. She furthered her artistic education at Byam Shaw School of Art and the R.A. Schools, before winning a French Government Scholarship enabling her to spend 1968-1969 in Provence. She taught Design at the English National Opera Company during the early 1970s and has also worked professionally as an art therapist. She has exhibited widely, including shows at the South London Art Gallery and at the Birmingham Museum & Art Gallery.

STOODLEY, *Peter* (b.1920)
Born in Bournemouth, Stoodley trained in painting at Bournemouth and Goldsmiths' Schools of Art, 1946-47. He took pottery and bookbinding as craft subjects at Camberwell, where Jacob Drew* taught him from 1947-48. He started a pottery centre at Barnet, Herts., which lasted about two years. In the early 1950s he worked at Poole Pottery, before beginning a teaching career at Bournemouth College of Art lasting until his retirement in 1980. In the 1950s he began making plant pots and has continued ever since. His major exhibitions include shows at the V & A; Suffolk Crafts Society, Aldeburgh; Terrace Gallery, Worthing; Craftsmen Potters' Association and at the Bohun Gallery, Henley-on-Thames.

STRONG, *Peter* (b.1932)
He originally studied Law, followed by National Service in the Royal Navy. He worked for two years as an assistant to Edward Payne (1906-1991), the stained glass designer in the Cotswolds. In 1958 he furthered his studies at Camberwell where he was particularly interested in wood-carving. Since leaving Camberwell in 1964, he has worked on various commissions which have included the decorating of concrete finishes for new buildings, mosaic and glass designs and repairs on roundels in Gloucester Cathedral. Other aspects of his career have included freelance stained glass designs and mural painting of both a secular and ecclesiastical nature. He married the sculptor Lesley South*.

STUBBING, *Newton Haydn* (Tony) (1921-1983)
After active war service he joined Camberwell in 1947, where the Principal William Johnstone* and Victor Pasmore* had the most influence on his painting. Within a year, he went to live in Spain and continued his study of painting in his fortunate appointment as one of the copyists at the Prado, the exercise sharpening his understanding of the techniques of the Old Masters. In 1949 he became a founder member of the School of Altamira, and his work veered towards the Abstract Expressionists' concepts of the period. He remained in Spain until 1954 when he took up residence in Paris. To pay his way, he worked on numerous commissions for theatre and ballet, and by the early 1960s his work was being shown in London and New York. His work is in public and private collections throughout the world, including the Museum of Contemporary Art (Madrid), Museum of Modern Art (New York), the Chase Manhattan Bank (New York and London), the Tate Gallery and the International Art Archives of France.

SUMNER, *Judith Mary* (*née* Holman) (b.1928)
She attended Camberwell 1943-48, where she was taught by Ayrton*, Gowing*, Minton* and Vernon Shearer*. Her work was never shown until the 1970s when she had a one-woman exhibition in Maine (U.S.A.). Very many famous portraits of her

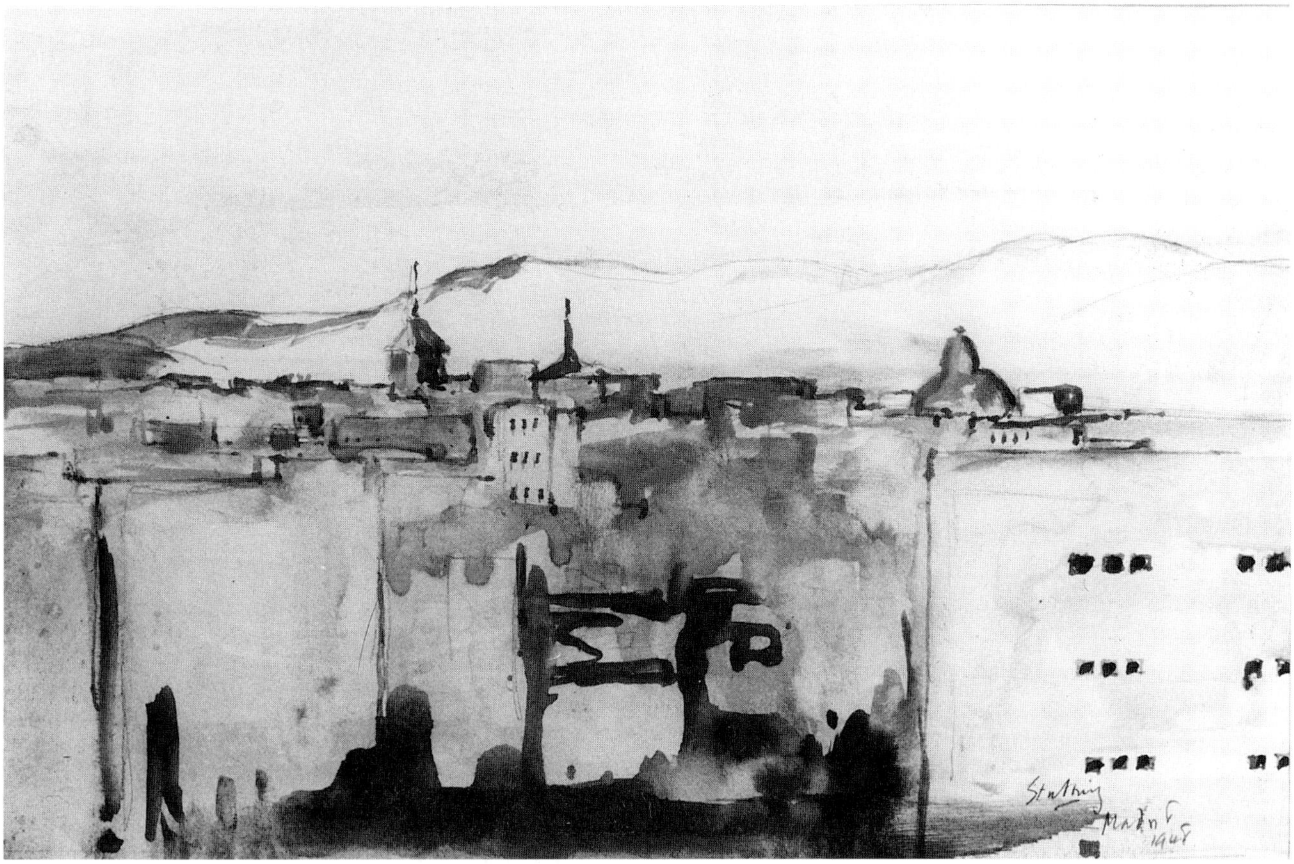

NEWTON HAYDN STUBBING. *Cityscape*, 1948 (inscribed 'Madrid'). Watercolour, 5½in x 8¼in. Private collection.

exist as during her time at Camberwell she was a popular model for the senior lecturers; amongst the most well-known being 'Judith at Sixteen' by Lawrence Gowing*, in the collection of the Royal Albert Memorial Museum (Exeter).

SUNSHINE *Monty* (b.1928)

He first became a student at Camberwell in the war years of 1942-45. Following his National Service he rejoined as a mature student, where he remained until 1951. He was taught and befriended by Minton* and Pasmore*, who were his only influences. In the early 1950s he joined Chris Barber's Jazz band and became the group's clarinet star. By the early 1960s he had formed his own band playing New Orleans style jazz and has consistently toured all over Europe.

SWAN, *Neville James* (b.1931)

Student at Camberwell 1957-60. His main teachers and influences were Dixon*, R. D. Lee*, Frank Martin* and Medley*. He showed his work in several group exhibitions in the early 1960s and had his first one-man show at the Rimmel Gallery, St. Johns Wood, in 1965. Shortly after he left England to teach in Greece, where he now lives. He also had a one-man exhibition at the Campion School, Athens in 1977.

SYMONS, *Patrick Stewart* R.A. (1925-1993)

Born in Bromley, Kent, he was educated at Bryanston in Dorset, a county in which he was later to spend may years working. He attended Camberwell 1946-50, where his main teachers and influences were Dodgson*, Kenneth Martin* and Rogers*. In 1953 he returned to Camberwell as a tutor, starting with his friend and colleague, R. D. Lee*, by teaching an amateur evening class, but he was soon appointed to teach Intermediate Drawing, a position he held until 1961. During this period he also taught at St. Albans School of Art and Chelsea School of Art, where he went on to

ELSPETH SPOTTISWOOD.
Polperro Harbour, 1950.
Oil on canvas, 16in x 11in.
Courtesy of Mr and Mrs R. Sansom.

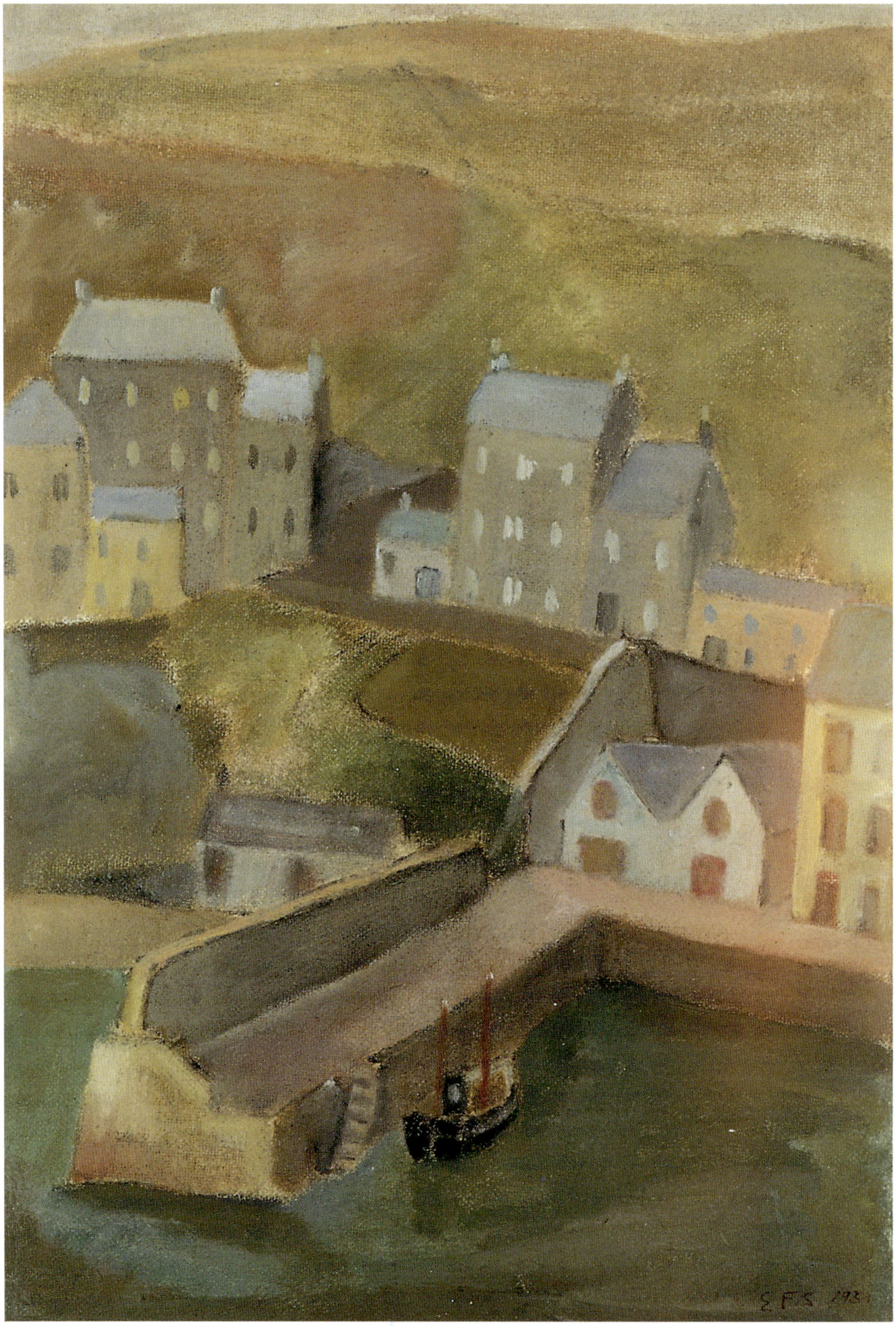

run the foundation course. He showed his work extensively and his early exhibitions included the L.G. and John Moores Exhibition. His first one-man exhibition was held in 1960 at the New Arts Centre. He was elected an Associate of the R.A. in 1983 and a full Member in 1991. He exhibited regularly at Browse & Darby, Cork Street, London. His untimely death in a road accident in Paris ocurred while he was accompanying a group of students on a visit to the Barnes Collection at the Musée d'Orsay. Examples of his work are in the collections of the Arts Council, Contemporary Arts Society and the Tate Gallery.

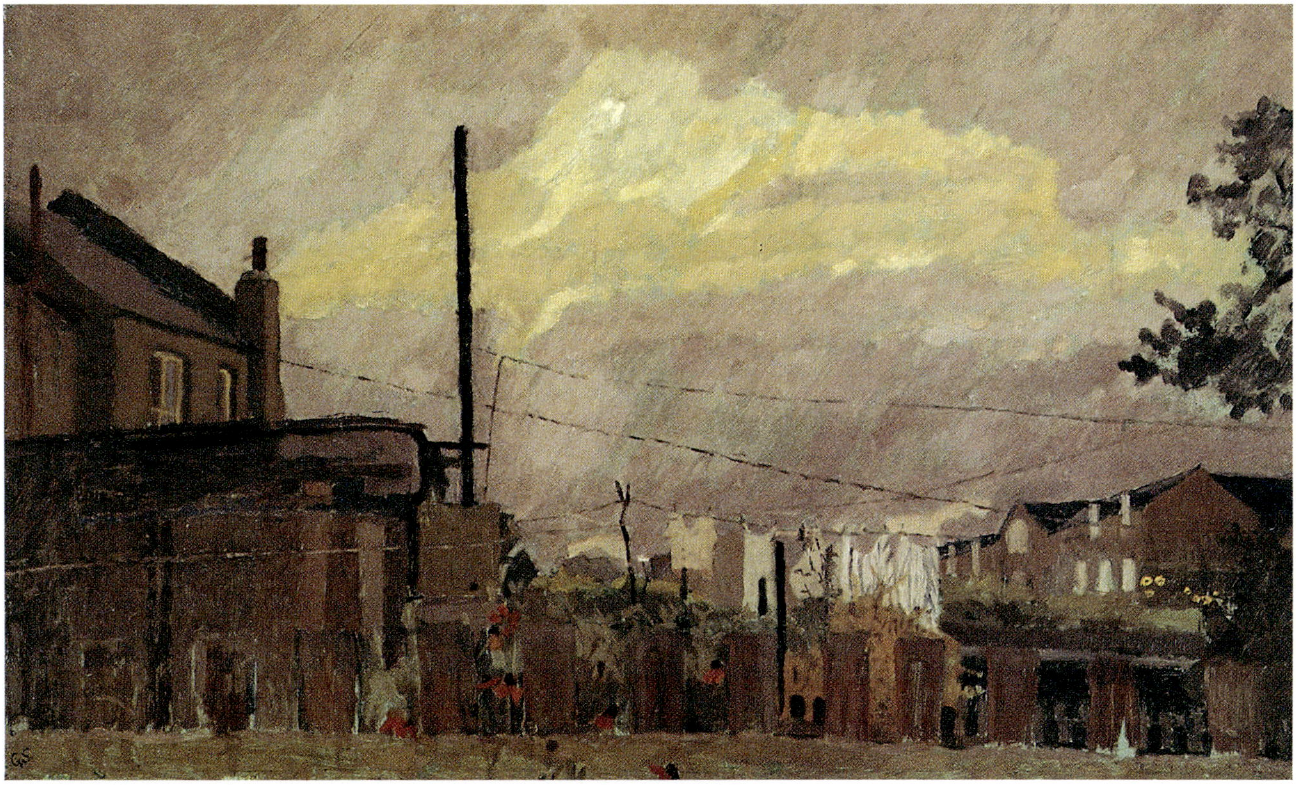

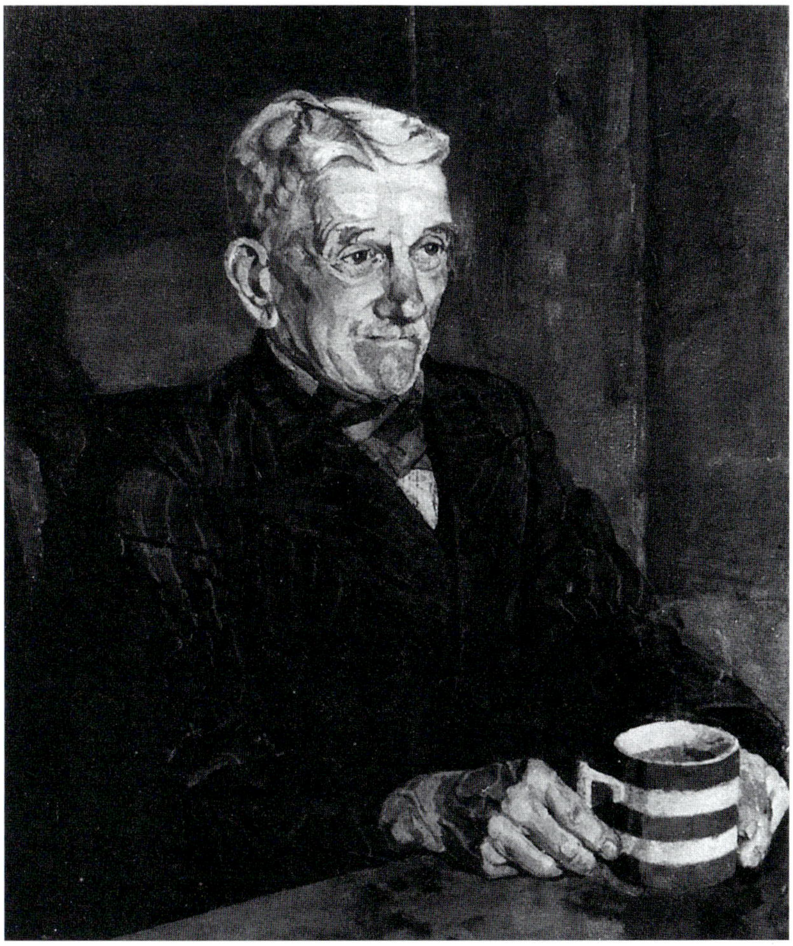

GLORIA STEEMSONNE. *Lower Sydenham.* Oil on board, 19in x 42in. Artist's collection.

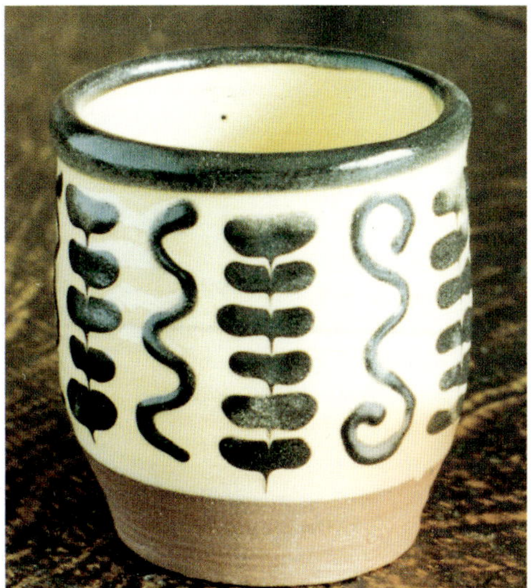

PETER STOODLEY. Red terracotta pot decorated under a transparent earthenware glaze, c. 1949. 3½in high. Private collection.

PATRICK SYMONS. *Jack Fox*, 1950. Oil on canvas, 22in x 18in. Courtesy of Nicholas Browne.

T

TARRANT, *Terence Richard* (b.1930)
A student at Camberwell between 1950-52, studying mainly commercial art, he is perhaps the only student to have become a medical artist. From the early 1950s, for over thirty years, he held such a position at the Institute of Ophthalmology and at Moorfields Eye Hospital (London).

TERBLANCHE, *Jacobus Filipus* (Philip) (1930-1985)
Born in Tzaneen in the Northern Transvaal, South Africa, he spent four years in London, having hitch-hiked all the way. During the period 1955-59 he attended St. Martin's School of Art, where Sir Francis Rose* taught him for a year. He joined Camberwell Art School at Rose's suggestion in 1956 where he studied painting and drawing under Eurich*, whom he found an enormous stimulus and help. On his return to Africa in the early 1960s, he was appointed Art Director with Rhodesian Television, prior to a short spell with the South African Broadcasting Service. He later spent ten years as a lecturer at the Cape Technical College and examples of his work can be seen in the South African Cultural History Museum in Cape Town.

THORNHILL, *Alan* (b.1921)
He did not commence his art studies until 1949, when he attended Camberwell for a two year period. It was here that he chose to do Pottery and was taught and greatly influenced by Kendall*. He has had numerous exhibitions of pottery, sculpture and drawings, beginning as early as 1955 at the Piccadilly Gallery. During the mid-1960s he showed his sculpture at the Drian Galleries and during the 1970s and 1980s he held one-man exhibitions at the Morley Gallery, the National Theatre and Brunel University. For most of the 1950s he ran his own pottery at Hawkley in Hampshire. During the 1960s and '70s he taught Pottery and Sculpture at Morley College, Lambeth.

TIDNAM, *Nicholas Rye* (b.1941)
A student at Camberwell from 1957-61, he was taught by Bullard*, Dunstan* and Michael Rothenstein*, amongst others. His work has been shown in numerous group exhibitions, including the Folio Society, Mercury Gallery (London and Edinburgh), Roland Browse & Delbanco, South London Art Gallery and he has also participated in the R.A. Summer Exhibitions; N.E.A.C. and the R.B.A. He has spent numerous years as a teacher, having been on the staff of Medway College of Design and Epsom School of Art.

TOWNSEND, *William* L.G. (1909-1973)
He studied at the Slade School of Fine Art under Tonks (1862-1937) and Steer (1860-1942) between 1926-30. He travelled extensively during the late 1920s and early '30s, visiting France, Italy, Tunisia and Egypt. In 1931 he first exhibited with the L.G., but he did not become a member until twenty years later, and in this same year, held his first one-man exhibition at the Bloomsbury Gallery in London. This was followed two years later with a show at the Wertheim Gallery. During the years prior to the Second World War he worked as a book illustrator and became seriously involved in Socialist politics, to the extent of being invited to stand as a Labour parliamentary candidate. Following the war he spent three years on the staff at Camberwell, before following his old friend Coldstream* to the Slade. By the beginning of the 1950s he was visiting Canada regularly and by 1951 had taken up the position of Guest Lecturer at the University of Alberta, Banff. He was to return on innumerable occasions to teach in Canada and became something of a spokesman on Canadian art. He was a prolific writer and in 1976 Andrew Forge* edited *The Townsend Journals – An Artist's Record of His Times 1928-1951* into a

most fascinating chronicle of British art. His work is represented in private and public collections throughout the world, including the Tate Gallery, the V. & A., the Arts Council of Great Britain, the municipal galleries of Birmingham, Bradford, Eastbourne, Leicester, Salford, York and the R.W.A., Bristol. His work abroad is to be found in the National Gallery of Canada, the Art Gallery of the University of Alberta, the National Gallery of Victoria, Melbourne, Australia and the City Art Gallery, Auckland, New Zealand.

U

UDEN, *Edna see* BIZON, *Edna*

UGLOW, *Euan* L.G. (b.1932)
He was a student at Camberwell 1948-51, where Coldstream* and Carter* were to become his great influence. In 1951 he furthered his studies at the Slade School of Fine Art where, in 1953, he won the Abbey Minor Scholarship. He began to exhibit his work in the mid-1950s with the L.G. and in 1960 was elected a Member He has held one-man exhibitions at Beaux Arts Gallery, Browse & Darby, and the Whitechapel Art Gallery. He was a prize-winner on two occasions at the John Moores Exhibition in 1961 and 1972. In the early 1960s he began part-time teaching at both the Slade School and Camberwell. His work is represented in many public collections, including The Tate Gallery, The Arts Council, Glasgow Art Gallery, Southampton Art Gallery, Ferens Art Gallery (Hull) and the South Australia National Gallery.

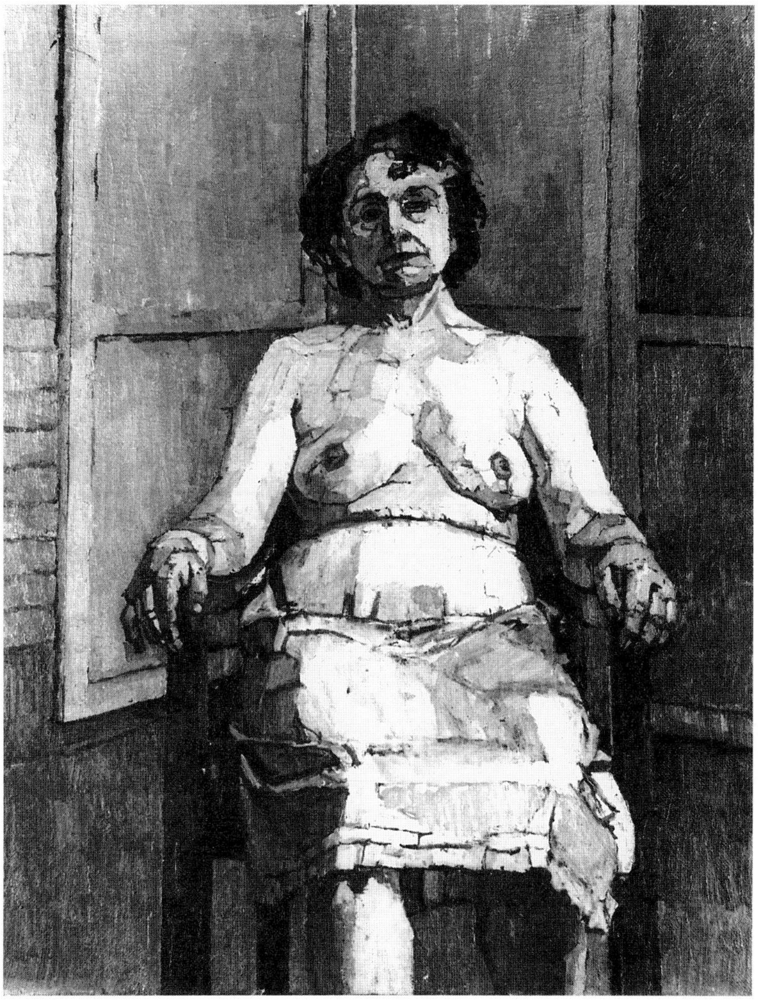

EUAN UGLOW. *Woman with White Skirt*, 1953.
Oil on canvas, 36in x 28in.
Private Collection. Photograph courtesy of Browse & Darby.

V

VAUGHAN, *John Keith* (1912-1977)

He was largely self-taught as a painter, never attending any formal art classes, his first job in fact being with Lintas, an advertising agency in the Unilever Group. In 1942 he held his first one-man exhibition at the Lefevre Gallery and continued to have one-man shows regularly on a national and international basis. His meeting with Graham Sutherland (1903-1980) influenced him greatly and a large period of his early work reflects in this admiration. Towards the end of the war, he was to meet John Minton*, Robert Colquhoun (1914-1962), John Craxton (b.1922), Prunella Clough (b.1919) and other Neo-Romantics. As a conscientious objector he spent the war years in the Pioneer Corps as a Clerk and latterly as a German interpreter at a P.O.W. camp. After leaving the Army in 1946 his friend Minton encouraged him to continue his career in art, and together they shared a house and studio. Minton also introduced him to William Johnstone*, who promptly engaged Vaughan as a

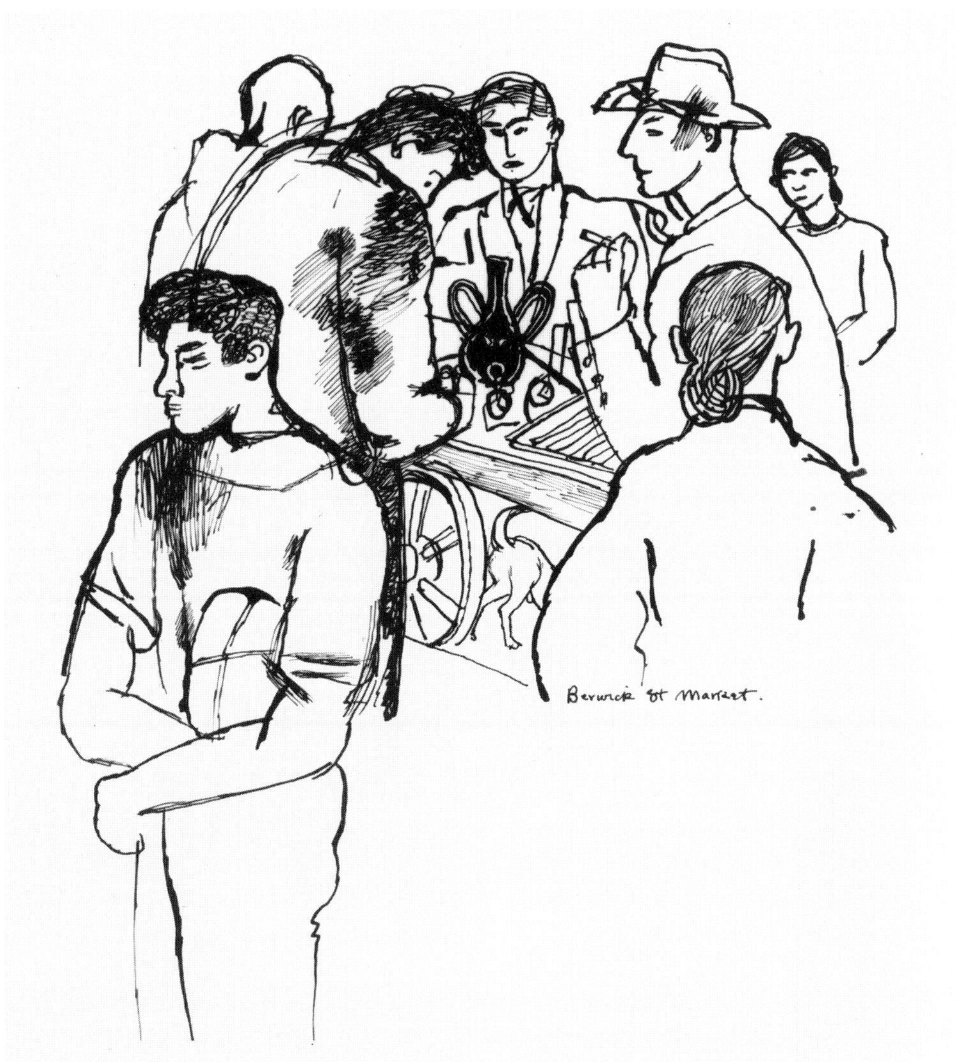

KEITH VAUGHAN. *Berwick Street Market.* Pen and ink, 10¼in x 9¼in. Private collection.

teacher of Illustration at Camberwell School of Art. He collaborated with Minton on the design and illustration of *Time Was Away*, written by Alan Ross who was later to publish Vaughan's *Journals and Drawings*. In 1948 he left Camberwell for the Central School of Art, where he again taught illustration. He exhibited his work in New York, Buenos Aires, Iowa, São Paulo, Los Angeles and Glasgow. He was visiting lecturer at the Slade School from the mid-1950s for approximately ten years. He exhibited many times during the early 1950s with the L.G. and his work is represented in private and public collections around the world. Shortly after his death in 1977 the Mappin Art Gallery, Sheffield, gave him a memorial exhibition.

VERSTER, *Andrew* (b.1937)
A student at Camberwell from 1955-59, where he was much influenced by Michael Salaman*. During this time he also briefly attended St. Martin's School of Art as a part-time evening student. A year at Reading University followed, before returning to his native South Africa, to take up a teaching post at Johannesburg School of Art. By 1963 he had been appointed a lecturer at the University of Durban. In 1974, he became Head of the Division of Art at Durban Technical College and in 1975 a retrospective exhibition of fifteen years' work was held at the University of Natal. It was about this time that he gave up teaching to concentrate full-time on painting and also at this time, he became an art critic and writer. Skilled in various techniques, his career has included numerous architectural commissions. Since 1967 he has had over thirty-five one-man exhibitions in Cape Town, Durban and Johannesburg and he has taken part in numerous group exhibitions in South Africa and overseas, including Austria, Israel, Greece, London, West Germany, Korea, Australia, Belgium, Holland and the U.S.A. His paintings can be seen in the public collections of the South African National Gallery (Cape Town), Durban Art Gallery, the University of Witwatersrand Gallery (Johannesburg), University of South Africa (Pretoria) and the Pietersburg Collection.

VOGEL, *Karel* (1897-1961)
Born in Budweisz, Czechoslovakia, he studied at the University of Prague 1916-22, gaining a doctorate in Classical Archaeology and the History of Art. From 1922-24 he attended the Prague Academy of Fine Arts, studying sculpture under Jan Stursa (1880-1925), before furthering his studies in Vienna with Professor Anton Hanak (1875-1934). He worked as a professional sculptor in Prague and for many years enjoyed in his own country a considerable reputation, producing many fine portraits, including one of Kokoschka (1886-1980). He declined an invitation by the University to become Professor of Sculpture because Hitler's armies were at the time massing in Central Europe and he chose instead to take up residence in England with his wife. Once in England, many distinguished people helped him with commissions until he was able to establish himself in a modest way as a sculptor. Some of his earliest British commissions included the Duchess of Devonshire and Dame Myra Hess. Along with many other émigré artists, he was interned at the outbreak of war but was soon released, taking teaching posts at Oswestry School of Art and Liverpool College of Art. It was in 1948 that he first met Leonard Daniels*, the Principal of Camberwell, through an introduction from Helmut Ruhemann*, who was at that time the Consultant in Picture Conservation at the National Gallery and, like Vogel, a fellow refugee from Nazism. That same year Vogel was invited to join the staff at Camberwell and within a few months was appointed Head of the School of Sculpture. A fine sculptor, a highly intelligent man and an exceptionally gifted teacher, he produced a whole generation of good and devoted students. In his early sixties he was stricken with a degenerative disease, dying at the age of sixty-four. A fine draughtsman, he exhibited not only his

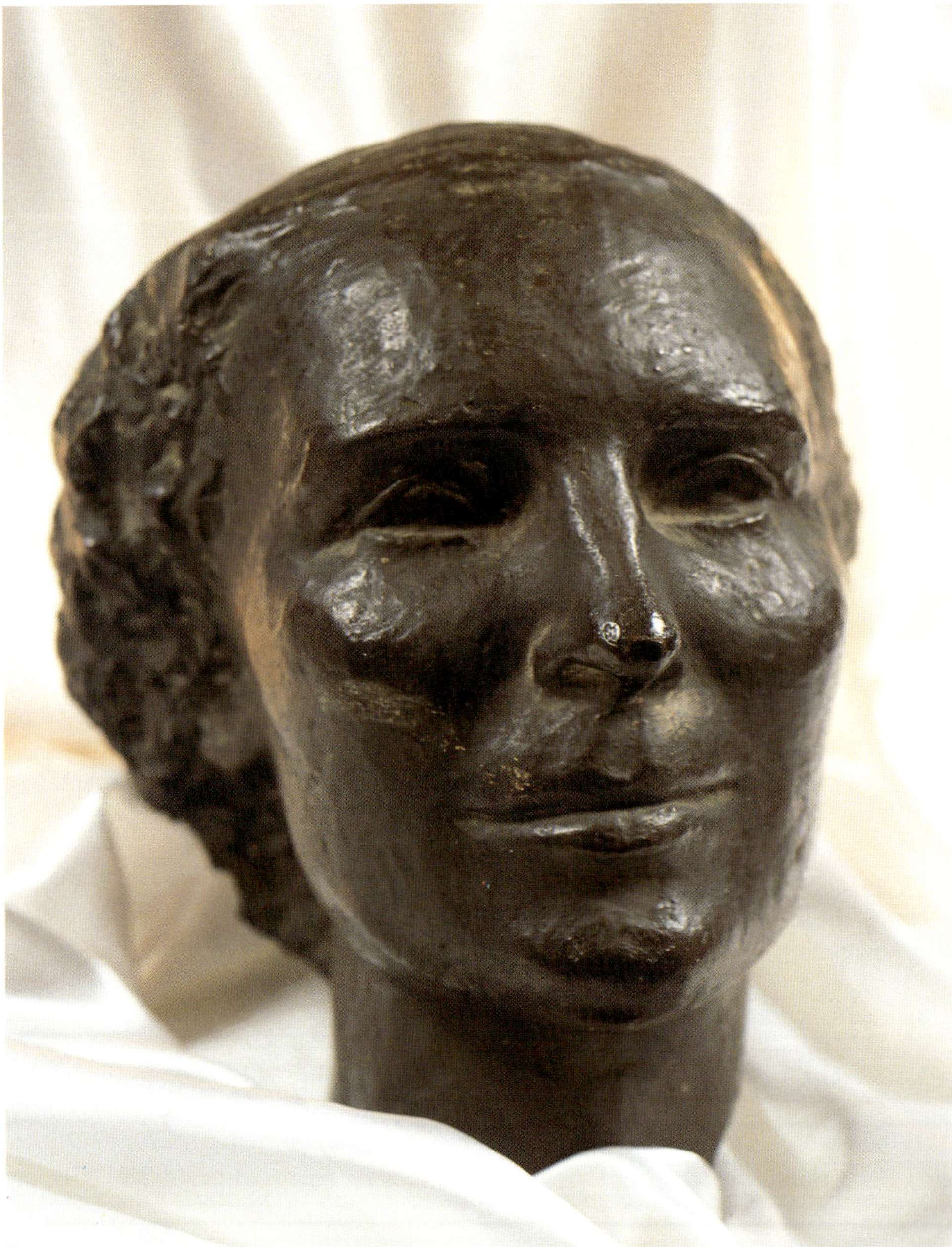

KAREL VOGEL. *Helen Watson**. Bronze, 11in high. Courtesy of Lesley South.

sculpture at many leading exhibitions, but also his drawings, which were often shown at the Leicester Galleries. His work can be seen in the State Museum (Prague) as well as the Nuremberg City Museum. Several of his sculptures are in public places in the U.K., in particular a fine figure study adjacent to St. Peter's Church in Hammersmith, as well as a figure group at Harlow New Town. Vogel exhibited at the Venice Biennale before the war and he also showed at the two Battersea Park Open Air Exhibitions in 1951 and 1960. Two of his last portraits included Alec Guinness and his Camberwell colleague, Claude Rogers*. A touring Arts Council retrospective exhibition of his work was held in London and Bradford in 1963.

(The author is indebted to Leonard Daniels, who helped with this information.)

W

WAKEFORD, *Edward Felix* A.R.A., R.B.A. (1914-1973)
He studied art at Chelsea School of Art and later during the early 1930s at the R.C.A. He taught at Camberwell 1956-58 and had many group and one-man shows, including the British Council, Jerusalem 1944; Brook Street Gallery 1946; Hanover Gallery 1953; Wildenstein, (group exhibitions 1948-62); Fieldbourne Galleries, Memorial Exhibition 1973; Abbott Hall, Cumbria 1986. Several of his works are in public collections, including the Glasgow Art Gallery, Shell-Mex, British Petroleum, Carlisle Art Gallery, Douglas Art Gallery, Isle of Man and the Imperial War Museum. The Chantrey Bequest purchased a painting for the Tate Gallery collection. He wrote his autobiography, *A Prize for Art*, published by Macmillan in 1961.

WALTERS, *Neville* (1922-1973)
The twin brother of Nigel Walters*, he attended the R.C.A. during its evacuation to Ambleside in the Second World War. During 1948, with his brother, he joined the staff at Camberwell lecturing in Industrial Design. He did not continue teaching and spent the rest of his life as a designer in industry.

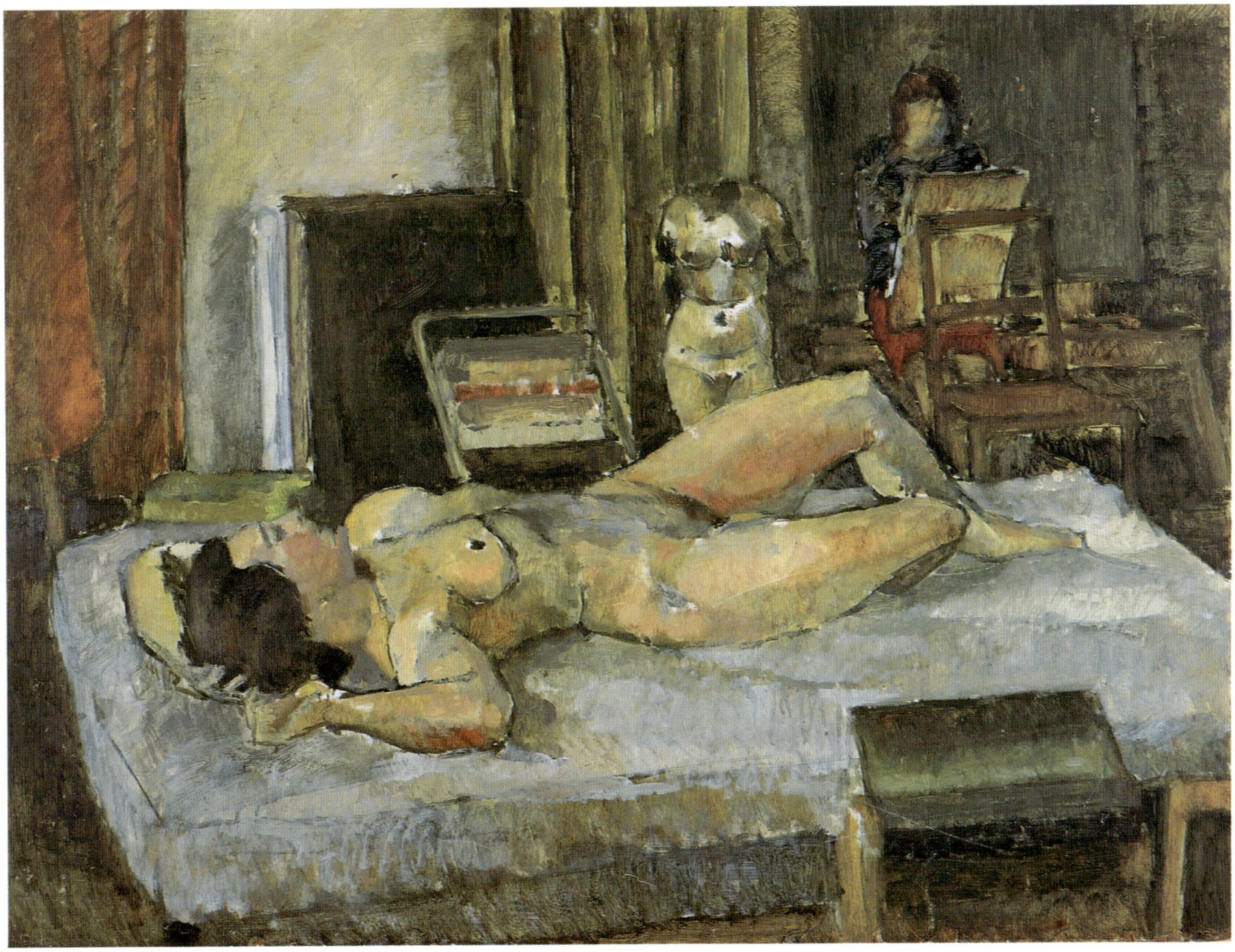

ROY WATSON. *Nude*, 1958. Oil on board, 28in x 36in. Artist's collection.

WALTERS, *Nigel Vincent* (1922-1988)
With his brother, Neville*, he was a pupil at the R.C.A. during its period of evacuation to Ambleside. In 1948 he joined the staff at Camberwell where he taught Industrial Design, before joining the Central School of Arts & Crafts, where he lectured on Furniture Design, eventually becoming Head of the Interior Design and Furniture Department. By the mid-1960s he had formed a design partnership with his wife, Sheila, after several years as a design consultant with the furniture makers F. Wrighton & Sons Ltd.

WATSON, *Helen* (b.1908)
Studied at Wakefield School of Art and during the 1920s at the R.C.A. She joined the staff at Camberwell in 1947, where she was to teach for the next twenty years. She has exhibited on several occasions at the R.A.

WATSON, *Roy Coulam* (b.1932)
He was a student at Camberwell 1954-58, where his main influences were Christopher Chamberlain*, Dixon*, Eyton* and Fry*. He has only begun showing his work recently and has participated in group shows in Cambridgeshire and Heidelberg.

WEAVER, *Peter Malcolm* (b.1927)
After leaving the Royal Army Medical Corps in 1947 he began to study at St. Martin's School of Art, where he stayed until 1950. A two year period at Camberwell followed, where he was most influenced and taught by Bloch* and Eurich*. In 1952 he furthered his studies at the Slade School of Fine Art for two years. From 1957 until 1987 he taught continuously at Camberwell. He has shown his work at the R.A. and the R.W.S., but mostly at exhibitions of the Printmakers' Council, of which he was a founder member.

WEBB, *Maureen see* RIPLEY, *Maureen*

WELDON, *Ronald* b.1925)
He attended Camberwell 1950-55, where his main influence was Martin Bloch*. Very few of his early works remain, as he abandoned painting shortly after leaving Camberwell. It is only in the last few years that he has recommenced painting and his work has been exhibited at the Royal West of England Society.

WESTWOOD, *Joyce Enid see* ARIMATSU, *Joyce Enid*

WHEELER, *Peter Timothy* (b.1941)
Following three years as a general engineering apprentice, he became a student at Camberwell in 1959 and was to remain there for the next four years, his main tutors included Eyton* and Fry*. His group exhibitions have included John Moores (Liverpool), L.G., and various shows in Germany during the early 1980s, as well as the R.A. Summer Exhibitions. In more recent years he has made a successful career in theatre, film and television as a model-maker, sculptor and prop designer, dividing his time between London and Italy.

WHITEHEAD, *Phoebe see* BULLOCK, *Phoebe*

WHITWELL, *Margaret* (1922-1966)
Following an education at Croydon High School, Margaret Whitwell served in the operations room at Biggin Hill in the W.A.A.F. 1940-45. At the end of the war she became a student at Camberwell for three years until 1948. She was strongly influenced by the Euston Road members, but following the completion of her

course in 1949 she left England for two years, travelling and working in Italy, painting only very occasionally. Hardly any of her work survives and she was never very prolific. She returned to England in 1951 and took up a job with the furniture designer Sir Gordon Russell as his personal assistant and was heavily involved in the organisation for the Festival of Britain. She married John Forge, the brother of the artist and writer Andrew Forge*.

WILLIAMS, *Denis* (b.1923)
Born in the West Indies, he came to England in 1946, enrolling at Camberwell soon after his arrival. He studied painting for over a year before beginning work as a civil servant to supplement his income. He held his first one-man exhibition at the Berkeley Galleries in 1949, attracting the attention of Wyndham Lewis (1882-1957), who gave encouragement to Williams. His second exhibition was held the following year at Gimpel Fils where he continued to show for some time. He was joint second prize winner with Heinz Inlander* in the *Daily Express* exhibition in 1955. He taught at the Central School throughout the 1950s.

WILLIS, *Victor* (b.1934)
A student at Camberwell from 1957-60, he was taught and influenced by Christopher Chamberlain*, Dunstan*, R. D. Lee* and Symons*. In subsequent years

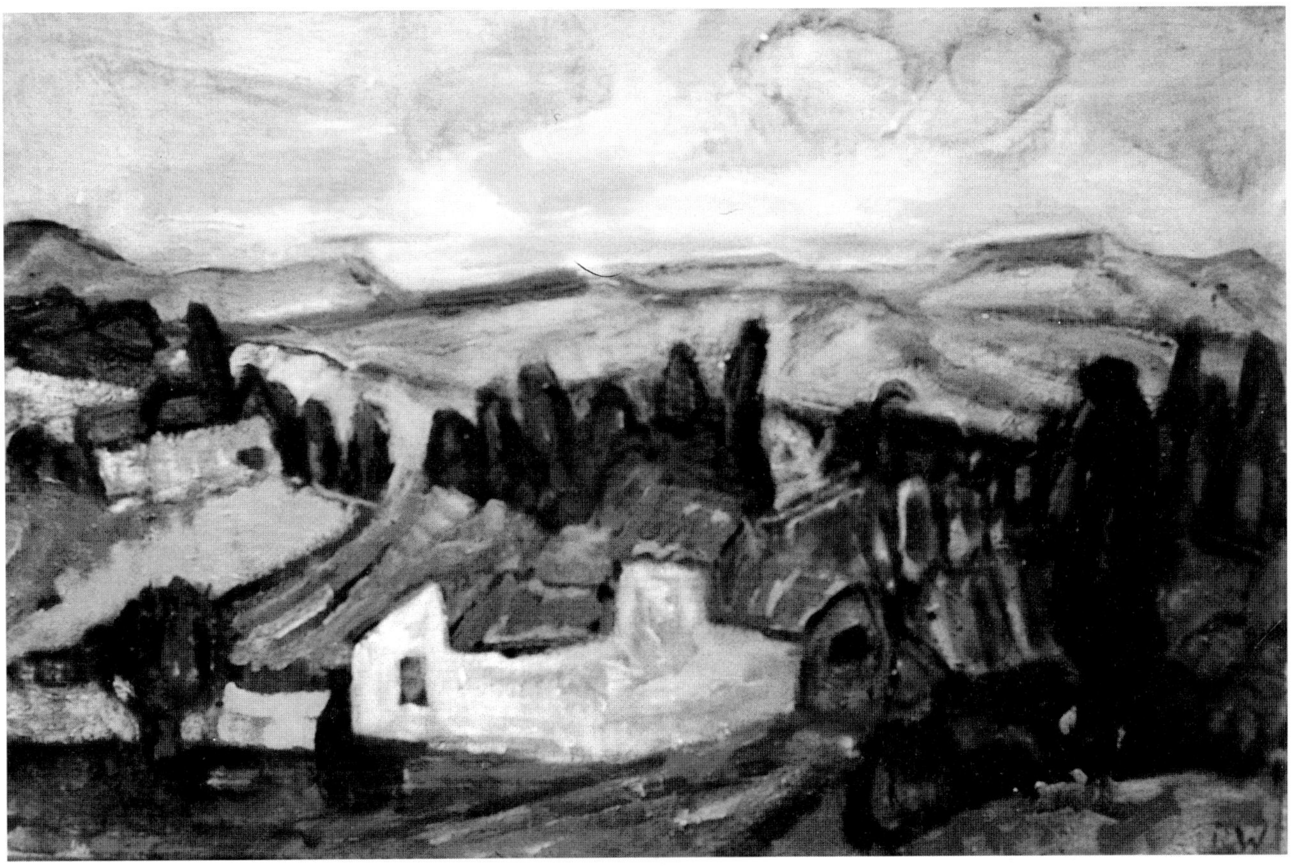

RON WELDON. *Farm at St Montant.* Oil on canvas, 16in x 24in. Artist's collection.

he also studied at the City & Guilds College and at the Sir John Cass College. He has exhibited in many group exhibitions, including Hayward Annual, South London Art Gallery, Camden Arts Centre, N.E.A.C., R.A. and a group exhibition in New Brunswick, Canada. He has held numerous teaching posts, and in 1983 was awarded an M.A. in Fine Art by Goldsmiths' College. More recently he has shown at Duncan Campbell Fine Art and has also written articles on night painting for art magazines.

WOLFERS, *Wanda Marcelle* (b.1930)

Known as Wendy, she studied at Camberwell from 1947-50, where she was most influenced by the Euston Road painters. She won a scholarship to the Slade School of Fine Art where, after three years, she received her Diploma in 1953. She taught art in private and state schools throughout the 1950s. During the early 1960s she lived and worked in Paris studying, amongst other things, lithography. For many years until the 1980s she was involved in film work as an editor and scriptwriter until she took up residence in New York, where she now lives and works. Her work has been shown with the L.G., and in 1960 she had a one-woman exhibition at the Galerie de Seine and more recently at a gallery in New York.

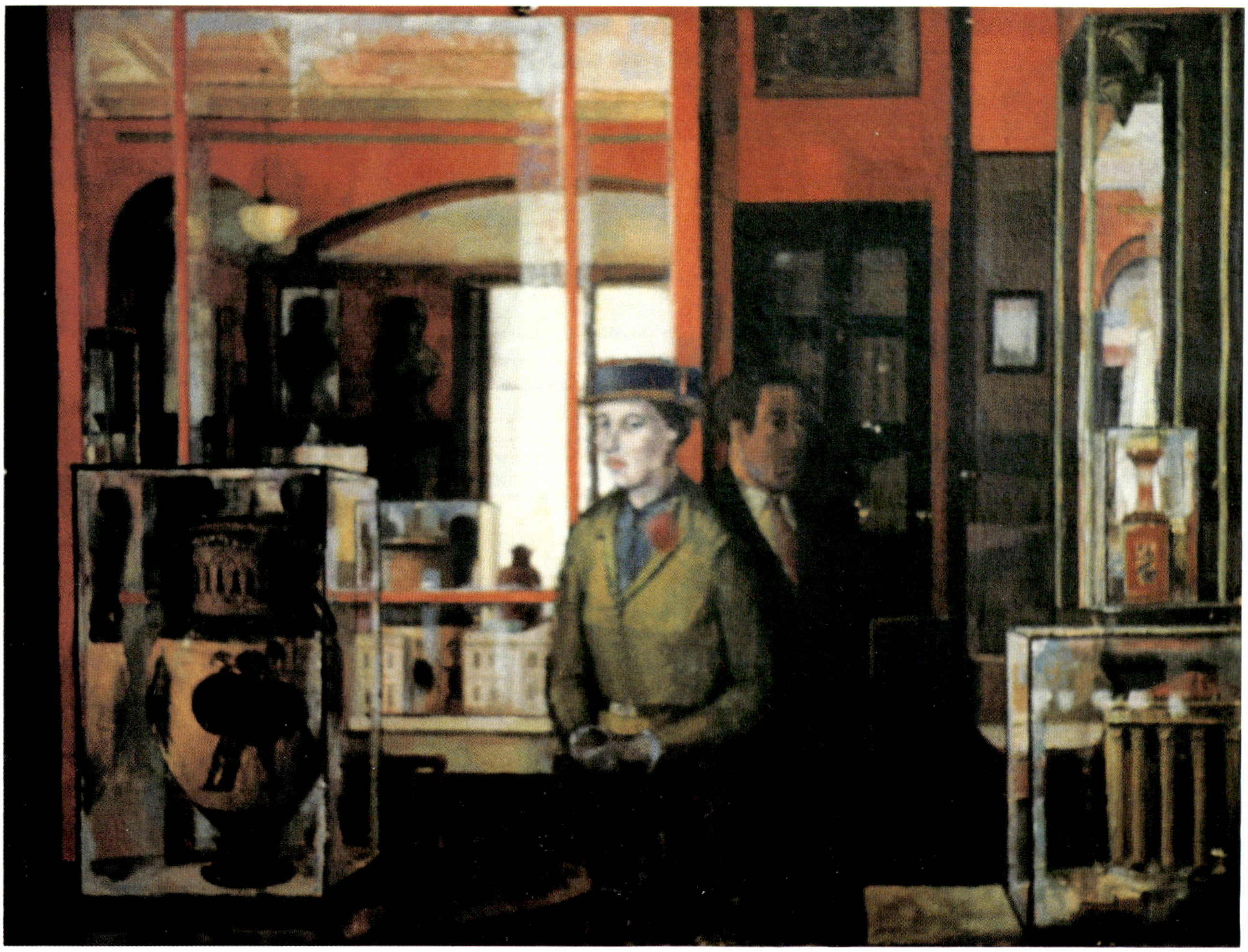

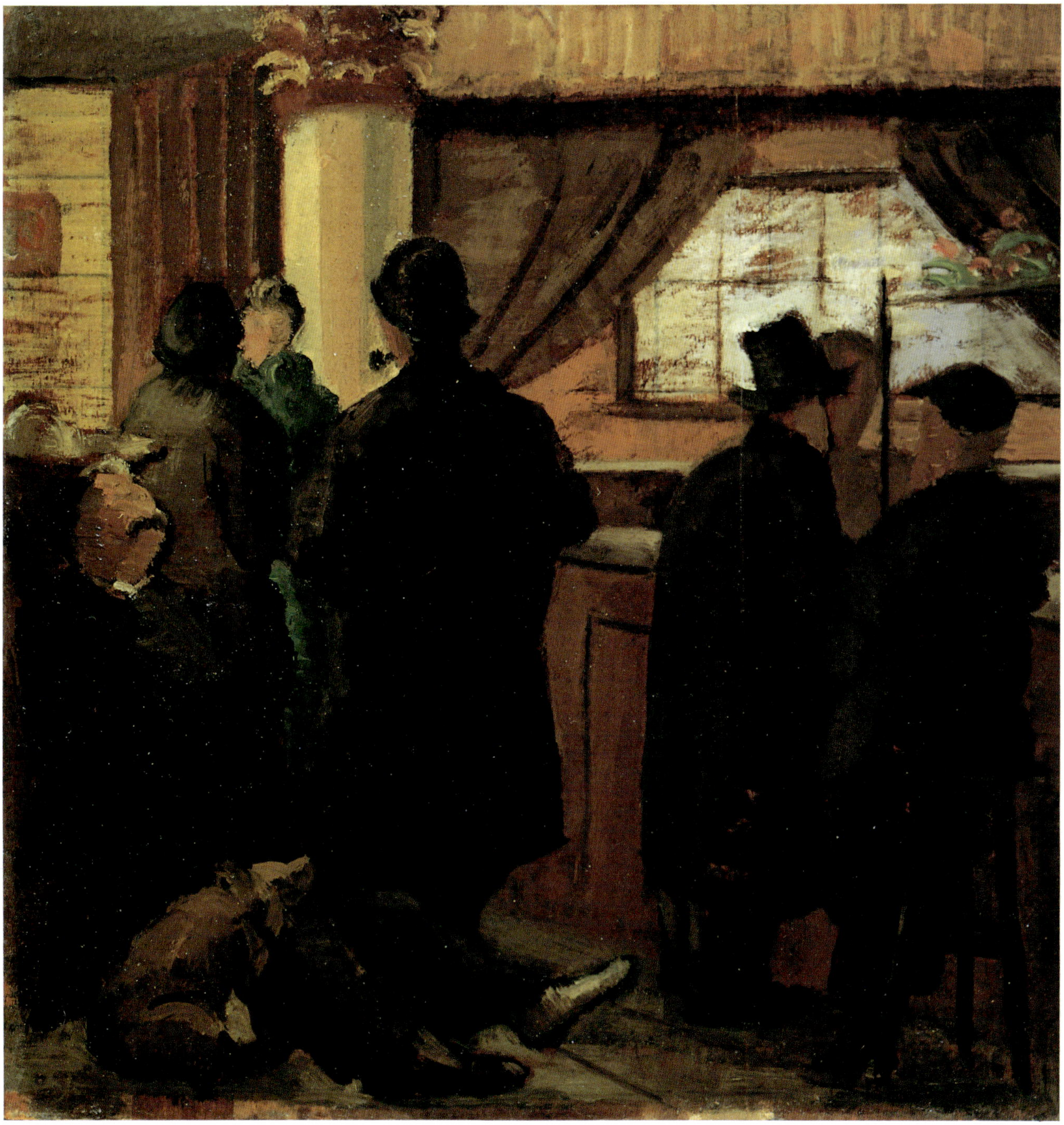

MARGARET WHITWELL. *Interior of Walmer Castle Pub*, 1947. Oil on canvas, 14in x 10in.
Private collection.

Left: PETER WEAVER. *The John Soane Museum, London*, 1951. Oil on board, 18in x 24in.
Artist's collection.

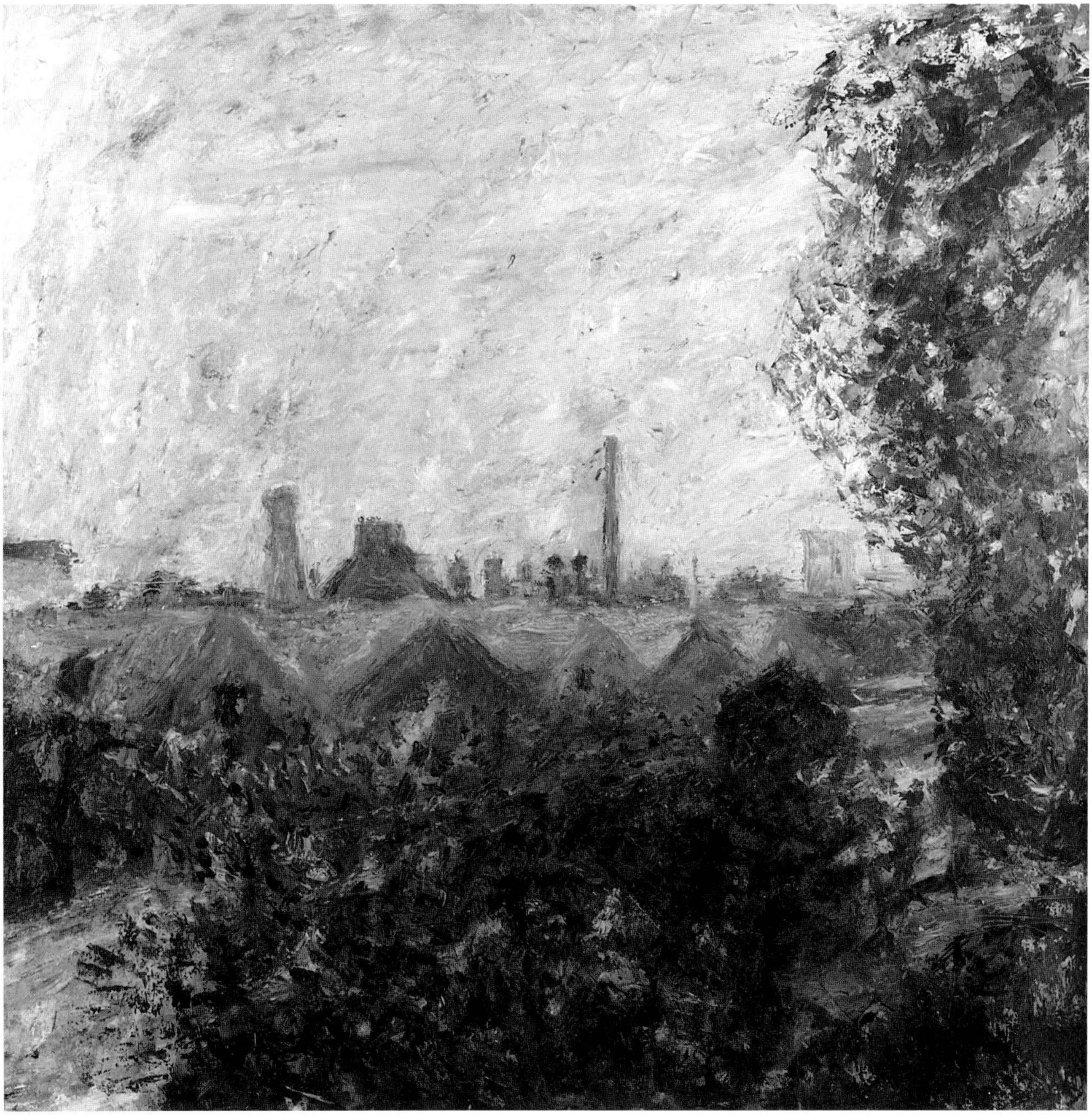

VICTOR WILLIS. *View from Addington Square Studio – Looking toward Camberwell*, c.1957. Oil on board, 36in x 36in.

WOLPE, *Berthold Ludwig* (1905-1989)
Born in Germany, he studied typography at the Offenbach Künstgewerbschule from 1924-28 under the tutelage of Rudolph Koch (1876-1934). He began teaching in the late 1920s at Frankfurt School of Art and by 1935 had taken residency in England. He joined the staff at Camberwell in 1948, where he remained for four years as a tutor in Graphic Design and Lettering. His other teaching posts include the R.C.A. and the City & Guilds of London School of Art. During his career he was responsible for the typography and design of countless book jackets for Faber & Faber, by whom he was employed from 1941-75. He also illustrated many books, including *Collected Poems* by Walter de la Mare. In 1968 he was awarded an

Honorary Doctorate at the R.C.A. A retrospective exhibition of his work was held at the V. & A. in 1980. Arguably his most famous typographic design was the Albertus typeface which he designed in 1934 for the Monotype Corporation. Wolpe did not draw the letters but cut them with a chisel. He then proceeded not to incise the letters but to painstakingly cut away the background leaving the letters as a raised design.

WOOD, *Owen Thomas George* (b.1929)
Known as 'Oska' to his friends, he studied at Camberwell 1945-48, where he was influenced by Einzig*, Minton* and Vaughan*. During the 1950s he exhibited at various mixed exhibitions, including the Young Contemporaries and with the L.G. and in 1956, with his Camberwell friends and colleagues Robert Hunt* and Peter Dunbar*, held a three man exhibition at the St. George's Gallery, London. His work has been shown internationally in Germany, Czechoslovakia, Italy, U.S.A. and Japan. He has had one-man exhibitions of watercolours at the Francis Kyle Gallery and at Chris Beetles. He has illustrated innumerable books and has also designed record sleeves for Decca and Philips. He has designed Christmas and greeting cards and has worked on murals, including the London Stock Exchange Public Gallery. The current series of banknotes from £1-£100 for the Clydeside Bank of Scotland were designed by Wood in 1969 and more recently, in 1980, he designed their £50 note. During the 1960s he taught Illustration and Graphic Design at Cambridge, Colchester and Norfolk Schools of Art.

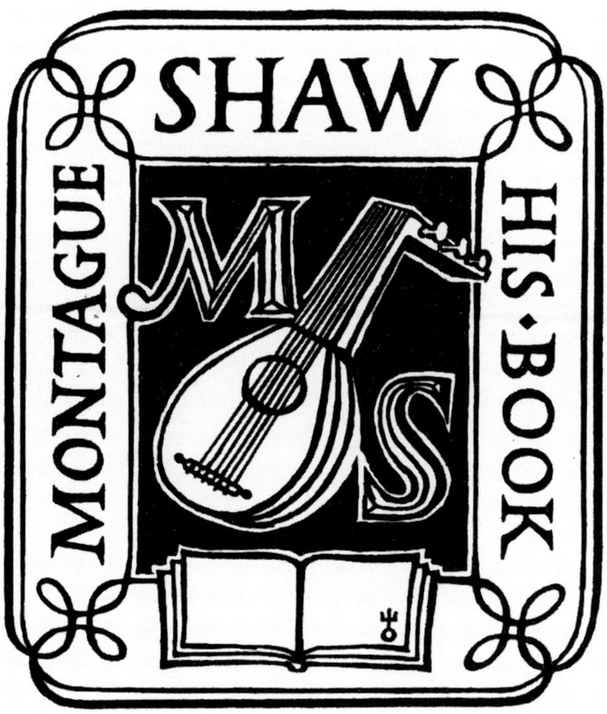

BERTHOLD WOLPE. *Supra* ex-libris for the Hirsch Music Library, commissioned in 1948. The design was cut on brass in three sizes: the largest to be blocked on folios, a medium size on quartos and the smallest on octavo size books.

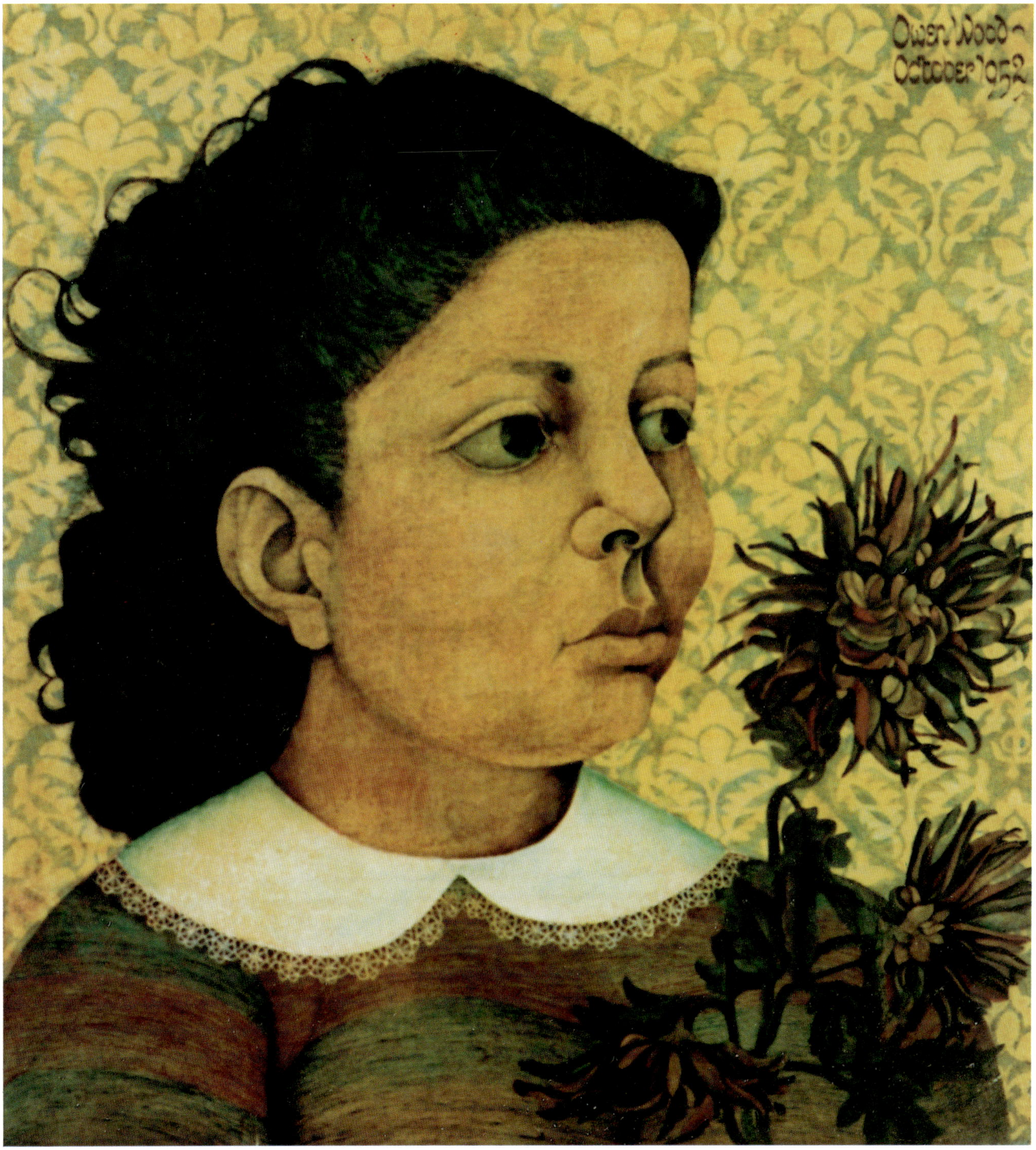

OWEN WOOD. *A Girl with Flowers*. Oil on board, 18in x 15in. Courtesy of Mr and Mrs James Mair.

WOOLWAY, *George Richard* (1879-1961)
Painter, who studied at the Royal College of Art 1899-1904. He was a friend of Philip Wilson Steer (1860-1942), who supported his application for the job of Principal of Clapham School of Art which Woolway held in the early 1920s. About ten years later he became Principal of St. Martin's School of Art, a position he held until his retirement from teaching during the Second World War. Briefly at the end of the

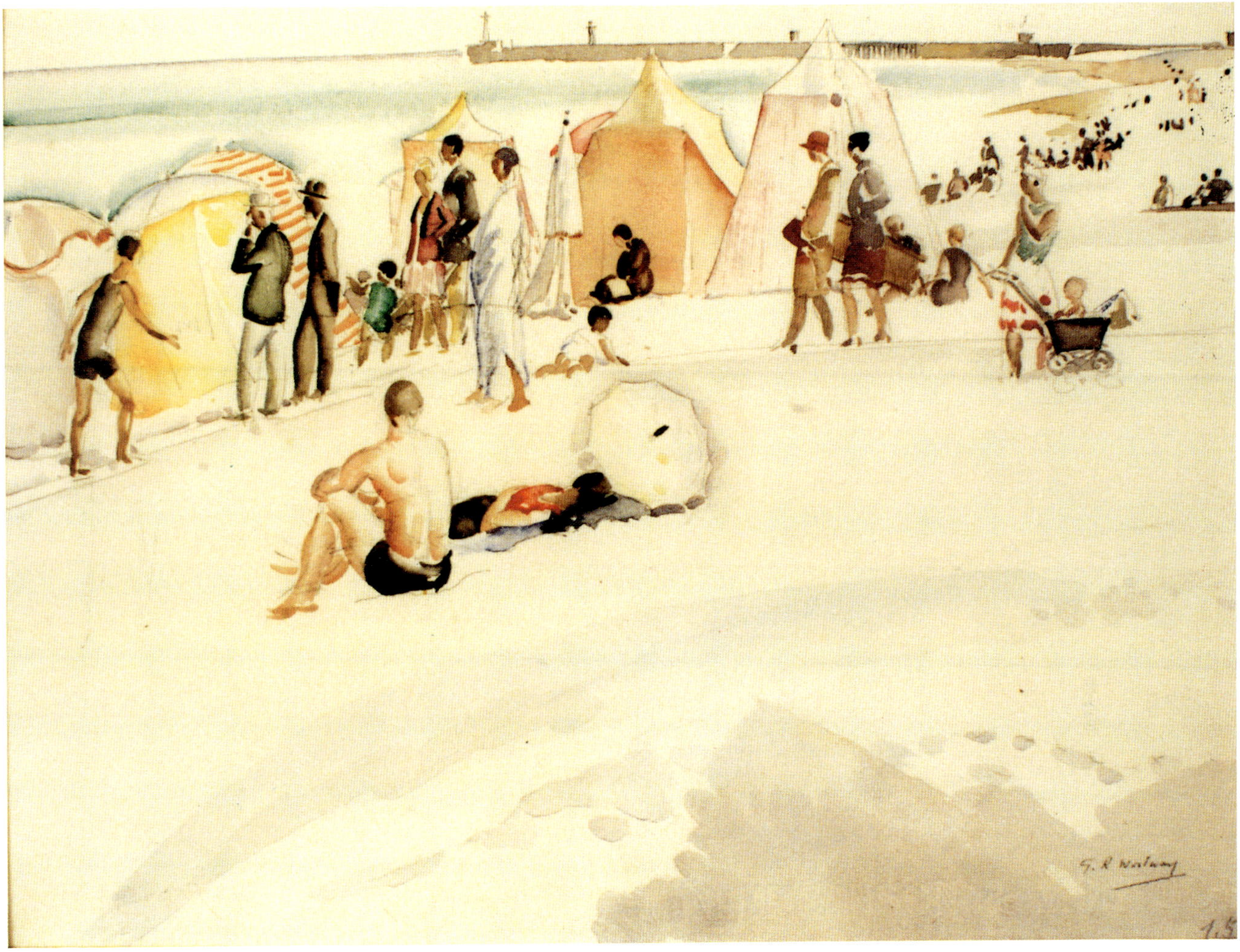

G. R. WOOLWAY. *Brittany Beach*. Watercolour, 10in x 12in. Private collection.

war he held the position of Principal at Camberwell following the departure of William Johnstone*. Although a fluent watercolourist, particularly of the French coastal towns of Brittany and Normandy, he was only an occasional exhibitor. He showed at the R.A. and at the Cooling Galleries. Chelsea Town Hall was the site of one of his successful mural compositions.

Y

YHAP *Laetitia* D.F.A. (b.1941)
Studied at Camberwell 1958-62, where she was influenced and taught by Auerbach*, Eyton*, Hoyland* and Uglow*. In 1962 she was awarded the Leverhulme travelling scholarship to Italy. On her return she attended the Slade School of Fine Art until 1965 when she was awarded a Diploma in Fine Art. She has exhibited several times at the Young Contemporaries Group Exhibitions and she held her first one-woman exhibition at the Piccadilly Gallery in 1968. In 1970 she was elected a member of the L.G. She has shown her work several times at the John Moores Exhibition at the Walker Art Gallery, Liverpool, and her work has also been seen at the Towner Art Gallery, Eastbourne, and at Hastings Museum and Art Gallery. She shows regularly at the R.A. Exhibitions, and her work can be seen in public collections, including the Arts Council of Great Britain, the Nuffield Foundation, Hastings Museum & Art Gallery, Rugby Museum, Contemporary Arts Society, Hove Museum & Art Gallery, The British Council, Tate Gallery and the Walker Art Gallery, Liverpool. She married the artist, Jeffrey Camp*.

YOUNG, *Dennis* (1917-1988)
He attended High Wycombe School of Art 1933-36, where he studied furniture design before winning a scholarship to the R.C.A., where he was to remain until 1938 studying architecture. He was much involved with the exhibition design for the Festival of Britain in 1951 and as a freelance designer was also responsible for creating exhibition stands in the immediate post-war years throughout Europe, including some of the first Western exhibitions seen in Russia. He joined the staff at Camberwell in 1952, where for five years he lectured in the Graphic Design department. His prowess as a designer is perhaps best remembered for his work on the design of office chairs.

YOUNG, *Louise see* REID, *Louise*

YOUNG, *Rosemary* (b.1930)
During the immediate post-war period from 1947-48 she studied at Camberwell under Coldstream*. She furthered her studies at Wimbledon School of Art before winning a Scholarship to the Slade School of Fine Art as a post-graduate student, studying sculpture until 1952. During this period, her work was shown in the Battersea Open Air Exhibition in 1951 and at the Hanover Gallery the following year. Shortly after the death of her husband, the sculptor Reginald Butler (1913-1981), she returned to the art of sculpting after an absence of many years.

Memories of Camberwell

On a questionnaire sent to the students and teachers, they were asked "what Camberwell meant to me". Here are some of the replies, not always flattering, which in the main are unedited.

Penny Allen (*née* Colman): "I wish I had been a few years older to have absorbed more of what was available. The greatest influence for me was William Johnstone, whose ideas and painting I found continually inspiring."

Frank Auerbach: "I thought Camberwell a splendid school with staff and students who had my respect and a tradition of unpretentious decency and goodwill."

Phoebe Atkins (*née* Hopson): "Camberwell meant freezing cold classrooms, Lancashire hot-pot in Lyons at Camberwell Green, buying two Weights cigarettes at a time, getting my first kiss in an abandoned graveyard from a fellow student, being madly in love with David Leach – the pottery teacher – carving a Madonna and Child out of a single matchstick, and painting a portrait in oils on a student's front tooth after it had been knocked out in a fight!"

John Avis: "As a very young student educated during the war years, I feel that my real education only began when I arrived at Camberwell. At this time, under William Johnstone, who terrified us youngsters, there was an incredible collection of staff, ranging from the Euston Road Group to the British Romantics; as well as some outstanding designers. Students included mature ex-service intakes, which helped the younger ones to grow up in attitude. Camberwell was also a centre of the jazz revivalist movement. A most enjoyable and inspiring place to be without the present divisions between fine art, design and craft; in fact it is what art schools should be like, but alas are no longer so."

Daphne Ayres (*née* Echalaz): "Thinking back, my student days at Camberwell have really always seemed quite the most contented and care-free four years of my life. Actually however, at the time I suppose that our emotions ran practically without cease. The incredible exhilaration if Mr Pasmore had given a passing word of praise to one's painting as he whirled through the life class. The endless despairing cries and moans for help to patient Mr Coldstream and Mr Rogers and so on *ad infinitum*. Anyway the teaching certainly gave us 'a new way of looking' and I think most of us in varying degrees are still at it."

Eve Baker (*née* McMullin): "Martin Bloch was for ever throwing out quotable one liners, one of the best being 'Watercolour painting! It is the English outdoor sport – every Colonel does it'."

Geoffrey Baker: "An oasis of inspiration and friendliness, vitality and intellectual enquiry, of egalitarianism and sanity."

Jean Barham (*née* Plummer): "When I went to Camberwell in the cold January of 1947 it was full of ex-Army, Navy and Airforce people trying to keep warm in uniform coats. To begin with we spent our time in the life drawing room. Mr Pasmore would occasionally come round and give an opinion. Mr Monnington and Rodney Burn would sit systematically at each donkey doing their best to instruct us in the art of life drawing. Lawrence Gowing saw me drawing the Venus de Milo and said that I could now start painting. This was a year after beginning life drawing

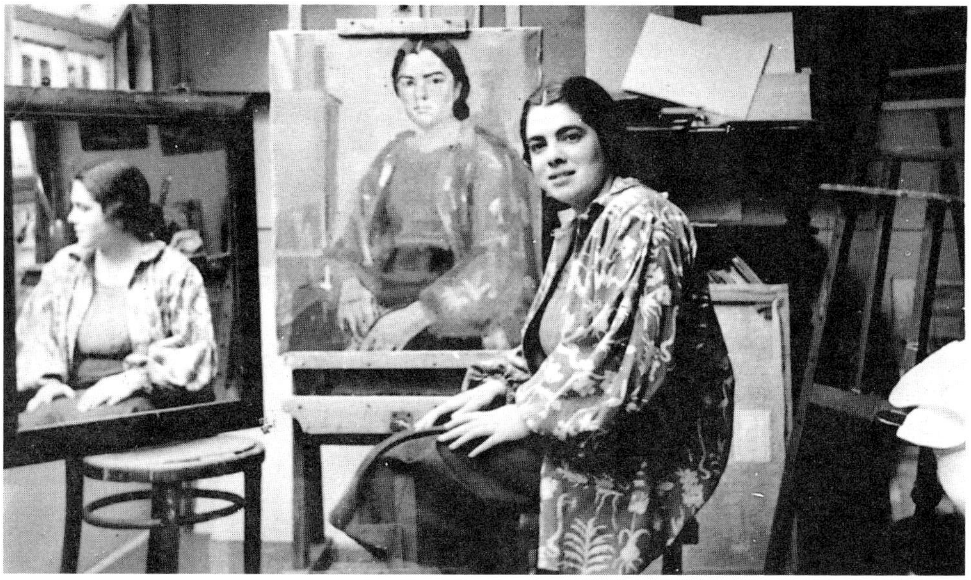

Elspeth Buchanan in her studio, c.1948.

classes. This gave me great joy. We were lucky to be amongst such a group of very distinguished painters/teachers but until I left Camberwell I found this inhibiting."

Victoria Bartlett (*née* Howitt): "It was a time when one could immerse oneself in work without the intrusion of other responsibilities. I am still grateful to the artists who taught us; they did not expect great talk or achievements; but they encouraged us to look, work, see and look again. It wasn't easy, but it has been useful."

Clifford Bayly: ".... the last two years at Camberwell studying painting were less structured than I had imagined. In fact we saw very little of the staff, and looking back I wonder just how much teaching some of them did... There was a good creative ambience, however, within which one could work, and this strongly influenced one's motivation. I have fond memories of John Minton at the 'Naughty Nineties Ball' dressed as a poor Victorian serving girl in black, carrying a bird-cage and singing 'My Old Man Said Follow the Van'. A student whose surname I think was Fox, when he became bored or frustrated with his work, would leave the life class and crow like a cockerel at full throttle very realistically in the corridor outside; he spoke for us all on occasions. For my sins, and due to the fact that no-one else was as daft as I, I allowed myself to be persuaded to take over the Chairmanship of the Students' Union. I soon found out that my main responsibility was to organise the annual Christmas party...some of my friends who worked hard with me at this time were Sandy Carmichael, Victor Belcher, Victor Poole, Henry Mundy, Rik Richards and all the Jazz-playing fraternity."

Dorothy Bevan (*née* Johnson): "The quarter sheet of Imperial per day led to obsessively disciplined drawing – non use of rubber most inhibiting. The joy of relationships with Victor Pasmore, Lawrence Gowing, Dora Batty and Michael Salaman last forever. Disgusting lunchtime meals leading to surreptitious consumption of jam doughnuts – hence my weight! The introduction to another dimension in music. Wally Fawkes gave me away at my wedding."

Edna Bizon (*née* Uden): "When I first went there it was still partly boarded up from war damage. Materials were still in short supply, one could only obtain a new sheet of drawing paper when both sides of an existing sheet were used up. Most other facilities were minimal but the quality of the teaching was superb. A strong emphasis was placed on drawing, especially from life and the Antique. The disciplines of this have always remained with me, so too has a feeling for the subtleties of colour which I attribute to the influences of the Euston Road Group so strong there at the time."

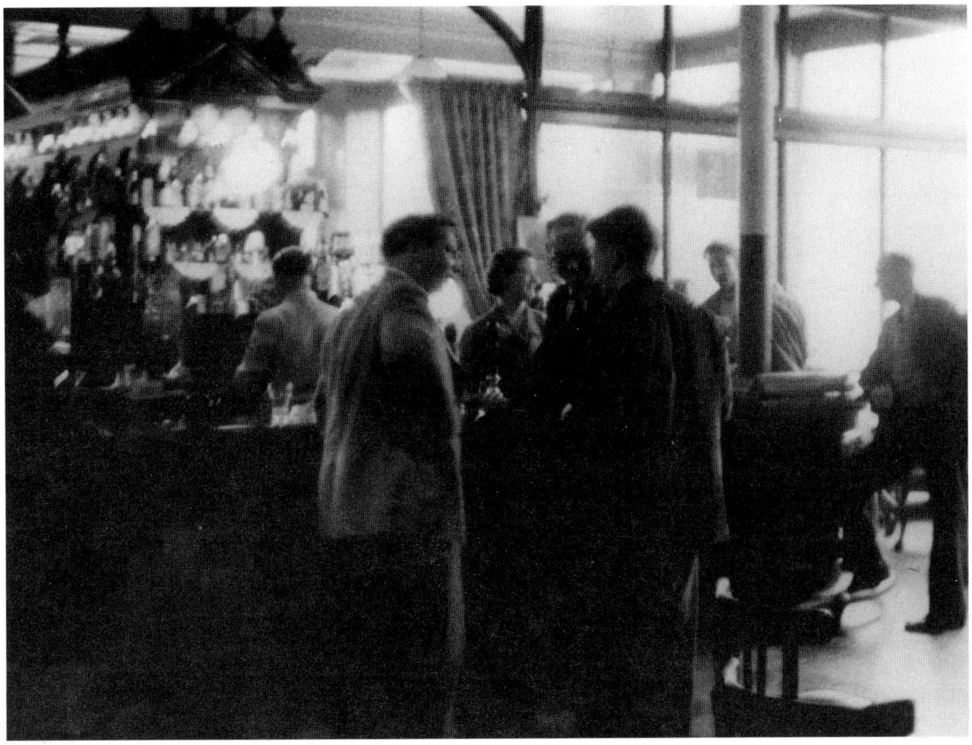

The Walmer Castle, 1955. From left to right: Leonard Daniels, E. A. A. Mynett (School Secretary), Gerald Hunt (President of the Students' Union).

John Brason: "It was a teaching job that enabled me to find my feet – meet the next generation – and convince myself that I was not a teacher. It was, at the time, the only art school in the country worth a second glance."

Elspeth Buchanan: "In London at the end of the war, I soon came to the conclusion that my war-work as a cartographer had estranged me from the life of the artist; so I signed up at Camberwell. Painting there opened up new worlds for me, although I was only there for one year, I worked very hard and the staff were most helpful, especially William Coldstream. The Euston Road Group had much the same point of view as the Edinburgh College of Art – abstract art was not encouraged and one developed realism. I remember few students but one that remains in my mind was Earl Haig (I suppose because he was Scottish). At every model rest time, he had to go and have a glass of milk, he had just returned from a German prisoner-of-war camp, and was in poor health."

Geoffrey Charlesworth: "Gilbert Spencer remains very much in my memory, he was such an eccentric, the effect was comic rather than influential. I sought only to find my own language, the excellent teaching staff taught me breadth. 'Don't niggle' was the splendid dictum."

Brian Chugg: "Camberwell's Principal at the time was a Mr Daniels, a calm, approachable person, whose influence lay behind the disciplined approach in the studio and workshop. The influence of the Euston Road School was kept alive by the presence on the staff of such artists as Claude Rogers. Individual as the staff were, there was undoubtedly a unified Camberwell style. The genial German expressionist, Martin Bloch, and his fellow refugee Karel Vogel – Senior Lecturer in the Sculpture Department – were exceptions that prove the rule. A welcome feature of the teaching programme was the lectures given by visiting experts in their fields, I well remember a Mr Lucas of the National Gallery, whose methods and materials discourses were always entertaining and sometimes hilarious. The History of Art lectures by Linda Murray revealed unsuspected depths in the middle reaches of European art."

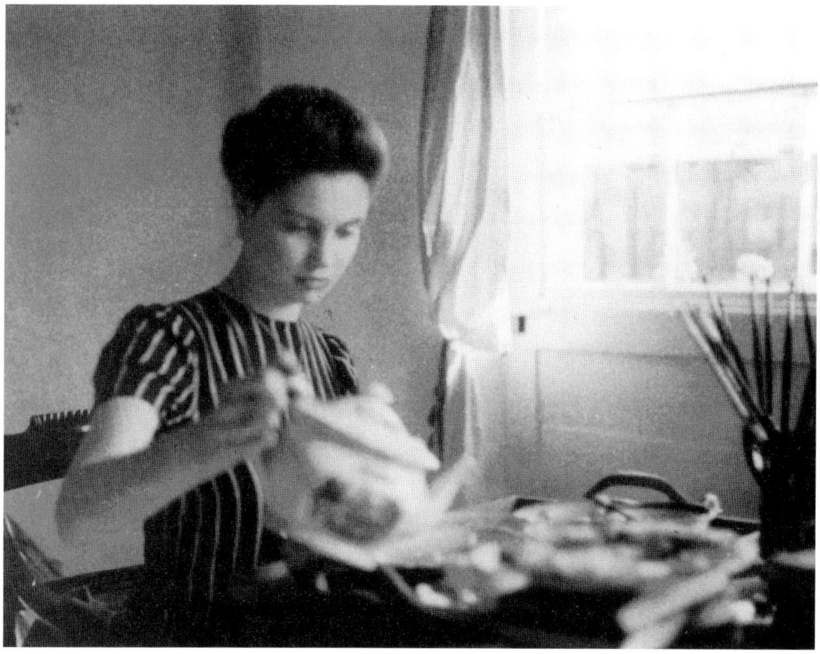

Dodie Masterman, c.1945.

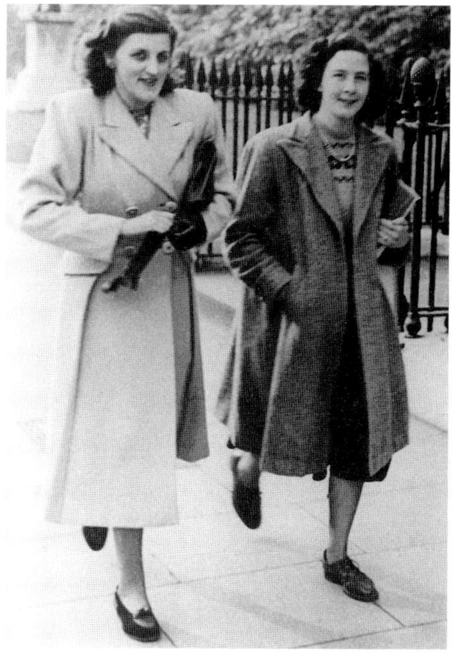

Patricia Martin (*née* Denniston) and Katherine Martin (*née* Hamp), 1948.

Joan Clare: "Victor Pasmore would burst into a class, exclaim pertinently on some point and promptly disappear. On one occasion the model wore a fur hat. 'If you see a beaver then damn well draw a beaver' he said. I did a sketch of William Coldstream dozing on a bench in the studio during a rest break, but was warned off by a student who told me the sleeper was a vicious character and I would suffer dire consequences!"

Michael Clipson: "Camberwell was to me a sort of paradise, I remember Dodie Masterman making me draw with observation. Joe Dixon, whom we all worshipped (Mr.Fix-it). The visits of Stanley Spencer (he stood on the table because of his size). I remember Dick Lee telling us to copy a Medici postcard upside-down. I remember Michael Rothenstein telling me that teaching was soul-destroying. Vivian Pitchforth, a master of drawing who, like many deaf people, heard very well when you thought he couldn't, but above all, Camberwell gave me a sound grounding in drawing and design and a questioning mind that takes nothing for granted. A colleague of mine (ex-St Martin's) swears that he can place me as an ex-Camberwell student by my drawing style – 'dot and carry'."

Peter Collingwood: "A good range of junk shops nearby, worth a weekly visit. A good yearly sale of pottery from the Ceramic Department. It was also nice to show one's new ideas to enthusiastic young students."

Lesley Cope: "Victor Pasmore, a hero of few words, stood behind me as I nervously drew, silent for ages, finally saying 'Why don't you make it sing?' It took me years before I could dance and sing through oil painting and then only sometimes. When at Camberwell I drew from life extensively, attending the day classes as well as the night. When this became too intensive, I would occasionally lash out at painting. The London horses fascinated me. I went into an attic and painted a white horse rearing. My fellow students urged me to show the teacher, so I shyly did. It happened to be Claude Rogers, who held it for quite a while, studying it, in front of a class of about sixty-five students, then came to a loud conclusion: 'Why, this woman is frustrated!'"

Richard Cowdy: "The Sculpture Department became a bastion of defence against

Modern Abstract art. For me it was, at first, a very solid training in the skills of clay modelling from life, but then became too monastic. I should have left earlier than I did."

Roy Cross: "My boyhood and early manhood and the start of my artistic career was steeped in Camberwell atmosphere. But my work centred around aviation and the sea. Camberwell School of Arts & Crafts was not ideal to teach me these special skills and backgrounds. Regarding technique, perhaps I should have persevered."

Leonard Daniels: "I was Principal for twenty-seven years. Obviously Camberwell meant a lot to me as much of my time, thought and action were centred there. I inherited, in 1948, a distinguished but ill-assorted staff. Over the years the mixture was changed until it seemed that one had got the mixture right, or nearly so. It was necessary drastically to reduce the number of subjects taught. There were changes, some wished for, some not; there was need for constant reappraisal and adjustment. Getting the right staff, not only good of their kind, but suitable to our particular needs, was one's chief preoccupation. Our purpose, generally, was concerned with aspects of the world about us. This involved the work not only of Painting and Sculpture, but of Graphic Design, of Textiles and Ceramics, in that Drawing was everywhere the basis of our study. Other approaches were possible and were exemplified in the work of some staff and many students, but basically we were concerned with aspects of reality from our study of the visible world."

Sheila Denning: "Tom Monnington said to me once in a life class 'What I admire about you Miss Denning, is the authority with which you make your mistakes...'"

Patricia Denniston: "To be in London was heady enough stuff for a colonial art student, despite rationing and the very cold winter of '47. But to find myself a student at Camberwell, just after the war, was the best part of all. It was the whole life of the place really, that splendid array of painters on the staff (I remember basking in the reflected glory of that), drawing day after day in the Life Room, unlearning the sleight of hand that had got me through three years of art school previously. 'Well, what have we here?' and Claude Rogers plonking heavily down on the donkey, knocking things flying as he did so. I remember him, Tom Monnington and William Townsend for the help they gave me, but how stimulating was the presence of Coldstream, Gowing and Pasmore, as well as those good students who I suppose had come because of them. I think most of all I learnt to look. A lot followed from that; it was a wonderful time for discovery and growth. We mustn't forget tea at the Winchester, sausage and chips for 10d at Camberwell Green. Enthusiasms shared with one's cronies – friendships which have survived distance and years."

The following is an extract of a letter dated 4th September 1949 written by Claude Rogers to Patricia Denniston, who had taken a job at the University of Cape Town for six months, teaching drawing:

"My dear Pat

It is natural enough, to begin with, to fall back upon the things you remember being taught, and in certain simple fundamentals this is more or less inevitable since the ideas trace back if not to Giotto at least to Leonardo; but if you don't mind me saying so I think it is worth remembering that the best teachers (in my opinion) teach from the stand-point of problems, indeed of the particular problem which interests them at the moment. This is what made Tonks so stimulating. Of course the old boy had terrific presence, and was armed with a battery of barge-poles for the presuming. He had wit of a sort and a sardonic tongue. But his real value was, that he was always bubbling with some enthusiasm, some interest (probably

From left to right: Geoffrey Monk, Leonard Daniels, John Brason, Gilbert Spencer, Karel Vogel and Joe Dixon, c.1953.

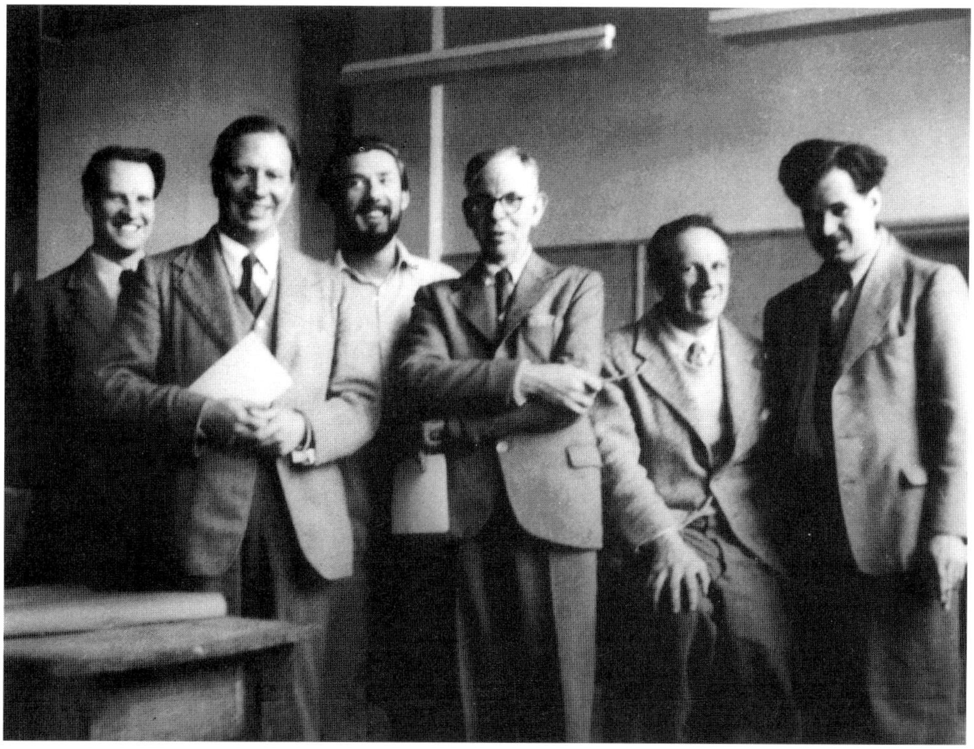

forgotten next day) some prejudice (usually vile and wrong); and, that he taught largely from these day-to-day excitements, with the result that he was stimulating and contradictory to the extent that he provoked students into rudimentary thought. Most of the things he did, in his work, were pretty frightful, and to follow his practice led close to perdition. But he was always working, always reading and thinking about painting; and many of the things he said were memorable, some of them if only because they were presented rather dogmatically and simply, and invited questioning and contraction – silent questioning and contradiction I need hardly say. Victor Pasmore has something of this divine gift of stimulating and provoking, though as I need not remind you his work is on a totally different level. What I am getting at is this; use the things you remember being taught as a standby for the moment if you like, but try to teach from your own experience and interests. Try to think out why you do what you do when you paint and draw; and what you mean by the technical terms you use – 'tone', 'colour', 'direction', 'proportion', 'silhouette', 'shape left' and the rest – in relation to your own work and your own interests and to what others have said or written about them. The whole fun of teaching (apart from the personal contacts) and the only way to keep alive at it and not to become a pedantic machine, is to do this. You will find that you presently develop little verbal tricks for explaining points to people. As soon as I become conscious of such a trick (and so a bit bored with it) I try to drop it and to find an alternative… and you must of course always criticise work in relation to the standard each student has achieved, besides your own personal, high-falutin' Leonardo-Rembrandt-cum-Cézanne (or whatever it is ideal!)."

Joe Dixon: "William Johnstone used to have a terrible habit of offering students more places than were really available for comfort. At the beginning of one term, students were jammed in the hallways and corridors and Johnstone called Halliwell to ask why this had occurred. Johnstone was not amused to be told that it was his fault for offering too many places. However, no-one to my knowledge was every asked not to attend, due to an excess of numbers."

Marianne Downing: "Friendship, warmth, sincerity. During the worst air-raids the tutors managed to arrive for evening classes. During the continuous raids of 1944/5

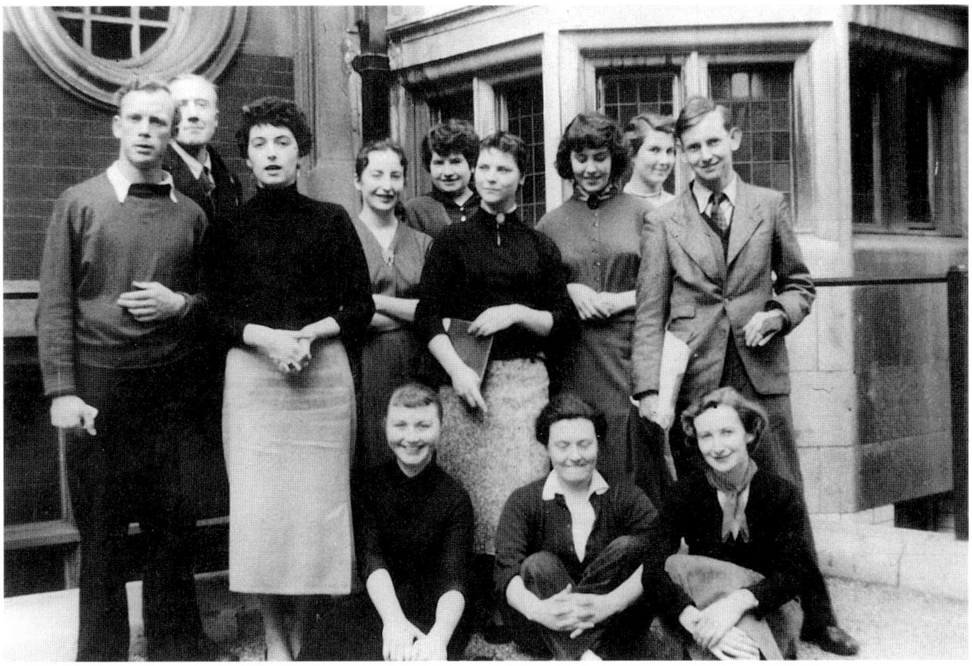

Intermediate group, outside the main building, Camberwell, 1950. Louise Hencke (centre, holding book) and Pip Macfarlane (seated front left).

there were many times when the models did not turn up, and only two or three students came to the evening life classes. John Minton arranged for students to take it in turn to pose, he himself would divide his time between teaching and posing. He would 'sign on' a student as a model and would divide the model's fee between us."

Bernard Dunstan: "I started teaching at Camberwell around 1950/51, having come back to London from Bristol the previous year. I had been teaching in Bristol at the West of England College of Art and had heard a good deal about Camberwell from George Sweet, the Head of my Department, a close friend of Claude Rogers, who engaged, while I was there, a Camberwell ex-student, Hilda Scott, to teach drawing. This was the first introduction I had to the 'point-to-point' measuring, the Camberwell way of drawing. I was impressed by its intensity and uncompromising attitude – no mere approximation or guessing – but appalled by its rigidity and desperate slowness. I had the same feelings on starting to teach a life class at Camberwell. Accustomed to a certain freedom and charm of 'touch' from the Slade and the Byam Shaw – even if I found it hard to imitate – I was baffled by students who drew in such a doctrinaire way; always sight-size; sometimes seeming to get no further than the collar-bones after a morning's work, going laboriously round the outline of, for instance, a foot, with no thought of the form coming towards you or receding. Much later on I remember saying to a student 'but why don't you put the eyes in?' to be told severely, 'I am not bothering about details'. There was a student painting a head, who made all the obligatory exact measurements from the knot of the model's tie. Naturally, every day the tie was tied slightly differently; so every measurement had to be re-made, but there was a certain rigorous moral principle, one felt, involved.

I began teaching 'Intermediate Comp.' – Composition classes for the Intermediate students. For the Intermediate exam, they had to produce a half imperial picture in gouache. I also took some evening drawing classes. This was, of course, at a period when there was a glut of students and it was comparatively easy to get a job teaching. Once in, you made yourself useful, and were given odd bits of teaching here and there. The evening life-drawing classes were straightforward, if slightly exhausting, if one had been in the School all day. They were mostly amateurs with a scattering of day students. One of my regulars was a Mormon lift attendant who used to wait for the model to appear; if not an attractive girl he would say 'Well, I don't think I'll stay this evening – a bit tired'. Intermediate Comp. was harder work. The students seemed mostly to have come up from the Junior School – an interesting invention of that period which took students of a very tender age so that by the time they came up to the Senior School they seemed to 'know it all'. They were tough, and back-chat and repartee was continual. Barry Fantoni and his cronies would paint nothing, it seemed, but jazz bands, whatever the subject set. I used to take the rather unruly class (though there were always some charming girls in it) out to draw in the mornings – Camberwell Green, Peckham Rye, tube stations – and they would paint in the afternoon. Life-classes with these students were harder work than with the amateurs, you had to try to stop them talking, for one thing, for at that time there was quite a strict rule that no talking went on while the model was posing, this was difficult for such articulate characters. We had to fill up the most complicated forms – hours worked, pay per hour, which altered according to the number of hours – in order to get any money at the end of the month, or rather several weeks after the end of the month.

Philip Matthews, then acting Head of Department, gave me my job, largely I think on the strength of a large ambitious picture I had shown at the New English Art Club exhibition, a criticism of which he wrote for *Arts Review*. The Principal at the time was Leonard Daniels, an extremely nice and urbane man whose pleasant and what would now be called 'laid-back' manner possibly hid a determined and very clear mind. Later on, I took over Claude Rogers' evening class in painting; but as a very subordinate member of the staff I never met any of the great men, Coldstream or Pasmore, and only slightly do I remember meeting Claude at Camberwell, though of course I did later on. Perhaps at that period, he was the only one left. The members of staff that I knew well were Richard Eurich, Martin Bloch, Karel Vogel, Chris Chamberlain, and Michael Salaman. Later, Gilbert Spencer became Head of the Department. Violently opposed to Bloch and not particularly in any case in tune with the students and their prevailing attitude to drawing, his appearances in the studios were on occasion explosive and seldom, I feel, very helpful to the students. But it was at a time of a certain confusion of aims. It was rather interesting to me to see the clash, or combination of Bloch's expressionist approach with the existing, but perhaps by now less all-pervasive, Camberwell drawing. Bloch had a powerful and persuasive personality; students are such sheep that they will follow any teacher with charisma, and he gathered round him a nucleus of devoted disciples (what a familiar situation all this is), while others remained firmly devoted to the pure doctrine. But somehow there developed a sort of drawing which combined the two approaches – diametrically opposed one might say – in an interesting way.

As a digression, I might put in here a theory that teaching in art schools can be very bad for the painter, although it has been assumed for a very long time in England that it is the only way he can stay alive and keep on painting. But the trouble is that he is likely to be influenced, almost unconsciously, by his fellow members of staff and even by his students, into an attempt to get on to whatever band-wagon is going at the time. Many good painters, I am convinced, have been tempted away from their natural path by this quite natural interest in 'what's going on', and subconscious desire not to appear an 'old fogey'. Life-drawing in particular became a sort of battleground in which each School or faction displayed its only stylistic banner. I can remember when it was possible to tell, with a certain accuracy, where a student had come from by the style of the drawing – dots and dashes from Camberwell; black charcoal rubbed so vehemently that it went through the paper from Bromley, or anywhere where the Bomberg influence prevailed; lines like a hedgehog's spikes going in all directions with a sharp edge defining each change of plane, from the Byam Shaw. How tiresome it all seems. What a relief it would have been to have seen a single student who simply looked at the model and, in love with the subtle ample lines, attempted to trace them on his

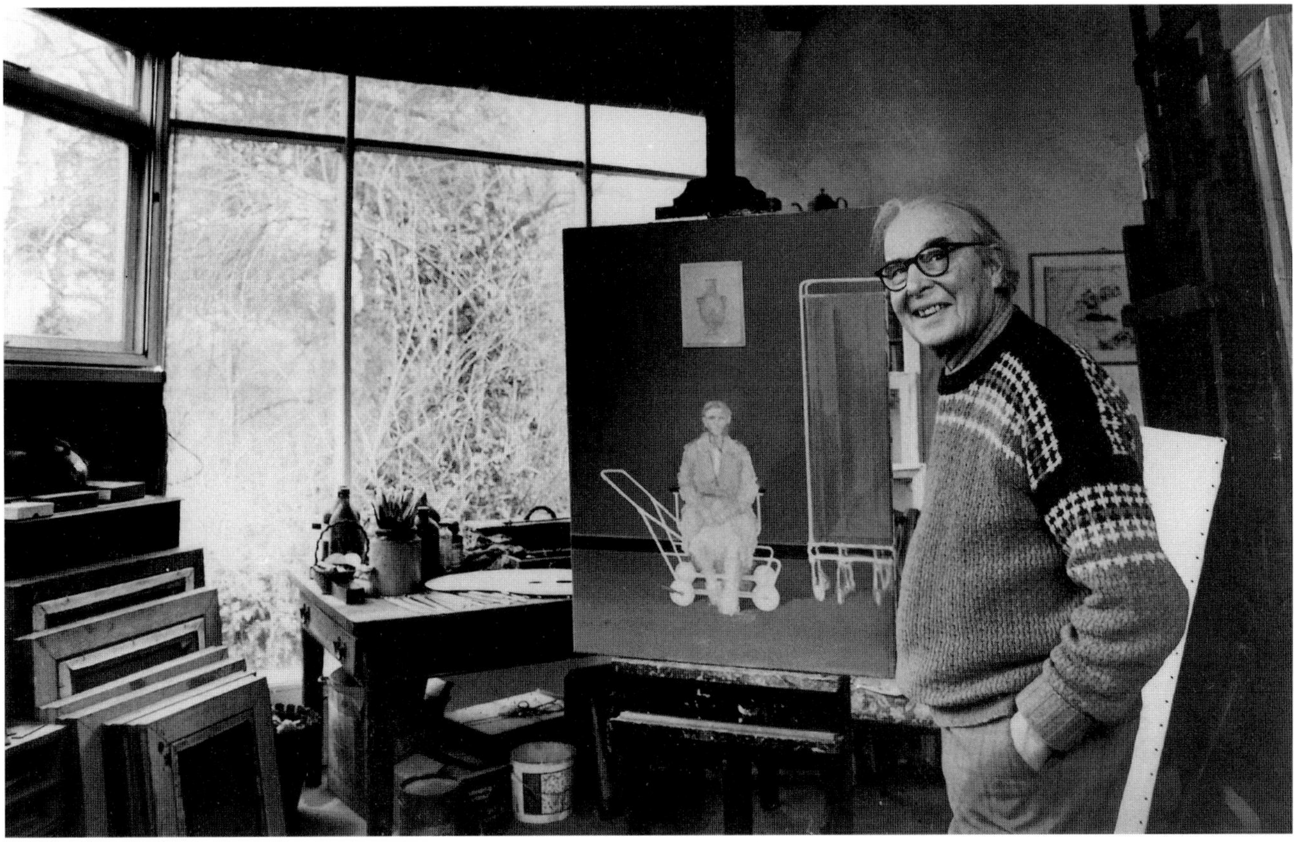

Michael Salaman, c.1960.

paper without the interference of any stylistic demands!

By the time Robert Medley took over as Head of Department, I was beginning to reduce my teaching at Camberwell and began to take on more at other schools; so I didn't take part much in the so-called 'Art School revolution' as it affected Camberwell. 'Intermediate' disappeared with much else, but unlike so many other art schools, life-drawing did go on. My teaching at this period dwindled to evening classes in life-drawing and general drawing as it was called, covering still-life and so on, and much attended by GCE students, until after the period of the exam, when the class suddenly diminished to a mere handful. I hardly saw any other members of the staff. Later still I became a member of the governing body as the R.A. representative with Leonard Daniels as the Principal in the new School building, and later on still under the Headship of Ian Tregarthen-Jenkin, until all my old friends – Philip Matthews, Dick Lee, Chris Chamberlain – either retired or died. The Governing body itself seemed to get bigger and more politically or ILEA dominated; when I too faded out and no longer took the 36 bus from Victoria."

Roy Turner Durrant: "The female models meant a great deal to me, as I remember it."

Harold Eldridge: "After more than forty years it's difficult to remember in detail, but suffice to say that one made the journey to Camberwell every evening and on Saturday afternoon after work in all weathers and particularly during air-raids – it must have meant a great deal."

Bernard Evans: "Martin Bloch attached great importance to drawing. His life-drawing sessions were divided into two halves. The first half consisted of quick poses, often the model was asked to take up a particular pose such as climbing a ladder or picking up a jug. He might ask the model to repeat the action from time to time while we were drawing, in order to maintain the spontaneity of the pose and

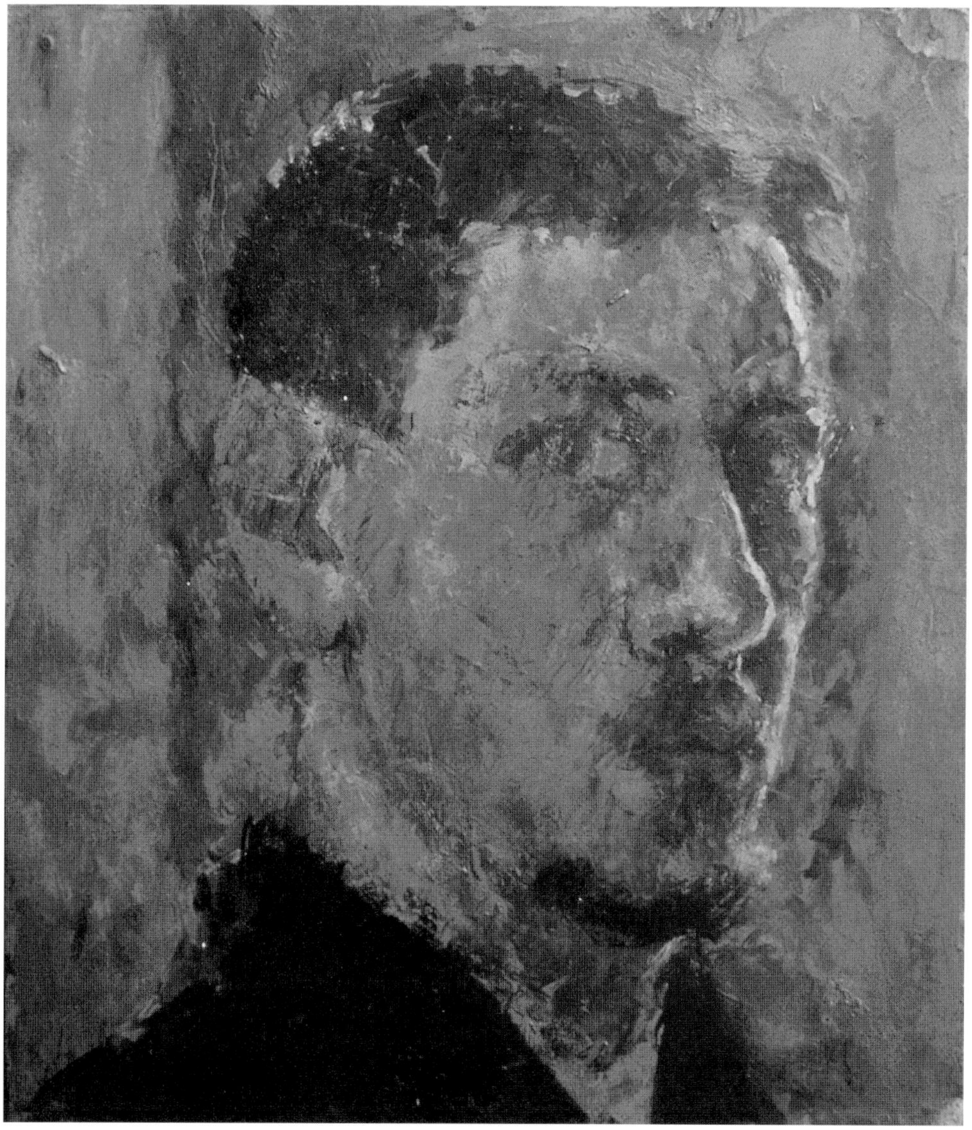

Barry Fantoni. *Self portrait*, c.1958. Oil on canvas, 18in x 12in. Courtesy *Sunday Times.*

the tension of the muscles. Malcolm Morley was a student during my time at Camberwell, and we became very friendly. I remember he was asked to do a composition based on the Flight from Egypt. The teachers were not amused when his painting showed Rommel in the desert full of tanks, fleeing from the advancing British Army."

Anthony Eyton: "It was a felicitous time in that many of one's fellow students had just returned from being in the Services, and so there was a very enthusiastic atmosphere with strong positive teaching from William Coldstream, Victor Pasmore, Claude Rogers and John Dodgson. The rigour of painting from the model, small in scale and dull in colour, was exacting. We believed in the particular and that pictures should be made according to our sensations, aided and abetted by measuring and carefully relating colours to each other. The emphasis on the value of drawing was a good rock bed. Victor Pasmore, on looking at a still-life with vegetables, once said ' the trouble with you is that you have no sense of art'."

Barry Fantoni: "Gilbert Spencer was a teacher at Camberwell during the early to mid-fifties. If anything, he was more eccentric than his more famous brother

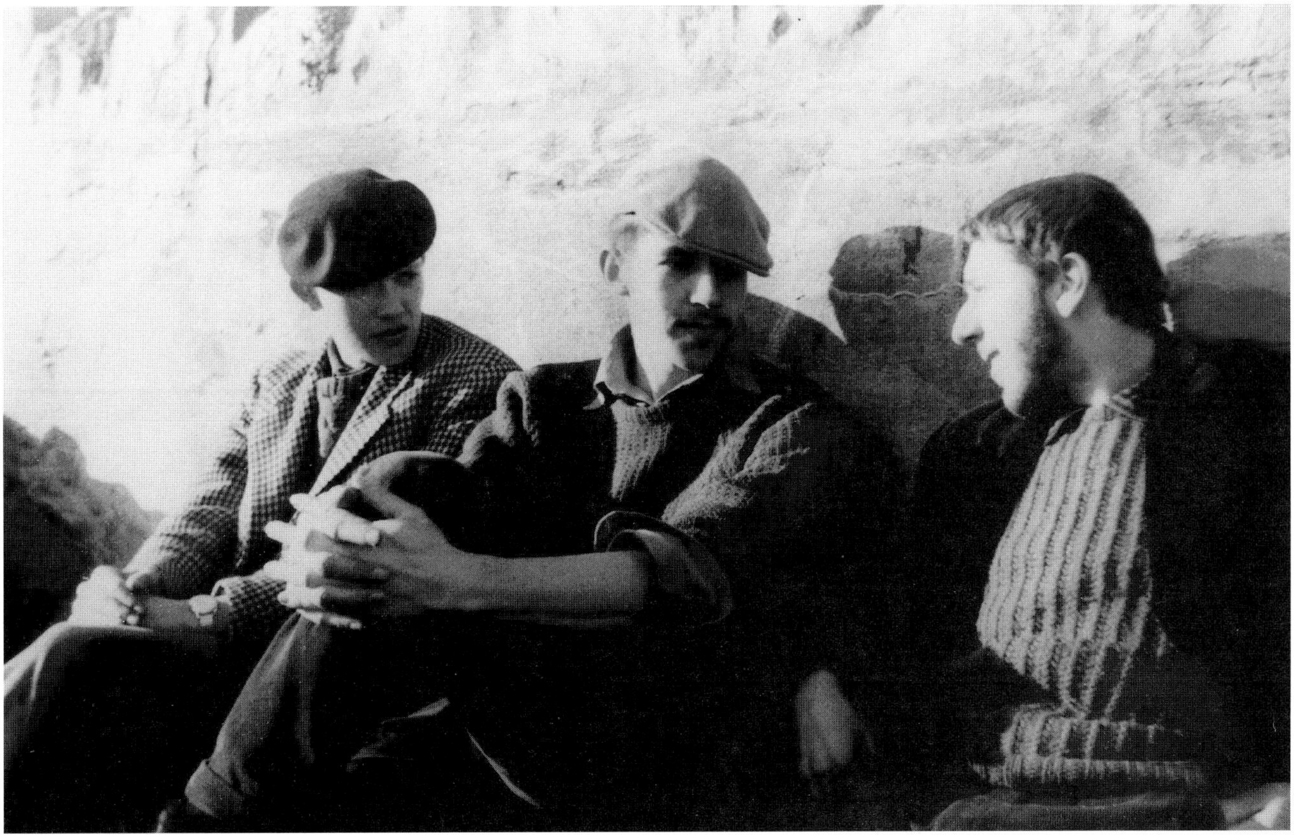

Port Isaac, Cornwall, 1957. Left to right: Tom Morgan, Brian Davies, Barry Fantoni.

Stanley, although on the surface he appeared more normal. I was once painting a view from an upstairs window which overlooked the main road from Camberwell to Peckham. It was an April morning and the rain, when it fell, came down in sudden heavy showers. As I struggled with the task of relating the shapes of the houses against the blossoming tress, I noticed Gilbert Spencer walking towards a letterbox, some two hundred yards away from the School. A man in his sixties, he carried a letter in front of him as if he were about to present it to someone. I watched as the rain began to fall heavily from an overcast sky. Totally unaware of the downpour, Gilbert inched forwards, his pace slow and deliberate. He reached the letterbox and passed it, the letter in his outstretched grasp getting soggier by the second. A dozen or more paces beyond the letterbox, he suddenly stopped and began walking backwards. When he finally drew level with the letterbox he shoved the lump of white pulp into its mouth and, turning round, trundled slowly back to the life class where wet and undisturbed, he continued teaching!"

Clifford Frith: "In 1942 I started teaching at Camberwell. William Johnstone was Principal and it was he who was responsible for bringing in such distinguished staff including Mervyn Peake, Michael Ayrton and John Minton, who brought a different attitude and influence into the School. Johnstone was a remarkable man, he looked a little like Picasso. I always felt he liked to emphasise the fact too. I and many other students and staff were terrified of him in a fascinated way, a totally unconventional head of School. On one occasion, I was summoned to his room to discover A. E. Halliwell draped in a uniform of an Army Colonel three sizes too big, posing for a commission on which William Johnstone was working. I was then ordered to 'lay in' the entire canvas while 'Picasso' paced up and down behind me issuing instructions to both of us. It was Johnstone who insisted we all sign a book on arrival, together with a written explanation for his lateness. Victor Pasmore, who was then living in Blackheath, on arriving a few minutes late wrote 'Fog in Channel'. We used to have an annual cricket match between Camberwell and Goldsmiths', which Philip Matthews and Joe Dixon used to organise. By this time I had also taught at Goldsmiths' and I had the greatest of difficulty deciding which team to play for. I remember sharing a life-class with Lawrence Gowing, there were so many students we couldn't get into the studio. The post-war boom!"

Terry Frost: "It was an opportunity to meet 'the Coldstream Guards'."

David Garbett: "Monty Sunshine – the jazz Clarinettist – who regularly played with his group at the end of term dances; his purity of tone and uninterrupted line with its likeness and singing quality was outstanding in its own right and heaven to dance to, especially after 'bitter and rum' at the Walmer Castle pub opposite. Art by contrast was confusion, with only hints of possibilities and still continues to be so up to a point."

Eleanor Gaussen Marks: "There was an exciting feeling of discovery and vitality and of group togetherness. The life drawing classes taken by Francis Hoyland opened up new vistas of possibility for me. There was a strong comradeship which passed the teacher/student syndrome, and led to lasting friendships. Philip Matthews was, in particular, a kind and helpful mentor."

Woolf Goldberg: "The one thing that really sticks in my mind about the School, in the old building in those days, was the appalling food in the canteen, provided by a very fat female cook who really imagined she was God's gift to our stomachs."

Alastair Gordon: "Five years of warfare in the Brigade of Guards. Then demobilisation and the number 12 bus down Peckham Road to Camberwell School of Arts & Crafts with a portfolio of drawings under my arm. Some change in life-style. William Johnstone examined my collection of work in silence while I stood to one side, diffidence and arrogance warring within me at the same time. I was accepted. Having returned to a strange London after protracted excursions through the Middle East and Europe, I consulted several wise old owls either in, or connected with, the art business. They were unanimous in saying 'Camberwell is the best place, dear boy'. One, bawdy and cynical, said 'plenty of sex but not much art'. The truth was that William Johnstone (as Principal) had been gathering together a teaching staff second to none: The Euston Road School – Victor Pasmore, Claude Rogers, William Coldstream, Lawrence Gowing, Tom Monnington (already an R.A.), John Dodgson, Elliot Seabrook, Rodney Burn (oldies), Kenneth Martin and the whiz-kid, John Minton.

My first day presented no fears: ex-service men and women were then quick to adapt to new, strange environments. (We had, after all, been doing just that for years). I knew little about the domestic art scene in London, and perhaps I had a secret snobbishness that the French for painting and the Germans for music, were far superior. Sensibly though, I watched and waited, making friends with pretty girls and men of my own vintage. Like all students, we collected into interchangeable groups, the difference being that many of us were in our middle to late twenties and anxious to make up lost time. The more gifted and intellectual students – Anthony Eyton, Andrew Forge, Anthony Fry, Patrick Symons, Patrick George, Henry Mundy and others, stood apart, not through conscious elitism. They were too dedicated to strike poses.

The painting and drawing school was spread between four large north-facing studios built in a stark Edwardian style. They comprised the life painting and life drawing studios, and below them a general purpose studio and the antique room.

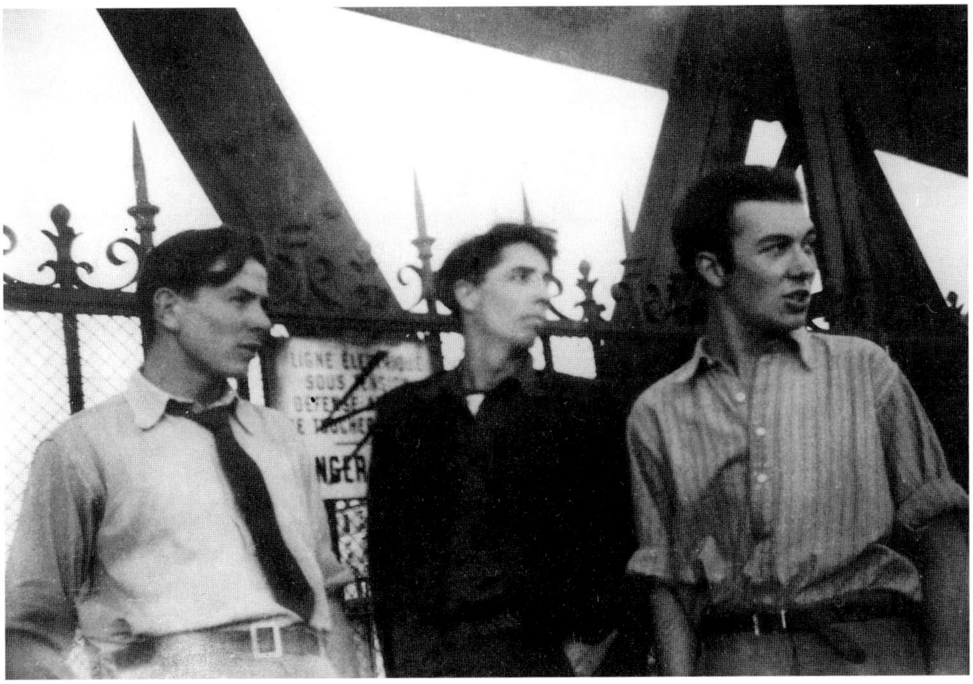

Eiffel Tower, Paris, 1948. Left to right: Peter Dunbar, John Minton, Robert Hunt. Courtesy of Marsh Dunbar and Robert Hunt.

In this latter there was occasionally a clothed model but usually it was deserted save for a few contemplative souls painstakingly working out their personal nirvanas in paint; except for one – Terry Frost – who made detailed and accurate drawings of the antique with an H pencil. Up in the life rooms a recurring selection of professional models stood, sat or lay in undramatic poses, the Euston Road ethos being that the nude human body was just another object whose structure must be analytically observed and transcribed unemotionally to canvas or paper. If this sounds flippant it is not meant to be. What I learnt at Camberwell was that meretricious reportage was a base art compared to the intelligent co-ordination of eye, mind and hand for translating the three-dimensional world on to a flat surface. Surely a sound base for students to work at for two years before launching (if they so wish) into the abstract, the fantastic, all the modern-isms, or...stay where they are. The human bodies we studied so earnestly belonged to a now almost extinct profession. Miss Murphy, secretary of the models' union (imagine!) and her husband were nudists anyway, ensuring a deep all-over tan, especially in a hot summer. One girl, Junoesque in build, was so prim that it was an effort to remove her dressing gown on the rostrum. Why she took up modelling gave rise to ribald speculation. Another girl looked straight out of Thurber until she posed, when all was grace and elegance. In those days male models wore a cache-sexe (Miss Murphy wore one in pale blue silk once a month for a few days). The male models all looked elderly, until in 1948 one arrived who looked like Father Time. Elliot Seabrook asked him how long he had been modelling for, and he replied that his first job was 'for Mr Millais as the boy in green in *The Boyhood of Raleigh*'. Since the picture was painted in 1865 he must have been over ninety...

I have mentioned the general-purpose room below the life rooms: I don't want to give the impression that the nude was all. It was in this room that students would work at still-lives of their own construction or bring in landscape sketches and work them up into paintings. I myself spent a week in Wapping doing sketches for a dockscape which provoked half-an-hour of fascinating soliloquy about the nature of art from Victor Pasmore, who was at that time going through the transition from figurative to abstract. Victor's internal workings-out found verbal form in the most alarming but brilliant statements to students, who had to sort out in their own minds which were eccentric discards and which were relevant to their own work. Kenneth

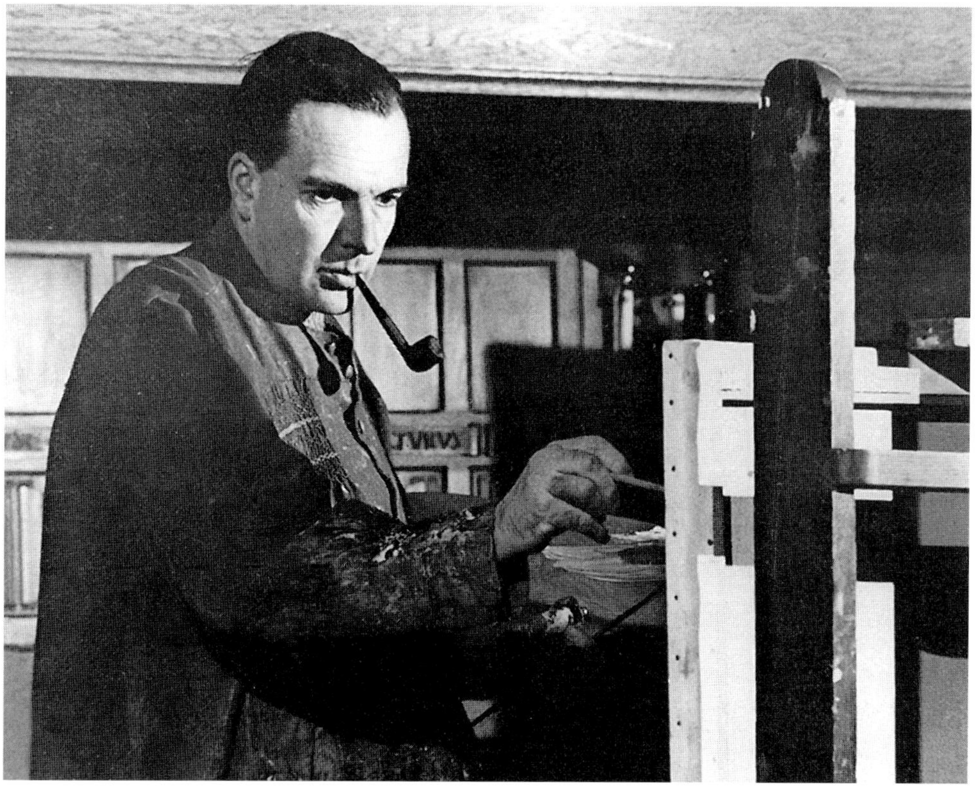

Earl Haig, c.1953.

Martin, on the other hand, also getting to grips with his mathematically calculated mobiles, kept his own counsel, confining himself to admirably pithy remarks like 'Don't let your shapes get flabby'.

At this time, just after the war, the London County Council committed itself to giving grants to thousands of art students, from which were expected to emerge only a handful with real talent and possibly a genius or two. Something like throwing ink at walls for years and by chance writing a symphony. The task for our teachers therefore was to concentrate on the obviously gifted and offer cursory but constructive advice to the rest 'You haven't quite realised that right buttock' said Claude Rogers loudly to one gushing girl, and hastily moved on. Compared to modern times, the teachers had it easy. We were after all, most of us, straight from years of military discipline and could readily take up the cerebral disciplines which painters such as William Coldstream and Tom Monnington regarded as essential learning. An airy-fairy girl, having waved brush-strokes all over the canvas, had inaccuracies pointed out to her, 'Oh' she said, 'but I'm just sketching it in', and got the crushing rejoinder 'Then why not sketch it in RIGHT'.

I say that our teachers had it easy, but I don't mean financially. Those who can, cast your mind back thirty-five years and remember the art market then was not geared to pushing talent at greedy 'investors'. There were the few discerning collectors, but they were too few to pay the bills, even of established painters. All of our teachers were respected by the cognoscenti, but none was a name known to the public. We were the privileged observers before the art boom carried some of them to national and even international fame. Oddly enough sculpture – the real English leader in the world market – was only just operational at Camberwell. There was a single room in the basement for sculpture classes, where some of us threw clay about once a week, moving the model around on her circular turntable according to the angle you fancied working on. Nothing remotely memorable came out of this room in spite of the enthusiasm of Huxley Jones' teaching. Elsewhere in the building there was a thriving pottery school (which had Alan Caiger-Smith as a student) and a graphics school to which on festive occasions student Humphrey

Lyttleton would bring his trumpet.

As part of the diploma course there were regular lectures on art history given by members of the Courtauld Institute. These lectures became so banal ('This painting' announced one girl showing a slide of a van Eyck 'has very good recession') that a group headed by Andrew Forge decided that we would give our own lectures, and scrap the Courtauld. This worked very well, since it gave the student lecturers the incentive to swot up particular subjects thoroughly; no-one wanted to make a fool of himself in front of fellow-students. In all this art education there was little instruction in knowledge and handling of materials. I suppose that observation and demonstration were considered enough. Plenty of art, but not enough craft. You stretched your own canvas, primed it as best you knew how from what you could pick up, brought brushes and paints to suit your own style and just got on with it.

I have hinted that the social life was in the form of concentric but overlapping rings. Six of us, three men and three girls (one of whom became my wife) lunched daily at the Kentish Drovers, a cosy faded Victorian pub now alas replaced by ugly shops. The landlord, Mr Morgan, was as Victorian as his pub, 'Will you be taking luncheon now, ladies and gentlemen?' We had our own table, kept reserved for us and no-one else. Our conversation was gossipy and no deep dialogue of anaesthetic turn marred the merriment. Occasionally we would invite friends to come down from London to join us. I cannot count the number of marriages and liaisons that developed over the two years, nor the enduring friendships, nor the alliances to make a purer aesthetic. What I do know is that I can look back now, later, and experience a warm glow of memories. Some agonies and loneliness, yes, but these recede into the background against that brave new world when British art started to pick up the bits and reassemble a structure which, if it led to other things – abstract, pop, minimal, post-modernism – was the soundly based catalyst from which all others grew."

Anne Gordon (*née* Barry): "Camberwell was a nice sociable rest centre, away from the dances and night-clubs! I remember Claude Rogers looking at an animal painting I had done and commenting 'draws horses – won't starve'."

Kenneth Gribble: "I went to Camberwell by accident, I had originally been accepted at the Slade as Randolph Schwabe was very taken with my drawings. He spoke of the art scene and gave such a glowing account of Camberwell saying 'we have some of our men there', (Coldstream and Rogers) that I spent an extra year there before taking up my place at the Slade. After the serenity of Harrow School of Art, Camberwell was bedlam; shortages of everything including easels. I remember Claude Rogers going bonkers – 'these bloody students' was all he used to say about the new intake. I also recall John Minton clearing up the debris of the blitz in the litho room and frantic activity with a levigator and Litho press. I think I was there when the first litho was printed by Minton. The place seemed to be constantly full of tobacco smoke and everywhere had an aroma of Balkan Sobranie and turpentine."

Pamela Haddon: "When the first euphoria of just being there had worn off, I found Camberwell most bewildering. Then eventually quite miraculously I made friends with some fascinating people, among them some energetic thinkers; and it meant that I became better educated and partly civilised."

The Earl Haig: "Lawrence Gowing, whose wide knowledge of painters of the past and whose professional approach to the practicalities of landscaping (whose preparations for the field, selection of equipment and subject matter would have earned him promotion in the army) was a strong influence...The places where our painting took place became trodden like battlefields after days of stamping about in the grass and nettles..."

Edward Hamlyn: "I was taught by highly motivated, practising artists. I was young and impressionable and it has taken me twenty years to turn my back... I still occasionally look over my shoulder."

Melville Hardiment: "...to be taken seriously by artists of the stature of Victor Pasmore and Claude Rogers was such a creative stimulus that the kick lasted all one's life...how many combinations can be arranged...from a corridor wall, a table top, a chocolate coloured knife box and a lemon, all multiplied by the number of colours available, the answer was my first still-life under Claude Rogers."

Donald Harris: "On arriving from South Africa in the immediate post-war years, I was an apostle of 'modernism', an attitude that has been modified by stages over the years. As an exponent – or rather one who was tending towards abstraction via cubism, I had limited experience of great art in the original and was overwhelmed by the National Gallery. I was also distinctly underwhelmed by the most recent work at the Musée de l'Art Moderne in Paris. This more than anything else knocked the bottom out of my world. When in addition, West End galleries were uninterested in what I had to show in my folder, I was somewhat shattered. I met Albert Garrett (the wood engraver) who recommended Camberwell as the place to go. I found the restrictions placed upon me by the Coldstream type disciplines irksome. It seemed to be generally thought there, that any mark appearing to have any vitality, spontaneity or assurance, was frowned upon. However, I accepted the discipline holding my own views in reserve as a challenge. The pain involved in this effort was to last many years, but was eventually to help me to clarify my notions and my own approach."

David Hepher: "Camberwell stopped one dead in one's tracks and made one look at the real world very hard. It was a very perceptual School, perhaps too much so. Cézanne was God and there was a general mistrust of twentieth century art. That was its strength, blinkered, narrow but sound. Its failure was to place too big a burden of the achievements of the past on to its students' heads and I think this often stifled and inhibited those who passed through. The 'mores' of Euston Road could so easily turn into a sort of constipated morality. The teachers and artists with more vision who were freer in this respect were Spencer, Eurich and Bloch and indeed the 'horse's mouth' himself – Coldstream – also had a much wider vision."

Barry Hirst: "We were very 'green' in 1950 and I remember being taken aback on the first day that I was there by Theo Mendez (then a student) asking me, within two hours of having arrived, 'if I was settling in alright?' Theo, I should add, was also drawing upon 'two hours worth' of experience...he was never short of confidence, this is my earliest memory. During those first two years Dodie Masterman made an impression, and it was at this time that I first encountered Dick Lee. Lee, apart from running a 'tight' Euston Road drawing class, is also remembered as having explained how to tune a ukulele against the phrase 'my dog has fleas' (an absolutely essential skill to possess). Drawing was all-important and the strict regimes for which Camberwell was primarily known at that time provided a firm basis for many of us. However, I am bound to add that I still often wonder whether the 'regime' was also responsible for stultifying the future of as many as it helped. Another phenomenon at that time was to perceive Uglow (a senior Student) proceeding to college in 'shorts', unheard of in those days and particularly in a south-east London urban setting.

It was towards the end of this first two year period that I unofficially absented myself from the prescribed classes to join those of the painting school run under the aegis of Martin Bloch. Bloch, in those days, represented the most diametrically extreme position imaginable when compared to the Euston Road. His strength as a teacher lay in his ability to 'fire' his students through his unwavering sense of commitment to painting and drawing, drawing of a very different kind to that practised by other staff. This total belief in drawing was coupled to a use of 'colour', which came as a merciful release to many of us. You can imagine the shock for a typical Camberwell student to be told 'Today is a pink day, paint as much of your picture pink as you dare let the paint flow' or again, 'do not draw with all these measurements, preserve the naive quality'. My parents had resisted my going to art school and there was never enough money for materials (grants were few and far between and I certainly did not have one). On one occasion I was painting a very small panel of (God knows why!) a man on his hands and knees stalking pigeons across a low pitched slate roof. I was trying to work with about three tubes of colour and no white. Bloch wanted to know why I was working in this very limited way, I said 'because I have not any colours'. Within one hour he returned with a carrier bag containing colour and brushes which he had purchased from the 'materials shop' at the foot of Rye Lane. "You have no excuse for painting such a dull picture now have you!". It should be remembered that he and his family were then living at Alma Studios (Herman had stepped in to offer them a temporary home). His main means of subsistence was his part-time teaching at Camberwell. He had very little and yet he had always been doing things like this. After Intermediate, came the Army. When I returned, Bloch was dead. Afterwards I often went to see Madame Bloch, but I do so much regret the shortness of the time that I was able to know Martin. Without any doubt whatsoever he is my fondest memory and it is he to whom I remain most grateful.

After the Army I became a painting student, I still had no grant and was living in a partitioned semi-basement at New Cross Gate. I earned £3/10s a week working as a doorman at the New Cross Odeon, opposite the Marquis of Granby... and that was it! Somehow or other Leonard Daniels, the Principal, never did come to me for fees. I also received an unofficial materials allowance which would mysteriously appear at my painting place. I do not know where it came from or who was responsible for providing it, but such things were possible and did happen at Camberwell. Other less charming examples come to mind, like arriving early in order to eat the still-lifes of the part-time extra-mural students. There was also a period where, in order to conserve slender funds, a group of us took to living in the roof (this was quite a good arrangement as one could enter and leave the building once it was locked by clambering from a window across the wall and out through the grounds of an asylum(?) next door). This episode came to an end when the caretaker caught us grilling the part-timers' still-life herrings on the model's fire. Yet again we were treated with a patience and generosity typical of the particular nature of Camberwell at that time.

Suffice to say...the virtues of Camberwell were that it was an institution which put its students first. It was run by people who believed in the subject. If you were lucky enough to have gone there then you were taught something, irrespective of whether you agreed with the philosophy or not. The staff were not the professional educators who are currently selling-out the subject, they were painters and sculptors whose first commitment was to painting and sculpture. I count myself fortunate to have been able to go to Camberwell, for whilst many contemporaries might have similar feelings about their own particular college, I do think that few

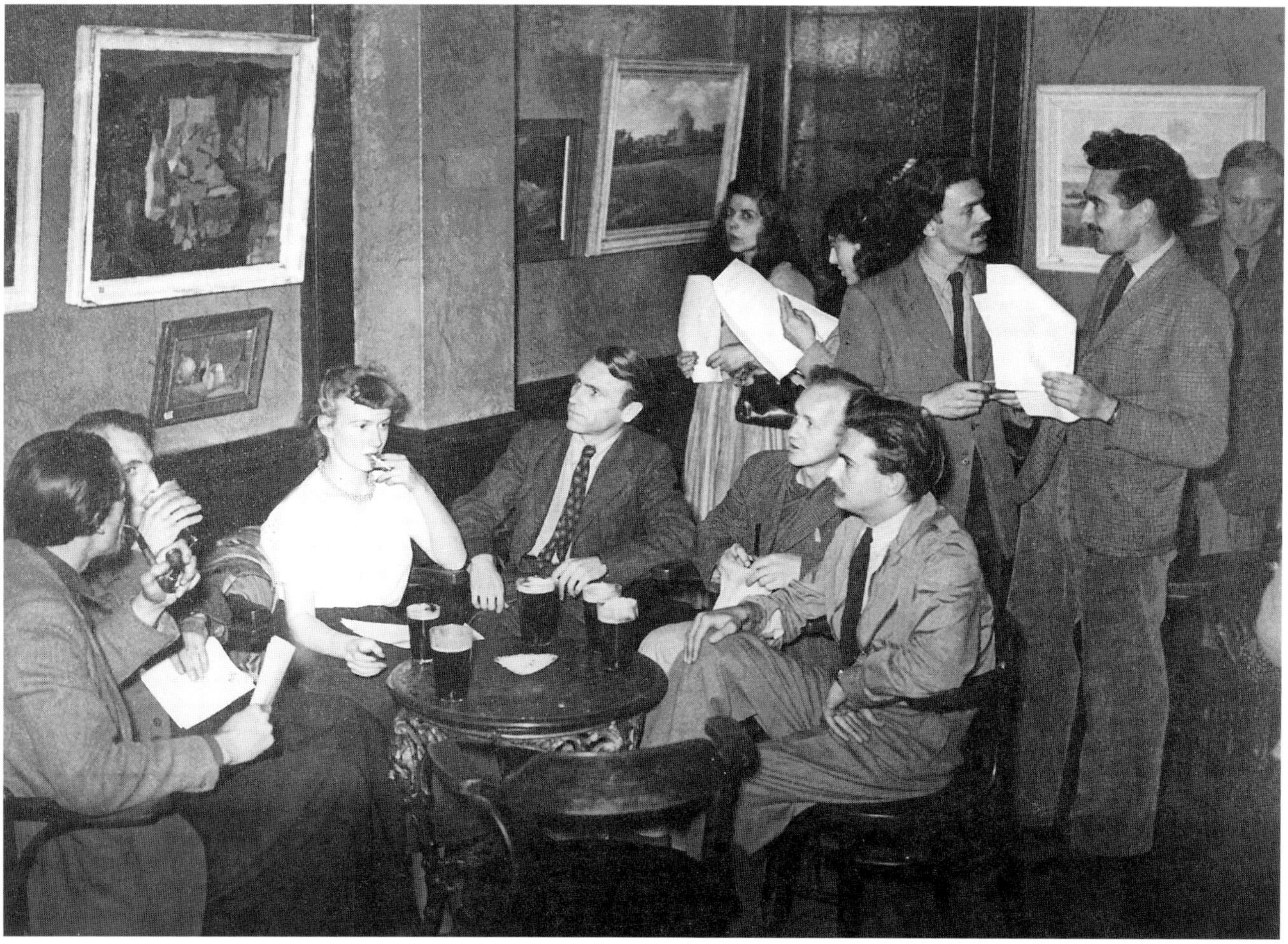

Exhibition of Camberwell students' paintings, Walmer Castle, August 1948. Seated at table from left to right: Gillian Ayres, Henry Mundy, unknown, unknown, Opal Echalaz (standing in front of painting), Elise Miers standing behind William Millar, who is talking to Anthony Eyton. The elderly gentleman on the right is Elliott Seabrooke.

colleges could have offered the formidable depth of experience available at Camberwell at that time. I sometimes wonder whether or how we, the beneficiaries, have fulfilled our responsibility towards today's students – I do not think it bears comparison."

Alexander Hollweg: I was interviewed late in 1959 by Philip Matthews and Robert Medley. Robert was a friend of my grandfather – Edward Wadsworth – who had drawn Robert's friend Rupert Doone, and he had suggested I went to Camberwell. They must have thought me a bit odd with a rather poor folder of work to show. I remember they were fairly unimpressed, but what stuck in my memory was that they both wore tweed jackets and highly coloured paisley ties. I said that I wanted to be an illustrator, but Medley said I should paint, as all the best illustrators were painters. They put me into the Intermediates for a year with Joe Dixon and Paul Bullard.

It was a most informative period, I learnt a lot in that year and would have been lost without it. The TRUTH Myth…ART was a dirty word…artistic demeaning criticism. I teased Euan Uglow, saying that 'artistical' was probably the true pejorative. It was not him personally but what he represented as the Camberwell ethic that I found frustrating. Slickness, style, a clear procedure appeared to be anathema. So, was picture making and story-telling abstraction or making things up? The truth was what one could see, observation the true way and objectivity the goal. This was art, what happened was that everyone took on one of the 'house styles', Coldstream and later Auerbach, and they assumed that they were doing Art! In fact, I learned a lot from Euan and employed his dicta with good effect as far as I could in my final examination for N.D.D. Medley was different, he would rush into the studio with nervous languidity, look at your picture, make a couple of gestures rather like describing a space or the angle between two planes, rush out again only pausing at the door to exclaim 'The penny will drop in two years time…'. But he encouraged me to follow my own personality and general exuberance. I took my dreary pictures to him one day and he remarked that the darkness was not for him – the bleak landscape of Peckham in the late '50s, Euston Road, Gowing and Bell. Medley encouraged me to try sculpture which I did, as this somehow let one off the painting hook and dispelled misguided student conceptions. I remember Rodney Burn's wife who taught modelling, at which she excelled, tale was that she refused to sit for Epstein as she was convinced he would seduce her.

Medley lectures on Poussin were the most important teaching I received. His theory of visual and literary metaphor was profoundly exciting and influential. The teaching of his friend, the American artist Charles Howard, was most informative, he would talk of the language of paint, and form and colour, 'If you make a horizontal it's like being by the sea – calm – you want to lie down. The vertical makes you sit up, stand tall, the diagonal confuses, creates nervous tension…' He also taught the dynamics of forms and shapes in relation to each other.

Fellow student and friend Chris Stephens, now a television director, decided to put on some plays. We gave the first British performance of Camus' *Caligula*, and also Anouilh's *Ring Round the Moon* with great success. The Principal, Leonard Daniels, and others, were shocked that painters should stoop so low as theatricals, Laetitia Yhap assisted with the costumes. Medley was encouraging, he understood, having previously been involved in the theatre. Certainly, it was a breath of fresh air, an attempt at some form of expression and performance. I certainly learnt a kind of looking… we drew from 9.30 a.m. to 9 p.m. some days.

Pop Art when it came, and abstraction and all American painting, as well as a lot that happened in Paris, completely confused me and I looked at it with Camberwellian scorn. Nine years looking and talking about contemporary painting with art students later changed some of that, as did meeting a lot of artists who had nothing to do with Camberwell and who just laughed when I said that I thought Coldstream was a good painter. One of my tutors was Richard Eurich. He once very diffidently showed me a photograph of a giant mural he had done for a Children's Hospital in the north of England. I was astonished and delighted by it but it had little influence over me at that time, the penny did drop several years later. I was at the time immersed in the other Camberwell ethic – Frank Auerbach. We all tried to draw like Frank but he would beat his head against the wall in frustration, as this was the last thing he wanted. He once sat beside me and did a slow considered Camberwell drawing of the head of the figure and said 'I do feel that you ought to find out what's there first'.

Sargy Mann and I went to a Kitaj exhibition, probably in 1960. Kitaj had been at the Ruskin at Oxford in the 1950s when I was drawing there. He did 'tit-bit' nudes as I thought of them then, and was a great guru for the other students. I realised he was not a painter like us, he was a picture maker. I understood the difference, but couldn't do anything about it and was quite jealous."

Opal Howard (*née* Echalaz): "Camberwell gave to me the unique chance of exposure to the enormously stimulating influences of a very diverse group of artists, gathered together for a brief period under one roof. Their discussions alone were an art education. For the students of painting, our instructors were benign tyrants.

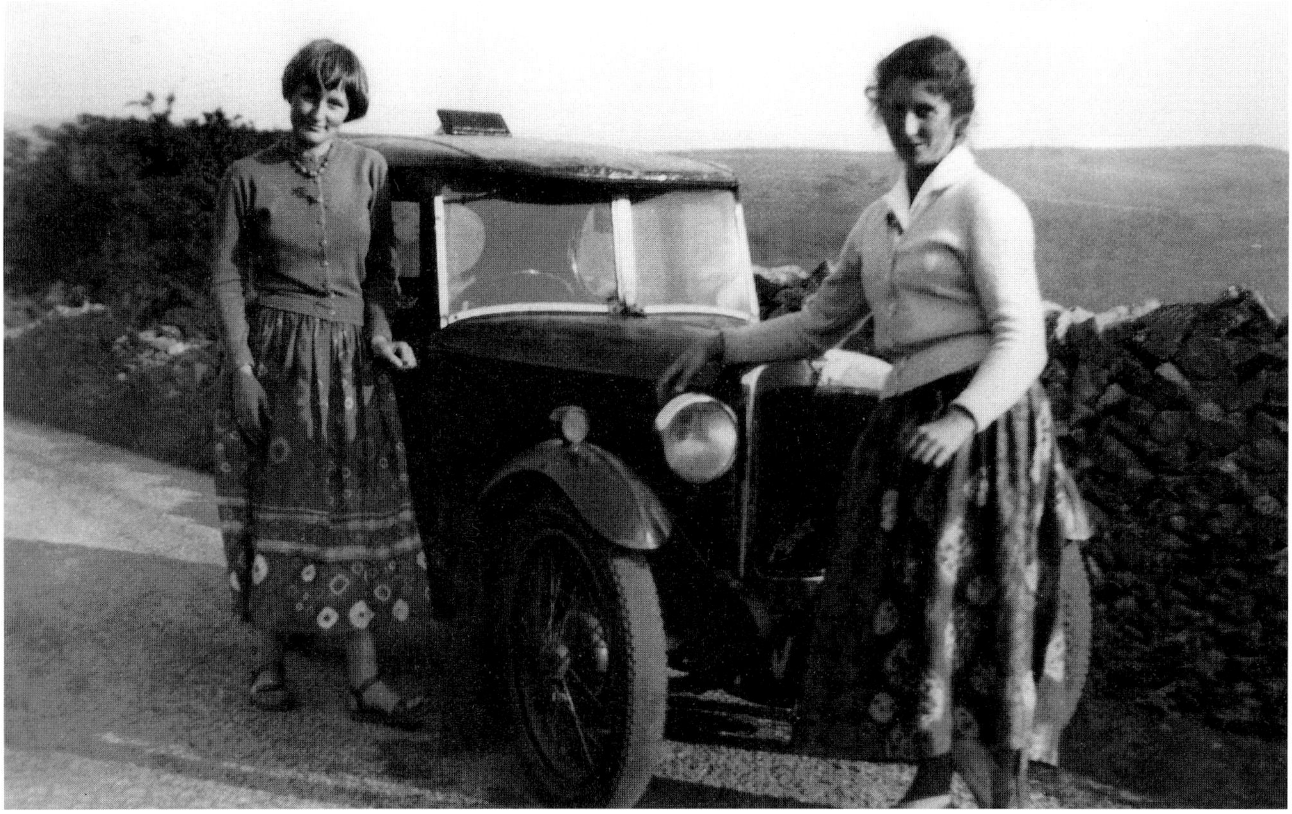

Jane Sewell (left) and Heather Watson, 1952.

Drawing and Design were our twin disciplines dinned into us from morning till night. Painting was drawing with paint and bright colour was frowned upon. Piero della Francesca and Ingres were our most revered Old Masters. Victor Pasmore's comments could be devastating, leaving many female students groping for their handkerchiefs. I was fortunate also to study under the charismatic John Minton who influenced a whole school of illustrators, while the gentle and charming Edwin La Dell gave me a lasting love for the craft of lithography. I received from these tutors and others a training in and understanding of art, which has immeasurably enriched my life and though circumstances have often prevented me from continuous practice, I have never taken up a brush or pencil without remembering, perhaps subconsciously, a valuable pearl of advice."

Francis Hoyland: "Camberwell meant hard work; learning a method which I afterwards found was geometrically impossible; respect for the Old Masters, and party spirit. John Dodgson taught me by far the most, a really marvellous approach to the whole of painting, encouraged my imaginative work and told me to trust my eye."

Jane Hughes (*née* Sewell): "There was a feeling of great optimism and all things seemed possible, and for us Art was without question the most important thing in our lives."

David Hume: "Camberwell showed me that serious painting need be neither abstract or academic. It meant looking at Piero rather than Michelangelo, Poussin, rather than Rubens, Cézanne rather than Van Gogh, Coldstream rather than Sutherland, and anything rather than the R.A.!"

Robert Hurdle: "Camberwell was a fresh start. Before the war I had studied at Richmond Art School, a very formative period. For two years, before being called up in 1940, I had rooms in Bloomsbury where I painted intensively in a highly

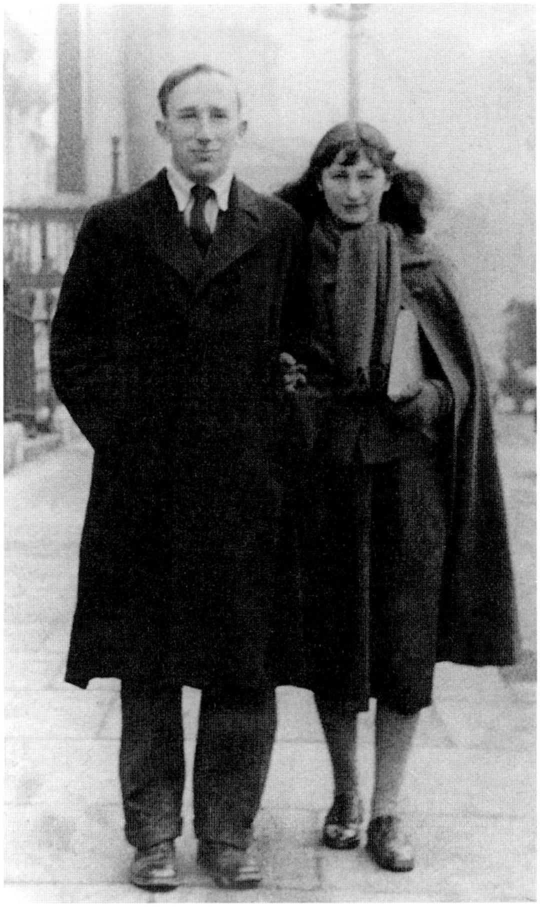

Patrick George and Jo Higson, 1948.

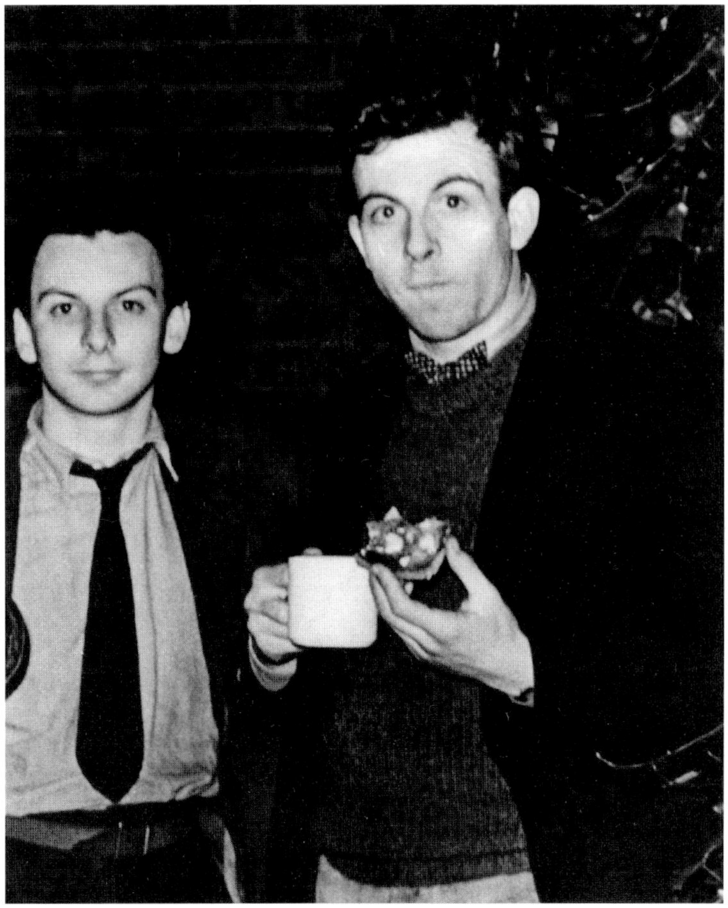

Tom Espley (left) and Patrick Symons at Tony Fry's Camberwell house, c.1950.

charged subjective manner. Although living so close to Euston Road, I was hardly aware of the existence of the Euston Road School. It was therefore a revelation to go, on the recommendation of Ralph Nuttall-Smith of the Slade, to Camberwell Art School and come directly under the influence of the Euston Road painters. It was not an easy experience. After six years of war service with all the frustrations of being unable to paint, it was difficult to go to this rather forbidding institution in South London and to enter into the life of an Art School again. I was surrounded by some very talented students who were far more involved with the Euston Road than I was myself. A daily acquaintance with students such as Patrick George, Andrew Forge, and Christopher Pinsent centred on Lower Marsh, had a considerable influence on my development as a painter. One of my tutors, William Townsend, happened to be my next door neighbour in Bayswater, so I became very aware of his painting, and he would drop into my basement flat and discuss my work. But I suppose, the most important influence Camberwell had on me was in the sort of drawing that was taught there. I accepted the tenets of Euston Road drawing; sight size, then plumb line. relative proportions, measurements, and the relation of space to picture plane. Drawing as taught by Claude Rogers and Kenneth Martin and many others helped me to re-learn drawing. It was this objectivity that became a watershed in my progress as a painter.

Other guests or inmates at the Marsh were Tony Fry, whose boyish appearance belied a mature ability to paint variations on the Euston Road method. Jo Higson held her own amongst the men, painting in her own style. Tony Eyton, demobbed from the Guards, brought an already mature facility. Patrick Symons and Dick Lee were both devoted followers and Francis Hoyland – a young hero-worshipper – hastened to make his mark. This was the group who, with other friends, gathered in the late '40s at Lower Marsh. Here much tea was brewed, meals prepared and painting theory declared around the board. Canvases of the inmates leaned against the walls, the views through windows, portraits, still-lifes, all imbued with the smoke and brick-dust of the Lower Marsh light. Back at Camberwell, Coldstream and Pasmore had great prestige. In the very large classes, they could only make personal contact with a limited number of students, these were either the most talented known to them, or those enjoying a more elevated social position. Coldstream would sit down by a student and discuss his or her work at some length, but being a quiet-spoken man his words were very rarely overheard. Pasmore's perambulations of the life room would be more rapid, concluding abruptly with some general statement addressed to the whole class such as, for example, avoiding the dangers of painting *trompe-l'œil*, or the importance of painting to the extremities. Rogers was always extremely helpful, he would make contact with a wide range of students, always generous with the demonstrative use of his pencil and brush. Gowing would engage in explosive dialogue with favoured students, while Monnington and Rodney Burn represented a more academic approach in their Life Room tuition. John Dodgson, Kenneth Martin, Elliot Seabrooke and Sam Carter were much more orthodox in the Euston Road sense. Colin MacInnes was the visiting lecturer in Art History. He would appear in the evening in a shabby sheepskin coat and discourse eloquently on painting from Giotto onwards.

At one time, a series of talks on periods of Art History would be delivered by individual students. These performances were as uneven as the audiences. The star performer was Andrew Forge, whose illuminating survey of the Bassano family of the Venetian School he managed to extend over two separate evenings.

The hiatus of the war had created a generation of older art students, many of them following pre-formulated styles of painting. There was however a particular group of students who could be called second generation Euston Roaders. Some had been at the same prep. school – The Downs – where their mentor, Maurice Feild, had directed them towards the Euston Road."

Prudence Ingham Clark (*née* Makower): "One of my strongest memories must have been in my first term. I caught the bus every morning and...one particular morning I noticed one remaining passenger on top of the bus with me. He alighted at the same stop as I did, and after several mornings we began to pass the time of day with each other. Finally, one morning, we started a conversation. I was asked if I was a student at Camberwell School of Art, what course I was attending, and who taught me. His questions intrigued me, so I decided to find out more about the middle-aged kindly man who wore thick country tweeds and looked like a gentleman farmer. I asked him the same questions he had asked me. Not getting very satisfactory answers, I finally said to him, 'Well, what do you do at Camberwell then?' to which he replied, 'Actually I am the Principal!' after which we became firm friends."

Don Jarvis: "I did painting at Camberwell, in those truly wonderful days. Not so much for the staff, nearly all of whom I held in contempt – nor for the 'teaching' which was (fortunately) inept, thus forcing us to learn from each other and the Old Masters. For the last two years I played truant each Friday, spending the whole day and more drawing at the V & A, National or Tate Galleries. When not 'at school' we met at each others' homes and talked about Life, Art and Politics – growing up together, getting drunk on cider at 6d (2½p) a pint, sick, partying, going to dances, especially at other art schools where the girls were better looking or more compliant...but above all, painting the days and nights away. Walking five miles home carrying heavy, framed canvases down Coldharbour Lane past the house where a future Prime Minister was a child. Cycling through Kent seeking the ghost of Samuel Palmer, camping, playing bad tennis, but making good paintings. In our clique everyone was a good painter. We gave each other nicknames: Laz (Bill Lazard), Toad (Ray Little), Wayne (Peter Andrews), Jack (Victor Tripp), Rick (Richard Hyde), Eegie (Paul Eagleton), Paddy (Patrick Lovely), Fan (Barry Fantoni)... mine was/is Don (David). Others included: Bill Clark, Maurice Irving, Tony Miller. The latter pair were doing furniture, but were certainly good painters. Yes, there were girls at Camberwell. As painters, Pearl Mason and the strange Julia Wilding stand out.

The prevailing style was Euston Road School. Some of the staff had been at the ERS, but Martin Bloch was a painter more to our liking. Sadly, he died in 1954. To our lecturers, French Impressionism was awfully avant-garde, but towards 1956 some of them seemed to grudgingly admit that Courbet was perhaps a sort of... well, might be a painter of sorts. Thus, they were only about a century out-of-date. I was savaged for having a Dali-ish thing in my portfolio. From about 1954 I had begun serious abstract paintings, so from such encounters I learnt to keep them from the staff's eyes. Fellow students knew about them. Even they needed some persuading.

Hanging over all male students was the threat of National Service – i.e. the war in Cyprus. Rick, Bill Clark, Eegie and Wayne eventually went there. I avoided it by prolonging my studies. Bill Lazard was a C.O., Toad was declared unfit. It was a disruptive force. Jobs were out of the question. They intended us to teach in secondary schools. Some did an A.T.C. course: Toad, Pearl, Eegie and I. Others just drifted into teaching: Laz, Paddy, Bill Clark. It may amaze people today, that with so much happening in the art world of the fifties the Camberwell teachers were so ignorant, or maybe wilfully dismissive? Tachism, Pollock, Fluxus, Cobra...Only Social(ist) realism and Kitchen Sink were derisively noticed. Yet, we were still to be found out on the streets with our drawing boards. Toad, Laz and I painted at the South Bank, on the site of the old Dome of Discovery, with our flimsy easels tied down, hung with a brick, blowing leaves off our palettes. Or again, on Waterloo Bridge late at night trying to get the right oil colours under sodium lights when the only thing you could do was read the label on the tube, all colours looked alike. I still have that 3ft x 2ft painting. It *is* surprising that someone doing E.R.S. type subjects would have cited Mondrian as a main influence; and Wols too!

Exhibitions during Camberwell days were held in the Walmer Castle. I once sold a figure painting for 30 shillings (£1.50). We all drank it. I won the Painting Prize in 1954, £5. We all drank it. The 5ft. x 4ft painting, 'The Return of the Ancient Mariner' was later destroyed. Thought to be too old-fashioned. It was a huge output; much of it I would burn, or scrape off. Foolish, but that's youth. After 1956 I exhibited with Toad, Laz and Eegie anywhere one did not have to pay for the space. The South London Art Gallery was part of the fabric of the art school."

Jennifer Kelly (*née* Somerville): Extracts from the artist's diary supplemented later with personal recollections: "I have been told to see William Johnstone as soon as I arrive. After knocking on his door he invited me into his office where we stood either side of the mantelpiece. I had the impression of a very warm man, with an open expressive manner. He talked in an animated way about Picasso, for about ten minutes. I responded equally enthusiastically but having no views of my own about any artist, all my comments being what I had heard from 'in-the-know' adults and books by Herbert Read. Mr Johnstone then said 'I will hand you over to William Coldstream'. I followed him downstairs to the entrance hall and long corridors, and up a winding turret where he told me to wait, while he went inside the Life Room. After feelings of apprehension and shyness which seemed to last a long time, the door opened, and Mr Johnstone came out saying 'This is Miss Somerville' and left. Mr Coldstream was standing inside the Life Room holding the door open. I held out my hand for him to shake thinking it was the right social custom to do, but he did not respond and I let my arm fall to my side with acute embarrassment. He stared at me for some time and looking back at him, I saw a small, very thin, neat man in brown trousers, a check jacket, and a blue and white polka-dot bow tie (which he almost always wore). His shoes were polished, and his fine brown hair brushed neatly to one side. His face was completely without expression, apart from one of profound unhappiness. He said (looking at the floor) – ' I will take you down to the Antique Room'. There he introduced me to a handsome young man called Sam Carter, who taught Antique drawing. Mr Carter shook my hand and found two chairs for me – one to sit on, and the other to place in front for the drawing board to rest on the back. Mr Carter lent me an HB pencil, and throughout my five years at Camberwell and the Slade, I found the softer grades of pencil were frowned upon – pastels looked on with horror – or using white crayon for highlights on coloured paper (equally disliked – author's note). My drawing board was large, about 24in x 15in, and I noticed all the other girls had smaller boards, and were doing small neat drawings. I started drawing very freely, filling the whole paper with an 'impression' of the plaster cast. Mr Carter came and sat down beside me and explained in the kindest way that I had not understood the form of the cast at all. He drew a diagram of the cast on my board. After a while I came to cherish all the drawings of the Camberwell teachers beside my own. When 1 o'clock came, most of the students went out for lunch, three or four remaining with their sandwiches. I was far too shy to go out to lunch by myself, as it was something I had never done, so I continued drawing a cast.

Just before two o'clock everyone returned and Gloria, a local girl from Peckham, came and sat by me and asked me if I would like to see her photos of film stars. I said I would very much, and she took out of her handbag glossy postcards of successful American film stars – the men all highly desirable but unattainable with glossy Brylcream hair. Just as I was admiring a photo of Cary Grant, and imagining him in love with me, the door swung open and to my horror I saw Mr Coldstream coming towards me. I suddenly felt ashamed of my interest in film stars and hastily threw Cary Grant back into Gloria's lap. Mr Coldstream still wore his expressionless face and asked me in his quiet voice if he could sit down and look at my drawing. He started working on the side of my drawing. He held the H.B. pencil in his right hand, but with the back of his hand lying on the paper and the palm uppermost with the pencil lying across it, resting between his second and third finger. The pencil mark was very light and hardly showed on the paper. He explained about 'fixed points' where after drawing a line you dug the pencil into the paper which constituted a fixed place from where you measured and plotted the next move, fixing 'points all over the drawing'. I later noticed several students had succumbed to this so called 'scientific way of drawing', their drawings resembling currant buns. I wasn't at all happy doing this, and my drawings throughout my art school days became worse and worse.

By 4.30 p.m. students started leaving the room to go home, I took a bus to Victoria along dismal and decaying shabby streets... My mother loved her work at the British Council and was exhilarated by it...then she asked me about my day at Camberwell and I told her in glowing terms about the lessons I had received from Coldstream and Carter. She said that she knew Coldstream and that he was a good, rather dull painter and that she would invite him to supper sometime. I used to arrive at Camberwell every day with 4/6d in my purse for fares and lunch. At 8.30 a.m. I would practice the piano in the art school and would enjoy the admiration of a man and woman who came early from Brighton every day and sat in the room listening. This bit of admiration pleased me, as I had none from the drawings I did or from my parents and it was difficult, having been the best artist at school, to being one of several hundred in an art school. We all had to sign on and form a long queue in the hall to do this. If you hadn't 'clocked in' by 10 o'clock, by giving your name to a man in a box with a book, you were marked absent. Humphrey Lyttleton used to bribe the man in the box in the hall with cigarettes as he was invariably a late arriver. Quite soon after I arrived, 'signing-on' was abandoned for a more humane way, by having a piece of paper in each room where you put your signature when you arrived, whatever the time in the morning.

The Antique Room was divided down the middle by hessian screens, one half forming a life painting class. I noticed that Mr Coldstream and Mr Carter had a very friendly and easy relationship together and that Mr Coldstream enjoyed teasing Mr Carter, who took everything very seriously. I felt an increasing affection for both of them and on the days that they didn't come (Coldstream didn't come on Wednesday) I missed them not being there. Mr Coldstream gave me a lesson most days.

I still didn't go out to lunch until, after a fortnight, two school friends came to study at Camberwell with me, Wendy Wolfers and Prue Makower. They were both extroverts and I got to know other students through them, and also we went out to Lyons at Camberwell Green for lunch...We were about the only students (out of several hundred) who ate at Lyons, we were well aware that it was a middle-class thing to do and real artists ate in workmen's cafes or Italian family restaurants. Almost every day a funeral procession would pass, everyone taking their hats off as the black horses driving the hearse came by. Camberwell Road was depressing enough anyway, with the obvious poverty of the people.

At five o'clock I used to sit on a long bench in the downstairs hall and watch all the staff and students come down the steps in the corridor and leave by the front door. Mr Coldstream wore his beige wool Captain's coat and a brown trilby hat and scarf and gloves.

Sam Carter suggested I tried life drawing one or two days per week. The life room was situated directly above the antique room. It was very crowded, and latecomers had no chance of a place, as there were three or four people deep. By coming early to Camberwell, I was able to be the first in the room and find a chair where I could sit with my back to the wall (so other students couldn't see what I thought were bad drawings). Mr Coldstream, Claude Rogers, Victor Pasmore, William Townsend, Rodney Burn and Lawrence Gowing all came in together. It was clear that Mr Coldstream was the leader. He always took the initiative and was the spokesman... Victor Pasmore's presence always caused a murmur of admiration among the students, as he had quite a lot of publicity at that time and Kenneth Clark had bought the lovely painting of Pasmore's wife. When coming into the life room, Pasmore's beard would enter first, then lots of untidy black hair, a hidden face and a body bent forward from the waist and hands clasped behind his back. He was one of the few teachers who looked like an artist and wore shabby clothes, and baggy corduroy trousers. He had a rather vague manner when teaching and if he couldn't find the right words would wave his arms about instead. I loved his paintings at that time and saw the Elephant & Castle underground station in a Pasmore haze. I was unable to see there was no form at all in his pictures. I wished I could imitate his hazy style. A student told me Pasmore pressed wet newspaper on his wet pictures to obtain the 'vague' look.

My mother asked me to look in at the British Council offices in Portland Place on the way home as she had a picture of Mr Coldstream's to show me. It turned out to be his *Hands Around the Cat* which was going on exhibition. I thought it was absolutely lovely and it reminded me of Raphael. I was later told by a woman student, who was in love with Mr Coldstream, that Raphael was one of his favourite painters. Men students were a bit envious of Mr Coldstream's winning ways with women and complained that he hardly ever gave men students lessons, and that he was a ladies' man who used a 'bedroom voice' when talking to women. Mr Coldstream certainly seemed to induce feelings of respect, closeness and compassion in women – partly because he looked very unhappy (I can't ever remember seeing him smile) and his remoteness inspired feelings of respect. Exactly the opposite was Claude Rogers, who wore his heart on his sleeve. He was popular, as you always knew where you were with him, he would say exactly what he thought but no one took offence, as it was said with warmth and friendliness. Men students used to imitate Claude giving a life painting lesson and frequently using the word 'breast' pronouncing it 'bweast' as he couldn't say the letter 'R'! Once I was starting a life painting when Claude came up and criticised it saying 'You must be bolder, it's all too hesitant', I said 'But I am afraid of painting badly', he said in exasperation, 'Well, if you are afraid you will never do anything well' and walked away. I knew he spoke the truth.

Prue, Wendy and I got to know Sam Carter well, he was always such a steady influence and was invariably good humoured and courteous, so we were happy to approach and talk to him. We used to ask him why Mr Coldstream was such an enigma and had such a detached air about him. He said that Mr Coldstream had no close friends and never let anyone near him, though he, Sam, was very friendly with him but not in a possessive way. He said he inspired love and respect in people, but had this 'Don't come up to me, I will come up to you if I want to' look about him. One morning, upstairs in the life room, I had just been given a lesson by John Dodgson, a very nice man, when in walked Mr Coldstream. John Dodgson said 'Hello Bill', I had never heard Mr Coldstream called Bill before and it was rather a disappointment to me, as I didn't think he looked like a Bill at all. I had always thought that people who knew him well would call him William.

In the divided antique room, I started a life painting behind the hessian screens. The model, in her thirties, sat on a wooden chair with her one arm resting on the back of the chair over which her bright pink dressing gown was placed. She had dark hair and a golden skin and when Mr Coldstream came to start me off, he made me aware of the beauty of tone and colour of the screen, pink dressing gown, gold skin, and dark hair. I was too shy to ask what paints I should use as I thought I was expected to know, also I did not know how to mix paints or what medium to use. I never asked. Behind the screens, painting from life, were Andrew Forge, Christopher Pinsent and Patrick George. They were known collectively as 'The Marsh', as Christopher Pinsent owned a terraced house in Lower Marsh, Lambeth and Andrew and Pat each had a floor to themselves. Tony Fry and Francis Hoyland and Patrick Symons were also part of the group of very nice and clever students. Some of them had been at the same prep school together, The Downs School at Colwall, where their painting master had been Maurice Feild, a friend of Mr Coldstream's.

My school friend, Prue, got on very well with 'The Marsh', particularly Andrew Forge, and they invented nicknames for some of the students. One woman in her forties was a plague to Mr Coldstream as she was continually pestering him several times a day to see her pictures. Andrew and Prue called her 'The broken umbrella' as this was very apt when you saw her. Her pictures were what is politely called 'the naïve school of painting' which was in vogue at the time, and Mrs Langley had some success in selling her works in London galleries. She was always to be seen painting in the corridors and rushing up staircases after Mr Coldstream to ask him how much she should charge for her pictures. Once I met him in the corridor, breathless, and he asked me 'which way did Mrs Langley go' and when I told him, he quickly rushed off in the other direction. My feelings at this time alternated between Coldstream and Gowing, the latter also bringing out strong maternal feelings in women. When Gowing sat down to look at your drawing, saliva would gush out of his mouth and drip onto the paper, the more he talked – and he talked a lot – the more saliva would puddle the drawing. He was totally unconcerned and would take out a large coloured handkerchief from his top pocket and wipe it away without turning a hair. This made me feel very tender for him. 'The Marsh' told me that Lawrence Gowing was a genius and that although only in his thirties he had already written books on art, besides being a brilliant painter. The men students didn't care for Gowing and one student who was jealous of my concern for Gowing took me into the corridor where we peered through the glazed upper part of the door into a large room, the student told me that Gowing's mistress was working in the room and that Gowing had done many fine portraits of her. My warm feelings for Gowing left me the day he came into the upstairs life drawing room and complained to another teacher that he had to walk from Peckham in the rain and had forgotten his galoshes. An artist who complained about getting wet and wore galoshes was beyond the pale.

Prue, Wendy and I had made friends during the breaks with some boys of our own age who studied with John Minton learning illustration. We were fascinated by their open conversation, one of them told us John Minton was in love with him. They all went to hear Humphrey Lyttleton play at a jazz club in Oxford Street. They made it clear that girls like us were not welcome at the jazz club. Lawrence Gowing saw us talking to the 'jazz boys' and told someone he knew who knew my parents, I felt very bitter about this and never spoke to Lawrence Gowing again. Gowing and Claude Rogers didn't like each other at all. When they were together in the same room you could feel the hostility. Students would look at each other wondering if 'the fur would fly'. Usually it was Claude Rogers who would skulk out of the room.

One morning, whilst drawing in the antique room, Sam Carter came over to me to tell me that a still-life that I had recently painted had been put into a students' exhibition in the upstairs life room and that Bill Coldstream had given it third prize. I was amazed as I didn't even know about the exhibition and thought that the still-life was dreadful. Sam told me that Coldstream was put out that I wasn't there, he came into the antique room looking irritable and annoyed. He always pretended he was looking for something when he did this, lifting up bits of paper in a nervous way.

By some thoughtlessness on my part I found myself one day completely in Coldstream's bad books. Coldstream approached me one morning and asked me if I was coming to the lecture on Renaissance Painters that was being held that afternoon. I foolishly said without thinking that I was not going as 'The Marsh' said that the lecturer wasn't very good. Coldstream went red in the face and abruptly left the room. I later learnt from Andrew Forge that the lecturer was Coldstream's current girlfriend with whom he was having a very close relationship at the time. No wonder he was annoyed. The next morning I had started a life painting in the small upstairs room, and as there were so many students the model posed in the centre of the room with the students arranging their easels all round her. I was in the worst place, with my back to the door, Coldstream entered and started criticising the fact that my easel was placed away from the light. He said 'You should know that you can't possibly paint with your back to the light'. The tone of his voice was irritable and annoyed and he went on to complain about the angle of the easel and every small detail. As I had no confidence in myself I didn't defend myself, and when he passed on to another student I went into the locker room in the basement and burst into tears. I knew he was angry because of my remarks about his student girlfriend. Andrew Forge later said that Coldstream didn't speak to any of them for a fortnight. After that episode I sought sanctuary in the antique room with Sam Carter, who was always a brick and a great stabilising influence. Some time later Coldstream came to give me a lesson and was very nice, so I felt that I had been forgiven.

One group at Camberwell were called 'The Hockey Sticks' by 'The Marsh'. They were a group of girls in their late twenties who had been in the W.R.N.S. Coldstream obviously enjoyed their company and it was clear that one of them was in love with him. He was evidently attracted to her and saw her away from the school. Later, he realised he had taken on more than he could handle and tried to avoid her. She would be seen piteously running after him in the corridors, desperate to see him alone. I used to go to the National Gallery most Saturday mornings, and often in the canteen there I would see Bill Coldstream having lunch with one of his student girlfriends. I once saw all the Euston Road Group together in the National Gallery, by this time Bill Coldstream had purchased a new hat, a navy one with a large brim instead of his old traditional brown trilby. Claude Rogers wore mittens. Coldstream always wore his poker face and pretended not to notice students if he saw them in the Gallery.

The day came when my mother invited Bill Coldstream to supper. When he arrived he seemed quite shy. He noticed my dark blue dress and commented on how lovely it was, calling me Jennifer for the first time. My mother insisted on showing him paintings that I had done at five years of age; faded and crumpled drawings were in a pile under a metal framed bed. I felt very ashamed and unhappy that Mr Coldstream had seen that I had no bedroom of my own. After supper, my mother talked about Stanley Spencer and both my parents started being abusive about Daphne Charlton, who at the time was involved with Spencer. However I was most impressed to hear Coldstream defend Daphne. I thought it showed very great strength of character to stand up for absent friends. As usual, Bill Coldstream never smiled the whole evening. The next day he came up to me as soon as he arrived in the antique room and seemed to adopt a kinder more tender attitude towards me. I knew he was appalled by my home life, Sam Carter told me some time later of this. The following week I was painting in an upstairs life room where Bill was giving me a lesson. He told me to look through the window at the trees in back gardens, saying that you should always look through glass when you are painting, as it leaves flat patterns like a Cézanne painting and it cuts out detail. I noticed that looking through glass looked like a Pasmore picture.

A brilliant caricature had been done by a student of all the Euston Road Group for the end of term Christmas party. Claude Rogers was portrayed as a fat policeman and Bill Coldstream as a clergyman. It was exactly like them. I didn't see much of Coldstream the next term as he spent most of the time in the offices on administration and therefore did little teaching. I saw him one day in Regents Park after it was known that he was going to be Slade Professor. He said he would like me to come to the Slade but it would have to be three days per week for the first year as it would create jealousy amongst many Camberwell students who wanted to migrate to the Slade with him. He told me that he was going to the Courtauld Institute and would I like to join him. We walked down Baker Street and met Anthony Blunt, who showed us around the Institute, pointing out and discussing Impressionist paintings. Coldstream eventually left me at the entrance to Baker

Street underground, and I hardly ever saw him again."

Margaret Kerr: "When I entered the Pottery Department in 1950, Dick Kendall, who had succeeded Jacob Drew, was Head of the Department. Dick and Honora French were the only full-time members of staff with the exception of Geoff, the technician who prepared clay and lead, rather a troglodyte existence in a dark subterranean basement, filled with sacks of clay and glaze materials – some of the latter unlabelled and spilling contents on to the floor. Kendall was a superb craftsman and regarded by one and all with warm affection – we always found him approachable and ready to give us his time and expertise. Administration and organisation were definitely not his forté … trying to get him to make a decision was like trying to put a jelly in a bag.

On the bus travelling to Camberwell on my first day, a lady spoke to me enquiring if I knew the stop for the Art School. I replied that I too was going there. After a long pause she enquired to which department I was going, then volunteered that she was making her way to pottery. Having not the faintest idea who she was, I asked if she had done much pottery – there was an even longer pause before the entirely characteristic reply 'Yes, a little'. This was Norah Bradon, of all the staff, she was arguably the most distinguished. She had made a reputation as one of the early pioneers of studio pottery in Britain, firstly through her work at St Ives with Katherine Pleydell-Bouverie when they studied under Bernard Leach. Secondly, and perhaps more importantly, she was known for her research with Pleydell-Bouverie into the effects of wood ash on the colour, texture and behaviour of high-fired stoneware glazes. Teaching students in the contents of a busy workshop was unhappily not Norah Bradon's métier. She was so modest, so self-effacing and so exceptionally shy that she found it difficult to become part of the scene. Between students and teachers there was easy rapport and a good deal of friendly badinage with the occasional flare-up and flying sparks, all of which seemed alien to Norah Bradon. Occasionally, she would refer to Bernard Leach as 'Rikkiti' – evidently a nickname from her early days … I think it pained her when we called him 'Bernard' or referred to his potters book as 'The Bible'. Norah would always be ready to discuss the making-up of a particular body or the modification of a glaze – but with the protestation that she really knew very little about them. In general her response to questions was that her knowledge was very limited and she could not be of much help. On the rare occasions when you could get her on her own, she would tentatively, and with the utmost hesitation and diffidence, make perceptive and valuable comments about one's work. I once asked with some hesitation what it was that held her back from ever showing anyone how some problem might be solved. She said that she felt that it was quite wrong for her to influence our work in any way. It is very much to be regretted that she felt unable to make what might have been a unique and important contribution to the department.

Honora French must have been known to generations of students. She fired the kilns and taught, with Jock Purdie, the adult evening classes. In her younger days she had worked for Charles Vyse, whose ceramic work is today much sought-after. She was a real enthusiast and always had work of her own in hand and told us how she had sat up in bed the previous night to finish incising some decorations on a piece of porcelain. Attired like a hummingbird in brilliant shades of scarlet, shocking pink, lemon yellow and emerald green, she was a startling figure and her hats and earrings were memorable. Long after she had retired, I occasionally met her in the Greenwich antiques markets, where she was known to all the jewellery stall ladies. I would drive her to her home, where she had a positive Aladdin's cave of treasures – pots by Bernard Leach, Shoji Hamada, Michael Cardew, Hans Coper,

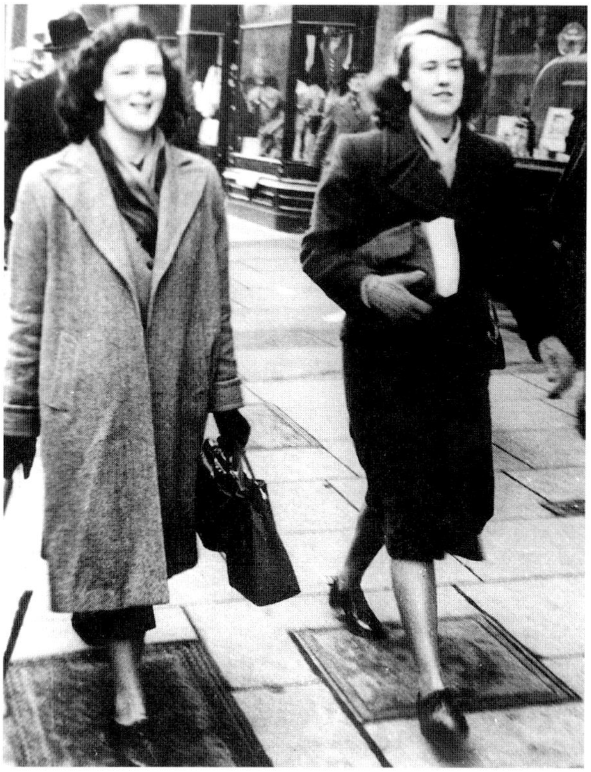

Katherine Martin (*née* Hamp) and Mary Laughton (*née* Shields), February 1949.

Lucie Rie, Ian Godfrey and many others, together with Casa Pupo rugs, woven hangings by Barbara Sawyer and Peter Collingwood and a collection of vividly coloured or delicately patterned iridescent rocks and shells. 'Frenchie' had the welfare of the school very close to her heart. She died in March 1992 at the age of ninety-one.

Jock Purdie was, by 1950, a post-diploma student who stayed at the school to do his own work and teach. It was vitally important to know what 'hat' he was wearing as he had a famously explosive temper and an ulcer. He was over forty and regarded by some of us with awe. He was very inventive and excelled as a decorator, selling his work privately. In the late 1950s he retired to Scotland to set up his own pottery on the Isle of Arran. Jock gave me a great deal of help when I first started teaching. When 'Frenchie' died, I tried to contact him but his name was no longer in the telephone book.

In a courtyard outside the pottery at Camberwell, Ralph Nuttall-Smith had a two-thirds life-size female figure on which he was working. Now and again he came out to examine this figure from all angles through half closed eyes. Taking up his mallet and chisel, he would remove an imperceptible fragment, dust with his sleeve and palm, examine it again, and then return indoors. One bitterly cold day in a snowstorm of whirling flakes, someone glanced outside to see him with his overcoat collar turned up chipping away – we all crowded to the windows, impressed by such dedication.

The History of Art lectures were often given by competent people from the Courtauld Institute and usually no more than mildly interesting. Karel Vogel's lectures were another matter altogether – they were wonderful joyous occasions when he shared with everyone his own passionate interest in classical sculpture. Impervious to considerations of time and even subject matter, and ignoring trifles such as inverted or double images, he would enthusiastically reveal to us the subtleties and delights to be enjoyed in the study of sculpture. His lectures were illuminated by penetrating insights and sometimes personal anecdote. To one lecture – part of a series in Renaissance sculpture – he brought by mistake slides of the lively vigorous drawings made by a mentally-handicapped Dutch child, who had lost her capacity to draw when painstakingly taught to read. In the middle of this, there suddenly appeared an image of the Hermes of Praxitalese – greeted by Dr Vogel with a happy cry. He told us that it had been discovered by his very own teacher and when as a student he was taken to see it, he had cried. Karel Vogel was a life-enhancer and much loved by students."

George Knox: "I think I may have been the first person to teach art history on a regular basis at Camberwell – a weekly lecture for 32/6d (£1.63p). I well remember being interviewed by Gilbert Spencer before starting and his telling me 'now I do not want you to fill up students' heads with a lot of nonsense about Matisse and Picasso'."

Gloria Laser: "A real culture-shock coming out of a Victorian approach to art into what seemed post-war re-evaluation and emergence of abstract art thinking. The place was full of cosmopolitan groups of students from Scandinavia and Egypt.

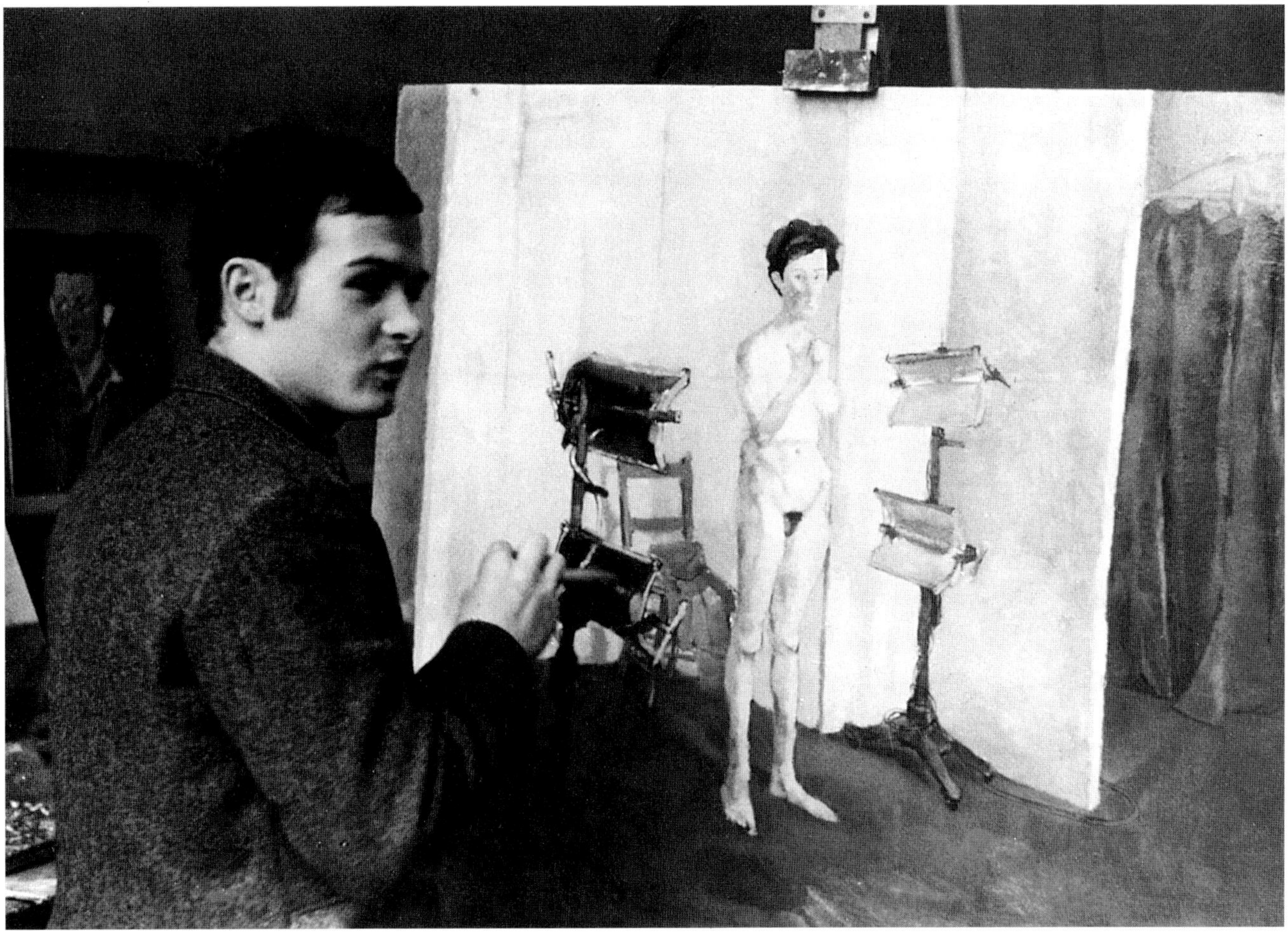

Patrick Lovely, 1952.

Having the availability of galleries and museums was only surpassed by being taught by already recognised names; especially the genius, sensitivity and understanding of John Buckland-Wright."

Mary Laughton: "Since 1949, Camberwell has meant to me some good and interesting friends. At the time, I knew too little about art and was too immature and shy to take advantage of what was offered. Any artistic personality I may have had was submerged, so that while I remember the place with affection as some kind of working jungle, I think it was the wrong school for me. Victor Pasmore's Saturday morning visits were my week's highlight, because he always showed interest in imaginative paintings, however strange, and took them seriously, in marked contrast to some other teachers, or so it seemed to me at the time. He would saunter in, hands behind his back, often saying nothing, but a friendly nod or grunt meant encouragement and 'that's a try, yes, that's a try' meant approval. He once told me that a tree with which I was having trouble was 'not logical within the picture – it just wouldn't be there' Eventually I took it out and he was right, so I consider what he said whenever I have serious trouble with a picture now."

Dick Lee: "I was there as a student at a marvellous moment. I made a number of life-long friends and was influenced by them, probably still am. (Andrew Forge, Francis Hoyland, Tony Fry, Tony Eyton). I was incredibly lucky to be given a teaching job. I didn't qualify for an ex-serviceman's grant because I was a Rhodesian! Joe Dixon, Philip Matthews and Helen Watson eased me into classes, where I met so many interesting, talented and wonderful people off and on for the next thirty years. I was sorry when the Euston Road painters departed to the Slade, but looking back it could well be that I might not have been so lucky as regards

Susan Einzig and John Minton, c.1950.

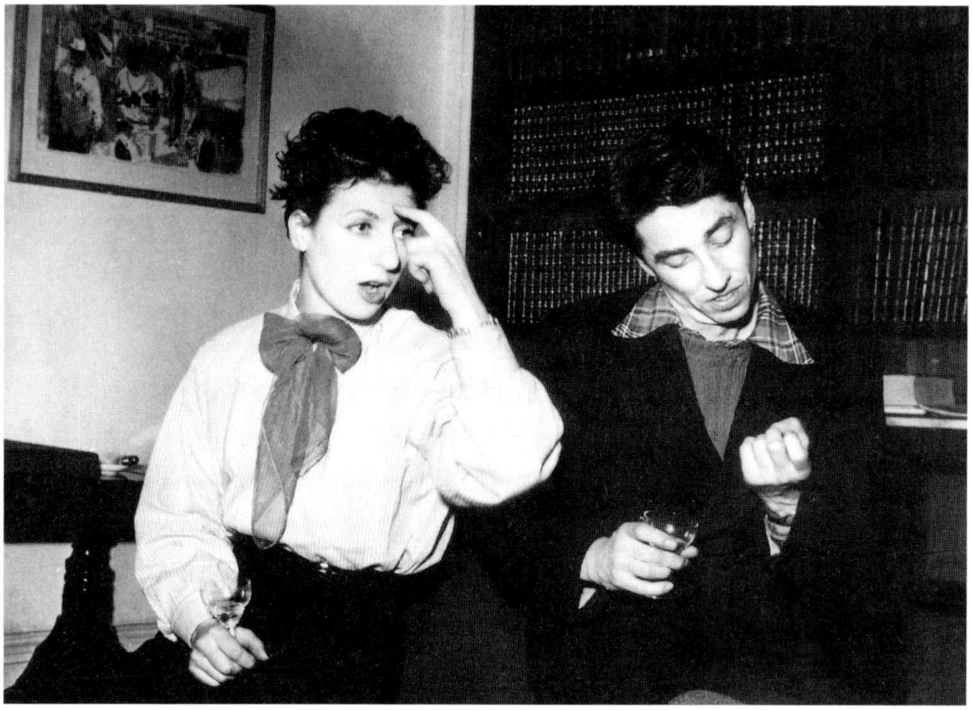

teaching at Camberwell had they not done so."

Adrian Lewis-Evans: "The damp cupboards for individual pots (in) those days were a wall-high collection of stacked biscuit tins painted with names and symbols to show ownership of contents. Antique wheels in the throwing rooms to which Norah Bradon would carry a half-hundredweight bag of clay from the vaults below, her delicate voice and build belying her strength. Taciturn, tall and bearded Scot, Hugh (Jock) Purdie and round-faced and horn-rimmed 'Frenchie' packing the equally archaic gas kilns installed perhaps half a century earlier."

Patrick Lovely: "Considering my horrible early childhood and education, to be suddenly released into a world where a nude woman dominated the classroom – well, what more can I say!"

Jack Lugg: "To have large numbers of visiting artist/lecturers coming into Camberwell throughout the week was very confusing; especially as there appeared to be a very large gap in the standard of ability and quality of the teachers for imparting knowledge. Spencer's profound and only words when looking at one of my paintings were 'compose compose!!' He of course was quite right."

Humphrey Lyttleton: "Camberwell can be summed up in two words – John Minton. My main interest was illustrating and cartooning. Life classes under Pasmore and Coldstream were interesting, but since I was also starting my career as a musician, I played truant from many other classes, such as architecture and the history of art. John Minton and Susan Einzig had the most influence on me as a cartoonist – they were also contemporary figures who visited us (myself and Wally 'Trog' Fawkes) in our habitat – the London jazz clubs."

Erica MacDonald: "I joined Camberwell when William Johnstone re-opened it in the autumn of 1943. We were an odd assortment of students, being either very young (far younger than would be allowed nowadays), wounded ex-servicemen and refugees. I personally owe much to Johnstone and Michael Ayrton, who was then aged twenty-one. In two terms in a badly bombed, badly lit, cold school, they taught me to draw – really draw. The thrill and excitement of that! Later the Euston Road Group came on to the staff and the Neo-Romantics, Ayrton and Minton, were

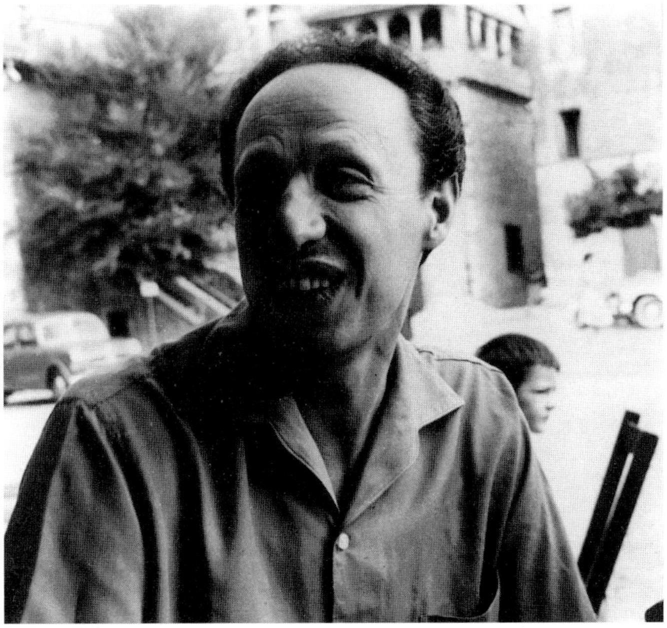

Heinz Inlander, c.1955.

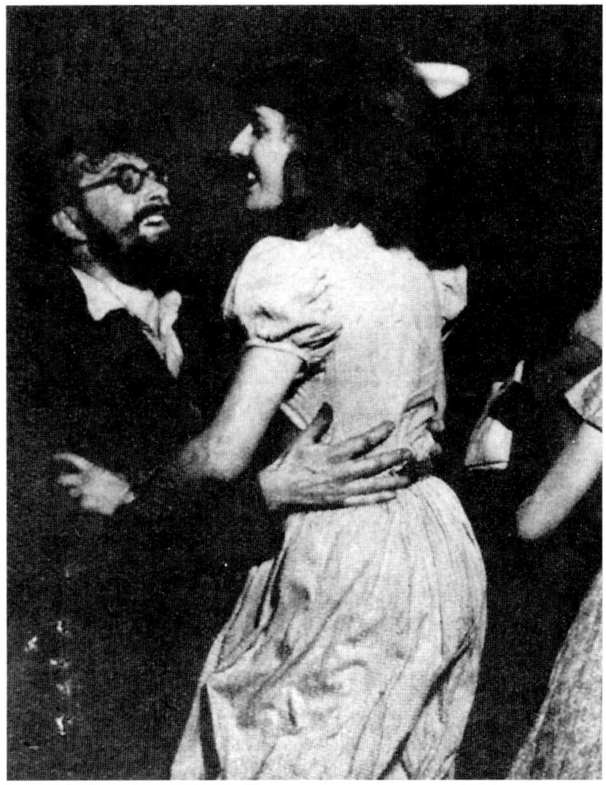

Philip Matthews dancing with an unknown Camberwell student, c.1952.

hugely scorned. The newcomers to the staff viewed my fluency and ease in drawing with grave suspicion, especially as I was only aged fifteen. I thought they totally disapproved of my work. Pasmore decided to teach me to paint and one day set up a still-life in a room of my own for five hours. When he returned I had finished my first ever painting, bottle labels, highlights and all and enjoyed every minute. Pasmore's reaction was one of absolute fury – 'you've made painting easy and it should be difficult', was the burden of his objection. After a night of tears, the only conclusion I came to was that my crime was enjoying painting and working too fast. So I took a whole term on my next picture and in my report, Pasmore wrote 'Erica is slow but no need to worry'.

Life classes were just as miserable for me, it was I who labelled the Euston Road Group 'Dot and Carry One School of Drawing'. Cautious drawing with many dots where they had pause for thought. In the '70s Claude Rogers told me that they had actually prized and collected my discarded drawings but, at the time, they had succeeded in demoralising me into retreating from painting into the illustration department where John Minton was a most sympathetic person. I never cared for his work – too mannered – but he encouraged wide and diverse reading, and was kind beyond words."

Andrew Maclaren: "Camberwell gave me an enduring foundation for my work, but perhaps above all, a sense of relationship with a particular strand of English painting. The rigour of the teaching has always remained a yardstick to measure one's efforts against. The values handed down to us have proved to be a great help at times when what often is lauded is incompetent and impoverished. I look back and feel very privileged to have been a part of it."

Arthur Maderson: "The centre of the social universe was 'The Walmer Castle' down the road. I also have fond memories of a weekly trip to the Pie & Mash shop to restore one's sometimes flagging (I had a nine foot college scarf) proletarian credentials."

Trata Mahoney (*née* Drescha): "The Austrian Trio - Inlander, Eisenmeyer and

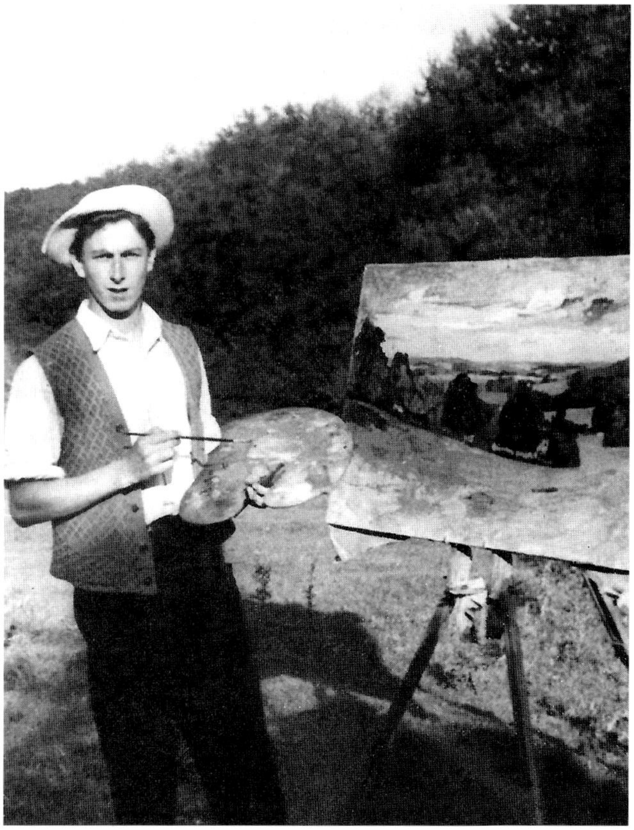

Terry Scales at Michael Salaman's country home, Bucklebury, Berkshire. Summer 1950.

Doitch, in earnest discussion with Pasmore – the intellectual elite, so to speak."

Elizabeth Massey (*née* Breeds): "During my period at Camberwell an interesting project, organised principally by Pasmore, to furnish Holloway Prison with six paintings of London scenes was attempted and my picture of Victoria Station was amongst those selected. However, later on the scheme was unfortunately abandoned. I won a prize (two canvases from Sickert's studio) for a landscape painted in Spain during one of the summer holidays. Many years later, I had the top surface of one of the canvasses removed to reveal a painting which Claude Rogers surmised to be by Thérèse Lessore (Sickert's third wife)."

Philip Matthews: "I suppose I was about thirty-ish when I was offered some teaching at Camberwell. It was in the Secondary Art Department, known generally, as the Junior School. I was ushered into a large room furnished with rows and rows of high benches, more like a Science Lab. than an Art room. 'Teach 'em industrial design' I was told. I was a bit taken aback at this, as I had never heard of such a thing. 'I'll approach it through drawing', I thought. I looked at the work the class had been doing. It appeared to be restyling electric irons, and there were many strange-looking streamlined objects purporting to do this. 'I shan't last long at this', I thought, 'a few weeks at the most. They'll find out I know nothing about irons'. The general idea was debased Bauhaus.

One day I was summoned to the Principal's office. 'This is it' I thought, feeling relief. The Principal, William Johnstone, was a formidable man, closely resembling James Cagney. Some years spent in California aided the illusion. 'Matthews', he said tersely, Cagney-ishly, 'I see from y'papers y've had the rudiments of some sort of schooling'. This was not what I was expecting. 'Yes, sir', I said cautiously. 'The man teaching general subjects has gone sick', he said. 'I want you to take over his work for a week or two. Teach 'em some history, geography, English, arithmetic etc.' In vain did I protest. 'Get up there now and start', he all but shouted, almost reaching for his shoulder-holster. I lost no time in quitting his office. 'I'll approach it through drawing', I thought. So we did a great deal of English Literature, as that could be illustrated. Scenes from Shakespeare were acted and then drawn. Readings from the new translation of the Odyssey were illustrated. Arithmetic was more difficult. Quite apart from the fact that I could hardly add up myself, there seemed little scope for drawing. Geometry seemed the only possible answer. So we did geometry. History and geography I let slide rather. The class used to get very restive at about 3 p.m. Fighting would break out. Confiscation of weapons became routine. At the end of a week I could not literally speak; so hoarse had I become. I could not find a way of re-channelling the fighting into drawing. So I organised the fighting! Three minute rounds of wrestling took over the last hour of the day; two freefalls, with a look-out posted in the corridor I could see why the previous man had gone sick. He never came back. Owing to the incredible topography of Camberwell, staff had to pass through my room to get to the canteen. At odd intervals the top brass would file through, Gowing, Rogers, Pasmore, Johnny Minton, the elegant Elliot Seabrooke, Tom Monnington. 'Good morning, Mr.Chips', they would invariably say. I got to like my pupils very much. They were a lively lot; experienced and sophisticated teacher-baiters. Two in particular I remember. They had strangely contrasting yet euphonious names – Euan Uglow, Terry Scales…"

(The author is indebted to Natalie Giltsoff and Miranda Pearce for access to papers of the late Philip Matthews.)

Michael Millman: "William Johnstone was perhaps the most important influence, he said that after having had the feeling of success… sales and exhibiting in the Royal Academy, it was perhaps a little late to waste time taking the course! My own feeling was that I was looking for a real serious atmosphere."

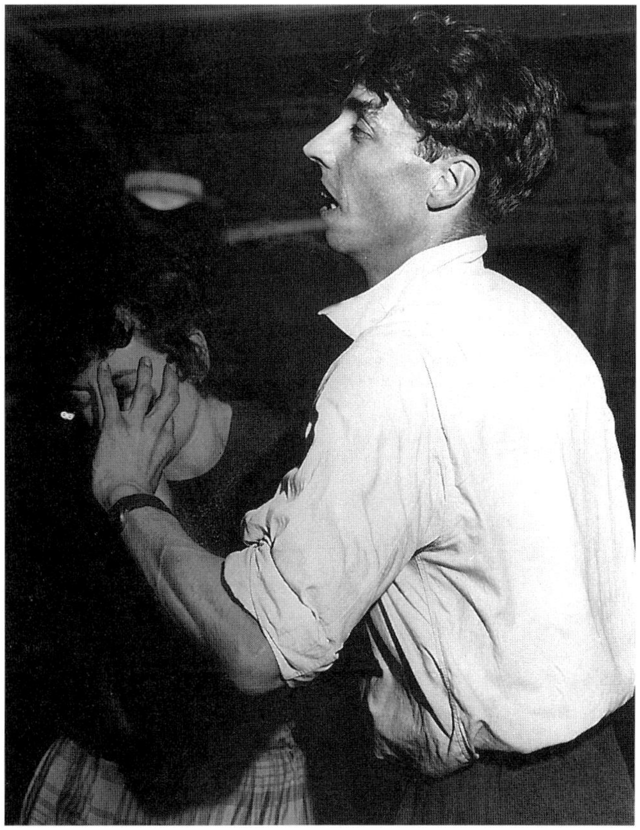

John Minton dancing, c.1953.

Geri Morgan: "The most important single quality that affected me was the atmosphere of hard work and commitment to art. Craft subjects (I did Ceramics as a subsidiary) helped painters to be makers, doers, and this practical approach has helped many of us to survive as artists. There was a dialogue between the Romantics (Minton, Ayrton etc.) who were largely involved with illustration and the painters of the Euston Road School and the Royal Academy like Tom Monnington. Against the background of a post-war Britain where euphoria deriving from the Labour victory of '45 had not quite given way to disillusion, politics and art were constantly discussed. Many students were mature often ex-service people and no doubt this was of the greatest importance in determining the seriousness and excitement of the atmosphere."

Glyn Morgan: "I am afraid that Camberwell was a great disappointment to me. I went there attracted by the illustrious names, but the place was so overcrowded (I counted seventy people in one life class) that it was difficult for it to function properly. Though painting was what I always wanted to do, I soon switched to illustration where I was happier and received some worthwhile teaching. I particularly remember John Minton, a charming man, and a most energetic and inspiring teacher. After two terms I spent my first long summer at Cedric Morris's and I realised that this was the real thing at last."

Christine Morley: "As a Fine Art student, I think I was unfortunate to be there in the hiatus between Gilbert Spencer's last year and Robert Medley's appointment. It seemed to me that the latter had no interest in the students he had inherited as his second year cohort."

Malcolm Morley: "At Camberwell, I realised that I liked girls who went to art schools better than girls who didn't."

Bernard Myers: "I first met Camberwell students and staff at the Bexleyheath Rhythm Club with Lyttleton, Fawkes and Minton in 1947. I started a design course, but a painting lesson from Tom Monnington persuaded me to join the painting school. Ralph Nuttall-Smith was a teacher of sculpture at the Slade, and he also taught part-time at Camberwell. It was his regular practice to cycle from University College across Trafalgar Square to Camberwell. On one particular evening, whilst cycling across the Square he got caught up in some form of peace demonstration and got off his bike to have a look. In amongst all the jostling of the crowd, out of his rucksack fell a sculpting pick and hammer. An attendant policeman saw this and arrested him for carrying dangerous weapons. No-one would believe he was a sculptor until he made a 'phone call and several students beat a hasty path to bail him out!"

Richard Negus: "My awe of the 'artist' disappeared during the day I was working with John Minton on illustrations for the *Radio Times*. I got the size wrong, and Minton said 'Well, just draw some more leaves and fill the space'."

Rachel Patterson (*née* Richards): "Four years of great pleasure... My fellow students included ex-servicemen on grants, this gave a far wider range of experience and feeling to otherwise adolescent groups of students. Everyone benefited, staff and students alike. Apart from the great discipline of life drawing and the teaching of various crafts, we were very fortunate in experiencing a broad spectrum of other arts, particularly music. Jazz, classical music and film groups were set up by both staff and students."

Christopher Pinsent: "A poem on retiring from teaching at Camberwell, June 1986:

This School in '86 A.D.
Is not the place it used to be.
Some forty years I'll take you back
If I can cultivate the knack.

Scared to be three minutes late
We hurried through the Queen Anne gate,
We drew from models all the week,
And only in models' rests dared speak.

Male models never quite undressed,
But had to pass an acid test,
They posed three feet above the floor
And stayed erect from nine till four.

The students wore dull natural locks,
And flying boots and oatmeal smocks,
They 'ranged the easels round the throne,
And drew until the thing was done.

Some in the front would place a chair
For a closer look at you-know-where,
The teachers were an ill-dressed lot
Who argued seriously on art.

Great Coldstream at each easel paused
To show how measurements are caused;
And if your painting you couldn't do
Claude Rogers finished it for you.

And when it came to hands and feet,
And getting them to look alright,
"Stop!" cried great Pasmore, hand aloft
"Useless to do these drawings soft

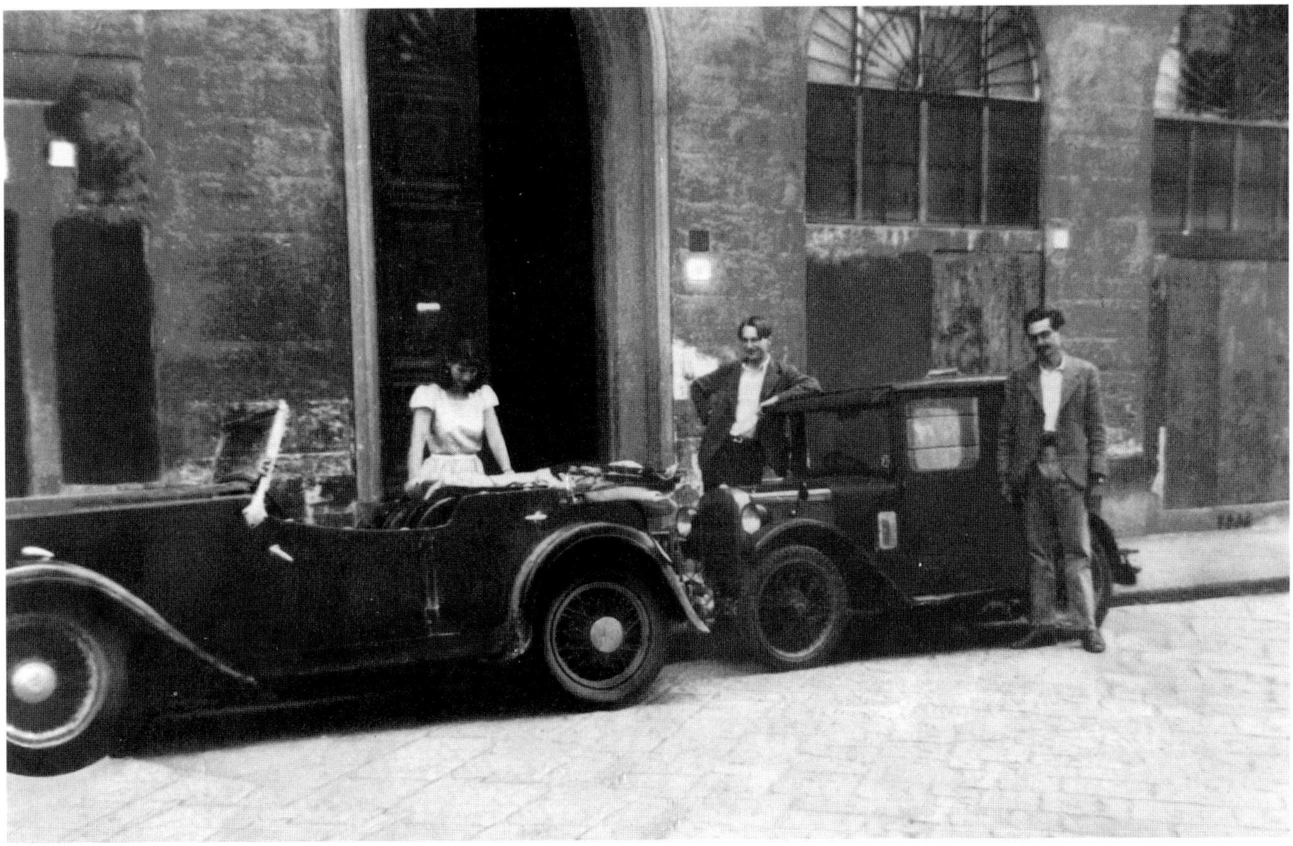

From left to right: Jo Higson, Christopher Pinsent and Anthony Eyton, Florence, c.1949.

Look at how Rembrandt painted fingers
Extremities are where art lingers".

Twelve thirty now, so it was then
The hour perennial for the din.
Not as now a healthful lunch
But direly on some junk to munch.
Dare any call permissiveness
An educational success.

Things come and go we all know this
As surely as my name is Chris
What matters most the friends we have
And how we'll miss them when we leave.

Though all my life I've been a dreamer
I still have a ticket for the steamer
And you who stay thank everyone,
For all the kind things you have done.
And you who stay God Bless you all,
May He preserve you in the fall*.

What Renoir painted with, my friends,
Is very much to do with ends;
Tip of the brush must praise the world
Before the final flag is furled."*

*Christopher Pinsent is referring here to anticipated staff cuts, due to Government cut-backs.

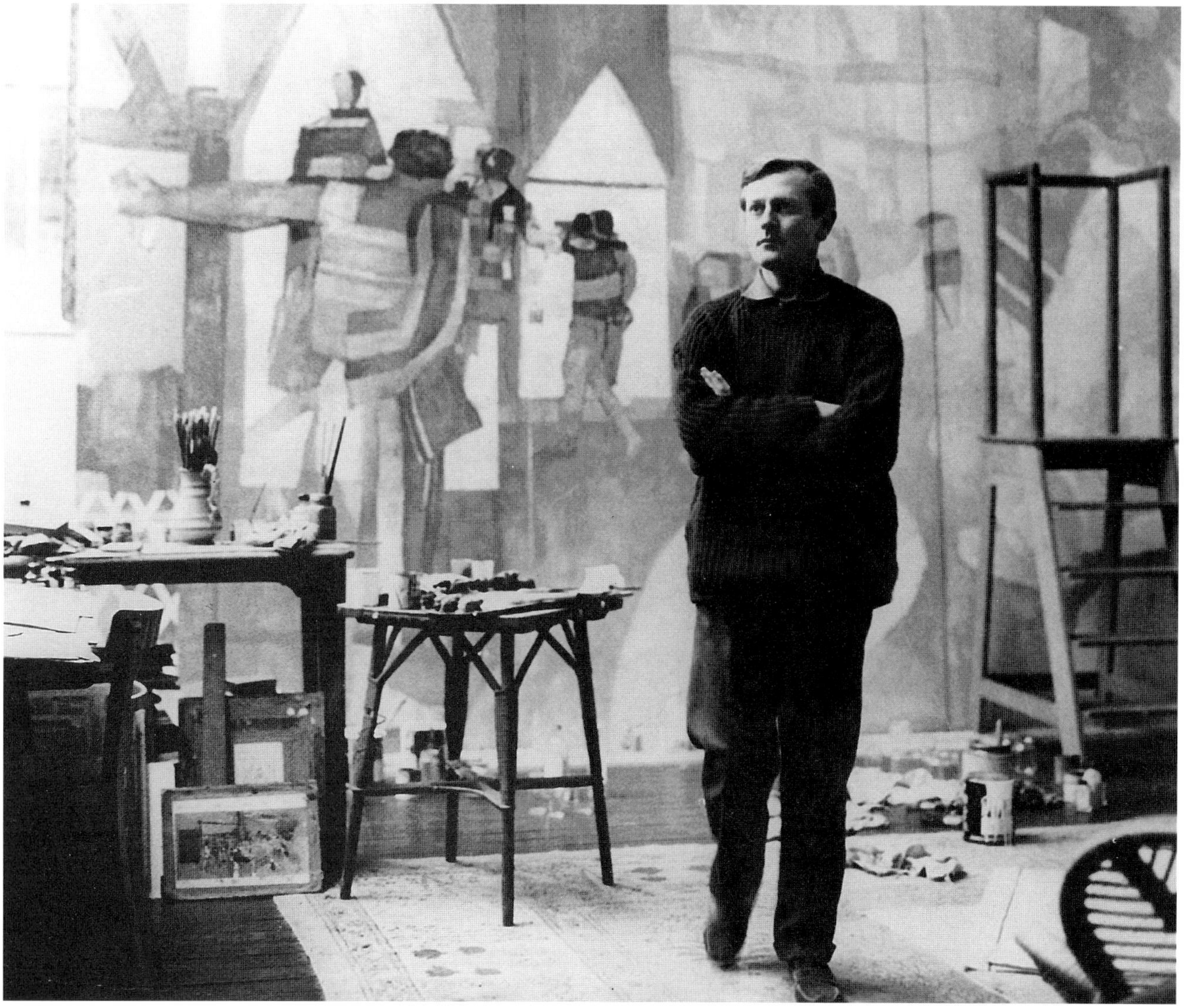

Leonard Rosoman, c.1950.

Jennifer Proctor (*née* Calver) "I arrived at Camberwell aged seventeen years with my knees knocking and terrified to find the School full of experienced ex-service students. My favourite class during the first two years was lino-cutting and wood-engraving with John Buckland-Wright. I think we spent as much time philosophising as working. The best student in the class was Gordon Davies, who was a very talented illustrator, mostly pen and ink drawings. He was very influenced by John Ward. I also found Richard Eurich most kind and sympathetic and I remember having long conversations with him – usually at the bus-stop outside the School."

Terry Raybould: "Although Frank Auerbach exerted a dynamic influence on all who were taught by him, some of my lasting impressions are of the other teachers. During a life drawing evening class, I was having particular difficulty in trying to draw the twist in the body of the model. Chris Pemberton sat with me to help. He started a drawing next to mine on the paper. He worked at a steady pace to start with but gradually speeded up, then stopped, and took off his jacket, started again building up the drawing in quick spurts – dots and short lines dashing about, stopped again, took off his sleeveless jumper to reveal braces, loosened his tie and off he went again! Gradually the marks accumulated to make a beautiful, sensitive, knotty drawing of the figure. He then breathed an exasperated sigh and said 'well I

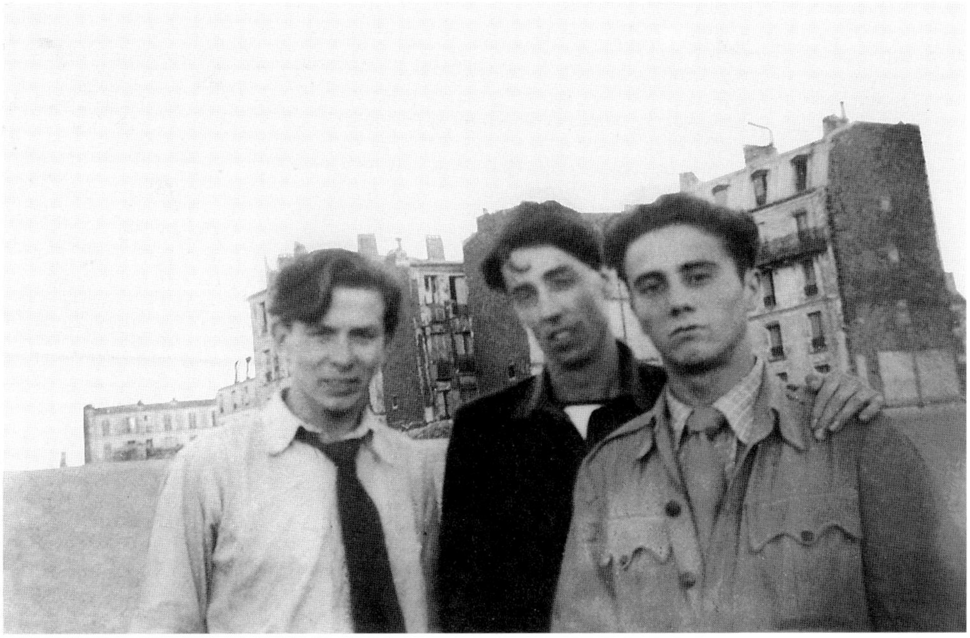

From left to right: Peter Dunbar, John Minton and Eric Verrico, France 1948. Courtesy of Marsh Dunbar.

can't do it either!' So perhaps neither of us had been able to express the precise twist in the model. But I had been treated to a demonstration of drawing at the highest level.

What lasting character Camberwell will be attributed with, I can't say. For my part I count myself extraordinarily lucky to have been a part of the history of the best art school of its day. Its attributes, to me, have been a caring community; the greatest seriousness for the activity of art, laced with joy and humour."

Louise Reid (*née* Young): "There was a cross little man in the office who was never very helpful, but every now and then he would come puffing up the stairs and along the corridor into our silent painting room and approached a particular student saying 'telephone for you Sir' – we all wondered why he should get such special treatment, then we found out it was Earl Haig's son. I remember John Minton, who was very helpful and who taught me in Illustration classes. I also remember Victor Pasmore, who was very silent and mostly sat puffing his pipe. If we needed help, we had to go out in the passage where they would all be sitting, but they were always willing to give advice or a 'crit' on a painting. I often feel that the training I got was excellent but so academic that it has been quite hard to shake off. But the seriousness of the 'looking' has become part of my life."

Richard Robbins: "The most important lesson I learnt during those years at Camberwell was the example of Joe Dixon. His dedication to the students was absolute. His was an example to inspire thought, one's attempt to follow it must and has fallen far short."

Leonard Rosoman: "Two occasions stand out in my mind during my time at Camberwell. I shared a class in Illustration with Johnny Minton and it was a fairly rowdy noisy lot of some thirty students. Johnny would stand the racket for so long and then scream at them at the top of his voice – this silenced them for a while and he would take advantage of it by taking out a pen and doing a vigorous drawing for the *Radio Times*. The other is a story that Keith Vaughan told me of William Johnstone interviewing him as if he were a prospective student. Johnstone's opening remarks were 'So – you want to come here and learn to paint like Victor Pasmore eh?' Vaughan, being a timid and nervous man, said 'yes' and listened patiently to a short lecture from Johnstone on how hard work on Vaughan's part

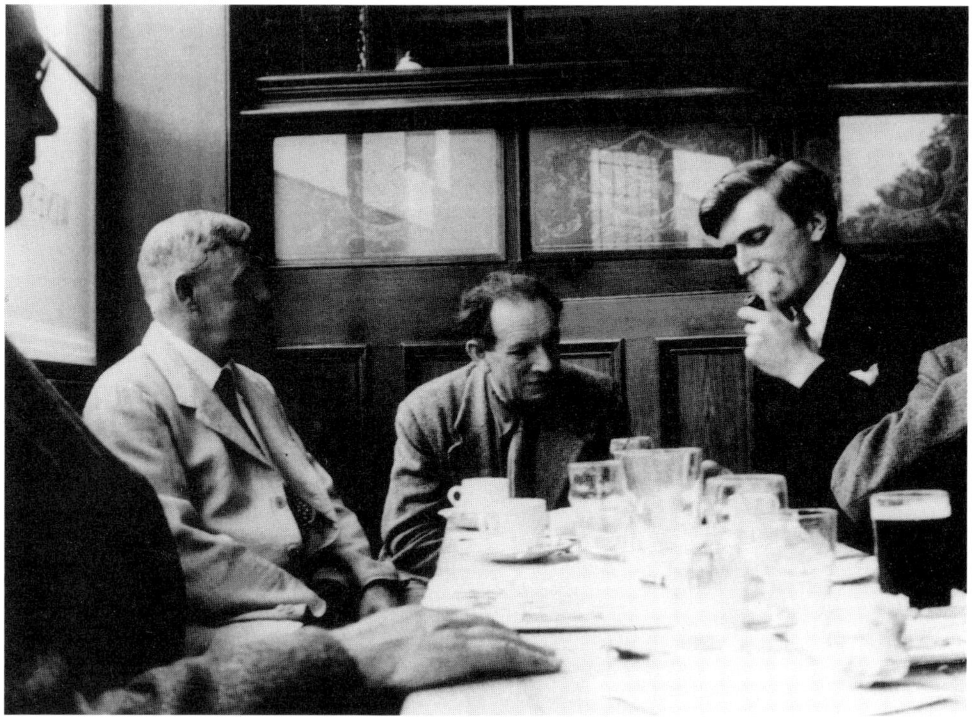

From left to right: Michael Rothenstein, R. V. Pitchforth, Karel Vogel and Richard Macdonald, Walmer Castle pub, Camberwell, c.1953.

would probably turn him into a good artist. Vaughan left the room and was quite prepared to go downstairs and enrol as a student if he hadn't been stopped by one of his colleagues, so powerful was Johnstone's force and presence."

Michael Rothenstein: "I had a like/dislike relationship with Camberwell, the like part of course involved the many interesting teachers and students – Pinsent, Uglow, Kitaj, Gillian Ayres, and Agathe Sorel. The dislike was that I always felt that printmaking was the poor relation. Classrooms and print rooms tended to be isolated, and the very word printmaking caused raised eyebrows. I recall one instance when a young dusky model, I think maybe of Persian origin, was recruited to the life class, but no amount of persuasion by the teachers would induce her to undress. The class was full of many young men at the time who, in the morning session, were greatly disappointed. However, this dusky maiden was invited to the pub for lunch and after plying her with a few glasses of whisky, the male members of the afternoon class were more than satisfied. There was no opposition to her undressing!"

Godfrey Rubens: "It was quite enterprising of Leonard Daniels to give jobs to refugee artists like Vogel and Bloch. Their ideas were so entirely different from the rest of the staff. It was actually illegal at the time to start a Students' Union, but the activities at the School that were organised by the students may have helped with the removal of that ridiculous ban. My chief memory of Camberwell, as far as the teaching was concerned, was of the division between the 'Euston Road-ers' and the rest, of whom Martin Bloch was, in my view, the most outstanding. It was he, for example, who encouraged us to go to the great Munch exhibition at the Tate, when the 'Line and Dot' teachers advised us against going. It was Bloch too who had a better understanding of Turner than anyone else there and an enthusiasm that he succeeded in communicating to his students. Bloch, unlike all the other teachers at Camberwell, did not go round the classrooms but had his own atelier in what had been, I believe, the gymnasium. A number of kindred spirits gathered there to work with him. The yearly exhibitions organised by the students at the local pub – the Walmer Castle – were very successful."

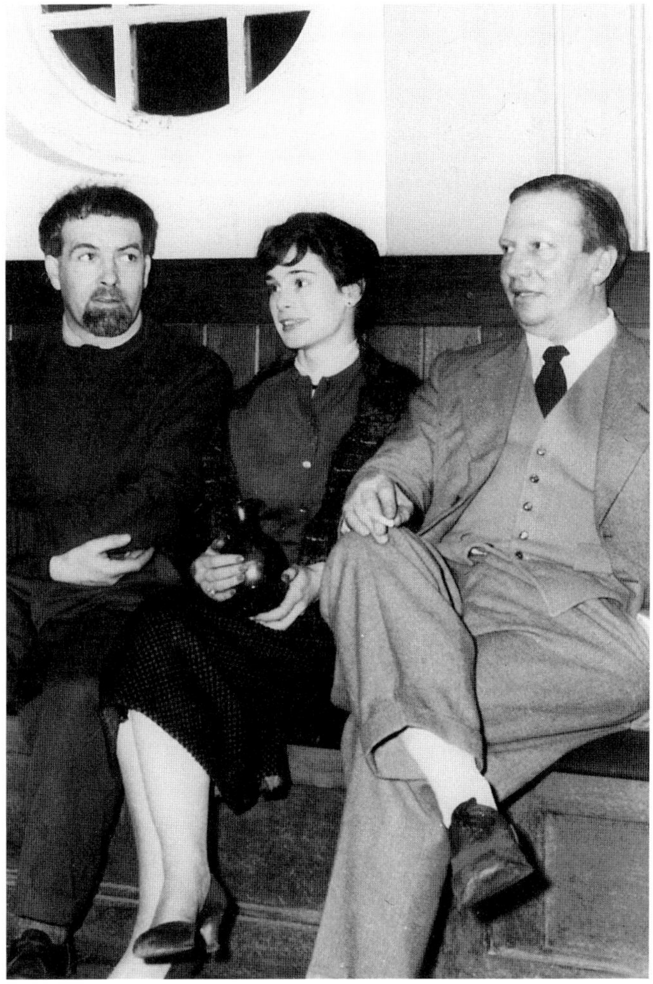

From left to right: Vernon Shearer, Walburga Shearer and Leonard Daniels, c.1955.

Terence Scales: "Being at Camberwell as a thirteen-year old junior was an extraordinary experience. To be given not five but maybe fifteen minutes by masters who would draw on paper what was in their minds, was such a unique thrill. I listened to everything and everyone with avid attention, practising every evening what I had learned during the day. The fact that the staff passionately disagreed with each other, made it all the more real. The Neo-Romantics and the Euston Road painters would take witty swipes at each other, Johnny Minton being particularly good at this. The students tended to follow one or other of these two groups, but overall there was a great hunger for knowledge and a desperate need to see, practice and discuss painting. In the lunch hour hectic games of football would take place behind the bombed rear of the South London Art Gallery, students arriving back in front of the life model with hands shaking trying to control their pencils. Camberwell has always been very down to earth, robustly independent of passing fashions, it has produced a stream of makers and its reputation of being steeped in tradition has not prevented a long line of former students being at the forefront of new developments. Not all the teachers were conventional by any means. I remember an elderly man called Norton who taught Architecture, Perspective and Anatomy. His Anatomy lessons often involved his painting in brush and poster paint on the body of a model, a male I might add, to emphasise muscle tone and anatomical structure. The class were amazed, and the model didn't seem to mind."

Vernon Shearer (supplied by his wife): "...the last bastion of civilised culture: i.e. proper drawing."

Elizabeth Sidonio: "I do not give my date of birth on any papers connected with art – because to me that was when my life began, it was a complete and stimulating entry into an entirely new world from my previous background and the realisation of the wonderful privilege to be taught by the cream of contemporary artists. I loved Camberwell."

Geoffrey Smedley: "I can certainly think of other ways of being introduced to the visual arts; but Camberwell served for me. I rate the experience highly, particularly Sam Carter's introduction to drawing as an unabashed scrutiny of appearances. I remember getting through the grapevine the electric news that Pasmore had gone abstract. I can also remember Kenneth Martin selling a broadsheet on Abstraction in the life room. At the time it seemed a clandestine thing to do."

Denis Smith: "Charles Johnson introduced me to painting. I met him in the queue at the Aldwych. He invited me to his Lectures at the National Gallery and suggested I took some lessons in painting, which I did at Beckenham School of Art. My teachers there were Carel Weight and Henry Carr. This idyllic period was abruptly

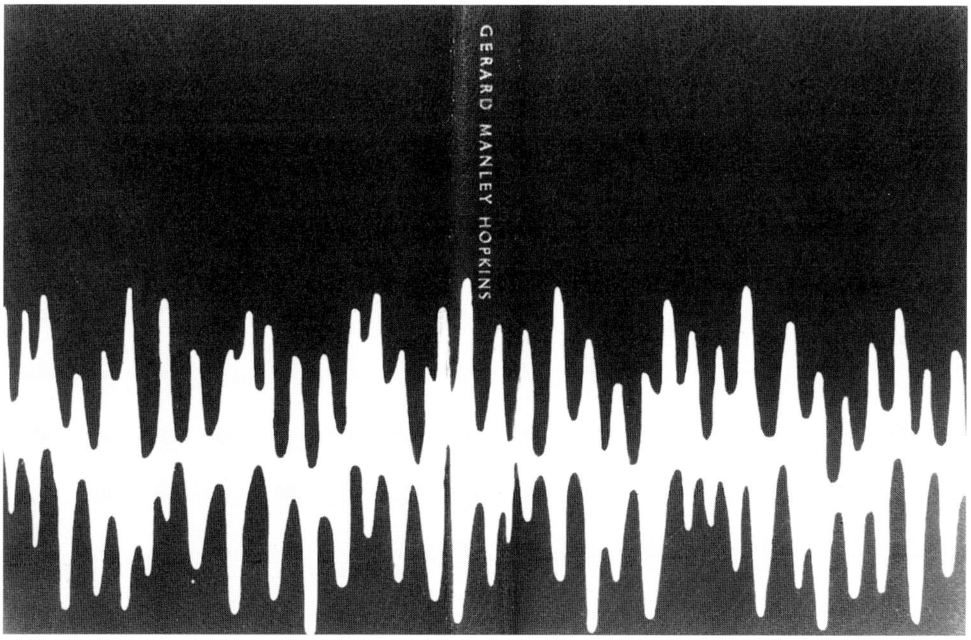

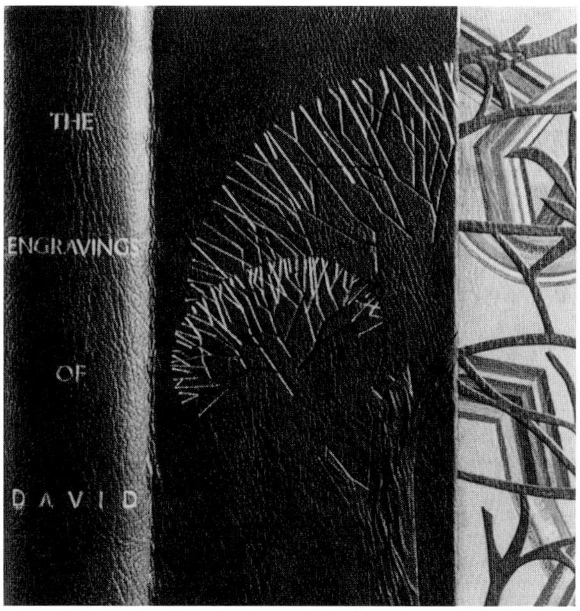

Above: SALLY LOU SMITH. Bookbinding. *Poems of Gerald Manley Hopkins.* Dark brown goatskin with recessed onlays of fair calf. Private collection.

Left: SALLY LOU SMITH. Bookbinding, 12½ in x 9½in. *The Engravings of David Jones.* Black goatskin with recessed panels of multicoloured onlays, gold and blind tooling. Courtesy of Mrs G. Chipperfield.

terminated by war service. Camberwell some years later was, for me, a rekindling of the enthusiasm engendered by Carel Weight, and Clifford Frith was here the inspired teacher. Many of his students will recall struggling along from Camberwell Green with enormous sheets of hardboard to capture his arrangements which generally contained a generous supply of fruit and flowers with the model. Very important, too, were the drawing classes under Nuttall-Smith, always packed full, as many day students remained for the evening sessions leaving little space for the late arrivals."

Sally Lou Smith: "I remember very well the canteen, the food was not good. It was the only place I had ever eaten where they could produce mashed potatoes that were stringy. They did a very good spotted dick, though. The apprentices were students only one day a week, at that time they still had to do hand book-binding and I learned quite a lot from overhearing instructions for the kind of work I was not doing, but it was useful to know how it was done. It took the best part of half a year to understand what many of them were saying because they had a fairly heavy Cockney accent, which was strange to my ears, and I became embarrassed because they would say something to me and have to repeat it two or three times. I finally became so embarrassed, I just sort of smiled. I remember the day-release boys who were rather mischievous. If I was doing some gold tooling and having a leaf of gold laid out on a gold cushion, they often liked nothing better than to come along with a big piece of board and waft it over the gold, sending it fifteen feet in the air."

Lesley South: "I had not made up my mind whether to attend Camberwell or Chelsea, both of which at the time had fine reputations for their Sculpture schools. From where I lived I could take either the 36 bus to Camberwell or the 12 to Chelsea. The 36 happened to arrive first, and that was my decision which shaped the rest of my life. Karel Vogel enjoyed his journey to the school every morning. He often told me how he enjoyed looking at interesting heads of the people travelling on the tube with him. He would study them for the length of the journey making mental sketches which he might put into practice. One morning on such a journey, so engrossed was he by this wonderful head sitting opposite him, that he failed to notice that it was his fellow teacher Helen Watson. It was only when she virtually shouted at him that he came out of his trance and realised he had been staring at someone he had known for some years."

Derek Southall: "I was and still am profoundly anti-Euston Road, but I am grateful that I had something worth working against."

John Spencer: "What Camberwell meant to me? A good question. The companionship of others trying to do the same thing, that was very important. The great kindness of some of the teachers was another. I remember when first I had a picture accepted by the Royal Academy, Richard Eurich wrote to congratulate me. His letter ended with the words 'most of my friends would not be seen dead in the R.A.'* Most of the teachers were so wonderfully encouraging – their dedication, both to their own art work and to the work of their students, was very impressive. Edward Ardizzone spoke of a student who said of him 'Ardizzone is a nice chap, but I wish he wouldn't leave snuff all over my drawings!' It is somewhat disturbing thinking of times long past. I have just been reading of Groucho Marx after watching some early films of his remarking 'I didn't realise I was so talented and agile then'."

*Author's note – how times have changed!

Andrew Verster: "Our work always looked dull in comparison with St. Martins and Chelsea, we noticed this especially when we took ours into the Young Contemporaries, and usually had it rejected. Camberwell was not greatly adventurous but it was a good training, one which gave you a good basis for later development. I liked the idea that through a 'laying on of hands' we had a direct link with the Impressionists; the people who taught us had been trained by someone who had been taught perhaps by Dégas or some of his associates. Perhaps that explained why we had our feet stuck in the 19th century and were not at home with the Moderns. Cézanne hung heavily over us and life was unthinkable without him. It was only when the exhibition of New American Painting came to the Tate that any of us began to really feel for contemporary art. I remember being moved by the Rothkos and thinking that Grace Hartigan held many answers.

We had disciplined training, my respect for the way colour operates was born in my third year when we began in the Painting School. We were given a palette of yellow ochre, black and Indian red and then a still-life with bright lemons, cloth, vases and other Cézanne-ish things, and told to paint this as accurately as we could. Weeks, maybe months later, when we felt we had exhausted the possibilities of these colours, we were allowed another one or two, but we had to make out a case for any new colour we wanted. In Composition, the vertical/horizontal grid dominated our eyes, so obsessive was it that I remember well during one lunch hour in the Common Room watching a fellow student – Andrew Aarons – adjusting his foot so that it composed well with the squares of the Marley tiled floor. Truth to appearance was equally obsessive. Alan Love, Christopher Addison and myself once shared a still-life group of some fish on a plate on a checked table-cloth on a round table. Because these particular fish were important and because we painted very slowly, we tried all sorts of things to keep them from going off, including varnishing them. We felt betrayed when someone suggested Cézanne had used wax fruit – in fact we didn't believe he would have done so. Equally, the mark we made was sacred, the closer it resembled Cézanne the happier we were. The result was that most of our work was interchangeable. We used the same colours, described objects in the same way, had the same subject matter and generally conformed to the Camberwell way of doing things. It was difficult later to throw off the style.

Museum study meant amongst other things painting in the National Gallery, we were hopeless but felt flattered by two things; Americans who wanted to buy our copies of Titian and the rule of the Gallery that a copy had to be fractionally different in size, even if only an inch from the original. The idea that they felt that there was any chance of us getting close to the original was heartening. Once Gilbert Spencer brought Stanley to talk to us, we were over-awed at meeting one of our gods and we were too shy to ask questions. He looked like a schoolboy with a string tie, country clothes and untidy hair. He was bewildered by the attention and the numbers and said nothing, I think he was frightened of us. He probably wanted to get home quickly! One of the other lecturers I remember well, was Sir Francis Rose, he had a run-down but glamorous air. He talked about famous people he had known, Clare Booth Luce who had written articles for *Life* magazine and had been paid, he said, a hundred pounds per word; Chaim Soutine whom he had known in Paris and Christopher Wood, for whom he had posed naked as a young man, showing us the actual painting. He taught us almost nothing – we taught him how to prime hardboard with P.V.A."

Roy Watson: "I remember finding some difficulty on one occasion and asking advice from someone who responded by suggesting that I go to see Christopher Chamberlain – 'He has a lot of practical common sense to offer.' It surprised me then to hear of art spoken of in those terms, but the clarity with which my problem was solved confirmed my adviser's faith."

Peter Weaver: "I remember Sir Francis Rose running a class which he called 'Monoliths' but of course, he meant monotypes. Sir Francis once asked Vernon Shearer what glue he could use for making a maraflage. Vernon said 'You mean sticking a piece of canvas to a piece of board?', 'Yes', replied Sir Francis. 'Well, (pulling Sir Francis's leg) you must make a flour and water paste but the flour must be compost grown and stone-ground'. Sir Francis failed to find any grocer who stocked such stuff – but later when talking to the Queen Mother!! she was the only one who could tell him where he might get it."

Tim Wheeler: "At the time I felt it was rather a narrow place, especially after Pop Art and the Americans… although now, I would describe myself as a Camberwell painter."

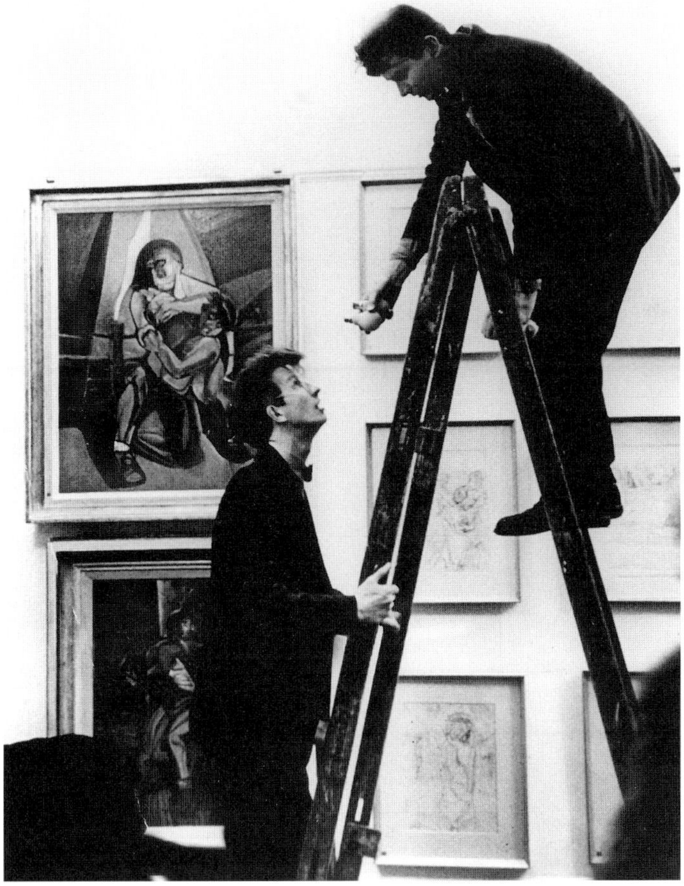

Owen Wood (left) with Peter Dunbar, June 1955.

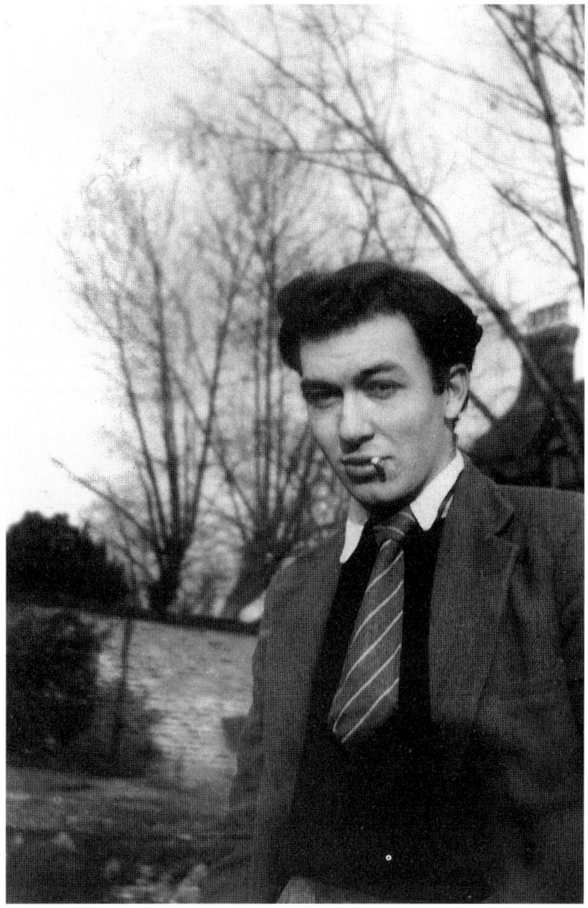

Robert Hunt, spring 1949.

Marcelle (Wendy) Wolfers: "I owe my grasp of the elements of drawing to Sam Carter, whose infinite patience as a teacher was, I hope, in my case, partially rewarded. Kenneth Martin used to advise us when trying to teach drawing – 'You see, you've got to see the thing as flat as a pancake' – in his resounding Yorkshire drawl that we neophytes found hilariously funny and used to imitate."

Owen (Oska) Wood and Bobby Hunt in conversation with the author:
Hunt: "I remember a Picasso exhibition at the V & A towards the end of the war which was much discussed back at Camberwell, but only by Pasmore and by the likes of, I recall, Johnny Minton. The rest of the staff felt that Picasso was not traditional and therefore could be a bad influence on art students."
Wood "I was painstakingly slow in my painting and I still am today for that matter! I remember a most beautiful model and she would pose for us every day. As time progressed the class painting her got less and less as they finished their work. Eventually, I became the sole student in the class, and there she was posing for me naked, and all I had achieved after six weeks was the completion of her head. I was so engrossed in the detail, I had not noticed the rest of her body."
Hunt "In those days, you had to be sixteen years of age to go into a life class, but I remember John Dodgson pushing me through the doors at the ripe old age of fourteen. The shock of seeing pubic hair for the first time was unbelievable! The jazz movement at Camberwell was amazing in those days. I never knew how we found time to study art as we seemed always to be playing jazz. I remember one day going into the 'Music Room', which was really the boiler room at Camberwell, where we had been relegated to play our instruments so that we could not be heard by the rest of the school. I recall Oska being down there and playing his trombone

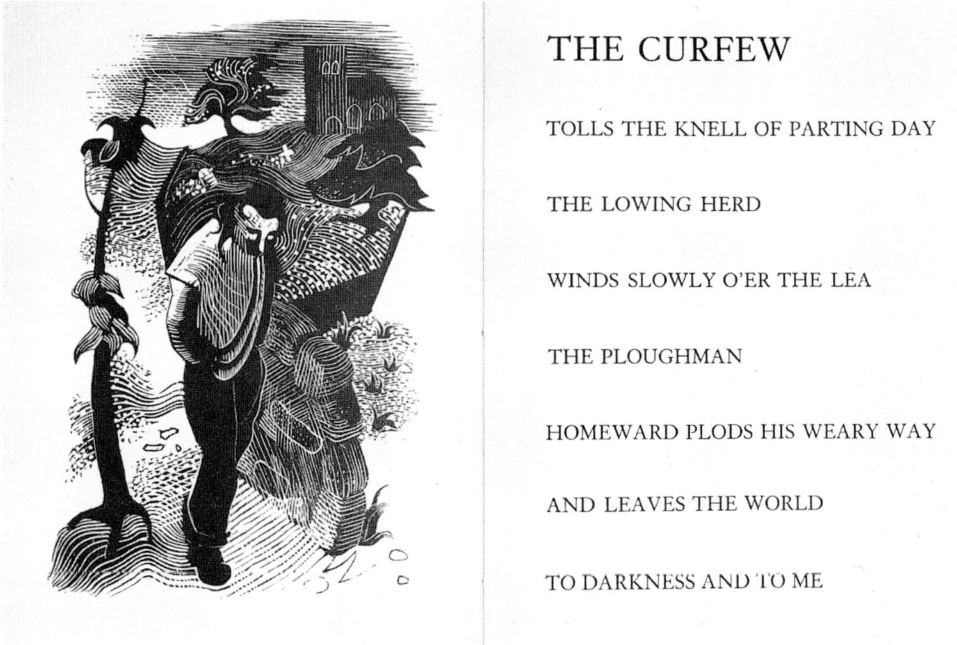

Above and opposite page: Lithographs by an unknown Camberwell artist, 1946. Author's collection.

and this new face was standing there handling my trumpet. I rather indignantly said that it was my property and would he kindly leave it alone. The new face asked if we were keen on jazz and would we like to go and see George Webb's Dixielanders. We were thrilled at the opportunity and we were given tickets. By now we had guessed that this new face was probably involved with the band but we weren't that interested. Of course, on the night we soon found out that the donor of the tickets was Humphrey Lyttleton."

Wood "Of course it was Bobby Hunt who taught Monty Sunshine some of his first musical notes."

Hunt "The Annual Balls were amazing. I think it was 1945 when we had the Hayseeds Báll, each year was a different theme, with students doing some of their best work in the way of painted murals, paper sculpture and wonderful advertising posters. In 1946 the theme was the Naughty Nineties. I recall Toni del Renzio coming dressed as Toulouse Lautrec, but can you imagine the Can-Can being performed by men? I think we also had a performance of the Swan Lake ballet, with Denis Piper as the Prima Ballerina! That was the year that John Minton gave us a song and also the year that Rik Richards smuggled in a barrel of beer (alcohol was banned); his father ran a pub I believe."

Wood "One of the party pieces when the jazz band was playing at these balls was when a gorgeous young female student, whose name I cannot recall, but who had amply proportioned breasts would go on stage when Bobby Hunt was about to play a trumpet solo. Instead of using a mute, she would adroitly muffle the sound of Bobby's trumpet with whichever breast was nearest at the time."

Hunt "There was the time, of course, when Oska nearly died. One year at a party, we had the most incredible chicken rolls. They were the talk of the moment. Oska stood up to give his trombone solo and nearly blew his head off as, unbeknown to him, someone had rammed a chicken roll into his trombone. Poor Oska, he had a headache for two weeks!"

ELEGY
WRITTEN IN A
COUNTRY
CHURCHYARD

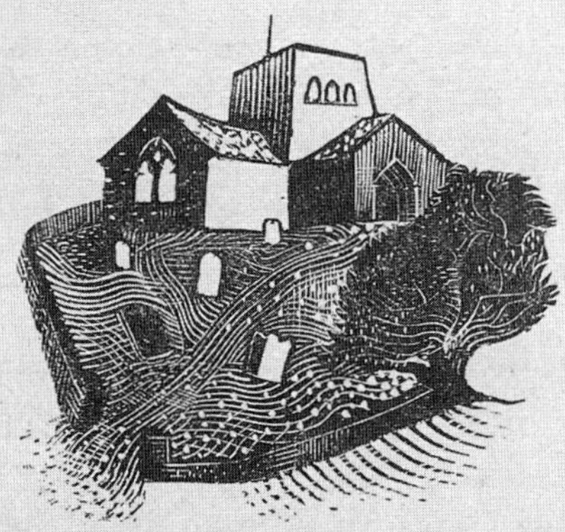

THOMAS GRAY

Absent Friends

During my research at Camberwell, the archives produced a number of names of reigistered students which do not appear in this book, either because I failed to make contact with them or because, when I had made contact, they chose not to assist. However, since the records show these people attended the school during the period 1943-60, I record them here for the sake of completeness.

Because of the difficulty of interpreting the records (for instance, when only a surname and initial appear it is not even possible to determine the sex) some of the students or teachers listed here may possibly have been working in disciplines not covered by this book.

Hopefully, a second edition will fill many of the gaps and answer some of the questions, and I would be grateful if any former students at the school during 1943-60 would send me information about their careers, as well as any memories and anecdotes, to add to those already published.

Adamovich, Adam
Addison, Christopher Edward
Ahmed, Amena
Akehurst, Norman
Allan, Roger William
Allen, George Blake
Allen, Janet Ruth
Andrews, Peter W
Anjunag, Narendra R
Appleton, Reginald John
Arnold, Frederick Sidney George
Arnold, John Robert
Arthurs, Terry
Ashok, Bhaleraq

Baer, Sigrid Alison
Ball, Susan
Bantock, Terry
Barker, Barry
Barnes, Jean A
Barrett, Eileen J
Beadle, John
Bebb, Roy H
Belcher, Sidney Victor Henry
Bennet, Lilian
Berger, Iris A
Berry, Herbert
Berry, R
Bhalerne, Ashock
Bill, James
Birch, Michael
Blakeley, Charles
Blinkworth, John C
Bliss, Brenda V
Blunden, Brian H
Bonel, Phyllis
Bosanquet, Pamela
Bowden, Leonard
Box, Simon
Bradley, Margaret
Brady, Barbara
Brand, Paul
Breeds, Norman Victor
Brown, Cynthia Barbara
Brown, Joyce
Brown, Pamela
Buckley, Bridget
Burn, Dorothy
Bury, Roland Finucane
Butler, Ken
Butterworth, Michael

Campion, Oliver
Canning, Elizabeth B
Carlton, Corina
Carlton, Trilby
Carter, Daphne
Chamberlain, Kenneth
Checketts, Norman F
Cheetham, John Roger
Clark, William F
Clarke, Sylvia

Clarkson, Chris
Clipson, Christopher
Clipson, Gordon
Cohen, Sydney
Coleman, Francis
Conti, Paul
Cooper, Derek
Cottingham, Kenneth
Cowan, Madeline
Cox, Albert W R K
Cranmer, Robert J
Croney, John Edward
Crugten, Joan van
Cruickshank, M
Cuff, Robert R

Dance, K
Davies, Gordon
Davies, Thomas Richard
Davis, Brian George
Dawson, A G
De La Mere, Helen
Debney, Beryl
Denney, Jacqueline
Dickinson, Frank Holdsworth
Diggens, Rodney Ian
Diggle, Stanley V
Doig, Sally
Dover, Margaret E
Dyke, Kenneth

Edinburgh, William A
Elliot, Michael J
Elliot-Lord, Pamela Rose
Elmslie-Owen, G E
Eriksson, Anthony M
Errington, Winifred M

Faulkner, Enid L
Fender, James Homer
Fern, Jane
Findlay, D G
Fiorini, G
Fischl, Renate
Fisher, W H
Fletcher, Nicola Hamilton
Fortnum, Eve
Foster, A
Foster, Caterina
Foster, Heather
Fox, Roy
French, Honora
French, John A
Furlong, Barbara

Gale, Richard
Gentilli, Jeremy Edward George
Ghaffar, Abdul
Gillows, Solomon
Glover, Peter Frederick
Goodman, Ann
Green, Stephen
Greetham, Geoffrey
Grierson, Ronald
Groves, John M

Hannen, Kenneth
Harney, Arthur
Hart, D
Harvey, Margaret A
Hawker, Albert A
Hill, Patricia
Hilton, Margaret
Hoad, John
Holden, Barbara
Holding, Robert
Holdsworth, Peter
Hooper, John
Hopkins, Henry L
Hough, Jean
Howard, Nicholas
Hughes, Reginald Arthur Jeffrey
Hunt, Kay

Ilani, Ruth

Jellyman, John
Johnston, Graeme
Jones, Eryl Mai

Kearsley, Roy
Kennington, Patricia Ann
Kenwood, Margaret Mary
Kerwood, Margaret
Khan, Cyril
Kitching, Gerald
Koppenhagen, Maureen

Lack, Barbara D
Larking, Ernest A R
Law, Robert Alan
Leman, Jacqueline Daphne
Lemon, Hazel
Lester, Adrian

Lewcock, S
Lewis, Douglas
Lidzey, John F
Lindsay-Berry, E
Linford, Victor
Little, Raymond Robert C
Lomas, Eve
Loth, Ann
Love, Alan
Lucas, A W
Lynch, James F

MacFarland, Elsie
McFarland, Elizabeth P
McGowan, Thomas E
McMullen, Eve
Mallam, Jenifer
Marston, Frank W
Martin, Jess
Martin, Lynton Hugh
Martin, Thomas Ashton
Mason, Pearl
Mee, Greville R
Meller, Ann Rosalind
Middlehurst, F
Millard, Anthony J
Mills, Alan J
Mitchell, Valerie J
Moore, John H
Morgan, Patrick Thomas
Morris, Jean D
Morton, Douglas Gibb
Mossman, Derek A
Moulner, Michael B
Mussi, Susan Jane

Naish, William R K
Naji, Kassim
Neville, Eleanor Charlotte M
Nicholson, Ian
Noak, Richard Alfred Paul

O'Brien, Antonia
Ocleppo, Nick
Old, Ashley G
Olds, W
Oosthuizen, Daniel Jacobus J
Orpin, Joan
Orrock, Edmund

Paramor, James
Paris, June
Parker, Mollie A
Patten, Doris Ethel
Pavlides, Pauline
Pearce, Jean Erica
Pegram, Roy
Pell, Robert Leslie
Pennell, Jennifer Edwina
Peppiate, David B
Perry, E T
Phillips, Alison M
Phillips, William
Pickersgill, Howard
Platt, Michael
Polten, Rae
Pool, Vincent James
Poulden, Sylvia Marion
Prentice, John Tattersall
Price, Ursula Diana Nye
Purdy, Jock (Hugh)

Quinn, Mary

Rawdah, Shermine
Reeve, Michael
Reeves, Anne
Reynolds, Ottoline
Riley, Eileen
Ritchie, Isobel Evelyn
Roberts, Joan
Roddis, Peter
Rowe, Victor
Russell, Victoria
Rutherford, Ian
Ryder, G

Sampson, Bretonneaux H G
Savage ?
Scharenguival, Inez
Scholfield, Geoffrey M
Scholton, Mary C
Schwarzova, Sonja
Schweizer, Audrey L
Shaberman, Ralph B
Sherwood, Irene O
Sneider, Evelyn Gladys
Snoader, Anthony B
Somerville, Moira
Starkey, Anthony R A
Steel, Barbara Louise
Steggle, Sidney
Stewart, Robert Seymour
Stone, H R

Stocks, Josephine
Straker, Edwin
Streames, Roy Victor
Stretch, Heather R Stanton
Sultan, James Edgar
Sutton, James

Tabor, Ann
Thatcher, Janet
Thomas, Peter Lewis
Thompson, Ralph
Thorogood, Marika
Tossell, Pamela Jean
Treherne, Robert
Trimble, Charles James
Truman-Cox, Walter
Tyrell, Miles

Varkonyi, Lajos
Verniquet, Etienne Wilfred
Verrico, Eric
Vicary, Richard
Vesty, Jane

Walton, Keith
Watson, William
Webbe, Diana E
Weighill, Dorothy M
Werner ?
West, David Richardson
Weston, John G
Wetmore, Robert
White, Philip
Whiteing, Victoria R A
Whitley, Kenneth A
Whittaker, May
Wight, Clifford
Wilmott, Dorothy
Winding, Peter J
Wright, Macvyn

Yarri, Shaya
Young, Margaret L L

Zoeftig, Alan

Bibliography & Further Reading

(in Chronological order)

Elegy written in a Country Churchyard, Thomas Gray.
A booklet containing four wood engravings composed in Granjon on the Linotype and printed in the Typography Department of the L.C.C. Camberwell School of Arts & Crafts, 1946. Artist unknown.

Jubilee: Camberwell School of Arts and Crafts – 1898-1948, commemorative booklet with text by Leonard Daniels, 1948.

The Euston Road School and Others, Brighton Art Gallery exhibition catalogue with introduction by William Townsend, 1948.

Arts News & Review, 26th February, 1949, p.15, 'The Camberwell School of Arts & Crafts – A Cultural Centre of South London'.

The Artist, pp.67-69, November 1951, 'The Camberwell School of Art'.

Camberwell – Past and Present Students, South London Art Gallery exhibition catalogue, February 1957.

Terry Frost Retrospective Exhibition, The Laing Art Gallery, Newcastle-upon-Tyne, exhibition catalogue with introduction by Philip James, 1964.

A Painter's Diary, Francis Hoyland, pub. Educational Explorers Ltd., 1967.

John Dodgson 1890-1969, South London Art Gallery exhibition catalogue, June 1971.

Claude Rogers, Paintings and Drawings 1927-1973, Whitechapel Art Gallery, exhibition catalogue with introduction by Andrew Forge, April 1973.

Euan Uglow, London Arts Council, exhibition catalogue with introduction by Miles Murphy, 1974.

Dictionary of British Artists: 1900-1950, Grant M. Waters, pub. Eastbourne Fine Art, *Vol.I*, 1975, *Vol.II – Plates*.

University Challenge, Barry Fantoni & Quentin Blake. Their Thesis on Camberwell School of Art, *Punch* magazine, pp.1080-1083, 8th December 1976.

The Townsend Journals: An Artist's Record of his Times – 1928-1951, ed. Andrew Forge (Tate Gallery Publications, London), 1976.

Daily Telegraph, 'Lively Talents Bred at Camberwell', exhibition review by Terence Mullaly, 4th December 1978.

Everything but the Kitchen Sink, Campbell & Franks exhibition catalogue, 1978.

Points in Time, William Johnstone, pub. Barrie & Jenkins, 1980.

Anthony Eyton Retrospective Exhibition, South London Art Gallery, exhibition catalogue with introduction by William Packer, May 1980.

Patrick George, Paintings and Drawings 1937-1980, Serpentine Gallery, exhibition catalogue with introduction by Lawrence Gowing, June 1980

Art & Artists, 'The Golden Age of Camberwell', Alastair Gordon remembers his student days at Camberwell School of Art, pp.16-18, September 1983.

Drawn from the Life... A Memoir, Robert Medley, pub. Faber & Faber, 1983, pp.214-227.

Lawrence Gowing, Serpentine Gallery, exhibition catalogue with introduction by Stephen Spender, pub. The Arts Council of Great Britain, 1983.

The Story of the Artists' International Association 1933-1953, A.I.A. catalogue of exhibition organised by Lynda Morris and Robert Radford at Museum of Modern Art, Oxford and touring, 1983.

The Euston Road School, Bruce Laughton, Scholar Press, Aldershot, 1986.

TROG – Forty Graphic Years – The Art of Wally Fawkes, foreword by Raymond Briggs, pub. for Fourth Estate, 1986.

Camberwell Artists of the '40s and '50s, Belgrave Gallery, exhibition catalogue with text by Irving Grose, May 1988.

Arts Review, 'Artists of Camberwell of the '40s and '50s', review of the Belgrave Gallery Exhibition, by Max Wykes-Joyce, pp.332-333, 20th May, 1988.

Painting the Visible World – Painters at the Euston Road School and at Camberwell School of Arts & Crafts: 1930-1960, Austin/Desmond Fine Art, exhibition catalogue, 1989.

Terry Frost – Works on Paper 25 years...1947-1972, Austin/Desmond Fine Art, exhibition catalogue, October 1989.

Camberwell Painters, Austin/Desmond Fine Art, exhibition catalogue, September 1990.

Eyton, Lee, Mann & Pemberton – Works on Paper, Cadogan Contemporary, exhibition catalogue with text by Christopher Pinsent, October 1990.

The Paintings of William Coldstream 1908-1987, text by Lawrence Gowing and David Sylvester, Tate Gallery Publications, touring exhibition catalogue, October 1990.

Anthony Eyton Paintings 1938-1975, 'A Sort of Touchability', Austin/Desmond Fine Art, exhibition catalogue, 1990.

Bernard Leach, Hamada and their Circle, Tony Banks and Cornelia Wingfield Digby, 1990.

Dick Lee, Cadogan Contemporary, exhibition catalogue with text by Christopher Pemberton, February 1990.

A Dictionary of British Studio Potters, Pat Carter, pub. Scholar Press, Aldershot, 1990.

Dance till the Stars Come Down – A Biography of John Minton, Frances Spalding, pub. Hodder & Stoughton, 1991.

Camberwell Painters II, Austin/Desmond Fine Art, exhibition catalogue, September 1991.

Claude Rogers: Paintings and Drawings, exhibition catalogue written by Jenny Pery, The Ben Uri Art Gallery and the Royal West of England Academy, 1992/93.

Terry Frost, A Personal Narrative, David Lewis, pub. Scholar Press, 1994.

Together Again, South London Art Gallery, exhibition of ex-Camberwell Students with Introduction by Philip Matthews, date unknown.

Index

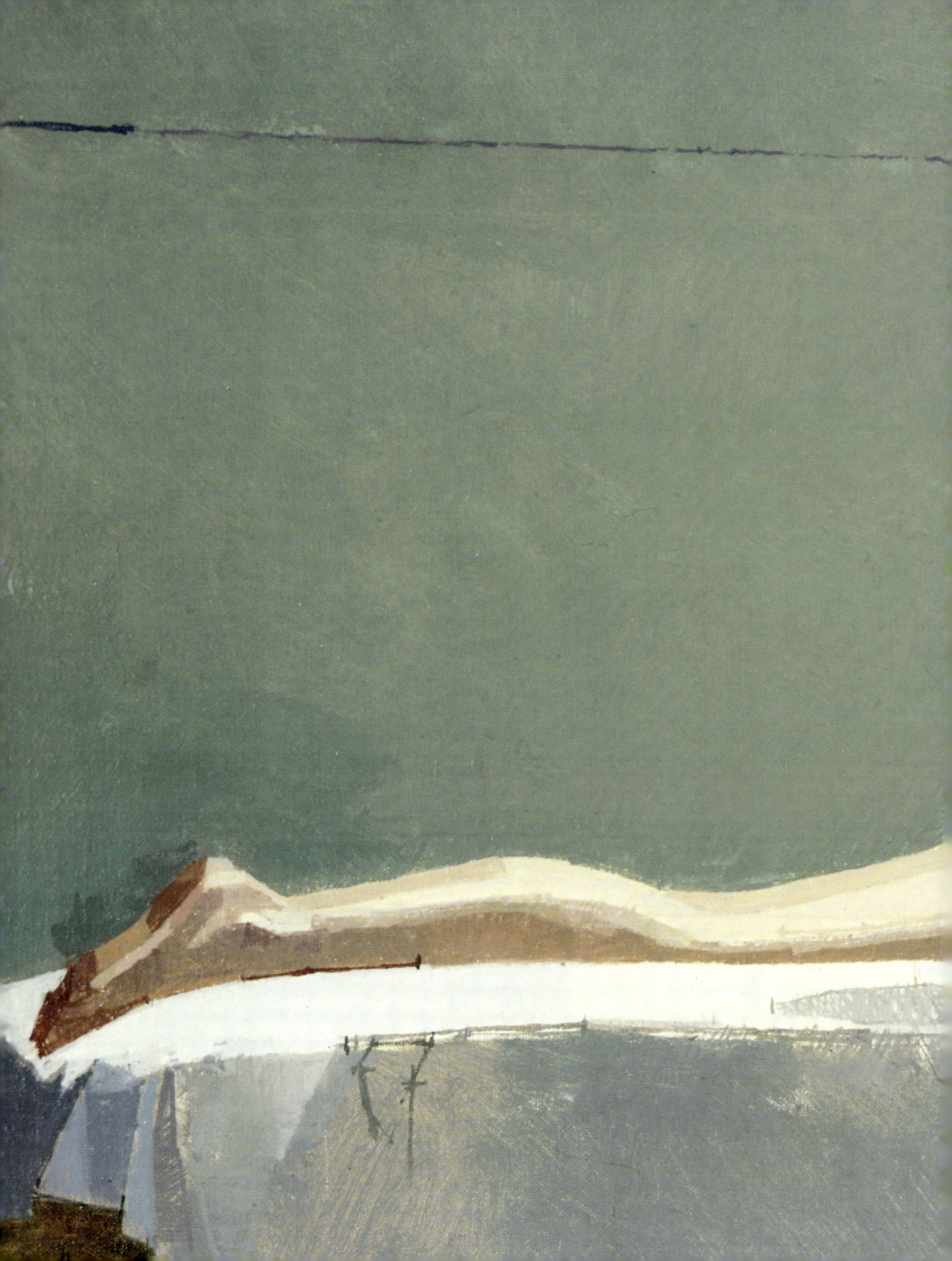